Francis Bacon and the Tradition of Art

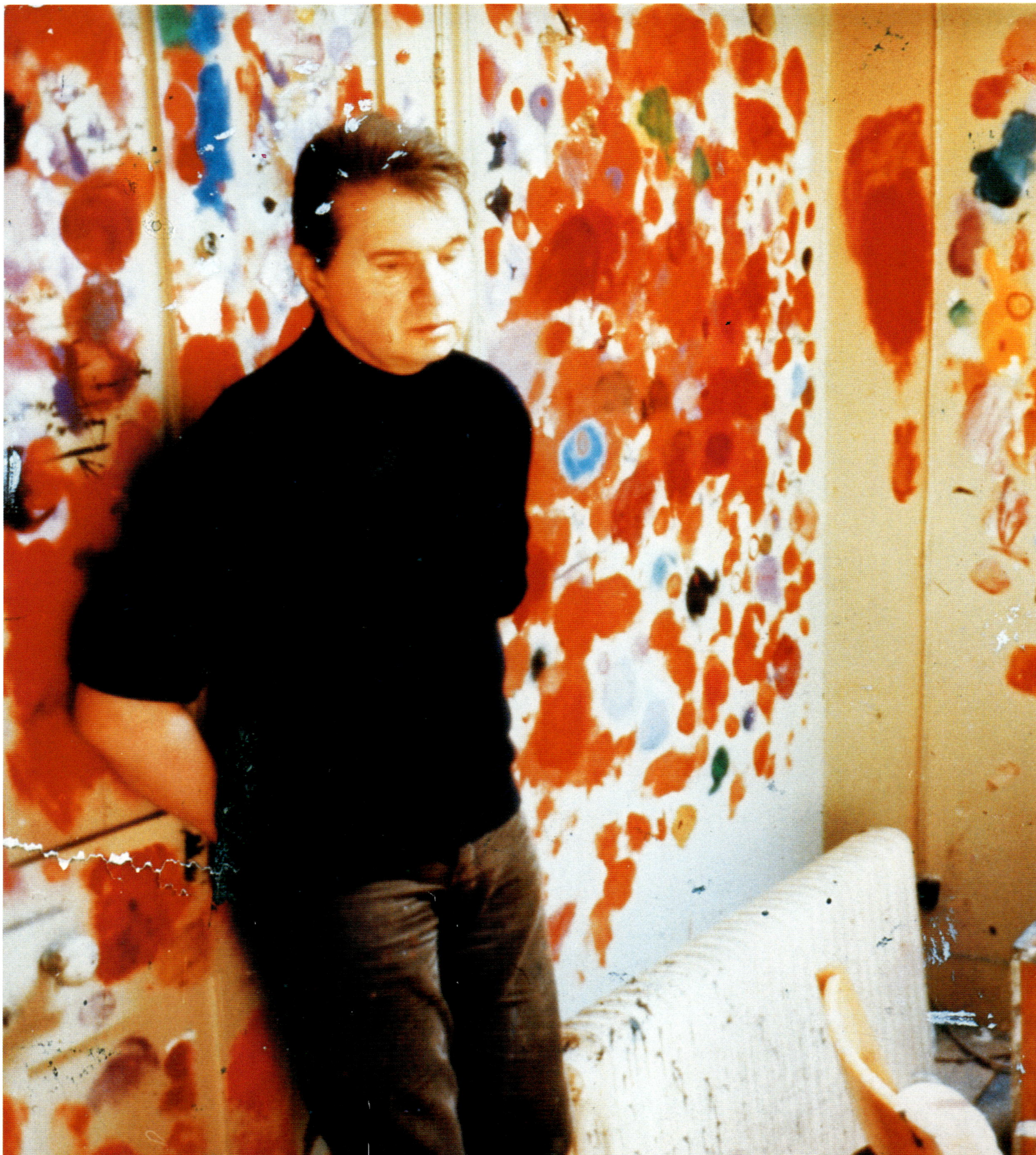

An Exhibition of the Kunsthistorisches Museum Vienna
in Co-operation with the
Fondation Beyeler, Riehen/Basel

Francis Bacon and the Tradition of Art

Edited by
Wilfried Seipel
Barbara Steffen
Christoph Vitali

Kunsthistorisches Museum Wien
Vienna, 15 October 2003 to 18 January 2004

FONDATION
BEYELER

Fondation Beyeler, Riehen/Basel
Riehen, 8 February to 20 June 2004

SKIRA

Editorial information on the catalogue

Owner and Publisher:

Generaldirektor
Prof. Dr. Wilfried Seipel
Kunsthistorisches Museum Wien
A–1010 Wien, Burgring 5

Barbara Steffen, MA
Barbara Steffen Art Advisory
48 East 66th street
New York, NY 10021

Direktor
Christoph Vitali
Fondation Beyeler
CH-4125 Riehen/Basel

Catalogue Design:
Skira editore

Graphic Design:
Stefano Tosi

Text Graphics:
Marco Abate

Realisation:
Lorena Biffi

Editorial Board:
Barbara Steffen
Verena Gamper
Alexandra Hennig
Felicitas Kunth

Proof-reading:
Elisabeth Herrmann-Fichtenau
Annette Schäfer
Karin Zeleny

Translations:
Christopher Roth
Joshua Stein
John Winbigler

First published in Italy in 2003 by
Skira Editore S.p.A.
Palazzo Casati Stampa
via Torino 61
20123 Milano
Italy
www.skira.net

Printed and bound in Italy.
First edition

ISBN 88-8491-721-2

Distributed in North America and Latin America by Rizzoli International Publications, Inc. through St. Martin's Press, 175 Fifth Avenue, New York, NY 10010.
Distributed elsewhere in the world by Thames and Hudson Ltd., 181a High Holborn, London WC1V 7QX, United Kingdom.

Front cover illustration:
Cat. no. 14

Back cover illustration:
Cat. no. 13

Illustration on p. 2:
Cat. no. 152, detail

Illustration on pp. 8 and 9:
Cat. no. 14, detail

Illustration on p. 10:
Cat. no. 73, detail

Illustration on p. 12:
Cat. no. 60, detail

Illustration on p. 14:
Cat. no. 104

Short Title:
Francis Bacon and the Tradition of Art
Exhibition Catalogue of the Kunsthistorisches Museum and the Fondation Beyeler
Vienna and Riehen/Basel 2003
ISBN 3-85497-070-6

Exhibition

General Direction:
Wilfried Seipel
Christoph Vitali

Idea:
Wilfried Seipel

Concept:
Barbara Steffen

Curator:
Barbara Steffen

Assistant Curator:
Verena Gamper

Curatorial Assistance:
Alexandra Hennig
Felicitas Kunth

Exhibition in Vienna

Project Management:
Franz Pichorner
Barbara Steffen

Exhibition Organisation:
Gabriele Stöger
Verena Gamper

Public Relations and Media Affairs:
Annita Mader
Magdalena Pfeifer
Ruth Strondl
Julia Weitzer

Exhibition Architecture:
Blaich + Delugan

Exhibition Graphics:
Angela Hartenstein

Restoration Services:
Elke Oberthaler
Barbare Eble
Monika Strolz
Robert Wald

Guided Tours:
Gabriele Helke
Cäcilia Bischoff
Konrad Schlegel
Daniel Uchtmann

Audioguide:
Christoph Paidasch
Natalie Lettner

Exhibition in Riehen/Basel

Project Management:
Verena Formanek
Barbara Steffen

Structures, Lighting and Design:
Ben Ludwig
Dieter von Arx

Organisation of Material on Loan:
Nicole Rüegsegger
Tanja Narr

Supervision of Restoration:
Markus Gross
Friederike Steckling
Ahmed Nabbech (assistant)

Public Relations:
Catherine Schott

Corporate Communication:
Claudia Carrara
Andrea Schaller

Guides and Audioguide:
Philippe Büttner

Sponsors for Vienna:

Die Presse

ORF 1 ÖSTERREICH 1 CLUB

Sponsors for Basel:
Gemeinde Riehen
Kultur Basel-Stadt
Basler Zeitung
MANOR
Novartis
Sarasin&Cie AG
UBS

Lenders

Aberdeen, Art Gallery & Museums Collections
Aix-en-Provence, Musée Granet
Amsterdam, Stedelijk Museum
Basel, Riehen/Basel, Fondation Beyeler
Basel, Galerie Beyeler
Belfast, Ulster Museum
Bergamo, Accademia Carrara di Belle Arti
Berlin, Staatliche Museen zu Berlin, Neue Nationalgalerie
Berlin, Staatliche Museen zu Berlin, Nationalgalerie, Sammlung Berggruen
Brussels, Private Collection
Chicago, Art Institute of Chicago
Chicago, Museum of Contemporary Art
Des Moines, Iowa, Des Moines Art Center
Dublin, City Gallery The Hugh Lane
Frankfurt/Main, Städelsches Kunstinstitut und Städtische Galerie
Freiburg/Breisgau, Institut für Grenzgebiete der Psychologie und Psychohygiene e. V.
Lisbon, The Berardo Collection – Sintra Museum of Modern Art
London, Arts Council Collection and Hayward Gallery
London, The Estate of Francis Bacon
London, The National Gallery
London, Tate Gallery
London, Private Collection
Los Angeles, Collection Franklin and Susanne Konigsberg
Lyon, Musée des Beaux-Arts
Madrid, Fundación Collección Thyssen-Bornemisza
Madrid, Museo Nacional Centro de Arte Reina Sofia
Melbourne, National Gallery of Victoria
Minneapolis, Minneapolis Institute of Arts
Montauban, Musée Ingres
Napa, California,/Bern, Hess Collection
New Haven, Connecticut Yale University, Center for British Art
New York, Solomon R. Guggenheim Museum
New York, The Museum of Modern Art
New York, Collection of Samuel and Ronnie Heyman
New York, Collection of Mr. and Mrs. J. Tomilson Hill
New York, Private Collections
Norwich, University of East Anglia, Sainsbury Centre of Visual Arts
Otterlo, The Netherlands, Kröller-Müller Museum
Paris, Musée National d'Art Moderne, Centre de création industrielle Centre Georges Pompidou
Paris, Musée Picasso
Philadelphia, Philadelphia Museum of Art
Rouen, Musée des Beaux-Arts
Switzerland, Private Collections
Vaduz, Marlborough International Fine Art
Vienna, Albertina
Vienna, Kunsthistorisches Museum
Vienna, Leopold Museum – Privatstiftung
Washington D.C., Hirshhorn Museum and Sculpture Garden, Smithsonian Institution

Table of Contents

Catalogue

Appendix

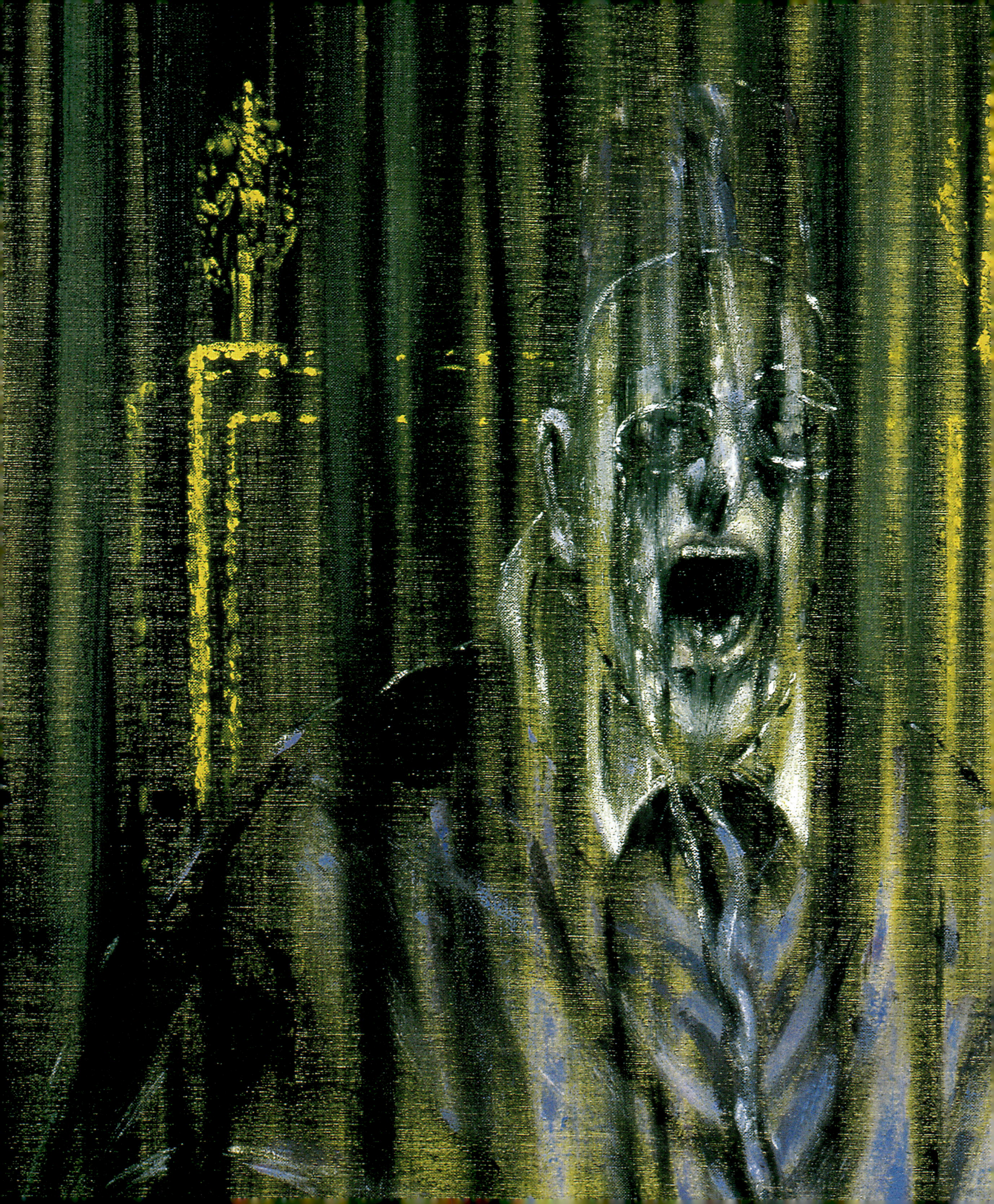

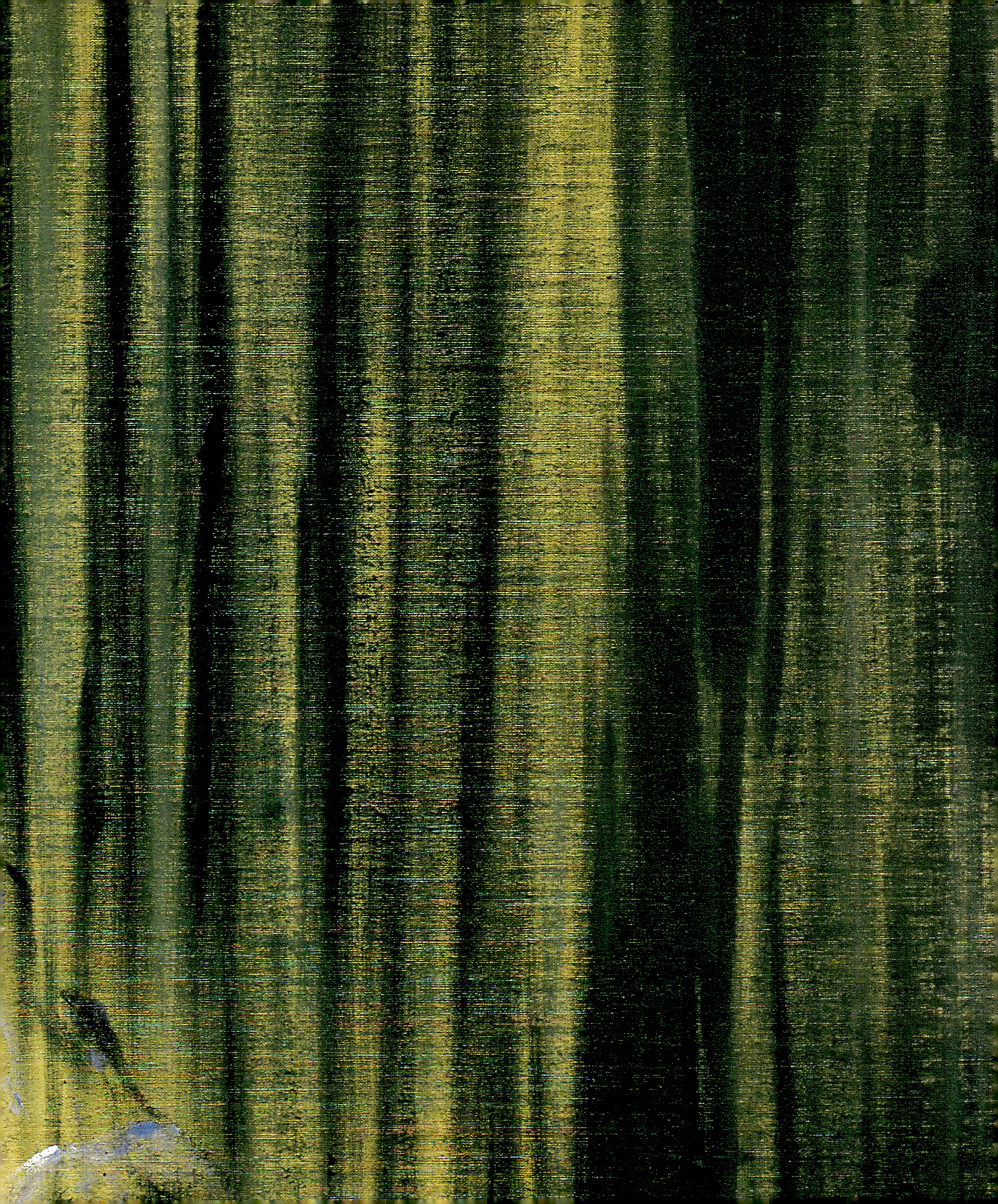

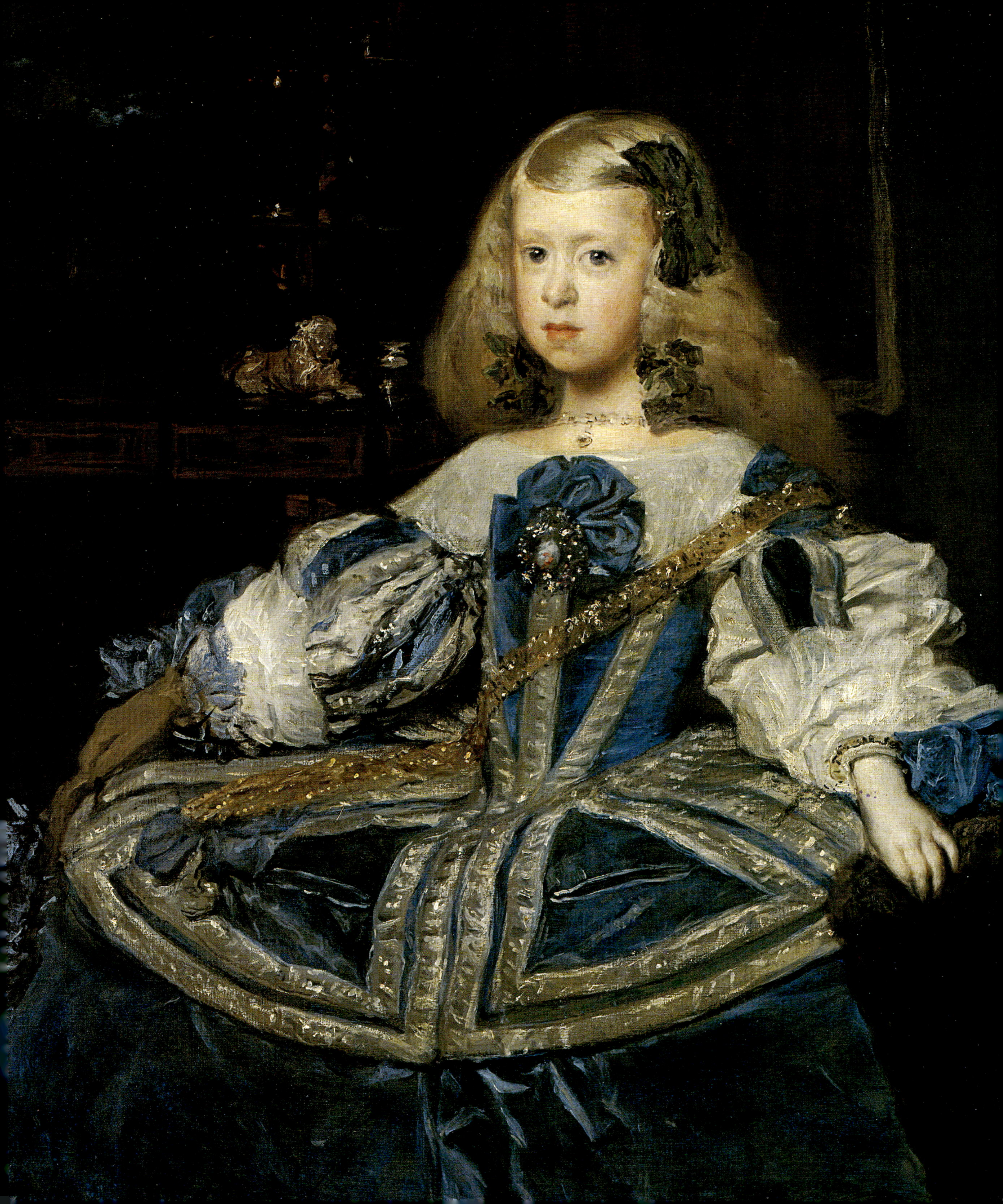

Foreword

Francis Bacon is represented in Vienna, indeed Austria, only by a single painting, a portrait in the Museum of Modern Art. While Bacon has in recent years and decades been the subject of retrospectives and large-scale exhibitions in Germany, France, Great Britain and especially the United States, his work has yet to be shown in Austria in a representative or even a smaller show.

There can be no doubt that Francis Bacon was one of the most important painters of the twentieth century. To document this with a major exhibit specially conceived for Vienna has been a project of particular importance to me for many years. The difficulties associated with realizing this plan were clear to me from the outset. Indeed many years of reflection, consideration and waiting past before, by fortunate coincidence, I found in Barbara Steffen someone who was prepared to take on the task. As curator she has been able to broaden and expand the exhibition concept, making the Kunsthistorisches Museum not only the appropriate but the ideal venue for the first Francis Bacon retrospective in Austria.

Presenting Francis Bacon's work in the context of the painterly tradition, exploring the visual heritage of his works in specific areas, and drawing on the corpus of material with which he worked, developed into a fascinating project. Indeed, at its inception I would have hardly dared hope for the realization of the exhibition in its present scope. Barbara Steffen's concept convinced not only many private and public lenders, but also institutions which preserve objects that were an important source of inspiration for Bacon and thus for the subject of the present exhibition.

Upon reading the opening lines of Ms. Steffen's essay, "Painterly Tradition and Coincidence in Francis Bacon," one may well ask whether the juxtaposition of Bacon's works and his models, which he generally comprehended in a merely associative way, really reflects Bacon's intentions, ideas and respect for the artistic tradition. In 1985 Bacon himself acted as curator for an exhibition at the National Gallery in London. For this show he selected the works from the museum that he considered most important and displayed them in the manner he deemed most appropriate. He declined for whatever reason – be it insecurity or respect – to hang these works side by side with his own, as had originally been planned. The study, which has only recently become possible, of Bacon's "inspirational material," innumerable illustrations culled from art books and magazines, photographs and sketches that he kept in his atelier, provided the concept for the Kunsthistorisches Museum's retrospective.

I should like to express our thanks to the numerous lenders for the exhibition, including the Solomon R. Guggenheim Museum, New York, which has provided us with Bacon's 1962 triptych, Three Studies for a Crucifixion, that has not been shown outside the United States for many years. Special thanks are due to private lenders who have agreed to part with important works from their collections for a lengthy period.

I should similarly like to express my appreciation to the staff of the Kunsthistorisches Museum, and in particular to Franz Pichorner, Gabriele Stöger and Annita Mader, who made such an exceptional effort to bring this exhibition to fruition. Of course, our greatest debt of thanks is due to exhibition curator Barbara Steffen, who has here realized her most impressive magnum opus.

I am particularly pleased that out of our original request for a loan from the Beyeler Collection evolved the idea of presenting "Francis Bacon and the Tradition of Art" at one of the most magnificent museum buildings of our time in Riehen, following its run at the Kunsthistorisches Museum. I am very grateful indeed to Ernst Beyeler and Christoph Vitali for their cooperation and generosity in lending objects for the exhibit.

Wilfried Seipel
Generaldirektor, Kunsthistorisches Museum

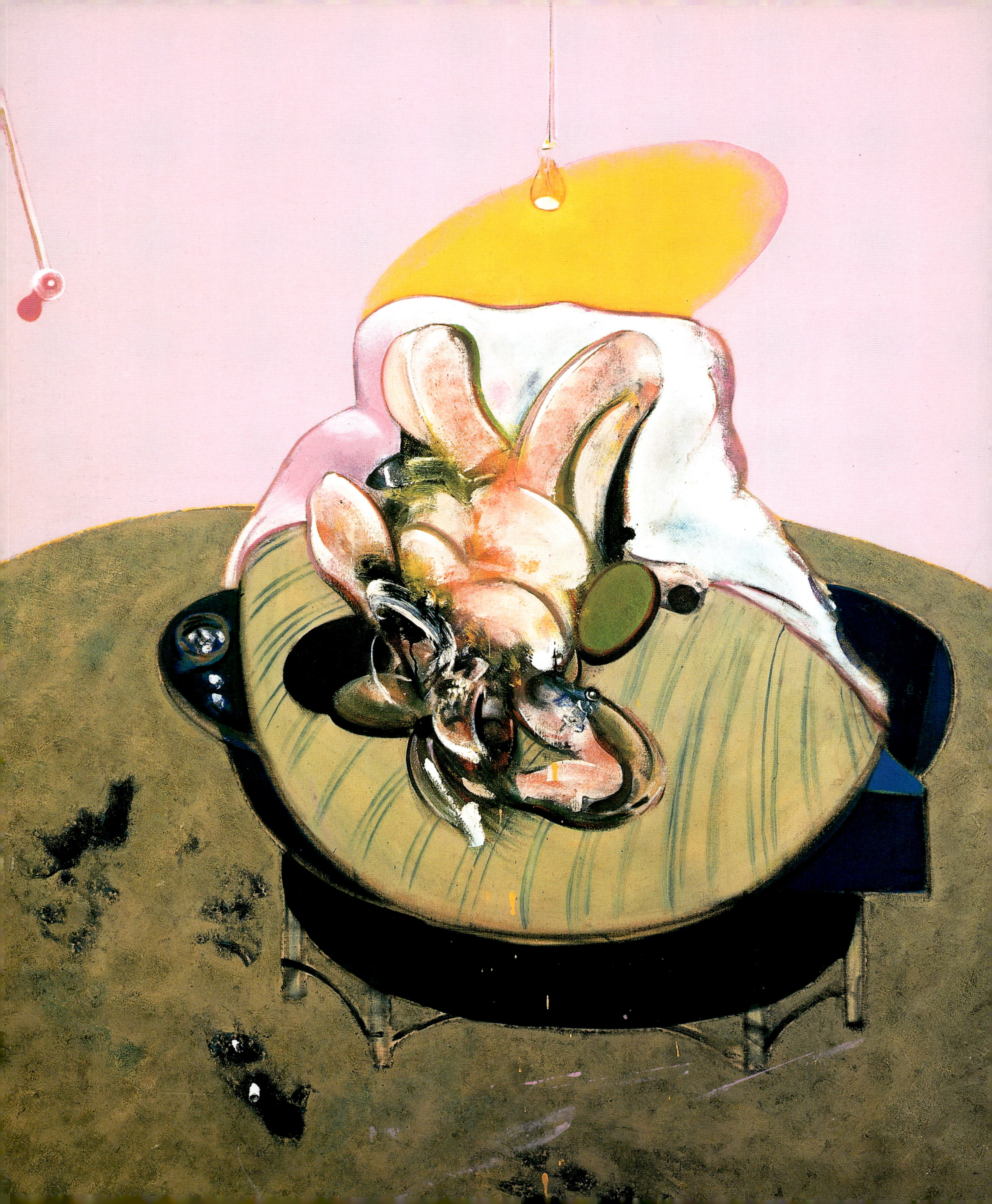

Observations on Francis Bacon

When I first saw the works of Francis Bacon in the 1950's they struck me as that of a surrealistic Baroque painter. He painted brutal subjects in soft, precious colours, and had something of a twilight Mannerism. When years later I met Bacon personally he seemed very reserved, sensitive, controlled and cultivated, but with characteristics that bespoke tremendous tensions. One sensed that he was an artist whose work was difficult to approach, and that among his contemporaries he was absolutely unique as a painter.

Upon the first encounter with the pictures of Francis Bacon one is taken aback by the apparently banal evidence of corporeal conditions, only to be immediately spellbound by the powerful statements of figures that move and float as though in a space ship, of lines that support a cage or a ramp so as to simultaneously highlight and isolate the portrayed, and also by the invariably genial concordance of content and form. Bacon wrestles again and again with unreality to create a reality that makes the viewer uneasy and insecure. On this Bacon said, "I think that Realism must be reinvented. It has to be continually reinvented. In one of his letters van Gogh speaks of the necessity of making changes in reality that become lies which are truer than the pure truth. That is the only way a painter can recreate the intensity of the reality he attempts to capture. I think that reality in art is something profoundly artificial and that it has to be created anew, otherwise it would be merely an illustration for some purpose and thus in fact hearsay" (Sylvester, 1997, p. 174).

The joint effort with Wilfried Seipel of the Kunsthistorisches Museum in Vienna and the curator of the exhibition, Barbara Steffen, has given us a unique opportunity to document with original works Bacon's network of association with the great masters who he admired – from Titian to Velázquez, Rembrandt, Degas and Picasso – reproductions of whose work he displayed on the floor of his atelier. In this way he was able to create his pictures in the context of a continuous dialogue with art, and place them on a new existential level. Christoph Vitali and I would like to thank Prof. Dr. Wilfried Seipel, Dr. Franz Pichorner and the curator, Barbara Steffen M.A., for making possible this presentation of the world of Francis Bacon and for the ideal spirit of co-operation in which we have worked together on this fascinating project.

Ernst Beyeler
Fondation Beyeler

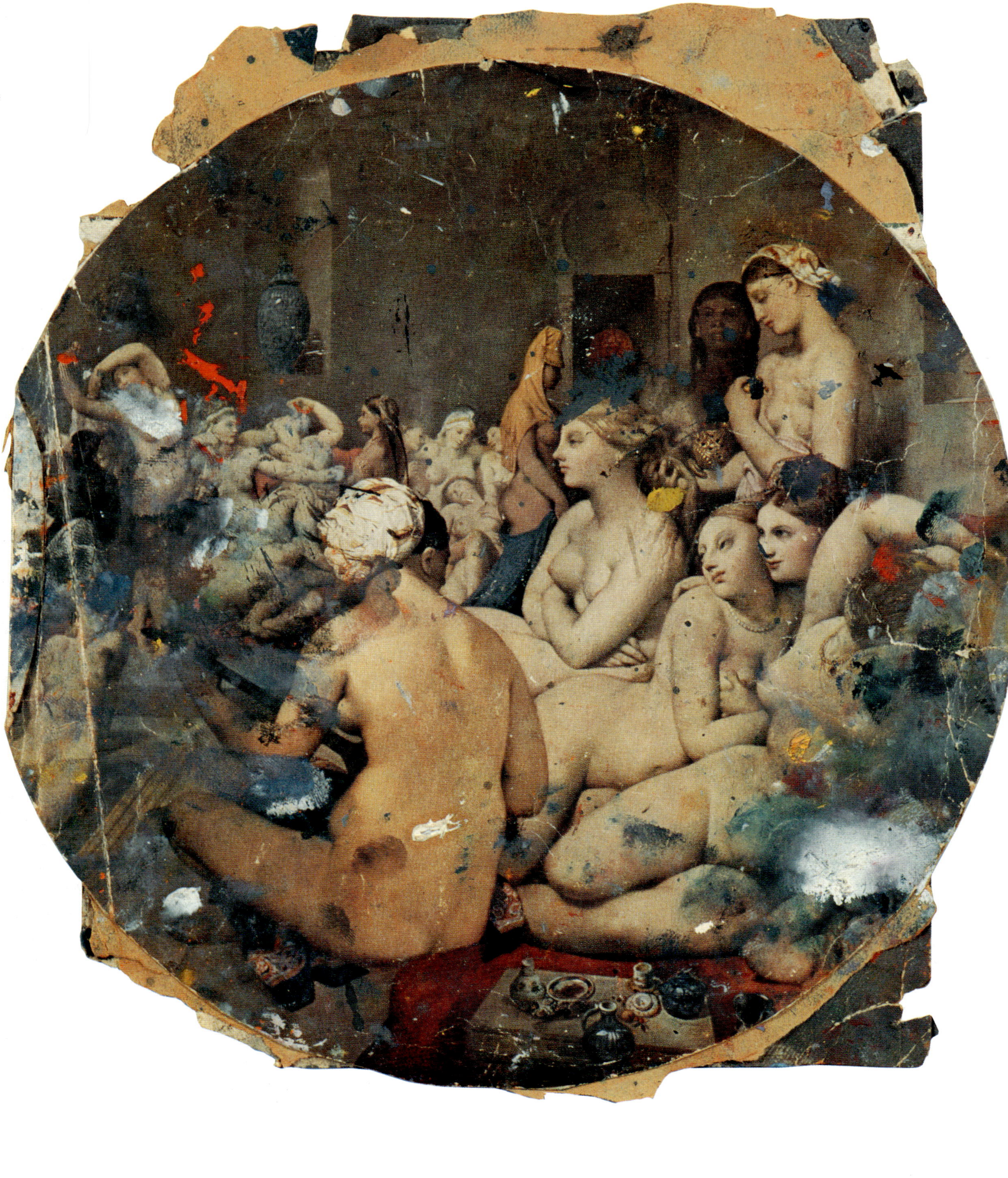

Introduction to the Exhibition

The exhibition Francis Bacon and the Tradition of Art *will be presented in the Picture Gallery of Vienna's Kunsthistorisches Museum, which also has paintings by Titian, Velázquez and Rembrandt in its collection. Thus it is possible to present Francis Bacon's works next to paintings that served as models and sources of inspiration to him. In contemplating the title of the exhibition,* Francis Bacon and the Tradition of Art, *visitors to the museum will also wonder what is meant by the term "tradition of art." The expression is drawn from art theory and denotes the transmission of the cultural heritage of artistic skills and knowledge, and a holding fast to works of the past, especially in painting. A break with this tradition manifests itself in an artist's conceptual and visual progress. Famous artists of Modern Art such as Mondrian and Kandinsky began their careers as figurative painters and evolved in the course of their artistic development into Abstraction. A significant break can be discerned in their works when they freed themselves from tradition and created something new in art.*

The case of the English painter Francis Bacon, who was born in Dublin in 1909 and died in Madrid in 1992, is different. Bacon's first experiments as an artist were in the tradition of German Bauhaus decorative art and furniture design. His early efforts were close to Surrealism of the twenties, and he frequently remarked that it was Picasso's work of that period which moved him to become a painter. Bacon was self-taught. He never attended an art school and his sole artistic mentor was the Australian painter Roy de Maistre. Although Bacon had no academic training, he had a consuming interest in the works of other artists, as well as in literature, film and music. He spoke French fluently, knew Greek and Spanish, read T.S. Eliot, James Joyce and Ezra Pound. Bacon also became an expert on film and was intimately acquainted with the genre from Eisenstein to Visconti, and collected books about film directors. His great passion though was painting and sculpture. He kept books in his studio about Velázquez, Rembrandt, Ingres, Van Gogh and Soutine, Greek sculpture and Egyptian art. Bacon never became an abstract or geometric painter. He did not think much of Abstract Expressionism; instead he went his own way, independent of the prevailing artistic currents of his day. In a way he remained an outsider his entire life. While he maintained close friendships with other artists, among them Lucian Freud and Alberto Giacometti, his circle of friends was composed mainly of eccentric bohemians with whom he drank through the night in bars and pubs.

The more Bacon immersed himself in the tradition of painting and sculpture, the more intense did his paintings become. He is certainly the only twentieth-century artist, who over many years created a series of paintings inspired by Velázquez's famous portrait of Pope Innocent X. Bacon was fascinated by Van Gogh, Ingres and Rembrandt as can be clearly seen in his interpretations. However, it was Picasso and Giacometti who were of particular importance as artistic sources for Bacon and who changed his work. Francis Bacon was a recognised artist as early as the late 1940's. His works were acquired by the Museum of Modern Art in New York and London's Tate Gallery shortly after his first great successes in the late forties and early fifties. Few painters have expressed their opinions so convincingly about the work of other artists from the most varied periods as did Francis Bacon. He was interviewed on several occasions between 1962 and 1986 by art critic David Sylvester. Reading these published conversations one can learn much about Bacon's preferences, interests and his relationship to artists of other epochs. Bacon left many questions about how he stands in relation to his own work unanswered, or replied only superficially so as to evade the critic's probing. Even as an understanding of Bacon's method and his obsessive fascination with artists like Velázquez and Picasso may be gleaned from details, he leaves considerable room for fresh interpretations.

Bacon found inexhaustible sources of inspiration in the tradition of art – that is the tradition of painting, sculpture and drawing – as well as in the visual impulses of the everyday world such as advertising, photographs of animals, anatomical studies, sports photos, and snapshots of friends. In fact, any picture that depicted the unusual, special or horrible fascinated him. This exhibition is not intended as a retrospective of Bacon's work similar to those staged by a number of major international museums like the Centre Pompidou in Paris and the Tate Gallery in London. The complex concept that underlies the present exhibition is to trace Bacon's statements and place his works in the context of his predecessors so as to illuminate his relationship to tradition. This exhibit is the first opportunity to examine his works side by side with the artists who inspired him, and in this way to cast at least some light on how he conceived and devised his paintings.

Seldom in the history of twentieth-century art has it been possible to analyse in such detail the influence of one artist upon another as here with the works of Francis Bacon and the artistic tradition. Not only did works by Velázquez, Soutine and Picasso serve as a source of inspiration for Bacon, but also the material that he kept in his London studio. Complementing the paintings at this exhibition are documents that illustrate Bacon's method and the creation of his works. These include over sixty-five objects, from newspaper clippings to art books, overpainted photographs and partially torn pictures, which were part of Bacon's documentary material. These artefacts have been selected from the reconstruction of his studio at the Hugh Lane City Gallery in Dublin. This "studio material," as I call it, was of great importance for Bacon and thus deserves an appropriate place at this exhibition. Indeed, this material is the missing link between the tradition of art and Bacon's oeuvre. Only careful study of these images, altered and distorted by Bacon, permits an insight into his creative process. The artist manipulated these photographs and advertisements with paper clips, by slashing and overpainting. The viewer will see that Bacon was inspired not just by original works by Velázquez, Rembrandt or Picasso, but that he used reproductions of their works, as he had modified them, as the model for his own paintings. Bacon adopted the motif from the tradition, but the subsequent treatment of these images, which is reflected in his oil paintings, was executed by Bacon himself.

To define the various areas within Bacon's oeuvre more closely, the exhibition has been divided into sixteen thematic groups, including the pope series, the motif of the scream, cage, meat and the Crucifixion, and mirror, as well as the juxtaposition of Bacon's works with those of Velázquez, Ingres, the Surrealists and others. Each thematic group brings together works from the artistic tradition (Titian, Velázquez, Ingres, etc.), Bacon's oil paintings and studio material. All three areas should be studied with equal interest for each presupposes the other. In so doing the visitor will understand why the Kunsthistorisches Museum is the first location for this exhibition, in which tradition defines the modern. In 1973 Francis Bacon spoke with David Sylvester about the paintings of Titian and Velázquez in the Kunsthistorisches Museum, saying "I can see the unbelievable quality of Titian. The Lucretia and Tarquin in Vienna, for example, is considered, I believe, to be one of Titian's greatest works. When you place it next to the Philip Prosper that is also there however, Velázquez seems so much realer and so much more revealing" (Sylvester 2000, p. 239). The second location at which the exhibition will be shown, the Fondation Beyeler in Riehen near Basel, is a museum of the Modern Art. It houses wonderful paintings by Cézanne, Picasso, Giacometti and many other artists, particularly exponents of Impressionism and modern art. Upon a visit to the museum I saw Picasso's work exhibited in one of the museum's largest galleries. At a single glance Picasso's world opened itself up to me. It was easy to understand why an artist like Francis Bacon decided to become a painter after having seen a work by Picasso for the first time in Paris in 1928. The valuable artworks lent for this exhibition by the Fondation Beyeler help to further flesh out the relationship between the tradition of the Old Masters, Modern Art and Bacon's work. This exhibition thus seeks to present Bacon's oeuvre in a new context, allowing visitors to immerse themselves in the various artistic traditions from the Old Masters to Impressionism to twentieth-century sculpture to films of the 1920's and to advertising photographs and cuttings of daily newspapers.

Barbara Steffen, MA
Curator of the Exhibition

Cat.no. 14A
Francis Bacon
Study after Velázquez
1950
Oil on canvas, 198 × 137.2 cm
London, The Estate
of Francis Bacon
(© The Estate of Francis Bacon / VBK, Vienna, 2003)

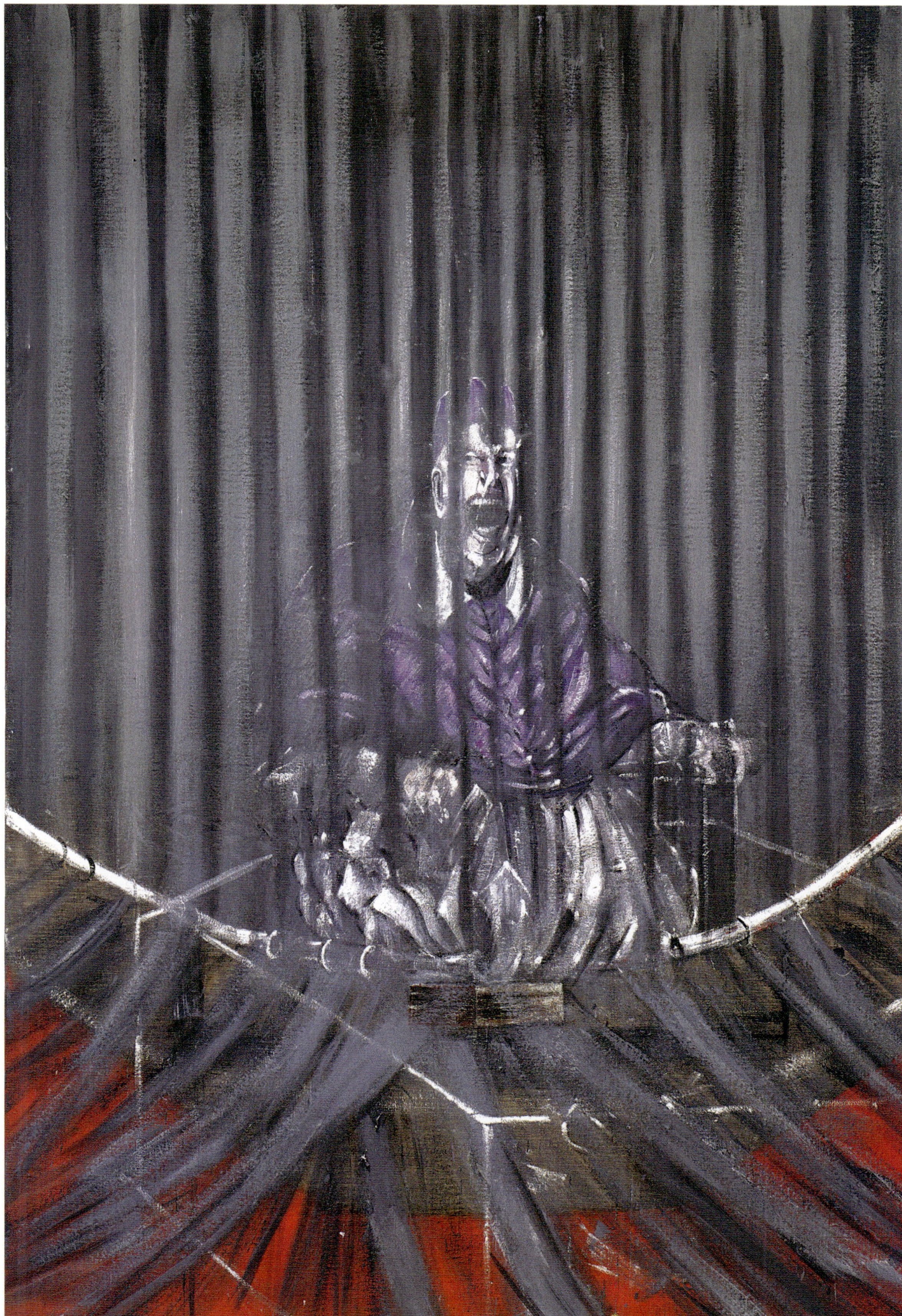

Cat. no. 14A

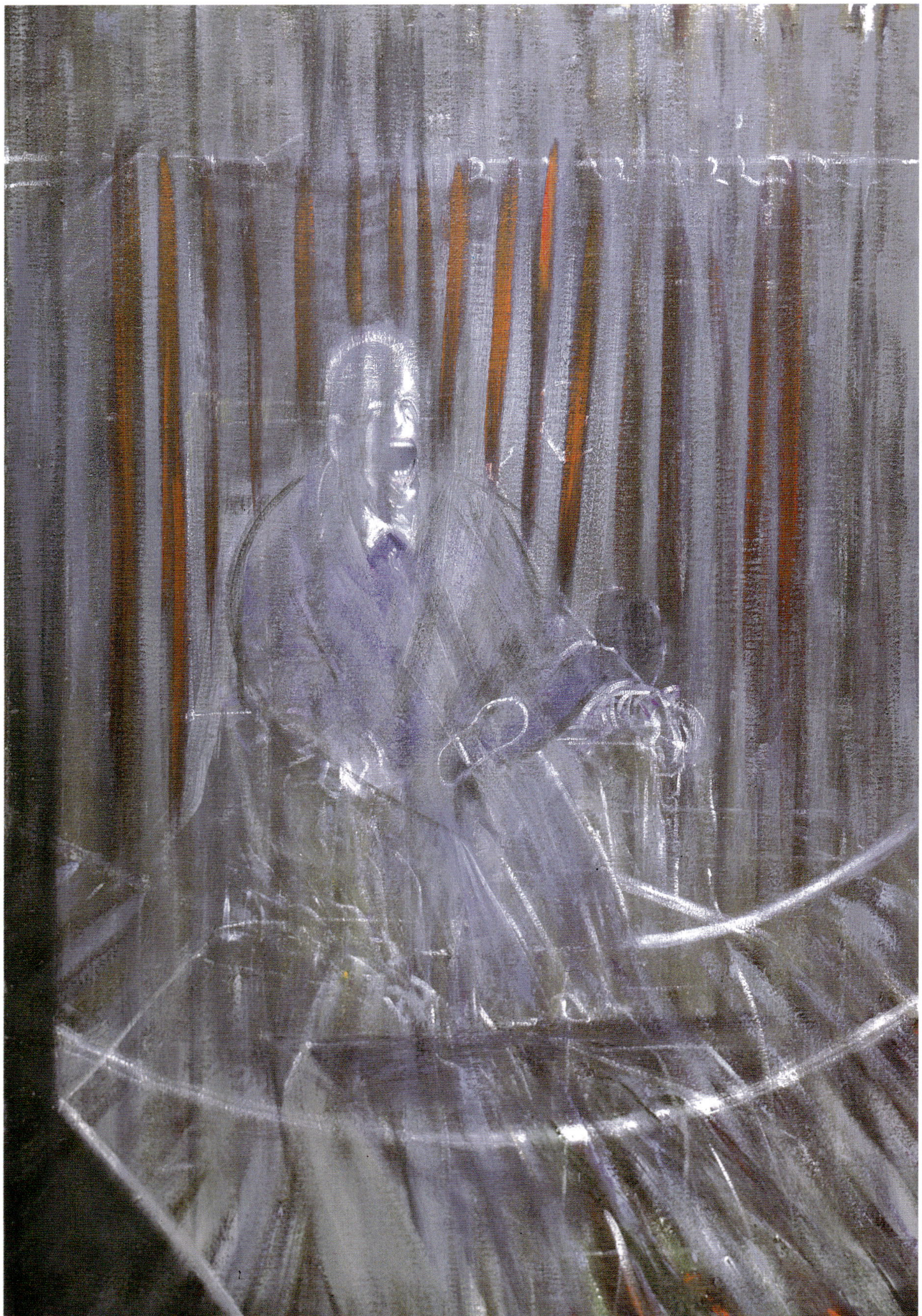

Cat. no. 14B

Cat.no. 14B
Francis Bacon
Untitled (Pope)
1950
Oil on canvas, 198 × 137.2 cm
London, The Estate
of Francis Bacon
(© The Estate of Francis Bacon
/ VBK, Vienna, 2003)

Acknowledgements

Over the almost three years that it has taken to organise this extensive exhibition and the accompanying publication, I would never have been able to manage alone all the various tasks involved, from design to logistics and catalogue production. It was Wilfried Seipel who gave me the confidence to realise this project; he invariably supported my ideas and promoted the venture with tremendous energy. I am indeed indebted to him for making this exhibition possible; he was untiring and surmounted all the hurdles encountered with ease. Franz Pichorner was from the inception of the project a partner who played a central role and with whom I was able to discuss all of my considerations and concerns. His enthusiasm and diplomacy helped to make this plan become reality. Without the cooperation of major museums and private collectors, we would not have been able to secure the many loans of works from around the world. Here I would like to express my appreciation to all those who have been so generous in lending paintings to the Kunsthistorisches Museum and the Fondation Beyeler for this exhibition. Although all are named in the list of lenders, I would like here to mention a number of them for special thanks, as well as other persons who assisted in securing individual loans.

Ernst Beyeler's boundless passion for art led to his not only becoming the most prominent lender of the exhibition, but also its host starting in Switzerland in February 2004. Christoph Vitali, the new director of the Fondation Beyeler, drew on his extensive experience to mount the exhibition in Switzerland. Verena Formanek represented the foundation efficiently and coordinated the venture most professionally. I would further like to thank Paul Asenbaum, Vienna, Heinz Berggruen, Berlin, Ivor Braka, London, Leonard Cuenod, Bern, Lisa Denisson, chief curator of the Solomon R. Guggenheim Museum, New York, James Demitrion, director of the De Menil Collection in Houston, Tomilson Hill, New York, Thomas Krens, director of the Solomon R. Guggenheim Museum, New York, Margo Leavin, Los Angeles, Hans-Jürgen Papies, curator of the Berggruen Collection, Berlin, as well as Susan L. Talbott, director of the Des Moines Art Center. A special note of thanks goe to Margarita Cappock, curator of the Hugh Lane City Gallery of Dublin, who researches and manages the material in Francis Bacon's reconstructed studio in Dublin, and provided me with much helpful information about the artist. To her as well as to Ernst van Alphen, Olivier Berggruen, Norman Bryson, Michael Peppiatt and the other contributors goes my appreciation for the inspiring essays in the catalogue. The intensive preparation of the project by the Kunsthistorisches Museum would not have been possible without Annita Mader and her Public Relations Department, as well as Gabriele Stöger.

Karl Schütz and Wolfgang Prohaska of the Kunsthistorisches Museum's Picture Gallery assisted in curatorial advice for the exhibition. For the support in preparing the illustrations for the catalogue I would like to thank Stefan Zeisler and Thomas Ritter. The exhibition catalogue would never have been produced in time were it not for Elisabeth Herrmann. For the publishing of the catalogue we are indebted to Skira, especially to Massimo Vitta Zelman, Manoli Traxler and Marzia Branca of Milan. The informative audio guide was prepared by Christoph Paidasch and Natalie Lettner. The task of designing the exhibition was taken over with great enthusiasm by Dieter Blaich and Kai Delugan. The realization of the exhibition concept, research, organisation of loans, editing of the catalogue, and the concept of the installation was only possible with the help of my curatorial team. I would like to express my appreciation to my curatorial assistant Verena Gamper for her enormous energy, as well as to Alexandra Hennig, Felicitas Kunth and Benjamin Dobler whose assistance was invaluable. I am personally indebted to Professor Friedrich Teja Bach of the Department of Art History at the university in Vienna for his perceptive advice and suggestions.

This publication is dedicated to my parents Professor Carl Steffen (1918–89) and Margarethe Steffen.

Barbara Steffen, MA
Curator of the Exhibition

Essays

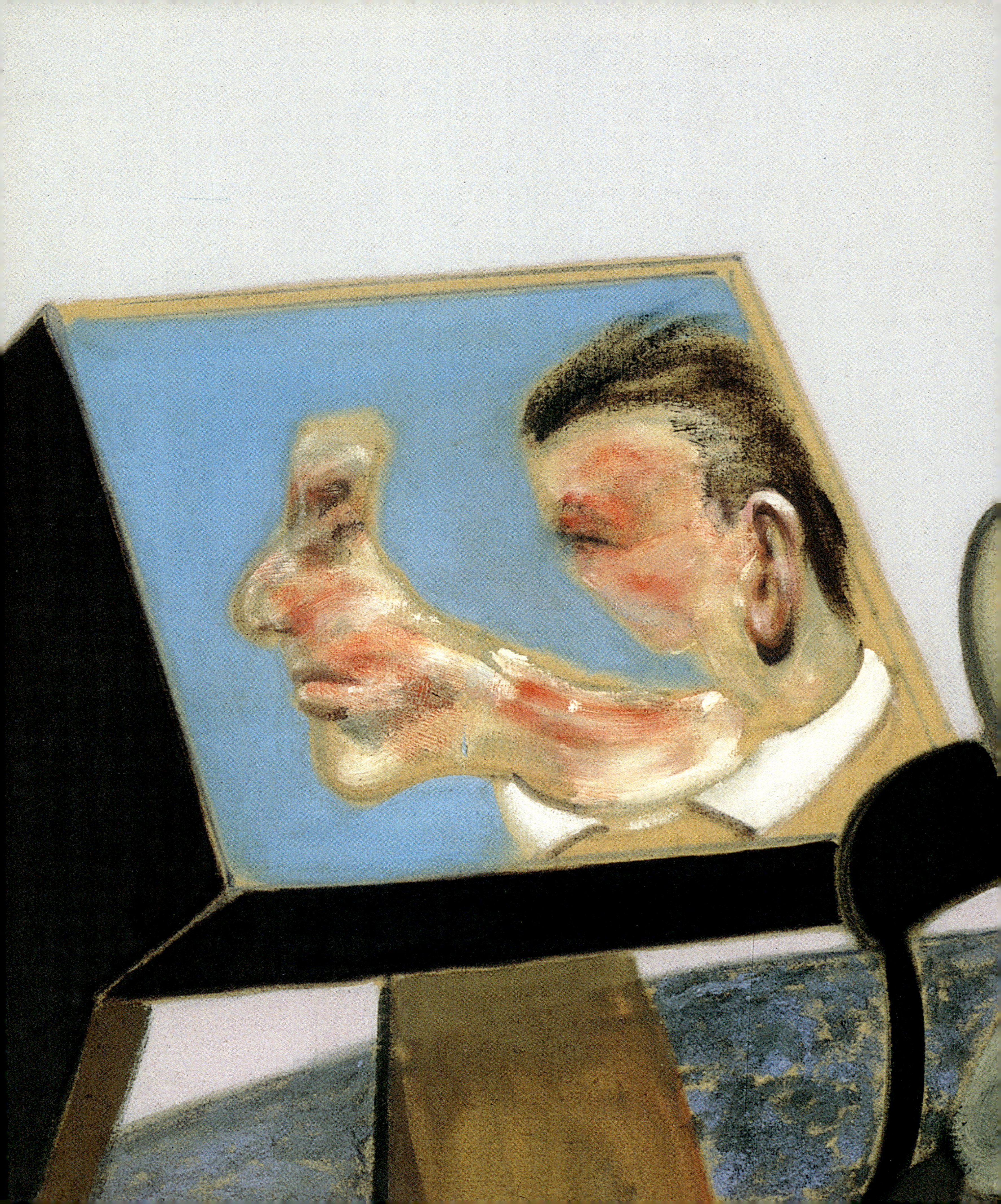

Barbara Steffen

Chance and the Tradition of Art in Francis Bacon's Work

The Exhibition "The Artist's Eye"

On October 23, 1985, the National Gallery in London opened an exhibition by Francis Bacon. The artist had been invited by the museum to select and present the works from the collection of the National Gallery that meant the most to him. At that time the artists R. B. Kitaj, Howard Hodgkin and David Hockney had already served as curators at the request of the National Gallery. Bacon was thus the fourth artist to curate an exhibition in the series *The Artist's Eye*. Each of the artists had been requested to integrate one or more of his own works into the respective exhibition. But Bacon was adamant in his refusal to present his own pictures in this context. The director of the National Gallery, Michael Levey, then cancelled the exhibition, and it was only after David Sylvester intervened with the museum association that Bacon was allowed to assemble the show under his own conditions.

From the collection's masterpieces Bacon selected 18 paintings, dating from the 15th to the 20th century. This selection reflected his interest in artists whose work had influenced his own. In the foreword to the catalogue Michael Levey wrote: "What he would select among favourite paintings in the National Gallery was, predictably, going to be both stimulating and revealing – if by no means always foreseen. He has not wished to be led into commenting on these paintings, whose greatness is perhaps the sole factor they share. [...] Borrowing the artist's eye, we are permitted to see a concentration of the very greatest paintings from several centuries."[1]

Bacon's selection, which is testimony to the quality of his artistic eye, was Masaccio's *Virgin with Child and Angels*, Michelangelo's unfinished *Entombment*, Velázquez's *Portrait of Philip IV of Spain* and *The Toilet of Venus*, two *Portraits of Margaretha de Geer* by Rembrandt, Goya's *Don Andrés del Peral* as well as Ingres's *Madame Mortessier Seated*. The other paintings were Turner's *Rain, Steam, and Speed*, Van Gogh's *A Cornfield with Cypresses* and *The Chair and the Pipe*, Degas' *Woman Drying Herself*, Cézanne's *The Grounds of Château Noir*, Manet's fragments of *The Execution of Maximilian* and four works by Seurat: *Bathers*, Sketch for *Bathers, Asnières*, *Study for Sunday Afternoon on the Island of La Grande Jatte: Man Fishing*, and *Man Fishing from a Boat at its Moorings*.

In his selection of paintings Bacon concentrated on the depiction of the human figure – for example Masaccio's enthroned Madonna – or on the representation of the naked body in Michelangelo's *Entombment of Christ* as well as on the bather in Degas' pastel of the *Woman Drying Herself*. The manner in which the paintings were hung and arranged was remarkable. It was not chronologically based on the sequence in which the paintings were created, because Bacon was primarily concerned with the relationships of the figural motifs. He placed Manet's fragment, for example, next to the *Portrait of Madame Mortessier* by Ingres, Masaccio's *Virgin* next to Seurat's *Grand Jatte* and Michelangelo's *Entombment* between Degas' pastel of a *Woman Drying Herself* and Van Gogh's *Chair and Pipe (Plates 2 and 3)*. Bacon did not write an essay for the catalogue, but he did make a short statement as an introduction: "I am not writing a foreword – I have often tried to talk about painting but writing or talking about it is only an approximation as painting is its own language and is not translatable into words. The Manet I have chosen I know is completely changed from what Manet painted but I very much like the montage that has been made of the fragments. The question of fragments is a fascinating and endless subject. Would the Elgin Marbles have been so beautiful to us if we had them now in their original state?"[2]

Despite the unusual way the pictures were hung, the newspaper reviews were astonishingly good. The London newspaper The Observer wrote, for example, "It's easy enough to spot symbolic and formal affinities by shuffling National Gallery postcards. Regrouping the originals, outside their usual Schools and eras, is a different matter. Disparities of scale and handling, as well as subject-matter, make for difficulties. The chance to juxtapose paintings normally kept apart has been given to few so far and Bacon is the first to let the paintings speak for themselves without even an

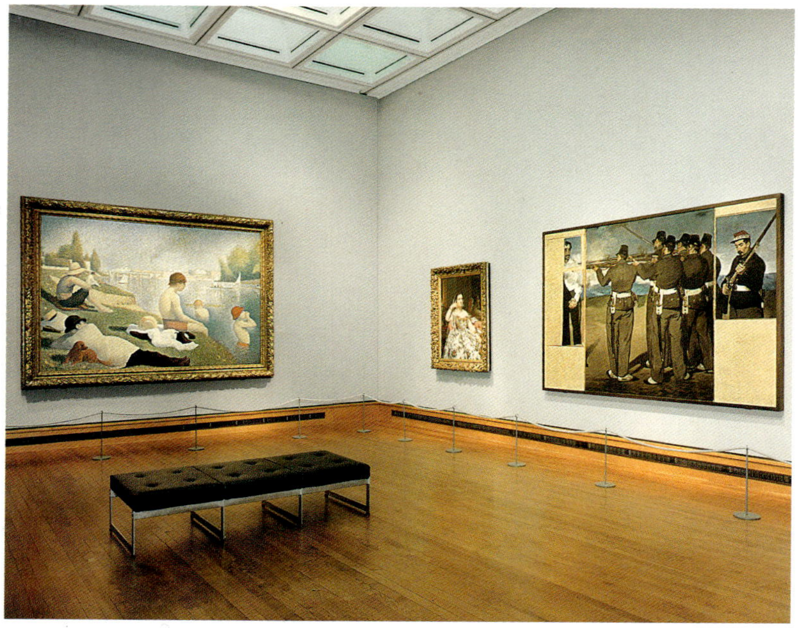

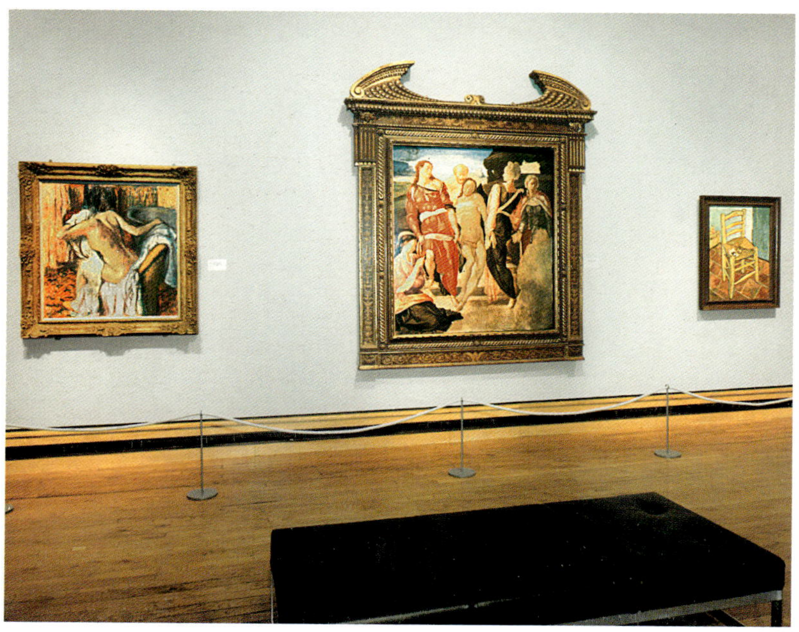

Plate 1 on p. 22: Francis Bacon, Study of George Dyer in a Mirror, detail. 1968 (cat. no. 120).

Plate 2: View of the exhibition The Artist's Eye, 1986. Seurat, Ingres, Manet. (©: The Estate of Francis Bacon/Dublin, Collection City Gallery The Hugh Lane.)

Plate 3: View of the exhibition The Artist's Eye, 1986. Degas, Michelangelo, Van Gogh. (©: The Estate of Francis Bacon/ Dublin, Collection City Gallery The Hugh Lane.)

example of his own work introduced to speak for him."[3] According to Sylvester, the reason why Bacon refused to show his own paintings in the exhibition next to those by the Old Masters was that Bacon "did not believe his work to be worthy of such a context."[4] The question remains, however, whether the artist meant that literally or whether his rejection was related to the problem of his proximity to his sources. As is well known, Bacon – like Manet – did not work from original artworks but mainly from photographs taken from art books and reproductions from magazines and catalogues.

The Borrowing of Motifs

The art historian Richard Wollheim describes the phenomenon of the artistic "way of borrowing" using Edouard Manet as an example. He refers to Harold Bloom, who in *The Anxiety of Influence* investigates the theme of an artist's fear of artistic influence as found in British and American literature. Wollheim explains this fear as resulting primarily from two factors: from the rivalry that exists between the present and the past, which is, of course, a natural condition, and from the fact that artists are always more likely to "borrow" motifs and compositions from other artists that they admire and esteem. The element that links rivalry and admiration is envy. "Envy, it is crucial to see, will not arise from rivalry alone: it requires admiration – finding the rival good – as additive. But whether any particular mixture of admiration and rivalry will, in the case of a particular artist, give rise to envy depends on the rest of the psychological constitution."[5] Envy, adds Wollheim, creates fear and insecurity, which the respective person begins to resist. He pursues this thought further, coming to the conclusion that envy hinders creativity: "Envy of such an order makes creativity impossible."[6]

One may assume that artists such as Manet, Picasso and Bacon were very aware, on the one hand, of their rivalry with and simultaneous admiration for other artists, and that each of them reacted to it very differently in his work. But the kind of envy that Wollheim describes is not evident in this manner. He adds, however, that there is also fear of envy, and that uncertainty and confusion are employed in order to reduce it, as in the case of Edouard Manet. His compositions are frequently based on works by such artists as Rubens, Rembrandt and Velázquez, as a comparison of Manet's *Tragic Actor* of 1865/66 with Velázquez's *Pablo de Valladolid* of 1632–35 reveals *(Plates 4 and 5)*. Manet's borrowing of motifs from tradition, his "way of borrowing" in order "to compensate for the poverty of his imagination"[7] has essentially two aspects. On the one hand, this borrowing usually does not result from a

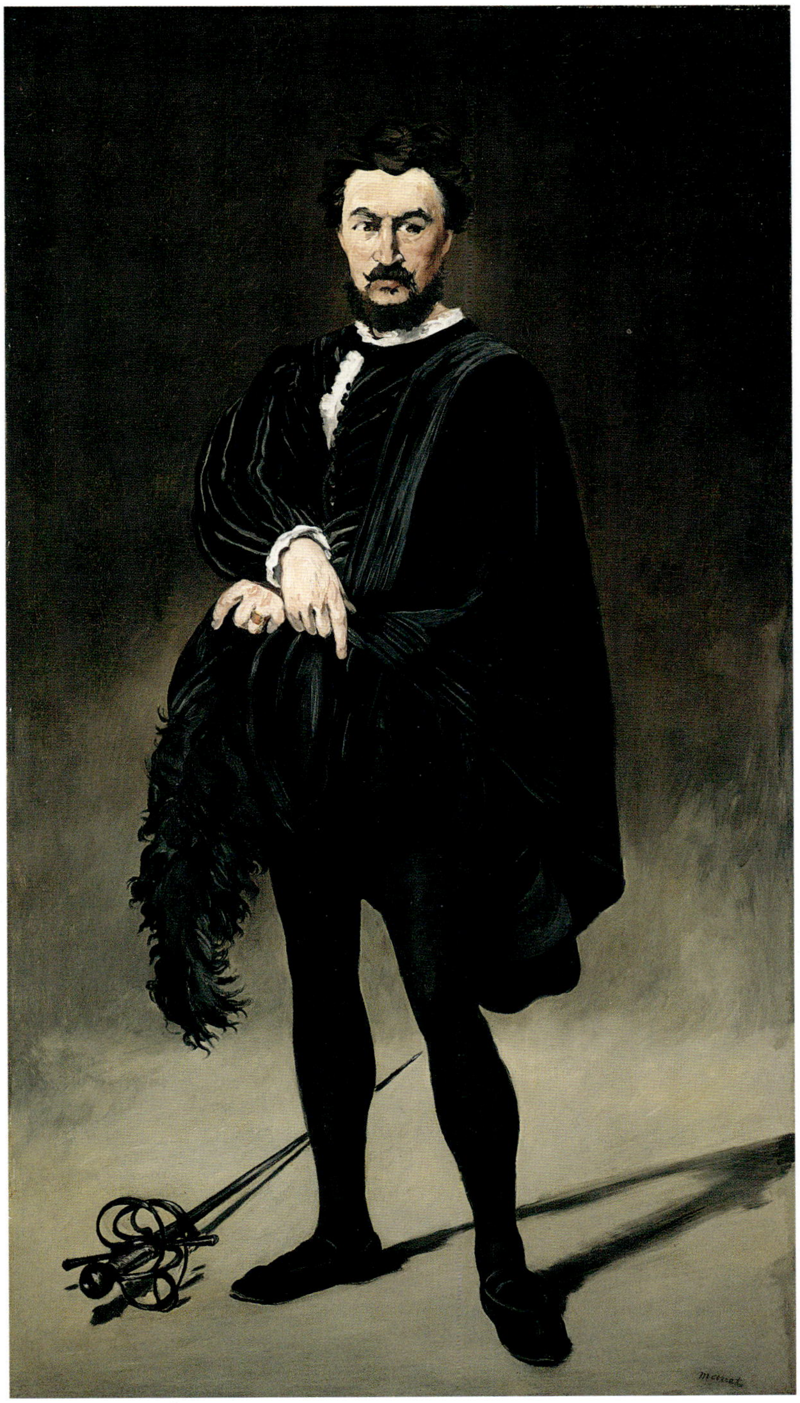

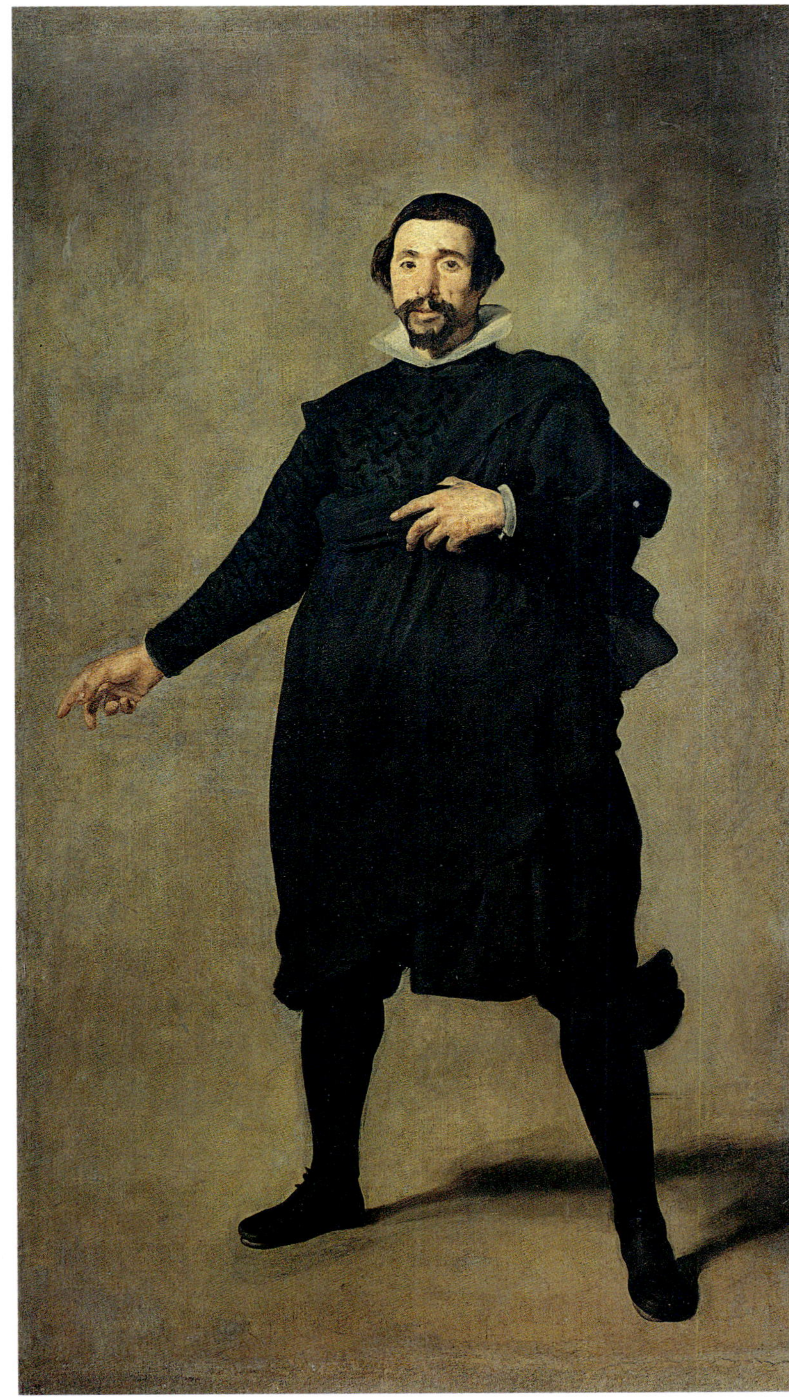

Plate 4: Edouard Manet, The Tragic Actor (Rouvière as Hamlet). 1865–66. Oil on canvas, 187.2 × 108.1 cm. Washington, The National Gallery. (©: Washington, The National Gallery.)

Plate 5: Diego de Silva y Velázquez, The Jester Pablo de Valladolid. Around 1632/34. Oil on canvas, 209 × 123 cm. Madrid, Museo del Prado. (©: Madrid, Museo del Prado, photo: Peter Willi – Artothek.)

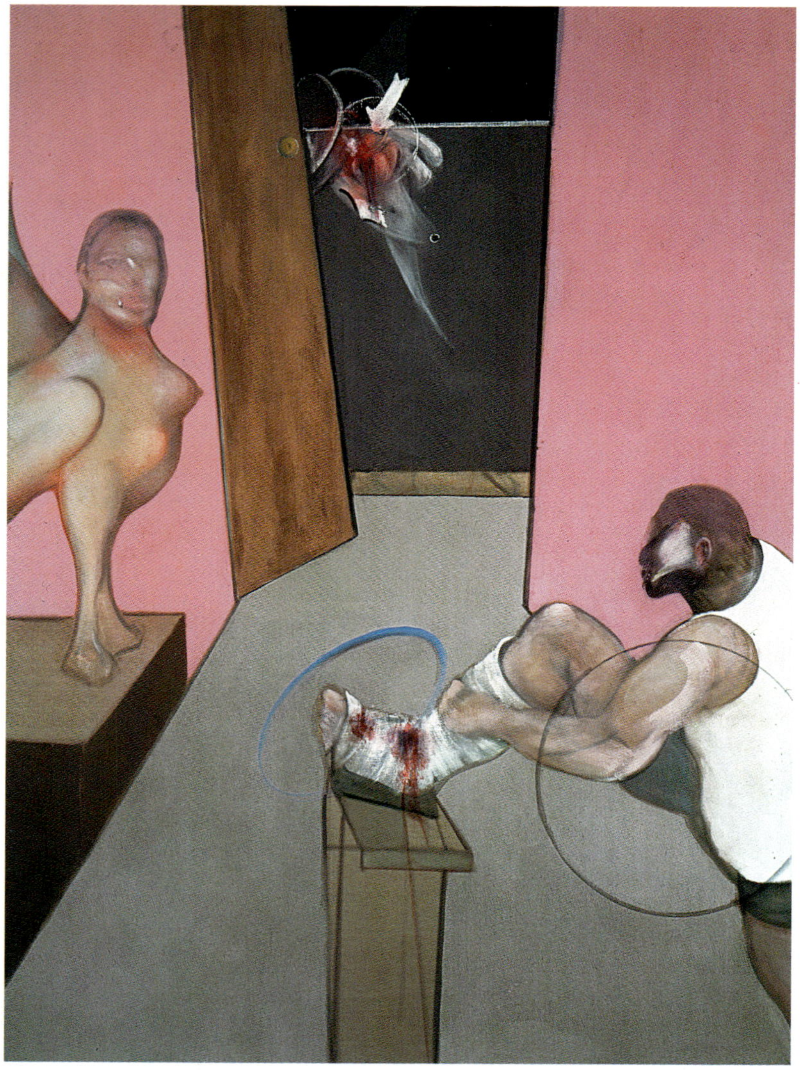

Plate 6: Francis Bacon, Oedipus and the Sphinx after Ingres. 1983 (cat. no. 97).

study of original artworks but of illustrations, frequently from Charles Blanc's *Histoire des peintres de toutes les écoles,* Paris 1861–76. On the other hand, Manet often did not focus on a single source but rather created a collage from several pictorial motifs by different artists. Manet admired the artists he used as models for his work and created even closer relationships to them in order not to be overwhelmed by them.

Bacon painted his version of *Oedipus and the Sphinx* of 1983 after Ingres's *Oedipus* painting of around 1826/27, which is on display in the National Gallery in London *(Plates 6 and 7).* Two other versions of Ingres's picture are in the collections in the Louvre in Paris and the Walters Art Gallery in Baltimore. The Louvre version is among the reproductions of Ingres's paintings collected by Bacon. In this case, Bacon borrowed not only the mythological theme but also the general composition from his model. Thus Oedipus is shown in profile, standing at the right side of the picture, his body cut off by the right edge. His right leg is raised and bent at the knee, in a position similar to the figure in Ingres's work. But in Bacon's painting both the lower leg and foot are wrapped in a white bandage through which blood is seeping. In contrast to Ingres's painting, Oedipus is not naked, but wearing an undershirt and dark training shorts. The Sphinx is on a plinth at the left side of the painting. Her head is held at a slight angle to the painter's view, and her facial features are blurred. There is no eye-contact between the Sphinx and Oedipus. While the Ingres painting opens to a light landscape, Bacon's scene takes place in a room with an open brown door at the centre rear of the painting, providing a view of the blackness of night. A Fury covered in blood is in the doorway, with a white arrow pointing to her.

Bacon's vocabulary is unmistakable in this picture: the background of broad, flat surfaces leading to an undefined space, the positioning of symbols such as circle and arrow that emphasise certain elements, and the strong contrast of colours that the artist repeatedly used in his late work. Here Bacon borrows the subject of Ingres's work as well as his composition with regard to the two figures but speaks a completely independent pictorial language in his painting. David Sylvester remarks on the different role of Oedipus: "Where Ingres makes Oedipus dominant, holding the centre and boldly closing in on the Sphinx, Bacon turns a winner into a loser."[8]

Another work that was created on a model by Ingres is *Diptych: Study from the Human Body; Study of the Human Body – From a Drawing by Ingres* from the years 1982–84 (cat. no. 102). Bacon first painted the female torso, the right panel that originally was to have been part of a triptych but remained unfinished. A second panel with a male torso after Ingres was bought at the time by Michel Leiris for the Centre Pompidou. Bacon suggested hanging the panel of the female torso together with that of the male. When the museum was unable to buy that panel, he decided to paint a new panel with a male torso, which today is the left part of the diptych hanging in the Hirshhorn Museum in Washington. Bacon took the female figure from Ingres's work *Turkish Bath,* of which he had a small cut-out reproduction. The many traces of paint on it suggest that he must have used it very frequently (cat. no. 104).

The female figure lying to the right in the foreground is holding her arms crossed above her head and has her right leg crossed over her left. Particularly conspicuous is the round, feminine shape of her hip. A pencil sketch on transparent paper found in Bacon's studio served as a preliminary drawing for the panel with the female torso. It shows that Bacon originally gave far more emphasis to the curvature of the body and hip than is found in the painted version. Viewing the two torsos makes it clear why the artist so admired the fragmentary nature of the Elgin Marbles in London.

Chance in Dadaism and Surrealism

Hans Arp was one of the first artists in the group of Dadaists to integrate accident and chance into the process of creating an artwork. In the collage he created around 1917, *Arranged According to the Laws of Chance,* for example, he allowed small pieces of paper to fall to the floor and then fastened them to a sheet of backing the way they had come to rest by chance. Marcel Duchamp's *3 Standard Stoppages* (three threads glued to three painted canvas strips) of 1913 is another well-known, somewhat earlier example of chance in art. In the original description, "A straight horizontal thread one metre in length falls from a height of one metre onto a horizontal plane ..." three times. The artist then fixed the threads on the canvas in the shape that had come about by chance. "I performed this experiment in 1913," said Duchamp, "in order to capture and preserve forms that had occurred by accident."[9] Thomas Zaunschirm made the following comment on this work: "The action of dropping is not one of releasing but of permitting: it is called chance."[10] From this time on, the integration of chance began to play a central role in the history of 20th-century art. For art, the permitting of accidents meant a new openness and at the same time an opening of new dimensions through the admission of the unforeseeable to an artwork.

Herbert Read describes Bacon's early work of the 1930s as "critical paranoia painting," a painting from the subconscious that is close-

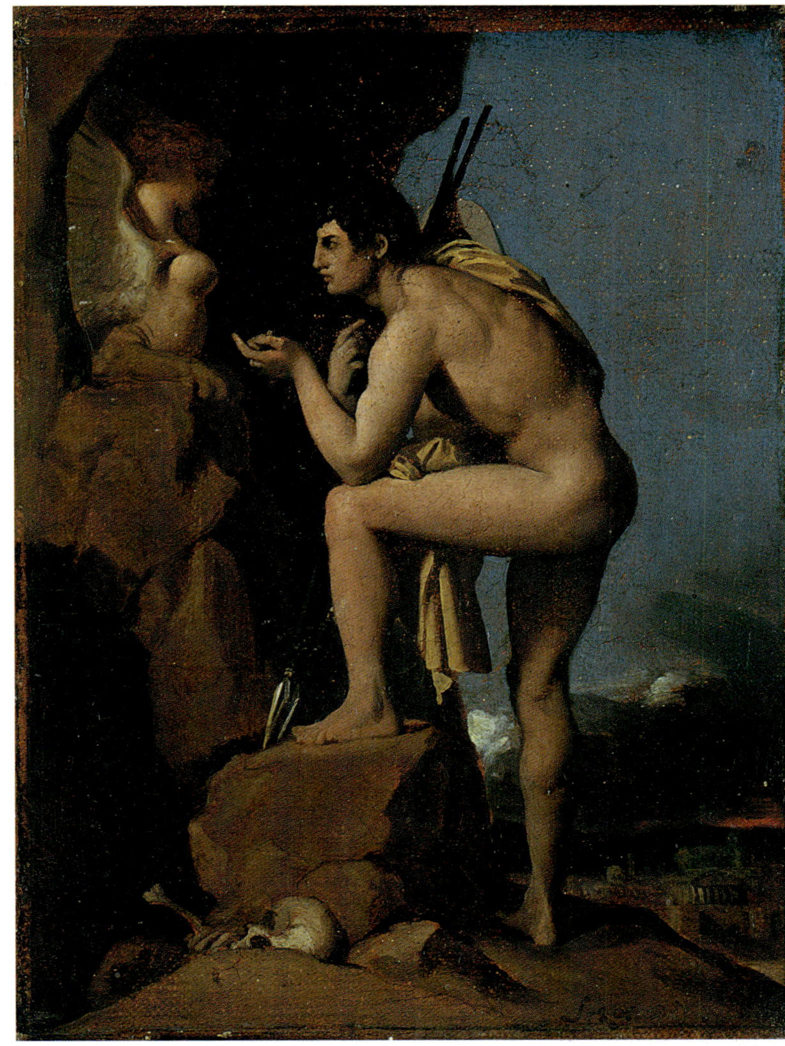

Plate 7: Jean-Auguste-Dominique Ingres, Oedipus and the Sphinx. Around 1826/27 (cat. no. 120).

Plate 8 on p. 29: Francis Bacon, Study for Head of Isabel Rawsthorne. 1967. Oil on canvas, 35.5 × 30.5 cm. Private collection. (©: The Estate of Francis Bacon/VBK, Vienna, 2003.)

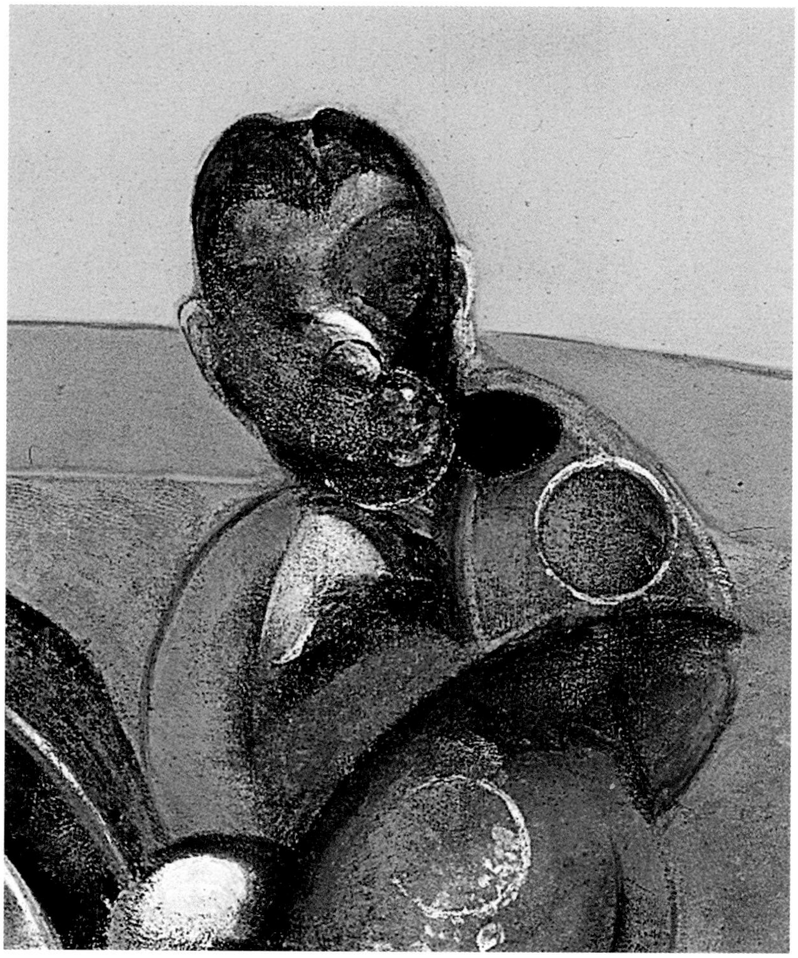

Detail, plate 9.

ly related to Surrealism. Beginning in the mid-1930s, spontaneity in the creation of artworks became an element of substantial importance to the Surrealist artists. Chance played an important role in this and became established as an artistic principle and programme. Such artists as Yves Tanguy, André Masson, Hans Bellmer and Max Ernst investigated various processes involving chance.

In the interviews that Bacon's friend, the art historian David Sylvester, conducted with him over the years, Bacon always insisted that his pictures had been created purely by chance. "And that is why in a way it is very wearing, because it is really a complete accident. [...] Because I don't know how the form can be made. For instance, the other day I painted a head of somebody, and what made the sockets of the eyes, the nose, the mouth were, when you analyzed them, just forms which had nothing to do with eyes, nose or mouth; but the paint moving from one contour into another made a likeness of this person I was trying to paint."[11] [...] "You know in my case all painting – and the older I get the more it becomes so – is accident. So I foresee it in my mind, I foresee it, and yet I hardly ever carry it out as I foresee it. It transforms itself by the actual paint. [...] Perhaps one could say it's not an accident, because it becomes a selective process which part of this accident one chooses to preserve. One is attempting, of course, to keep the vitality of the accident and yet preserve a continuity."[12]

The White Blotch

While Duchamp individualised and subjectivised chance, it has a different effect in Bacon's work than in that of the Dadaist and Surrealist artists. His "accidents" occur in a different, and in particular, in a calculated context. They are generally different from the arbitrary occurrences found in the work of Duchamp or Ernst and have greater significance than being simply unforeseen and playful.

A characteristic element in Bacon's use of chance in his painting is a white blotch, as found, for example, in *Study for Head of Isabel Rawsthorne,* 1967, *(Plate 8), Study of George Dyer in a Mirror,* 1968 *(Plate 1)* and *Study for Bullfight No. 2*, 1969 *(Plate 9)*. In these pictures Bacon throws thick white paint at the canvas: at the face of the figure, at the bull, at the centre of the painting. The resulting white blotch looks as though the undiluted paint had been accidentally added to the painting by hand or with a thick brush or cloth. Sometimes it remains where it landed; sometimes it is drawn with the brush to adjacent points in the picture. But first Bacon simply adds the white blotch, whether or not it fits into the painting.

The Spanish painters of the 17th century, especially Velázquez,

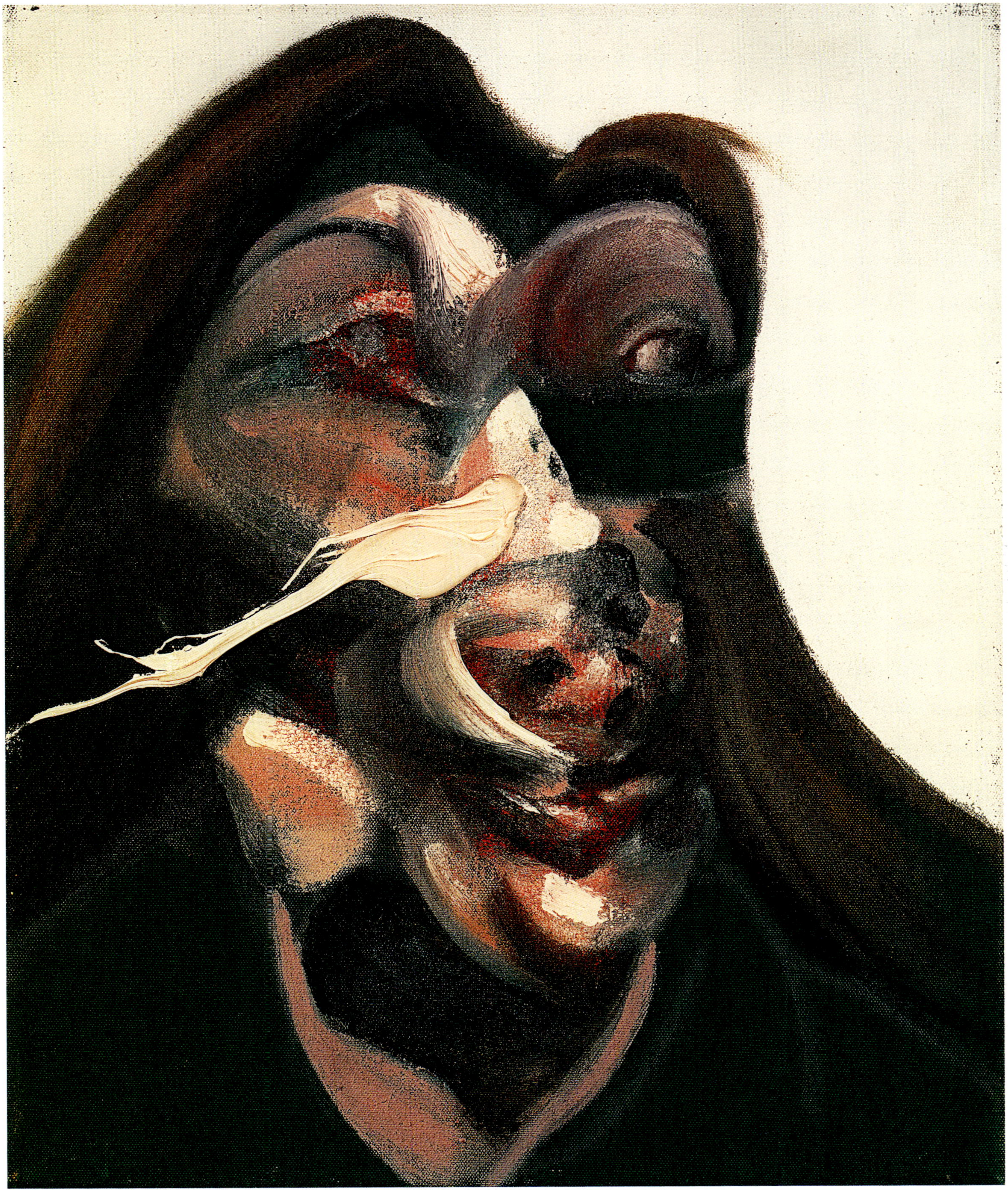

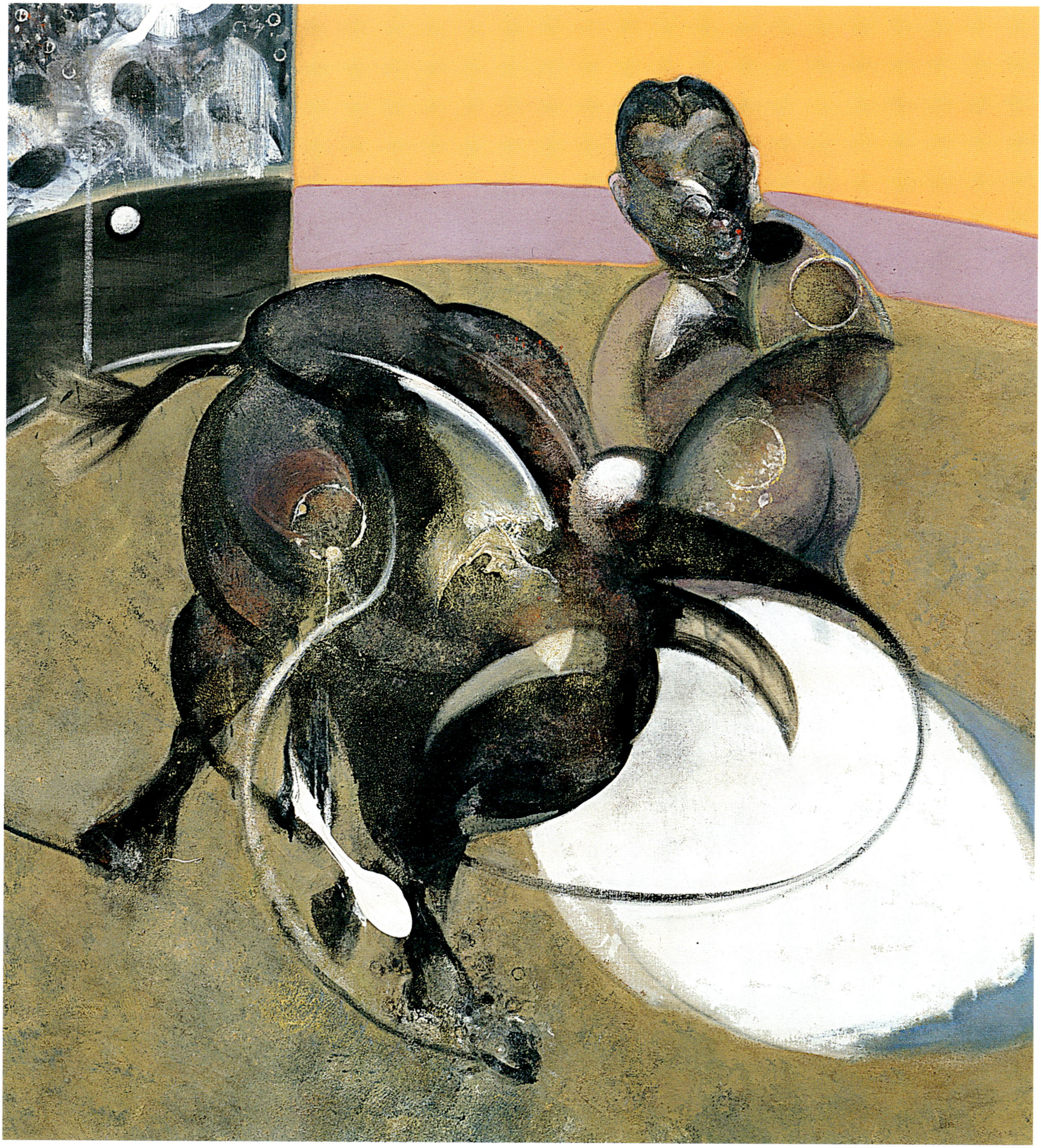

made use of the technique of *borrones* – spots of thickly applied paint. The ornate clothing of the royal family of Philip IV was painted by Velázquez with a full, wide and free brushstroke, with the quick addition of dabs of paint. Velázquez's biographers, the painters and art theoreticians Francisco Pacheco and Vicente Carducho, described this special manner of painting in their treatises on art. In Pacheco's view, it was derived from late works by Titian and El Greco. Vicente Carducho associated the *borrón* – the thick spot of paint – with Venetian painting. In the late work of Velázquez – the *Portrait of Infanta Margarita Teresa (Plate 10)*, for example – this dabbed technique is especially evident in the blue bows in the princess's hair as well as in the round brooch with white spots and dots at the neckline of her dress. Similar white, abstractly placed dots of the kind in Margarita's jewellery are found again three hundred years later in Bacon's paintings.

In Bacon's explanation of the meaning of the white spots and splashes that he added to the canvas so abruptly and almost thoughtlessly, he speaks of "pure accident," of "instinct," and that the picture almost paints itself. He says that the subconscious is finding expression in his work. In the third interview that Sylvester conducted with him, Bacon speaks in detail about his technique of lending expression to chance. He explains that he throws the paint onto the canvas by hand rather than using a brush. "I can only hope that the throwing of the paint onto the already-made image or half-made image will either re-form the image or that I will be able to manipulate this paint further into – anyway for me – a greater intensity."[13] Often Bacon also used cloths or brushes to apply the paint, in which case the cloth hanging thick with paint left behind a network of spots and traces of paint on the canvas. In response to Sylvester's question of whether his throwing of paint was really accidental and whether someone else could do it for him, Bacon answered: "I know the part of the canvas I want to throw at, so I would have to tell them what part of the canvas to throw at, and, since I've thrown an awful lot, perhaps I'd know how to aim better onto that part. [...] For instance I would loathe my paintings to look like chancy abstract expressionist paintings, because I really like highly disciplined painting, although I don't use highly disciplined methods of constructing it."[14]

Sylvester argues that throwing the paint is "conscious manipulation"[15] and part of a calculated work process. This manipulation – or as Bacon calls it, instinct or inspired accident – leaves many open questions, despite the artist's explanation. Is not the act of throwing – the decision to apply paint accidentally to the almost-completed paintings – a carefully considered and conscious act by

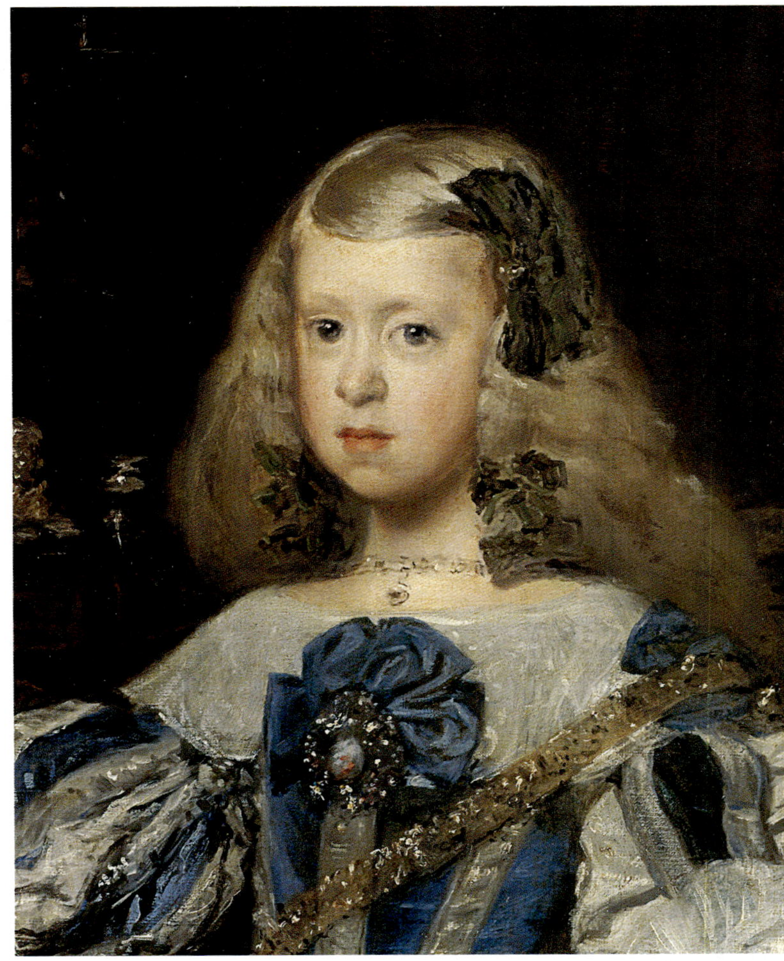

Plate 9 on p. 30: Francis Bacon, Study for Bullfight No. 2 1969 (cat. no. 61).

Plate 10: Diego de Silva y Velázquez, Infanta Margarita Teresa in a Blue Cloth, detail. 1659 (cat. no. 73).

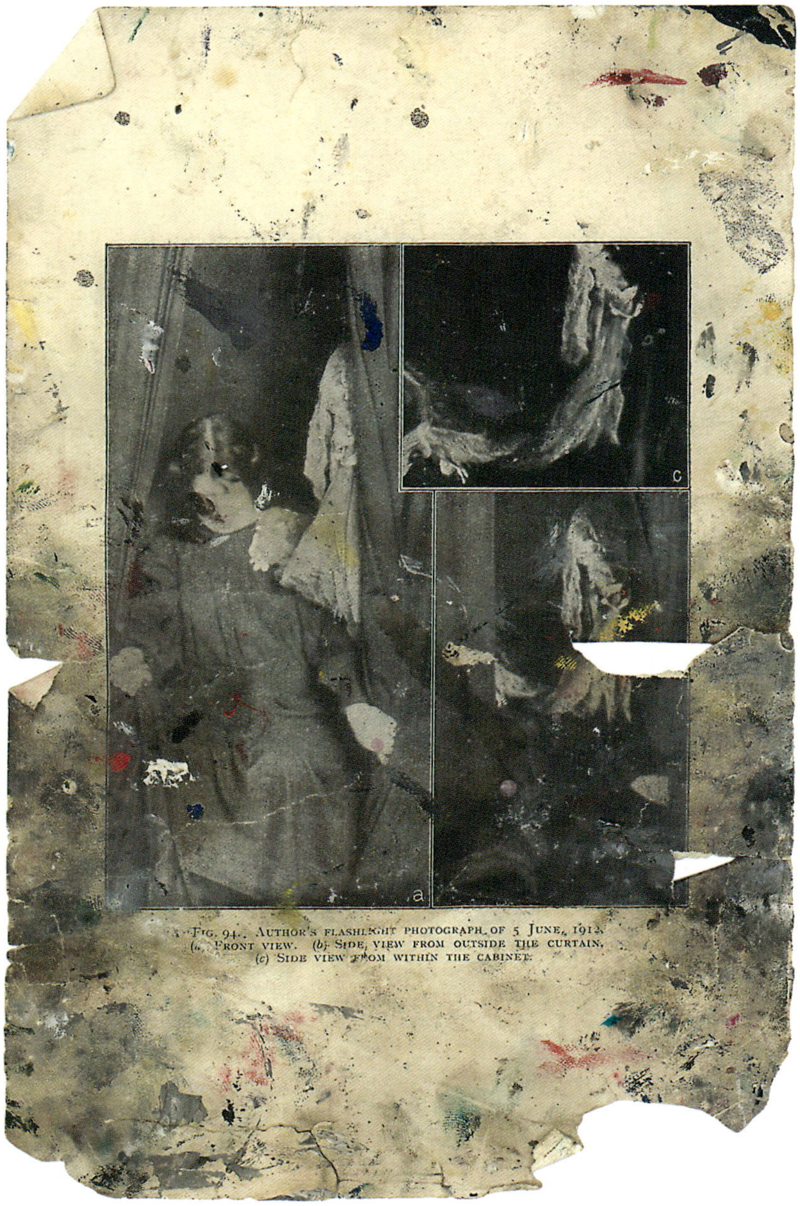

Plate 11: Page from the book: Albert Baron von Schrenck-Notzing, Phenomena of Materialisation, London 1920 (cat. no. 21).

the artist? Does it not seem that Bacon wants to give viewers the impression of a calculated accident because he wants, in order to create a further dimension of intensity, to distract them from the familiar motifs of a composition that he has worked out to the last detail? In this case, wherein lies the accident? There is a proximity to Pollock's drip paintings, about which Harold Rosenberg says: "What was to go on the canvas was not a picture but an event."[16] Is Rosenberg's "event" comparable to the "greater intensity" Bacon achieved by throwing paint? It should be noted in this connection that Leonardo da Vinci in his *Treatise on Painting* says "[...] by throwing a sponge soaked with various colours against a wall to make a stain, one can find a beautiful landscape"[17].

Da Vinci's approach to chance and his interpretation of a blotch that occurs in this manner must be understood differently from that of Bacon. Bacon's blotches remain abstract; they cannot be read as landscapes or objects. On the contrary, they usually appear abruptly in the painting, do not fit into the composition, and "disturb" the depiction of the figures. On Bacon's use of the white blotch, Michel Leiris writes: "Bacon uses various means or forms of portrayal, probably for the same purpose as the round or elliptical blotches and the white spots of uncertain form that he sometimes adds to his figures or other areas of the canvas in order to further emphasise the obvious density of the figure."[18]

Although Bacon rejected every form of spiritualism, he was convinced of the radiance and energy of a person and sought to depict this energy or aura. Thus the white blotch in Bacon's paintings becomes an "emanation" in two senses. On the one hand, these blotches, which are added by chance to a largely finished canvas in an eruptive gesture, are direct emanations or radiations of the artist himself (realised through his movement of throwing). On the other hand, they should be understood as emanations from the person depicted on the canvas. While the scream in the early Pope paintings was the manifestation of the psychical state and aura of the figure, and the emanations were hindered in their utterance (as represented by the cage and other boundaries), the figure in later paintings is liberated from its suffering and pain; the emanations are allowed to escape. The inner tension of the figure or of the person depicted is released; the tense and distorted body is liberated by the flow of energy to the outside.

Bacon's Esotericism and Emanation

In 19th-century France and Germany, scientists, photographers, doctors and parapsychologists developed so-called fluid or occult photography. In 1895 Wilhelm Konrad Röntgen discovered the fluorescent rays later known as X-rays that were produced by electrical discharges through gases in a tube. Later experiments were conducted in occult circles with X-ray photography, and seances in which the invisible became visible fascinated such groups in Paris and Munich. Doctors such as Hippolyte Baraduc and Jules-Bernard Luys tried to photograph the fluid emanations of subjects under the influence of hypnosis. In the following years the terrain of the invisible was expanded to include spirit and thought photography. Bacon owned a copy of the book *Positioning in Radiography* by K. C. Clark from the year 1939, which contains photographs showing people in various positions in an X-ray machine (cat. no. 68). Bacon used many of these photos as sources for his portraits. "I've also always had a book that's influenced me very much called *Positioning in Radiography*, with a lot of photographs showing the positioning of the body for the X-ray photographs to be taken, and also the X-rays."[19]

When Bacon's studio was moved from London to Dublin's Hugh Lane Municipal Art Gallery in 1999 and reassembled there, among the books found was found a copy of *Phenomena of Materialisation*[20] *(Plate 11).*

The general practitioner Baron Albert von Schrenck-Notzing had published this book in 1914, causing a sensation in German and French parapsychology, but it also attracted criticism. Schrenck-Notzing, who had learned the technique of hypnosis, frequently invited spectators to his office in order to convince them of the reality of the phenomenon of materialisation that occurred during these sessions. He either performed the hypnosis himself or had a female hypnotist hypnotise a usually female medium, who sat on a chair behind a curtain *(Plate 12).* Schrenck-Notzing made the acquaintance of "Eva C.," as he called Marthe Béraud, later his French medium, while he was a guest of the sculptress Juliette Bisson in Paris, where the group held occult sessions starting in 1912. Bisson, who herself was enthusiastic about the phenomenon of materialisation, took photographs of her friend Béraud while she was under hypnosis (cat. no. 19). The medium was first dressed in a black costume in order to be sure that she had concealed nothing in her clothing. Placed into a kind of deep sleep, the medium then began – with the curtain half open – to emit amorphous shapes from the openings of her body, mostly from her mouth and nose. These shapes could be net-like forms that streamed from her mouth, or textiles such as socks, remnants of fabric, and threads that came from her head or from behind her ears. Faces of dead people drawn on fabric-like tissue were also emitted from the medium. With up to nine cameras distributed around the room, Schrenck-Notzing took photographs of these forms, which he called "teleplasma." He was convinced that

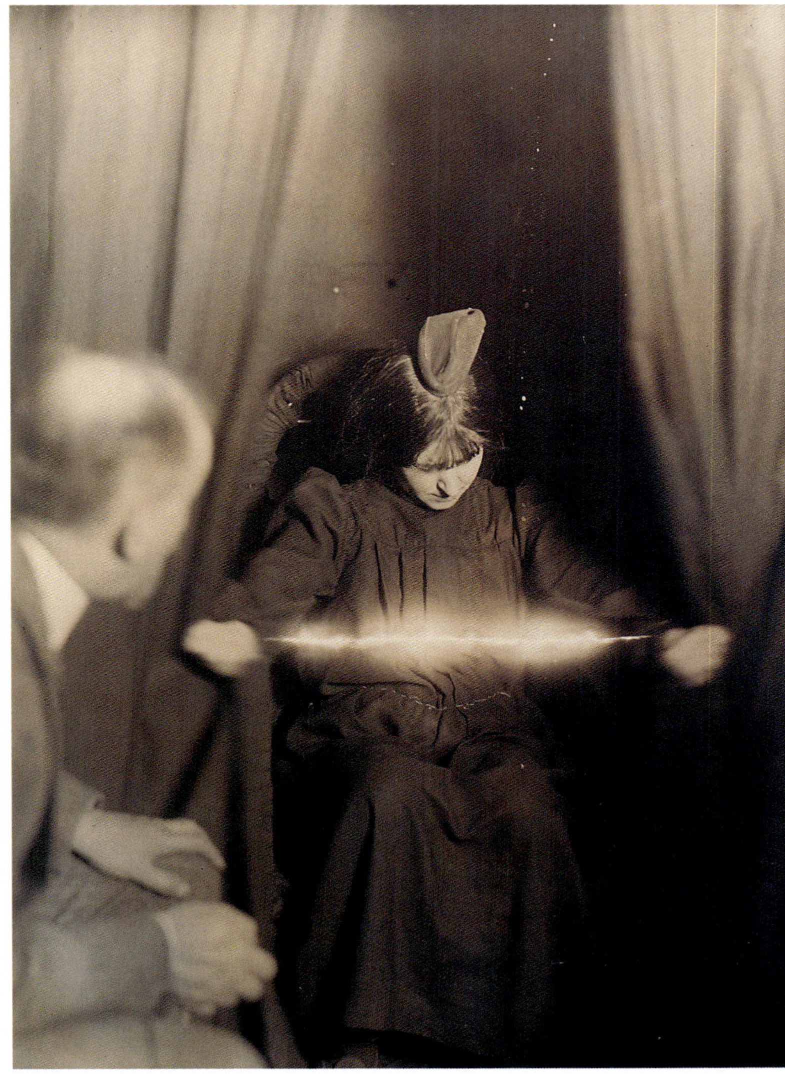

Plate 12: Albert von Schrenck-Notzing, Phenomena of Materialisation with Eva C., Munich, 17 May 1912 (cat. no. 18).

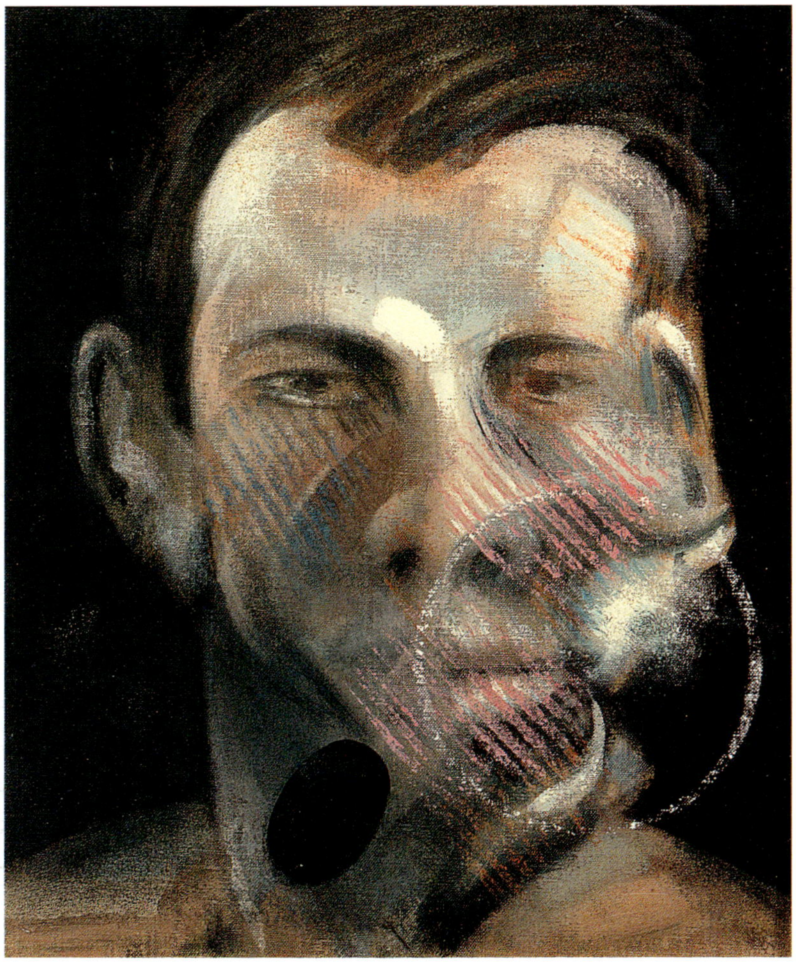

Plate 13: Francis Bacon, left panel of the triptych Three Studies for a Portrait (Peter Beard) I. 1975. Oil on canvas, 35.5 × 30.5 cm. Private collection. (©: The Estate of Francis Bacon/VBK, Vienna, 2003.)

Plate 14 on p. 35: Francis Bacon, Three Studies for Portraits, Including Self-Portrait. 1969. Oil on canvas, each panel 35.5 × 30.5 cm. Private collection. (©: The Estate of Francis Bacon/VBK, Vienna, 2003.)

these teleplasmas were spiritual pictures of sensory materiality. At the same time that Schrenck-Notzing was conducting his sessions, many critics were attempting to prove that materialisation was pure fraud.

In interviews with Francis Bacon the conversation sometimes turned to trance-like conditions. David Sylvester once asked Bacon whether he sometimes fell into a trance-like state when he was using chance in his painting. "I don't like using the word trance-like nowadays, because it comes too near to modern mysticism, which I hate. I also think, perhaps, it sounds slightly pompous to say it's a trance-like state [...]," answered Bacon[21]. He was convinced that it was a kind of instinct: "[...] all art surely is instinct, and then you can't talk about instinct, because you don't know what it is."[22]

Thus it is likely that Francis Bacon was more interested in the visual representation in Schrenck-Notzing's photographs than in their spiritualistic content. He basically rejected every kind of occultism and also had no faith in attempts at spirit photography. But he was interested in the pictures as sources for his work and in the radiant energy they claimed to show.

In the German version of the interviews with David Sylvester, these forces are called "energies," while in the original English edition Bacon calls them "emanations." He told Sylvester: "The sitter is someone of flesh and blood and what has to be caught is their emanation. I'm not talking in a spiritual way of anything like that – that is the last thing I believe in. But there are always emanations from people whoever they are, though some people are stronger than others [...] with their face you have to try and trap the energy that emanates from them."[23]

What Bacon means by emanation is the psychic energy, the radiance of a person. Signifying a discharge, an outflow, the term emanation gives central meaning to the metaphor of flowing in Bacon's work. The concept of *emanatio,* which is rooted in the traditions of classical antiquity and Christian theology, migrated to occultism and pseudo-religions after being officially rejected by the first Vatican Council (1869–70). In its secularised form "emanation" no longer signifies a flowing out from God or the divine, but rather a kind of expansion, a radiation or charisma that comes from all living things and thus also from people. The nature of a person is contained in his or her radiance or outflow. In the case of artists such as František Kupka, who himself was a medium, or Wassily Kandinsky, emanation became the materialisation of the spiritual, which they tried to make visible in their art. Jean-Claude Lebensztejn describes the phenomenon of emanation in Bacon's work with the words: "Emanation is for him of a material, individual nature and

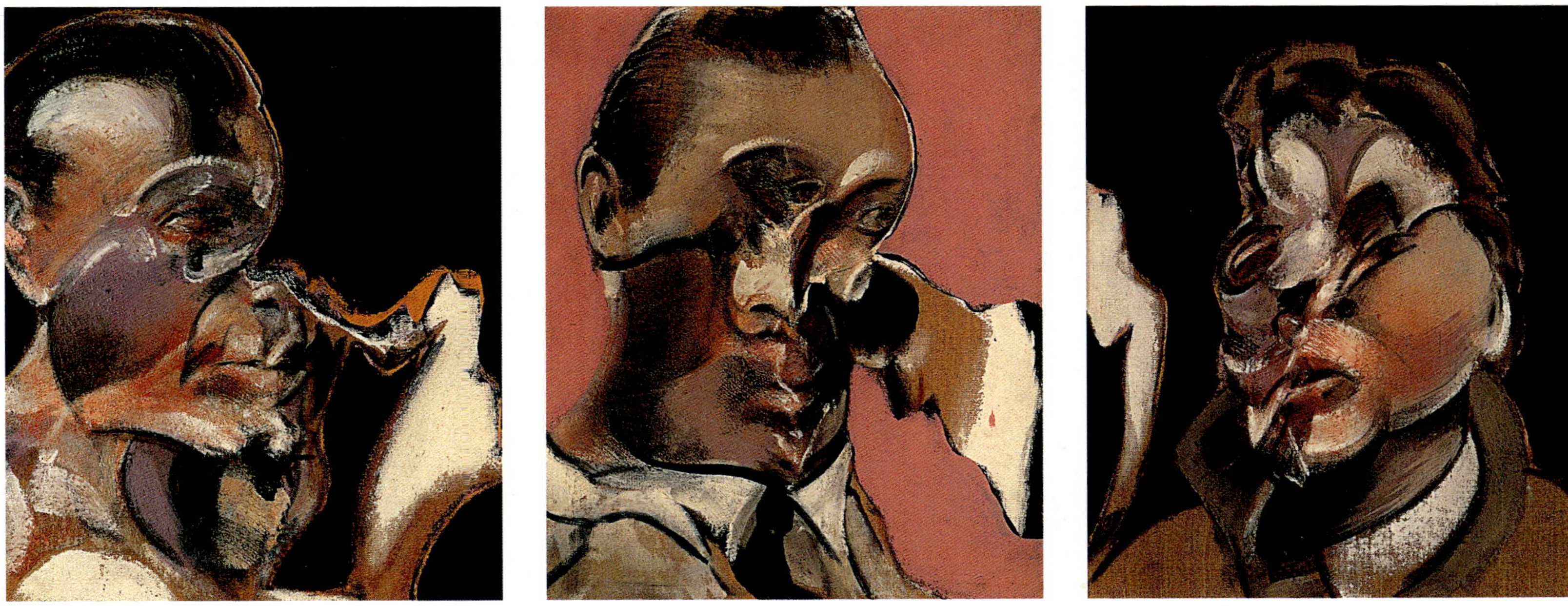

can be understood only instinctively. Bacon believes that he possesses this clairvoyance; to him, his ability as a painter is not a gift but rather a certain receptivity."[24]

In seeing himself as a "medium for chance and accident"[25], Bacon places himself at the centre of events; emanations come on the one hand from him himself and on the other hand have to be captured by him. The energy flows from the interior of the body to the outside; the body virtually flows out, the fluid aspect emerges from it. The amorphous mass, which Lebenszstein compares with ejaculation, flows from the body of the figure and manifests itself in Bacon's paintings in the form of abstract blotches and splashes of paint, shadows and similar elements. Some of his pictures suggest a very direct influence of Schrenck-Notzing's materialisation phenomena on Bacon. One example is *Head II* of 1949 (cat. no. 26), in which there is a white set of teeth growing out of an indefinable head, and a white blotch beneath the head on the right stands out from the black fragment of the figure. The head also appears between the two halves of a curtain, in a very similar manner to the way the usually female figures sat behind a half-opened curtain while in Schrenck-Notzing's hypnotic trance. The left panel of the triptych *Three Studies for a Portrait (Peter Beard) I* of 1975 *(Plate 13)* shows the easily recognisable face of his friend. In comparison with the other portraits, this depiction is very carefully elaborated and only slightly deformed. However, over the mouth and the left cheek there is a white circle in which a white, thick blotch appears to being growing out of the cheek. It could be understood as a sort of light source but also as a fabric-like form, an apparition of light surrounded by the circle. This becomes even more evident in the small triptych *Three Studies for Portraits, Including Self-Portrait* of 1969 *(Plate 14),* in which white, amorphous forms extend into the face from outside and constantly change. The emanation or radiance becomes part of the figure; the invisible is made visible. Bacon sometimes speaks of making his figures not more realistic but rather more real. This reality includes the emanation, aura or radiance, even though this is not visible in everyday life. Bacon's manner of painting propagates a new way of seeing by pointing out the psychic powers of human beings. Seen in this light, Bacon, as he himself says, is not devout but still receptive to a corporeal radiance, which comes from the subject and which he tries to make evident in his paintings.

The Materiality of Photography as Chance

After Bacon's heirs gave his studio to the Hugh Lane Municipal Art Gallery in Dublin in August 1999, the employees there catalogued some 7500 photographs, books, drawings, sketches, newspaper cuttings and notes that the artist had used over the years as sources of inspiration for his paintings. This collection of materials had been piled everywhere in his disorderly, chaotic studio: on the floor, in drawers, on wooden shelves and in small boxes. Many of these sources were previously known, e. g. the reproductions of Velázquez's *Pope Innocent X* and Muybridge's photographic studies of the body. A large part of the collection, however, was still little known at the time and provided more precise information about Bacon's manner of selecting motifs and his style of painting. There are, for example, photos of his friend George Dyer, of whom he

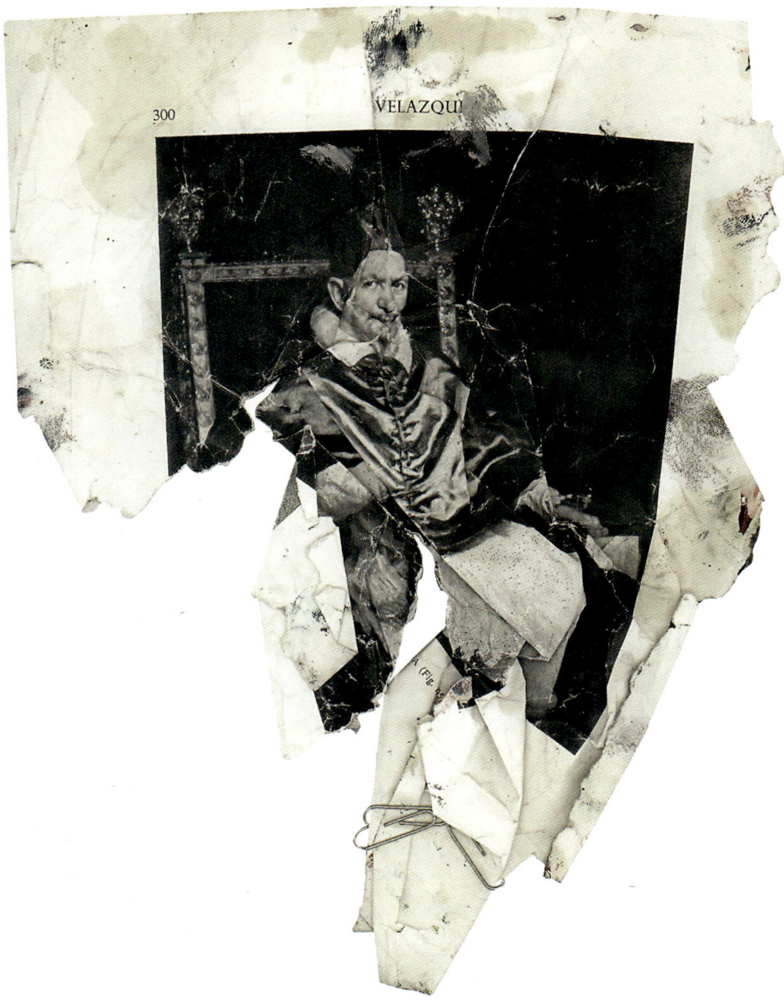

Plate 15: Black-and-white illustration of Pope Innocent X, 1650, by Diego Velázquez. Page from an unidentified book (cat. no. 11).

frequently painted portraits, as well as Isabel Rawsthorne, Lucian Freud, Henrietta Moraes and other contemporaries. Bacon owned many art books, and he cut and tore illustrations from them. Included in his estate were reproductions of works by Ingres, Rembrandt, Van Gogh and Picasso, photos of wild animals, film, sports and war photographs, illustrated medical books as well as a collection of pictures of Egyptian and Greek sculpture and photos of political leaders and dictators. So far, few examples from this trove of images has been shown at Bacon exhibitions in Britain, Holland and Portugal. If one compares the figures and compositions of the paintings with the corresponding source material, one begins to understand Bacon's fascination with Van Gogh and Velázquez, for example, and the way in which he newly interpreted their paintings.

In these new interpretations of the pictorial tradition, the meaning of Bacon's figural motifs is, of course, often difficult to comprehend, and sometimes a clear reading is impossible. That is the case, for example, with his entwined bodies, which are often making love or fighting while lying on a bed, or with his papal heads obscured by veils or stripes, where the expression is focused primarily on the depiction of the scream. There is significant variation in Bacon's manner of painting, pointing to a number of various processes, one of which will be more closely investigated here. If once examines the photos and models from his studio more precisely and then tries to understand how Bacon used them in practice, one notices, among other things, a correspondence between the photographic models and the paintings, which is more than simply a matter of the depiction of the figures or of the space. There is a black-and-white photograph from a book about Velázquez, for example, of his *Portrait of Innocent X (Plate 15).* This catalogue page is in relatively poor condition. The lower half of the paper has been torn and is held together only by a paper-clip, so that the body of the portrait subject is only partially visible. If one compares this model with papal pictures such as *Study for Portrait VII,* 1953, and *Study after Velázquez's Portrait of Pope Innocent X,* 1953 *(Plates 16 and 17),* one sees that Bacon outlined the body of the Pope with short, broken blue lines in the area of the shoulders and upper arms. The folds of the Pope's cope are accented in light-blue paint that only partially suggests the shape and does not extend to the outline of the shoulders. Only a relatively small part of the upper body is fully painted; the rest is either suggested by the contour or the black background shines through it. How did Bacon come to use a white dotted line to extend the Pope's right shoulder? The model photograph with its tears and folds in the paper also shows

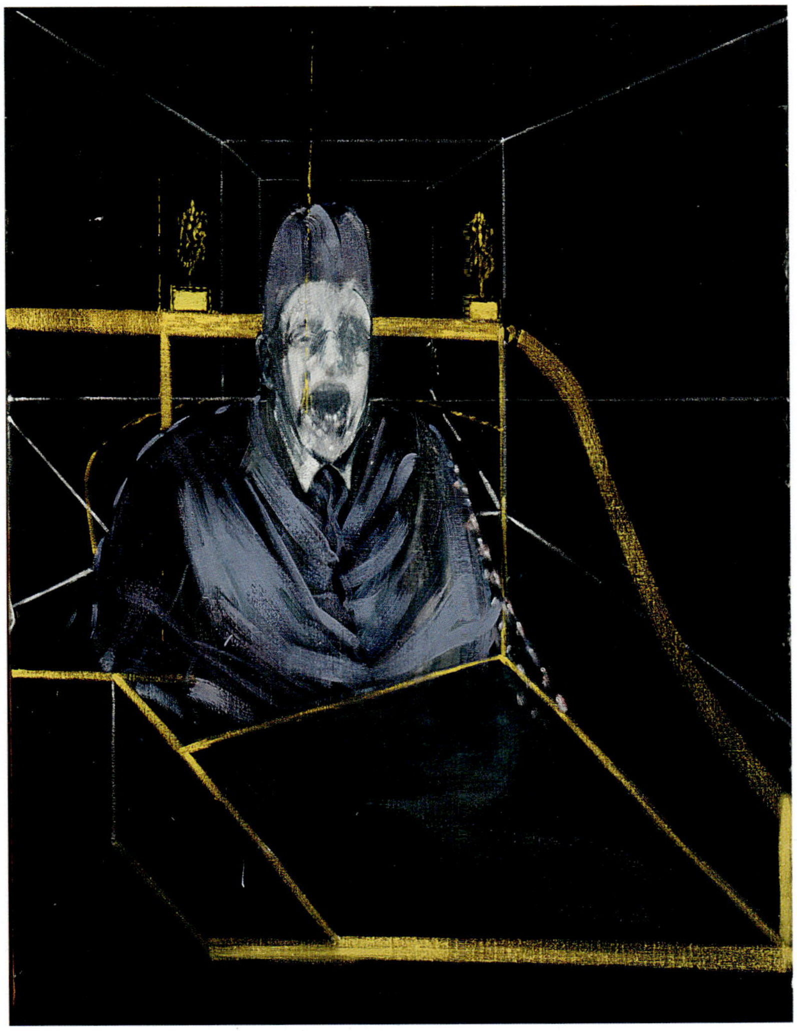

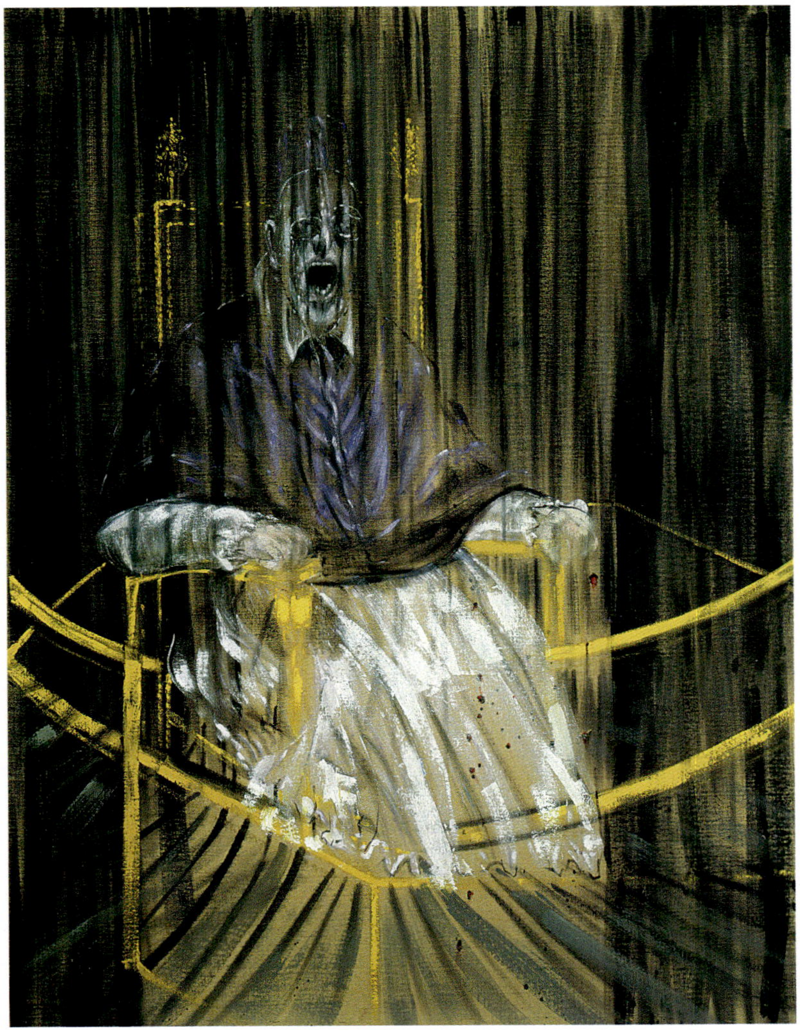

Plate 16: Francis Bacon, Study for Portrait VII. 1953 (cat. no. 7).

Plate 17: Francis Bacon, Study after Velázquez's Portrait of Pope Innocent X. 1953 (cat. no. 14).

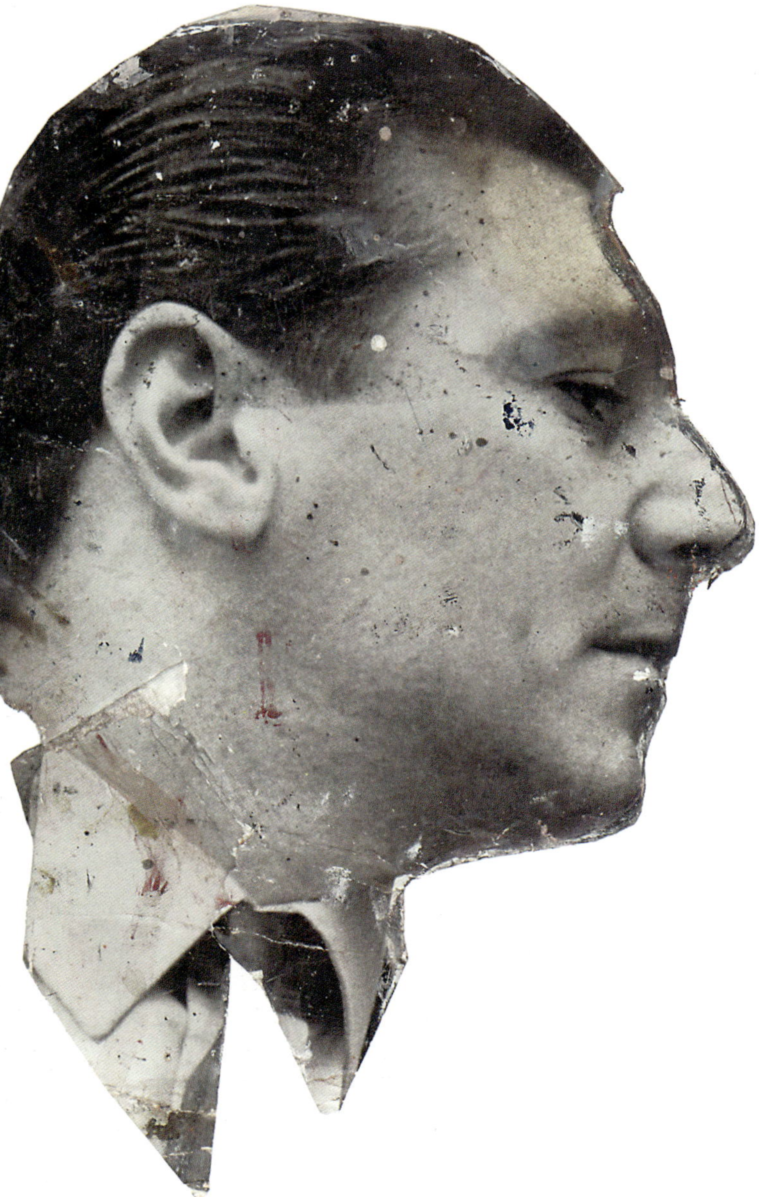

Plate 18: Cut-out head of black-and-white photograph of George Dyer, taken by John Deakin. Mid-1960s (cat. no. 122).

Plate 19 on p. 39: Francis Bacon, right panel of: Three Studies of the Male Back. 1970. Oil on canvas, 198 × 147.5 cm. Zurich, Kunsthaus, Vereinigung Zürcher Kunstfreunde. (©: The Estate of Francis Bacon/VBK, Vienna, 2003.)

only parts of the Pope's cope, and it is evident that the folds and tears in the paper correspond with the lines and contours in Bacon's painting. In *Study after Velázquez's Portrait of Pope Innocent X* the Pope's white cassock is somewhat uneven and torn, and several places along the hem are bordered in wavy black lines. These lines correspond with tears in the photograph. Like many other models, this photo has many small spots, which are either spots of paint (Bacon must have left the photo lying for some time next to his paint-pots and brushes) or changes in the paper itself that occurred because of other circumstances. The small red dots on the cassock in Bacon's study of Innocent X are also found on the photograph. Thus Bacon not only adopts the figural subject in his work, he also sees the subject through the medium of photography and as influenced by its material condition and transfers components of both form and content in the model to his canvas: he takes both as his subject.

Speaking in his second interview with David Sylvester about the use of photographs, Bacon said: "And 99 per cent of the time I find that photographs are very much more interesting than either an abstract or figurative painting. […] I think it's the slight remove from fact, which returns me onto the fact more violently. Through the photographic image I find myself beginning to wander into the image and unlock what I think of as its reality more than I can by looking at it."[26] The medium that conveys the "facts" also contributes to this reality. *Portrait Isabel Rawsthorne Standing in a Street in Soho* (cat. no. 59) is a striking example of this factual situation. On the black dress of his subject Bacon has again added a thick white blotch that extends in two directions. In the model photograph, there is a tear in the photographic surface at the same point on Rawsthorne's dress and jacket so that the background of the photographic paper shines through (cat. no. 70). The torn corner and the blank areas of the photograph also correspond to areas in the background of blue and beige surfaces, which have an abstract appearance.

There are many such examples of accidents that came about through the borrowing of accidental additions to the sources Bacon used as models. As can be seen in the portrait photo of George Dyer, Bacon sometimes also changed the photograph itself. In this case, he did so by exactly cutting out the contours of the profile; by folding the paper he then created a line that runs past the ear to the cheek *(Plate 18)*. In the right panel of the triptych *Three Studies of the Male Back* of 1970 *(Plate 19),* which shows Dyer's reflection in a mirror, the described line is replaced by a white blotch with strokes running from it.

In preferring to portray his protagonists using a photograph as his

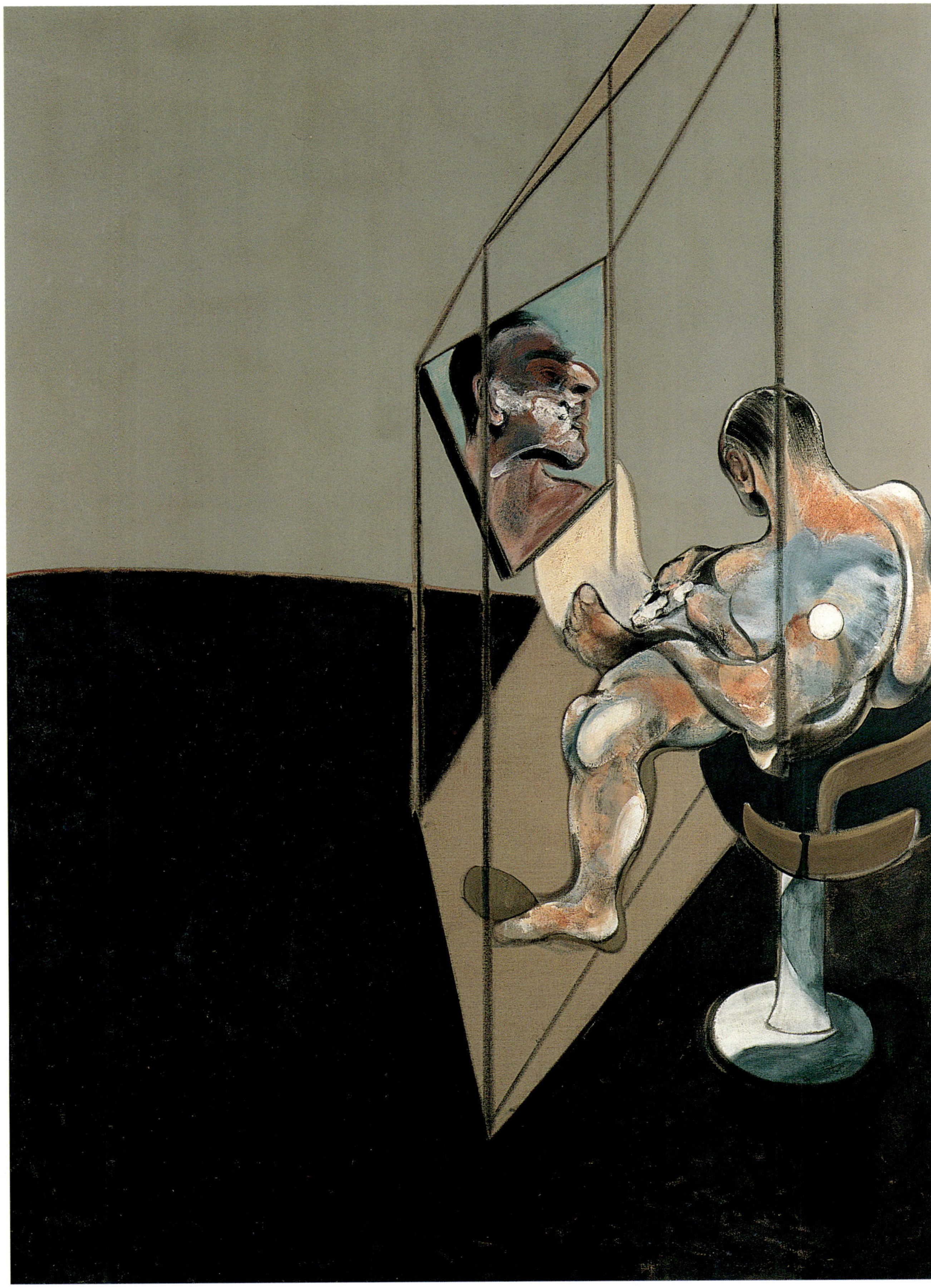

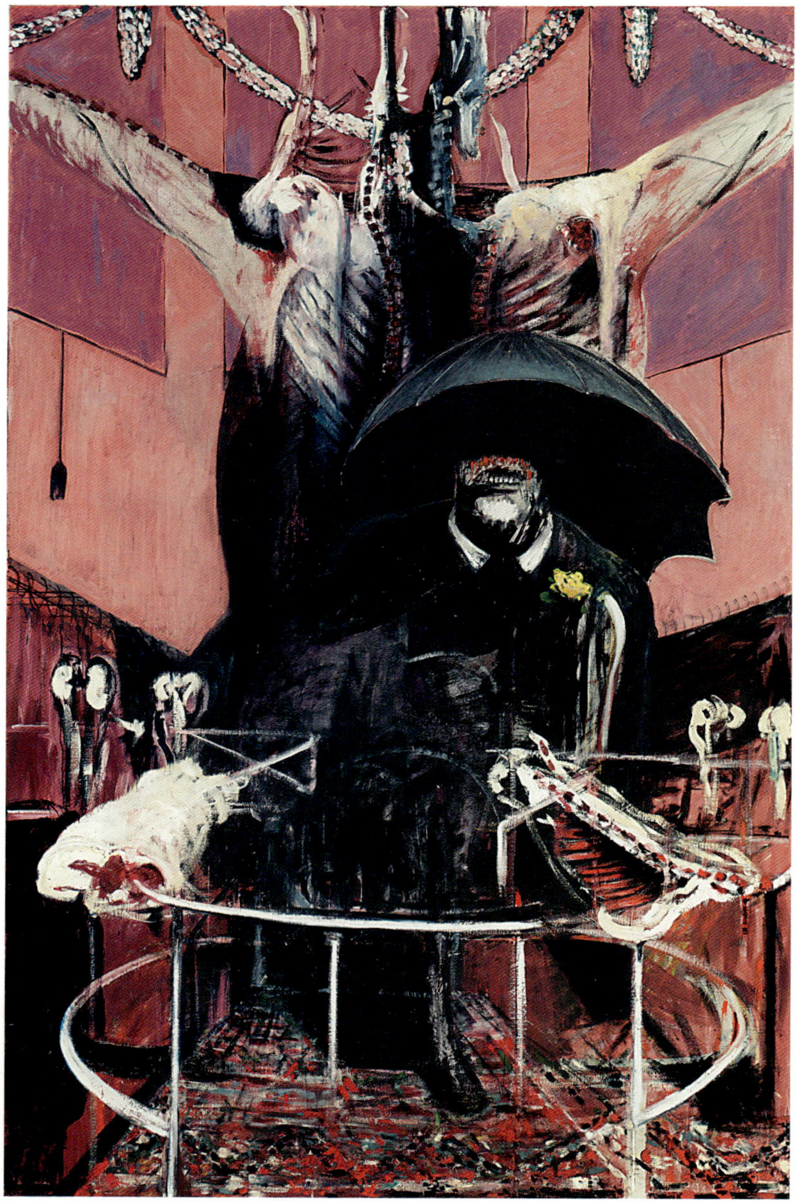

Plate 20: Francis Bacon, Painting 1946. Oil and tempera on canvas, 123 × 105.5 cm. New York, The Museum of Modern Art. (©: The Estate of Francis Bacon/VBK, Vienna, 2003.)

source, Bacon's concern is not only to distance himself from reality but also to recognise the composition in its abstractness, to which the sensual quality of the paper also contributes in that its material texture flows into the painting. Here we find the kind of accidents that fit Duchamp's definition of chance. In Bacon's work it is not just the seemingly accidental paint spots that lend his paintings the dimension of chance but also, importantly, the borrowing of accidental changes to the material condition of his source. The white paint blotches, which are more or less integrated into the painting, are thus not so much an expression of the unforeseen; on the contrary: Bacon knows exactly where he wants these thick marks to appear. They are in keeping with Sylvester's "conscious manipulation" but take on a life of their own as soon as they are applied to the canvas and drawn out in various directions.

In addition to the methods described here of placing the "white blotch" consciously and then in some cases drawing it out, as well as the stimulation the artist received from rips, folds, paint drippings or water spots that occurred accidentally on his source material, chance is also manifested in Bacon's painting in a motific-thematic regard. This can be seen in his departure from an idea or in the shifting from one motif to another. Bacon describes the creation of his work *Painting 1946* in the following manner *(Plate 20)*: "One of the pictures I did in 1946, the one like a butcher's shop, came to me as an accident. I was attempting to make a bird alighting on a field. [...], but suddenly the lines that I'd drawn suggested something totally different, and out of this suggestion arose this picture."[27] The bird became an umbrella, the motific selection in the painting changed completely by "complete accident"[28], which for Bacon was proof of the unforeseeable and accidental in his painting.

The face consists of abstract, accidental forms of which Bacon said: "Because this image is a kind of tightrope walk between what is called figurative painting and abstraction. It will go right out from abstraction but will really have nothing to do with it. It's an attempt to bring the figurative thing up onto the nervous system more violently and more poignantly."[29]

"Also, I think the man now realizes that he is an accident, that he is a completely futile human being, that he has to play out the game without reason [...], and what is fascinating now is that it's going to become much more difficult for the artist, because he must really deepen the game to be any good at all."[30] Bacon wants a "very ordered image," but also wants it to "come about by chance"[31]. But to what extent does Bacon grant his paintings enough space for them to occur by accident? On the one hand he counts on chance by opening himself to the creative process when he adds white blotches of paint to the canvas and then either allows them to run or draws them out and when he accepts the quality of the photographic paper as it is and transfers it to his painting. On the other hand, he understands very clearly the models he uses, the content of the series he creates, and which motifs and spatial qualities he uses in his pictures – such as cage structure, monochrome background and figural arrangement. One almost has the feeling that Bacon first has to create his network and his co-ordinates in the painting – that he has to feel that he is on safe ground, so to speak – in order to then allow the "accident" to happen. Thus one can speak in his case of a controlled and limited accident, to which the painting is not indebted for its whole creation but which is restricted to formal guidelines determined by the artist and which can only spread and develop within these co-ordinates. Thus Bacon exercises strict control over his paintings and motifs, although he constantly strives to circumvent and evade it. When one considers the photos from his studio or sees the reconstructed studio in Dublin, one must first imagine the frightful chaos in which the artist worked for years on end. But at the same time one discovers a certain system in the manner in which Bacon sought and found his motifs and visually realised his concepts, in the way he created order in a painting and left a place for the unforeseen only within this order. Cicero in his *De divinatione* remarked sceptically on the possibility of perfection occurring in art by chance: "Carneades used to tell that once upon a time, in the quarries of Chios, a stone was split open and the head of a little Pan appeared; well, the bust may not have been unlike the god, but we may be sure that it was not so perfect a reproduction as to lead one to imagine that it had been wrought by Scopas, for it goes without saying that perfection has never been achieved by accident."[32]

[1] Exh. Cat. London 1985, p. 4.
[2] Exh. Cat. London 1985, p. 4.
[3] The Observer, 24 November 1985.
[4] Sylvester 2000, p. 252.
[5] Wollheim 1987, p. 231.
[6] Wollheim 1987, p. 232.
[7] Wollheim 1987, p. 235.
[8] Sylvester 2000, p. 164.
[9] Holeczek 1992, p. 29.
[10] Holeczek 1992, p. 26.
[11] Sylvester 1999, pp. 11, 12.
[12] Sylvester 1999, pp. 16, 17.
[13] Sylvester 1999, p. 90.
[14] Sylvester 1999, p. 92.
[15] Sylvester 1999, p. 97.
[16] Quoted from Lachmann 1992, p. 506.
[17] Chastel 1990, p. 212.
[18] Leiris 1989, p. 17.
[19] Sylvester 1999, p. 32.
[20] I thank Margarita Cappock, who drew my attention to this book.
[21] Sylvester 1999, p. 96.
[22] Sylvester 1999, p. 97.
[23] Sylvester 1999, pp. 174, 175.
[24] Exh. Cat. Munich 1996, p. 45.
[25] Sylvester 1999, p. 140.
[26] Sylvester 1999, p. 30.
[27] Sylvester 1999, p. 11.
[28] Sylvester 1999, p. 11.
[29] Sylvester 1999, p. 12.
[30] Sylvester 1999, p. 28, 29.
[31] Sylvester 1999, p. 56.
[32] Schäublin 1991.

Norman Bryson

Bacon's Dialogues with the Past

David Sylvester: "Well, of course, there's not all that number who are painting the figure today. But I think it does more. And people seem to feel in looking at your figures that they are seen in moments of crisis, moments of acute awareness of their mortality, moments of acute awareness of their animal nature – moments of recognition of what might be called elemental truths about themselves. [...]"

Francis Bacon: "[...] One is particularly aware of it in Velasquez, of course. I don't know whether it's because of Velasquez's tremendous sophistication. Obviously, he was a profoundly sophisticated man living in the society of the Court, and he was probably the only really sophisticated being existing around the Court at the time; that was the reason the King insisted on keeping him near him, because he was the only man that at least enlivened for a moment his day. But one feels in all his paintings the whole poignancy that Velasquez must have felt – even in those beautiful things where the figures have this wonderful structure and yet at the same time have the colouring of a Monet. You feel the shadow of life passing all the time."[1]

Of all Bacon's complex entanglements with the art of the past, his dialogue with Velázquez stands out for its intensity and its central position within his development. In the interviews with David Sylvester, Bacon is largely dismissive of the works he made prior to his encounter with Velázquez' paintings: he claims that "the analytic side of my brain" had not yet switched on,[2] that he was a painter without a true subject – and that "without a subject you automatically go back into decoration."[3] It is Bacon's fascination with the portrait of Pope Innocent X that pushes him forward: "I became obsessed by this painting and I bought photograph after photograph of it. I think really that was my first subject."[4]

Bacon's recorded remarks on Velázquez are tantalising in that they never spell out what it was that drove the obsession. In the passage quoted above, the key terms "sophistication" and "poignancy," and the maddeningly vague phrase "attitude to life," point in the general direction of Bacon's thought and feeling, but they do little more than that. Bacon is an artist whose dealings with tradition are formative and crucial: one thinks of Ingres' obsession with Raphael, or Gericault's with Michelangelo. But beyond a certain point, reading the conversations with Sylvester doesn't help. As a viewer, you are on your own. Looking closely at Velázquez is the only way into this terrain of "influence."

But who influenced whom? Mieke Bal has written persuasively about the folly of conceiving relations between artists in terms of a historical or linear series, that is, following a model of causality or determination.[5] If we were to think this way, we would have only a one-way street, from sender to receiver, master to disciple, early to late. In its place, Bal proposes a revisionary possibility: that the later artist generates or produces the earlier one, through a "preposterous" logic of reversed influence. Although Bacon stated that his paintings were "after" Velázquez, perhaps we can turn the preposition around: what is Velázquez after Bacon?

It is something to do with flesh, and faces, and power. Velázquez is indeed a painter of life at court, which is to say, life as it is governed by a highly evolved system of manners and social coding. And Velázquez apparently does little to disturb the proprieties of this society. In contrast to Goya, whose portraits of the court tend toward emotional ambivalence and at times outright caricature, Velázquez' attitude toward his social surroundings is impassive, or inscrutable. More precisely, Velázquez makes images that almost require him to declare his hand: Does he think of Philip IV as a monster, or doesn't he? Does he think the Infanta Margarita is pretty, or just plain bizarre? But then the painter withholds the answer to the question his own image has raised. Perhaps this is something that Bacon touches on in his word s o p h i s t i c a t i o n: Velázquez' images contain a complex array of attitudes toward their subject matter, but they do not display the need to reach any kind of final decision or essence. It is not that Velázquez is without opinions – the sense is quite the opposite – but he is not about to declare them. In the emotional economy of the paintings, this is not a necessary step. The non-declaration, the withholding

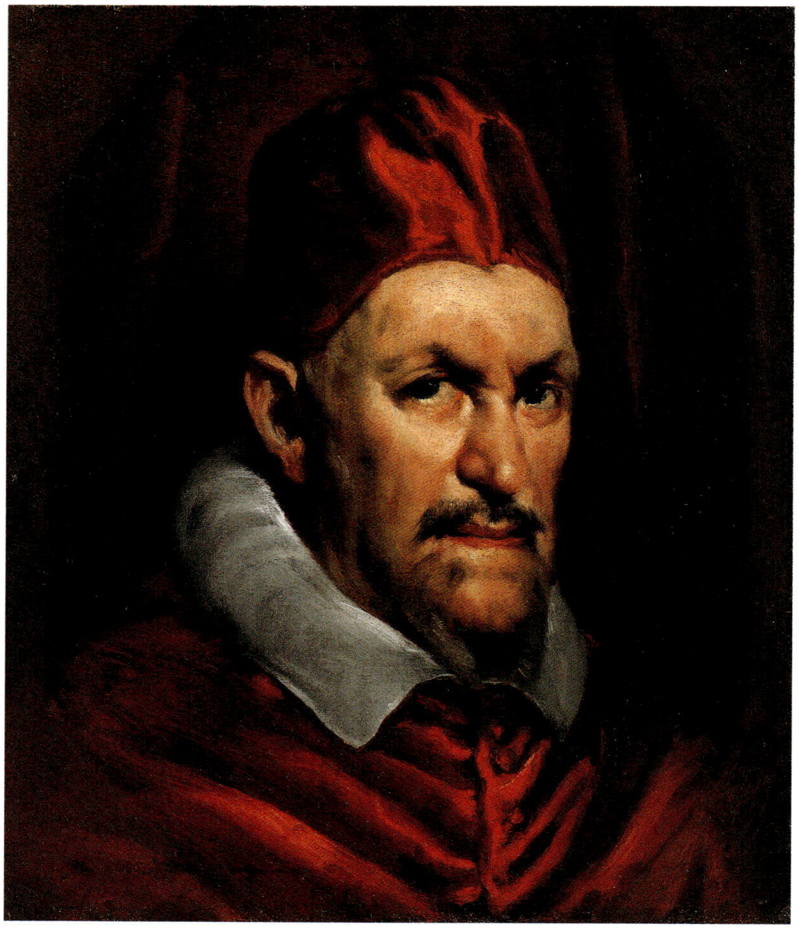

of judgement, is about keeping response to the world open, not closing it down, not limiting the self or simplifying the visual field through final determinations. Velázquez' inscrutability implies a whole ethics of maintaining the openness of the self and of the social field, almost by abstention.

Bacon's revisionary relation to Velázquez looks more closely at this openness or abstention; his impulse is to analyse it, dissect it, break it apart. In the process, Bacon alters the conditions of our own viewing of Velázquez by making the question of Velázquez' attitude toward his sitters, and the act of painting them, almost the central issue of Velázquez' works. There are certainly times when Velázquez' impartiality or suspension of judgement seems merely to coincide with the normally conservative and flattering aims of court portraiture. In the Prado's equestrian portraits (Philip IV, Count Olivares), for instance, the impassivity of the elevated figures can take the guise of formality and social distance: "These people are not for us to judge, they exist beyond the scope of our judgement, their inscrutability – and that of the painting – measures the distance between power and powerlessness." But in all the most interesting cases, Velázquez' withholding of judgement is more radical: a strategy of willed suspension of attitude that allows the most complex and contradictory forces to flow beneath the impassivity of the picture's surface. Below the decorum of the likeness of Innocent X lies a commentary (we hardly need Bacon's help to see it) of exceptional complexity: that the sitter is benign, that he is demonic, that he is intelligent and also unscrupulous, diplomatic, feral, pious, astute, veiled, transparent, opportunistic, rigid *(Plate 2).* By fastidiously maintaining his openness or equipoise, Velázquez opens the picture's surface to a circulation of intense, multiple affects that variously collide and harmonise in the ongoing temporality of viewing.

At its most fascinating, Velázquez' abstention or suspension generates a new kind of image in court art, in which so many of the conventions of normal portraiture are being observed that the final image can bypass the censor and pass as a straightforward likeness. This is a process of contraband that works entirely by manipulating the codes of manners, by appearing to observe the proprieties while in fact smuggling in highly subversive goods. (It may demonstrate one of the affinities between Bacon and Velázquez that at a time, long before the Wolfenden Report, when same-sex eroticism lay totally beyond the pale of British art, Bacon nevertheless managed to smuggle into the arena images of such an extreme sexual charge that they are still startling today. How did he get away with it?)

Plate 1 on p. 42: Diego de Silva y Velázquez, King Philipp IV of Spain, detail. C. 1652/53 (cat. no. 82).

Plate 2: Roman School (?), Copy after Velázquez, Pope Innocent X. 17th century (cat. no. 3).

When Bacon says that what drew him to Velázquez was a certain "attitude to life," it is not necessarily an attitude observable on the surface, but at a much deeper level, in the body and the drives, and in the affects generated by the body and the drives. For Velázquez, the social field is governed by power relations that operate in a more profound register than words such as "decorum" or "manners" may imply. All of Velázquez' sitters have their place in the social hierarchy etched deeply into their flesh. If "manners" and "decorum" suggest a mask, a polite surface held up to the world, Velázquez is more brutal: power does not lie on the surface, it shapes flesh and bone. Consider the blacksmiths in *The Forge of Vulcan,* whose muscles and postures are the pure products of their work and their milieu, bodies made lean and taut by hammering, by sweat, by a level of constant exertion, a particular diet, a particular temperature in their environment. And compare their wiry, dynamic bodies with the divinity who visits the forge, courtier, scion of a higher class, with his ultra-white skin and muscular slackness, his comfortable measure of subcutaneous fat, product of a life of ease, of giving orders, of a different diet and habits, of a softer environment and cooler temperatures. There is nothing contractual or juridical about power in Velázquez: the social overlaps with the physical. Or consider the women in *Las Hilanderas:* the distant Athena next to her royal tapestry, imperious, theatrical, and aggrieved; and, in the foreground, the entirely different bodies of women who labour, whose eyes and hands are led by the minute tasks of spinning, whose bodies have long since settled into shape around their work, industrious, companionable, fully absorbed. Think of the woman in *Old Woman Poaching Eggs,* whose skin and taut facial muscles indicate a long life of strain, of struggle and exposure, of limited tasks and small satisfactions; or of the labourers in *The Feast of Bacchus,* brown from the fields, whose entire life as a class is summed up in the way they are drinking.

In Velázquez, fate lies in the flesh: rank becomes physique. Fate's mark is the scar, the scarring of flesh by class, and the myriad details of life in a society governed by strict caste groupings. Even the royals do not escape: the Infanta is, in a sense, as scarred by her social position as any of the peasant faces and bodies *(Plate 4).* For hers is a body entirely given over to the function of display, deformed by display, her hair frozen, her body fused with the hoops and scaffolding of her prosthetic dress, a body geared to projecting across vast distances of space and time (even we feel the effect of that projection, centuries later) a certain message about the genetics of royal blood, the wondrous Habsburg DNA. Surely one of the many inner games in *Las Meninas* is the strange rhyme it forms between

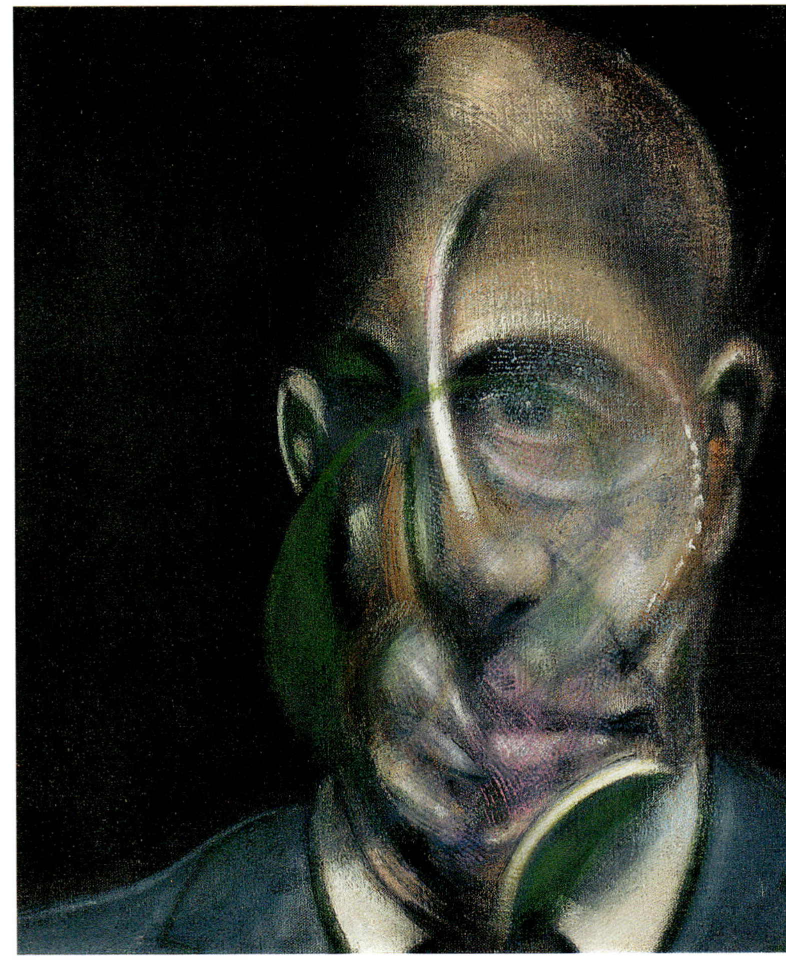

Plate 3: Francis Bacon, Portrait of Michel Leiris, 1976 (cat. no. 83).

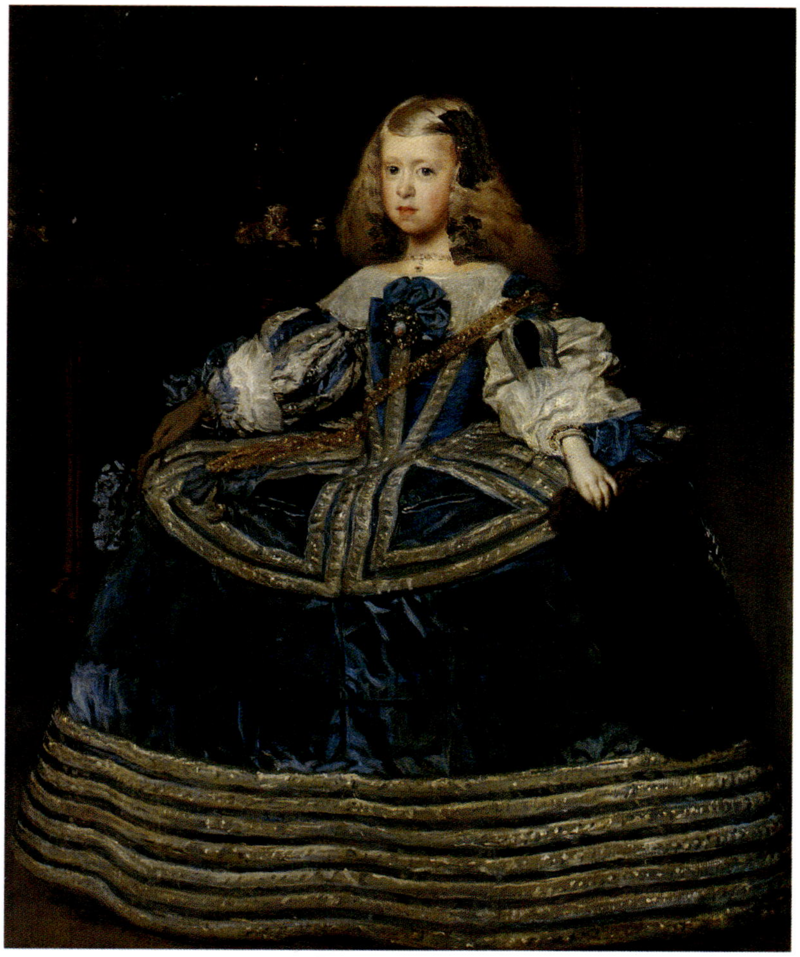

Plate 4: Diego de Silva y Velázquez, Infanta Margarita Teresa in Blue. 1659 (cat. no. 73).

the Infanta and her court dwarf, La Barbola: squat, pug-faced, absurd, isn't La Barbola the measure, the yardstick of the Infanta's own deformity, her secret sharer?

If, in Velázquez, power is always incarnate and never abstract, then the qualities of supreme power that belong to such men as Innocent X and Philip IV are properties resident in their very flesh, emanations of the body. Going beneath the strangely neutral surface of Velázquez' portrait of the Pope, Bacon finds a body instilled with powers of life and death, the bio-power of the absolutist state, implacable and demonic. Bacon's own operation on Velázquez' portrait is to peel back the picture's neutrality of surface as a surgeon might remove skin from a face. In a sense, Bacon's relation to Velázquez is intensely cruel: he takes Velázquez' own most personal achievement, his bracketing or withholding of judgement, and annuls it. The late-coming painter finally figures out that the apparent blandness or impartiality of Velázquez' surfaces in fact conceals a tense and highly volatile circulation of forces and affects – and he destroys that surface. If we accept that Velázquez' abstention is of the order of an ethical discipline – the self-discipline of remaining open to all responses, even with such formidable beings as Innocent X and Philip IV, then Velázquez' *ascesis* is truly impressive: to remain neutral, to withhold judgment – even in the presence of supreme power, even in the presence of what may be monstrous. What is stunning about Velázquez in these works is that he never for a moment relaxes the discipline of his abstention, that he never slips into simplification or foreclosure of his own multiple responses and affects. But it is precisely this *ascesis* that Bacon is out to dismantle, crushing the precursor and making his image over in his own likeness and in his own name.

Who, after looking at Bacon for any length of time, can fail to find that the portraits of the King in the Prado look more like Bacon than Bacon, *plus royaliste que le roi?* Piece by piece, the Habsburg face falls apart *(Plate 5):* it is no longer a unity, simultaneous with itself; its surface breaks up into the sub-areas and non-communicating zones that characteristically subdivide the face in Bacon. The painterly stroke of the *arc* that Velázquez brushes around the eye socket and chin of the Habsburg face becomes the *slice* with which Bacon is compelled to carve the human face. Even the signature of that stroke is appropriated, colonised by Bacon's own signature style.

This may be the subterranean connection between Bacon's own sadism as a painter, in his violent disfiguration of Velázquez' portrait of the Pope, and the power and monstrosity he finds or reveals in the sitter. Bacon presses on Velázquez' equipoise, applying to it more and more pressure, until it breaks open: Velázquez' Pope becomes a howl *(Plate 6);* the face of Philip IV disaggregates, breaks open before your very eyes. Surely we are dealing here with parallel fields of power: the power of absolute monarchy, as a force in the historical world; and the power of master painting and the master painter, as forces in the history of art. Bacon does not "represent" power, he taps into power, he becomes complicitous with it. The power to create and destroy (cities, armies, men) that belongs to rulers is diverted or re-routed by Bacon, transformed into the painter's capacity to create and destroy the Image of power: Bacon's power to create and destroy Velázquez, disfiguring him at the very point of his greatest strength (the abstention, the suspension of judgment) and re-creating him again in Bacon's own image.

It would be easy to say that this is all about killing the father. The regime of masculinity is revealed as, in the end, a murderous violence between ancestors and sons. To spell it out: the figure of the Father (everyone's father, yours, mine – not the real father, but the image or force behind him) is contemplated in the form of a supreme power (Philip IV, Innocent X) that is vanquished by the son in a drastic *coup d'etat.* What motivates the simplicity of this Oedipal tale is Bacon's own susceptibility to the Father's allure. In the crucial interview with Sylvester, Bacon is at first evasive, then wonderfully frank, then evasive again:

DS: "Do you think your involvement in [Velázquez] had something to do with feelings about your father?"

FB: "I'm not quite sure what you're saying."

DS: "Well, the Pope is *il Papa.*"

FB: "Well, I certainly have never thought of it in that way. But I don't know – it's difficult to know what forms obsessions. [...] My father was very narrow-minded. He was an intelligent man who never developed his intellect at all. As you know, he was a trainer of racehorses [...] I think he liked my younger brother, who died when he was about fourteen. He certainly didn't get on with me."

DS: „And what were your feelings toward him?"

FB: „Well, I disliked him, but I was sexually attracted to him when I was young. When I first sensed it, I hardly knew it was sexual. It was only later, through the grooms and people in the stables I had affairs with, that I realised it was a sexual thing towards my father."

DS: "So perhaps the obsession with the Velázquez Pope had a strong personal meaning?"

FB: "Well it's one of the most beautiful pictures in the world – I think I'm not at all exceptional as a painter in being obsessed by it. I think a number of artists have recognised it as being something very remarkable."[6]

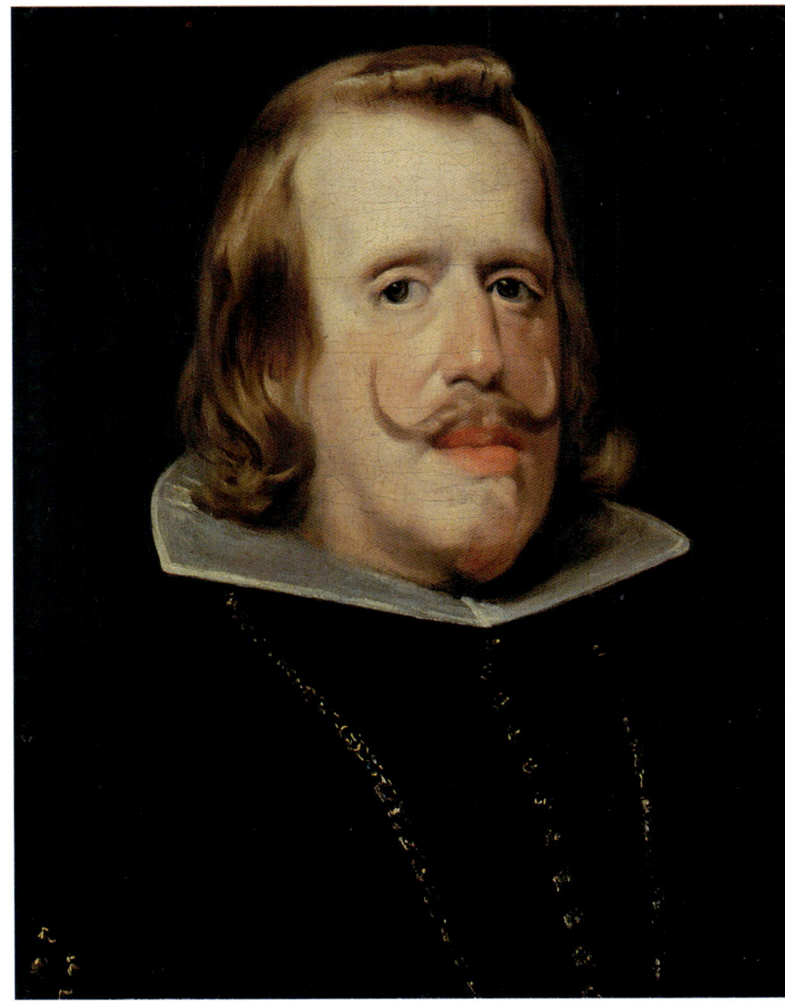

Plate 5: Diego de Silva y Velázquez,
King Philipp IV of Spain.
C. 1652/53 (cat. no. 82).

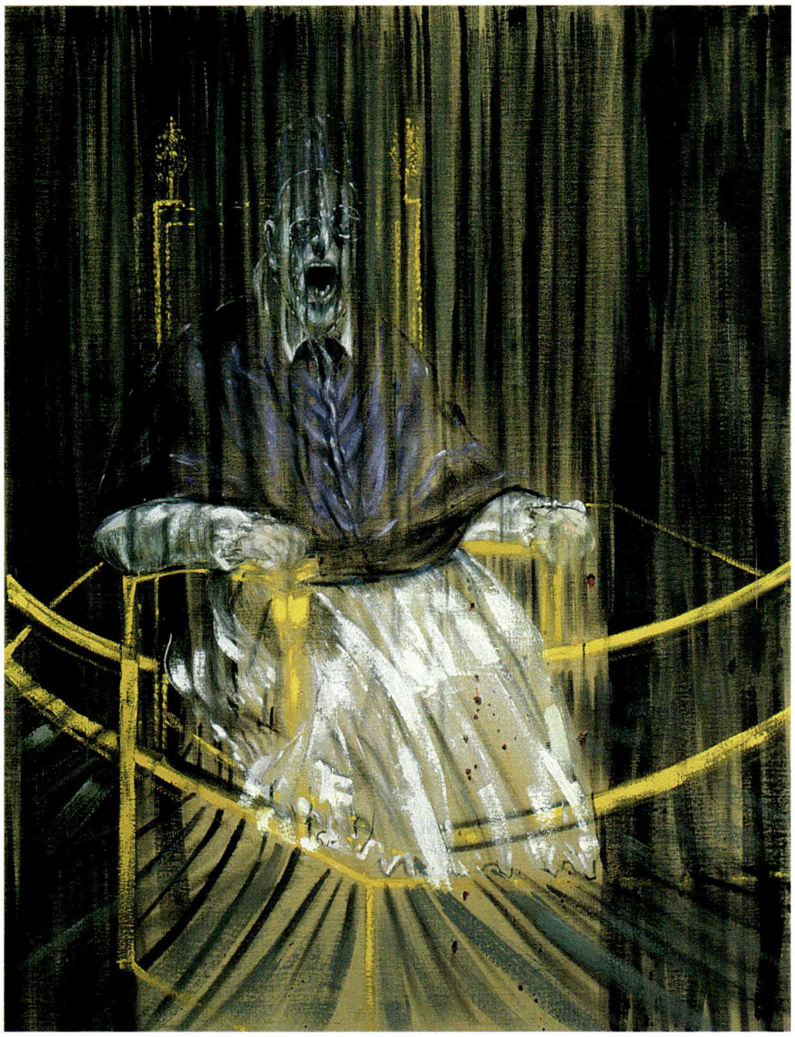

Plate 6: Francis Bacon, Study after Velázquez's Portrait of Pope Innocent X. 1953 (cat. no. 14).

It would, I think, be wrong to take Bacon's remarks – and Sylvester is certainly "leading the witness" here – as any kind of key to decipher his dealings with Velázquez. But his disclosure concerning the sexual allure of the father may point to a way in which Bacon responded to the aspect of carnality in Velázquez, and to the carnal brutality of power that subtends the polished manners of the courtier. For both of them, power resides in flesh: flesh is its true residence – not the abstract relations of law or diplomacy or the state. "L'etat, c'est moi" is here literally true: the body (of the king, of the princess, the dwarves, peasants, beggars) is less the effect of power than its ultimate cause and source. Rather than close our inquiry down, let us leave it vague: the Velázquez relation is something to do with flesh, and faces, and power, the power that incarnates in flesh and especially in the portrait, and the fluctuating currents of attraction and destruction that always play around power and flesh in Bacon's universe. Where else, in Bacon's dialogues with tradition, might similar forces and feelings come into play? Let us turn to Ingres.

In the case of Ingres' female nudes, an amalgamation of which forms the basis of Bacon's *Diptych: Study from the Human Body; Study of the Human Body – From a Drawing by Ingres (Plate 7),* the underlying fantasy that Bacon locates in his work would seem to be that of a body so pliant, so responsive to the excitement that arises on the "inside" of bodily experience through touch, that it offers no resistance; lacking internal structure, the figure becomes pure surface and pure elasticity. The Ingres study is exceptional in Bacon's work in that there is no sense of the body as possessing an interior, no sense of "meat" (or of violence, of cutting). The Ingresian skin is unbroken; it forms an even contour, a registering of skin and the sensations immediately beneath and around skin, but with little of the torsion or twisting that normally appear in Bacon's handling of the body. It is skin without bone. And if we come to Ingres through Bacon's revision, it is possible to see what Bacon is driving at: Ingres' desire for a body that is all contour, all touch, a body that is projected entirely by line and from the surface of the skin, without reference to interior anatomy, and least of all to bones and joints.

Consider the hand of *Madame Moitessier,* with its total softness and absence of rigidity, as though it were less a hand than a squid, a polyp, a jellyfish *(Plate 8).* It is in this area of the painting that Ingres defines the core fantasy which in the case of the nude figure will pervade the entire body – a circulation of erotic energy that flows as series of waves, a "wave form" that differs radically from the "crash form" (pain, sudden intensity) or "projectile form" (ejaculating, vomiting, defecating) that Bacon tends to follow elsewhere.

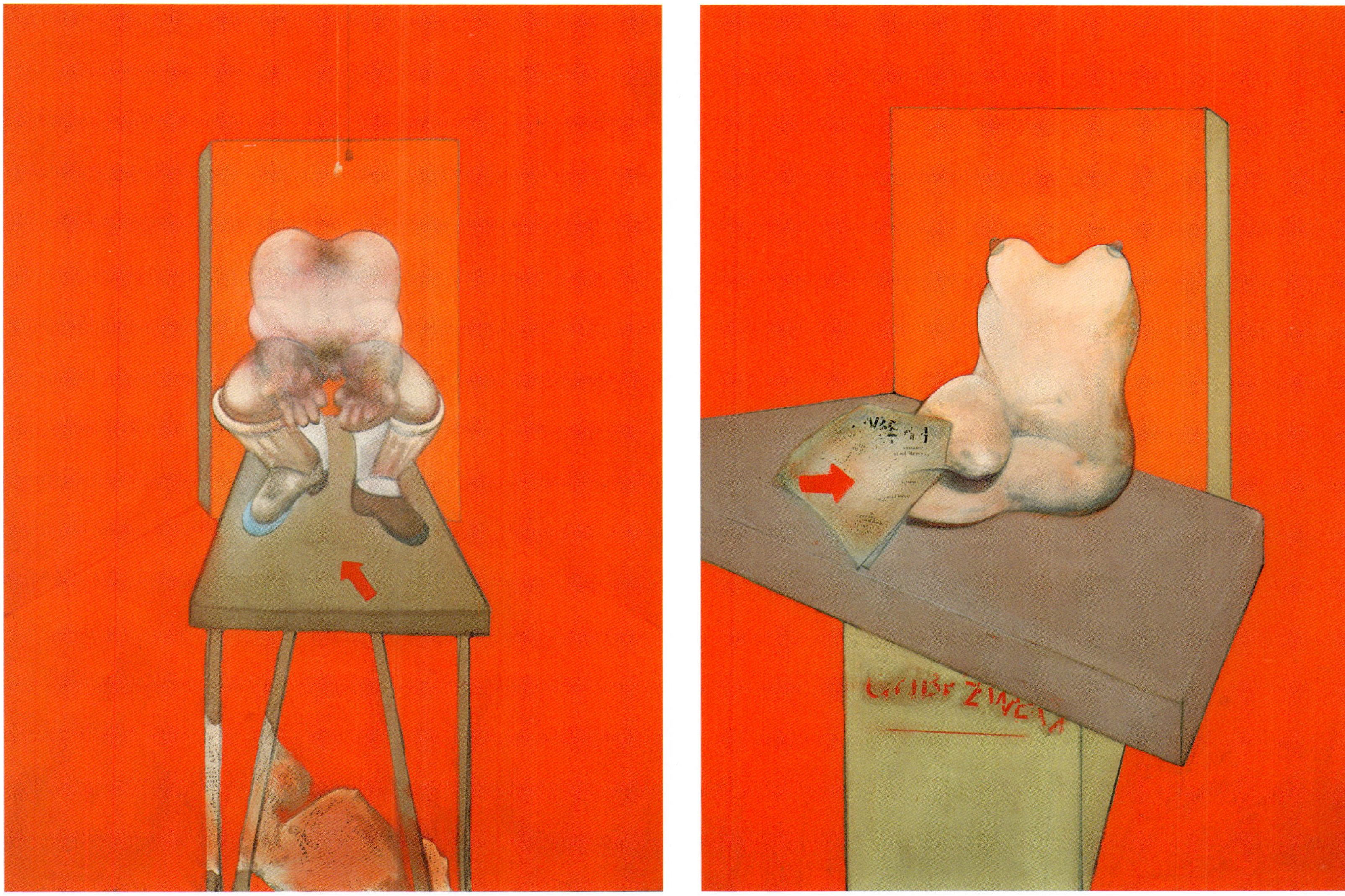

Plate 7: Francis Bacon, Diptych: Study from the Human Body; Study of the Human Body – From a Drawing by Ingres. 1982–1984 (cat. no. 102).

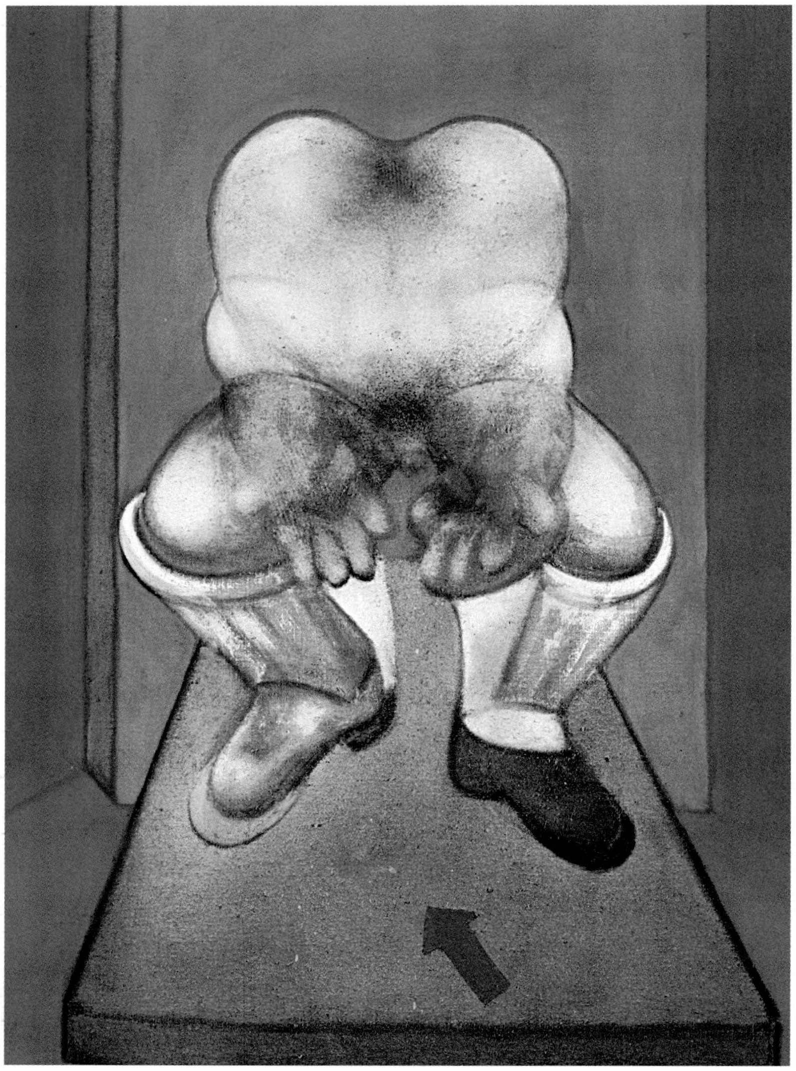

Detail, plate 7.

Which points to what may be the defining feature of Bacon's study after Ingres: that it is an exercise in exploring and inhabiting a mode of libidinality different from, and in some ways antithetical to, his own. What is obvious to Bacon is that under the guise of realism, Ingres smuggled into the arena of art (this is a similar case of contraband to Velázquez, or Bacon himself) a totally different kind of body, not based on the external view or anatomical understanding, but instead on internal sensation, the dermal and epidermal sensations of sensual pleasure. Bacon sees in Ingres a kindred spirit – and yet at the same time Ingres' sensibility, the waveform of pleasure in his work, is quite alien. Bacon has to think his way into these works, whose organisation of sexual energy is so different. As different as a female body from a male.

The Ingres study is a work that involves a radical alteration of all of the temperatures, rhythms and dynamics that constitute Bacon's habitual structuration of the libidinal field. Desire, in Ingres, is pretty unswervingly directed toward the female body – for once, Bacon has to shape-shift his own desire into a configuration *away* from the male body. But in a sense this is already what Ingres was always doing: imagining a totally different body from his own, imagining the erotic response of the female body from the inside, radically shape-shifting into a body that r e s p o n d s to the masculine. Despite the resolute heterosexuality of Ingres' object choice, what complicates the libidinal field is his need to think of the female body as though his own, masculine body did not exist: the women of *Le bain turc* or the *Valpincon baigneuse* or the *Odalisque à l'esclave* exist in their own world, a world of intense sensual pleasure, but with the men somehow absent. Think of the *Odalisque a l'esclave:* she is in the throes of pleasure, but alone (the male attendant, a eunuch, does not count). Ingres' imaginary theatre of desire always resembles a seraglio that men may not enter. The only route of access is via empathy, an empathy amounting almost to identification: to b e c o m e the object of desire, to feel its distinctive wave of sensation, the touch of the absent or invisible lover, becoming her touch, feeling as a woman, coming as a woman.

Look at the legs of the figure on the left panel of Bacon's diptych, with its odd shoes, one female, one male. Bacon seems to sense in Ingres the necessary bisexuality entailed by his object choice, that in order to love as a man, he must become a woman, become invertebrate, become the starfish or octopus of Madame Moitessier's hand, just a wave, an undulation.

Bacon's reworking of Ingres says a great deal about his approach to past art: his method involves going "behind" the historical image to the libidinal field that it seems to organise and express, and joining the image there. Bacon is not, in the case of Ingres, detained by the specifics of any particular image – his homage combines a broad range of nudes in a fluid aggregate whose function is to lead *past* the surface to the erotic imaginary that is its source. The manner in which 'influence' is felt here is less like competition or combat and more like dowsing or divining, conjuring out of Ingres' paintings a particular rhythm of nervous and sensual energy, and then absorbing that rhythm into his own. The alienness of Ingres' eroticism and of its heterosexual organisation of desire is expressed through the duality of the diptych form, with male on the left, female on the right. Yet what Bacon detects in Ingres is that, deeper than the structure of sexual difference, there is an impulse of fluidity and transformation, in which active merges with receptive and back. At this level it may be possible to find in Bacon's diptych a line of connection between the sensual pleasure of the female body in Ingres' heterosexual economy and the male body in its receptive state, in a same-sex organisation of desire. Ingres' ability to empathise (to the point of identification) with female sensation and excitement is transposed into a fluid masculinity that knows about penetration "from both sides." Bacon does not represent this fluidity, he taps into it, in the act of making the painting: "influence" takes the form of an impersonation, a doubling, where the shape-shifting of becoming Ingres, and the shape-shifting of becoming "woman" (or penetrated male) are made to rhyme.

Bacon's excursus into Ingresian territory is unusual in his work in its foregrounding of erotic passivity – the kind of same-sex economy that is dominant in his painting tends to be less interested in occupying a liminal state between masculine and feminine (or active and receptive), and much more concerned with male/male interaction, the interplay of virility. In order to become Ingres, Bacon must in fact radically restructure the anatomy of flesh and sensuality, removing all torsion and contortion, removing the bone from the meat. Yet this famous "meat" of Bacon's is easily misunderstood. It is natural for the viewer of Bacon to be reminded of the tremendous flayed carcass in Rembrandt; formally there is so much in common – the sense of the exposed spine and ribcage, the violence of the relation to the real, the appalling colours of meat, red, brown and blue. And yet, looking at the Rembrandt, you see at once the difference: Bacon's meat is *living* flesh, Rembrandt's is truly dead, a ruin, and the tone is one of elegy and mourning. It is similar with Soutine *(Plate 9),* where meat is an object of suffering and pity, of pains and torments that have now ceased, and are honoured and remembered. Although Bacon retains some of this, what is missing is the tone of mourning or melancholy. Far more than

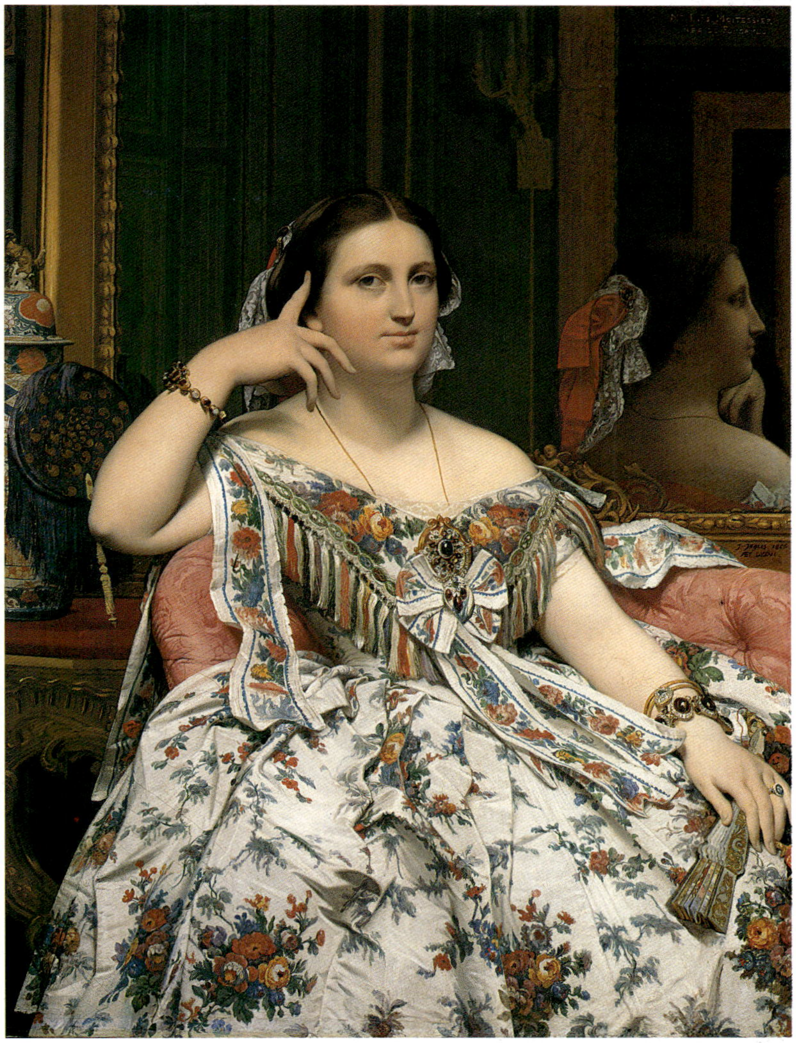

Plate 8: Jean-Auguste-Dominique Ingres, Madame Moitessier. 1856. Oil on canvas, 120 × 92.1 cm. London, National Gallery. (©: London, National Gallery.)

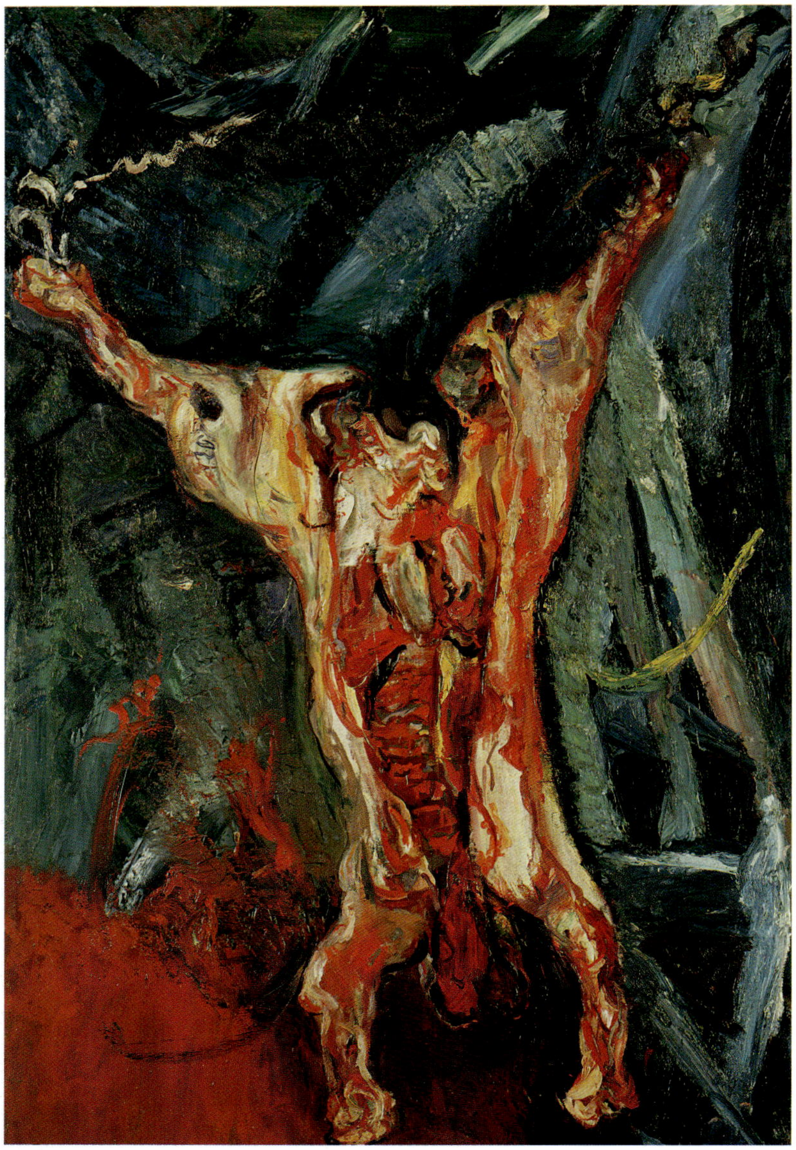

Plate 9: Chaim Soutine, Carcass of Beef. 1925 (cat. no. 135).

Plate 10: Edgar Degas, After the Bath: Woman Drying Herself. C. 1888/92. Pastel on Paper mounted on cardboard, 103.8 × 98.4 cm. London, National Gallery. (©: London, National Gallery.)

with Rembrandt or Soutine, in Bacon meat is alive with the colours of living flesh; meat is not the condition to which we are eventually reduced, but the condition we are in now, the condition of life itself. To put this another way, Rembrandt deflects the image of destruction and death into a cadaver, away from the land of the living – and this move offers consolation and simplification: death is not part of life. With Bacon, the death-drive is not deflected or warded off into a safely separated zone, it inhabits life from the inside, at the deepest level of the body's tissue and bone. Death is i n flesh; not posthumously, but intrinsically.

It is meat with bone: articulated, dynamic, forceful. Bacon's admiration for Degas' *After the Bath (Plate 10)* is relevant here, in that what Bacon notices is not only the voluptuousness and ease of female flesh (the de-ossified, passive flesh of Degas' teacher, Ingres) but also the spinal column: „You will find at the very top of the spine that the spine almost comes out of the skin altogether. And this gives it such a grip and twist that you're more conscious of the vulnerability of the rest of the body than if he had drawn the spine naturally up to the neck. He breaks it so that this thing seems to protrude from the flesh."[7]

Bacon's observation may seem capricious or perverse, until one recalls the extraordinary precision with which Degas renders joints and bones, not just in this painting, but throughout his work. In a room full of dancers, each performer assumes a precise attitude that is unlike all the others, a specific balance that is the outcome of kinetic forces acting across the points and muscles. In Degas' dancers (but also horses, bathers and bourgeois sitters) muscles, perhaps for the first time in the nineteenth century, have "origins and insertions;" Degas has almost a chiropractor's sense of how bones rotate in the sockets of the joint, how they become heavy or tense, how the body's centres of gravity are multiple and not just one, and how these centres form a dynamic constellation of points as they move through space. Degas returned to the body the bone structure that Ingres had spirited away. Bacon's response to Degas is, again, to go past the surface of the image to the libidinal organisation that lies behind it, where the vitality of the body is felt – kinaesthetically – as the pull of muscles and tendons against the bones into which they insert.

This pull, this contraction of muscle as it moves, is essential in Bacon; it is the mode of the body's greatest fascination for him: pumping, spasmodic, abrupt. In the history of art, the locus where these qualities are perhaps most dramatically felt is Michelangelo, who emerges in Bacon as a constant and pervasive force ("I've always thought about Michelangelo").[8] What is Michelangelo after Bacon? Primarily a draftsman, since it is in the drawings that the

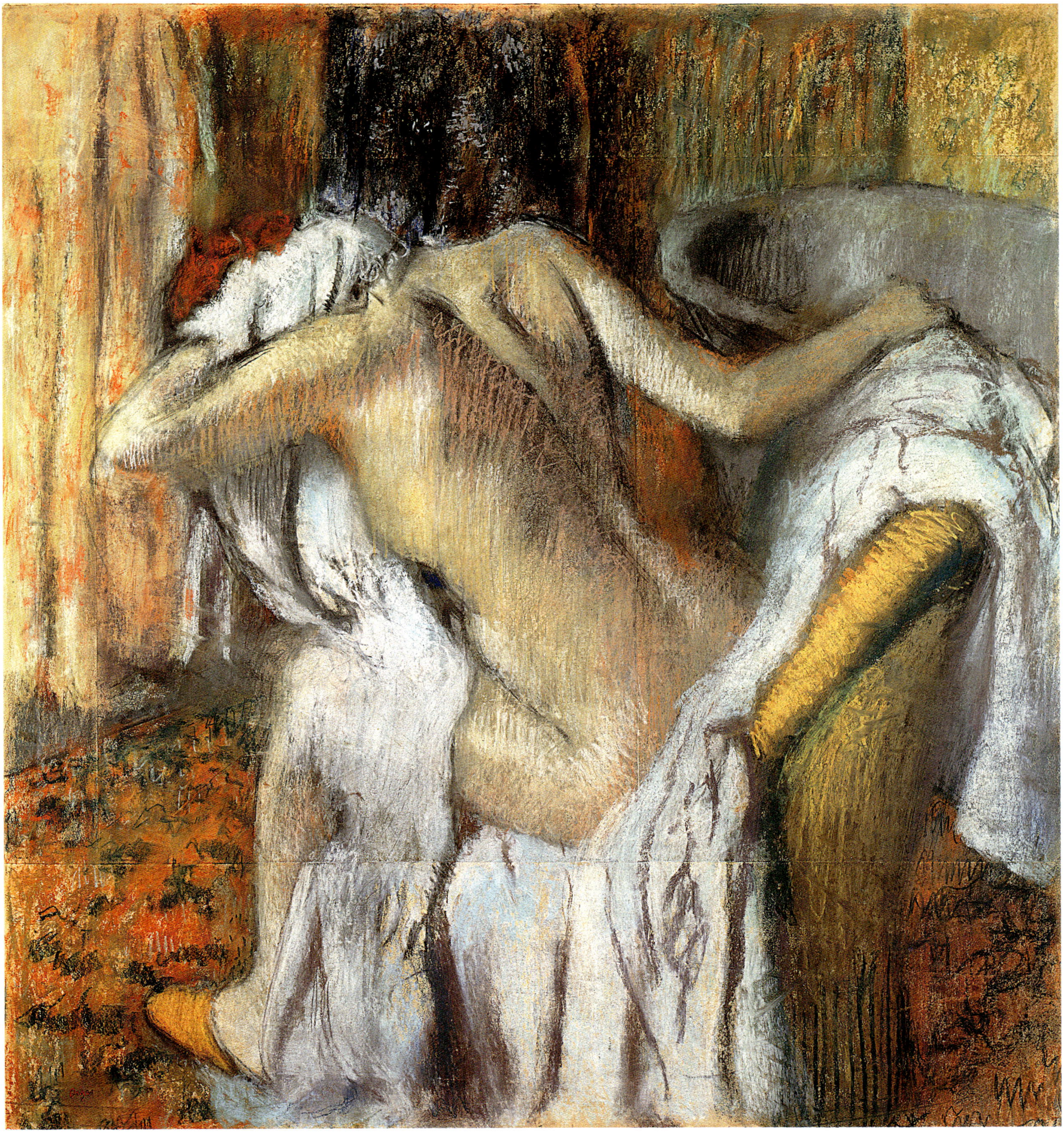

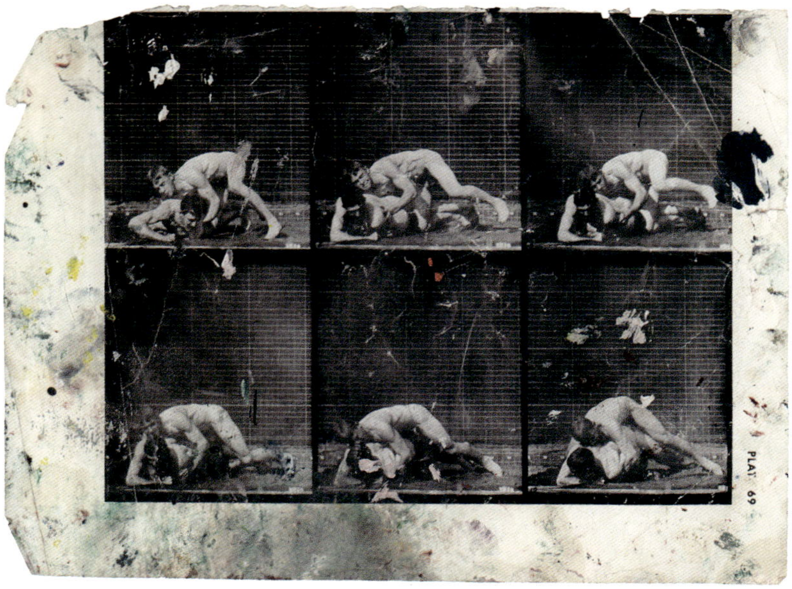

Plate 11: Black-and-white images of two wrestlers. Leaf from book, Eadweard Muybridge, The Human Figure in Motion, Philadelphia, 1887, London, 1901 (later edition) (cat. no. 144).

accuracy and precision of muscular action becomes so clear. Michelangelo's drawing of the hand of the Libyan Sibyl, gripping a bar sideways (1511–13),[9] can seem like a complete body by Bacon, a full figure study. Just as, after Bacon, the hand of Madame Moitessier is like a part-object summing up Ingres' entire sense of the invertebrate body of his desire, so the Michelangelo hand sums up his desire for a body exerting force to the maximum, in many directions at once, a body where muscle and bone form a complex torsion system, a body of twists and knots of kinetic force.

Bacon's feeling for Michelangelo was fused, according to his own account, with the photographs of Muybridge.[10] The interplay of influence gets complex here, as the dialogue shifts to three voices. It is as though Muybridge, read through Michelangelo, acquired a monumentality that Muybridge's figures (which are often close to comedy, or slapstick) lacked on their own; and, conversely, Muybridge opened up in Michelangelo a far greater sense of movement and struggle. The Michelangelo Captives, Slaves and Pietàs are, after all, centralised, pedestal forms. The genuinely off-balance quality that is present in Muybridge's wrestlers *(Plate 11)* opens them to a much wider and at the same time more dynamic space. Muybridge and Michelangelo form two interconnected channels of libidinal energy and rhythm that Bacon's work is constantly circling around: a body that is convulsive, with movements discontinuous and powerful.

Bacon adds to Michelangelo – Muybridge, as he does to Ingres and Velázquez, the particular range of rhythms that lie at the core of his work, for his figures are almost always inhabited by a life force that seeks a condition of shattering, of bursting the bounds. Within the external, "anatomical" body that others see, resides a body that is felt as an intense surge of vital force, an *élan vital* that is far more fluid than the anatomical body, since nervous excitation changes its form, pulling it into shapes that go against the forms known by the eye. In Ingres, the surge is a sine curve, a contour that never breaks, but holds its form dynamically, like a "standing wave." In Bacon, the surge is felt as a spasm; its key points are the body's openings – penetrating, vomiting, excreting. Already in Michelangelo, the pull of muscle against bone, and the knots or nodes that are formed by torsion, constitute a kind of purified erotic body. But Bacon changes the current entirely, by joining the torsion of muscle, with its erotic charge, to the spasms where the boundaries of the body break open to the outside, where inside and outside flow into each other and the body is opened up (like meat). Distortion in Bacon is fuelled by the feeling of the body's vitality increasing internally to the point where it has to break the body open and escape. Though loosely correlated with the muscular body, this body of spasmodic energy follows a very different logic, of thresholds or intensities rather than specific anatomical zones – muscular force and torsion are the base line from which the surge of libidinal energy arises, but as the surge increases it comes to redesign the body according to its own needs and rhythms, where different zones of the body can become displaced or condensed, as in a dream; where a mouth can become an anus, or an eye. Bacon's dark and menacing shadows, pulled beyond recognition as belonging to a body in any normal or anatomical sense, state in extreme form the rhythm that runs through his figures: not a curve but a jolt, a shock, a trauma, the point where flesh opens up to the outside air and throbs with a life-force that is thoroughly inhabited by its own destruction.

In Bacon's many interactions with tradition, perhaps the most striking feature is the absence of what Harold Bloom called "the anxiety of influence." He seems never to feel that to exist as an artist within a long tradition is a burden, that the tradition is already so replete that it has become crushing or oppressive. What enables Bacon to approach Velázquez or Michelangelo (or Géricault, or Picasso) with such equanimity is that he posits behind their work something else, a libidinality that exists in a configuration that is not his own, but can become is own. Behind Velázquez' Philip IV appears a regal-paternal body that incarnates power, that is power made flesh, and in that flesh appears Bacon's own personal rhythm, disjunctive, spastic, full of caesuras. Behind Velázquez' Innocent X appears the rhythm of life-energy peaking at such intensity that it has to escape through the body's opening, as a howl. Ingres is inhabited in a different way: Bacon modulates his own rhythm, adjusts it to fit the sine-curve of Ingres' female body, which is at the same time made into a variation on a masculine rhythm. With Michelangelo and Muybridge, the line of contact is different again: the erotic pull of muscle against bone is intensified into the contraction of a body about to shatter, to open up as meat. At the centre of Bacon's work lies rhythm, less in the musical sense than as a property of the living organism, organised around the leaps of intensity that occur in extremes of pain and pleasure. Bacon looks at the body, and at the history of painting, through the lens of the drive, the constellation of life-force whose most vital expressions are, for him, sexual; and at that level, all the masters of past art become his contemporaries.

[1] Sylvester 1999, p. 80, 81.
[2] Sylvester 1999, p. 71.
[3] Sylvester 1999, p. 199.
[4] Sylvester 1999, p. 71.
[5] Bal 1999.
[6] Sylvester 1999, p. 71, 72.
[7] Sylvester 1999, p. 47, 48.
[8] Sylvester 1999, p. 114.
[9] Michelangelo, Study for the right hand of the Libyan Sibyl for the Sistine Chapel, red chalk. Oxford, Ashmolean Museum.
[10] Sylvester 1999, p. 114–116.

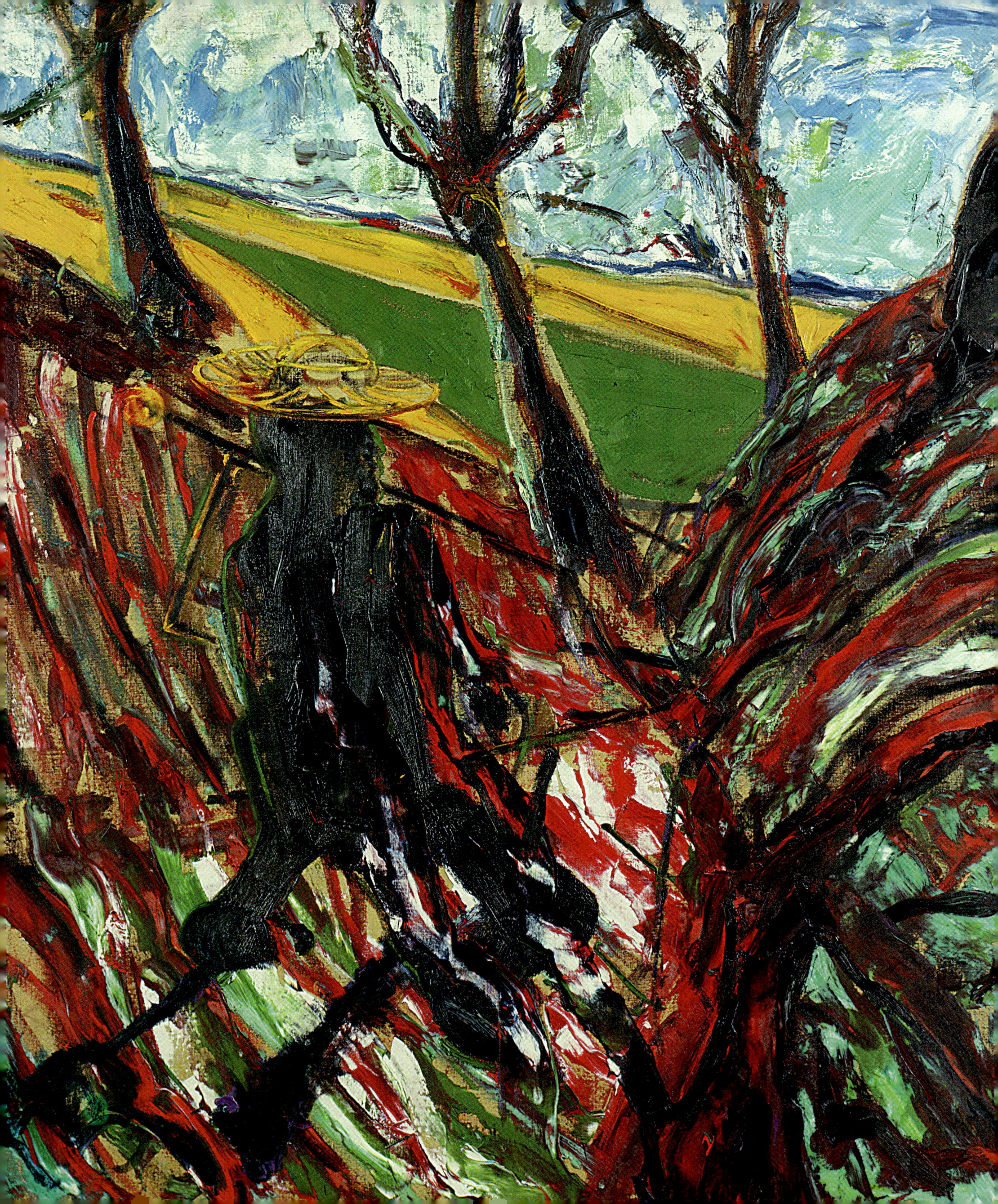

Ernst van Alphen

"Reconcentrations:" Bacon Reinventing his Models

"Influence" is one of the key concepts in traditional art history and art criticism. In order to understand an artist's work, critics place it within artistic genealogies. In publications about Bacon's work the same influences are reiterated again and again: Bacon has been influenced by the work of Velázquez, by Rembrandt's and Van Gogh's work, and of course, by the serial photographs of Edweard Muybridge. Such genealogies are constituted according to the mechanisms or principles of a family tree. They grow organically and they are hierarchical: the older artist plants the seed which is received by the younger artist. Young artists feed on older art. Important features of the work of the young artist can be deduced from the work of the older artist, as if a kind of DNA has been passed on from past to present.

This traditional notion of "influence" is amazingly persistent. Although the logic of influence has been deconstructed and reversed by several critics during the last seventy years, many people cannot resist its attraction. The main opponents of the notion "influence" are first of all T.S. Eliot, next the art historian Baxandall and last but not least the cultural analyst Mieke Bal. In 1919 in his essay "Tradition and the Individual Talent", Eliot challenged the kind of temporal order implied by influence in the following modest and careful way: "Whoever has approved this idea of order [...] will not find it preposterous that the past should be altered by the present as much as the present is directed by the past."[1] Eliot maintains the traditional idea that the past directs the present. He complicates this one-way-traffic notion of historical change by proposing the reverse mechanism, not instead of it, but next to it: the past is also altered by the present.

Michael Baxandall is more impatient. He ends his critique of the notion of "influence" with the following words: "But influence I do not want to talk about."[2] The argumentation, which has lead to this radical concluding statement, runs as follows. In the first place, "influence" is a curse of art criticism primarily because of its wrong-headed grammatical prejudice about who is the agent and who the patient: it seems to reverse the active/passive relation which the historical actor experiences and the inferential beholder will wish to take into account. "If one says that X influenced Y it does seem that one is saying that X did something to Y rather than Y did something to X. But in the consideration of good pictures and painters the second is always the more lively reality."[3]

Baxandall argues here that the later artist *actively* produces the "influence" by choosing to respond to the older work. At the same time he suggests that if the mechanism of influence exists, it is only at work in the case of bad artists: only bad artists let themselves be influenced. In the case of a good artist it is not only he/she who is the agent instead of the patient, but the kind of activity which he performs on the work of the predecessor is much more diverse and complex than what is implied by the shallow term "influence:" "If we think of Y rather than X as the agent, the vocabulary is much richer and more attractively diversified: draw on, resort to, avail oneself of, appropriate from, have recourse to, adapt, quote, differentiate oneself from, assimilate oneself to, assimilate, align oneself with, copy, address, paraphrase, absorb, make a variation on, revive, continue, remodel, ape, emulate, travesty, parody, extract from, distort, attend to, resist, simplify, reconstitute, elaborate on, develop, face up to, master, subvert, perpetuate, reduce, promote, respond to, transform, tackle ... – everyone will be able to think of others."[4]

The complex ways in which art acts upon predecessors suggests that it is not so much the present but rather the past which is conditioned by a perpetual flux. It is precisely this idea that is elaborated by Mieke Bal in her book *Quoting Caravaggio: Contemporary Art, preposterous History* (1999). Reading contemporary art works in their relation to Caravaggio or other baroque works, she demonstrates the idea that art's engagement with what came before it, involves an active reworking of the predecessor. "Hence, the work performed by later images obliterates the older images as they were before that intervention and creates new versions of old images instead."[5]

If we take Eliot's, Baxandall's and Bal's critique of the idea of influence seriously, it entails a major shift in the discourse of the proliferating writings on Francis Bacon's works. First of all, we should no longer deal with Bacon's works as the outcome of an art-historical process. Instead we should deal with them as the starting point for a reconsideration of the artists whose work was important for Bacon in one way or another. The kind of questions which become central then, are the following:

– How do we look at Velázquez after we have seen Bacon?

– What kind of Rembrandt emerges thanks to Bacon? Which features are foregrounded in Bacon's works and revise our conception of Rembrandt?

– Do Géricault, Ingres, Rembrandt, Degas, Velázquez, Van Gogh, and Muybridge, have something in common, which would explain why they were all important to Bacon?

These questions are already a lot more exciting than the reiterated search for great predecessors.

We should, however, not just reverse the traditional hierarchical relation of influence. It seems meaningless just to bestow on Bacon the kind of authority and agency that was previously ascribed to his predecessors. Although, when we want to understand the relation between his work and that of his predecessors, we are better off starting rather than ending with the work under consideration, in this case Bacon's, his work must also be read, that is actively and critically engaged. As obvious as this sounds, it is far from being standard practice. For one of the major problems in Bacon scholarship, is the authority granted his own voice in the numerous interviews with him.

Bacon is, as we all know, one of the best, most intelligent and articulate commentators on his own work. He was a self-conscious and vocal artist who has not refrained from strong and repeated statements about his work. Many of these statements are enormously helpful for understanding that work. But under certain conditions only – one of which is a sensitivity to their performative nature and force, rather than their often deceptive constative content. For, at the same time, or rather because they are so intelligent, his statements have a rather different function. First of all, without expressing his boredom or annoyance with the predictable, unintelligent questions of some of his interviewers, he will always answer politely. But his polite answers should in many cases be read as elegant refusals to answer the questions that he did not respect. In fact, his answers imply something like: "Don't expect an answer from me to such questions: look for yourself."

But this is not the only reason why we should be cautious about taking the interviews as a transparent way to access an understanding of his work when we approach Bacon's work and its relation to his predecessors. The second reason is that Bacon's place in the history of art is, to a large extent, constituted by himself in his interviews. His utterances are extraordinarily self-designing, even self-promoting. As Bernhart Schwenk has remarked, Bacon keeps almost the whole of twentieth century art at bay. He claims not to have any special affinity with his contemporaries. He presents himself in his interviews as a lone genius. It is only the dialogue with the most canonical artist which he allows. He will only dwell on the work of geniuses like Michelangelo, Velázquez, Rembrandt, Poussin, Van Gogh, Degas, Picasso.[6] Bacon may do this with more than little of irony, an irony that is, however, always two-sided. But still, heeding his statements in this respect so obediently is an insubordination to his injunction, expressed in the polite answers, to look for yourself.

The best way to put the authority of Bacon's own statements into perspective is by looking at them – as well as the paintings – quite closely. Let me focus for a moment on those remarks that are supposed to provide a better understanding of the artists or images that influenced him. In the interviews with Michel Archimbaud[7] Bacon makes the following remarks on the influence his predecessor Picasso has had on him:

„At a certain time in my life I was very much influenced by Picasso. Perhaps 'influence' isn't quite the right word, I certainly don't think Picasso would have used it. Let's say perhaps that Picasso helped me to see. [...] No not to see, it isn't even that. [...] Whatever it is, I admired Picasso greatly. For me, he was the genius of the century. Everything of his that I saw at that time had a huge effect on me. It changed me a lot. It was, as I told you, seeing an exhibition of his work at Rosenburg's that made me decide to begin to try and paint. Later on, I don't know. I think I've been influenced by everything I've seen. But it's true that Picasso was also influenced by everything. He was like a sponge that soaks up everything. That's what I am thinking of when I talk about influence; something like this phenomenon of a sponge that absorbs everything."[8]

Although it was seeing a Picasso exhibition that made Bacon decide to become a painter, Picasso loses his special role in Bacon's development when the latter declares that the former was influenced by everything he has seen. And in a following move of his answer Bacon reverses the active/passive relation in this historical process. Bacon like Picasso was the sponge that absorbed everything. He was not the passive recipient of influences, but the active absorber of images around him. It is in that aspect, not in the way he paints, that he is like – was influenced by, perhaps – Picasso.

Michel Archimbaud, not noticing Bacon's subtle deconstruction of the notion of influence, continues stubbornly with the follow-

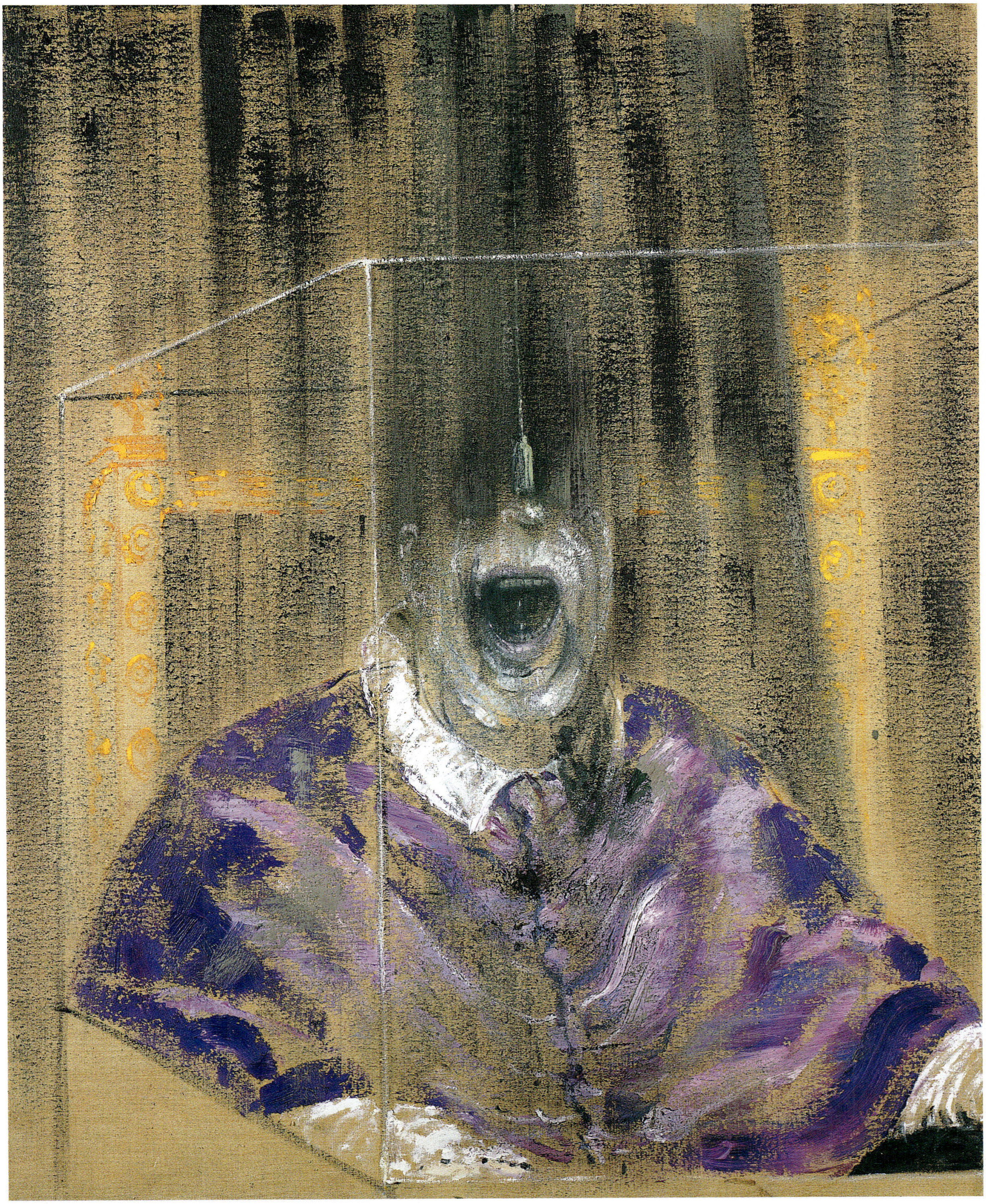

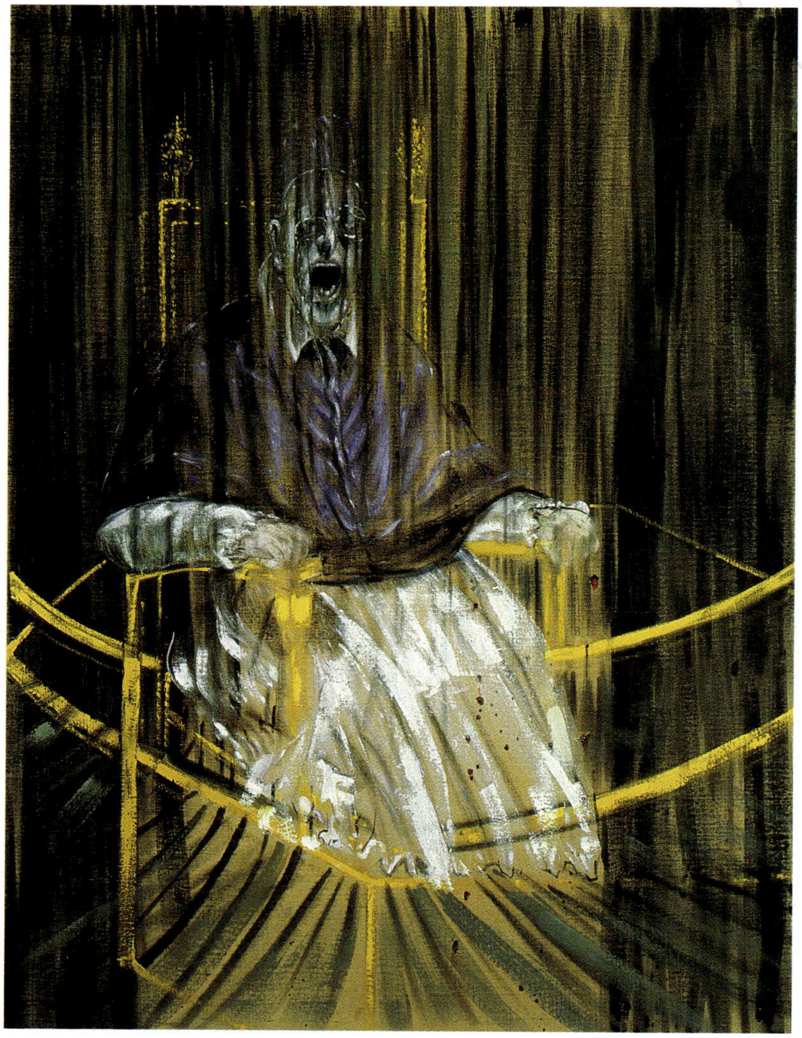

Plate 1 on p. 56: Francis Bacon, Study for Portrait of Van Gogh VI. 1957 (cat. no. 129).

Plate 2 on p. 59: Francis Bacon, Head VI. 1949. Oil on panel, 93.2 × 76.5 cm. London, Arts Council Collection and Hayward Gallery. (©: The Estate of Francis Bacon/VBK, Vienna, 2003.)

Plate 3: Francis Bacon, Study after Velázquez's Portrait of Pope Innocent X. (cat. no. 14).

ing question: "And apart from Picasso, who else has influenced you?" Bacon's answer is: "I have been influenced by everything that I've seen."[9] Bacon's answer – an answer he has now given twice – can be read as a polite rejection of the question. He rejects the conventional notion of influence. By saying that he has been influenced by everything that he has seen, he has totally emptied out the content of the word "influence." For the traditional notion of influence implies difference and hierarchy: some images have influence, others do not; and some images have more influence than others. If Bacon has been influenced by everything, the idea of influence has lost its relevance. Then, all images are equal and undifferentiated.

In another conversation with Michel Archimbaud, Bacon further elaborates the reversal of the active/passive relation between the artist and his predecessor. As an answer to a question about relativity of perception he says the following: „Yes, it's always like that when you look at a picture. But each person of course, translates it in his own way. The effect that the portraits by Ingres have on me is quite different from their effect on someone else, and it's not just because I'm a painter and the other person isn't. It's the same with the face of someone you pass in the street. You get an impression and you make all sorts of analyses based on these impressions and you can make all sorts of analyses based on these impressions and someone else, seeing the same face, will come to a totally different conclusion."[10]

According to Bacon, perception is never passive, it is by definition productive. In a conversation with Hugh Davies and Sally Yard, he draws the consequence of that insight for the production of art: "Great art is always a way of concentrating, reinventing what is called fact, what we know of our existence – a reconcentration [...] tearing away the veils that fact acquires through time. Ideas always acquire appearance veils, the attitudes acquire of their time and earlier time. Really good artists tear down those veils."[11]

This remark also has its implications for how we should evaluate Bacon's relation to his predecessors: not in terms of influence, but in terms of reinvention. This reinvention of the predecessor Bacon formulates with the word reconcentration. This implies not only a reversal of the active-passive relation, but also a different mode of articulating the relation between artist and predecessor: not in terms of what they have in common, of what the later artist shares with the earlier one, but in terms of how the artist is different from the predecessor on whom he allegedly modelled himself. For, reinvention implies difference as well as sameness. The pertinent neologism "reconcentration" gives the reinvention a specific edge: the emphasis, focus, stakes, and thrust is shifted.

The most obvious case to start with is Bacon's relation to Velázquez, or, we should say now, his reinvention of Velázquez through reconcentration. Probably Bacon's most famous painting, already indicates its source in the title: *Study after Velázquez' Portrait of Pope Innocent X (Plate 3).* This painting of 1953 is a reworking of Diego Velázquez' extraordinary painting of 1650 of the powerful and unscrupulous pope who duplicitously took the name "Innocent" for himself *(Plate 4).* As Hugh Davies remarks, when this painting was painted, this pope was arguably the most powerful man in the world.

„He sits confidently on the papal throne, [...] as God's representative on earth. The true brilliance of Velázquez's accomplishment in this painting is to have satisfied his demanding papal client with a flattering, beautifully rendered portrait while at the same time passing on for the ages the unmistakable hint of corrupt character and deep-seated deceit that well ordered and stern façade."[12]

This duality in Velázquez' painting of the pope is indeed striking: the pope does not only look powerful, heroic, self-confident, but at the same time, corrupt and even evil.

Bacon himself says the following about this painting: Velázquez came to the human situation and made it grand and heroic and wasn't bombastic. He turned to a literal situation and made an image of it, both face and image at the same time. The pope is like Egyptian art: factual, powerfully formal and unlocks valves of sensation at all different levels.[13]

First of all it is important to notice that according to Bacon's perception of Velázquez' painting *Pope Innocent X* is striking not because of his unique personality, his inhumanness, the combination of heroic power and corruption, but because of the opposite of uniqueness: of what he has in common with other human beings. Bacon calls this the "human situation." Thus he concentrates the representation on something quite different from the personalized portrait.

In Bacon's re-inventions of this painting, he does focus on the duality of the pope's representation. But the nature of the duality that emerges in his series of pope paintings is of an altogether different kind. We see the pope no longer in a powerful position, as heroic. He is now rather isolated, lonely, and primarily in extreme pain (as in *Study after*) or as a kind of average bore (as in *Pope I*) *(Plate 5).* The papal portraits of 1953, the *Studies for Portrait I–VIII* (cat. nos. 6, 7, 8) show a whole range of other common human emotions between the extremes of great pain and boredom or dullness. Thus it is thanks to Bacon's papal portraits that we can now have a different kind of perception of Velázquez' painting. It is due to Bacon's papal portraits that in the case of

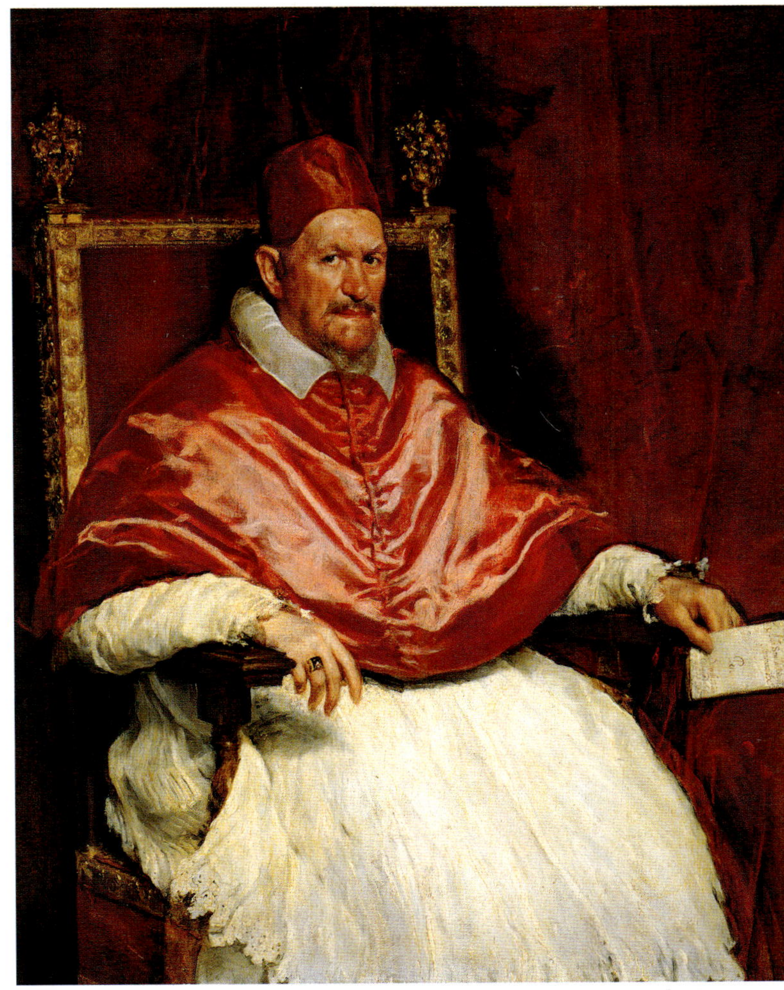

Plate 4: Diego Rodriguez de Silva y Velázquez, Pope Innocent X. 1650. Oil on canvas, 141 × 119 cm. Rome, Galleria Doria Pamphilij. (©: Rome, Galleria Doria Pamphilij.)

Velázquez' pope we no longer accept the aura of authority the pope radiates.

This aura was mainly an effect of portraiture as a conventional genre. As I have explained elsewhere, the painter of an artistic portrait does more then just documenting or illustrating somebody.[14] The portraitist proves her/his artistic originality by consolidating the self of the person portrayed. Although the portrait refers to an original self already present, this self needs its portrayal in order to secure and reconfirm its own being. The portrayer has enriched the interiority of the portrayed subject's self by bestowing exterior form on it. For, without outer form, the uniqueness of the subject's essence could be doubted. The artistic portrayer proves her/his own uniqueness by providing this proof.

The traditional portrait in this equally traditional view seems to embody a dual project. Two interests are intertwined in this genre. The first interest is quite obvious: the portrait's investment in the authority of the portrayed. The most innocent reading of portraits would be that the sitters were portrayed because they had authority in the first place, in whatever field of society. But since our insight into the past distribution of authority is mediated, among other things, through the portraits of historical figures to which we attribute authority because they have been worthy of portrayal, this intuitive acceptance of the "real" authority of the sitter is actually the reverse of that other activity, namely placing authority in them through the function of the portrait. From the perspective of the viewer this innocent reading is a case of analepsis, of chronological reversal. It is because we see a portrait of somebody that we presume that the portrayed person was important, and the portrayed becomes the embodiment of authority in whatever way. Thus, authority is not so much the object of portrayal, but its effect. It is the portrait that bestows authority on an individual self. The portrait, especially when it is framed by a place like the National Portrait Gallery or a comparable institution, expects us to stand in awe, not so much of the portrait, but of the portrayed.

Bacon, however, has radically deconstructed this authority-bestowing effect of the genre of portraiture. He did this through his "reconcentration" on pain and loneliness and boredom, aspects that make authority almost laughable in comparison. The duality that comes about in his portraits, the one between being isolated, lonely and in pain, or boring and bored, is now, as an after effect, also present in Velázquez' painting. But we first needed Bacon's pope portraits in which he undid the genre's conventional effects, before we could look at Velázquez in this more "humane" mode. After we have seen Velázquez' pope in this more humble, human way, it is

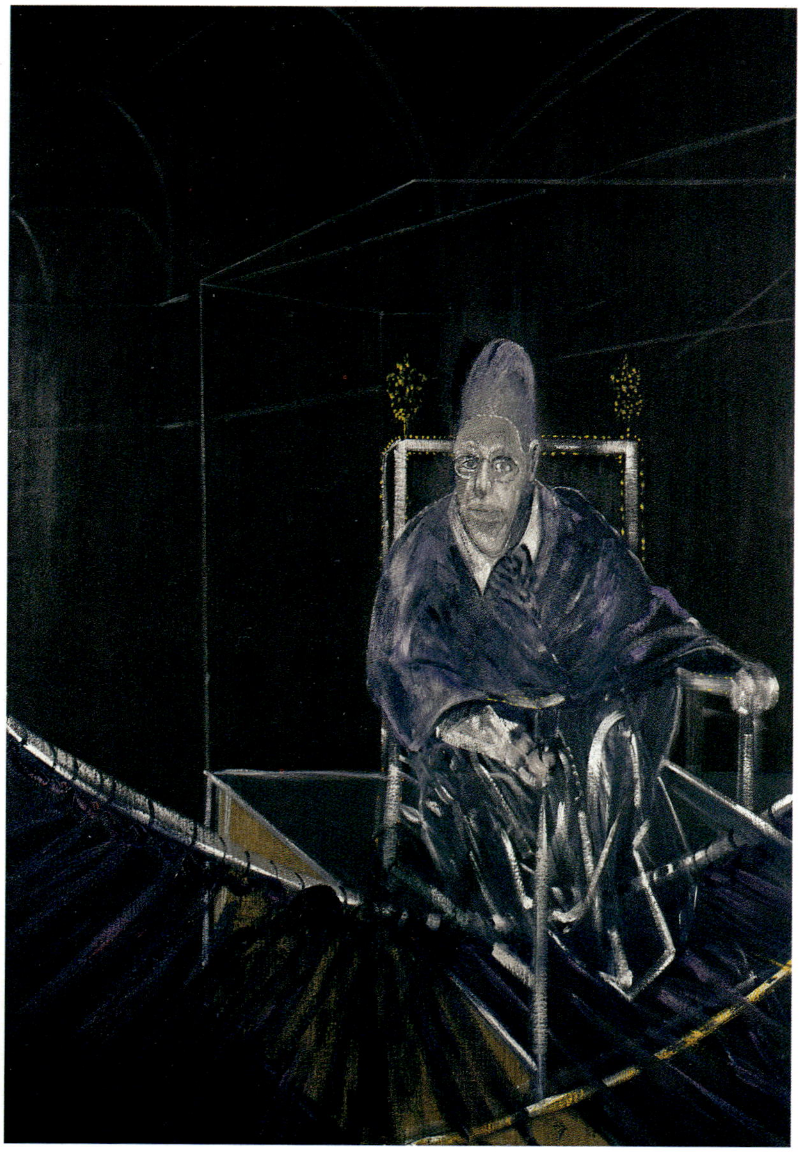

Plate 5: Francis Bacon, Pope I (cat. no. 4).

almost impossible to go back to the mode of looking that bestowed heroic authority on this figure.

Bacon's engagement with predecessors he admired, quite literally consists of deconstructing or taking away, effects of representational conventions which block our view of the represented person, like a censoring veil. In the interview from which I already quoted, he described these veils which cover the painting and which should be taken away. Let me quote this passage again: „Great art is always a way of concentrating, reinventing what is called fact, what we know of our existence – a reconcentration [...] tearing away the veils that fact acquires through time. Ideas always acquire appearance veils, the attitudes acquire of their time and earlier time. Really good artists tear down those veils."[15]

The tearing away of those veils, which are produced by representation itself, is a kind of painterly violence quite explicitly thematised in Bacon's work, including in his papal portraits. In this respect one could say that in his painting Bacon again and again comments on the function of painting, that of tearing away the veils that block our sight from really seeing predecessors.

Let me explain the way he foregrounds and destroys the veils of representation by dealing with these portraits as a series in which a telling development takes place. In the painting *Pope I,* 1951 *(Plate 5)* we see a relaxed pope, quietly sitting in his armchair. He is surrounded by a black space. There is no death or violence in this portrait. The black background is quiet, especially in comparison with the moving, uneven paint over-layering the pope in the *Study after Velázquez.* At the bottom of the former painting we see the representation of a curtain, this time no curtain of paint, but a painted curtain. This curtain is closed and the pope seems to be happy, or at least not in pain. This figurative representation of a closed curtain seems to have the opposite effect on the pope to that of the moving curtain of paint in *Study after Velázquez.* But, the paint handling tells us, it is not the curtains that are problematic; rather, it is the representation as curtain that is.

In *Head VI, 1949 (Plate 1)* there is again a curtain of paint in movement. But there is another striking detail in this work. Between the covered eyes of the pope there is an object that can be seen as a hanging light switch or as a curtain-tassel. This light switch/curtain tassel is a recurrent motif in Bacon's work. In his early work the motif is ambiguous: it seems to refer to the act of turning on the light as well as to the act of closing or opening a curtain. In his later work the second possibility disappears. The switch/tassel becomes an unambiguous light switch, sometimes hanging, sometimes fixed on the wall, most of the time in combination with naked bulbs. (See e.g. *Triptych May – June 1973* (cat. no. 131), *Three Studies of Figures on Bed, 1972,* cat. no. 138.)

In the painting *Head VI, 1949* the ambiguity is, therefore, significant. The light switch/curtain tassel covers or replaces the figure's eyes. This is striking because sight traditionally refers to the idea of perception as detection and revelation, as do lamps that are switched on or curtains that are opened. In fact perception, as well as representation as revelation, is foregrounded in a convention of seventeenth-century Dutch painting according to which half-opened curtains represented on the canvas reveal the depicted scene behind the curtains.[16] We can only see the represented object when the curtain is removed, and this half-opened curtain reminds us of the once-closed curtain, hence, its emphasizing the act of revelation. In the case of Bacon's painting, however, the sight of the pope seems to be blocked, cancelled out by this index of detection and revelation.

In contrast to *Pope I, Head VI* does not have the quiet, black painted space; there are strokes of paint on an almost naked canvas, strokes that signify movement. If taken together, the two paintings give rise to a logic that seems to allegorise representation. In *Head VI* representation appears as an act of detection or revelation. The curtain is being opened, the veil torn away, or the light switched on, whereby the opaque haze disappears. This act is clearly presented as a violent act: it shows the figure in its naked truth: isolated, lonely, in pain: not heroic, but as radically human. Hence, the allegorical and meta-critical meaning of these paintings can be formulated as follows. Bacon develops a mode of portraiture that does not consolidate the self of the portrayed person, but, on the contrary, lays bare an unsettling, disrupting force under the human skin.

The function of the curtain or veil in Bacon's papal portraits differs radically from the way the curtain functions in the famous portrait of Filippo Archinto by Titian *(Plate 6).* In that case we see a half transparent curtain or veil covering the right side of the pope. First of all, this veil is not being torn away, it is at rest. And it is more or less transparent, so it does not really cover this pope. While Bacon's pope portraits suggest that the act of revelation, of representation, is a violent act, in the case of Titian's portrait such a meta-reading seems not to be at stake at all.

My example of the papal portraits also suggests Bacon's fundamental distrust of representation and of what representation does to the represented model or object.[17] Bacon's distrust motivates him to look carefully at those predecessors who are not subservient to the medium of representation in which they work. Those painters are able to work against the deforming and deceptive effects of representation. Notwithstanding the deceitful nature of representation, they are able to show a truthful human condition. For, ultimately

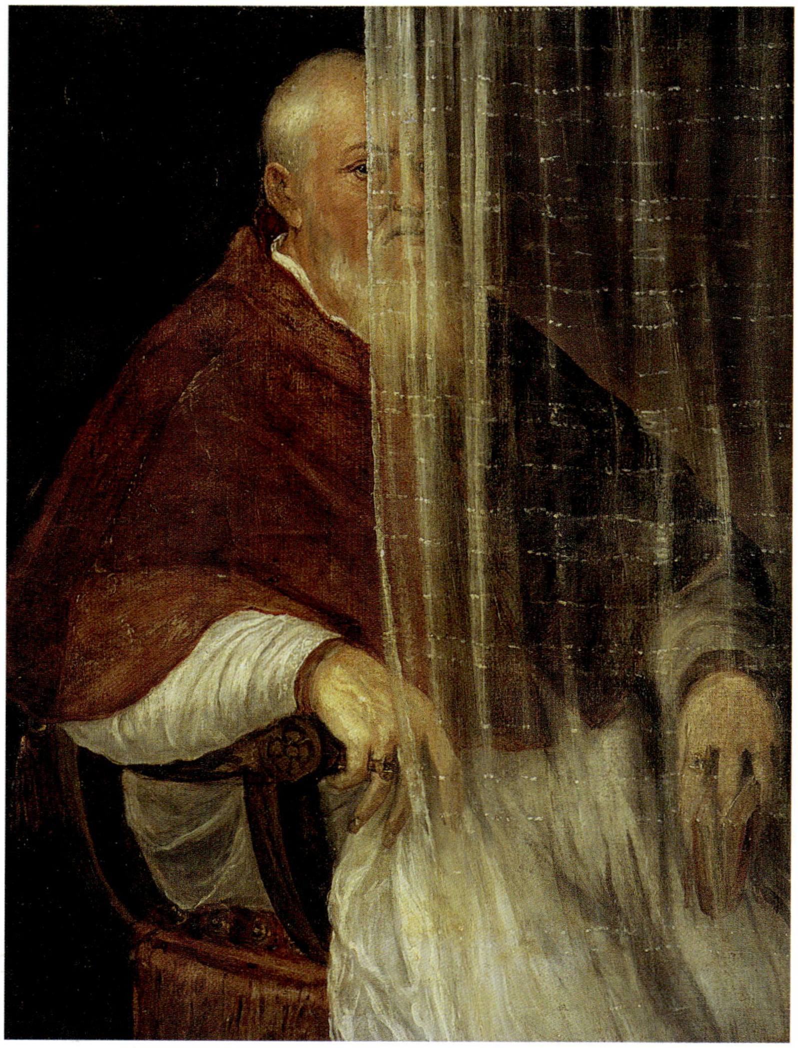

Plate 6: Tiziano Vecellio, Portrait of Cardinal Filippo Archinto (cat. no. 13).

Bacon is a realist, not in his mode or style of painting, but in his philosophy. His thought is not represented, let alone illustrated, in images. The visual image, including the way it represents and the way it is materially made, produces thought. Bacon's vision of the human condition and the deceptions against it wrought by traditional painting is precisely such a thought, a thought that is entitled to the name of philosophy.

Bacon articulates the naked truth of the human condition in a striking manner in his comments on the French painter Géricault (*Academic Study of the Nude*, c. 1816; cat. no. 108). He says the following about this predecessor: "The impressive thing about Géricault is the sense of movement in everything. Especially the representation of the human body and of horses; everything is captured in an incredible sense of movement. But when I talk about movement, I don't mean the representation of speed, that's not what it's about at all. Géricault somehow had movement pinned to the body. He was fascinated by it."[18]

The movement Bacon talks about is a movement internal to the body, not a movement of the body. Gilles Deleuze's reading of Bacon is very successful in providing an understanding of the nature of this internal movement in Bacon's work and in those art works he admires. According to Deleuze, Bacon's project consists of dismantling the face, that is, to rediscover the head not as the locus of a personality, but as something bodily. The body, then, is considered as flesh or meat. Of course the body also consists of bones, but bones are only a spatial structure. In the case of meat it could be said that the flesh hangs from the bones, while the bones hold up the flesh. In Bacon's work the body is revealed only when the bones no longer support it, when the flesh ceases to cover the bones. He strives to achieve a pictorial tension between flesh and bone. "Meat is the bodily state in which flesh and bone are in confrontation instead of forming a structural whole."[19] It is this condition of meat, which is at the same time the condition of all human beings who suffer. They cannot rely on the "support system" of their bones.

Within Bacon's bodily architecture the mouth and the teeth occupy a special role. (See especially *Study for the Head of a Screaming Pope,* 1952 (cat. no. 28), *Study after Velázquez's Portrait of Pope Innocent X,* 1953 *(Plate 2)* and *Head II,* 1949 (cat. no. 26). "They are small bones. But there is an affinity between the mouth and its interior, with meat, to the point where the open mouth has become nothing more than a section of sliced artery. The mouth then acquires a general power, which turns all meat into a faceless head. The mouth is no longer an independent organ, but a hole through which the whole body escapes, and from which the flesh hangs

[…]. Bacon calls this the Scream, the whole body's response to the immense pity that meat provokes."[20]

Bacon's notion of meat and the body can also be recognized in his admiration for Rembrandt's late self-portraits. According to him, these self-portraits resemble blocks of flesh with no bones to support it. He points out, for instance, that Rembrandt's head in his final self-portrait has no eye sockets. It just consists of flesh, which is in convulsive movement because it has to hold itself up without supporting bones. The "fleshy" nature of this Rembrandt self-portrait is also, albeit in a less radical way, at stake in Rembrandt's self-portrait in the Kunsthistorisches Museum in Vienna *(Plate 7)*. As right as this sounds to us now, it took Bacon's "reconcentration" to make this aspect of Rembrandt noticeable.

I propose to extend Deleuze's reading of Bacon's architecture of the body, of its malfunctioning support system, to the spaces in which his figures are located. Many critics have noticed the artifices in Bacon's painting that isolate the subjects in space: the boxes, platforms and cage structures. (See *Study for Portrait,* 1949, cat. no. 50; *Portrait of Isabel Rawsthorne,* 1967, cat. no. 59; *Diptych: Study from the Human Body, Study of the Human Body – From a Drawing by Ingres,* 1982–84; (cat. no. 102); *After Muybridge – Study of Human Figure in Motion,* 1965, cat. no. 57.) They are usually read as a means of short-circuiting the development of action, hence of narrative. But here there is more to say about these isolating spaces. The boxes and cage structures are always ambiguous. Something is wrong. The edges of the boxes never form a real, realistic space. They form impossible, non-existing spaces. So, like the bones, these real architectural spaces also fail to provide support for the figures placed inside them. The figures cannot be framed by the cages or boxes. The figures cannot find their location unambiguously in relation to these spaces, because the cages are impossible. So Bacon strives after a pictorial tension not only between flesh and bone, but also between figure and space. Both tensions undermine any idea of a support system for the subject. It is this lack of support systems that explains the pinning down of movement to the body.

It is especially in Bacon's series of Van Gogh paintings from 1957 that the relation between figure and space is undermined in the most complex way. These canvases were based on Van Gogh's destroyed *Painter on the Road to Tarascon* from 1888 *(Plate 8)*. Normally, and more extremely after 1957, Bacon's figures are painted in impasto, whereas the surrounding space is evoked by a strikingly flat surface. In the Van Gogh paintings both the figures and the space are painted in heavy impasto. But there are more differences in comparison to his other work. As Andrew Brighton

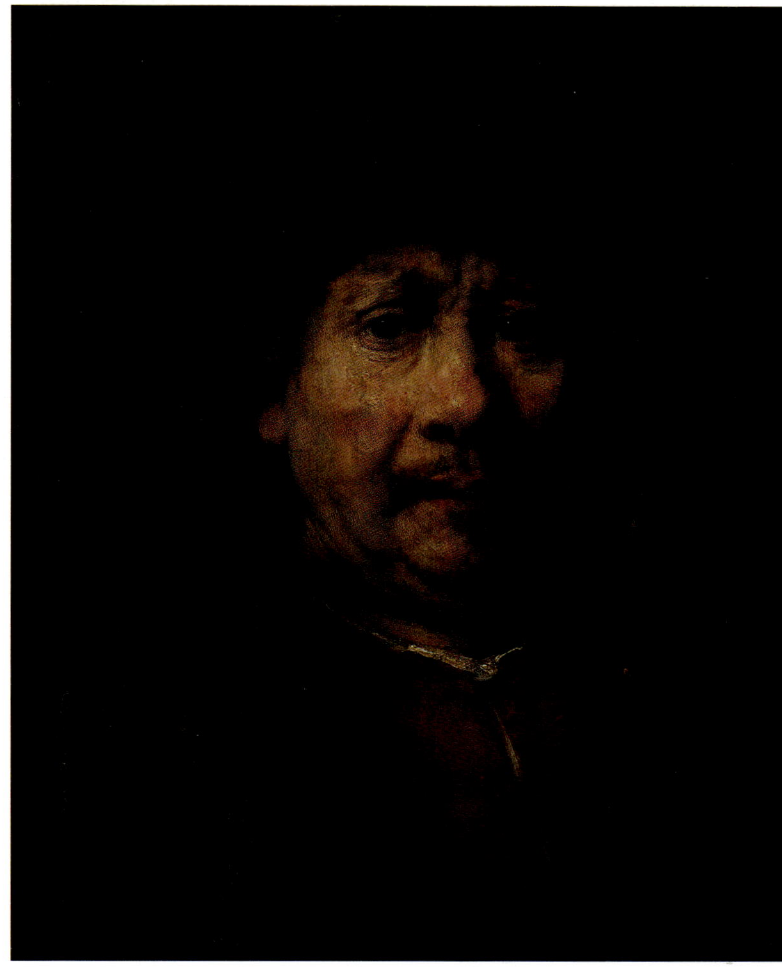

Plate 7: Rembrandt Harmensz. van Rijn, Small Self Portrait (cat. no. 80A).

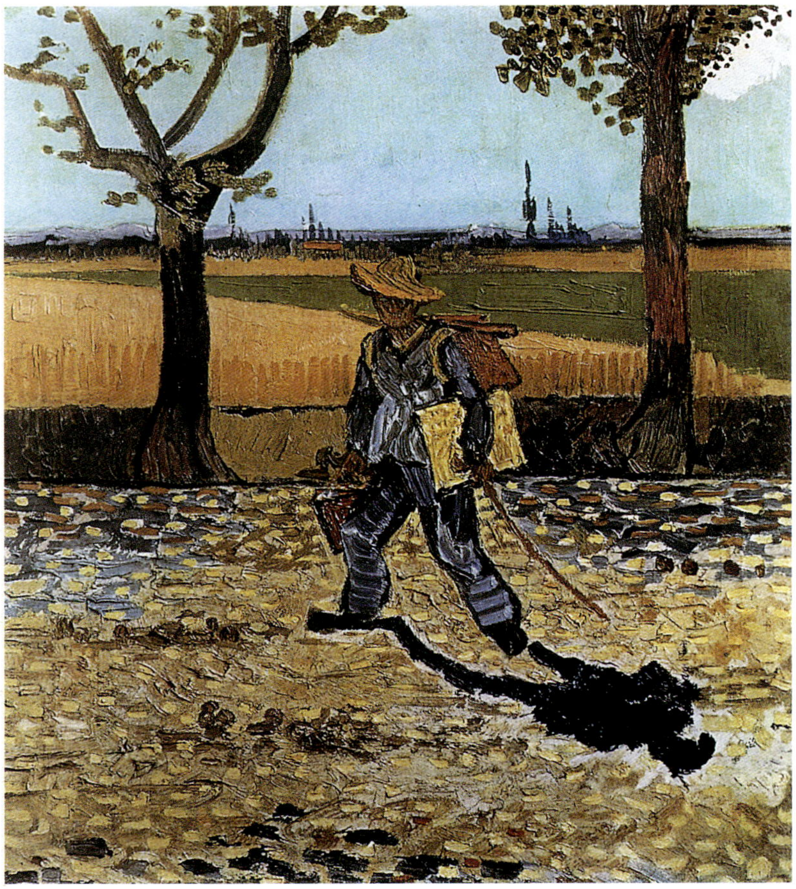

Plate 8: Vincent van Gogh,
The Painter on the Road to Tarascon.
July 1888. Oil on panel, 48 × 44 cm.
Destroyed, formerly Magdeburg,
Kaiser Friedrich Museum.

describes them: "In these paintings tone was subordinate to colour. Previously light and dark had described depth and rotundity, and colour provided incident or emphasis within the tank of darkness. In the Van Gogh paintings, rather than describe bodily movement, intense hues laid over each other in explicit brush strokes created a rhythm across the canvas, emphasising the surface of the painting."[21]

One could argue that the role of colour and impasto in Bacon's Van Gogh paintings is inspired by his model: by Van Gogh's paintings, especially by *Painter on the Road to Tarascon*. This would imply that Bacon is not reinventing the predecessor, but just following him. But it is not that simple. Van Gogh's use of bright, pure colours is usually explained with reference to impressionist ideas about subjectivity and the senses. According to 19th century empiricist psychologists like Ernst Mach or William James, objects of perception are not complex entities, but just bundles of sense impressions. The eye does not perceive objects but colour impressions. It is only in the brain of the perceiver that those impressions are mixed into objects. Van Gogh's later work seems to be an almost literal demonstration of this idea that colour is the most elementary unit. He does not paint objects but the colour impressions as they appear on the retina.

This kind of contextual knowledge about the second half of the 19th century is, however, rather irrelevant when we look at Bacon's perception of Van Gogh. Bacon is not at all interested in the empiricist ideas of perception. He is fascinated by the painterly effect of these ideas when they are embodied in paint, at least in the case of Van Gogh, and, to mention one other case, Seurat. The application of pure colours next to each other, instead of mixing them, creates a painterly "skin" that looks as if it is in movement or even turmoil. While Bacon is usually not a great lover of landscapes, Van Gogh's landscapes are an exception. But he looks at them as if they are bodies. And he sees movement "pinned to" these bodies. His comments on Van Gogh in one of the interviews with David Sylvester is telling in this respect: "Van Gogh is one of my great heroes because I think he was able to be almost literal and yet by the way he put on the paint give you a marvellous vision of the reality of things. I saw it very clearly when I was once in the Provence and going through that part of the Crau where he did some of his landscapes, and one just saw in this absolutely barren country that by the way he put on the paint he was able to give it such an amazing living quality, give that reality the Crau has of just plain bare land. The living quality is what you have to get. In painting the problem is to find a technique by which you can give over all the pulsations of a person."[22]

Again, this statement is surprisingly precise and deserves to be read with careful attention. Talking about the living quality of Van Gogh's representation of the landscape of the Provence, Bacon makes an imperceptible transition to the "pulsations of a person" as the most crucial problem for painting. In his own Van Gogh paintings we see precisely this: the pulsations of a person in – that is, embodied in – the landscape. This is Bacon's reconcentration of Van Gogh's work.

The Baconian term "reconcentration" is exactly adequate, more so than reinvention. For, through Bacon's agency upon Van Gogh, the landscape in the latter's work becomes a bundle of "pulsations of a person." In *Study for Portrait of Van Gogh VI (Plate 9)* we see Vincent standing still on a road. The road is composed of large strokes of thick paint. The impasto technique is even more strikingly used in painting the road than in painting the figure. Vincent is painted in very dark blue and black. These colours and the grimace on his face turn him into an embodiment of death. His body is not bodily at all, whereas the road is extremely body-like. The red, green and white strokes of paint turn it into a meat-like surface. It recalls the slaughtered oxen in *Three Studies for a Crucifixion,* 1962 (cat. no. 147), *Figure with Meat,* 1954 (cat. no. 136) and *Crucifixion,* 1965. After having seen Bacon's reconcentrations of Van Gogh it is almost impossible to look at Van Gogh without being influenced by Bacon's bodily reading. Although the painterly skin of his paintings will never look like meat, the turmoil that characterizes his way of applying colour is forever associated with internal movements of the body.

But there is more to be said about Bacon's Van Gogh paintings. In Van Gogh's *Painter on the Road to Tarascon* the figure is beautifully framed by the two trees: the painter is in the centre, one tree is to the right of him, the other to the left. This stable, static composition of the landscape provides the figure with a space in relation to which he can easily, and safely, locate himself. That situation has changed radically in Bacon's paintings. First of all in most of the paintings of the series, the composition is oblique instead of frontal. The two trees, although still framing the figure, are leaning over to the left as if a heavy storm is going on. The space is characterized by violence and turmoil. Earlier I compared the spaces in which Bacon's figures are located with the architecture of his figure's bodies. Neither the bones of the bodies, nor the markers or edges of his spaces provide support to the bodies/figures. This now seems to be the case also in Bacon's reinvention of Van Gogh. As if to compensate for this failure, in some paintings of the series he has added the artifice we know of so many from his other paintings: the cage or box. But they don't help. The figure remains caught up

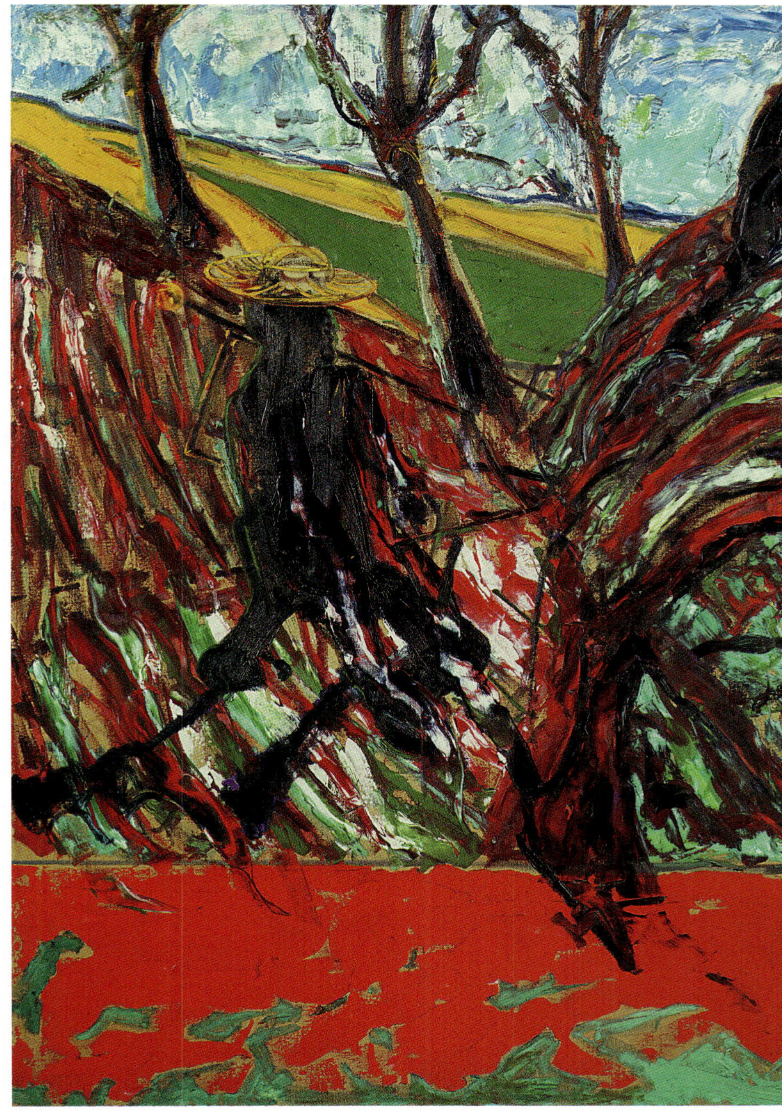

Plate 9: Francis Bacon, Study for Portrait of Van Gogh VI. 1957 (cat. no. 129).

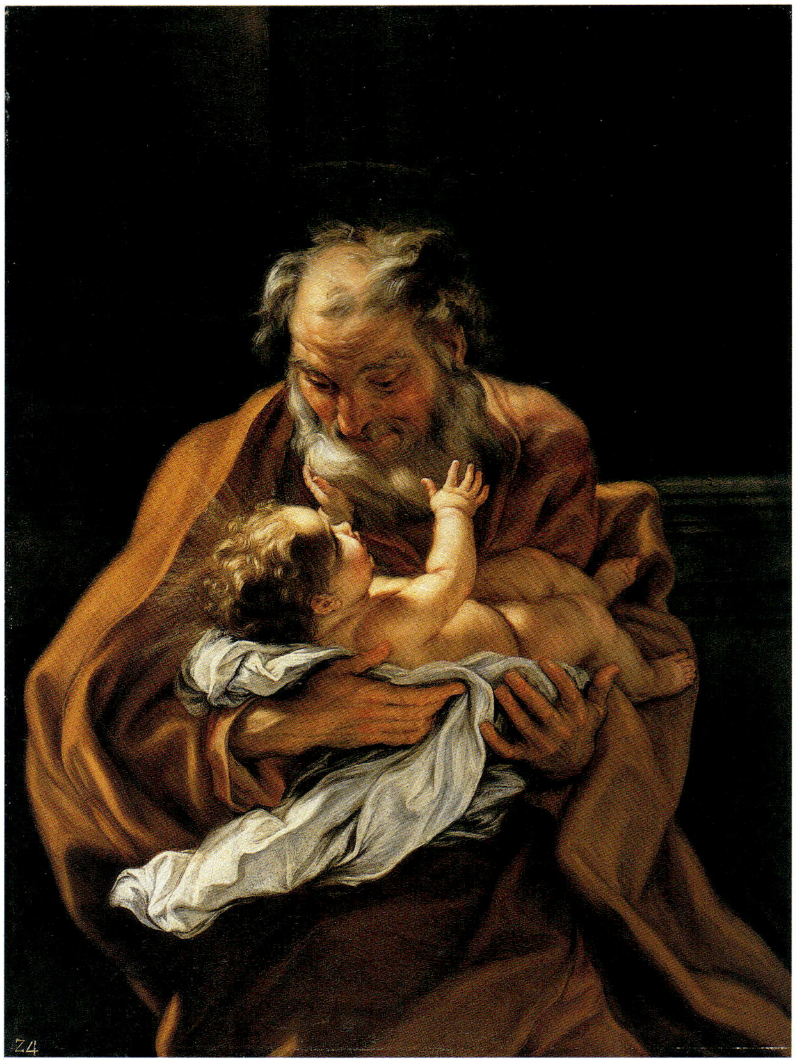

Plate 10: Giovanni Battista Gaulli (called Baciccio), Saint Joseph and the Infant Christ. C. 1670–85. Oil on canvas, 127 × 97.2 cm. Pasadena, The Norton Simon Foundation. (©: Pasadena, The Norton Simon Foundation.)

in a space which is fundamentally ambiguous and which obstructs self-experience.

Earlier, when I argued how to read Bacon's work in relation to his predecessors, I said that it is not particularly meaningful just to reverse the traditional hierarchical relation of influence. We should not endow Bacon with the kind of authority and agency that was ascribed to his predecessors in the traditional notion of influence. Although it is necessary to start, instead of ending, with his work when we want to understand the relation between it and that of his predecessors, his work must also be read, that is, actively and critically engaged with. It is also necessary to refuse the kind of individualism that is implied in the traditional notion of influence. For, it only makes sense to speak of influence if there has been contact between an artist and another artist or the work of another artist. Influence seems to suggest a contact-relation in one form or another.

In the wake of T.S. Eliot, Baxandall and Bal, as well as of Bacon's visual philosophy of the portrait, I propose we not only reverse the relation between predecessor and later artist, but also open up the notion of influence by refusing its inherent individualism. This enables us to begin by looking from the perspective of Bacon's work at art works he has probably never seen. Bacon has not only reconcentrated specific art works of specific artists. More specifically, he has reinvented our way of looking at art. His work helps us to relate to older art in a way that was unthinkable before we had seen his works. Let me finish with one example of this philosophy of looking that Bacon's paintings elaborate.

As far as I know Bacon never saw *Saint Joseph and the Infant Christ* (1670–85) *(Plate 10)* by the Italian painter Giovanni Battista Gaulli, also called Baciccio. This painting is in the collection of the Norton Simon Museum in Pasadena in California. It is a quintessentially baroque painting. First of all the subject of this painting is remarkable. Whereas the history of western art has countless examples of Mother Maria and child, examples of Joseph and Child are relatively rare. More remarkable, however, is the excessively baroque style. The folds of Joseph's dress are intensified by a mode of painting that seems to build up the painting by folds as such. The flesh of the child is built up by exceptionally generous quantities of grey, shooting through the pink and bringing it into movement, in addition to establishing similarity with the greying old man. In addition, the foreshortening brings the father closer to the picture plane whereas the child, whose feet recede in a rudimentary form of linear perspective, moves into the space where the father sits. Finally, the white cloth that covers the back of the child is strongly nuanced in grey, forming a continuity with the beard of the father, so that the child is made continuous with these two elements between which he lies.

The bodies of the father and child are not closed off, not sealed. They are folded and through the folds our gazes can enter them. The apparent openness of these bodies is caused by the "movement pinned to the body." Because of the turmoil which defines the way these two figures are painted, they also lose their boundaries. Their bodies are becoming entangled and confused. The selves of Saint Joseph and of the Infant Christ get lost in each other.

In terms of Bacon's philosophy of bodylines, of humanity, but also of looking at what came before the present, we can now say that Giovanni Battista Gaulli has clearly been influenced by Francis Bacon.

[1] Eliot 1975, pp. 37–44.
[2] Baxandall 1985, p. 62.
[3] Ibid., p. 59.
[4] Ibid., p. 59.
[5] Bal 1999, p. 1.
[6] Bernhart Schwenk, Francis Bacon aus heutiger Sicht, in: Exh. Cat., 1996, p. 72.
[7] According to me, the interviews with Michel Archimbaud are much more subtle and informative than the more canonical and esteemed interviews with David Sylvester.
[8] Archimbaud 1993, pp. 31, 32.
[9] Ibid., p. 35.
[10] Ibid., p. 170.
[11] Davies – Yard 1986, p. 23; emphasis added.
[12] Hugh Davies, in: Ext. Cat. San Diego 2001, p. 12.
[13] Davies 1978, p. 110.
[14] Ernst van Alphen, The Portrait's Dispersal: Concepts of Representation and Subjectivity in Conteporary Portraiture, in: Woodall 1997, p. 239–258.
[15] Archimbaud 1993, p. 23.
[16] According to Wolfgang Kemp this convention was inaugurated by Rembrandt. See for example Rembrandt's painting *The Holy Family with painted frame and curtain* (1646) which is in the Gemäldegalerie in Kassel. Kemp provides an elaborate discussion of this painting. See Kemp 1986.
[17] See for a more elaborate argumentation of this reading of Bacon's work: van Alphen 1992.
[18] Archimbaud 1993, p. 41.
[19] Deleuze 1989, p. 34–40.
[20] Ibid.
[21] Brighton 2001, p. 58.
[22] Sylvester 1987, p. 173, 174.

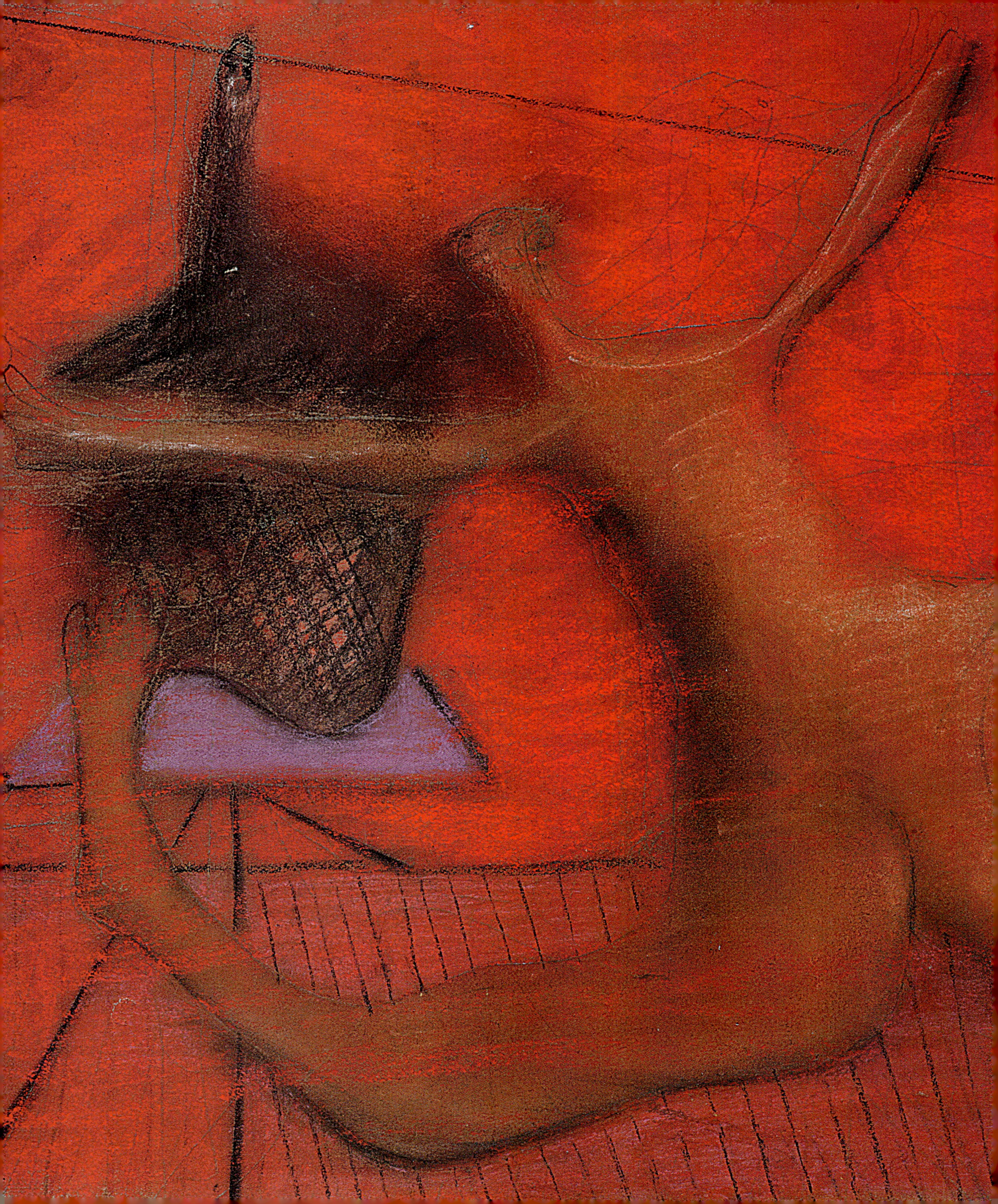

Olivier Berggruen

Picasso & Bacon: Painting the Other Self[1]

At first glance, the story of the relationship between Picasso and Bacon seems beyond dispute. The young painter first came across Picasso's work during a visit to Paul Rosenberg's gallery in 1927.[2] There he saw over a hundred drawings, most of them done in the classical style of the early 1920s. In later years, Bacon recalled his enthusiasm: "They made a great impression on me, and I thought afterwards, well, perhaps I could draw as well."[3] And in conversation with Jean Clair, Bacon declared: "Picasso was an extraordinary man. He is to me the greatest genius of our century."[4] However, Bacon rejected the notion that Picasso played an exclusive role in shaping him, likening himself to "a sponge that absorbs everything."[5] And although Bacon's work, at least in its early stages, betrays a close connection to Picasso's, it is my aim to discuss this relationship in terms of shared concerns, rather than try to reconstruct specific patterns of influence. Both artists were conscious of the psychological impact a painting exerts on its spectator, yet the ways in which these paintings connect with the viewer –including the artist as beholder of his own work – point to different solutions. Both artists were also keenly aware of the act of painting in terms of process, and this I want to review as well. Above all, Bacon and Picasso had a deep affinity in questioning the integrity of the self through the art of portraiture, but in offering distinctive creative paths, their differences are perhaps more enlightening than their similarities.

It is the revelation of Picasso's Surrealist, biomorphic works that further propelled Bacon under the Spanish painter's spell. In these works, created in Cannes and Dinard during the summers of 1927 and 1928, Picasso drew on his Cubist innovations and subjected his female bathers to a seemingly inexhaustible series of formal and psychological manipulations. Among them were a group of pen-and ink drawings of organic, bone-like forms; Bacon most likely saw them reproduced in Christian Zervos' article for *Cahiers d'Art* "Picasso à Dinard, Été 1928" in the early 1929 issue.[6] These forms proliferate with dangerous facility; such works have the gift of bewitching us by appearing so believable yet they are firmly situated in the realm of the imaginary. Bacon's early paintings feed off Surrealist visions of this type. His *Crucifixion* of 1933 can be directly traced to a drawing in the biomorphic style of the same subject by Picasso which was published in *Minotaure (Plate 2).*[7] More works from this period were shown at Alex Reid & Lefèvre's retrospective exhibition *Thirty Years of Pablo Picasso* in June 1931 in London. There Bacon saw such paintings from Dinard as *La Plage* (1928) and *Baigneuse* (1929).

All in all, Picasso's influence on the young Bacon has been taken for granted and has mostly focused on the revelatory force of his Surrealist phase. Yet Picasso's own connection to Surrealism is not without controversy, as he was inclined to switch styles without firmly committing himself to one particular genre. And he always remained on the margins of various Surrealist factions. But he realised that Surrealism held a considerable promise, as it drew freely on art's capacity to confuse the viewer, to induce in him various states of mind close to psychosis. Picasso set out to create plausible images of surreal elements brought together in an assemblage-like manner, thus blurring the borders between imaginary and real. The question of Bacon's connections with Surrealism falls outside the scope of this essay, as does the investigation of his acquaintance with Surrealist ideas. But there is little doubt that he felt stimulated by the Surrealists' emphasis on transformative processes in painting through accident and suggestion. Bacon's use of accident and chance, his natural acceptance of the motivating powers of the unconscious, are related to Surrealism, although he is only intensifying what Dawn Ades has termed "the already unpredictable behaviour of the fluid medium of paint."[8] Witness, for example, the splash of paint added or scraped at the last minute, as an afterthought. Paint is applied, yet not necessarily wedded to a form. It is dynamic rather than static. It seems that both Bacon and Picasso, at least during his Surrealist phase, saw painting *as process,* without too much thought interrupting the flow of gestural and instinctual responses to an emerging and by no means fixed configuration –

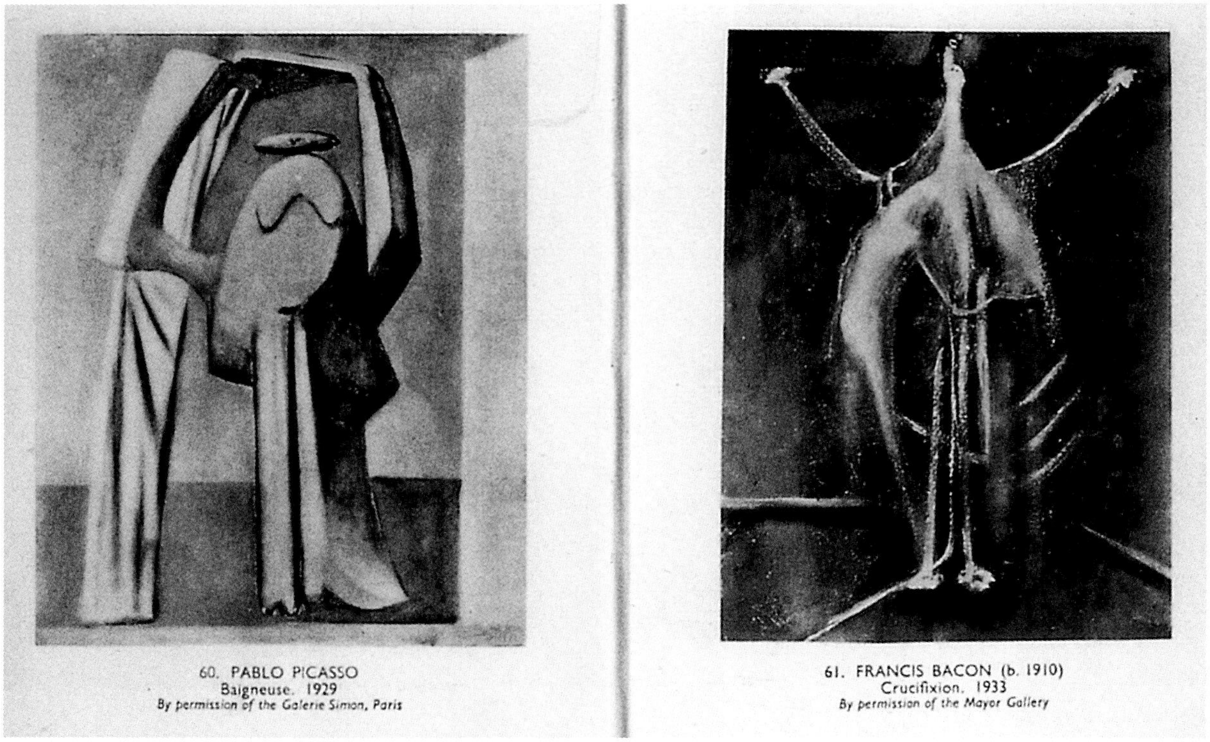

Plate 1 on p. 70: Francis Bacon, Studio Interior, detail. C. 1934 (cat. no. 44).

Plate 2: Francis Bacon, Crucifixion. 1933. Oil on canvas, 60.5 × 47.5 cm. Placed opposite Picasso's Bather in Herbert Read's Art Now, published in 1933.

a tacit acknowledgement that there is something irreducible about the medium; it is inescapable and thus places the artist within the bounds of the flat picture-surface. But already here a difference emerges between the two artists: Picasso's approach takes into account the possibility of formal manipulations – some of it instinctual –, whereas Bacon appealed to the notion of faithfulness to his feelings.

Therefore we should recognize that Bacon's commitment to transformative processes does not lie in a theory about the unconscious – and the recognition of its liberating effect – as much as in a general prevalent attitude which favours emotion and intuited response over intellect and concept formation. For Bacon, the work of art produces sensations in the viewer rather than intellectual stimulus. The artist wants to elicit in us a response in which our senses are virtually assailed. As such, life is never very far from the act of painting: sensations from everyday life are the ones which are given a pictorial expression. According to Sylviane Agacinski, Bacon's artistic practice eschews both representation and abstraction; such a conception leaves neither room for mimesis nor for staging ideas through the work of art. Bacon once said to David Sylvester: "How can one do this so that the mystery of the appearance is captured by the mystery of its making?"[9] There is no wish to represent appearances in Bacon's art; they belong to the domain of the ineffable. But there is a strategy, a presentation of something often derived from what is most banal – a photograph or a postcard – and thus transformation becomes all-important. The idea of transformation is at the centre of Bacon's art, and in this respect it is surely related to Picasso's example.

Transformation involves first and foremost the human body. Couldn't paintings, in particular portraits, provoke ambivalent feelings as to what constitutes the self? Often we feel that we are confronted by other bodies not unlike our own, i.e. not a dead thing acting through *reference* but a living thing that takes on a shape, organic or otherwise, through the organization of paint marks. Looking at these pictures brings us into contact with another embodied person. In Picasso's depictions of the artist's studio of the late 1920s appears the idea of metamorphosis, of the "self becoming other."[10] This aesthetic of the embodied other culminates with the series around the Minotaur, the mythical half-beast and half-human Dionysian creature in which Picasso delighted *(Plate 4)*. For Picasso, the Minotaur symbolized the innermost aspect of his personality, the dark regions of the psyche, or, as Lydia Gasman put it, "his persistent aspiration to vie with primarily dark external forces."[11] That the myth of the Minotaur appealed to Picasso is evident from his obsessive pursuit of the theme in the 1930s. Needless to say, the Dionysian, orgiastic forces of desire, the psychological creature is the glorification of uninhibited desire. We can already see the story of the Minotaur, albeit in a different form, as the paradigm of the mutated body in Bacon's work.

Between the two artists, some general differences emerge. With Picasso, the image reaches a fair level of organization and realization in terms of its potentiality, whereas with Bacon the image has not necessarily reached that state of completion. It is obvious that the younger painter was primarily concerned with the emotional resonance of the image rather than with formal investigation. John Russell, in his classic monograph on Bacon, articulates the difference as follows (with reference to the portraits from the 1960s): "The initial donnée in these portrait-heads is not so much distorted as contorted. We do not feel, as we do with some of Picasso's more bloody-minded rearrangements of the female head, that the features could never reassume their conventional appearance. We feel, rather, that we have penetrated to the inmost of human behaviour [...]."[12]

To use a term derived from Neoplatonic philosophy, couldn't we say that the subject of the painting is derived from an initial, potential and primitive state and is then allowed to *revert onto itself*? It is like a progression through different stages of organic mutation. From their initial condition Picasso's women appear to have reached a fairly stable level of being, whereas Bacon's screaming Popes are still moving through various stages of mutation; they are frozen in a state of intermediary mutation. Thus for both artists the painting exhibits the signs of an ongoing process: the human form appearing out of the void, transformed and mutilated, until that presence is returned to the abyss, the invisible ground that defines it. The demonstration of the corporeality of the human form is taken to an extreme in Bacon. His figures are subject to their own splitting up, dissolution. At times, they point towards erasure; absolute silence is written on the face, as in the *Study for Portrait II (After the Life Mask of William Blake)* from 1955 *(Plate 5)*. Obviously, representation is tied to presence and absence. The funerary mask leaves the traces of an absence.

But perhaps there is another level of comparison between Picasso and Bacon: both have a similar conception of the role of painting, or more accurately, are committed to a similar notion of the role of the artist – not as observers of the world probed as an outside object but as active participants in its rituals. The world is not primarily seen as the unfolding of an objective outside reality that remains forever elusive through mimesis, but appears as a web of relations integrated within an organized whole. The creation of the universe finds its echo in the creative act performed by the artist: he is not so much an observer, detached and rational, as the participant in a process of identification with visible nature through the act of painting. An act of exorcism is necessary to chase away some of the inner demons. This ritual can be observed

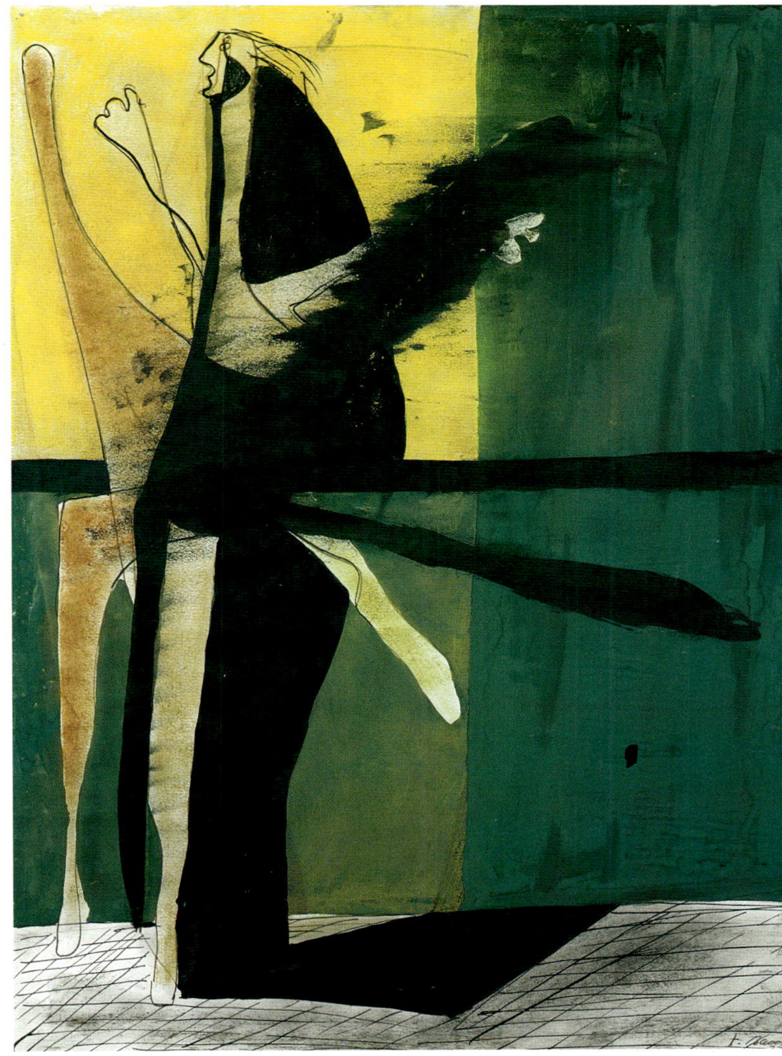

Plate 3: Francis Bacon, Composition (Figure), 1933 (cat. no. 42).

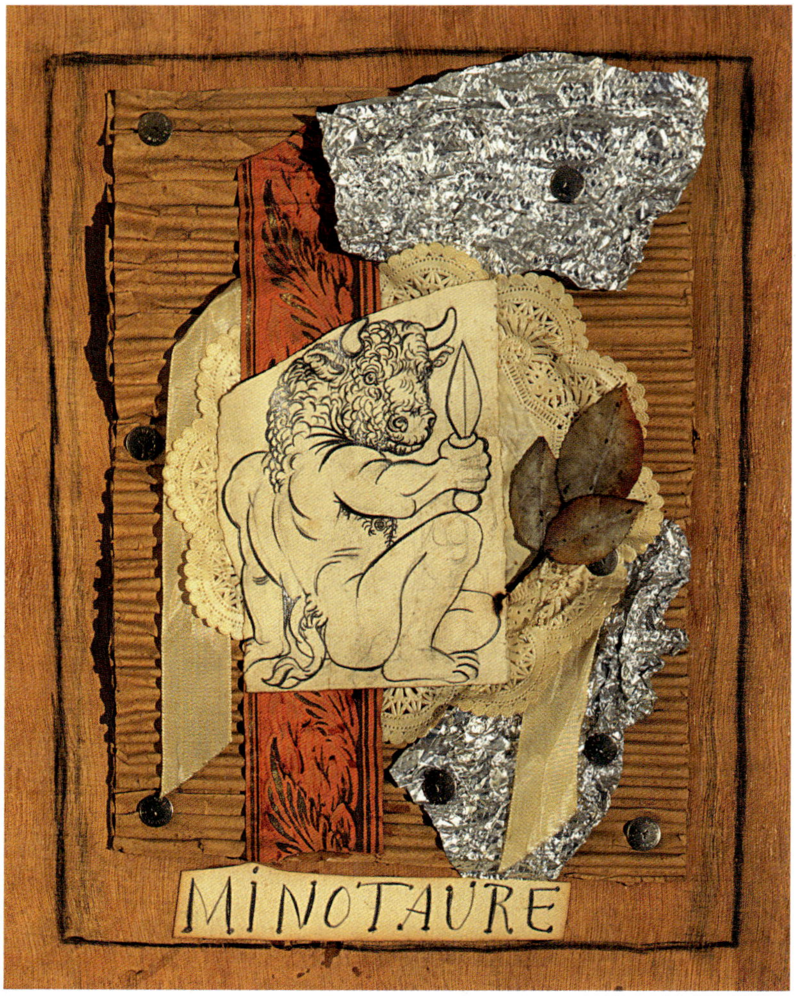

Plate 4: Pablo Picasso, Minotaure. Cover of issue no. 1, 1933. Collage, 48.5 × 41 cm. New York, The Museum of Modern Art. Gift of Mr. and Mrs. Alexandre P. Rosenberg. (©: Succession Picasso/VBK, Vienna, 2003.)

Plate 5 on p. 75: Francis Bacon, Study for Portrait II (After the Life Mask of William Blake). 1955. Oil on canvas, 60 × 51 cm. Private Collection. (©: The Estate of Francis Bacon/VBK, Vienna, 2003.)

in Picasso's later years, with his obsessive reworking of perennial themes such as the painter and his model. In Bacon's case, a state of drunken intoxication was conducive to his quasi-ecstatic painting practice. However, catharsis remained elusive, and the act of painting had to be repeated again and again. It could be argued that Bacon, in an almost obsessive fashion, paints the same work over and over again; hence his predilection for serial sequences, of which the Popes are the most famous. This again points to their common conception of painting not as an isolated object of enquiry, but as participating in all aspects of life. Thus the compulsion to repeat the process of portraiture speaks to something which lies outside of the painted surface, the performative act of the portrait.

A contradiction lies at the heart of Bacon's art: on the one hand, the absence of narrative, what Gilles Deleuze termed the path of "defiguration,"[13] the removal of the figure from conventional meaning; but on the other hand, unlike other artists of his generation, he avoids purging painting of anything but formal experience. This is perhaps the reason why Bacon eschews the specter of abstraction. Instead, the painted marks carry along their own force, but a force wedded to the presentation of the human form. The subject matter of the painting is its emotional resonance. It is through manipulation of images that the artist reaches a level of intensity. The intensity is derived from the way in which Bacon's paintings are usually constructed, with a background that points to a void, painted in neutral colours, or in shocking pink in later life, and a foreground which is that of the loaded archetype, the human figure: this is where the surface is tactile, almost palpable to the eye and to the sense of touch. The violence of the paint thus becomes the subject of the painting. Textures and outlines seem to attack or threaten the nervous system. The Surrealist technique of smearing paint, of giving it an almost liquid quality, brings us closer to the physical experience of the painter. Bacon's paintings are devoid of pathos, of existential lament.

Apart from Picasso's Surrealist works, Bacon felt most attracted by his depictions of crying women from the 1930s. To Jean Clair he spoke admiringly of the portraits of Marie-Thérèse Walter: "There's tremendous pathos in them."[14] In 1938, *Guernica (Plate 6)* went on show at the New Burlington Galleries near Piccadilly, along with countless related studies. The exhibit was later transferred to the Whitechapel in London's East End.[15] Parallels have been drawn between *Guernica*, its studies and Bacon's *Three Studies at the Base of a Crucifixion (Plate 7)*.[16] Bacon was struck by the emotional resonance of Picasso's new work, a presence that seems to shine through with unusual vigour, whereas portraits

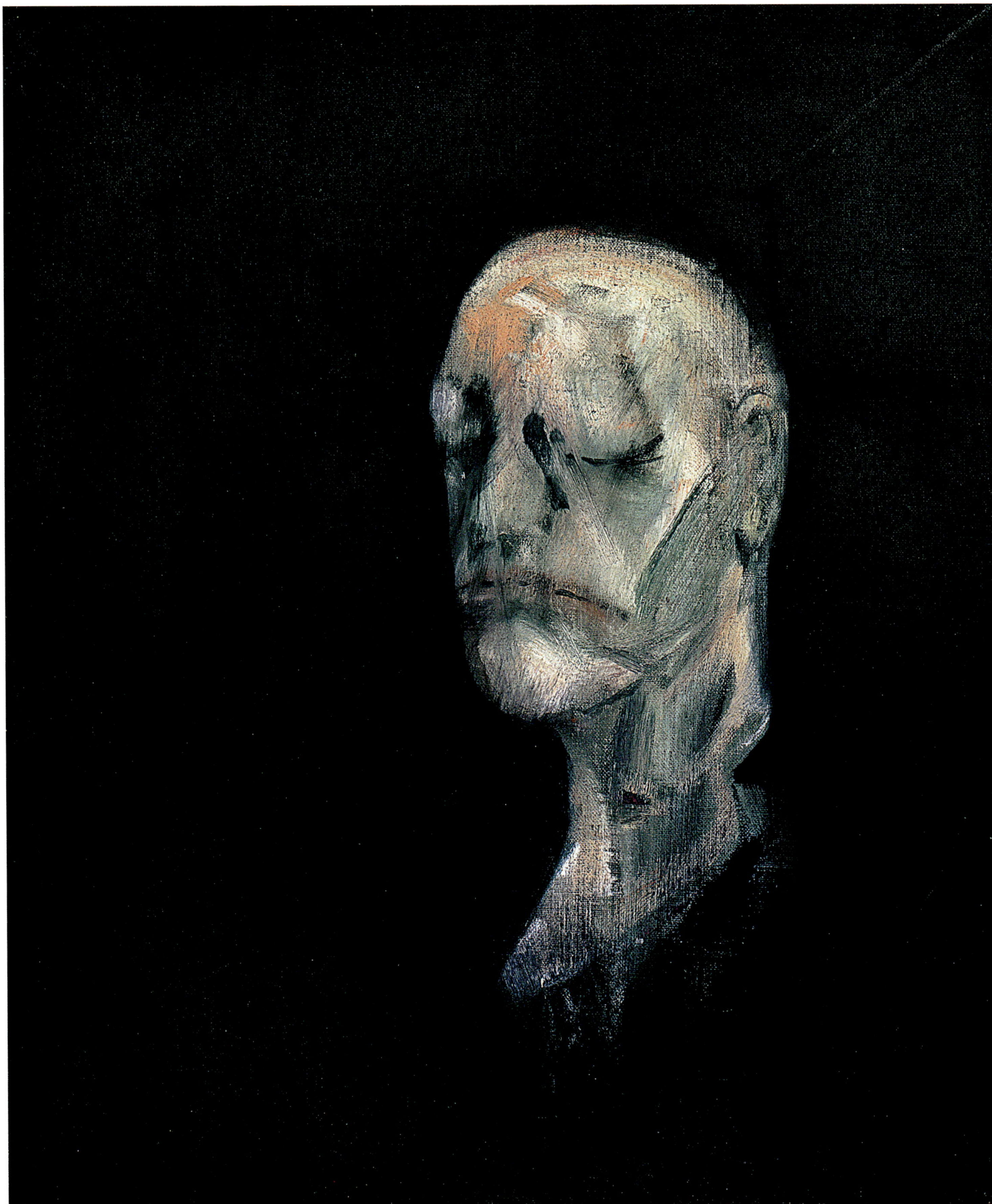

have a tendency to conjure up dead things rather than life. At the same time, Bacon was fascinated by the implied violence of such "serene" depictions as those of Marie-Thérèse. Picasso treated Marie-Thérèse's radiant beauty to a series of transformations which moved from conventional playfulness to obsessive metamorphosis. Of course Picasso felt a strong empathy towards a model who was his lover. Her various depictions give us a glimpse into the peculiar dialectic of exchange between artist and model: from loving identification to uncompromising de-figuration. Distance, emotional and formal tearing apart are achieved through the dislocation of the female body. The Minotaur, too, became an instrument for Picasso to articulate his distance or closeness to Marie-Thérèse, with images of the dying beast bearing testimony to the cessation of love.

Needless to say, Picasso resorts to various strategies in subjecting the human body to distortions. One is predominantly anatomical, in which different parts of the body are given an unusual prominence, without compromising the verisimilitude of the anatomical model. Another, more radical one features the notion of "assemblage" in which different body parts are taken out of context and reassembled in a seemingly random way. This points to an aesthetic of anatomical fragments, a form of mutilation in which destruction and violence are associated with the unleashing of creative powers. As Georges Bataille wrote in *Documents*, fragmentation and dislocation are indeed forms of religious sacrifice.[17] Bataille's review refers to some ancient Greek cults, dedicated to Mithras and Dionysus, in which sacrificial ritual stressing the dismembering of bodies is a way of communion with the deity, or at least a way of appeasing it. In Picasso's paintings, various body parts are presented as non-living things, as if they were elements of a still life. But in Bacon, elements of the body are not subject to playful games: they are painted over and over as living things that have an unlimited potency.[18]

In the wake of Bataille's writings, it would be apposite to say that Picasso is engaged in a ritual act of creation. The ritual sacrifice confers upon the artist the superior powers of the divine victim. "Through primitive ritual sacrifice he repeatedly took over the sovereign powers of his enemy, Dionysus, the monstrous other dwelling within himself."[19] It is easy to think of Marie-Thérèse or Dora Maar subjected to the painter's disfigurements as part of this ritual act in which the violence done to the subject (the sitter) is then felt – as if through an echo – by the viewer. Such depictions seem to alternate between apparent fragility and unbridled violence. In his portraits of Marie-Thérèse and Dora Maar, the painter allows for the sitter's gaze to hold the space between the sitter and viewer. The direct glance – the blue of each eye spills out of its black boundary, giving her gaze a watery intensity – of *Woman Seated in an Armchair (Plate 8)* testifies to this sense of engagement. But as Ernst van Alphen has noticed about Bacon's work, there is for the viewer a sense of unease far removed from Picasso's disfigurations.[20] In other words the violence exerted towards the sitter through the ritual act of disfiguration is one which is replicated by the sense of disquiet experienced by the viewer. Van Alphen is right in writing that the *effect* of the work is not only related to its content, but to the relational aspect of the work itself. Textures, outlines, wiped paint, all these tend to act on our nervous system, and in this manner emotional conflicts, psychical states are released through perception.

With Bacon, painting has less to do with vision – striving towards illusion and mimesis – than with a loss of vision: the interruption of vision results in a discontinuity of form and presentation. Bacon's path of "defiguration," to use a term borrowed from Gilles Deleuze, is less the sign of a rupture between figure and narrative than the evidence of the painter's efforts to sabotage his own work, to mutilate it. According to van Alphen, "paint does not stand in but stands before the figure, not uncovering but hiding it."[21] In *Study for Portrait 1949 (Plate 9)*, the veiling of the image by means of vertical slashes is indicative of a dialectic of presence and absence: what is brought forth is also being erased or obscured. Following the Neoplatonic principle of forms reverting onto themselves, the work of art points towards an unfathomable void.

In his monograph on Bacon, Ernst van Alphen writes of a peculiar feeling of loss of self. Such a feeling can never be objectified; however, our reactions can be described in such ways that they point, somewhat indirectly (because language intervenes here in a rather clumsy way), to the aesthetic experience itself. Of course the goal of describing aesthetic reactions is not one of trying to discover the ineffable essence or meaning which the work is supposed to embody. But there is, it seems, a valid way of talking about art experience without falling into the trap of essentialism. It may be assumed for our purpose that the painted surface acts as a conduit for certain feelings which in turn will be felt by the viewer. Let us look at *Study for Portrait VI (Plate 10)*, one of Bacon's most celebrated early portraits. It falls within the period when Bacon was painting pictures of men in dark suits, shrouded in deep-blue backgrounds. The sitter finds himself in a state of suspended *effroi*, as if unable to lock himself out of the spasm that affects him. (Such images are even more explicit in later years.) In turn, the beholder is likely to experience a loss of identity (which is not the same as

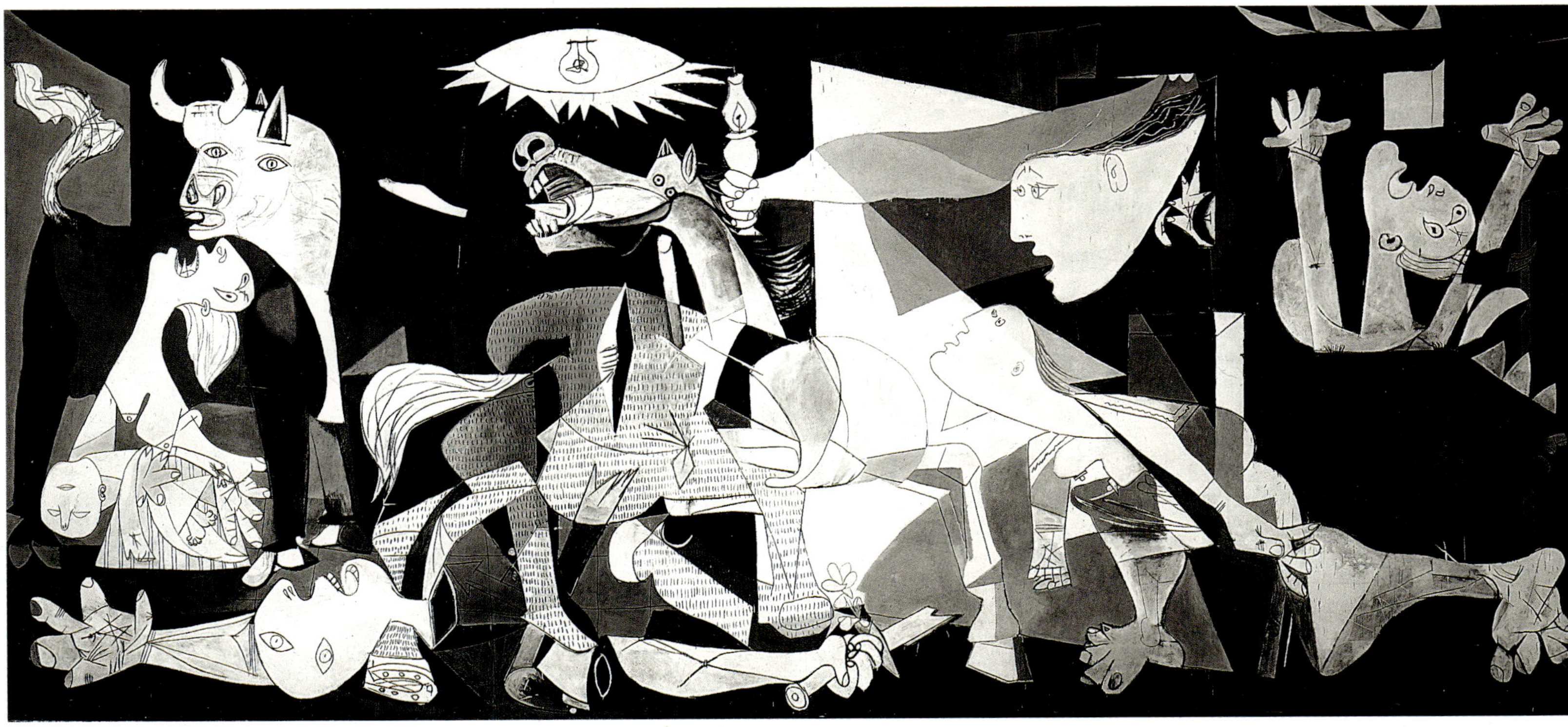

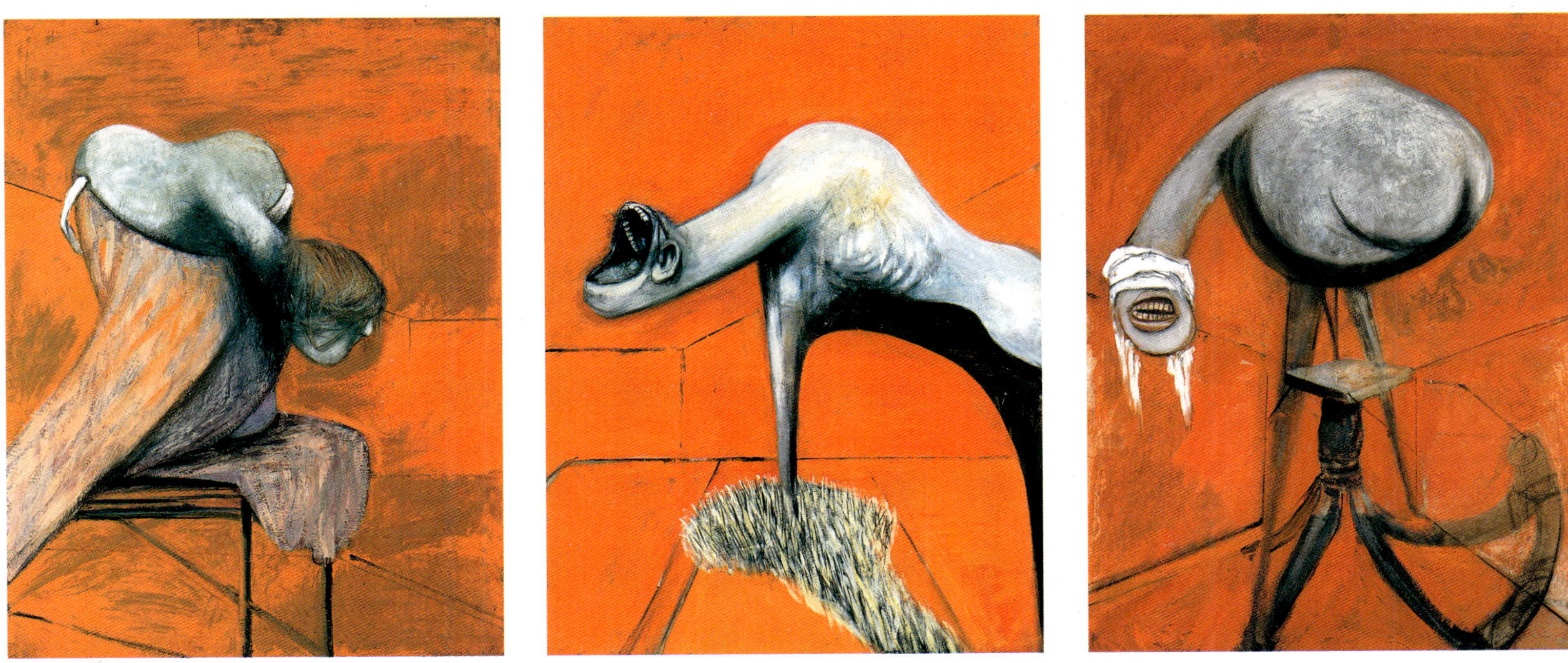

Plate 6: Pablo Picasso, Guernica. 1937. Oil on panel, 351 × 782 cm. Madrid, Museo de Arte Reina Sofia. (©: Succession Picasso/VBK, Vienna, 2003.)

Plate 7: Francis Bacon, Three Studies for Figures at the Base of a Crucifixion. 1944. Oil and pastel on hardboard, triptych, each panel 95 × 73,5 cm. London, Tate Gallery. (©: London, Tate Gallery.)

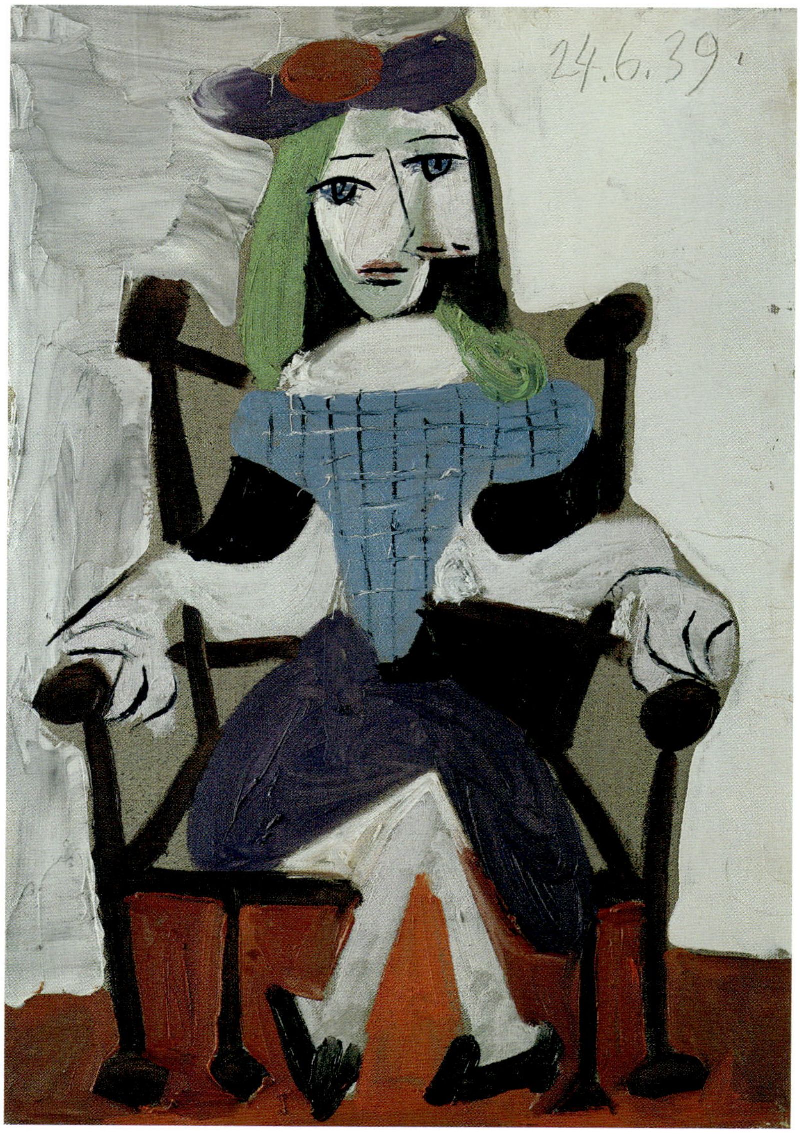

Plate 8: Pablo Picasso, Woman Seated in an Armchair. 1939 (cat. no. 92).

loss of self, for a different self emerges, perhaps not the one which constructs us as rational individuals): the disintegration of the body, the emphasis on such features as the mouth, the arrested state in which the individual, or rather the living thing, presents himself. All these resonate within us with particular urgency: we find ourselves redefined through the aesthetic experience, as a new identity emerges, that of *déchéance*, of lack of completeness, of loss of composure, as John Russell observed in his monograph.[22] But perhaps there is another way of reading the image. It is a peculiarity of Bacon's that he makes the viewer a witness of something disturbing rather than merely identifying with his subject. No other painter, not even Picasso with *Guernica,* seems to be able to provoke such unease in us.

This loss of identity, this stripping away of the layers of conventional selfhood, confronts us, as long as we are able to sustain the gaze, the presence of the other that the painting is. But within this form of participation disgust takes over. We find ourselves unable to turn away from the painting, for its creator puts us in the position of an accomplice. In this sense painting has less to do with representation than with active bodily engagement. And the question arises as to what kind of feelings such acts of transgression provoke in the viewer. Does he feel violated? Shame and revulsion, yet attraction: this all seems fairly standard in modern art, but I believe that it is Bacon's ability to put us in the situation of accomplice, not just voyeur, that sets him apart. The disintegration is not only the sitter's but also the beholder's. Bacon transforms the viewers of his canvases into partners in crime who are tempted to turn away from the scene, as does the painter himself. Thus some images need to be veiled or slashed: their violence has to be erased.

In Bacon's paintings, the confrontation between painter and model has the quality of directness. The external gaze, whether the artist's or the viewer's, confronts the painted figure with unabated violence and directness. In this sense Bacon creates an equivalence of purpose between maker and beholder. If the viewer turns away from the painting with a sense of unease, is it not because he feels embarrassed in being caught staring at something which is essentially private? But Bacon's portraits are representations of averted gazes; instead, the frontality of the subject lets us witness a subject who does not acknowledge us because he is being caught in the frenzy of his own convulsion. He is, to use an expression borrowed from Svetlana Alpers, herself referring to Rembrandt's *Bathsheba*, "not represented as complicitous in the performance required of him as a model."[23] Fragmentation, particularly in Bacon's later paintings and triptychs, is such that it is impossible to reach a comprehensive view of the subject. Picasso's dislocations, on the other hand, are the result of the painter's powers of projection, his magic or *Maya*. He demonstrates overwhelming control over his subject.

Picasso, on the other hand, encourages us to participate in an act of voyeurism; the witness can be found within the painting, looking at the scene over a curtain. The mirror image of the mutating beast is embedded in the Minotaur series and becomes a focal point of Picasso's own investigation of the self. A little-known drawing from December 1937 depicts a Minotaur with a woman holding a mirror. According to Lydia Gasman, "in holding the front of the mirror up to the Minotaur's face, she is performing the traditional role of virtue holding up the mirror to vice."[24] But the self's uncertain identity is embodied w i t h i n the picture: it does not reveal the ghost-like presence of a n o t h e r who is affected, possibly repulsed, by what is being painted. To a large degree, Bacon's images act like mirrors, albeit of a different kind. They are reflections of the beholder rather than a mere likeness of the artist or the sitter. At times, Bacon further blurs the boundaries of the self by painting a portrait within the picture, as in *Three Portraits: Posthumous Portrait of George Dyer, Self-Portrait, Portrait of Lucian Freud* (cat. no. 90). Images within paintings – metaphors for photographic objectivity – do little in clearing up the question of the identity of the self; rather, they serve to obscure it further.

At times Picasso infuses his work with an equally inescapable sense of compulsion; *Guernica, The Charnel House* and a few other works stand out as most revealing of this tendency. But in most Picassos, violence is ritualized and therefore integrated within a framework that makes them more acceptable. The ritual is emphasized by Picasso's deliberate placing of himself within the space of the picture. Towards the end of his Surrealist period, he embarked on a series around the theme of the painter and his model. Obviously he was interested in the dynamic between painter and sitter. Socrates held that the true self was not the body but the soul; and the name he gave this faculty is n o u s, distinguishing it thereby from the p s y c h e, which he held to be inseparable from the body and destined to perish with it at death. This notion finds a visual expression in the theme of the poet and his muse. And perhaps the poet is the symbol of the historical, mortal body, the muse the symbol of the timeless, immortal soul.

Beyond the violence exerted by the painting, there remains the question of the status of the work of art as an aesthetic object. Bacon's sitters are like a p p a r i t i o n s, and their glow can be grasped in purely aesthetic terms. We are faced with the work of an artist who avoids giving his creations an ethical purpose. But this does not exclude the painting having such a purpose for both

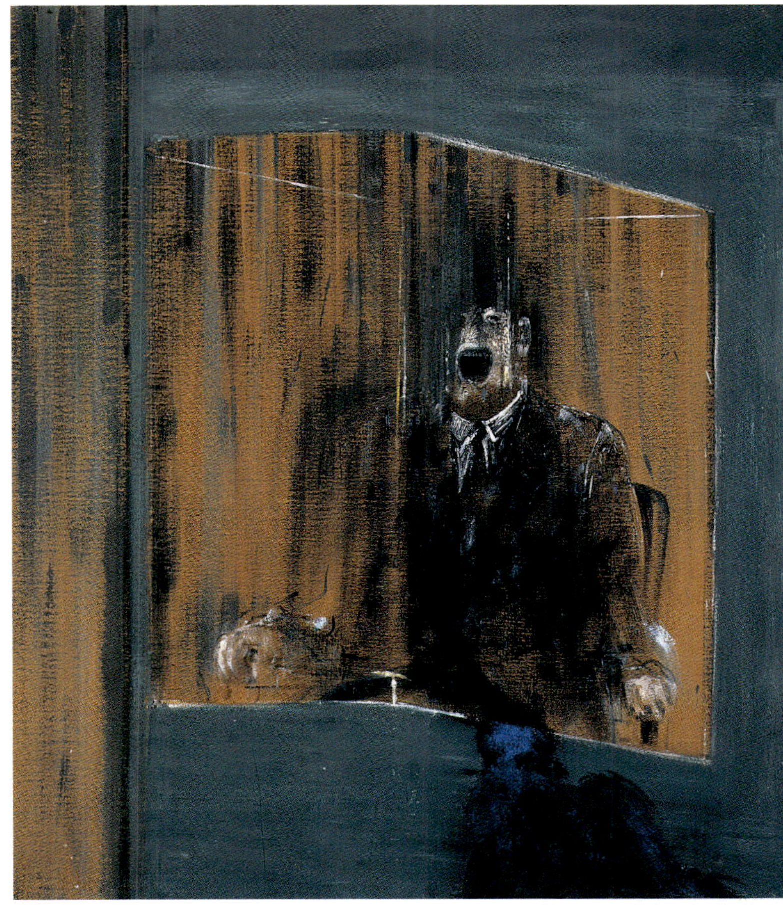

Plate 9: Francis Bacon, Study for Portrait. 1949 (cat. no. 50).

painter and viewer: it is linked to the belief that an aesthetic of violence does indeed fulfil a cleansing or purifying function. In this respect Francis Bacon said in conversation with Michel Archimbaud: "In a certain sense the Picassos that I like are violent, but not in their subject-matter, they are violent in the colours and forms that they use."[25] And so it seems that the scream of the Pope, the void of the mouth, could be an apt metaphor for the scream of the painting.[26]

According to Arthur Danto, the screaming Popes are bereft of psychology, since a scream "is not really the expression of someone's character;" it leaves no space for other expressions.[27] However, the work surely embodies psychological states, not so much the sitter's, but the artist's in his relation to his subject. Danto says that painting itself cannot be a scream, for the latter is an involuntary act (it "implies some loss of will"), and painting is largely a conscious process. But what involves loss of will is not the act of painting but our response to the work of art and the changing perception of ourselves it involves. If it cannot be made explicit, meaning nevertheless is manifested through embodied reactions of loss, disgust, malaise, etc. Thus the scream is verily the beholder's; an instinctive reaction that occurs within the instant of the first gaze.

The painting does not ask of the viewer to be given time; its violence lies in the immediacy of its impact; it acts as if a second look will not truly affect our initial response. This quality of the painting is also found in Picasso's work from the 1930s *(Plate 10).* Bacon blocks out anything that could detract from this impact: hence the paintings have a kind of uniformity, with the veiling of the image as a strategy to turn away from the force of the painting. One could argue that Bacon's strategy amounts to an impoverishment of the reach of paintings, concerned as he is with emotional violence. But at least Bacon's screams are slicing though the wall of silence that portraiture usually draws out. And Bacon, in an interview with David Sylvester, said that he wanted "to be able to paint the mouth like Monet painted a sunset."[28]

The theme of Bacon's work, its aim, rests in the method of projection, its psychological resonance (which is obviously unleashed through associations with certain subjects), the way in which known images perform a new role. This is where Bacon and Picasso meet, for Picasso gave the younger painter a powerful model: that of subject-matter seen as the pretext for something else, as in the representations of Marie-Thérèse and the crying women. That something else is a performance, a rehearsal of the same play again and again – the violence of the confrontation with a model (be it an abstract one), which is in turn reenacted through the gaze of the beholder. As mirrors of the self, paintings offer us images that

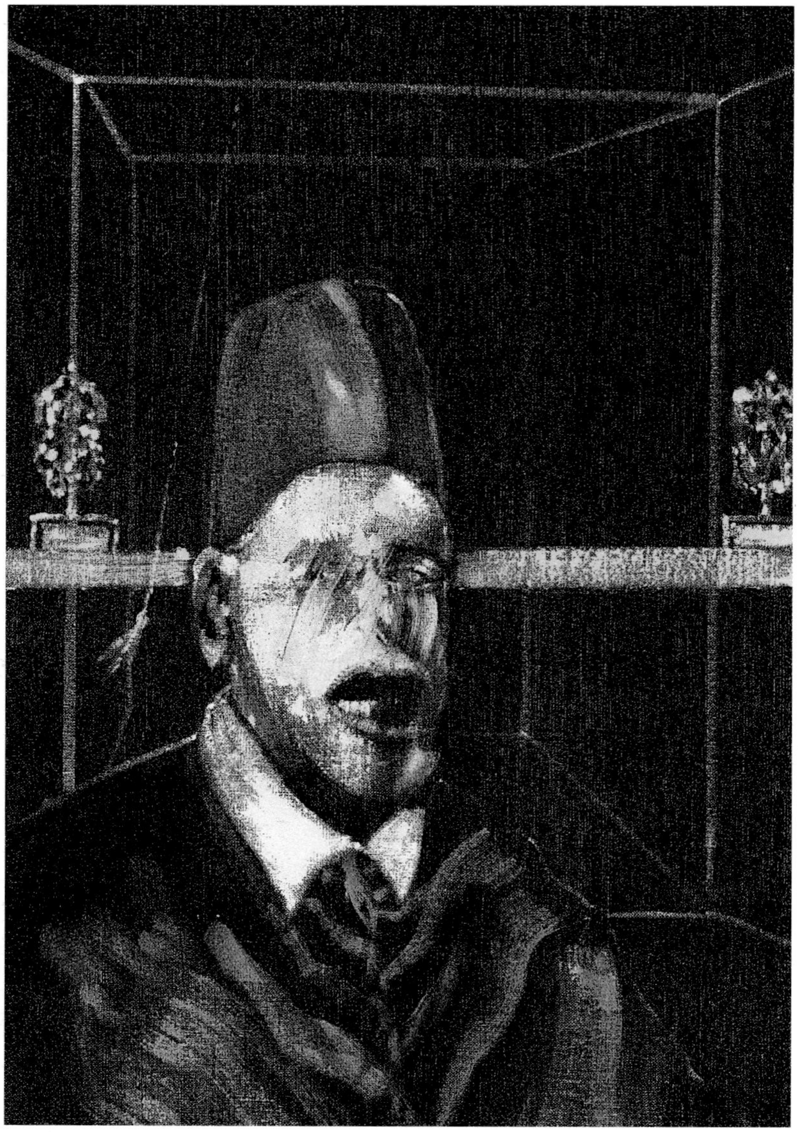

Plate 10: Francis Bacon, Study for Portrait VI and detail. 1953. Oil on canvas, 152 × 11·7 cm. Minneapolis, Minneapolis Institute of Art. (©: The Estate of Francis Bacon/VBK, Vienna, 2003.)

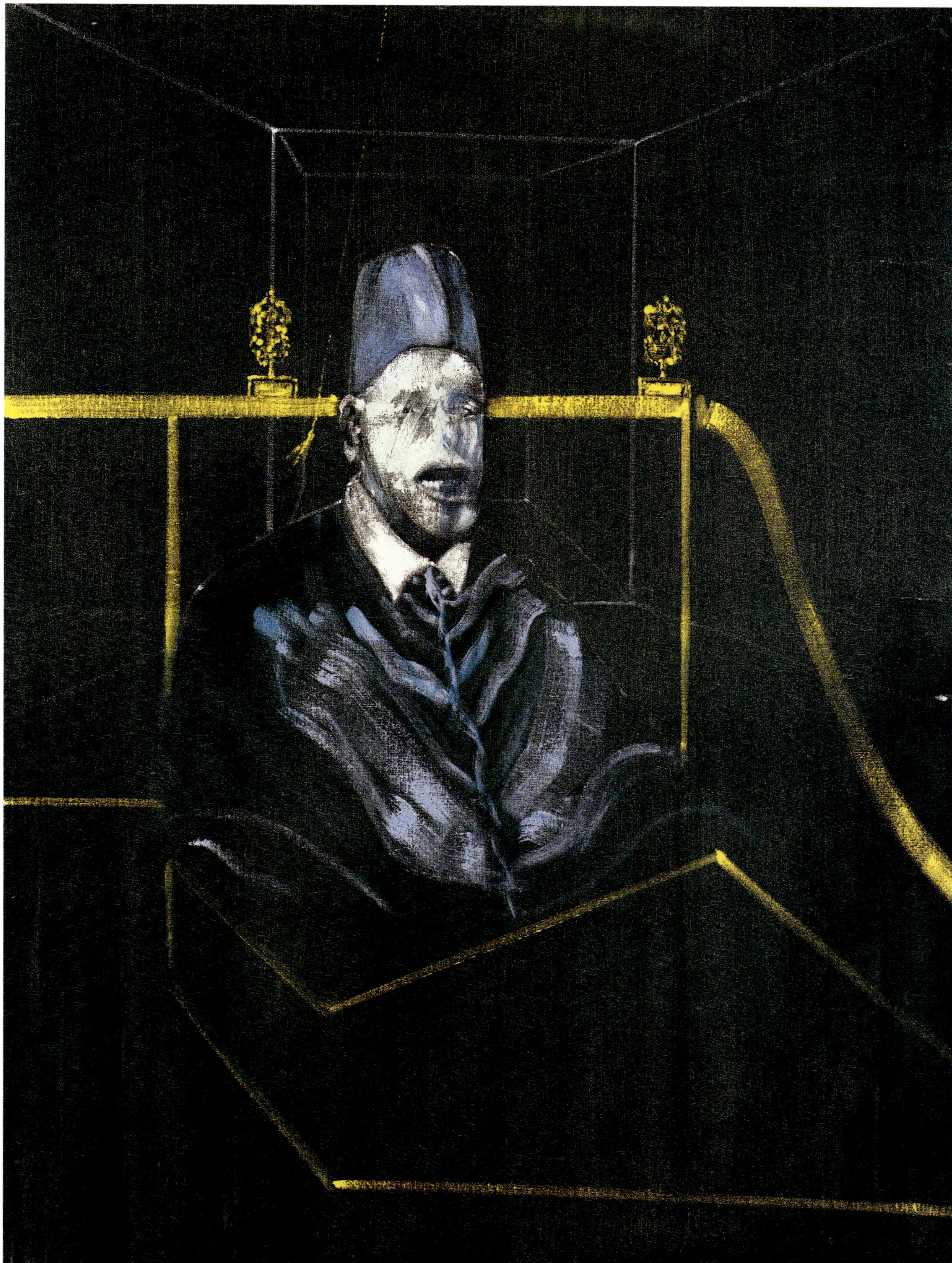

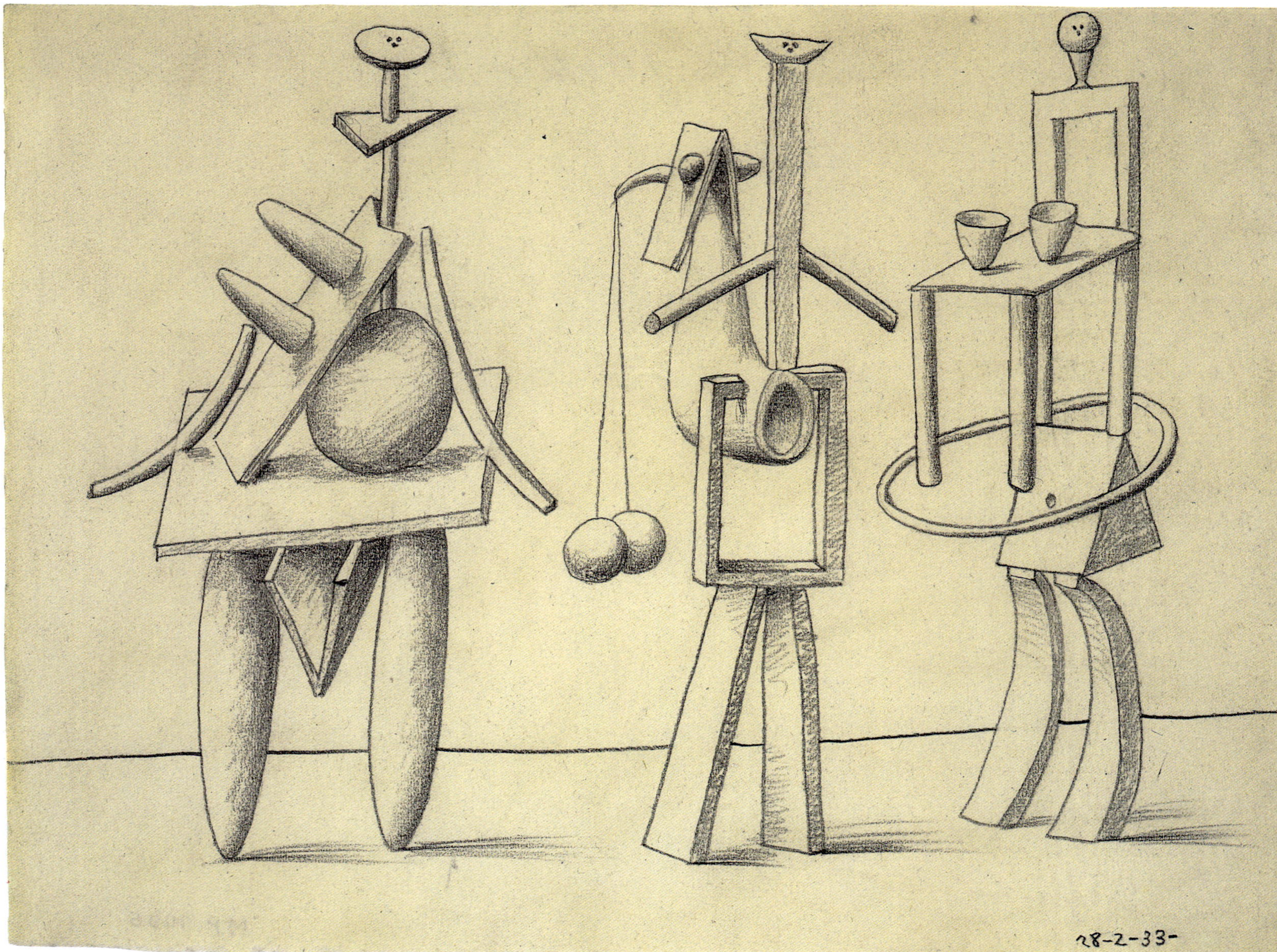

Plate 11: Pablo Picasso,
Une Anatomie: Trois Femmes.
28 February 1933. Pencil on paper,
197 × 270 mm. Paris, Musée Picasso.
(©: Succession Picasso/VBK, Vienna,
2003, photo: RMN – B. Hatala.)

appear to be distortions at first sight. The subject who sees himself in the painting starts to question the integrity of the metaphysical self that constitutes his everyday presence in the world. In this sense, the painting is capable of effecting a reversal between object and subject. Bodily presence becomes an object of enquiry, an enquiry that is prompted by none other that the subject – the sitter – of the painting. It is the moment of exchange – extending beyond the boundaries of the canvas – that gives Bacon's paintings their poignancy.

[1] I would like to thank Bettina von Hase, Nicole Root, John Richardson and George Condo for their comments and suggestions.
[2] *Exposition de cent dessins par Picasso*, Paris, Galerie Rosenberg, June – July 1927.
[3] Peppiatt 1997, p. 37.
[4] Jean Clair, *Pathos and Death*, in: Exh. Cat. Paris – Montreal 1992, p. 140.
[5] Bacon in conversation to Archimbaud: "But it's true that Picasso was also influenced by everything. He was like a sponge that soaks up everything. That's what I am thinking of when I talk about influence; something like this phenomenon of a sponge that absorbs everything." Archimbaud 1993, p. 32.
[6] "Picasso à Dinard, Été 1928." *Cahiers d'Art,* Paris, Editions Cahiers d'Art, 1929.
[7] Exh. Cat. Paris – Montréal 1992, p. 140. *Crucifixion* was first reproduced in Read 1933, pl. 101.
[8] Exh. Cat. London 1985, p. 12.
[9] Sylviane Agacinski, *Theoretical Excess: Transformations of Paintings*, in: Osborne 2000, p. 104.
[10] This expression is borrowed from Lomas 2000, p. 97.
[11] Gasman 1981, p. 1312.
[12] Russell 1971, p. 158.
[13] Deleuze 1981.
[14] Exh. Cat. Paris – Montréal 1992, p. 139.
[15] Exhibition under the auspices of the National Joint Committee for Spanish Relief. London, New Burlington Galleries, 4–29 October, 1938.
[16] Peppiatt 1997, p. 88; Read 1957, pp. 33–35.
[17] Documents, Paris, vol. II (1930), no. 8.
[18] Dawn Ades has suggested that Georges Bataille's review Documents is likely to have inspired Bacon, who was well-acquainted with French avant-garde publications. In *Documents'* famous Dictionary, under "Mouth," Bataille emphasizes the importance, the pre-eminence of the mouth in the life of animals, because "elle est la partie la plus vivante, c'est-à-dire la plus terrifiante pour les animaux voisins." In the Western world, the mouth has lost some of its preeminence, but its violence is there in a latent stage. Bataille writes: "Et dans les grandes occasions la vie humaine se concentre encore bestialement dans la bouche, la colère fait grincer les dents, la terreur et la souffrance atroce font de la bouche l'organe des cris déchirants." Documents, Paris, vol. II (1930), no. 5, pp. 299–300. Quoted in Exh. Cat. London 1985, p. 13. Bataille's entry was accompanied by Jacques-André Boiffard's famous photograph of a mouth.
[19] Gasman 1981, p. 1545.
[20] Van Alphen 1992, p. 10.
[21] Van Alphen 1992, p. 13.
[22] "What painting has never shown before is the disintegration of the social being which takes place when one is alone in a room which has no looking-glass. We may well feel at such times that the accepted hierarchy of our features is collapsing, and that we are by turn all teeth, all eye, all ear, all nose. The view out front ceases to be the only one, and our person is suddenly adrift, fragmented, and subject to strange mutation." Russell 1971, p. 72. Needless to say, the painting is the looking-glass.
[23] Svetlana Alpers, *Art as Representation and Expression*, in: Van Gerwen 2001, p. 174.
[24] Gasman 1981, p. 1365.
[25] Archimbaud 1993, p. 151.
[26] For a further discussion of this point, see Reinhard Steiner, *The Violence of Paint – Francis Bacon und das Rot der Prozessionen*, in: Steiner-Poeschl-Wegner, p. 177.
[27] Danto 1994, p. 99. The quote that follows is from p. 97.
[28] Sylvester 1975. It should be noted that in the wake of Herbert Read, Sylvester was the first critic to set up a comparison between Bacon and Picasso.

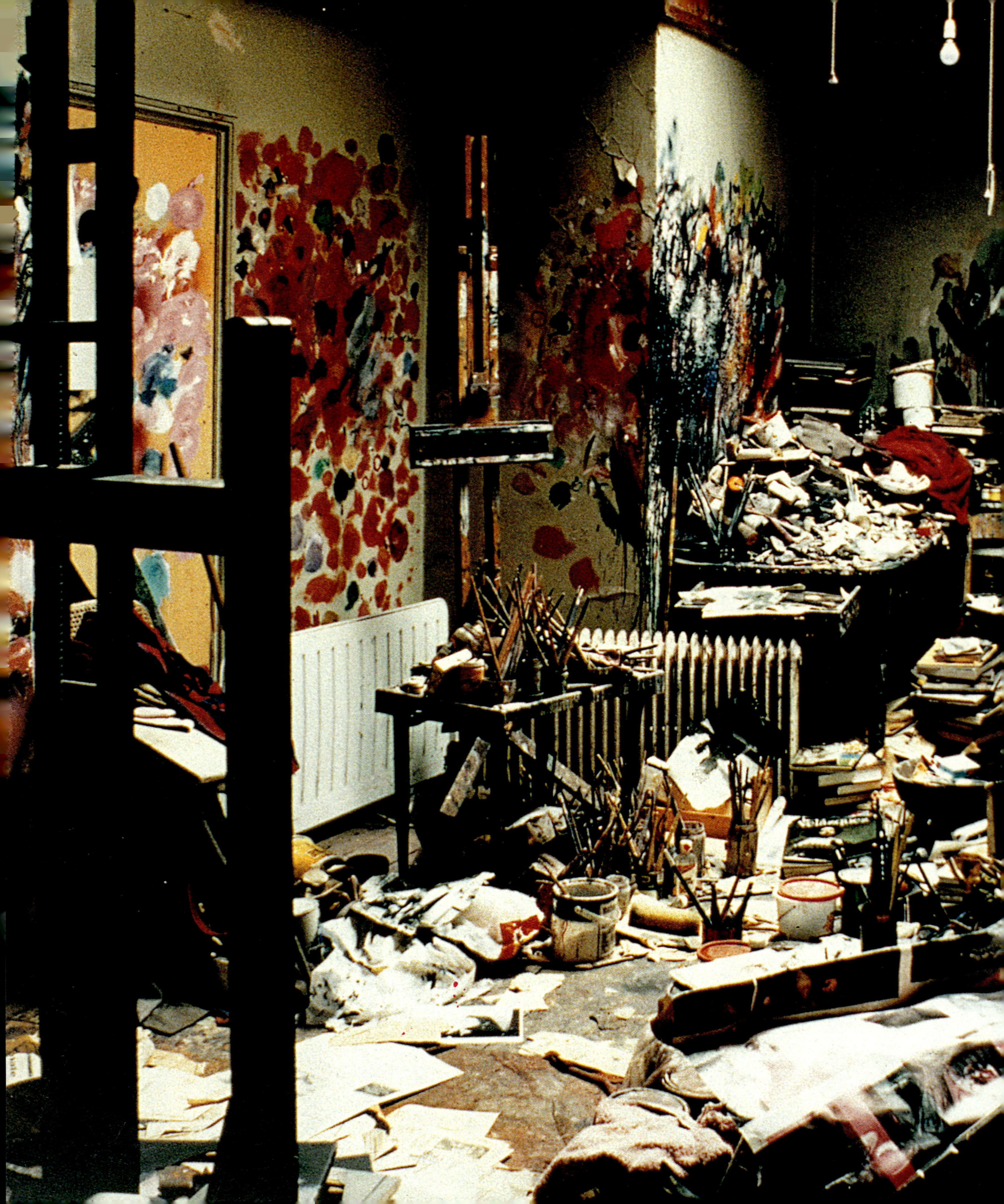

Margarita Cappock

"The Chemist's Laboratory" Francis Bacon's Studio

The reconstructed studio of Francis Bacon has been on view at Dublin City Gallery The Hugh Lane since May 2001. This unique gift to the city of Bacon's birth provides an unprecedented insight into the working methods of one of the most significant figurative painters of the twentieth century.[1] The studio was originally located in 7 Reece Mews, a modest mews dwelling in South Kensington, London which served as Bacon's principal residence and place of work from 1961 until his death in 1992.[2] The ground floor was entirely occupied by a garage space, which Bacon used for storage purposes. A steep wooden staircase, with a ship's rope for a handrail, led to the second floor where the artist's studio, bed-sitting room and unusual kitchen-cum-bathroom were located. In contrast to the spartan and orderly ancillary rooms, Bacon's studio was legendary for its masses of material, which the artist had accumulated over the years *(Plate 1)*. Some 7,500 items were found in the studio, including drawings, photographs, illustrations, books, catalogues, magazines, newspapers, paint materials, destroyed paintings and his last unfinished portrait. Bacon said himself of this cluttered space, "I feel at home here in this chaos because chaos suggests images to me."[3] From the confines of this room, he found the inspiration for some of the most powerful and emotionally-charged paintings of the past century. As he once remarked, it was rather like "the chemist's laboratory, which doesn't stop you imagining that some unexpected phenomena might appear; quite the opposite, in fact."[4]

The donation of the studio and its contents to the Hugh Lane Gallery in August 1998 marked the beginning of a unique project. The painstaking task of deconstructing the entire room and transporting it to Dublin for reconstruction was a daunting one. A team of archaeologists was engaged to undertake this work. Assisted by the Gallery's conservators and curators, they mapped the space, assigned codes to the objects and photographed and noted their positions. As the items were removed their nature, dimensions, condition and purpose was carefully noted. When the room was empty, the floors, walls, ceiling and doors were removed. The studio material was then transported to Dublin. In order to interpret the material fully, every single item found in the studio was recorded in detail on a specially designed computerised database. Each entry is accompanied by a digital image. This process of documentation took almost two years to complete. Nevertheless, it has resulted in one of the most comprehensive documentary archives of any artist, living or dead. It has also proved extremely rewarding in terms of scholarship on the artist and a number of important revelations have been made regarding the artist's life, inspiration, thought processes, unusual techniques and working methods.

Photography played a central role in Francis Bacon's work and a considerable proportion of the material found in the studio is of a photographic nature.[5] Photographs and photographic illustrations from books, magazines and newspapers provided Bacon with an immense visual library and by amassing multifarious images, new and familiar stimuli were accessible at any time in the privacy of his studio. By the time the artist had moved into Reece Mews in 1961, he had ceased working from the live model and preferred to work in isolation. During the 1950s, Bacon had occasionally worked from life but found the lengthy sittings and the physical presence of a model had an inhibiting effect on his work.[6] Even when he did paint from life, he looked at photographs of other subjects and filtered aspects of them in subtle and inventive ways. While posing for the artist in 1953, David Sylvester recalled observing Bacon studying photographs of wild animals, in particular a rhinoceros, at the same time. Similarly, a portrait of Lucian Freud was based on a photographic illustration of Franz Kafka and Bacon's memory of Freud's appearance.[7] When Freud arrived to pose for Bacon, he found the portrait almost complete.

From the early 1960s and with few exceptions, Bacon chose his closest friends as sitters, preferring to work from photographs and his own memory.[8] The artist felt that while painting friends he was practising an injury on them, something he had no desire to do in their presence. In their absence, he could twist their features and

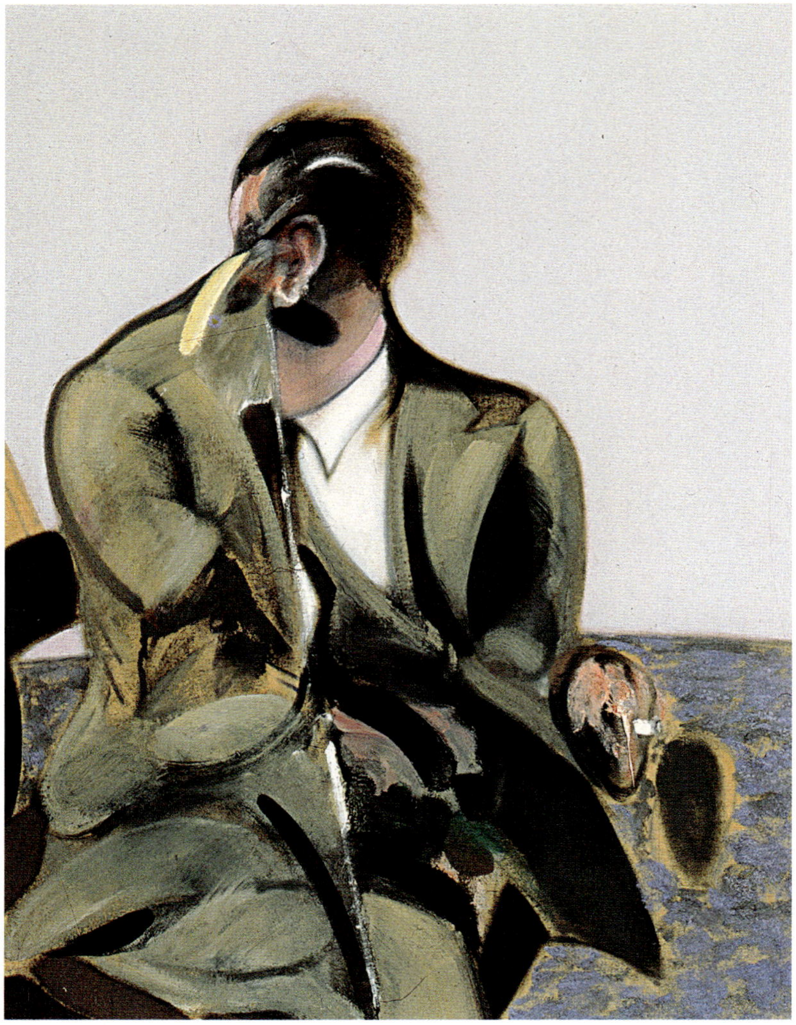

Plate 1 on p. 84: Colour photograph of Francis Bacon's studio at 7, Reece Mews. Photograph by Perry Ogden. Dublin, Dublin City Gallery The Hugh Lane. (©: Estate of Francis Bacon/Dublin City Gallery The Hugh Lane, photographic credit: Perry Ogden.)

Plate. 2: Francis Bacon, Study of George Dyer in a mirror, 1968 (cat. no. 120).

Plate 3 on p. 87: Lucian Freud sitting on a bed. Black-and-white photograph, taken by John Deakin. Early 1960s. A large vertical fold through the centre of the photograph is held by three metal paperclips. 272 × 217 mm. Dublin, Dublin City Gallery The Hugh Lane. (©: Estate of Francis Bacon/Dublin City Gallery The Hugh Lane.)

practise his "injuries" without having to contend with the judgement of the sitter. He needed photographs as "aides-mémoires" and to this end, commissioned the Vogue photographer John Deakin to produce several sets of photographs of Lucian Freud, Peter Lacy, George Dyer, Isabel Rawsthorne and Henrietta Moraes. Deakin's photographs played a crucial role in Bacon's portraiture from the first half of the 1960s onwards. Bacon had over 300 photographs by Deakin in his possession and while many of these are now in poor condition, their visual impact is still enormous. Most were taken in the period from 1960 to 1964 but several may have been taken somewhat earlier. While Deakin was a fine photographer and his distinctive technique appealed to Bacon, the artist maintained he was more interested in the subject-matter of a photograph rather than whom it was taken by. However, his views on photography were often contradictory and there are inconsistencies in his statements concerning his indebtedness to Deakin.[9]

Bacon's interest in photographs was not confined to what an image contained, he was also keenly receptive to its physical state. He was sensitive to the way that damage could alter an image irrevocably and said, "Well, my photographs are very damaged by people walking over them and crumpling them and everything else, and this does add other implications to an image of Rembrandt's, for instance, which are not Rembrandt's."[10] Bacon employed recurring pictorial effects in his work and the origins of some of these can be found in the tears, creases and paint accretions on the photographs and book pages littered across the studio floor. The large broken white line running down the centre of the figure in *Portrait of George Dyer in a Mirror,* 1968 (*Plate 2*), is based upon a crease in a photograph. This also explains why part of the figure seems to disappear and why the left shoulder is higher than the right. The face represented in the mirror may also be based on a torn photograph of George Dyer. Bacon was attracted to the work of the French artist Ernest Pignon-Ernest, who employed similar effects, and illustrations of Pignon's work were found in the studio.[11]

Bacon frequently manipulated photographs and created his own distortions, often using paperclips to hold the creases in place. A desire to isolate and confine particular motifs is evident in these interventions. In a photograph by Deakin of Lucian Freud seated on a bed, *(Plate 3),* Bacon folded the photograph so that one of Freud's legs was obscured and the other was emphasised. The creases are held in place with three paperclips and the smudged paint fingerprints on the left side of the photograph indicate extensive handling while the artist painted. Bacon repeatedly used

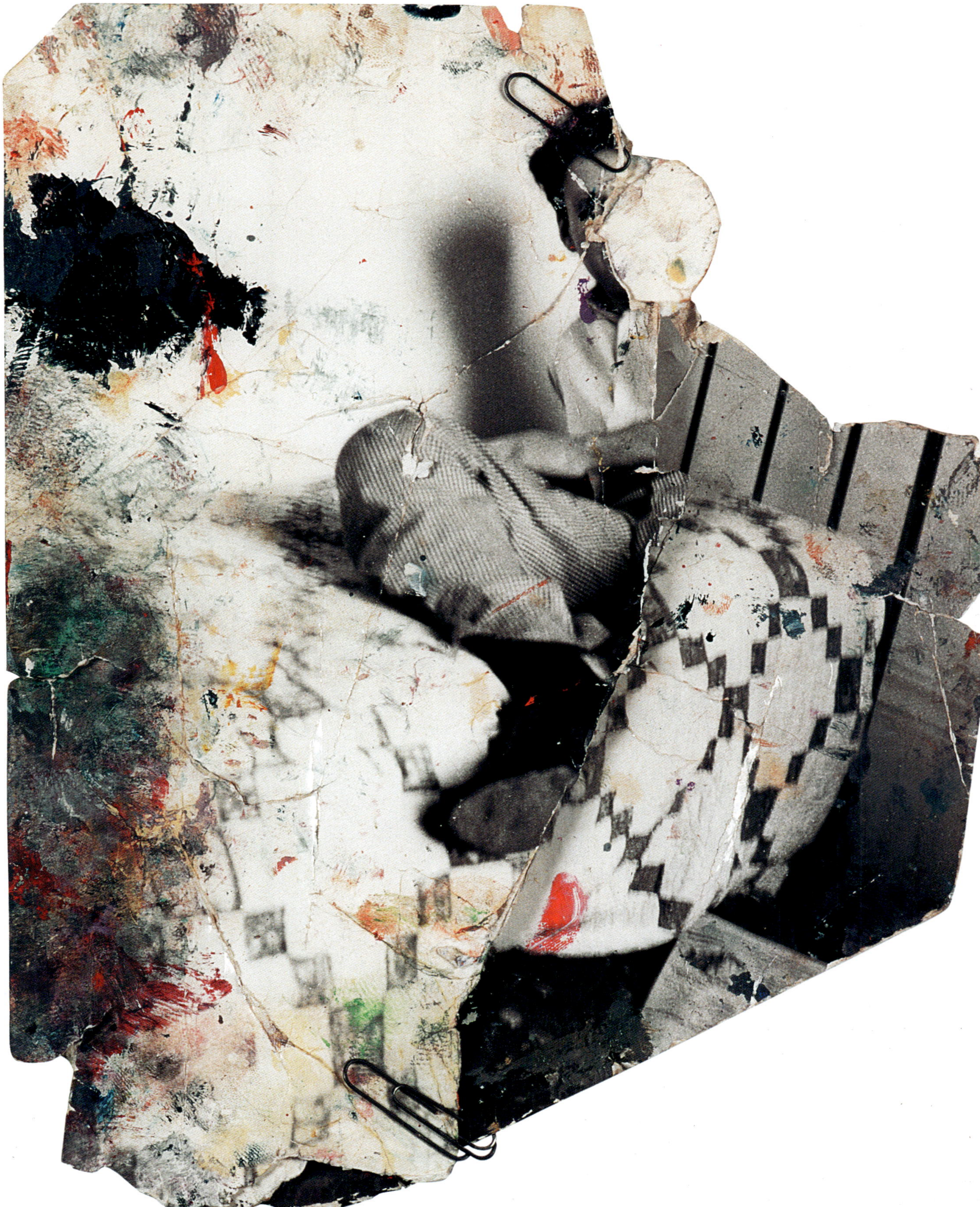

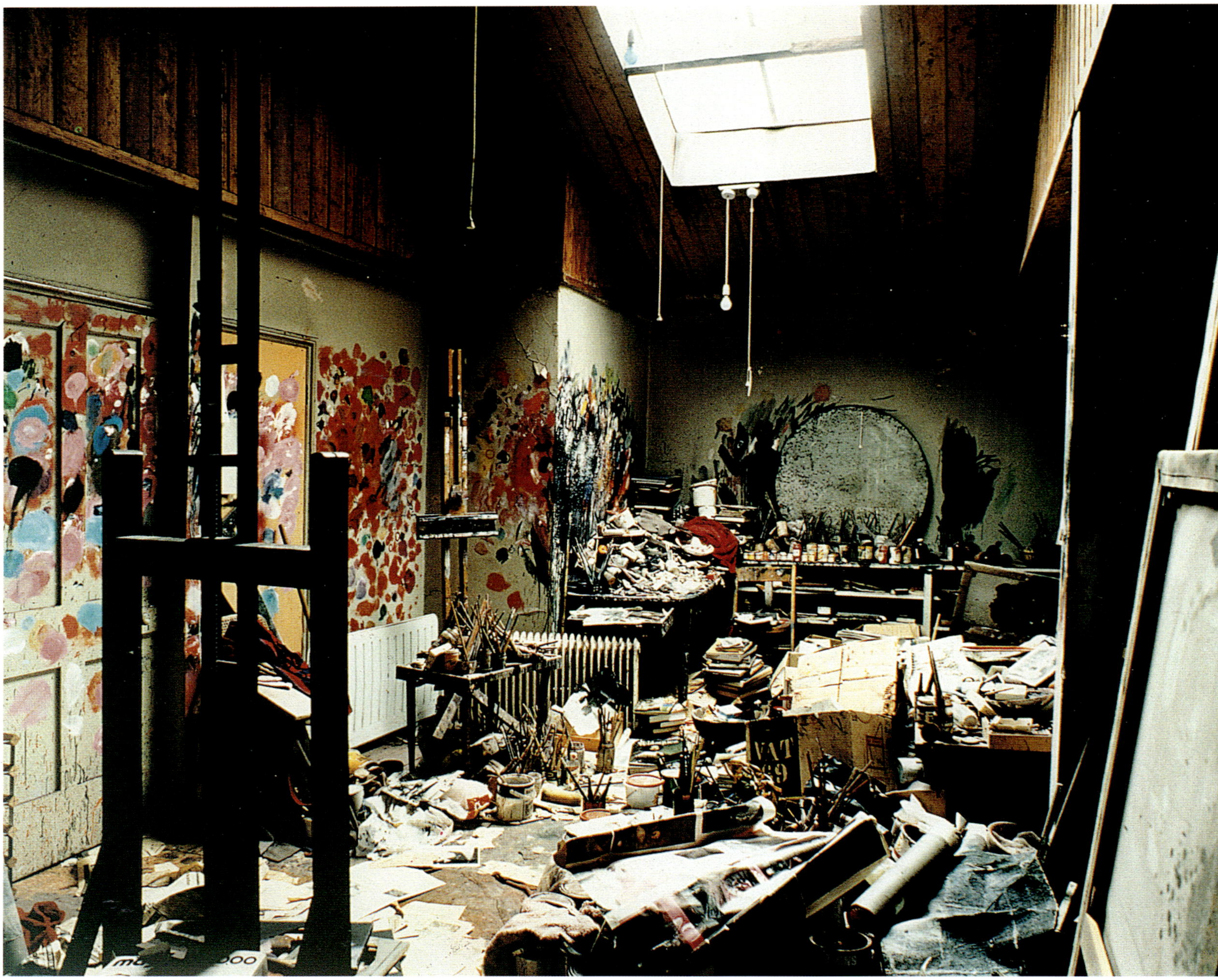

Plate 4: Colour photograph of Francis Bacon's studio at 7, Reece Mews. Photograph by Perry Ogden. Dublin, Dublin City Gallery The Hugh Lane. (©: Estate of Francis Bacon/Dublin City Gallery The Hugh Lane, photographic credit: Perry Ogden.)

the position of Freud's leg in this manipulated photograph in many portraits of the subject, for example, in the right-hand panel of *Three Studies of Lucian Freud*, 1969 and the right-hand panel of *Three Portraits, George Dyer, Self-Portrait, Lucian Freud*, 1973 (cat. no. 90). Indeed, it also appears in self-portraits, for instance, the right-hand panel of *Study for Self-Portrait – Triptych*, 1985–1986.

While Bacon eschewed the notion that his work was solely dependent on photographs, on occasion he could be remarkably faithful to the source. One perceives this in the case of the photographs of George Dyer, a former petty thief, whom Bacon met in late 1963.[12] Bacon painted portraits of Dyer obsessively, both during Dyer's life and after his tragic death in 1971. His distinctive features are omnipresent in Bacon's paintings from the mid-1960s to the late 1970s and intermittently from then on. The first major work to portray Dyer in all three panels is *Three Figures in a Room*, 1964.[13] Dyer is seen in profile in many paintings, such as *In Memory of George Dyer*, 1971 (cat. no. 121), *Triptych August 1972* (cat. no. 132) and *Triptych May – June 1973* (cat. no. 131). Bacon cut out the image of Dyer's head from one of the Deakin photographs. Due to the presence of a number of pinholes in this and similar cut-outs and the traces of paint around their outlines, it seems likely that these were used to trace head profiles onto the canvas.

Photographs of friends were not only used as the basis for portraits, they were also employed as components within full-length figure studies. A series of 23 nude photographs of the artist and art historian Lawrence Gowing have immediate resonances with many of Bacon's paintings of the 1980s, with their savage abbreviations of the human body. In 1976 Gowing began producing large pictures in which he traced the outline of his own naked body stretched on the canvas, the paint being applied by an assistant. It is possible that a series of mainly colour photographs found in Bacon's studio of Gowing in a variety of poses recorded part of one such performance. They are dated November 1978. In a number of the photographs his reflection is seen in a cracked mirror *(Plate 5)*. Gowing's truncated and distorted body strongly call to mind the headless and armless figures in Bacon's late paintings such as *Study from the Human Body – Figure in Movement*, 1982. The blurred, smeared effect created in these photographs clearly appealed to Bacon.

Many amateur and professional photographers took photographs of Bacon posing in his studio but rarely of him at work. These photographers included Henri Cartier-Bresson, Jorge Lewinsky, Michael Pergolani, Peter Stark, Michael Holtz and Jean-Loup Cor-

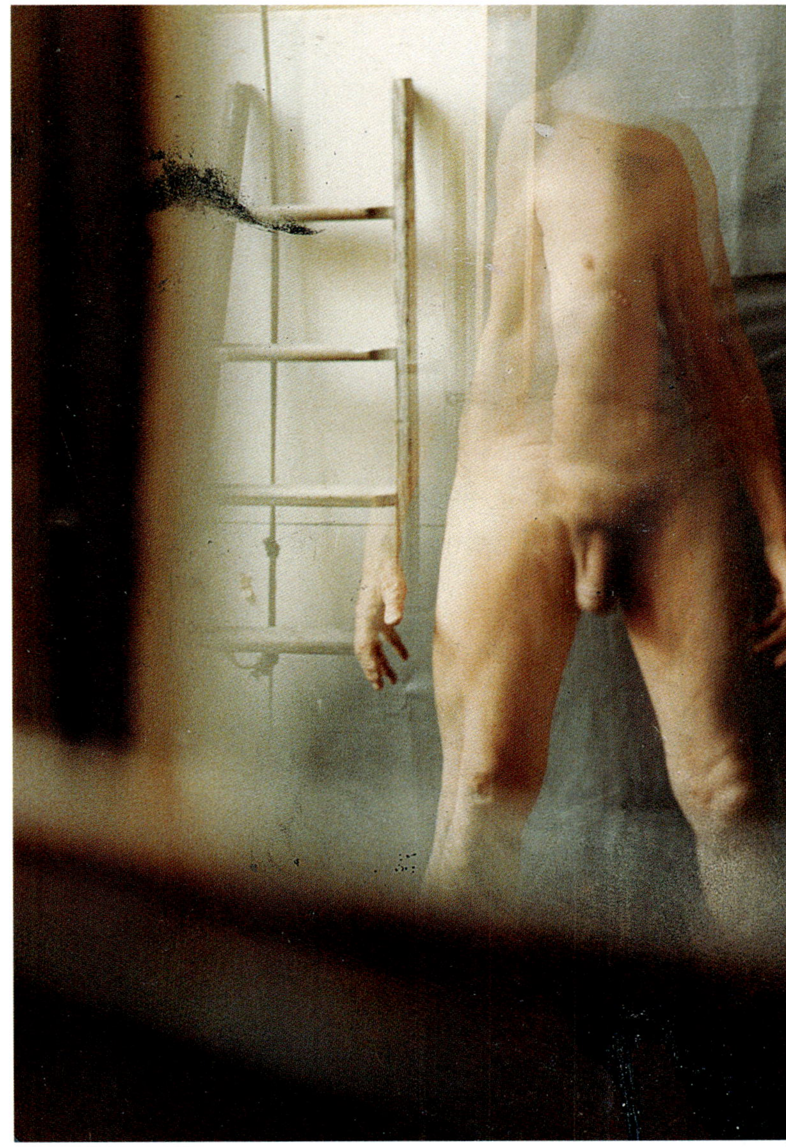

Plate 5: Standing Male Nude. Colour photograph by Sir Lawrence Gowing. November 1978. 88 × 129 mm. Dublin, Dublin City Gallery The Hugh Lane. (©: Estate of Francis Bacon/Dublin City Gallery The Hugh Lane.)

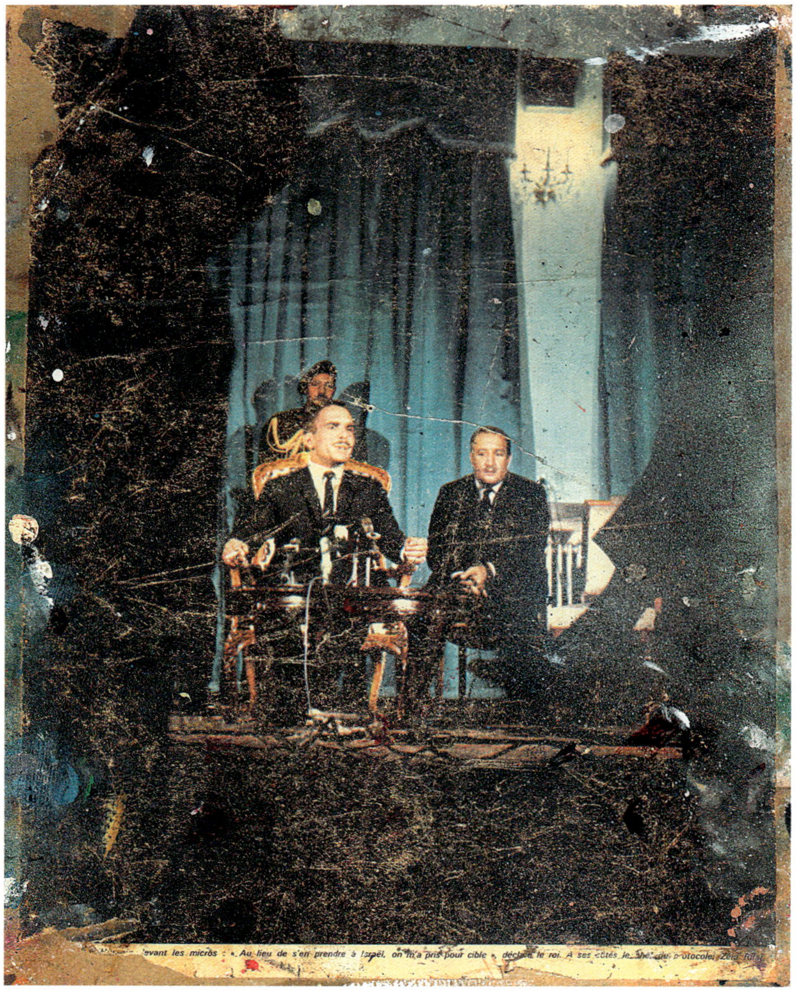

Plate 6: Image from the 1960s of King Hussein of Jordan (1935–1999), on a podium with a bank of microphones in front of him, mounted on card. 280 × 292 mm. Dublin, Dublin City Gallery The Hugh Lane. (©: Estate of Francis Bacon/Dublin City Gallery The Hugh Lane.)

Plate 7: Francis Bacon, Crucifixion. 1965. Oil on canvas, triptych, each panel 198 × 147,5 cm. Munich, Pinakothek der Moderne. (©: The Estate of Francis Bacon/ VBK, Vienna, 2003, photo: Andreas Freytag.)

net. The artist appears to have enjoyed these photo sessions, the resulting photographs providing Bacon with a visual record of his moods and poses, which he habitually consulted while painting self-portraits. Bacon is caught in an astonishing variety of poses, from the effusive and demonstrative to the remote and melancholic. There are formal correlations between the Stark photographs and several self-portraits by Bacon from 1973.

Aside from the work of particular photographers, Bacon found inspiration in countless other sources. The increasing dissemination of printed imagery in the twentieth century fed the artist's appetite for the alarming and the unusual. His declared aim was to create a visual shock through his work and, to this end, he sought images which showed both humans and animals in extreme conditions. He looked closely at illustrated books, magazines and newspapers whose subjects ranged from art, sport, crime, history and cinema to photography, wildlife, medicine and even parapsychology. The extraordinary breadth of imagery found in the studio confirms Bacon's statement that, "In a way, one is continually working and thinking and looking at things which don't have any immediate bearing on what one is trying to do, but they seem to come up again. You make a vast well of images within yourself out of which things keep coming."[14]

While Bacon was remarkably wide-ranging in his choice of source materials, certain preoccupations do emerge. Some of these boldly manifest themselves in the paintings whereas others are more latent. Illustrated history books and political features from magazines offered a seemingly limitless supply of motifs and ideas. Images of political leaders also appear in the studio material. Bacon's fascination with these images is affirmed by his choice of books and torn and mounted leaves. His interest in leaders was not so much motivated by their politics as by their iconic status.[15] The aura of power and authority surrounding these figures may have attracted Bacon in the same way that he was drawn to Velázquez's *Portrait of Pope Innocent X.* The political theme is also evident in Bacon's early paintings such as *Figure Study I*, 1945 and *Study for Man with Microphones*, 1946–48, which present mysterious, distorted figures with clusters of microphones. In later works the microphone device is avoided and authority is conveyed by more subtle means. The figure is now isolated, formally attired and seated on an elevated chair within a framing box as in *Study for Portrait*, 1949 (cat. no. 50) and *Study for a Portrait*, 1953 (cat. no. 89). An image from the 1960s of King Hussein of Jordan, on a podium with a bank of microphones in front of him, contains elements in common with both Bacon's early and later approaches *(Plate 6).* The artist was sufficiently struck by this illustration to

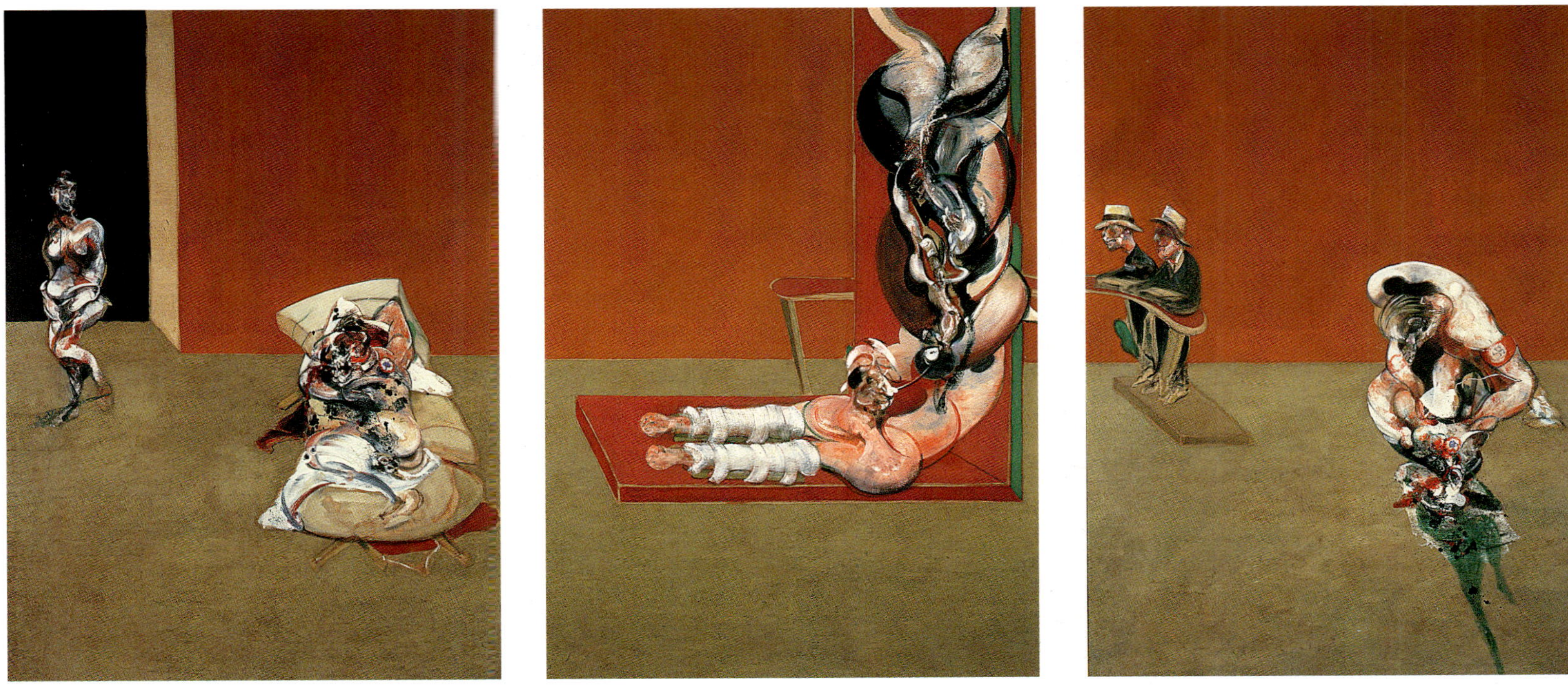

mount it on a piece of card. Another mounted image, this time torn in half, shows the lower part of the face of former US President Jimmy Carter, in front of a microphone. Occasionally Bacon made direct use of an image of a leader in his paintings. In the central panel of *Triptych, 1974 revised 1977*, the two figures on the curved background are based on distorted images of French President Raymond Poincaré and the English statesman, Austen Chamberlain. Bacon also closely modelled the figure in the left panel of *Triptych,* 1986–87 on an illustration of American President Woodrow Wilson.

Several books on Hitler and Nazi Germany were among the contents, though no image of the Führer has been connected with Bacon's paintings. Nonetheless Nazi imagery does appear in a number of works, most notably, *Crucifixion*, 1965 *(Plate 7)*. When questioned on his inclusion of a swastika on the armband of one of the figures, the artist explained that it was merely a formal device and that it should not be interpreted in a literal way. Bacon kept coloured photographs of Hitler and his entourage and was struck by the appearance of their red armbands.[16] It is possible that the colours and motifs of Nazism came to stand as a type of shorthand for alarm and terror and could thus be used as a ready means to shock and provoke. Bacon seemed to wish to tap into the violent associations of Nazism but was reluctant to accept that by doing so he might invite political interpretations of his work. It is an instance in which his desire to use a source for its visual force gets the better of his desire to skirt political debate.

Crime, above all violent crime, was another abiding interest of the artist. Some sections of Bacon's paintings immediately evoke the appearance of a crime scene. The central panel of *Three Studies for a Crucifixion*, 1962 is a notable example of this. Late paintings such as *Blood on the Floor – Painting*, 1986 and *Blood on the Pavement,* c. 1988 also imply that something violent and potentially deadly has just occurred. Bacon often made hand-written notes of ideas for painting, and these include a number of references to the "bed of crime", "scene of crime" and "pavement with blood." Several books on the subject of crime were found, most with missing pages, suggesting that the artist ripped out images of salient importance to him. Assassination attempts are a case in point. With the advent of high-speed photography and increased media interest in important political or religious figures, these events began to be caught on film. Images of assassinations were thus reproduced in mass-market photo-journalistic magazines such as Life International, Paris Match, Actualidad Española and The Sunday Times Magazine, of which Bacon had a large collection. Several loose leaves with features on the assassinations of Leon Trotsky, John F. Kennedy, Robert Kennedy and Martin Luther King were found throughout the studio. The attempted assassination of Pope John Paul II in 1981 appears on the cover of one of the Sunday Times magazines from 1985.

There is evidence that Bacon studied one assassination in detail, that of the Russian revolutionary Leon Trotsky, who was murdered with an ice pick. The artist had two copies of the same illustrated

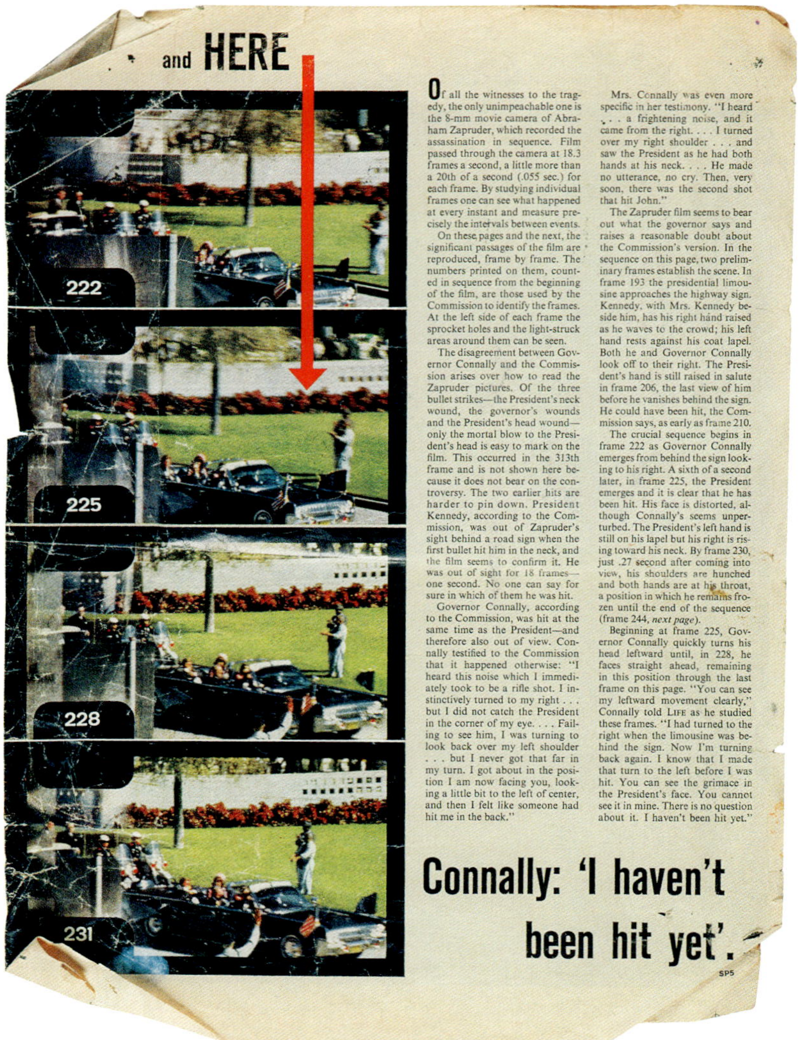

and HERE

Of all the witnesses to the tragedy, the only unimpeachable one is the 8-mm movie camera of Abraham Zapruder, which recorded the assassination in sequence. Film passed through the camera at 18.3 frames a second, a little more than a 20th of a second (.055 sec.) for each frame. By studying individual frames one can see what happened at every instant and measure precisely the intervals between events.

On these pages and the next, the significant passages of the film are reproduced, frame by frame. The numbers printed on them, counted in sequence from the beginning of the film, are those used by the Commission to identify the frames. At the left side of each frame the sprocket holes and the light-struck areas around them can be seen.

The disagreement between Governor Connally and the Commission arises over how to read the Zapruder pictures. Of the three bullet strikes—the President's neck wound, the governor's wounds and the President's head wound—only the mortal blow to the President's head is easy to mark on the film. This occurred in the 313th frame and is not shown here because it does not bear on the controversy. The two earlier hits are harder to pin down. President Kennedy, according to the Commission, was out of Zapruder's sight behind a road sign when the first bullet hit him in the neck, and the film seems to confirm it. He was out of sight for 18 frames—one second. No one can say for sure in which of them he was hit.

Governor Connally, according to the Commission, was hit at the same time as the President—and therefore also out of view. Connally testified to the Commission that it happened otherwise: "I heard this noise which I immediately took to be a rifle shot. I instinctively turned to my right . . . but I did not catch the President in the corner of my eye. . . . Failing to see him, I was turning to look back over my left shoulder . . . but I never got that far in my turn. I got about in the position I am now facing you, looking a little bit to the left of center, and then I felt like someone had hit me in the back."

Mrs. Connally was even more specific in her testimony. "I heard . . . a frightening noise, and it came from the right. . . . I turned over my right shoulder . . . and saw the President as he had both hands at his neck. . . . He made no utterance, no cry. Then, very soon, there was the second shot that hit John."

The Zapruder film seems to bear out what the governor says and raises a reasonable doubt about the Commission's version. In the sequence on this page, two preliminary frames establish the scene. In frame 193 the presidential limousine approaches the highway sign. Kennedy, with Mrs. Kennedy beside him, has his right hand raised as he waves to the crowd; his left hand rests against his coat lapel. Both he and Governor Connally look off to their right. The President's hand is still raised in salute in frame 206, the last view of him before he vanishes behind the sign. He could have been hit, the Commission says, as early as frame 210.

The crucial sequence begins in frame 222 as Governor Connally emerges from behind the sign looking to his right. A sixth of a second later, in frame 225, the President emerges and it is clear that he has been hit. His face is distorted, although Connally's seems unperturbed. The President's left hand is still on his lapel but his right is rising toward his neck. By frame 230, just .27 second after coming into view, his shoulders are hunched and both hands are at his throat, a position in which he remains frozen until the end of the sequence (frame 244, *next page*).

Beginning at frame 225, Governor Connally quickly turns his head leftward until, in 228, he faces straight ahead, remaining in this position through the last frame on this page. "You can see my leftward movement clearly," Connally told LIFE as he studied these frames. "I had turned to the right when the limousine was behind the sign. Now I'm turning back again. I know that I made that turn to the left before I was hit. You can see the grimace in the President's face. You cannot see it in mine. There is no question about it. I haven't been hit yet."

Connally: 'I haven't been hit yet'.

Plate 8: Life International magazine with colour photographic illustrations of the assassination of John F. Kennedy on 22 November 1963. November 28, 1966. 345 × 262 mm. Dublin, Dublin City Gallery The Hugh Lane. (©: Estate of Francis Bacon/Dublin City Gallery The Hugh Lane.)

book on Trotsky. In both copies, leaves were torn out from the final section covering his assassination in Mexico City. Several leaves from other books documenting the event were also discovered in the studio. One includes a photograph of the police reconstruction of the crime. Other images show the scene in the immediate aftermath of the revolutionary's death. Elements from that room, including a table lamp, a cabinet and pieces of newspaper or documents, are depicted in the right-hand panel of *Triptych*, 1986–1987. However, the body of the victim is absent and bloodstains on a cabinet are the only trace of his former presence. On this evidence, it would seem that Bacon's approach to assassination is indirect and surprisingly discreet. His pictorial interest rests more in the suggestion and implication of violent crime rather than in the action itself.

Probably the most famous and controversial assassination of the twentieth century was that of President John F. Kennedy on the 22 November 1963 in Dallas. Much of the debate surrounding his death has focused on 22 seconds of 8-mm film footage taken by Abraham Zapruder of the President's motorcade as it came under fire. Stills of this jittery footage, which Bacon had removed from three different publications, indicate that he was drawn to the subject on more than one occasion. A sheet of images of the incident from the 28 November 1966 issue of the magazine, Life International, contains superimposed red arrows that draw the viewer's attention to certain aspects of the crime *(Plate 8)*. Bacon would later use red arrows extensively in his paintings. Although there is no evidence to suggest that Bacon completed any paintings related to this event, he once drew Peter Beard's attention to a rail in the right-hand panel of *Triptych*, 1976, which he said had the same colour blue as that of "President Kennedy's assassination limousine".[17] Here, the reference to his source material is so oblique as to be only discernible to the artist himself.

An attraction to shocking and repulsive imagery is also evident in the artist's cache of medical imagery. Among the publications found in the studio, medical textbooks form a vital and distinct category. Particular areas of interest were X-ray techniques, skin disorders, forensic pathology and surgical procedures. Bacon seems to have been fascinated by disease and injuries from early in his career. While in Paris in the late 1920s, he bought a book on diseases of the mouth with hand-coloured illustrations. Although the book was not found in the studio, two fragments showing a mouth with a forceps on an abscess possibly belong to this source (cat. no. 39). The open mouth, whether that of primate or human, was a lifelong fixation. Skin and diseases of the skin were another enduring interest. Bacon observed that "[…] The texture of, for instance,

Plate 9: Leaf from unidentified book on skin diseases mounted on card with Sellotape. Date unknown. 330 × 203 mm. Dublin, Dublin City Gallery The Hugh Lane. (©: Estate of Francis Bacon/Dublin City Gallery The Hugh Lane.)

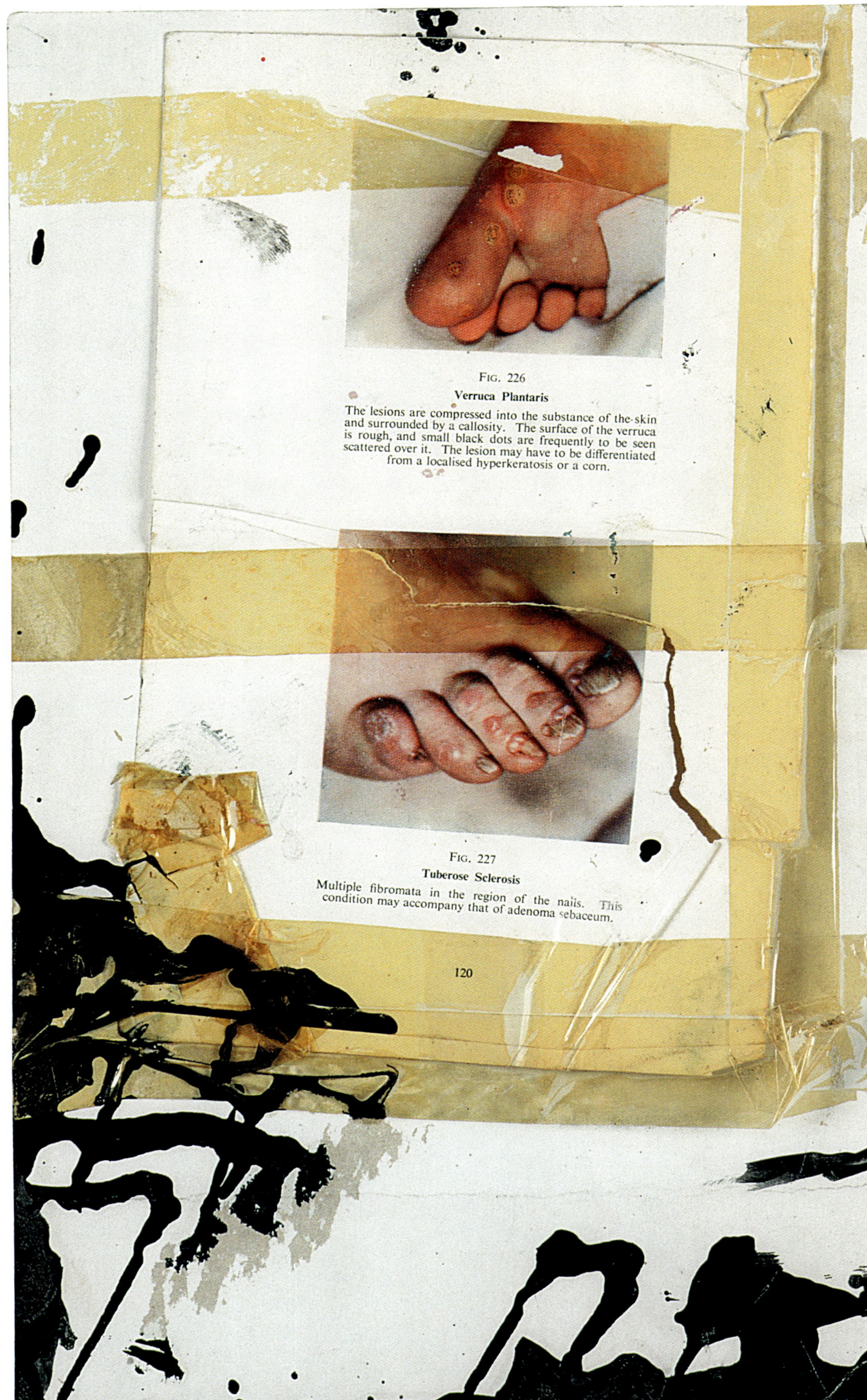

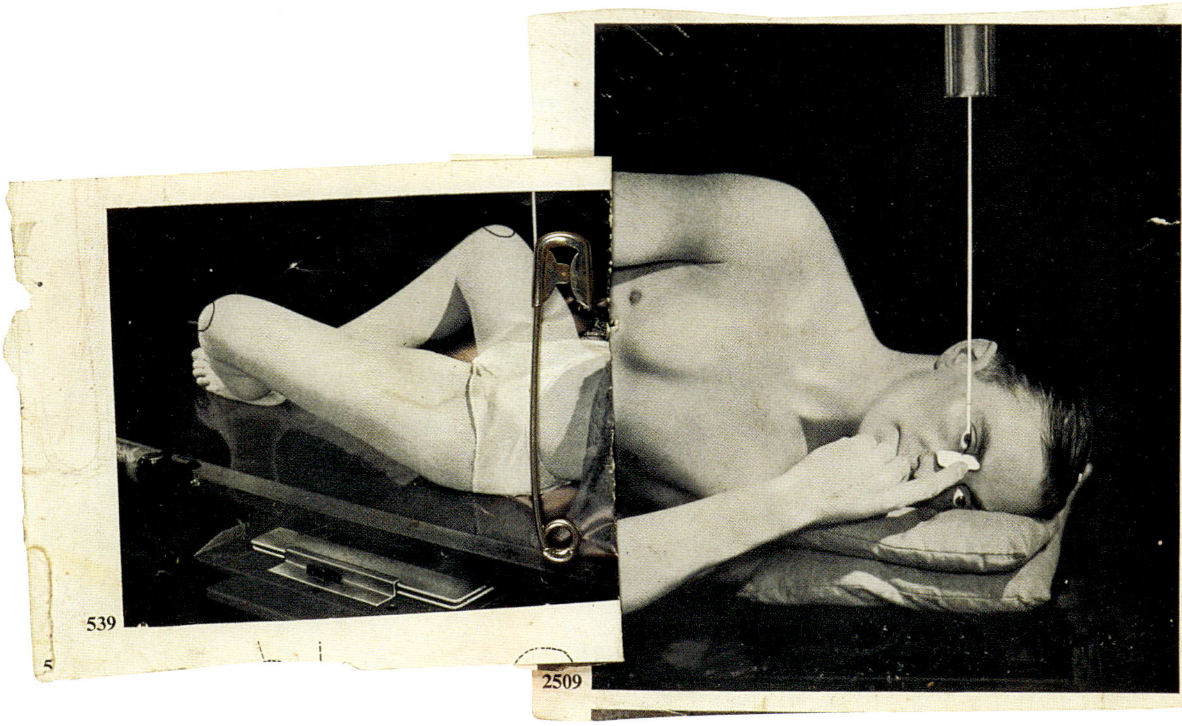

Plate 10: Two fragments from *Positioning in Radiography*, London, 1939 by K.C. Clark joined together with large metal safety pin. Bacon has juxtaposed two disparate black-and-white photographic illustrations to join a man's torso and a woman's legs. 110 × 188 mm. Dublin, Dublin City Gallery The Hugh Lane. (©: Estate of Francis Bacon/Dublin City Gallery The Hugh Lane.)

a rhinoceros skin would help me think about the texture of human skin"[18] and this preoccupation seems to have had its origins from the beginning of his career. In one of his early portraits from c. 1931–32, the figure has an outbreak of spots on one cheek.[19] An untitled book found in the studio illustrates virtually every skin disease and disorder imaginable. Bacon seems to have referred to it regularly and his characteristic trail of fingerprints in paint covers most of its pages. Several other leaves have been torn out and some were found scattered around the studio. Two images, both of diseased toenails, were cut out from this book and mounted on card with a view to working from the source *(Plate 9)*. The distortions caused by a skin disease may have informed Bacon's portrayal of skin in his paintings. In works such as *Head of a Woman,* 1960, the face of the figure is predominantly composed of bright red shades as if it were inflamed.

A key medical textbook for Bacon was *Positioning in Radiography*, by Kathleen Clara Clark and first published in 1939. The book contains over 2,500 black-and-white photographic illustrations, diagrams and texts on X-ray techniques, a subject that exerted a hold from early in his career.[20] The presence of a number of repeated motifs in Bacon's paintings can be directly linked to Clark's publication. These include a circular motif derived from circular illustrations and X-rays, and small directional arrows. On one occasion, Bacon used a safety-pin to combine two cut-out illustrations from this publication of a male torso and a pair of female legs *(Plate 10)*. Safety pins also occur as a motif in works such as *Study from the Human Body,* 1949. Bacon's use of this device has been linked to the work, *Tu m',* 1918 by Marcel Duchamp, where the artist plays with the notion of *trompe l'oeil* by including three actual safety pins to hold a tear together.[21]

Undoubtedly, one of the most significant books found in the studio is *Phenomena of Materialisation*, (London, 1920) by the German-born doctor Baron Albert von Schrenck-Notzing.[22] This eccentric textbook sets out to provide a systematic documentation of psychic phenomena. Adopting a pseudo-scientific approach, Schrenck-Notzing provides textual and photographic records of manifestations of spirits (ectoplasms) at seances directed by him. Visual documentation of these events is provided through photographs taken by Schrenck-Notzing, his patron Juliette Bisson and another person known simply as K. This book was probably acquired by Bacon in the 1930s[23] and its influence can arguably be discerned in *Crucifixion,* 1933. It became even more apparent in his paintings from the 1940s. It is almost certain that Bacon consulted the book at the easel. Despite its importance, and although he spoke at length about other sources, he never referred to *Phenomena of Materialisation* in any published interviews.

The book had both a pervasive and, in some cases, a very specific influence on his oeuvre. In several of the illustrations, white blobs of ectoplasm, the supposed viscous substance that exuded from

Plate 11: Leaf from *Phenomena of Materialisation*, 1920 by Baron von Schrenck-Notzing, with a distorted image of French statesman Raymond Poincaré. 245 × 163 mm. Dublin, Dublin City Gallery The Hugh Lane. (©: Estate of Francis Bacon/Dublin City Gallery The Hugh Lane.)

Plate 12 on p. 96: Leaf from book with black-and-white photographic illustration of an Egyptian statue on recto and text on verso. Date unknown. 365 × 295 mm. Dublin, Dublin City Gallery The Hugh Lane. (©: Estate of Francis Bacon/Dublin City Gallery The Hugh Lane.)

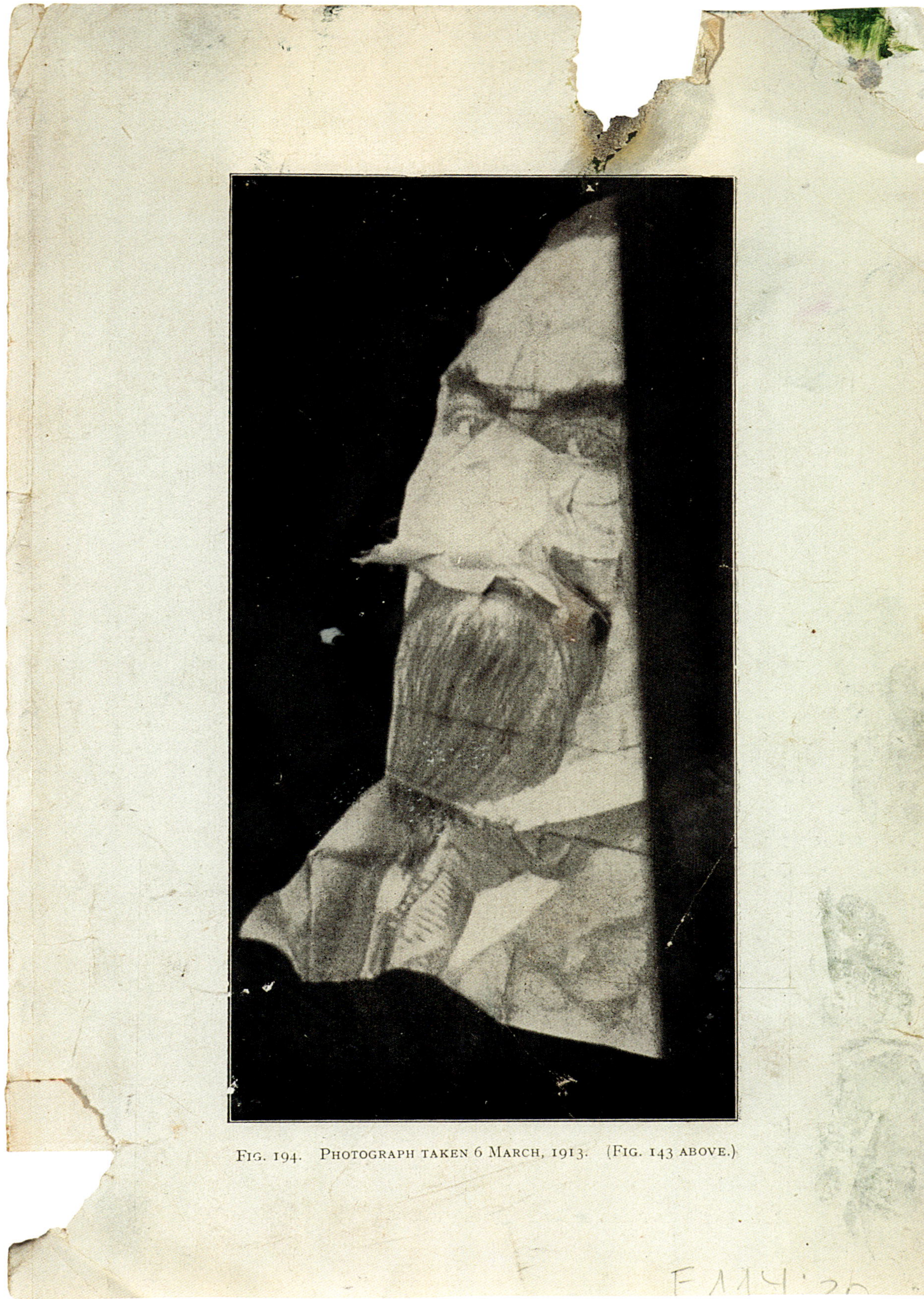

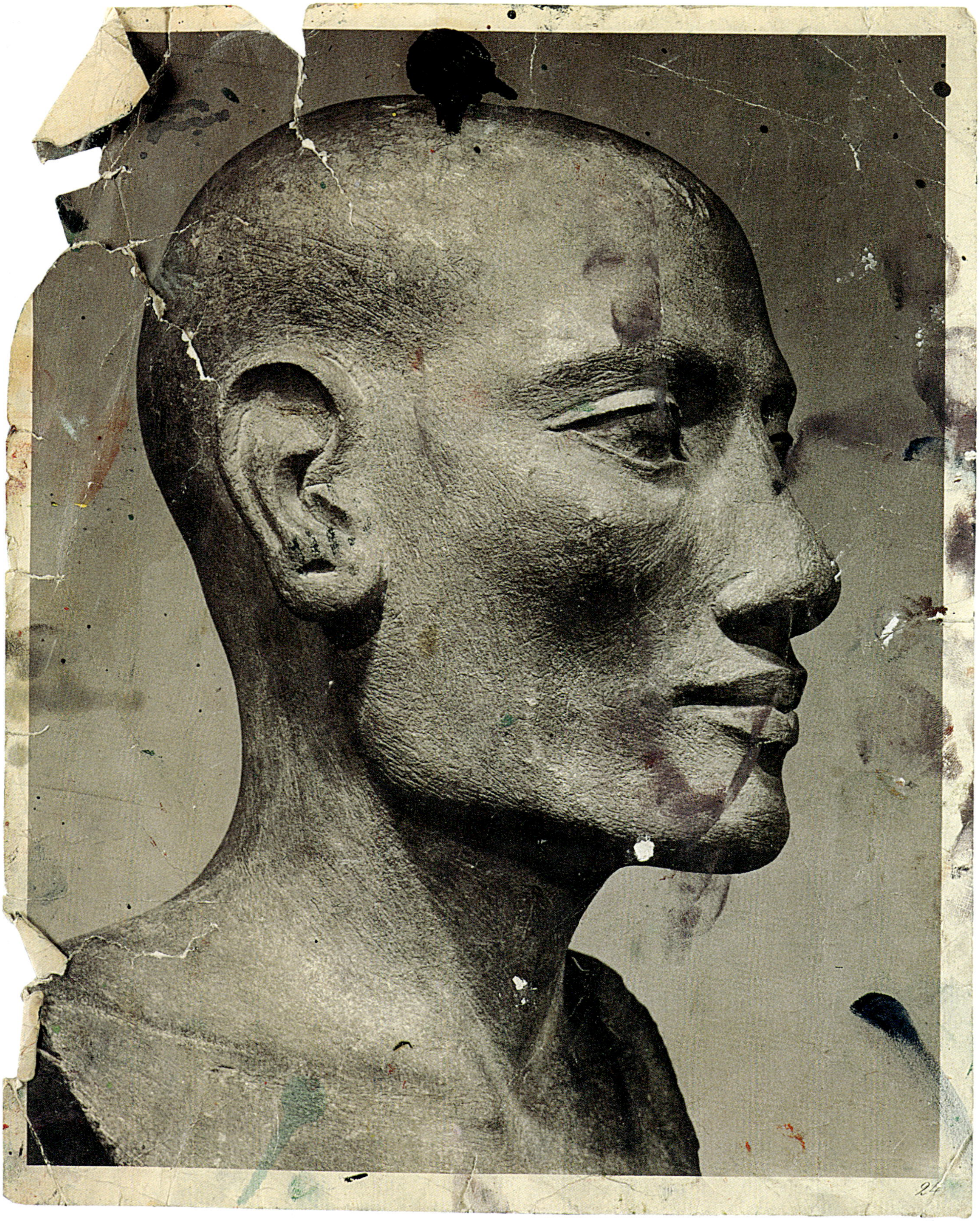

the spiritualistic medium during a trance, emerge from the mouths of mediums and even float freely across the air (cat. no. 20). The similarities with the blobs of white paint in paintings such as *Triptych May – June 1973* (cat. no. 131), *Portrait of George Dyer in a Mirror,* 1968 (cat. no. 120) and *Portrait of Isabel Rawsthorne Standing in a Street in Soho,* 1967 (cat. no. 59) are manifest. Bacon may also have consulted this book for new compositional ideas and there are striking similarities between the composition of paintings such as *The End of the Line*, 1953, *Two Figures at a Window,* 1953 and *Man with Arm Raised,* 1960 and images from Schrenck-Notzing's book. The seances at which the teleplastic phenomena occurred generally involved a single person who was seated in an enclosed, circular tent-like structure. The person is partially concealed. In most of the illustrations in *Phenomena of Materialisation*, a single figure is seen emerging from between curtains. The curtains in *Head II*, 1949 (cat. no. 26) and *Study from the Human Body,* 1949 (cat. no. 17) are clearly derived from the Schrenck-Notzing illustrations. The curtain motif also occurs in *Study after Velázquez's Portrait of Pope Innocent X,* 1953 (cat. no. 14), where the spectral image of the Pope is cast onto a curtained background and the image is partly lost where it falls on the darkness of the folds.

A comparison between Bacon's many paintings of Popes and the illustrations in Schrenck-Notzing's book is revealing. In certain instances, the influence of *Phenomena of Materialisation* on Bacon's Popes is remarkably direct. The head of *Study for a Pope III,* 1961 was based upon an image supposedly documenting the materialisation of an ectoplasmic form over the nose and mouth of French President Raymond Poincaré *(Plate 11).* Bacon transforms the figure into a Pope by placing a skull-cap on its head. The use of the Poincaré image is highly significant. Most of Bacon's paintings of Popes had been inspired by Velázquez's *Portrait of Pope Innocent X,* although he usually omitted the Pope's beard. In *Study for a Pope III,* Poincaré's beard is clearly discernible. The image of President Poincaré appears again in *Triptych 1974 – revised 1977* in the form of a face on a screen in the central panel. The similarity between the image in the painting and the image in the book is so pronounced that Bacon must not only have studied it closely, he must have had it directly before him.

In interviews given during his lifetime, Bacon professed great admiration for the work of artists such as Michelangelo, Ingres, Degas, van Gogh, Picasso and Giacometti. This is borne out by the number of books on these artists found in the studio. However, the studio also contained an impressive number of books and book leaves on Egyptian art and civilisation *(Plate 12).* Bacon believed that the achievement of Egyptian sculpture had scarcely been surpassed and even went so far as to say, "I think perhaps that the greatest images that man has made so far have been in sculpture. I'm thinking of some of the great Egyptian sculpture, of course, and Greek sculpture too."[24] His recorded remarks on the subject are generally short, but his high regard for the ancient world is clear. One of Bacon's most important source books on Egyptian art was *The Art of Ancient Egypt: Architecture, Sculpture, Painting, Applied Art* with an introduction by Hermann Ranke, which was published by Phaidon Press, Vienna in 1936. Fellow artist Lucian Freud acquired the German version of the book in 1939 and it is possible that he discussed it with Bacon. Freud has used it extensively during his career and based two recent paintings and an etching on plates 20 and 21, which show El-Amarna portrait masks.[25] Bacon was also intrigued by these masks and even traced around the features of a similar mask from the same book.[26] The influence of these face-masks is visible in the series of portraits he made of Lisa Sainsbury in the 1950s.

The influence of Egyptian and Greek sculpture can also be detected in Bacon's work in both the emphatic poses of his figures and the truncated limbs which frequently resemble the fragments of ancient sculpture. Here the intensity of the figures is enhanced by their fragmentary state. The bodies in Bacon's paintings are commonly bereft of normal limbs, or these limbs are reassembled in peculiarly disturbing ways. His comments on the Elgin Marbles are illuminating in this regard, "[...] the Elgin marbles in the British Museum are always very important to me, but I don't know if they're important because they're fragments, and whether if one had seen the whole image they would seem as poignant as they seem as fragments."[27] As with photographs, the damage that time inflicts on something, in Bacon's eyes, makes it more poignant, a word that he used at different times with reference to his own work and the work of other artists. Michelangelo's preparatory drawings of torsos and limbs also struck a chord with Bacon and it is likely that he found these abbreviated nude studies "poignant" in the same way he was moved by the broken fragments of ancient Egyptian and Greek sculpture. Fewer images of Greek sculpture were found in the studio, although Bacon was very drawn to Greek culture. He travelled to Crete and Athens in 1965 and had a life-long admiration for the plays of the great classical dramatist Aeschylus. A hand-written note in the studio indicates that he even tried to learn the Greek alphabet.

In the 1970s, Bacon expressed a wish to make his own paintings more sculptural.[28] In 1974, he remarked that he had been thinking about sculpture for several years. He also added, "I have very often used an armature to set off the image in paintings. I've felt that in sculpture I would perhaps be able to do it more poignantly."[29] Certain works have a strongly sculptural quality such as *Diptych: Study from the Human Body, Study of the Human Body – From a Drawing by Ingres,* 1982-1984 (cat. no. 102) and *Oedipus and the Sphinx after Ingres,* 1983 (cat. no. 97). Furthermore, the fictive platforms on which many of his bodies are placed resemble a plinth for a statue. While Bacon occasionally discussed the possibility of making sculptures though it would appear he never did so.[30] He was in contact with the Carlo Nicoli quarries in Carrara, Italy in 1978 and discussed the possibility of making sculptures based on his paintings but these plans were taken no further.[31] To the very end Bacon only ever succeeded in addressing his sculptural concerns in paintings, drawings and hand-written notes.

One issue, which has arisen since the artist's death, is the controversy surrounding his works on paper, such as drawings, interventions and hand-written notes. During his lifetime, Bacon placed heavy emphasis on the role of chance and accident in his work and denied using preparatory drawings. The evidence in the studio suggests that Bacon was certainly misleading on this point, and a considerable quantity of works on paper are in existence, the largest collection being in the Hugh Lane Gallery. The drawings were executed on a variety of media including tracing paper, lined paper, chain-laid manufactured paper and the blank end-papers of books. Some are cursory sketches executed in either pencil or ink and among these are several earlier drawings. Others are in ball-point or felt-tip pen and there are also some sketches in oil. Most are monochromatic and all are unsigned and undated. One of the best examples of Bacon's painted sketches can be found in the end-papers of a catalogue for an exhibition of paintings by Chaim Soutine held at the Museum of Modern Art, New York in 1950 *(Plate 13).* It shows a chair on a raised dais within a broadly described circular structure. Two owl-like forms are apparently perched on the back of the chair. The sketch cannot be conclusively linked with any one painting, though elements of it are found in paintings from the late 1950s and early 1960s.

The artist over-painted and traced over existing illustrations and photographs to define and explore motifs. The illustrations were sometimes of his own paintings and through these he sought to develop and improve works already out in the open. He also used existing paintings as the springboard for other works. "I very often find that I can work from photographs of my own works that have been done years before, and they become very suggestive."[32] Bacon had numerous reproductions of his own work both in the studio and pinned up on the wall in his kitchen.[33] In many of the hand-written notes, he urges himself to think of his earlier paintings. This personal form of artistic shorthand serves as an excellent record of Bacon's thought processes. His ideas for paintings were jotted down in a cryptic and allusive style, frequently invoking the imperative as if the notes were exhortations: "Think of crouching nude/1952/Three Studies on structures/With flesh coloured shadows"; "middle panel scene of crime from Triptych 1967 Center panel"; "Use photograph of own painting of man on couch against rail – the photo with figure in front with hands raised make the painting in circular setting with venetian blinds use the show in the photograph". The evidence of the studio suggests that Bacon was a more deliberate artist than he cared to admit.

However, while the drawings and hand-written notes demonstrate that Bacon was not the *alla prima* artist he pretended to be, there was room for spontaneity once he had started on a canvas. This is reflected in the destroyed and unfinished works found in the studio after his death.

Bacon was a ruthless editor and critic of his paintings. In 1942 he destroyed nearly all his earlier works and only ten canvases remain from the period 1929 to 1944. He emphatically dismissed, on a number of occasions, works that he had made prior to 1944 and he viewed his painting, *Three Studies for Figures at the Base of a Crucifixion,* 1944 as his point of departure. However, he continued to destroy a proportion of his output right up until his death. The artist spoke of the hypnotic effect a canvas had on him and of his urge to get them out of his studio as quickly as possible once he had completed them. He also said, "I think I tend to destroy the better paintings, or those that have been better to a certain extent. I try and take them further, and they lose all their qualities, and they lose everything."[34] While John Edwards destroyed the larger canvases at Bacon's behest, the artist liked to slash the small canvases himself.

One hundred incomplete or destroyed canvases were found at Bacon's Reece Mews studio after his death. They span some five decades of the artist's career, with the earliest known work dating from around 1946. The larger ones were stacked up against the walls and blocked out light from the two windows in the studio. Some of the smaller ones were found piled on shelves or discarded on the floor beside his easel. The human figures in Bacon paintings tend to be two-thirds to three-quarters life size; the majority of the large paintings are of figures, whereas the smaller paintings tend to be of heads. Over half the canvases found are in a small format. Some were used as palettes or have initial preparatory layers, whereas others carry portrait studies in varying states of completion. The artist may have used other canvases to test paint colours and tech-

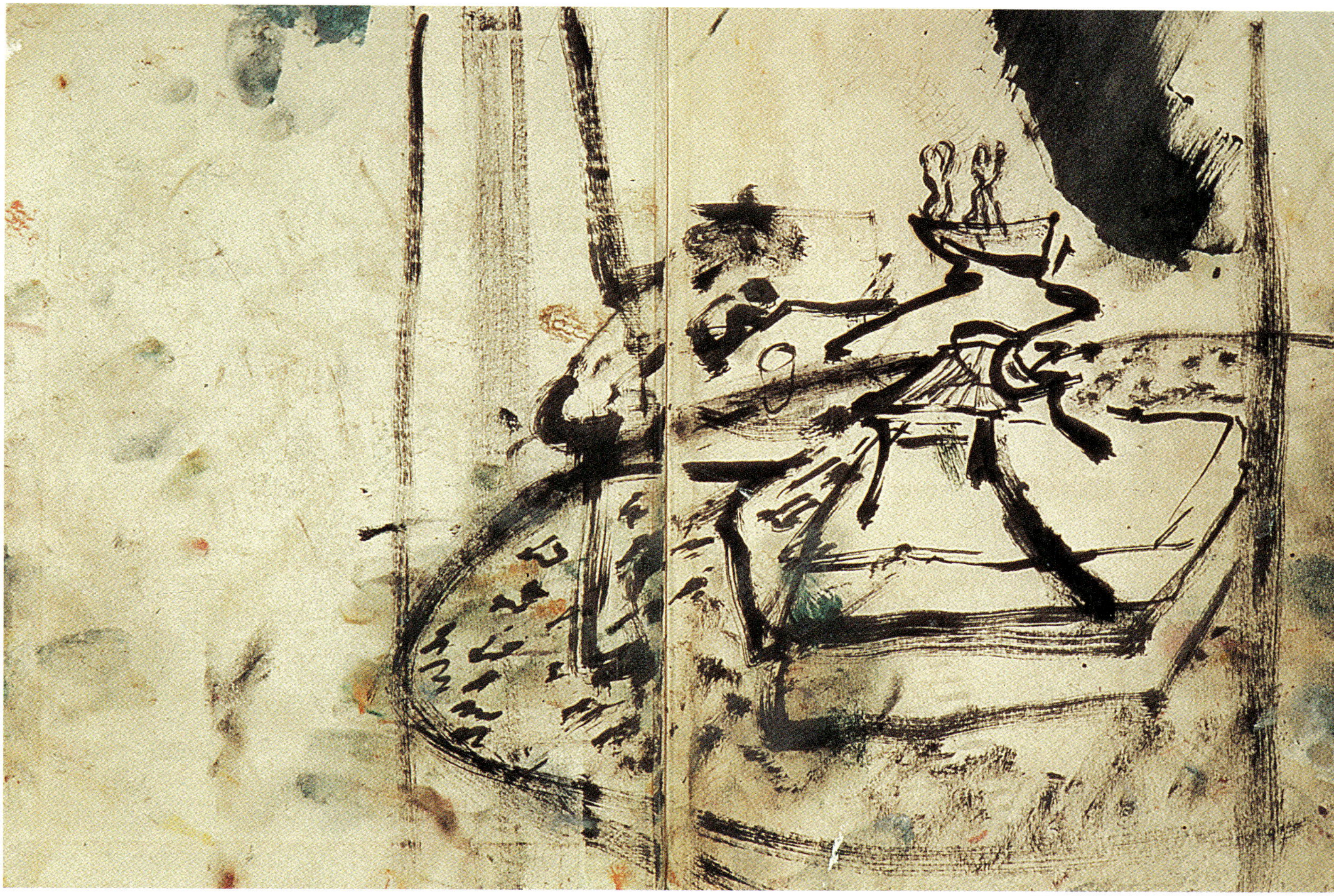

Plate 13: Chaim Soutine exhibition catalogue by Monroe Wheeler, Museum of Modern Art, New York, 1950 with sketch by Francis Bacon on end-papers at front. Drawing, circa 1950. 258 × 190 mm. Dublin, Dublin City Gallery The Hugh Lane. (©: Estate of Francis Bacon/Dublin City Gallery The Hugh Lane.)

Plate 14 on p. 101: Gorilla with Microphones. 1946–48. 145 × 127.8 cm. Dublin, Dublin City Gallery The Hugh Lane. (©: Estate of Francis Bacon/Dublin City Gallery The Hugh Lane.)

niques or possibly to clean his brushes since no conventional artist's palette was found in the studio. A more disturbing impression is given by the portrait studies. The head area of every portrait found in the studio has been cut out. Usually only a small area of the neck and outline of the head remain, making it difficult to identify the sitter. Nonetheless, some of these slashed studies can be linked to finished paintings of Lucian Freud, John Edwards, Isabel Rawsthorne and indeed self-portraits. Similarly, some of the larger paintings relate to completed triptychs or diptychs. A large destroyed figure study showing a semi-nude male seated in a red armchair bears close similarities with the right-hand panel of *Double Portrait of Lucian Freud and Frank Auerbach*, 1964.

These works, although destroyed, often show what a Bacon canvas looks like before completion. Bacon had no formal training as an artist and his unorthodox techniques are here revealed in their raw state. In most cases, a painting was taken to a relatively advanced stage before it was destroyed. In others all that exists are a few sketchily painted contours or preparatory paint applications. In the early 1950s, Bacon tended to apply thin washes of dark blue, grey or black paint as a preparatory layer and the composition was then executed over this, leaving areas of the preparatory layer to stand as the background colour. Some of the canvases found in the studio were executed in this way. Bacon's mode of working soon changed and instead, he tended to sketch figures, chairs and box-like structures in dilute paint directly onto the bare canvas. This drawing-like use of paint closely resembles sketches found in the studio. The artist would then build up the figurative elements of the composition and when he reached a certain point, would apply the background. In the later stages of painting, he would return to the figurative elements and build them up with thicker applications of paint. By contrast, some canvases indicate that the figures were relatively highly finished before the application of the background colours. While the figures were painted in oil, the backgrounds were executed using either acrylic or household paints, often applied with a paint roller.

Certain earlier works have very thick, complex paint films built up of multiple layers of different colours, many of which are not visible on the surface. This suggests that Bacon reworked the composition extensively as it progressed, something which tallies with the artist's own statements on his working methods. *Gorilla with Microphones,* 1946–48 is a good example of this tendency *(Plate 14).* The work was exhibited with the title, *Study for Man with Microphones* at the exhibition "British Painters Past and Present" at the Lefevre Gallery, London in 1946. It featured a distorted male figure, under a large umbrella, in front of a cluster of microphones and was similar to *Painting*, 1946. Bacon then reworked the painting about 1947–48 and in this new composition a crouched figure is seen from behind with a box-like structure outlined in white around it. This painting is executed on the primed side of the canvas. Bacon started working on the reverse side of primed canvases in the late 1940s, probably around 1947 or 1948.[35] *Head I*, 1948 and *Head II*, 1949 (cat. no. 26) are among the earliest examples of Bacon's works on unprimed canvas. *Gorilla with Microphones* is the only slashed canvas for which the two missing fragments of canvas were found in the studio. The presence of these fragments in 7 Reece Mews may mean that the work was slashed after 1961, and possibly much later. The paint along the edge of the cuts has a serrated edge, which would suggest that a considerable period of time had elapsed before the canvas was destroyed, as the paint was already dry. Bacon was clearly dissatisfied with the work and in the Alley and Rothenstein 1964 catalogue raisonné it was reproduced in the section on abandoned paintings.[36] The fact that the Alley and Rothenstein catalogue, drawn up under Bacon's supervision, divides the paintings into three categories – "Completed Pictures", "Abandoned Pictures" and "Destroyed Pictures" – is telling.

An unfinished work was found on Bacon's easel on his death in April 1992. His sister, Ianthe Knott, recalls seeing the same work on his easel during the previous November. Despite ill health, Bacon remained determined to attempt big works. The procedure he employed is familiar from his other large-scale works. The figure(s), sofa and framing device are sketched with paint upon the unprimed surface and one head has been brought halfway to completion. It is unclear how many figures the artist intended nor is there any firm indication that he had a final composition in mind. This is consistent with the artist's comments on the way he sketched onto canvas, "It never, never stays that way. It's just to get me into the act of doing it. Often, you just put on paint almost without knowing what you're doing. You've just got to get some material on the canvas to begin with. Then it may or may not begin to work."[37] In the final unfinished portrait, the brush is still groping to find the right pose(s) and the right arrangement of figure(s). In no other surviving work by the artist are several seated figures packed so tightly together. The large circle and fragment of an arc further concentrate the group. Possible sources for this motif range from K.C. Clark's *Positioning in Radiography*, 1939 to the circular mirror that faced him every day. As is typical of Bacon's procedure, the background has yet to be laid in. The head of the central figure is the most highly developed part of the canvas, but its identity remains elusive. At first, it was thought to be a self-portrait, an

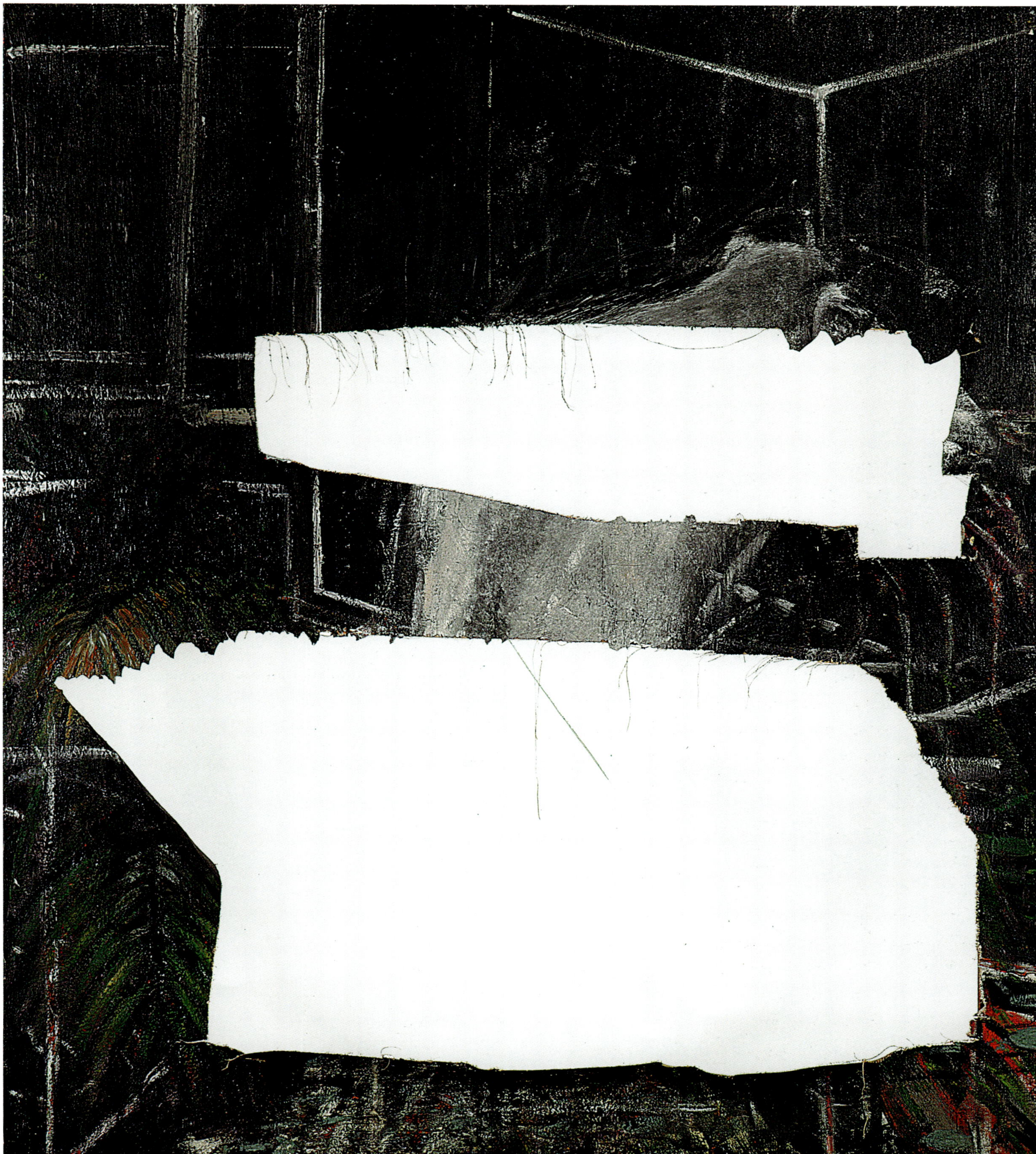

assumption consistent with the sitter's slightly protruding lower lip. However, the stark profile also resembles that of George Dyer and a further link may be made with an image found in the studio dating from 25 November 1965. This is the front cover of the Spanish magazine *La Actualidad Española*, with its four colour images of French President Charles de Gaulle. Using white paint, Bacon has circled around the profile of de Gaulle, almost as a photographer might circle an image on a contact sheet. Bacon sometimes evolved his paintings by a series of visual associations, a single portrait being the result of several stages and several different sources. In the final unfinished portrait these sources have yet to be resolved into a single identity, rather the features of Bacon, Dyer and possibly de Gaulle still vie for supremacy.

That lack of resolution was a defining attribute of the studio itself. New source materials were continually being brought into the room as older ones were recycled to near destruction. The artist once described the essentially accretive nature of the studio as being a form of autobiography. The processes that drove it have long since stopped but the space itself has been reconstructed as the artist left it. Examination of its contents has already deepened our understanding of the artist and new connections are being made all the time. Further study of the destroyed canvases may unveil more secrets and surprises just as his source materials continue to complicate the authorised account of a reckless and spontaneous master. The studio, with a labyrinth of memories and associations to its name has emerged to be the most mysterious and intriguing of all his creations.

[1] The studio was donated to Dublin City Gallery The Hugh Lane in August 1998 by John Edwards, Bacon's sole heir. Edwards first met Bacon in the mid-1970s and they remained close friends until the artist's death on 28 April 1992.

[2] While Bacon acquired new and grander places to work, he continually returned to the awkward but familiar studio at Reece Mews. In the late 1960s and 1970s he bought several properties including an impressive studio at Roland Gardens near the Old Brompton Road, a house in Wivenhoe, near Colchester in Essex, and a house in Narrow Street overlooking the Thames in Limehouse. He also bought a studio apartment on the Rue de Birague near the Place des Vosges in Paris in Autumn 1974.

[3] Sylvester 1999, p. 190.

[4] Archimbaud 1993, pp. 88, 89.

[5] 1,080 black-and-white photographs and 419 colour photographs were found in the studio after Bacon's death.

[6] Lisa Sainsbury sat for the artist once a week from late 1955 to early 1957 but Bacon also worked on these paintings in her absence. Of the eight portraits of Sainsbury that he commenced, only three survive. The photographer Cecil Beaton also sat for the artist but, on seeing the end result, was horrified and Bacon immediately destroyed the work. Beaton recalls this incident in his memoirs, *The Restless Years*, 1976.

[7] Sylvester 2000, p. 86.

[8] Bacon accepted portrait commissions from Giovanni Agnelli, Mick Jagger and Gilbert de Botton.

[9] In an interview with Sylvester from 1966, he openly spoke about the photographs he had commissioned from Deakin and how important they were to his work practice. Towards the end of his life it was a debt Bacon was occasionally reluctant to concede, at least in public.

[10] Sylvester 1999, p. 38.

[11] In an interview with the French newspaper Libération in 1988, when Bacon was asked which contemporary artists interested him, he mentioned the work of Pignon. Shortly after this interview, Pignon sent him some reproductions of work that he was doing in Naples. Bacon requested an enlargement of one section, showing a male figure with his head arched back and a large black arrow pointing at a *trompe-l'oeil* tear on the neck of the figure. The impression created is that the figure has suffered an injury. Bacon told Pignon that he had liked his work since first encountering it in 1976. I am grateful to Ernest Pignon-Ernest for this information given in correspondence with the author on 7 May 2003.

[12] Deakin took at least four different series of photographs of Dyer. One series shows him in front of louvred blinds, another in a street in Soho, another with Bacon in front of a delicatessen and a further series of Dyer in his underpants seated on a chair in the Reece Mews studio. None seem to have been stamped or dated.

[13] It was sadly prophetic that Bacon portrayed Dyer seated on a toilet in the left-hand panel. Two days before the opening of the Francis Bacon Retrospective at the Grand Palais in Paris in 1971, Dyer was found dead from a drink and drugs overdose on a toilet in the bathroom of the Hôtel des Saint-Pères in Paris. *Triptych May – June 1973* confronts the moment of Dyer's death.

[14] "Francis Bacon: Remarks from an Interview with Peter Beard," edited by Henry Geldzahler, in Exh. Cat. New York 1975, p. 17.

[15] Bacon appears never to have been a member of any political party. Unlike several artists and writers he counted as his friends, he had no allegiance with the Left and distrusted all brands of political idealism. His outlook was libertarian and he felt that the Right was "the best of a bad job." There is no suggestion in any of his works that Bacon wished to convey a political message and he repeatedly insisted that he did not.

[16] Sylvester 1999, p. 65.

[17] Farson 1993, p. 227.

[18] Sylvester 1999, p. 32.

[19] This portrait is illustrated (cat. no. 5) in Alley – Rothenstein 1964, pp. 26, 27. The authors note that it is wrongly described as a self-portrait but was done from imagination.

[20] In April 1933 Bacon exhibited as part of a group show at the Mayor Gallery, and in the same year *Crucifixion,* 1933 was reproduced in Herbert Read's book, *Art Now* and purchased by the collector Sir Michael Sadler. Sadler intended commissioning a portrait based on an X-ray of his skull, an idea that Bacon incorporated into another, more colourful treatment of the *Crucifixion* from the same year.

[21] Sylvester 2000, p. 56.

[22] Bacon may have been aware of other books by Schrenck-Notzing, who was also a renowned pioneer of psychiatry. *The Use of Hypnosis in Psychopathia Sexualis with Especial Reference to Contrary Sexual Instinct*, 1895 was one of his best-known psychiatric works. Schrenck-Notzing attempted to cure homosexuality through hypnotic suggestion and visits to brothels. These theories may have interested Bacon who remarked that "Being a homosexual is a defect. It's like having a limp." See Peppiatt 1996, p. 17.

[23] Sylvester 2000, p. 33. Sylvester offers no evidence for this statement.

[24] Sylvester 1999, p. 114.

[25] Exh. Cat. London 2002, p. 14.
[26] The presence of indented lines around this illustration indicates that the artist had attempted to trace the outline of the mask onto paper.
[27] Sylvester 1999, p. 114.
[28] Sylvester 1999, p. 114.
[29] Sylvester 1999, p. 108.
[30] Sylvester 1999, pp. 108–112.
[31] Telephone conversation between Carlo Nicoli and the author on 16 January 2003.
[32] Sylvester 1999, p. 37.
[33] He even mimicked this arrangement in a painting, *Study for a Portrait*, 1967 which shows three cursory illustrations of his own work pinned up on a wall in the background of the paintings.
[34] Sylvester 1999, p. 17.
[35] Bacon began to work on the reverse side of primed canvas in Monte Carlo in the late 1940s. He had run out of money and only had used canvases. He turned these around and discovered that he much preferred to work on the unprimed side. See Sylvester 2000, p. 33.
[36] A previous interpretation was that the first and second states reproduced in Alley and Rothenstein were, in fact, two different paintings. The Hugh Lane collection painting was thought to be the first state and the whereabouts of the second canvas, *Study for Man with Microphones* painted around 1947–48, was unknown. However, it would now appear that although Bacon supervised the production of Alley's catalogue raisonné, the black-and-white photographic illustrations of the first state and revised state of these paintings were transposed and the first state is actually the revised state. See catalogue number A5 in Appendix A Abandoned Pictures. I am grateful to Martin Hammer for this observation.
[37] Peppiatt 1989, reproduced in Domino 1996, p. 113.

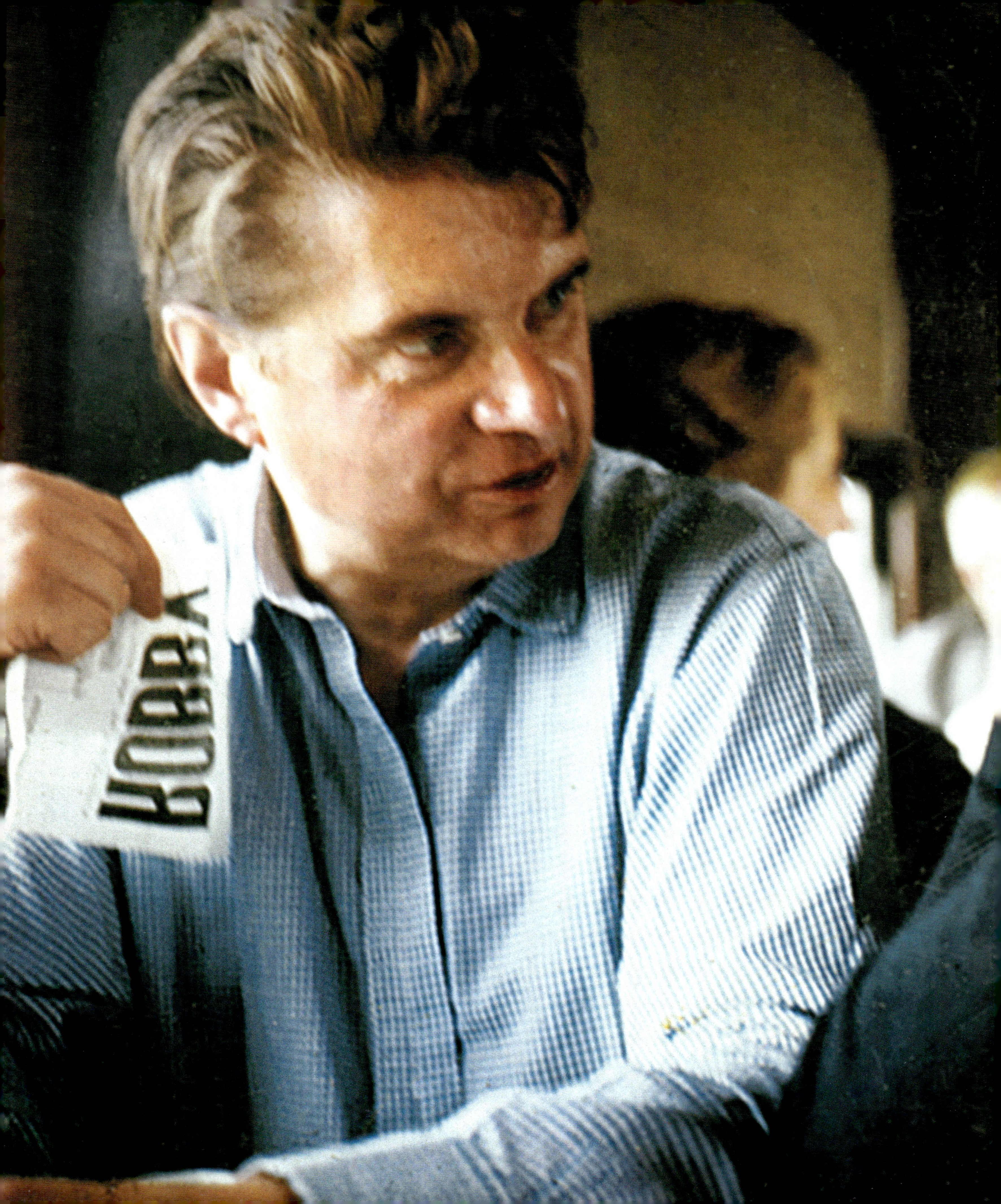
KOBRA

Michael Peppiatt
Bacon's Eyes

Whenever something caught Francis Bacon's attention, his normally genial gaze took on a cold, piercing intensity – like a bird suddenly spotting its prey. The look could come out of nowhere, at any time, provoked by a chance remark, for instance, a painting in an art magazine or the way someone walked into a restaurant. If you were unfortunate enough to have that look turned on you (and if you spent much time with Bacon, at some point it became inevitable), you had the sensation of being taken apart, swiftly and mercilessly. Whatever fear, guile or half-truth lurked within you had been analysed in a flash, minutely recorded and stowed away in a visual memory that forgot nothing, it seemed. It was the kind of scrutiny that took years to come to terms with, leaving you painfully self-aware.

What went on in the pale blue depths of that unwavering stare? Although he could be cruel and occasionally treacherous, Bacon was not a malevolent man. To the people he liked, he went out of his way to be generous and supportive; and those he disliked, he generally disregarded until they disappeared from his life. There was nevertheless something totally pitiless in that gaze. Was it the compulsion to tear off every veil, to lift appearance and look behind? Did Bacon feel that only the intensity of that look – the *mirada fuerte* that John Richardson mentions in relation to Picasso – could pierce the surface and lead him to a deeper, underlying truth. Certainly Bacon trusted his eyes to tell him everything he ever wanted to know.[1] Talking and reading, both of which he did with great appetite and flair, had proved to be extremely useful and illuminating, but it was what he saw that really counted. Vision was where all the senses and all experience converged in their most complete and potent form. And as I write this, I remember the look of terror I saw once in Bacon's eyes when (it was in Marseilles in 1976, just after his exhibition had opened at the Musée Cantini) we came abruptly face to face with a blind man with dark glasses and a white cane tapping his way down a dark side street behind the old port.

Those eyes, of course, spent a long lifetime dissecting everything that came within range. They had taken in animal and human life at an early age on a horse-training farm in Ireland, but they found their real focus in the densely populated centres of great metropolises. London, Paris, Berlin, and later to some extent Madrid, were the places that offered the most varied and abundant prey. There was no need for open landscape and the eruption of wild life when you could catch human nature in its essential bestiality trapped in the confines of a room. Bacon had, in fact, lived his life to excite and satisfy the hunger in his eyes as quickly and completely as he could. Love begun in bars, lulled in champagne, could only be fulfilled in the sadomasochistic arena, with its variety of harsher delights. There, more than anywhere, in the confusion of extreme pleasure and extreme pain, Bacon found access to a reality – the rawest emotion, the undisguised scream – that most situations in life disguised. And later, in his own version of "emotion recollected in tranquillity," Bacon was free to flay his lovers and himself on canvas with an abandon that would have proved fatal in real life, and for which he drew with supreme cynicism on medical textbooks, scientific photography and the entire history of figure- and flesh-painting in Western art.

Bacon's eyes took in not only the extreme situation, nevertheless, but whole sweep of daily existence. "What I love most in the end," he said to me once, when he was already quite old, "is simply being conscious. And all I ask of life these days is a body that will get me from place to place, and a mind that works." He watched with fascination as people's faces – above all, those he knew well – were transformed: hardened in hate, loosened by drink, intensified by desire. And from his portraits, I think it is clear that if he watched intently, like a predator, it was also with fellow-feeling and tenderness. Unsparing though he could be in his criticism of other people's art or characters, he was very indulgent towards the weaknesses and follies of those he cared for. Thus when the high-flown *Sturm und Drang* of sadomasochistic homosexual love proves overwhelming, Bacon aficionados turn instinctively for relief to the compassionate intimacy and insight with which the artist portrayed his circle of close friends.

"I am like a grinding machine," Bacon famously observed. "I look at everything, and everything goes in and gets ground up very fine." Along with photography and the history of art, as mentioned above, came virtually everything that had a visual existence, from newspaper print to desert boots and lipstick. I remember Bacon becoming transfixed, for instance, by a puddle of milk on a café table; he lifted his finger, as if to draw in it, then rather reluctantly abstained. And I remember thinking at the time (we were sitting appropriately enough at the Coupole in Paris) how vital the discovery of surrealism had been to Bacon. With its insistence on the importance of the unconscious and its fascination with the "chance encounters" of quite disparate things, surrealism – and Picasso at his most surrealist – was no doubt the single most important influence on his development, however much he distanced himself from the whole phenomenon later on. But, as with his other "borrowings," Bacon rapidly absorbed surrealist attitudes and techniques and turned them into something unmistakably his own.

Nor was it by any means only visual phenomena that attracted Bacon's interest. Everything, in a sense, from an Edith Piaf song to a line from one of Yeats' late poems went in and was ground up very fine, and there is certainly a study to be made of the effect literature had on Bacon. But more mundane things, details of the daily round – the chance shape of that puddle of milk, and the colour of bad wine drunk late at night – also left their traces. And from this extraordinary commingling all Bacon's images were born – chaotically and by the promptings of chance, but with a power of truth about our human condition that we are only just beginning to come to terms with.

What Bacon saw and how his imagination ground it up we will only ever know in part. That is surely one of the fundamental reasons why his images continue to haunt and taunt us. But the archive of his eye had a quantifiable, material existence in his studio. In many respects the two ran in parallel: the studio was a repository for what the eye had seen and selected, with old images serving to refresh the memory and trigger off new ones. And when the artist was alive, the experience of going in there, if only for a few minutes, was electrifying. The aura it derived from the scores of memorable paintings that had been created there was heightened by the sense that others still to come hung palpably in the air. It was almost as if the studio, set like a trap with every kind of suggestive mark and document, were itself capable of engendering new pictures all.

Once I had been fortunate enough to have gone in there at vari-

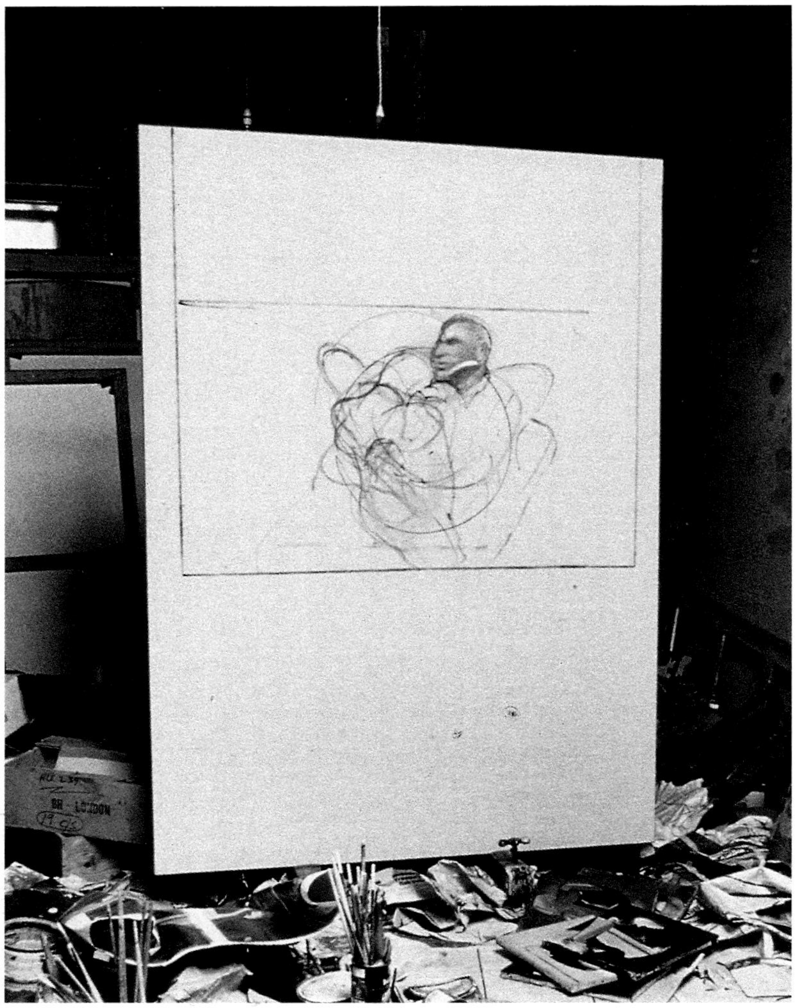

Plate 1 on p. 104: Colour photograph of Francis Bacon and George Dyer in the dining car of a train (possibly the Orient Express). Taken by John Deakin, 1965. Detail (cat. no. 155).

Detail of Francis Bacon's studio

ous times of the day and the night, the studio began to fascinate me almost as much as Bacon did. The Reece Mews studio came to seem like the artist's other self. It complemented all kinds of things that Bacon had told me about his work and his life; tantalisingly, its jumbled contents promised to fill in some of the many missing pieces in the jigsaw. If Bacon had really no interest in this or that painter, for instance, then why was an exhibition catalogue or reproductions of his work lying on the studio floor? Which new model (or lover, or both) were those fresh and barely crumpled photographs of, and why would a Greek phrase book have suddenly erupted out of the paint-encrusted rubble underfoot?

What Bacon said could often be evasive or subject to a passing mood or whim; he was also very aware, even when his guard seemed down and he was far gone in drink, of the impression he was making. In that sense, the studio was more reliable. It was a record of countless mornings of work, in elation or despair, the repository of so many sources, the mirror of the artist's mind. While Bacon was alive, I made extensive notes about the studio and wrote several factual descriptions of it. I should like to quote a relatively brief one here, written some twenty years ago, partly because everything that is written now about Bacon relates to the past, and this eye-witness account is still confidently couched in the present tense:

Bacon's London studio, inauspicious enough on the outside, is situated in a quiet, cobblestoned mews in South Kensington. Having negotiated a staircase to the upper floor as steep as a ship's ladder, the rare visitor finds himself in an ordinary rectangular room in no way predisposed for use as an artist's working space. It is just big enough to allow the painter to concentrate on one large canvas at a time; for this inveterate painter of triptychs, one might reasonably have expected a space three times as large, in which several paintings could be kept going simultaneously. Similarly, the light coming through the smallish opening overhead and one side wall hardly seems sufficient for the artist to gauge his acid suavity of colour. Many grander studios have been offered to him, but Bacon has not moved. He works best in that modest, familiar, cluttered room.

Sheer omnipresence of paint is what impresses most as one enters this highly fraught space. Coloured marks – accidental splats, brush wipes, trial runs of one hue against another – rainbow or cascade over the walls, turning them into giant palettes. Another pattern of chance blobs and trickles extends in an intricately coloured net over the book- and photo-strewn floor. Sticky masses of half-spent tubes, thickets of coagulated brushes rear up on all sides, amid old plates and pans used to mix colour, rollers, rags, tins and jars of

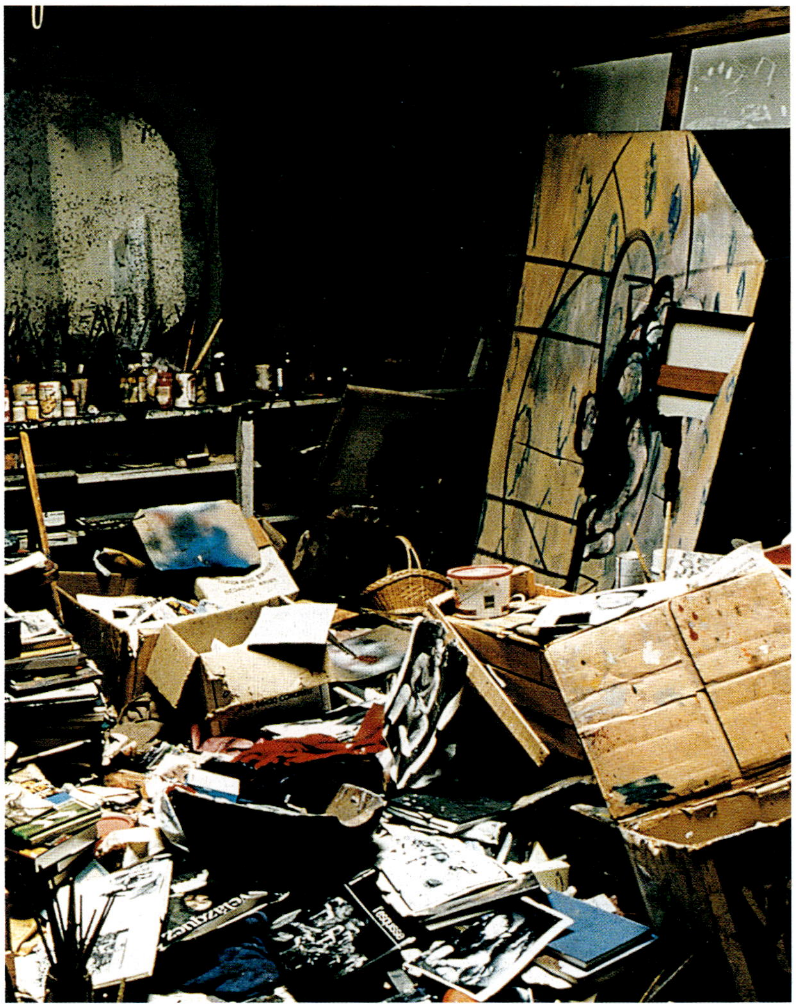

Plate 2: Colour photograph of Francis Bacon's studio at 7, Reece Mews. Photograph by Perry Ogden. Dublin, Dublin City Gallery The Hugh Lane. (©: Estate of Francis Bacon/Dublin City Gallery The Hugh Lane, photographic credit: Perry Ogden.)

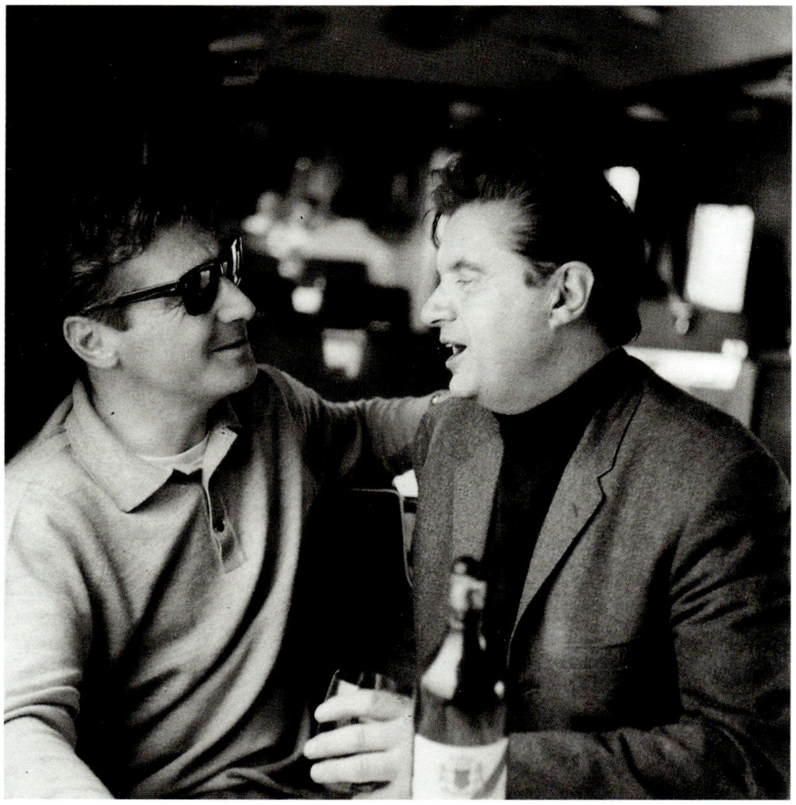

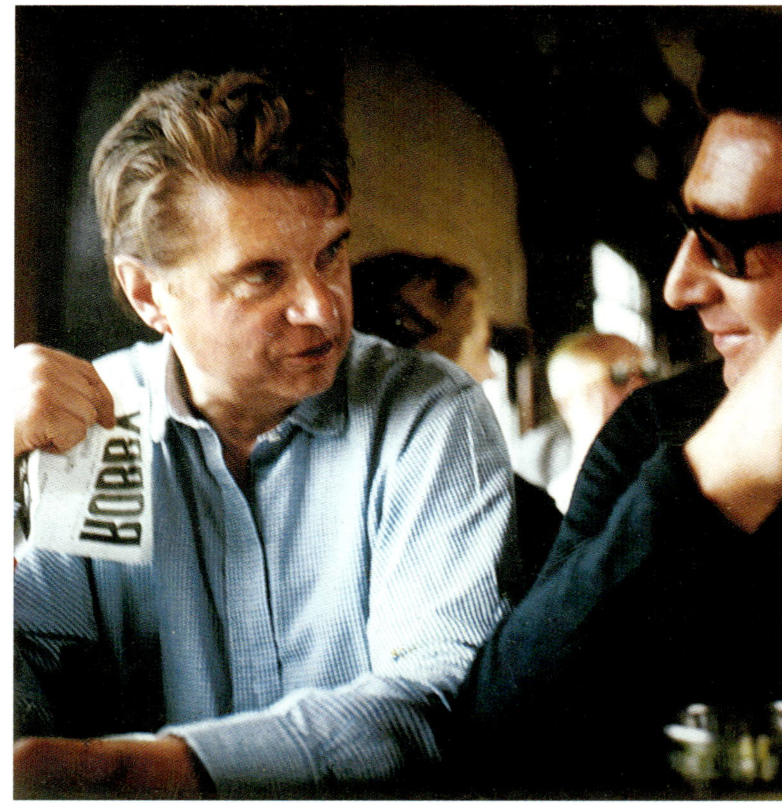

Plate 3: Black-and-white photograph of Francis Bacon and George Dyer on the Orient Express train on their way to Greece. Taken by John Deakin, 1965 (cat. no. 153).

Plate 4: Colour photograph of Francis Bacon and George Dyer in the dining car of a train (possibly the Orient Express). Taken by John Deakin, 1965 (cat. no. 155).

every description. An out-of-date passport or a single, shiny shoe occasionally heaves into sight like a drowning man, and is lost. Pinned to the wall are reproductions of Bacon's own, immaculate paintings, sprung out of this daunting mess. But the intense confusion also has something hilarious, even cheering, about it because it conveys utter disrespect for the ordinary rules of living and breathes a rare sense of freedom.

Then what catches the eye is the chaos carpeting the studio floor, which can be read as a kind of sourcebook for Baconian imagery. In it, paint-smeared and trampled, are newspaper items, books ranging from pre-Socratic philosophy to manuals on ape behaviour, an old T-square and dustbin lid, as well as several paint-soaked sweaters which Bacon has used to press on canvas so as to obtain a ribbed, chromatic effect. Above all, there are photographs of a spectacular diversity: snaps of friends, reproductions of works by Michelangelo, Velázquez and Rembrandt; scenes of disaster, car crashes and war reportage; studies of animals or athletes in motion; pictures of the Third Reich; Polaroid portraits of the artist himself. This image-jumble becomes most riveting when the artist moves from one end of the littered studio to the other, kicking up half-buried images that stay at the top of the heap for an instant to give new evidence – and perhaps fresh inspiration.

Yet to know that photographs of Goebbels lie cheek by jowl with the tragedies of Aeschylus, or that boxers stare into a page of T.S. Eliot, tells something only about the raw ingredients that may at some time, in some mingled or sifted form, have gone into Bacon's imagery. The essential, and most difficult, problem lies in determining how they have been transformed. Bacon has, after all, had the opportunity and the voracious visual appetite to look at virtually everything in existence; and his imagination has to the highest degree the power to blend the consciously remembered with chance recall of the kind that stalks our sleeping or daydreaming minds[2].

Since his death in April 1992, Bacon has rarely been out of the press. Indeed, he often seems to be more alive than ever, with his myth growing more extravagant by the year, as if his existence had been transformed, like a pharaoh's, into a vast archaeological dig, with "finds" being made regularly and reported to an eager public. Numerous paintings long thought lost or destroyed have now come to light; others have been found missing and must at least currently be catalogued with the chilling phrase: "Present Whereabouts Unknown." The paintings lost and found have, however, received nothing like the attention accorded to the voluminous batches of drawings that have surfaced. Here the shades of Bacon have been taken to task since, throughout his lifetime, the artist

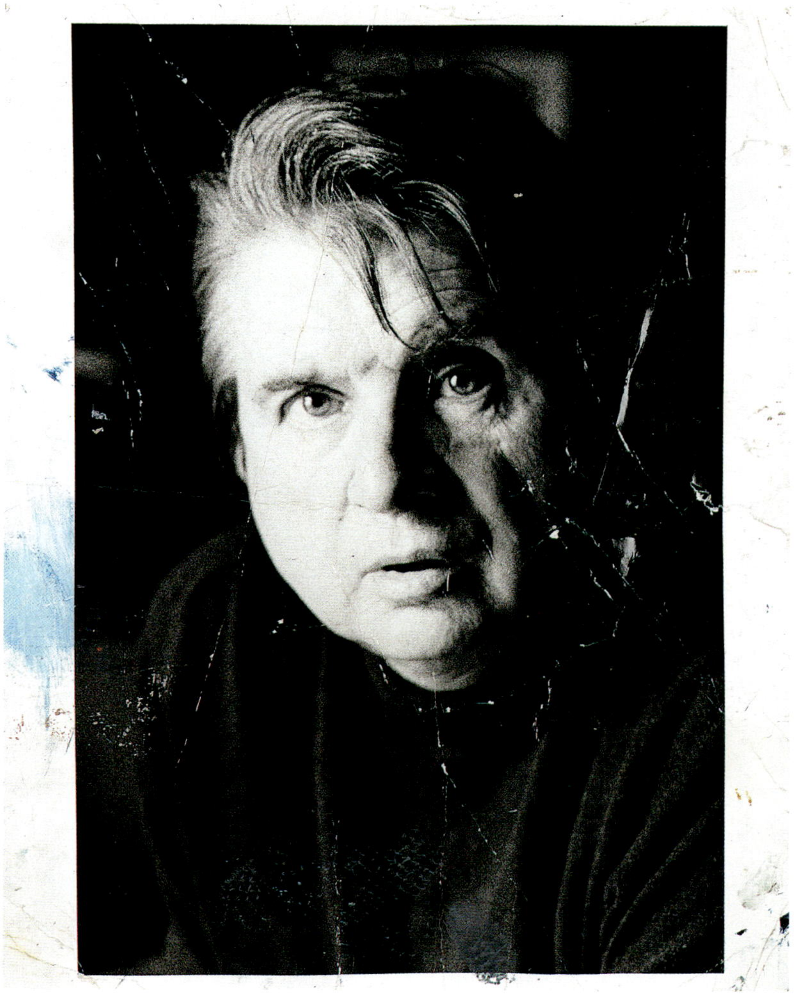

Plate 5: Black-and-white photograph of Francis Bacon in 7 Reece Mews. Taken by Peter Stark. Early 1970s (cat. no. 149).

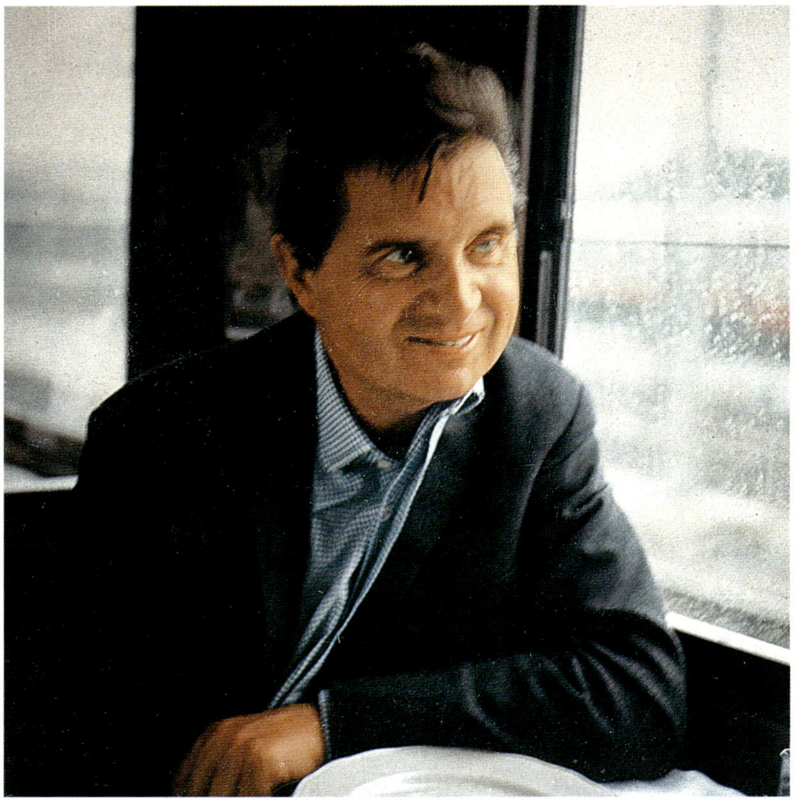

Plate 6: Colour photograph of Francis Bacon in the dining car of a train (possibly the Orient Express), taken by John Deakin. 1965. Photograph printed in September 1966 (cat. no. 154).

made a special point of repeating in interviews and to all those who would listen in private that he "never" drew. This was indeed somewhat misleading, but mostly because Bacon tended to talk in absolute terms; what he meant essentially was that drawing had no real relevance to the way he made images. True, Bacon roughed out odd sketches on scraps of paper and the end pages of books as a way of testing or noting down a potential image. More significantly, he often "drew" the outline of his central image with a paintbrush on the canvas as a run-up to actually engaging with a new picture. But unlike, say, Giacometti, for whom drawing was a central activity and the daily touchstone of his art, Bacon considered his drawings at best as notes, without interest or merit.[3] A mere fraction of these posthumously discovered "drawings" have actually been accepted as authentic and acquired by the Tate in London. The rest, including large numbers of overpainted photographs, continue to linger in limbo, despite widespread publicity, with a large question mark as to their provenance in some cases and their authenticity in others.

Another great upheaval in Bacon's posthumous world was the removal – lock, stock and barrel – of his studio from the South Kensington mews where he had worked for the last thirty years of his life to Dublin, the city where he had been born but to which he had no subsequent attachment. One result of this unexpected transfer has been the publication of numerous documents which once formed part of the great shifting sea of materials which Bacon kept underfoot as he worked. Many of the photographs and sources thus revealed were already known or resembled other documents previously recorded in the artist's possession. Certain others, however, offer new insights into the way Bacon's visual imagination gathered the most disparate fragments and used them either quite literally or – seasoned practitioner of surrealist techniques that he was – blended so closely with others as to become almost unrecognisable.

Among the thousands of studio items that have now been catalogued, for instance, is a curious book containing photographs of "paranormal" experiences. I knew that Bacon, for all the scorn he poured on any form of "mysticism," had been intrigued by W. B. Yeats' spiritualism; but I had put that down to his admiration for Yeats as a poet. I also remember him referring, with what seemed like amused scepticism, to Madame Blavatsky. But there may have been more to it than that, since some of these photographs, reportedly taken in mid-séance, reappear barely changed in certain of Bacon's paintings: one of them, notably, on the left-hand side of the central panel of *Triptych 1974,* a partly obscured head that also puts one in mind of Sigmund Freud. And while we are talking about this particular painting, it would be worth adding that, to my almost certain knowledge, the other head in this panel is a portrait of the writer Michel Leiris (a former Surrealist and close friend of Bacon's), while the horses cantering down the beach are clearly inspired by a similar scene by Bacon's much-beloved Degas[4]. But Bacon's mind worked in unpredictable ways, and it was certainly not because an image caught his attention that he believed in its underlying substance. Who might have thought, for instance, that among the artist's proven sources was a manual entitled *Fundamentals of Soil Science?* Transposing – not to say "lifting" – an image from it into a painting did not presuppose an expert knowledge of (or conviction in) irrigation techniques[5]!

Such clues to Bacon's imaginative processes and working methods will no doubt continue to emerge for many years to come. This is, after all, the stuff art history is made of, and it is both fascinating and extremely useful, allowing better-documented insights and interpretations of a work to evolve. At the same time, all the sources in the world, neatly analysed and cross-referenced, will never do more than illuminate the matrix out of which a powerful work of art has emerged. That is, no doubt, why Bacon remained quite secretive (locking certain key documents in a sea-chest he kept specially for that purpose) not only about his occasional sketches but also the full range of his interests and borrowings; he feared that his pictures might be reduced to the sum of the influences they had absorbed.

It already seems clear, despite the wealth of posthumous revelations outlined above, that Bacon's paintings resist this kind of interpretation, with the core of their mysteriously independent existence untouched; and this is a sign of their enduring fascination and power as painted images – what the painter and critic Lawrence Gowing once called "pigment-figments." But beyond their manifest and less-apparent appropriations, how do these images function? Ultimately, they seem folded in on themselves, like images in words that other words cannot undo. One thinks of Eliot at the end of the *Four Quartets:* "When the tongues of flame are in-folded/Into the crowned knot of fire/And the fire and the rose are one." Or the intricate imagery of the great Jacobean poets, where the entire universe is ransacked to stretch a particular thought or sensation into its fullest expression. Bacon was vauntingly ambitious. He had no interest in producing paintings that could be interpreted as having a specific, and hence necessarily limited, meaning. On the contrary, Bacon aimed at universality, at creating images that would infiltrate the imagination at every level and so perhaps, eventually, take their place beside the most evocative and potent paintings of the past.

[1] There was occasionally a look in Bacon's eye of taking everything he saw apart, like a clever, wilful child picking a toy to pieces.

[2] This extract comes from an essay published in Connoisseur (New York), September 1984, pp. 84–90.

[3] In some of the restaurants Bacon used to frequent, particularly in Paris, the chef would sometimes appear and intimate that if the "maître" (a form of address Bacon detested) had enjoyed his cooking he might like to leave a little drawing as a souvenir. "But I simply don't draw," Bacon would reply with some exasperation, then double the already excessive tip.

[4] I managed to find a copy of the Lemoisne catalogue raisonné of Degas' work for Bacon. Seeing the volumes paint-smeared and strewn over the studio floor was fairly dismaying until I realised how useful a sourcebook it had become for him.

[5] The image in question illustrates "irrigation by the corrugation method;" and it reappears, unaccountably enough, in a relatively little-known painting by Bacon, *Two Men Working in a Field* (1971).

Catalogue

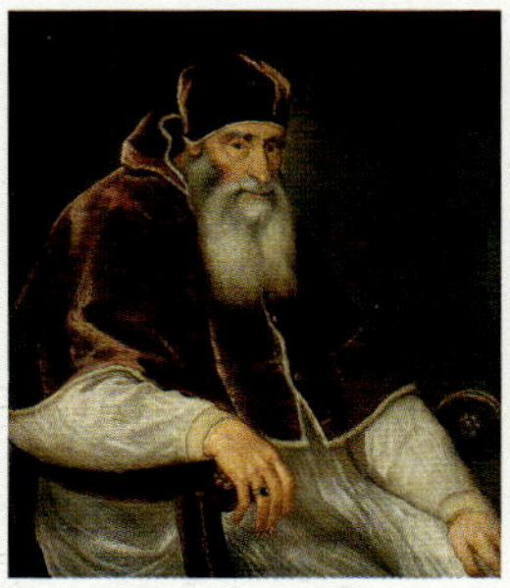
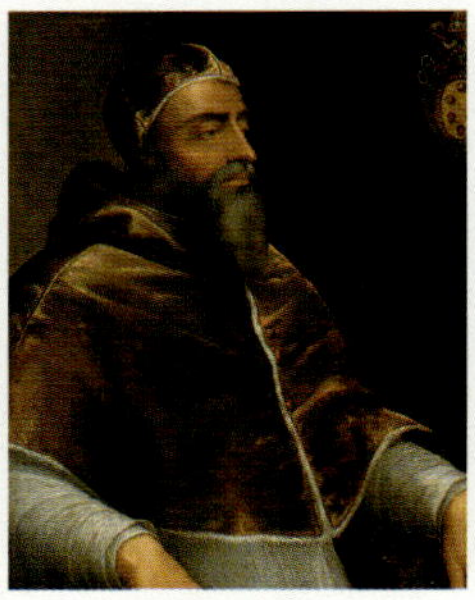
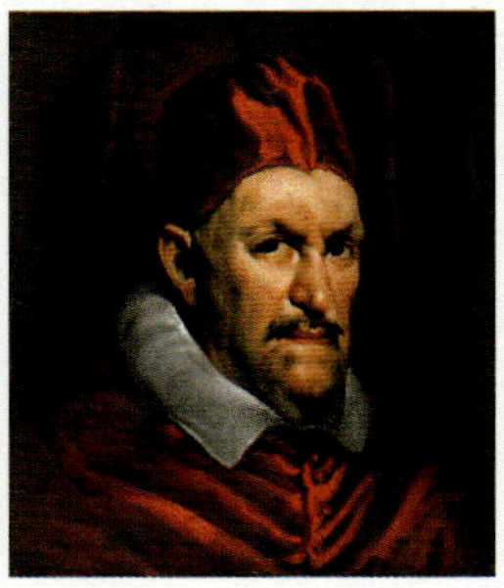
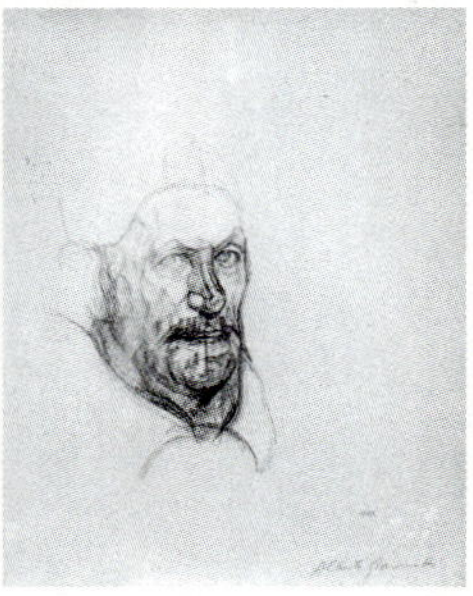
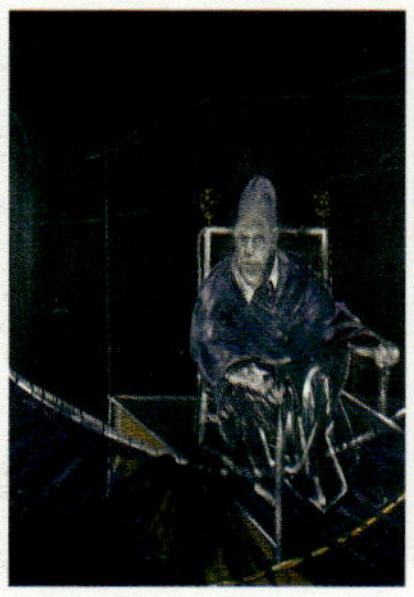
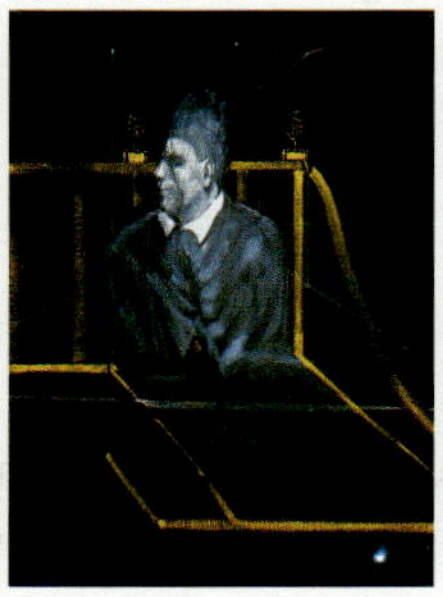
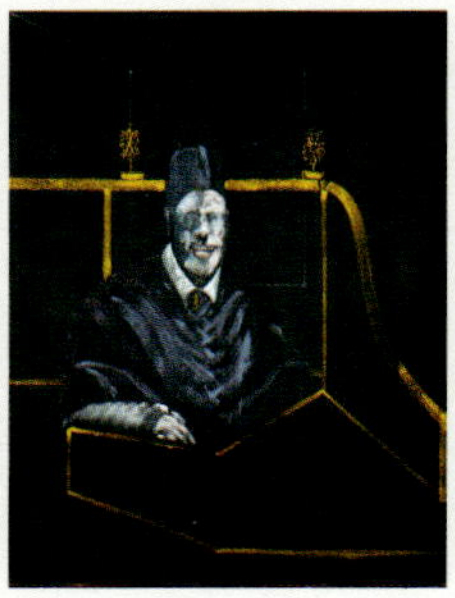
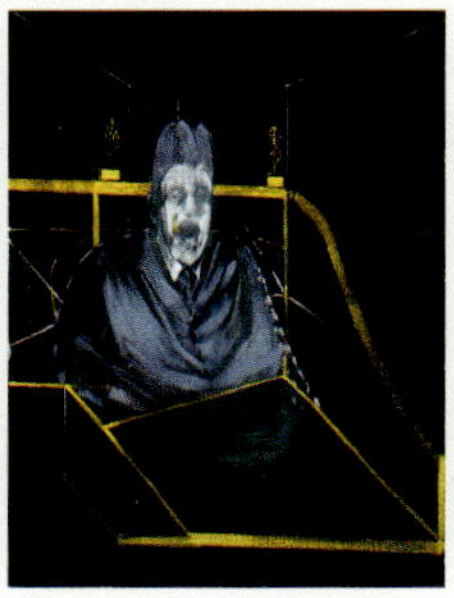
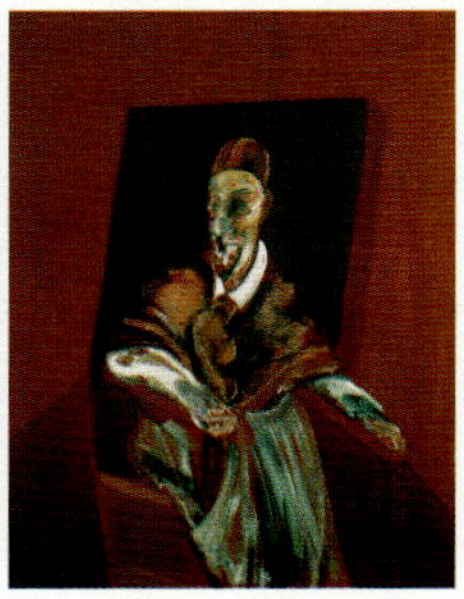
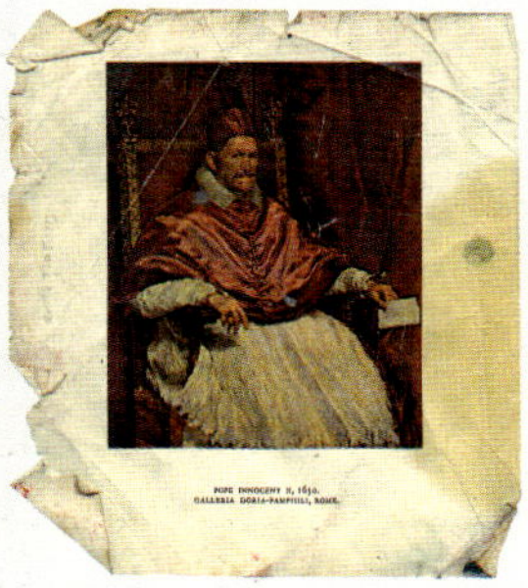
POPE INNOCENT X, 1650.
GALLERIA DORIA-PAMPHILJ, ROME.
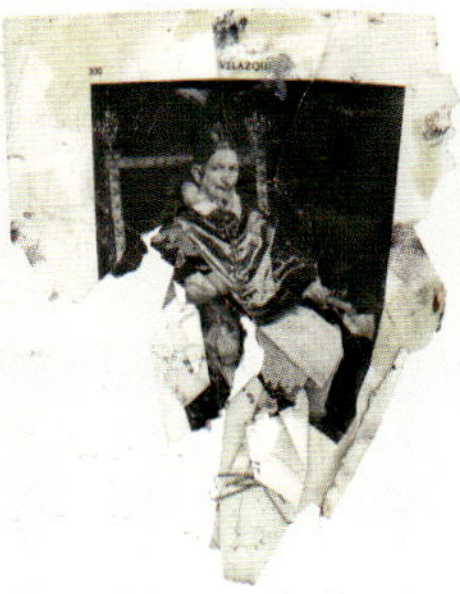
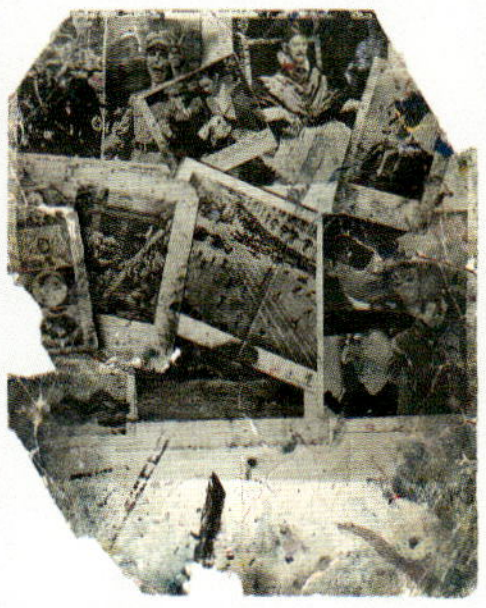

Barbara Steffen

The Papal Portraits

"It is true, of course, the Pope is unique, he is put in a unique position by being the Pope, and therefore, like in certain great tragedies, he is as though raised onto a dais on which the grandeur of this image can be displayed to the world."[1]

Papal Portraits in the Tradition of Painting

Francis Bacon occupied himself for many years with representations of the Pope in painting. He collected photos, purchased books with illustrations of papal portraits, stockpiled reproductions of the famous portrait by Velázquez, and over a period of twenty years he painted more than 45 pictures depicting the Pope.

Portraits of the Pope are portrayals of historical personalities and reveal a clear iconography of the Christian ruler. Over the centuries there has been a conspicuous shift from a narrative to a devotional depiction, to the external ideal of beauty in the figure of the Pope in the Renaissance, to the formal, state portraits of the 17th and 18th centuries. There are portrayals in which the Pope appears together with secular rulers in a comparison, as it were, of religious and secular power, depictions of the coronation and veneration as well as symbolic commemorative images. The state portraits that began to be painted at the time of Raphael depict the Pope in his strength and power as well as in active life – for example, giving his blessing, at an audience, as a mediator for peace, at the coronation of the emperor or as a promoter of the arts and sciences.

One group of papal portraits is of special interest in connection with Bacon: the portrayals of the Pope on a *sedia gestatoria* (portable papal throne), sitting on a raised platform or beneath a canopy. In all of these painted depictions the Pope is separated from the people and raised above them. We find this manner of presentation, with elevation, emphasis and, at the same time, isolation of the portrayed person in the works of Bacon as well, but he also used other elements to separate the figure or draw attention to it.

The portraits of the 16th and 17th centuries depict the Pope, in his exercise of power and as a representative of the Church, in the form of a three-quarter-length portrait. He is usually seated and has realistic features. So depicted, the Pope was supposed to represent the embodiment of power and splendour.

Between 1546 and 1568 Titian painted three *Portraits of Pope Paul III Farnese*, all of which were similar in structure. According to Vasari, the earliest of these paintings was in the palace of the Farnese family in Parma in the 17th century before it was acquired by the Museo Capodimonte in Naples.[2] The two other paintings are in the Kunsthistorisches Museum in Vienna and the Hermitage in St. Petersburg respectively. In the Vienna painting (cat. no. 1) the Pope is seated on his throne. With his head tilted slightly forward, his posture and beard suggest his advanced age and present him to the viewer as a rather tired, benevolent and almost sickly church dignitary. He is wearing the papal ring on his right hand. The mozzetta (short, cape-shaped garment) and the camauro (square cap with three ridges or peaks) are painted a crimson shade and create a strong contrast with the Pope's tunic and beard.

Of great importance in the history of papal portrayals is the *Portrait of Pope Clement VII* from the years 1531/32 from the studio of Sebastiano Luciani, byname Sebastiano del Piombo (cat. no. 2). It is also in the Kunsthistorisches Museum in Vienna. The artist, who was born in Venice, belonged to the innermost circle of Pope Clement VII, who appointed him to the post of *piombo*, or keeper of the papal seal, a position he held until his death. In 1529 Pope Clement VII returned from exile in Orvieto to Rome. There he met Sebastiano, who subsequently painted a series of portraits of him. A version painted on slate from this series is in the Museo Capodimonte in Naples, another in the Getty Museum in Los Angeles. In 1981 Michael Hirst[3] confirmed that the Vienna painting had been painted by Sebastiano himself, but the attribution has since been questioned. The Kunsthistorisches Museum's painting is a three-quarter-length portrait of the Pope, who is turned slightly towards a profile view and looking to the right. With his eyes

Plate. 1: Diego de Silva y Velázquez, Portrait Pope Innocent X, 1650. Oil on canvas, 141 × 119 cm. Rome, Galleria Doria Pamphilij. (©: Rome, Galleria Doria Pamphilij.)

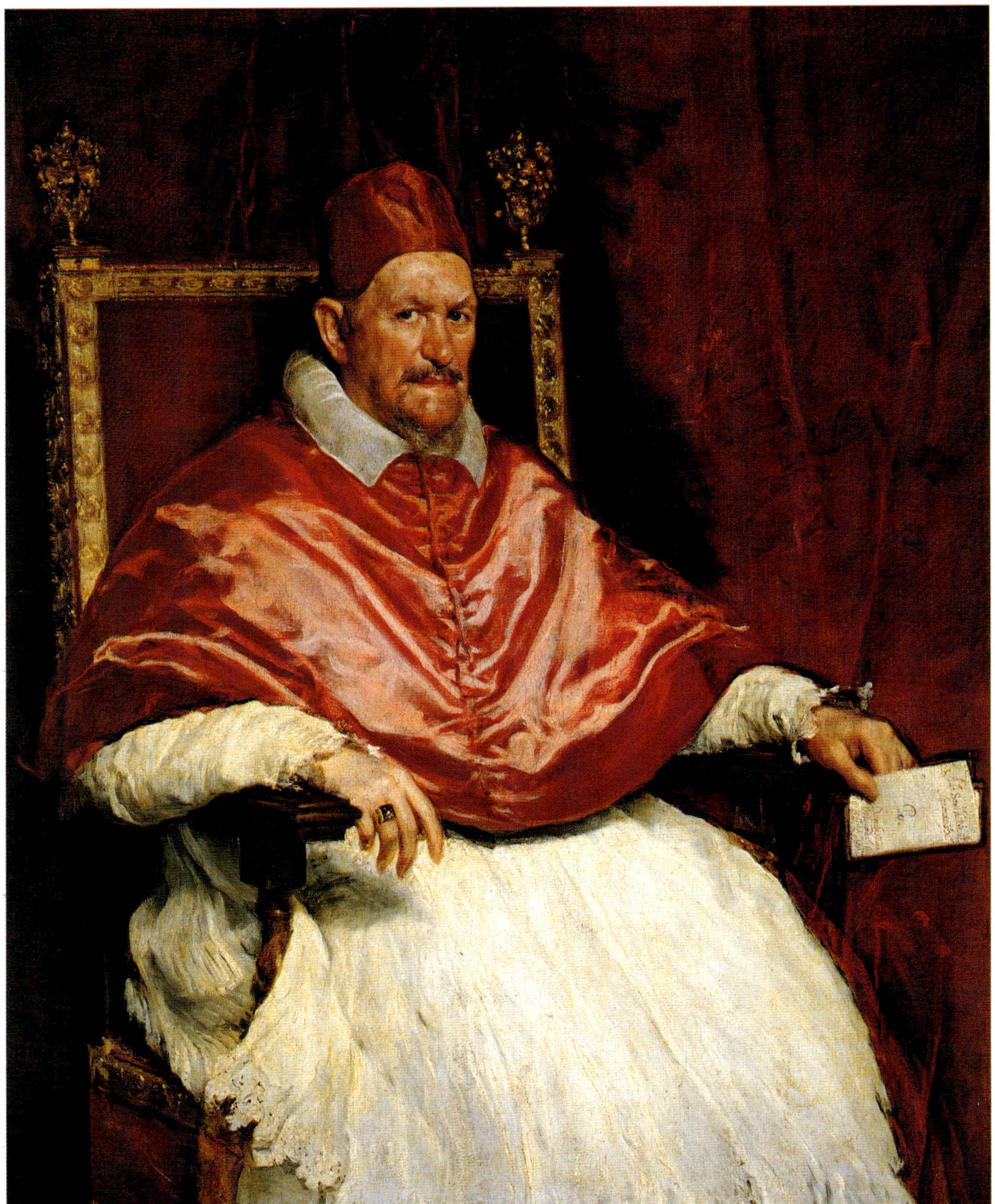

half lowered, Clement VII appears calm, dominating and self-confident. In comparison with Titian's *Paul III*, his upright posture gives him the grand appearance of a convincing representative of his office.

Giambattista Pamphili chose the name Innocent X when he was crowned as Pope in 1644. This was in memory of Innocent VIII, who had come to Rome because of the Pamphili family. His contemporaries described him as being "of tall, gaunt stature, with small eyes, large feet and sparse beard, his skin colour almost olive green, his head bare."[4] Innocent's physiognomy was so repulsive and his wrath and displeasure towards his subordinates was occasionally so great that some of the cardinals in the papal conclave had spoken out against his election.

In only a few sittings in Rome in 1650, Diego Velázquez painted the *Portrait of Pope Innocent X*, one of the most significant papal portraits in the history of European painting *(Plate 1)*. Seated on his throne and oriented to the right side of the picture, the Pope is gazing to the left, which creates tension in the painting. In his left hand he is holding a piece of paper with the inscription "Alla Santa di Nr. Sigre/Innocencio X./ Per/Diego de Silva/Velázquez dela Ca/mera di s. Mte Cattca. 1650."[5] A ring with a topaz dominates his right hand. The contours are painted with marked fluidity, and the broad spectrum of shades of red, yellow and white underscores the grandeur of the papal office. Velázquez avoided depicting the proverbial ugliness and severity of Innocent and painted the Pope in a highly lively manner. The chair, mozzetta and camauro as well as the curtain in the background are depicted in various shades of red that suggest the varying textures of the fabrics. Thus the dark, almost bordeaux-red curtain appears to be unbelievably heavy. It must have been made of rich velvet, lending the painting additional drama, while the camauro and the crimson mozzetta probably were made of stiffened silk. Bacon never saw the original of Velázquez's painting, but he collected many reproductions of the papal portrait (cat. nos. 10 and 11).

In addition to the main work, which is in Rome and not available on loan, there are other versions of the same subject by Velázquez and his circle: for example, the *Portrait Study of Innocent X*, which is a copy after Velázquez in the Accademia Carrara in Bergamo (cat. no. 3). This painting, which measures only 49 × 43 cm, very effectively depicts the severe facial expression of the Pope and his cynical look. Two other studies are at Apsley House in London and in the National Gallery in Washington respectively.

One might ask why Bacon was so impressed by Velázquez' papal portrait even though there are many other important and outstanding examples of such portraits. There were probably several reasons that prompted Bacon to focus his interest over the course of many years on this painting. On the one hand, there is the rich coloration, of which he often spoke admiringly, as well as the composition and the corporeal presence of the Pope. On the other hand, Bacon was probably also fascinated by the psychological depth of this painting. It depicts the Pope's almost audacious and crafty look and the narrow, determined lips that do not bode well. All of these attributes fill the viewer with respect, discomfort and fear – a kind of uncertainty about who or what is really hiding behind the figure. Among other aspects, these character traits must have made such an impression on Bacon that he adopted and intensified them in his Pope portraits. He went even a step further by making Velázquez's introverted but dangerously restrained Pope positively explode. He brought out into the open everything that was hidden and suppressed in the figure.

Francis Bacon and the Swiss sculptor and painter Alberto Giacometti were close friends from the beginning of the 1960s up to Giacometti's death in 1966. "I met him when he came to London for an exhibition of his work at the Tate Gallery. He was accompanied by his wife, Annette, as well as by Michel and Louise Leiris. He stayed at a hotel not far from here, and I remember that we spent a whole night talking to each another."[6] The two artists had much in common, and Bacon was not reluctant to sing Giacometti's praises: "Giacometti was not only the greatest draughtsman of our time but among the greatest of all time."[7] Both artists also set high standards in their art, leading them to destroy many of their works. But while Bacon worked from photos and other pictorial sources, Giacometti created his sculptures and paintings, particularly his later ones, using live models.

An early, rather untypical drawing by Giacometti also depicts *Pope Innocent X after Velázquez* (cat. no. 9). The literature dates it from 1936 when Giacometti visited a Cézanne exhibition in Paris. The elaboration of the face in this work on paper is reminiscent of Cézanne's drawing. While still a child, Giacometti copied earlier art such as Egyptian stone sculptures, works by Velázquez, Rembrandt, Titian, Cézanne and others. Speaking shortly before his death about copying he said: "Ever since I first saw reproductions of artworks, beginning in earliest childhood, [...] I have felt the need to copy those works that have attracted me the most. And I have never lost this desire to copy [...]."[8] Giacometti's drawing after Velázquez' *Pope Innocent X* depicts the same face that Bacon worked on for so many years. Giacometti's interpretation of Velázquez's painting, however, is completely different from Bacon's. In Giacometti's version the Pope's head is framed by the suggestion of the biretta and the fine contours of the collar. The face is elaborated the most clearly, with a focus on the nose and mouth. It appears as though Giacometti was primarily interested in the mouth and the moustache outlined above it as well as the wrinkles of the chin. His very fine hatching is reminiscent of Cézanne's networks of lines. It is not known whether Bacon was familiar with this Giacometti drawing.

The Significance of Velázquez's Papal Portrait for Bacon

We know that Francis Bacon never saw the papal portrait of Innocent X by Diego Velázquez in the original, and even when he was staying in Rome in the 1950s, where the painting was hanging in the Galleria Doria Pamphili, he never went see the original. The art critic David Sylvester repeatedly asked him about the reason why Velázquez's painting meant so much to him. "I think it's the magnificent colour of it,"[9] was the answer. And: "Because I think it is one of the greatest portraits that have ever been made, and I became obsessed by it. I buy book after book with this illustration in it of the Velasquez *Pope,* because it just haunts me, and opens up all sorts of feelings and areas of – I was going to say – imagination, even, in me."[10]

Distance was important to Bacon and led him to paint his own work from reproductions and not in confrontation with Velázquez's original. Bacon spoke of the fact that Velázquez also created a certain distance between his work and the painting that served as his source: "When I think of the Pope painted by Velasquez, of course he wanted to make it as much like a Titian as he could, but in a curious way he cooled Titian."[11] This "cooling" or distance, in turn, is clear throughout Bacon's work from the fact that he goes a step further than was possible for Velázquez by working from photos and reproductions and thus without having to deal with the texture of the original.

In his book about Bacon, John Russell emphasises the theme of deformation and the competition with the goal of renewal within a continuity: "In so far as he was 'influenced' by Velázquez, however, the influence was more subtle than the mere borrowing of a motif. [...] Velázquez's genius lay in the deformations which in his hands looked inevitable. Bacon was also moved by the element of continuity in Velázquez: the determination, that is to say, to vie with the state-portraits of Titian and remake them in the image of Velázquez's own time."[12]

The Pope Portraits in Series

In the autumn of 1951 Bacon painted a new series of Pope portraits, after having destroyed his first series of three paintings before the opening of an exhibition in the Hanover Gallery in London. These works, however, are not based on Velázquez but rather on a section of a photograph showing Pope Pius XII sitting on a *sedia gestatoria,*[13] the portable papal throne that was used for important ceremonies. The previous literature has not focused on the Pope in this photograph, but has mostly referred instead to Velázquez' papal portrait. It is thus interesting to take a closer look at this photograph (cat. no. 12). The art historian Sam Hunter, who wrote about Francis Bacon as early as 1952, made a photograph from the same period of Bacon's photographic sources, which were hanging as a kind of collage on the wall of his studio and which served as the source of many of his paintings. One of Hunter's photographs illustrates the motifs the artist was using in his work and the photos that inspired and influenced him. In recent years it has been reproduced several times in catalogues. It shows, among other things, a photograph of Velázquez's papal portrait, propaganda photos of Himmler and Goebbels, war photos as well as a picture of Baudelaire and stills from films. Less frequently reproduced is a second documentary photograph by Hunter showing another collage of paintings as well as motion studies by Muybridge, newspaper clippings with quotations from Hitler as well as the photograph of a papal procession, which depicts the Pope on a throne chair and raised above a crowd. Bacon used this photograph as a source for one of his first papal series, *Pope I, II, III* of 1951. Hunter describes the photographic collages as follows: "Bacon's studio has the character of a modern laboratory. On one side are his paintings, unique and extremely personal inventions. On the other side are tables piled high with newspaper clippings and photographs. [...] The only law that applies in Bacon's selection of visual literature is a kind of mysterious topical psychological pertinence. The common denominators of the photographs is violence."[14]

The works *Pope I, II* and *III* were painted for the exhibition in the Hanover Gallery in London. They are the first complete series that Bacon exhibited on a single subject. According to Ronald Alley[15] *Pope II* was painted first, followed by *Pope I* and then *Pope III*, which, however, was later destroyed and is now preserved only in photographs. In *Pope I* (cat. no. 4) the protagonist is seated on a *sedia gestatoria*, in a position similar to that of Pope Pius XII in the photograph mentioned above. In this painting the structure of the room is clear; the Pope is placed not only within a rectangular, geometric construction, which is perceived as a frame or cage, but also within the second architectural frame of a room with rounded arches intended to suggest the papal apartment. As in the later Pope portraits of 1953, two different architectural spaces provide the structure of the painting. While the rounded arches here clearly refer to the photographic source, the later paintings do not appear to connote a specific place. There the space is structured in squares, giving the Pope on his throne a strengthening system of co-ordinates as a frame and means of accentuation. In *Pope I* there are three spatial levels that place the figure in its "frame:" the architecture of the ceremonial sedan-chair with the suggestion of a canopy, the arched architecture in the background and the rope spanned, as it were, in front of the viewer, the "curtain rod." It, in contrast to the other architectural co-ordinates, provides a flat border to the painting, thus emphasising the space in the background. In the other Pope portraits we will often find the motif of a significant dividing line. *Pope I* depicts the Pope sitting on his throne, with a closed mouth and wearing glasses. In *Pope II* and *III* the glasses appear about to fall off his nose and his mouth is open in a scream. The motif of the glasses is taken from the still of the screaming nurse in Sergej Eisenstein's film *Battleship Potemkin*.

In 1953 Bacon painted a series of eight paintings that depict the Pope dressed in colours ranging from dark blue to black. This group is now spread across various museums and private collections in the USA. In the exhibition, *Study for Portrait II, V* and *VII* from this series are presented together (cat. nos. 5–7): Here Bacon depicts the Pope not on his throne or in a sedan-chair, but rather with his upper body enclosed in a system of rods, which can be interpreted as the head of a tubular metal bed. The figure is looking towards the viewer. Only in *Study for Portrait II* is the face depicted in profile; here it is looking to the left and is divided in two by strong lines running through the eye.

While the figure in *Study for Portrait II* appears rather restrained with its closed mouth and the motion of the body frozen, in *Study for Portrait V* and *VII* its appearance becomes a symbol of distorted pain. With the exception of *Study for Portrait I*, each painting in this series includes a cord with a tassel. In the later paintings this is often interpreted as the cable of a lightbulb hanging in the room. In a manner similar to the cubical framing, this cable divides the painting vertically, with the tassel touching the face or chest. One of the most expressive paintings is *Study for Portrait II*, in which the depicted figure in partial profile appears very flat, as though it were pressed against a mirror. In *Study for Portrait VII*, which like *Study for Portrait V* depicts an expressive face, the mouth is open the widest and the tassel is almost hanging into it, at the same time dividing the face with a vertical yellow line. It distracts interest from the portrayal of the head and directs it to the brushwork and especially to the linear composition. Here the figure of the "tragic hero," as Bacon called the role of the Pope, is shown less as a representative of power than as an isolated being, uniting and expressing all the suffering and existential pain of the world.

A later Pope portrait Bacon's is *Seated Figure* of 1960. It is part of a series of "red Popes" that were painted in the early 1960s. This painting also depicts a seated Pope; his lower arms and hands, however, rest more like those of an animal on the armrests of his throne and appear to be open mounds of flesh. They are reminiscent of Bacon's sphinx-like figures as well as his representations of dogs. The face of the Pope is painted with flowing brushstrokes in several shades of colour laid on top of one another. In the depiction of the dark, detailed eye and the succinct nose, it reveals the highly individual features of the subject. The artist has used white and light-green zones of colour to make the face almost three-dimensional and emphasise in a generous manner such areas as the cheekbones, the base of the neck and the nose, giving the face enormous liveliness and motion. The red, almost monochrome background as well as the mixture of colours and the dynamic brushwork further increase the intensity of the figure. This intensity is in contrast with the weakened corporeality revealed by the thin, haggard upper body, which is hidden beneath the papal robes. In a manner similar to Velázquez's portraying Pope Innocent as a malevolent, power-hungry pontiff instead of glorifying him, Bacon takes the "disfigurement" much further, making a pathetic creature of the Pope.

[1] Sylvester 1999, p. 26.
[2] Pedrocco 2000, p. 182.
[3] Exh. Cat. Vienna 2000, p. 234.
[4] Haidacher 1965, p. 596.
[5] Lopez-Rey 1999, p. 282.
[6] Archimbaud 1993, p. 70.
[7] Sylvester 2000, p. 200.
[8] Koepplin 1995, p. 3.
[9] Sylvester 1999, p. 25.
[10] Sylvester 1997, p. 25; cf. Sylvester 1999, p. 24.
[11] Sylvester 2000, p. 25.
[12] Russell 1971, p. 46.
[13] Ronald Alley pointed this out in his *Catalogue raisonné* on *Francis Bacon,* London (Thames and Hudson) 1964, p. 53.
[14] Hunter 1952, p. 12.
[15] Alley 1964, p. 54.

Cat. no. 1
Tiziano Vecellio and studio
Pope Paul III Farnese
After 1546
Oil on canvas, 89 × 78 cm
Vienna, Kunsthistorisches Museum, Picture Gallery, inv. no. 99

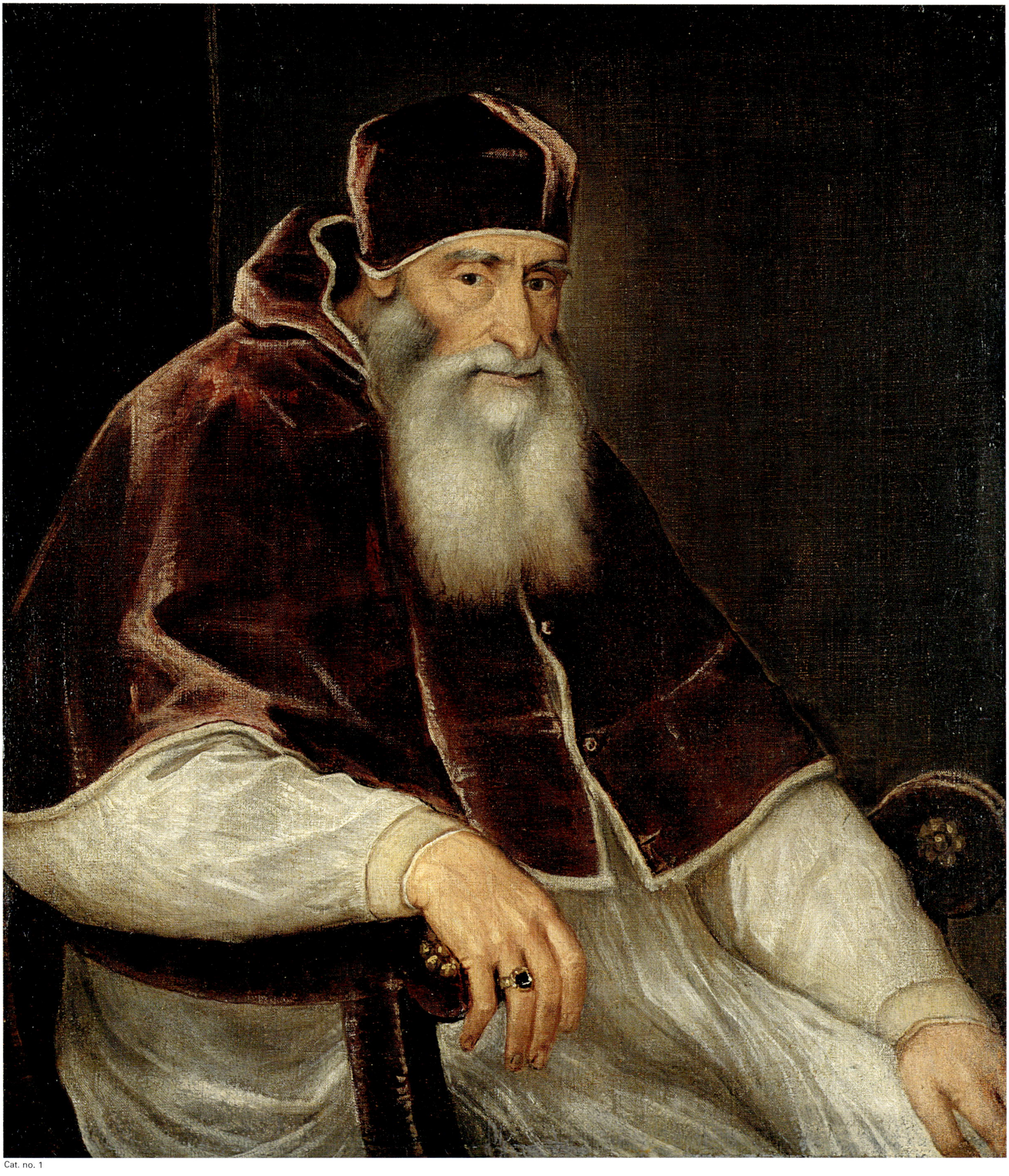

Cat. no. 1

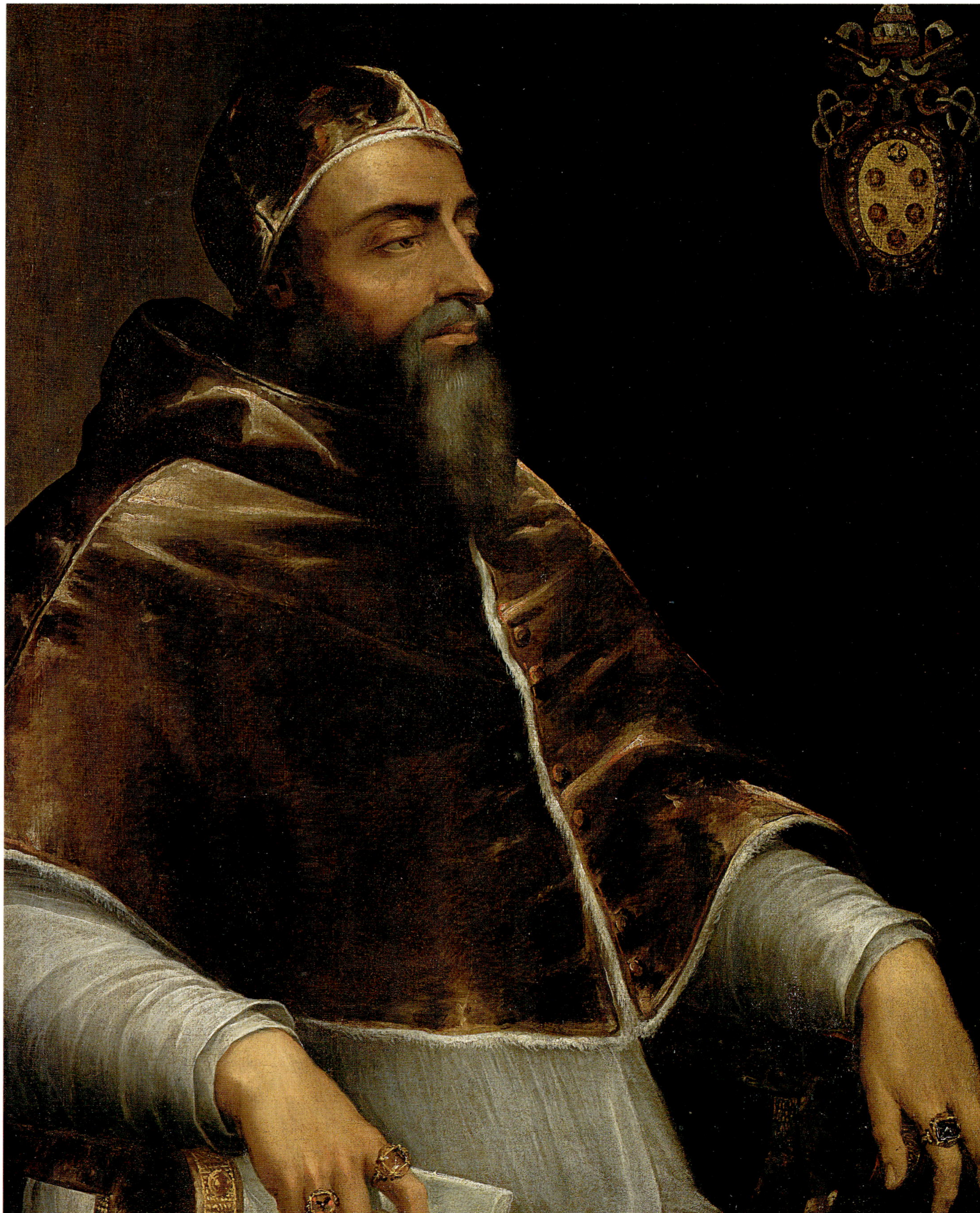

Cat. no. 2

Cat. no. 2
Sebastiano del Piombo's studio
Pope Clement VII.
C. 1531/32
Oil on canvas, 92 × 74 cm
Vienna, Kunsthistorisches Museum, Picture Gallery, inv. no. 6511; Schloss Ambras, Portrait Gallery

Cat. no. 3
Roman School (?), 17th century
Copy after Velázquez
Portrait Pope Innocent X
Oil on canvas, 49 × 42.5 cm
Bergamo, Accademia Carrara di Belle Arti, inv. no. 125

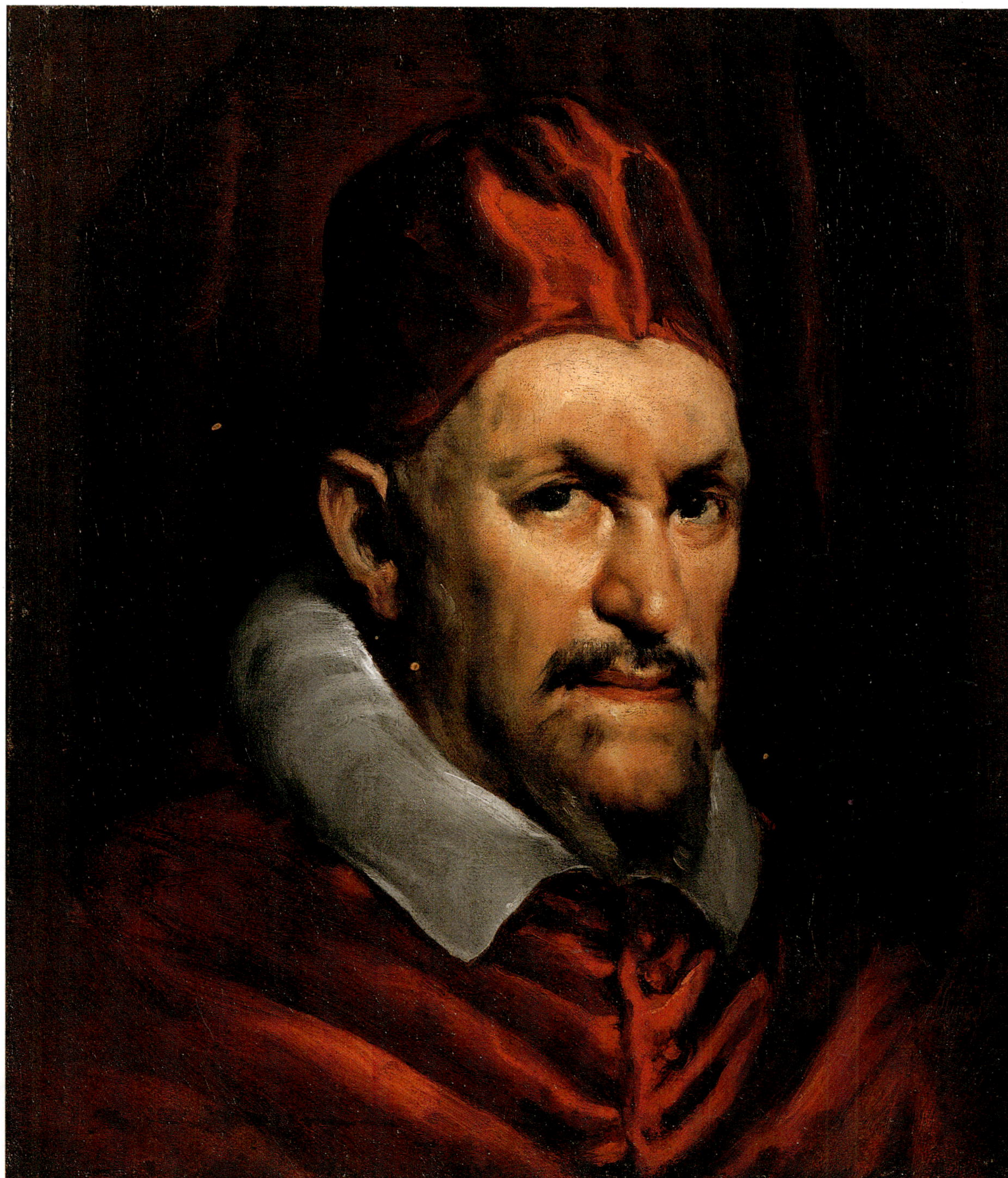

Cat. no. 3

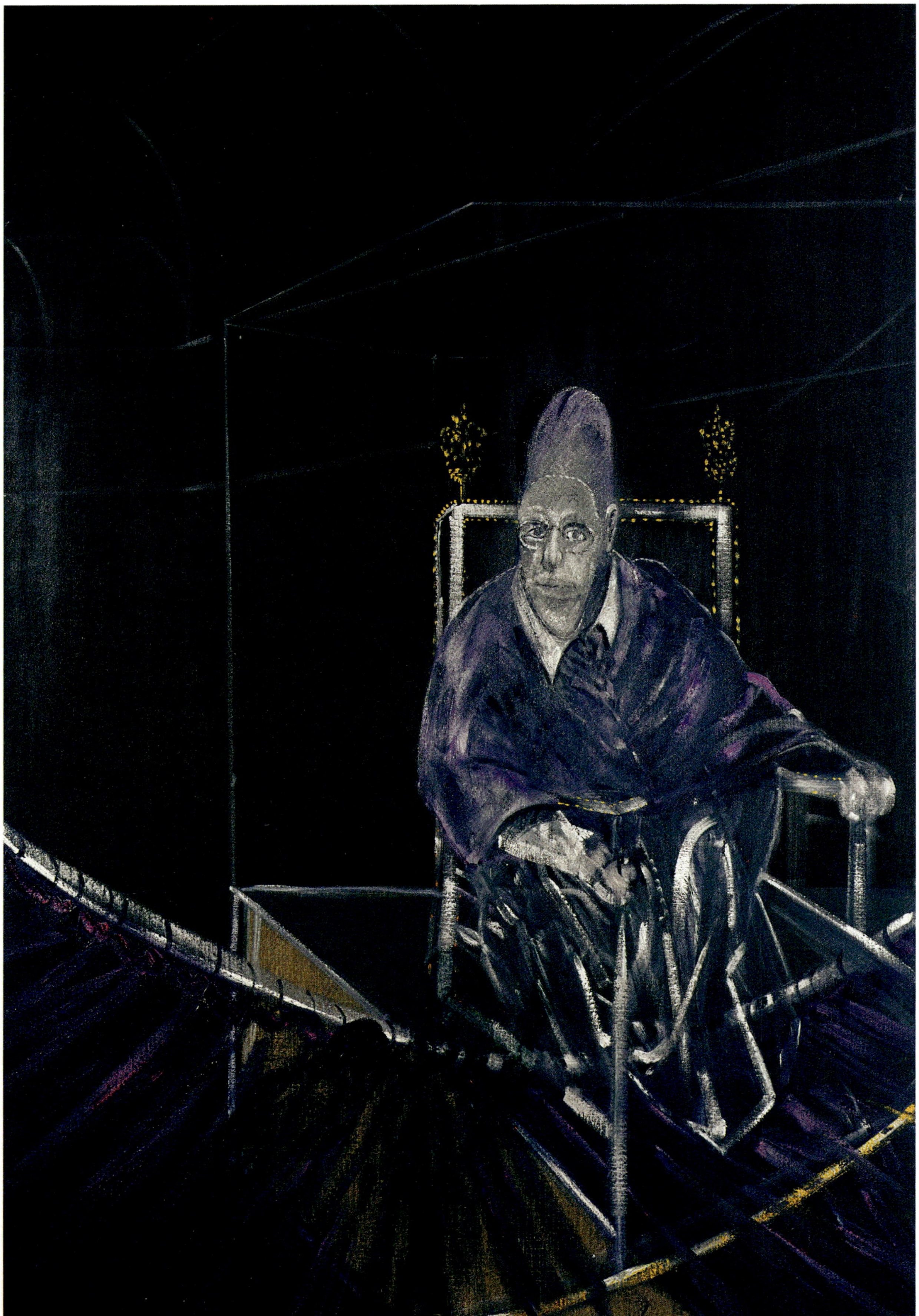

Cat. no. 4

Cat. no. 4
Francis Bacon
Pope I – Study after Pope Innocent X by Velázquez
1951
Oil on canvas, 197.8 × 137.4 cm
Aberdeen, City Art Gallery and Museums Collections

Cat. no. 5
Francis Bacon
Study for Portrait II
1953
Oil on canvas, 152.7 × 116.9 cm
New York, Collection of Samuel and Ronnie Heyman

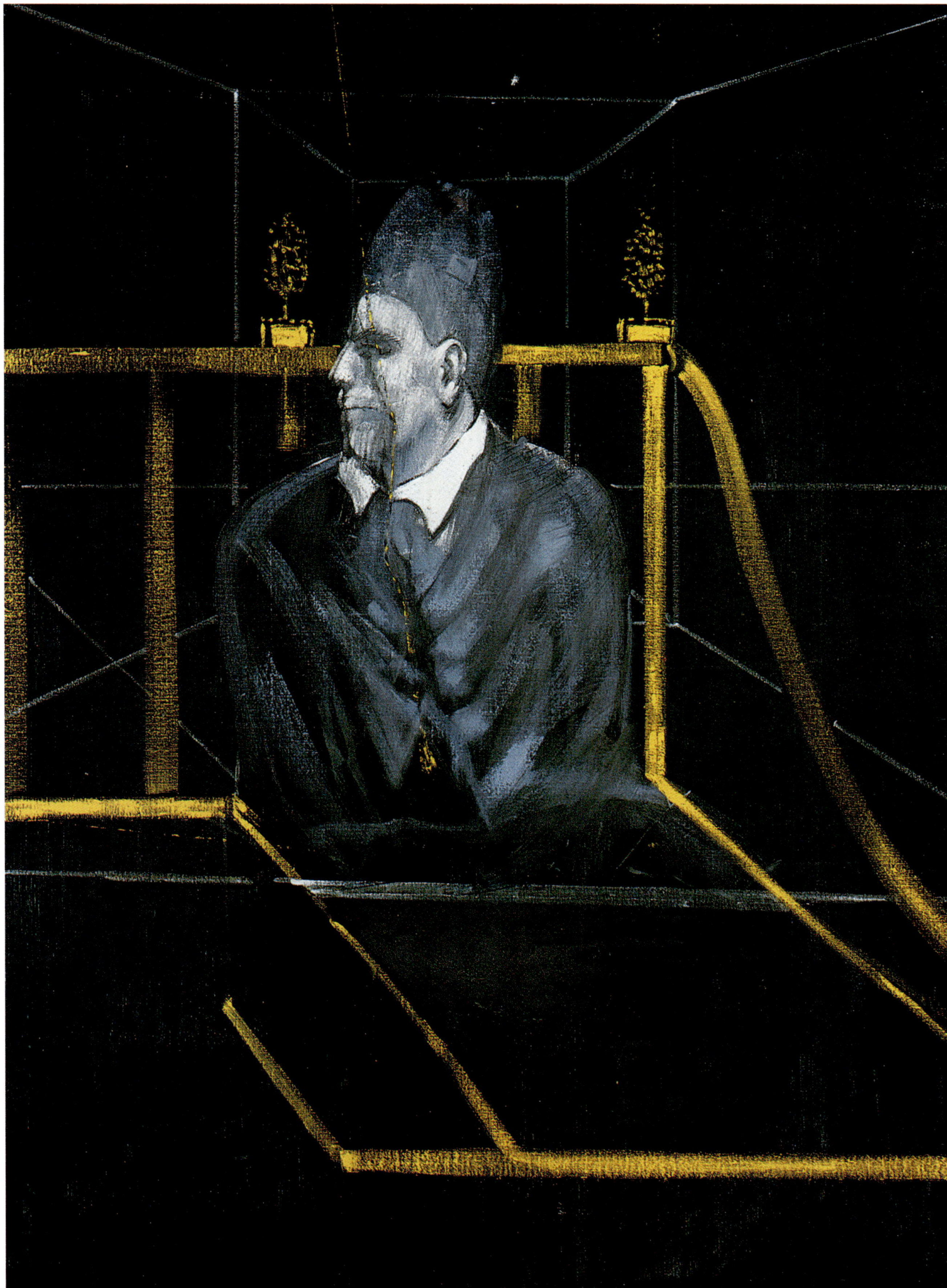

Cat. no. 5

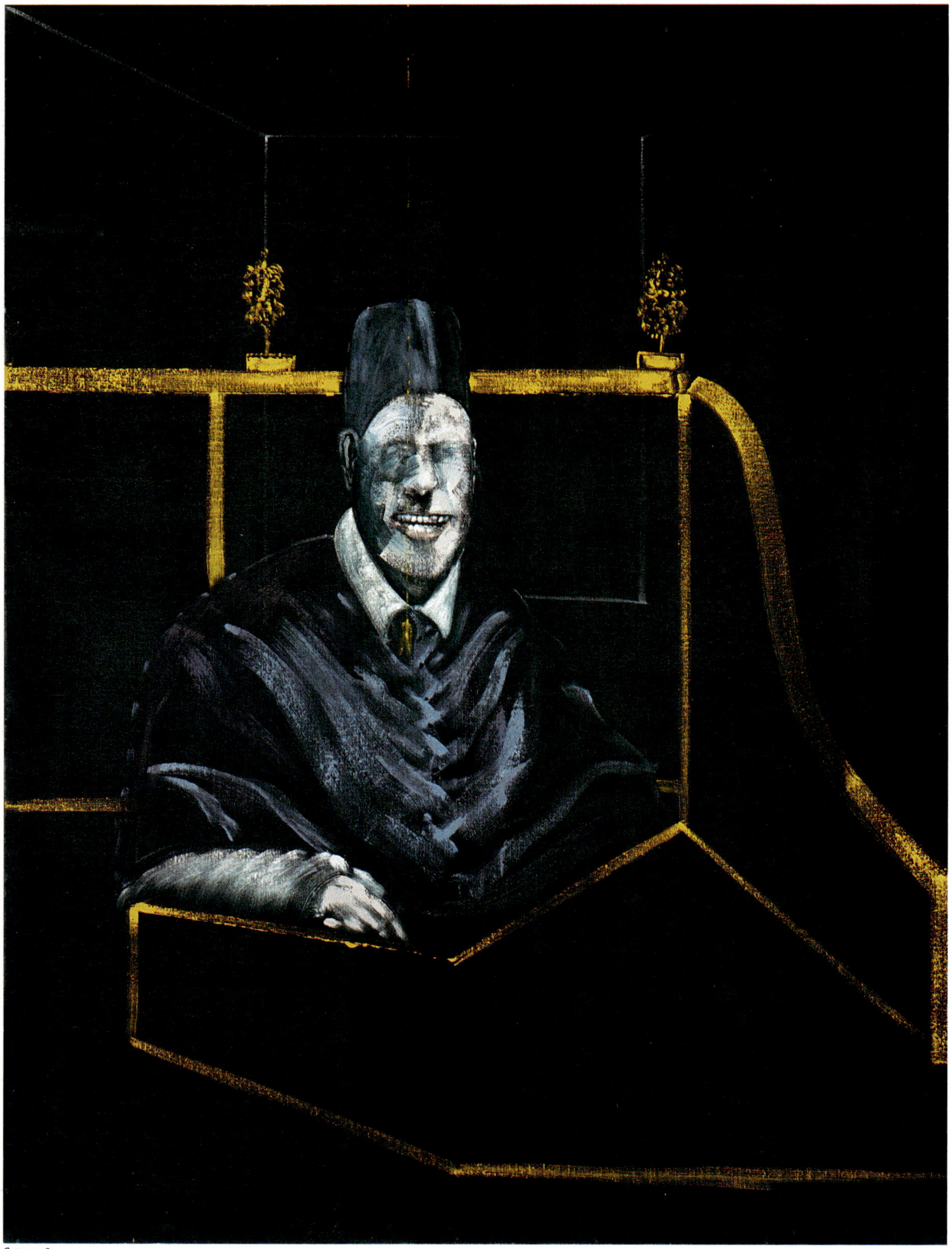

Cat. no. 6

Cat. no. 6
Francis Bacon
Study for Portrait V (Cardinal V)
1953
Oil and sand on canvas,
152.7 × 117.1 cm
Washington D. C., Hirshhorn
Museum and Sculpture Garden,
Smithsonian Institution, HMSG
66.183, Gift of the Joseph
H. Hirshhorn Foundation 1966.

Cat. no. 7
Francis Bacon
Study for Portrait VII
1953
Oil on canvas, 152.3 × 117 cm
New York, The Museum of Modern Art, Gift of Mr. and Mrs. William A. M. Burden, 1956

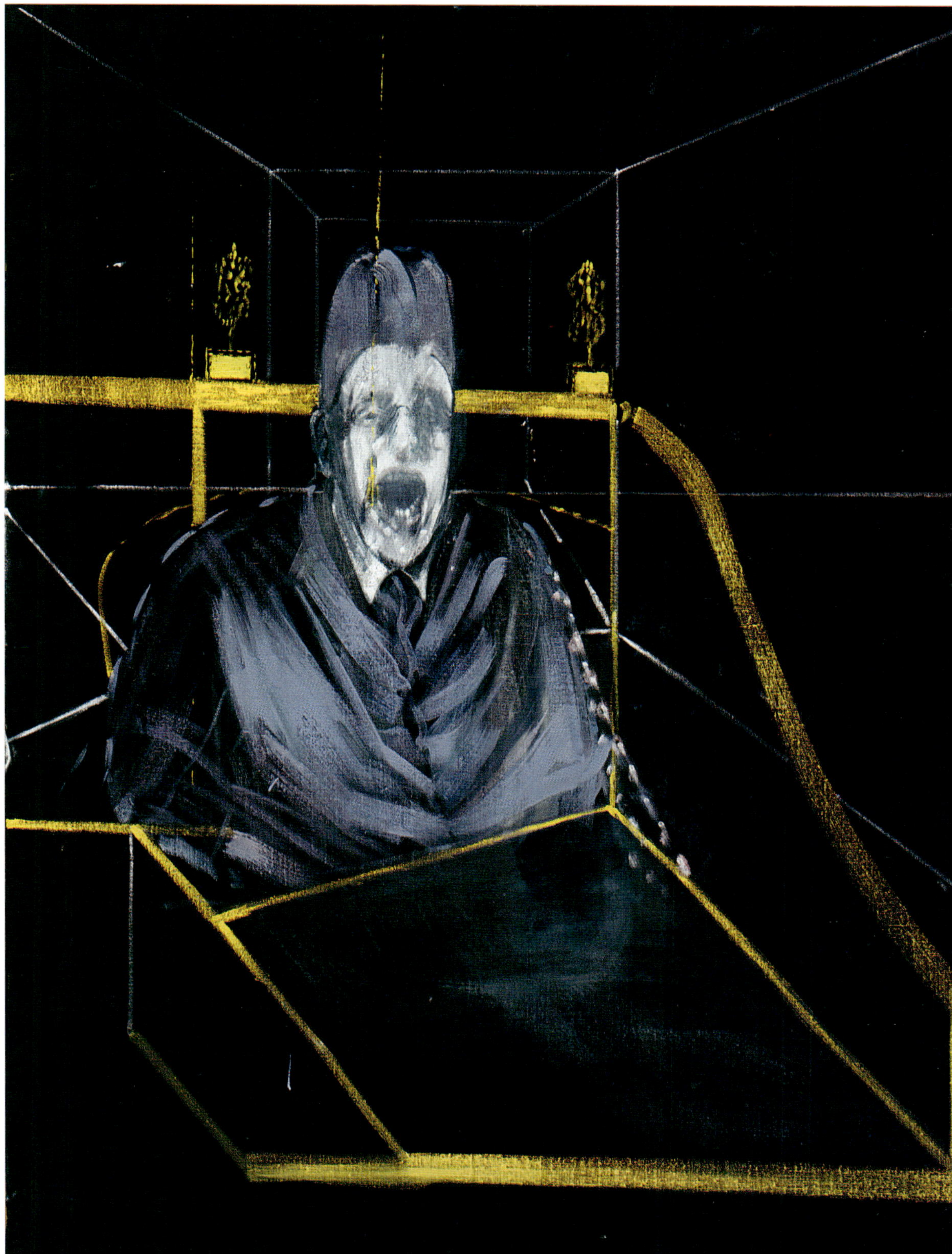

Cat. no. 7

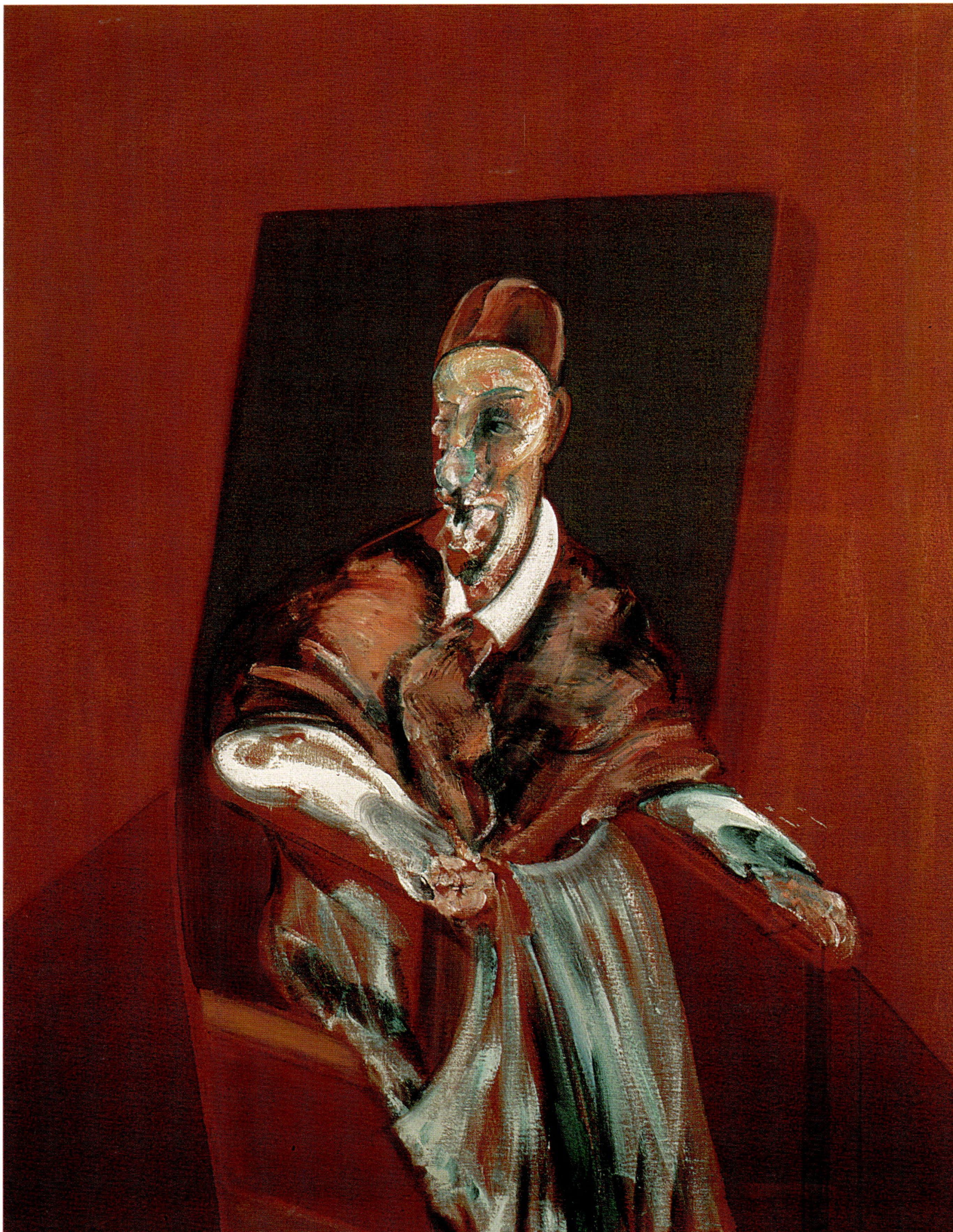

Cat. no. 8

Cat. no. 8
Francis Bacon
Seated Figure (Red Cardinal)
1960
Oil on canvas, 152.2 × 118 cm
Brussels, Private collection

Cat. no. 9
Alberto Giacometti
Portrait of Pope Innocent X.,
after Velázquez
1936 (dated 1942)
Pencil on paper, 210 × 260 mm
Paris, Musée Picasso,
inv. no. M. P. 3599

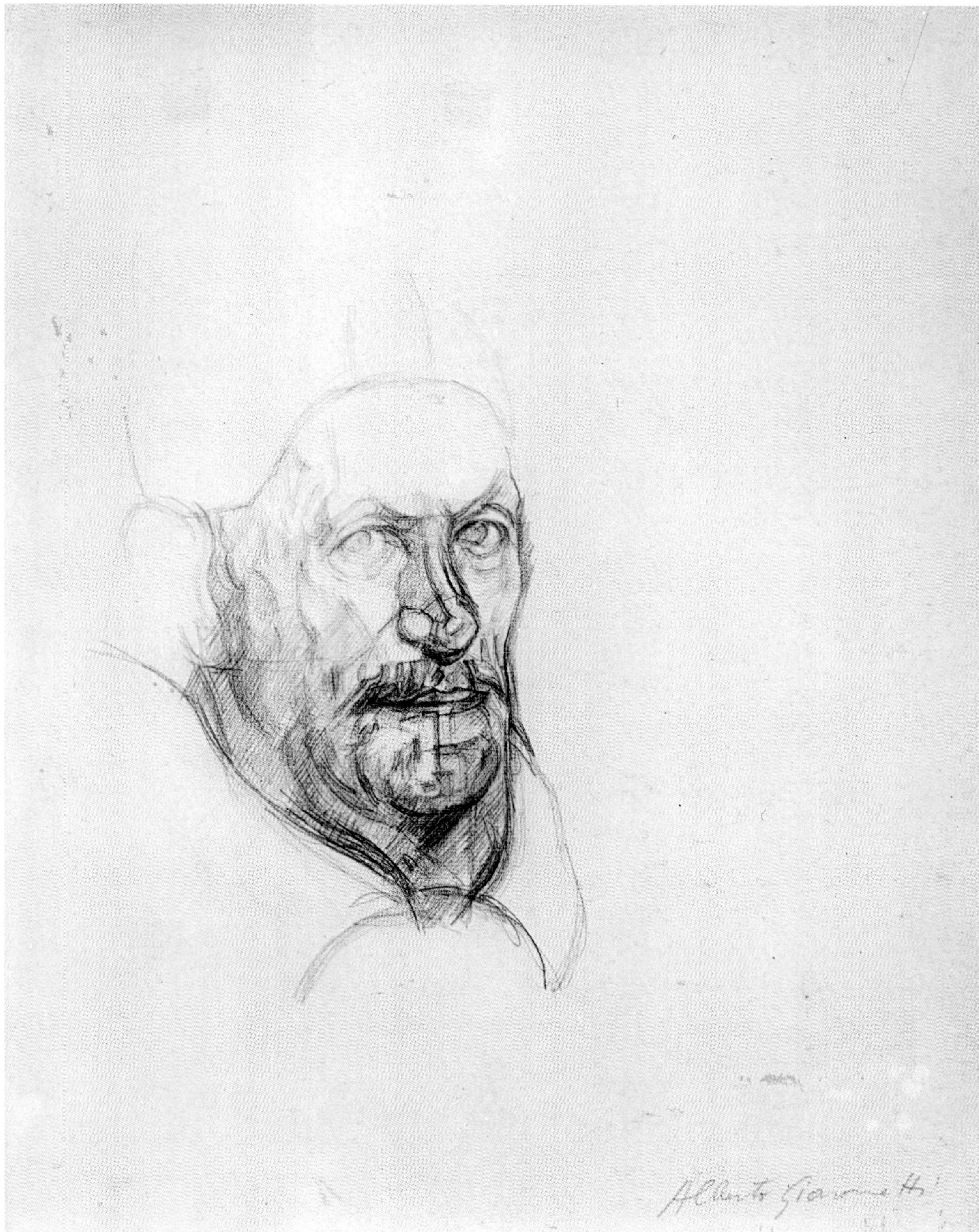

Cat. no. 9

Cat. no. 10
Colour plate of Pope Innocent X, 1650 by Diego Velázquez (detail). Leaf from unidentified book, 177 × 163 mm
Dublin, Dublin City Gallery The Hugh Lane, F105:113

Cat. no. 11
Black-and-white illustration of Pope Innocent X, 1650 by Diego Velázquez. Leaf from unidentified book. 280 × 223 mm
Dublin, Dublin City Gallery The Hugh Lane, F1:3

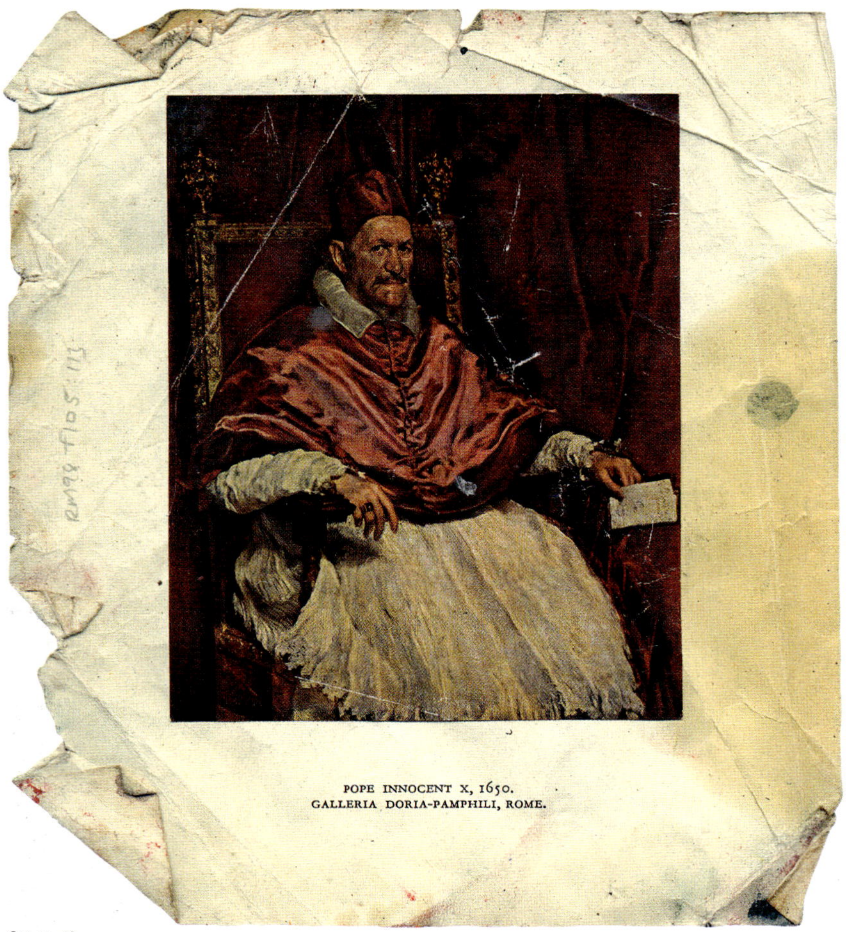

Cat. no. 10

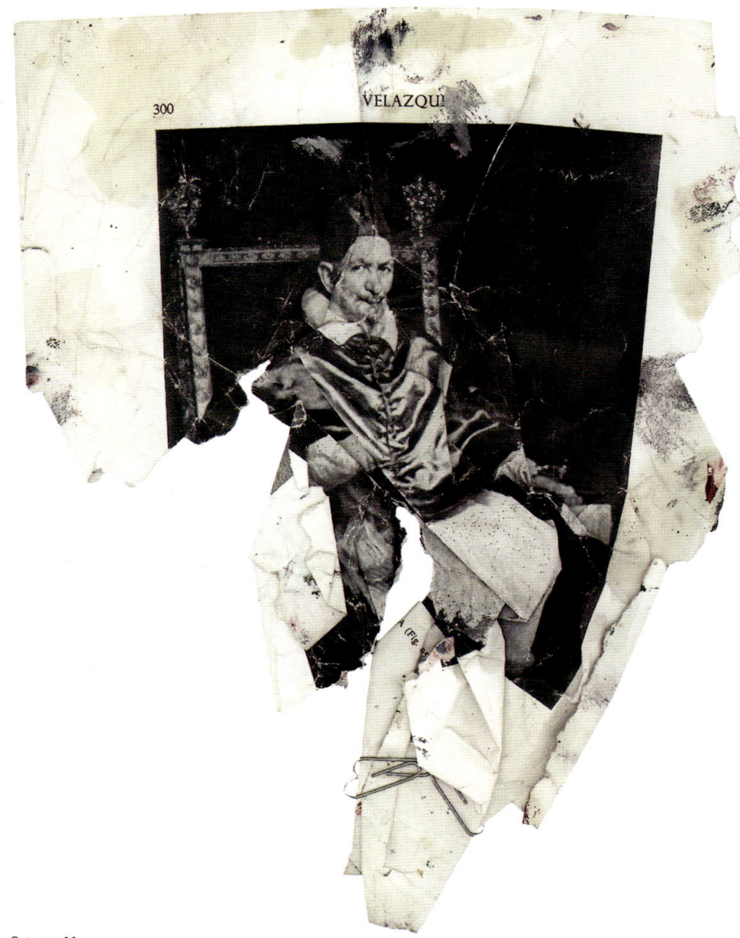

Cat. no. 11

Cat. no. 12
Black-and-white photograph of assemblage of photographs and torn leaves on wall of Francis Bacon's studio, taken by Sam Hunter. Summer 1950. 300 × 243 mm
Dublin, Dublin City Gallery The Hugh Lane, F1A:201

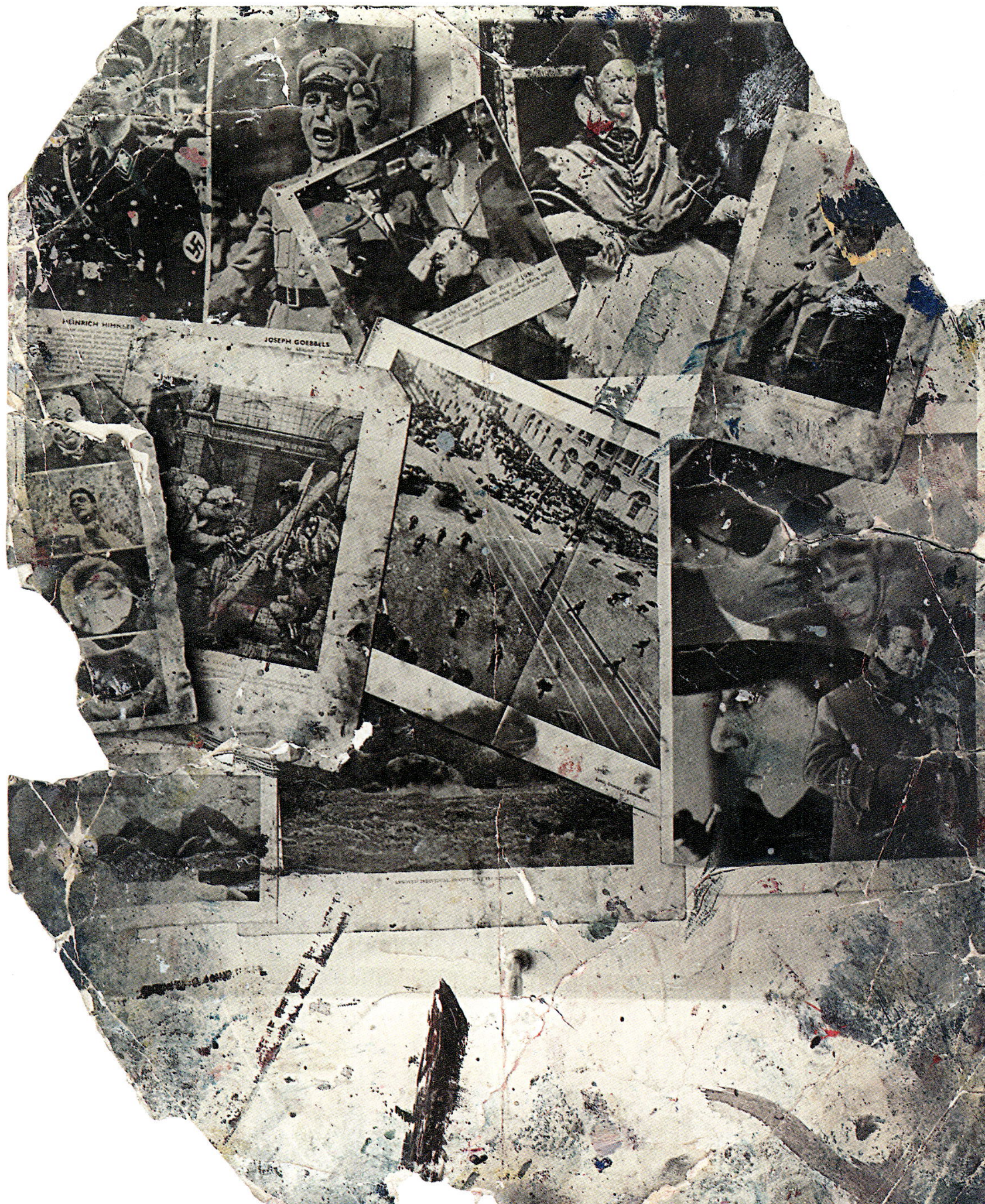

Cat. no. 12

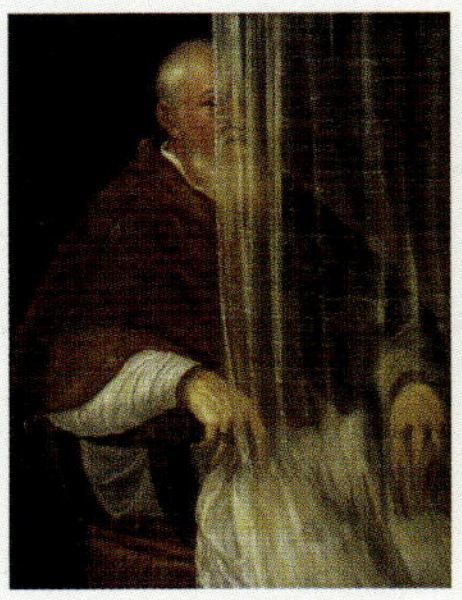
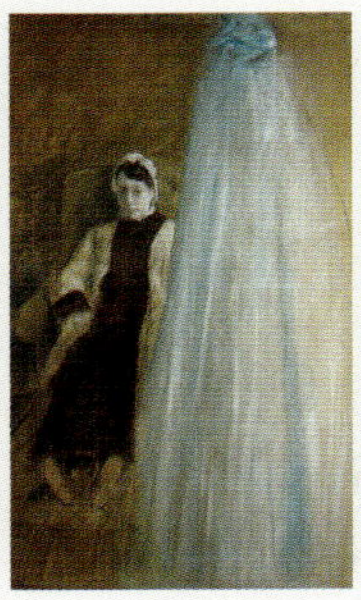
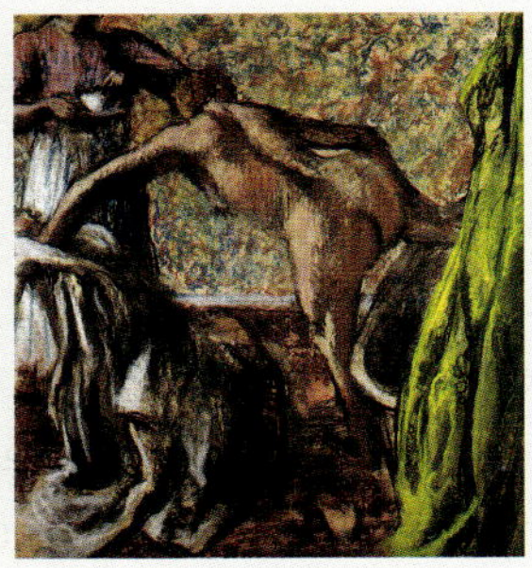
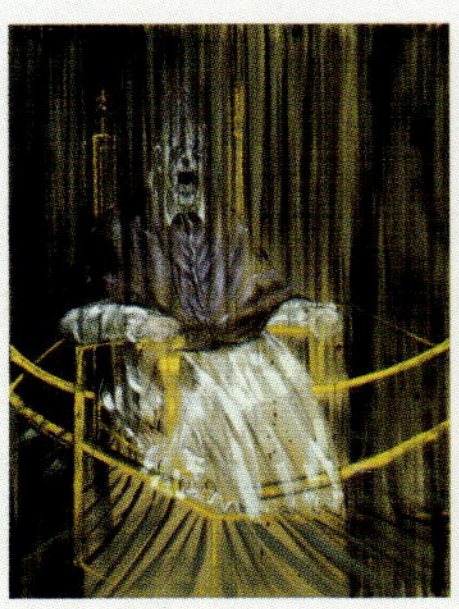
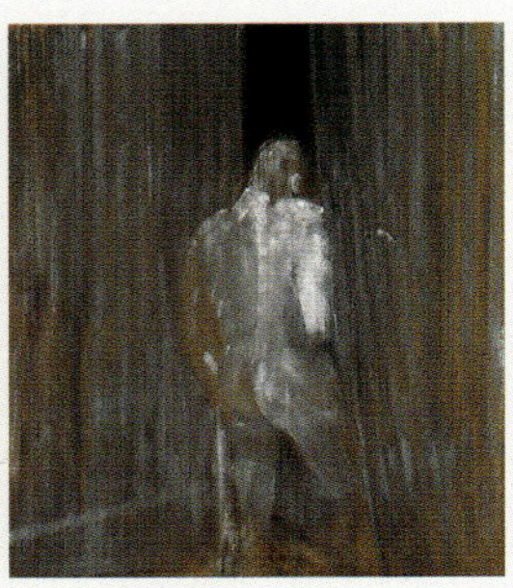
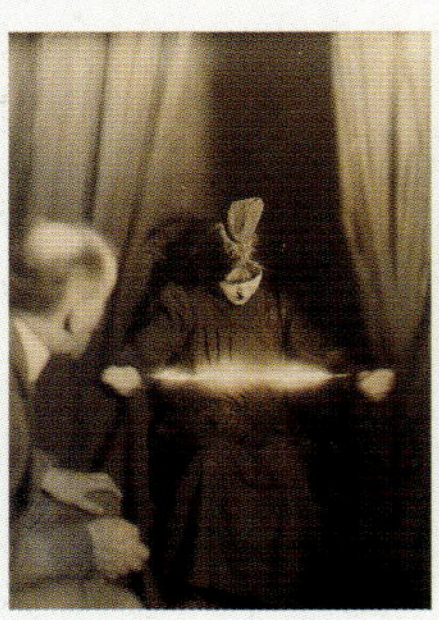
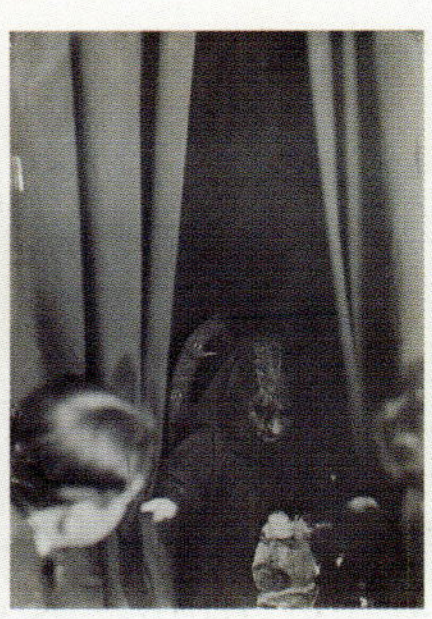
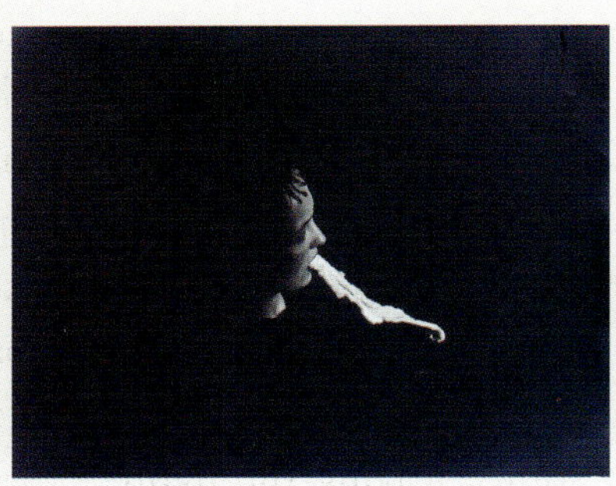
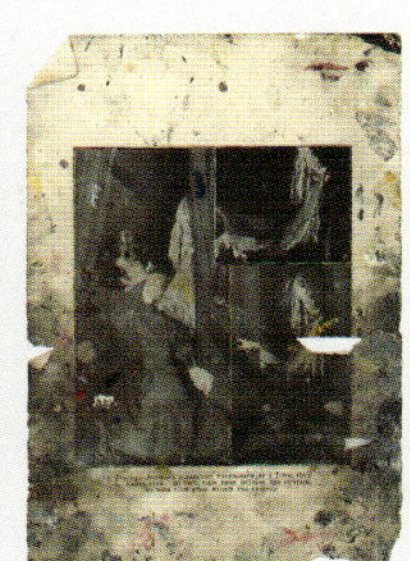
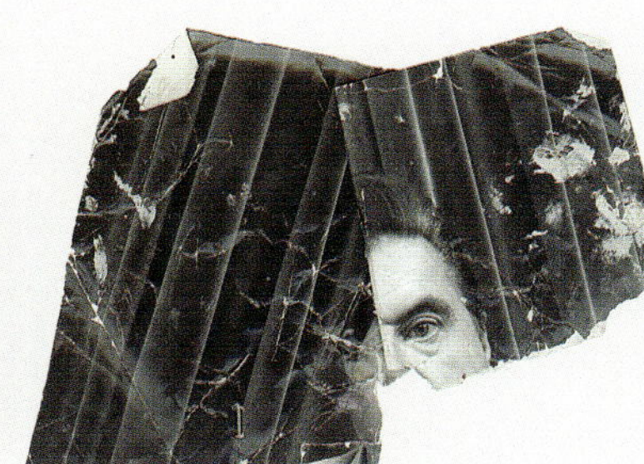
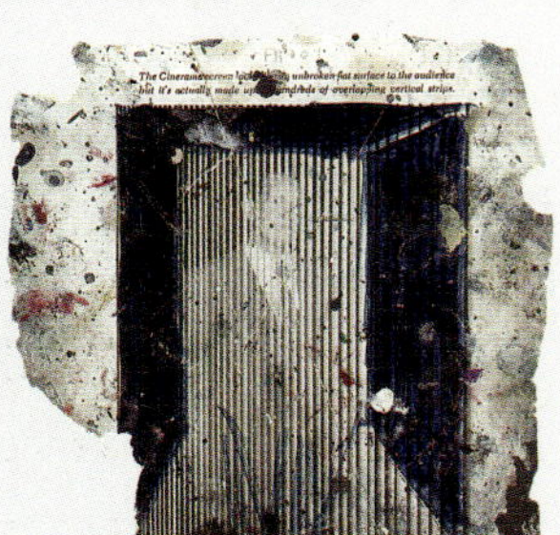

Barbara Steffen

Veils and Striations as Motifs of Isolation

Filippo Archinto was born in Milan 1495, studied law in Pavia and was sent in 1527 to Valladolid and then in 1529 on to Barcelona. In 1535 Pope Paul III convinced him to accept church office and subsequently appointed him governor of Rome. Archinto took part in the Council of Trent in 1546 and was papal nuncio in Venice from 1554 to 1556. In 1556 he was nominated to be bishop of Milan, but serious political controversies prevented him from taking up the position. He spent the last years of his life in Bergamo, where he died in 1558. In the 1550s Titian painted two portraits of Filippo Archinto. He depicted the clergyman seated with the episcopal ring on his right hand and a book in his left. This version of the painting, sometimes attributed to Leandro Bassano, is in the Metropolitan Museum in New York.

The second version, today in the Philadelphia Museum of Art (cat. no. 13), is the more interesting. In this work, which must have been painted around 1558,[1] the clergyman is depicted in the same seated position and with the episcopal ring and the book. The significant difference, however, is that half of the figure is concealed behind a transparent curtain that covers the entire right half of the painting. The edge of the curtain divides Archinto's right eye and leaves his right hand uncovered only as far as the ring finger, on which he is wearing the episcopal ring. His left hand, which is holding the book, is only suggested by Titian's open manner of painting. Because of the curtain, the portrait appears to be divided into two halves, which are painted in entirely different manners, permitting the portrait to be seen in two ways. Richard J. Betts 1967 explained Titian's decision to paint his subject partially through a curtain, thus partly obscuring his features, by suggesting that while Titian wanted to portray Archinto as a bishop, he created this visual difference because the latter in the end had not been able to assume office.

In 1963 Laurence Alloway for the first time pointed out the similarity between Titian's episcopal portrait and Bacon's papal paintings.[2] In this regard his *Study after Velázquez's Portrait of Pope Innocent X* of 1953 (cat. no. 14) deserves special mention. "I wanted to paint a head, as folded in on itself, like the folds of a curtain,"[3] said Bacon. While Titian covered the right half of the portrait of Filippo Archinto with a curtain, Bacon fills the entire surface of the painting with a hanging curtain marked with striations, leaving the figure behind it unrecognisable in part. The body dissolves in a network of colours, which in the area of the mozzetta and lower body is variously accentuated by the stroke and direction of the brush. Black striations run like streaks in various directions across the painting. The striations representing the curtain run from top to bottom to the end of the lower body and the Pope's white cassock. Other groups of streaks run in a slightly diagonal direction in the lower quarter of the painting, running from two sides towards the figure and the centre of the picture.

What is Bacon trying to achieve with these striations? On the one hand he uses them as a means of creating isolation, in order to make the Pope partially disappear behind the curtain in a manner similar to Titian. At the same time the other motifs (scream, colour, throne, framework) make his figure appear very immediate. On the other hand, the striations also play a purely compositional role by lengthening, stretching and distorting the subject in a manner similar to Giacometti's standing figures. But the striations also point deeply into the room, into the centre of the painting. They underscore the three-dimensional character of the space in which the figure is separated from the viewer and depicted as though in the vortex of a contracting space. Because he has omitted the background architecture, such as arches or a bed-frame, from this painting, Bacon uses hatching to create an extended system of co-ordinates.

A sketch from the 1950s (cat. no. 23) clearly illustrates Bacon's method of working: it is a depiction of a male figure with dozens of vertical lines laid across it, creating a grid-like system. Bacon found his source in a book on film technique, in which the construction of the Cinerama screen is explained. The screen was divided into many lines but appeared to the audience to have a smooth surface. Bacon marked his source with a blue felt pen by drawing a frame around the figure, but leaving it open in the lower third of the painting and drawing the ends of the contours diagonally towards the figure.

Some of the other sources that were found in Bacon's studio, such as the occult photographs of materialisation phenomena by Albert Schrenck-Notzing and Juliette Bisson from the years 1913–20 (cat. nos. 18–20) suggest the artist's interest in veils and curtains. So-called materialisation (or ectoplasm) is "rising" from the hypnotised medium, who can be seen in a trance-like condition through a half-open curtain. Photographs of such esoteric phenomena had a great influence on Bacon's paintings, such as *Study from the Human Body* of 1949 (cat. no. 17). Here he also portrays the protagonist in a trance-like state; he is isolated from the room and viewer and about to disappear behind the curtain. A fragment of a black-and-white photograph of Bacon himself and found in his studio shows the artist in front of a velvet curtain; the folds of the curtain symbolise the vertical components within the composition (cat. no. 22).

A late variant of the curtain motif from Bacon's collection of photographs is found in an ad for the British cigarette brand Silk Cut (cat. no. 24). Torn from a magazine, it depicts a purple-violet silk curtain, which is hanging on hooks and has folds like a stage curtain. Bacon must have been inspired to use this motif in many of his later works by the highly sculptural quality of the fabric, the vertical lines of the folds and the suggestion that something is hidden behind the curtain.

Another artist, working decades earlier, who used vertical lines and striation in a similar manner on the mainly female figures in his paintings was Edgar Degas. Bacon, who admired the French painter, spoke of him repeatedly: "It's his pastels that I particularly like. They are extraordinary. Especially the interiors with women at their toilet, the nudes rather than the dancers. [...] He really is the only artist to have known how to handle pastels like that, with those lines between the colours."[4] There is an entire series of late pastels by Degas that might serve here for purposes of comparison and which Bacon knew well, particularly since he owned several books on Degas' pastels, which he used as inspiration for his work. Various versions of *Woman after the Bath* show clear hatching (cat. no. 15). The largest pastel that Degas ever made, and which he drew on canvas, is *Madame Ernest May next to a Cradle* of 1881/82 or 1880.[5] It measures 130 × 80 cm and is now in a private Swiss collection (cat. no. 16). This is a preliminary study for a work commissioned by the art collector Ernest May, but it was never completed and signed because May withdrew his commission for the oil painting, and Degas broke off work on the study. Degas' pastel depicts the female figure in a relaxed pose at the left of the painting, sitting on a chair with her legs extended. She appears to be minding her child, asleep in the cradle. Rather than the child and the cradle itself, only the curtain of the cradle can be seen on the right. The folds of the fabric dominate the upright format of the picture, creating in its material texture the real theme of the painting. Although Degas is presenting a traditional genre theme here, he focuses not on the content of the scene but rather on the chromatic values as well as the graphic and compositional representation of the curtain. The blue-white striations are painted in an open and free manner, allowing the canvas to shine through. Bacon's view of Degas' art is clear in his formulation: "The very great Degas are the pastels, and don't forget that in his pastels he always striates the form with these lines which are drawn through the image and in a certain sense both intensify and diversify its reality. I always think that the interesting thing about Degas is the way he made lines through the body: you could say that he shuttered the body, in a way he shuttered the image and then he put an enormous amount of colour through these lines. And having shuttered the form, he created intensity by putting this colour through the flesh."[6]

In the works of Degas and Bacon, the

hatching and lines that veil the depicted body or screen it as though it were behind a curtain symbolise in a certain manner the clothing as well as the layers lying beneath it – the skin and flesh, but also the immaterial aspects of the psyche and the unconscious. Bacon, who was both cynical and at the same time seeking to reveal the existential, worked through these layers to reach his own self and inversely also protected and isolated himself with layers of veils by over-painting strata of colour on one another, which then create the atmosphere of the painting.

[1] Wethey 1971. In his dating, Wethey follows the research of Richard J. Betts, who in set the date as 1558. This was based on his theory that the clergyman was portrayed after he was nominated to be bishop, and thus after 1556.
[2] Cf. Sylvester 2000, p. 50.
[3] Exh. Cat. San Diego 2001, p. 13.
[4] Archimbaud 2000, p. 42.
[5] Ronald Pickvance proposes 1880 as the pastel's date. In: Exh. Cat. Vienna 1996, p. 96.
[6] Sylvester 1999, p. 176.

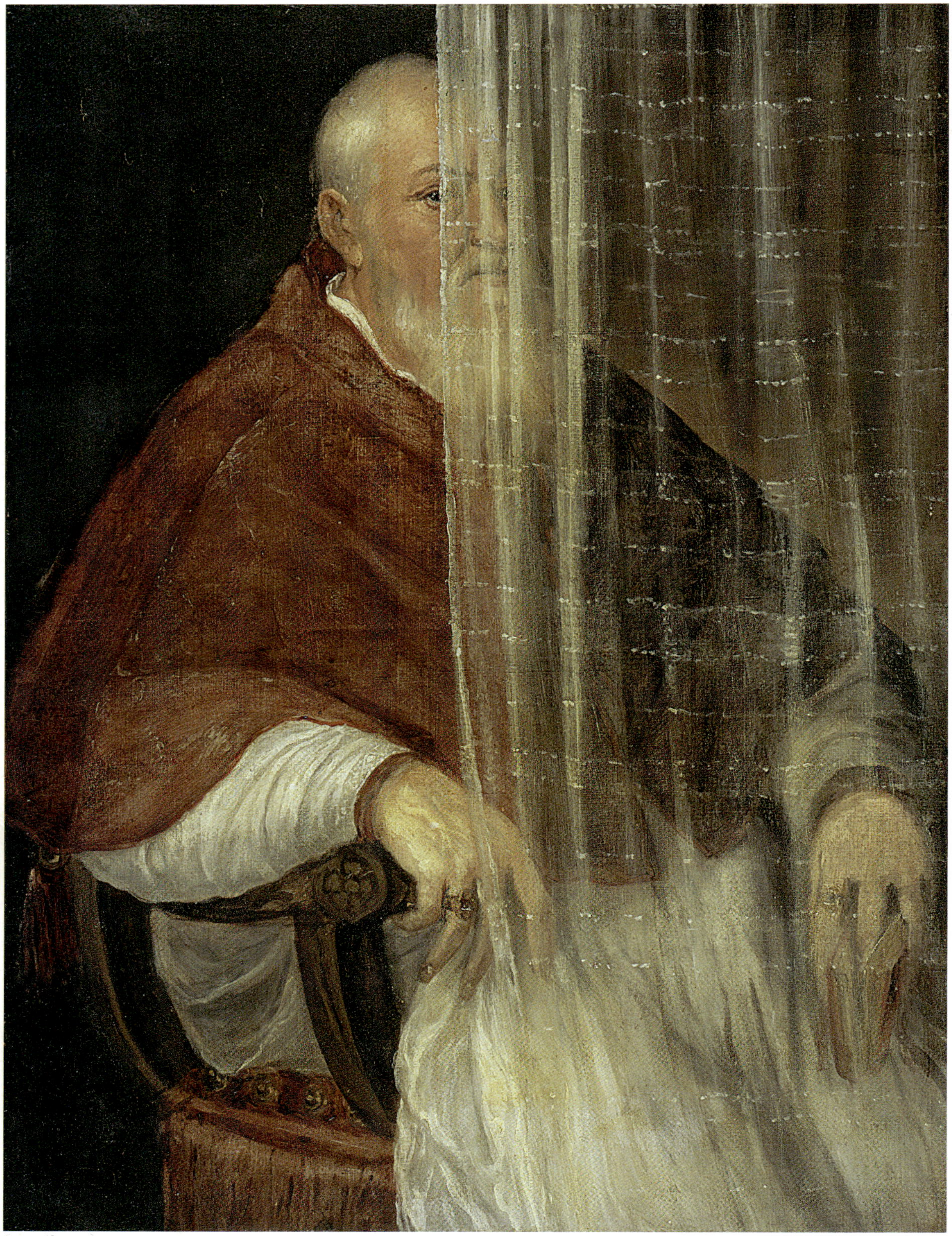

Cat. no. 13

Cat. no. 13
Tiziano Vecellio
Portrait of Cardinal Filippo Archinto
C. 1551/62
Oil on canvas, 114.8 × 88.7 cm
Philadelphia, Philadelphia Museum,
The John G. Johnson Collection

Cat. no. 14
Francis Bacon
Study after Velázquez's Portrait
of Pope Innocent X
1953
Oil on canvas, 153 × 118 cm
Des Moines, Iowa, Des Moines Art
Center, purchased with funds from
the Coffin Fine Arts Trust, Nathan
Emory Coffin Collection of the
Des Moines Art Center, 1980

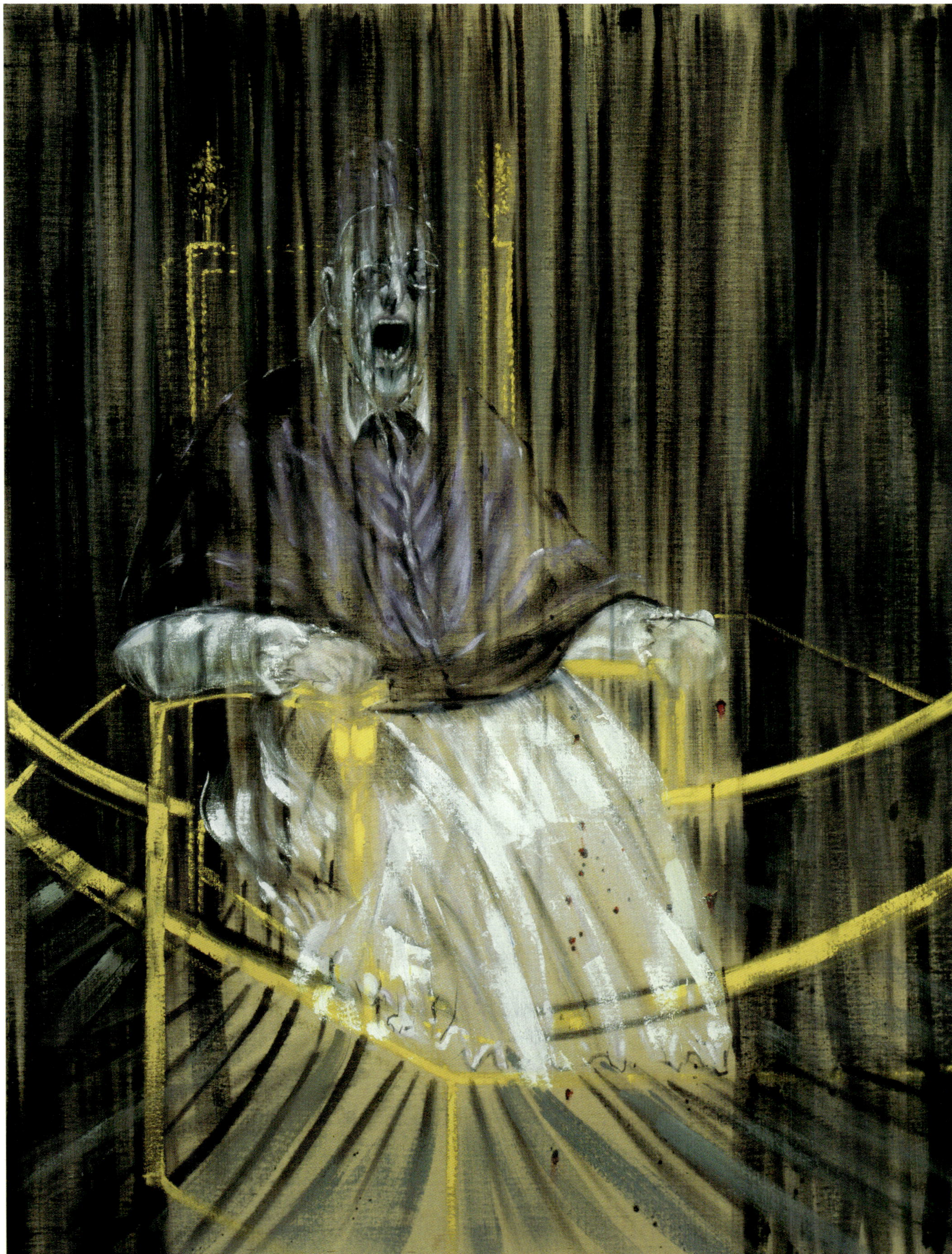

Cat. no. 14

Cat. no. 15
Edgar Degas
The Breakfast after the Bath
(The Bath)
C. 1895/98
Pastel on paper on card,
825 × 790 mm
Riehen/Basel, Fondation Beyeler

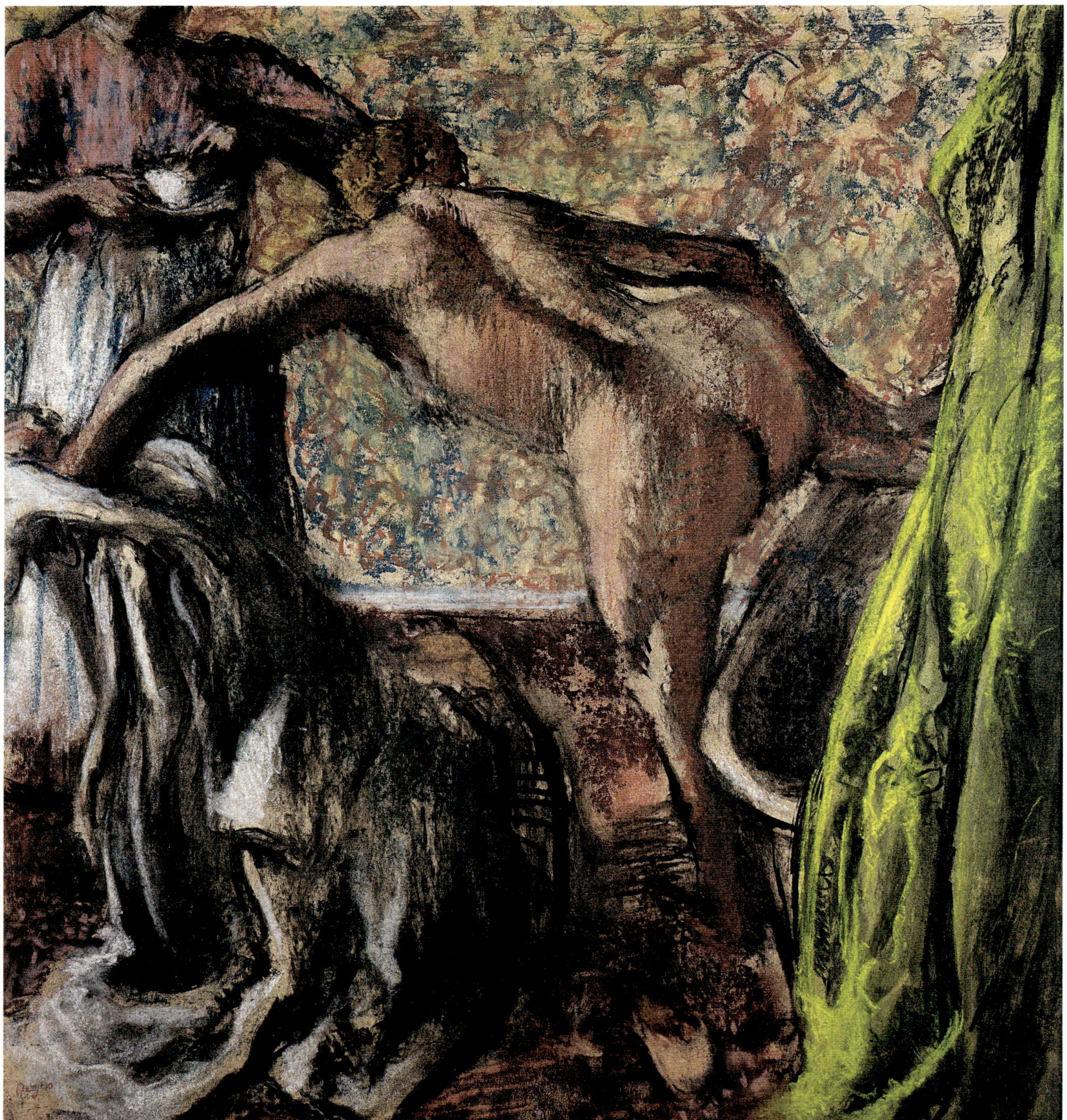

Cat. no. 15

Cat. no. 16
Edgar Degas
Madame Ernest May beside a cradle
1881/82
Pastel on canvas, 130 × 80 cm
Switzerland, Private Collection

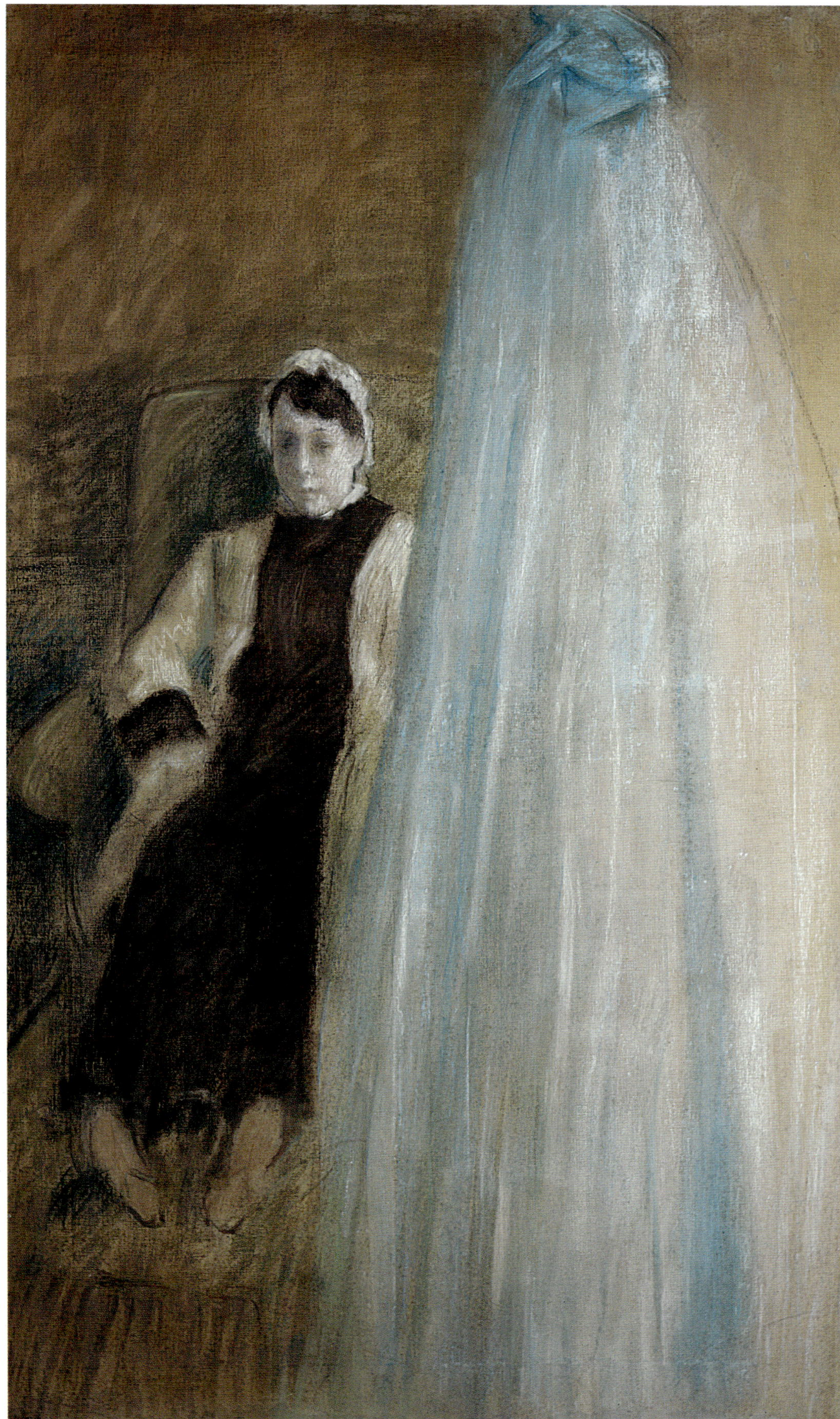

Cat. no. 16

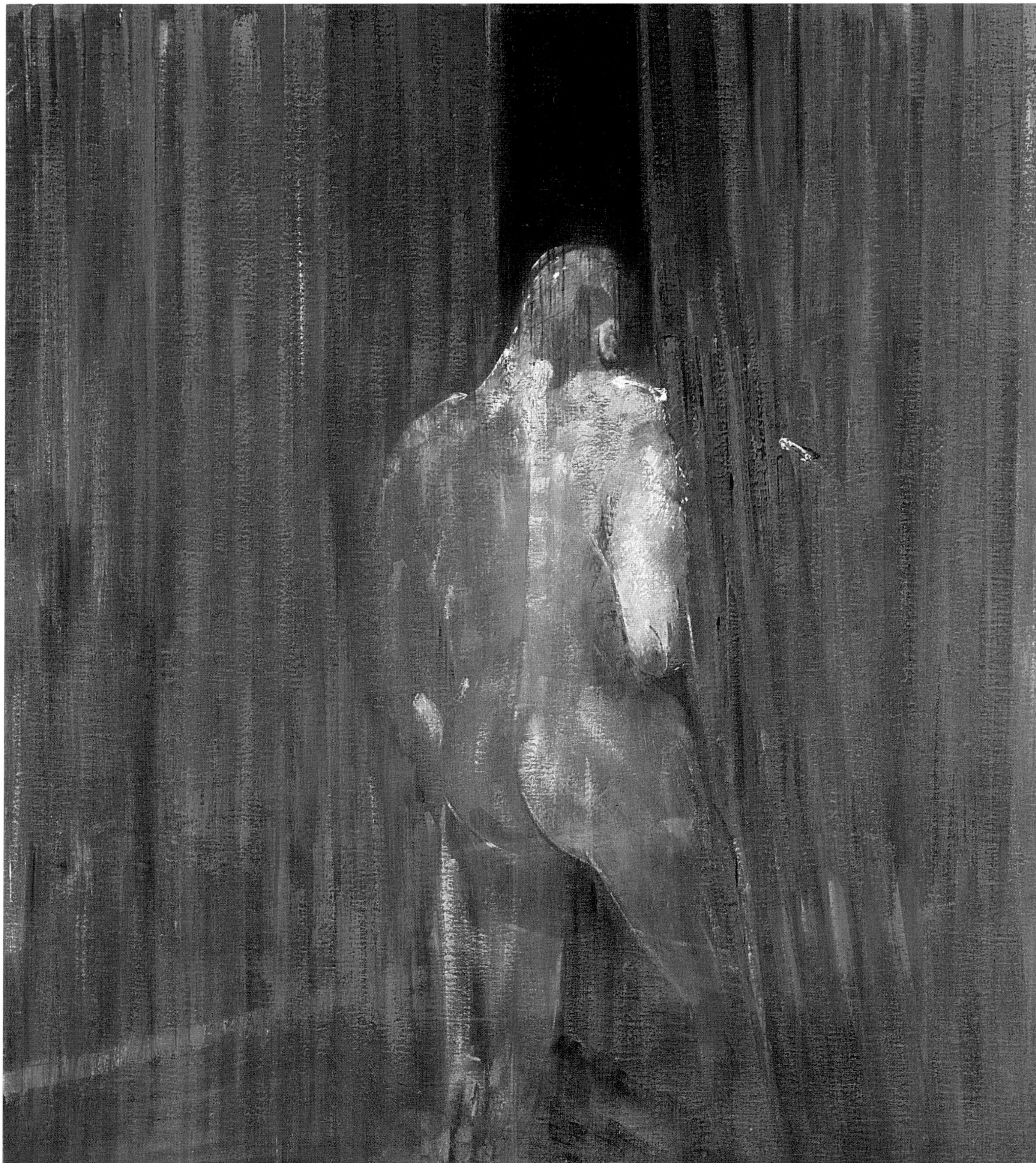
Cat. no. 17

Cat. no. 17
Francis Bacon
Study from the Human Body
1949
Oil on canvas, 147 × 134.2 cm
Melbourne, National Gallery of Victoria, purchased 1953

Cat. no. 18
Phaenomena of materialisation with Eva C.
Munich, May 17th, 1912
Photo by Albert von Schrenck-Notzing
240 × 180 mm
Freiburg/Breisgau, Institute for Interdisciplinary Subjects in Psychology and Psychohygiene, Estate of Albert von Schrenck-Notzing

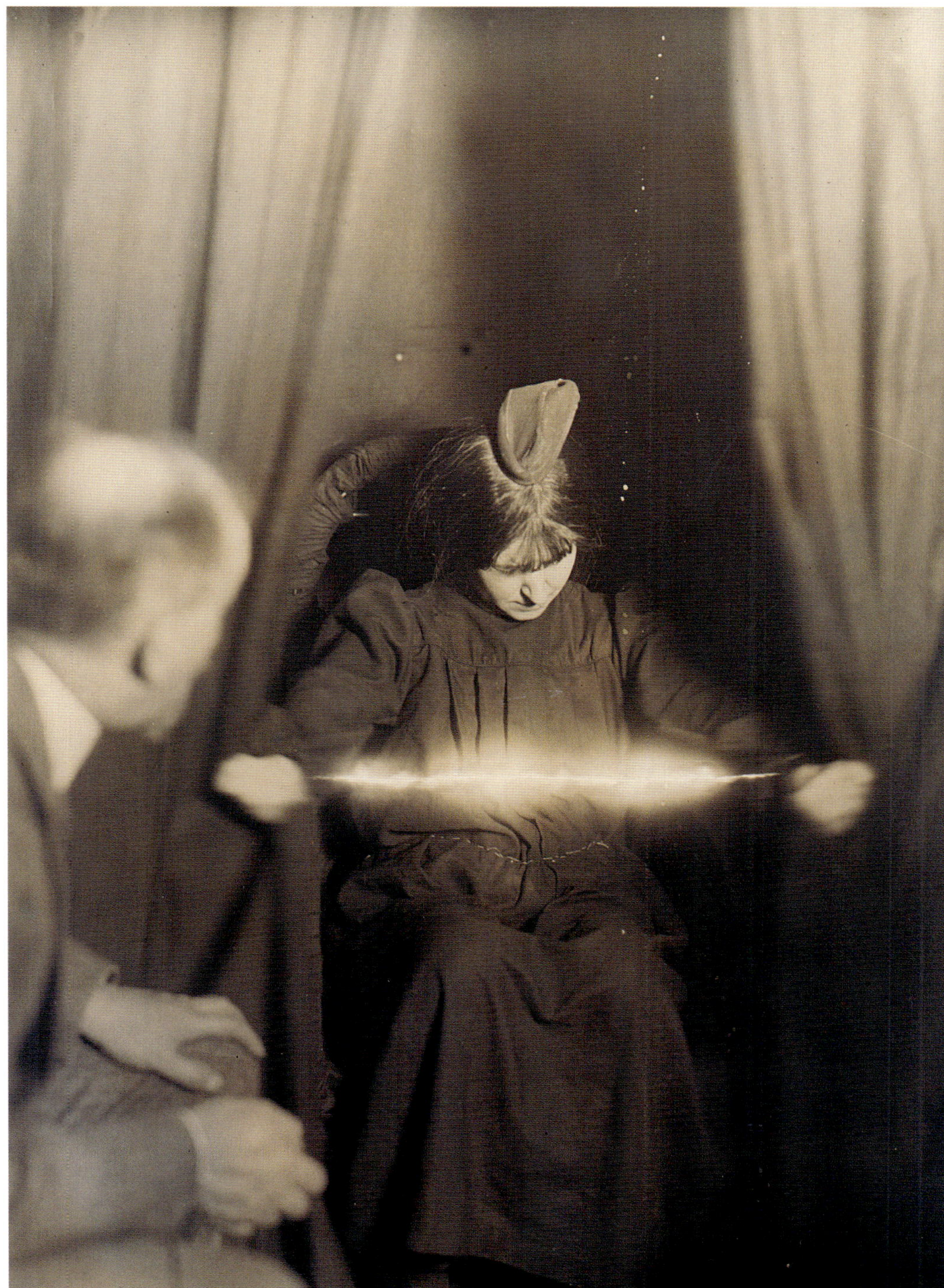

Cat. no. 18

Cat. no. 19
Phaenomena of materialisation
with Eva C.
Paris, May 2nd, 1913
Photo by Juliette Bisson
230 × 170 mm
Freiburg/Breisgau, Institute for Interdisciplinary Subjects in Psychology and Psychohygiene, Estate of Albert von Schrenck-Notzing

Cat. no. 20
Phaenomena of materialisation
with Stanislawa P.
Munich, January 25th, 1913
Photo by Albert von Schrenck-Notzing
89 × 119 mm
Freiburg/Breisgau, Institute for Interdisciplinary Subjects in Psychology and Psychohygiene, Estate of Albert von Schrenck-Notzing

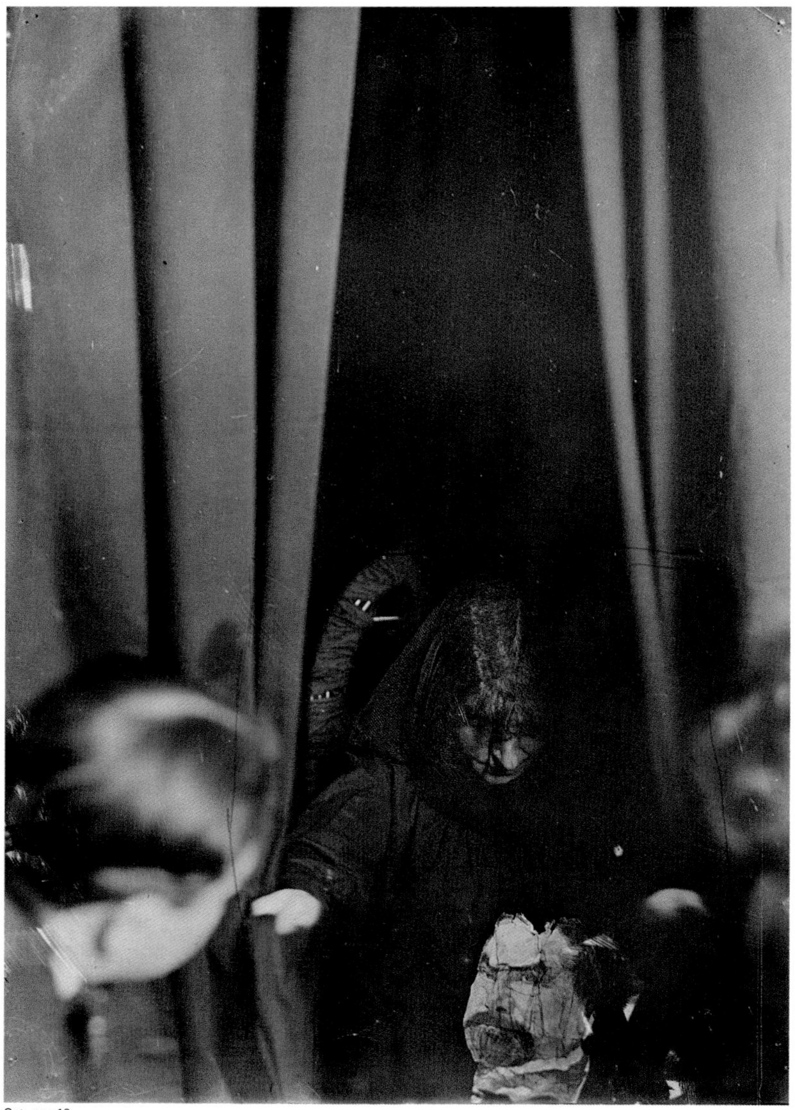
Cat. no. 19

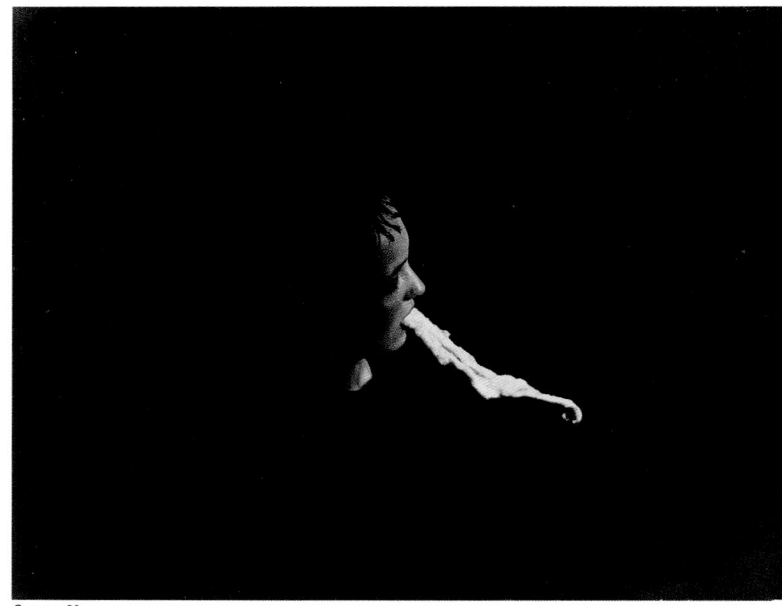
Cat. no. 20

Cat. no. 21
Leaf from Baron von Schrenck-Notzing, Phenomena of Materialisation, London 1920
246 × 162 mm
Dublin, Dublin City Gallery The Hugh Lane, F23:55

Cat. no. 22
Torn fragment of black-and-white photograph of Francis Bacon in front of curtain, taken by John Deakin. 1960s. 164 × 240 mm
Dublin, Dublin City Gallery The Hugh Lane, F16:295G

Cat. no. 23
Intervention by Francis Bacon in dark blue paint on a cutting from a Cinerama booklet. Early 1950s. 166 × 172 mm
Dublin, Dublin City Gallery The Hugh Lane, F17:109

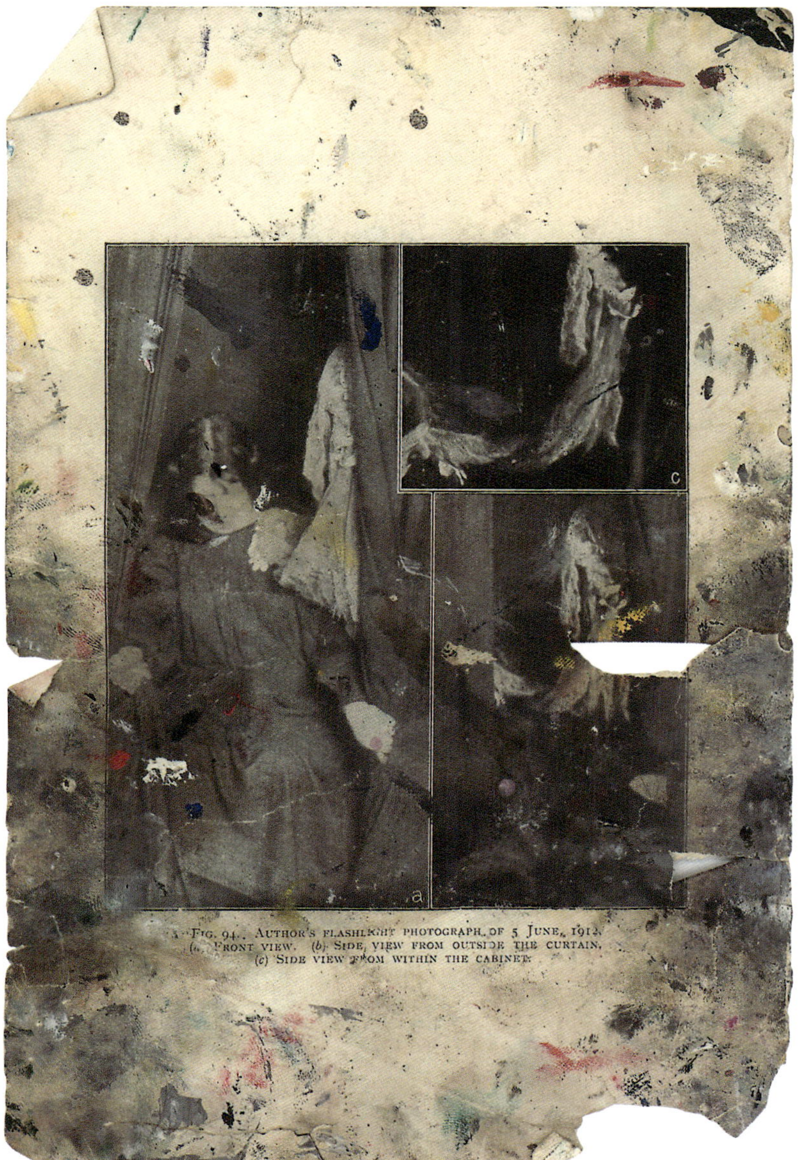

Cat. no. 21

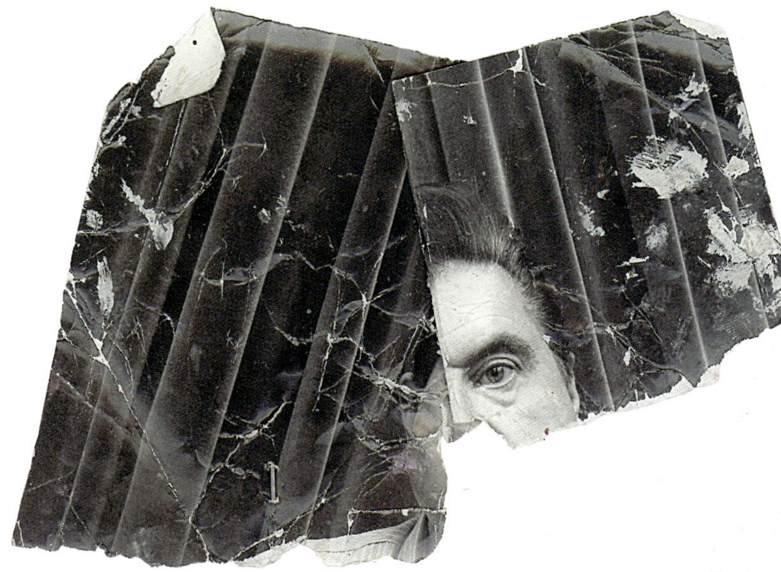

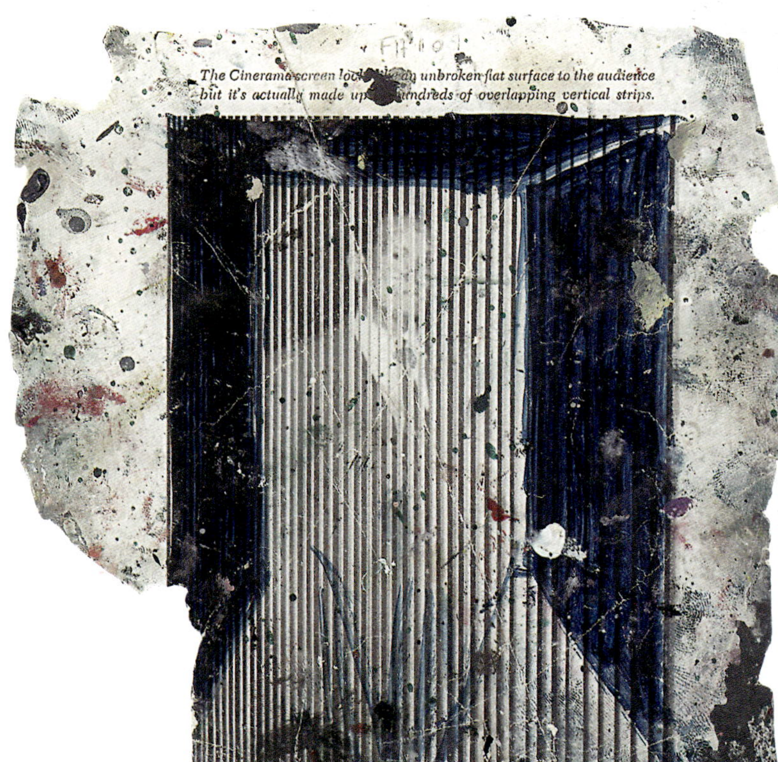

Cat. no. 23

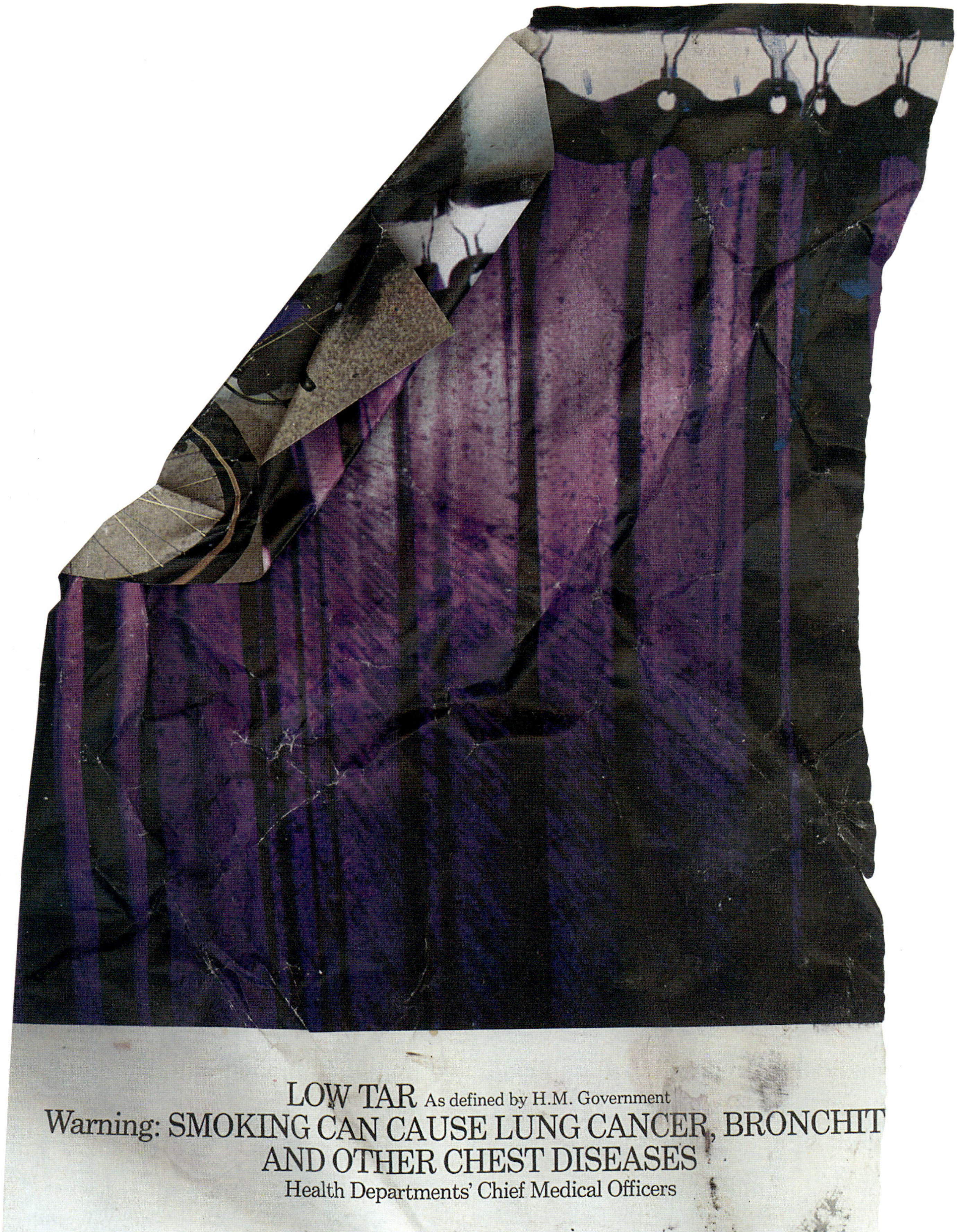
LOW TAR As defined by H.M. Government
Warning: SMOKING CAN CAUSE LUNG CANCER, BRONCHIT
AND OTHER CHEST DISEASES
Health Departments' Chief Medical Officers

Cat. no. 24

Cat. no. 24
Leaf with colour advertisement for Silk Cut cigarettes, torn from unidentified magazine. 1980s/early 1990s
295 × 228 mm
Dublin, Dublin City Gallery The Hugh Lane, F103:26D

Cat. no. 25
Alfred Werner, Degas Pastels, London 1969
285 × 270 × 22 mm
Dublin, Dublin City Gallery The Hugh Lane, F114:141

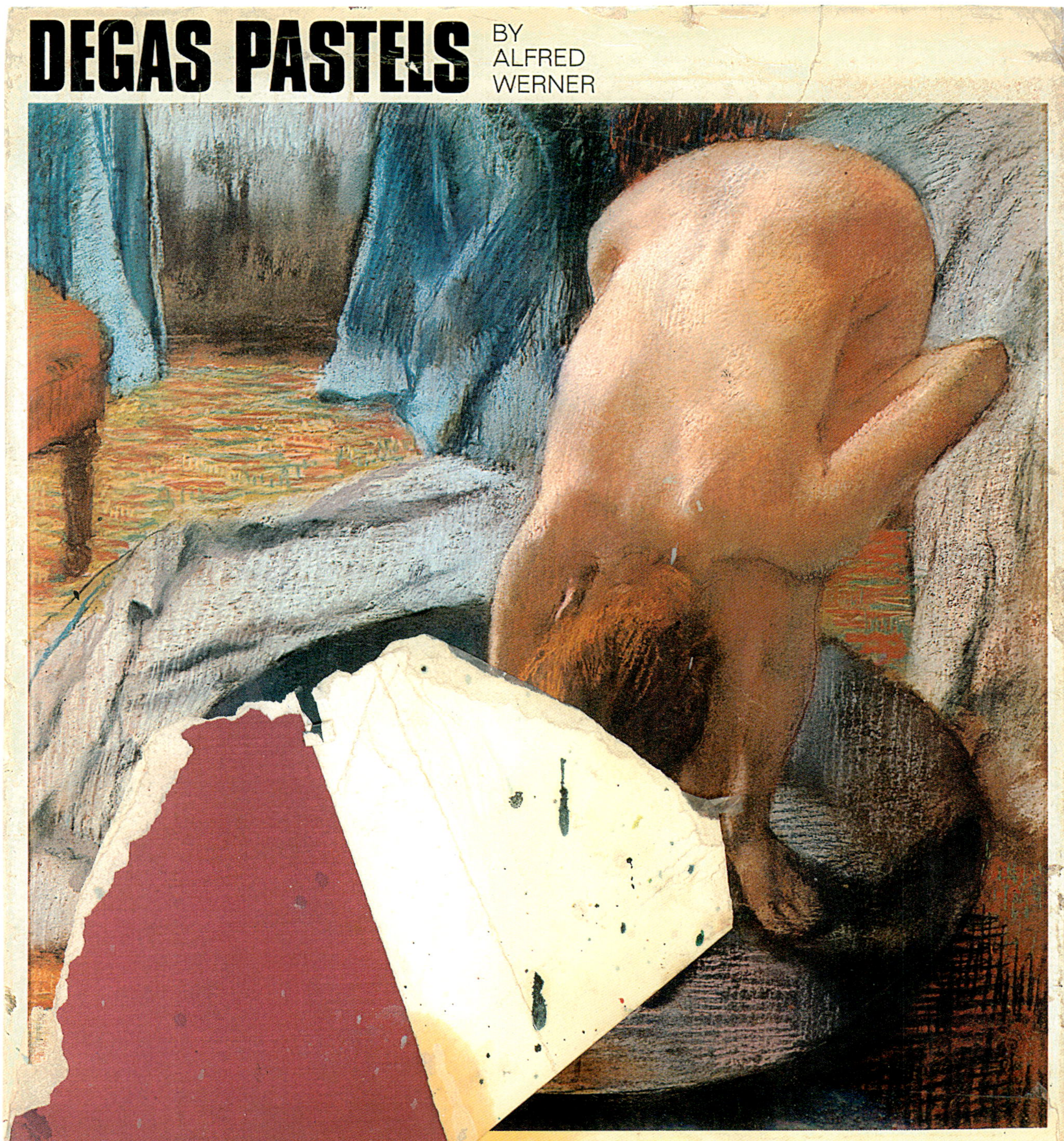

Cat. no. 25

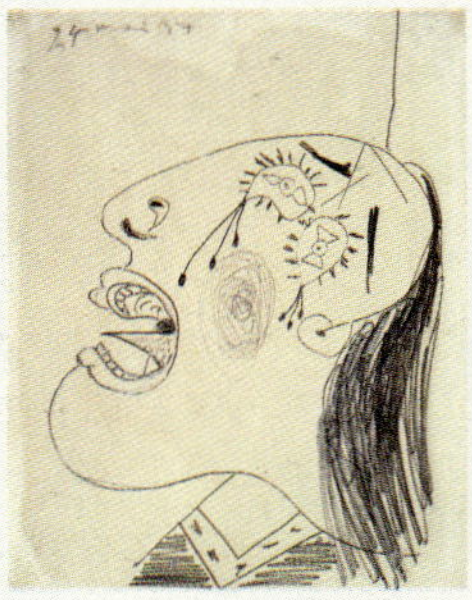
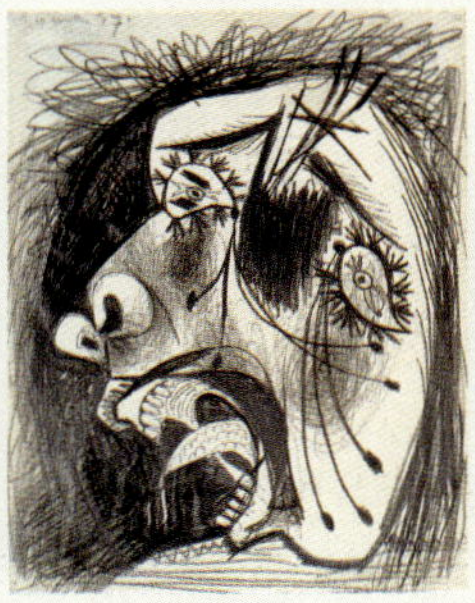
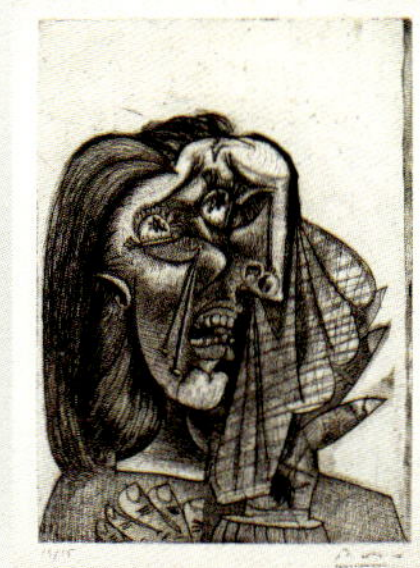
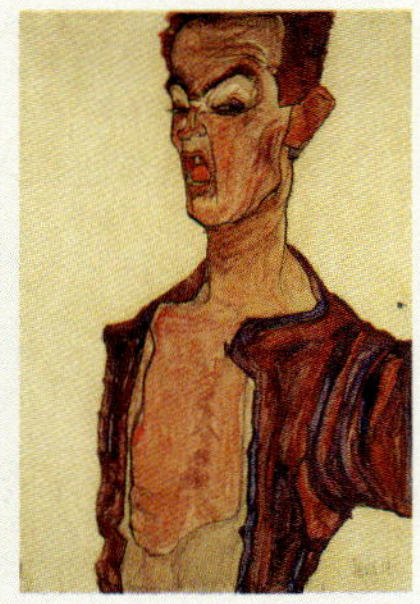
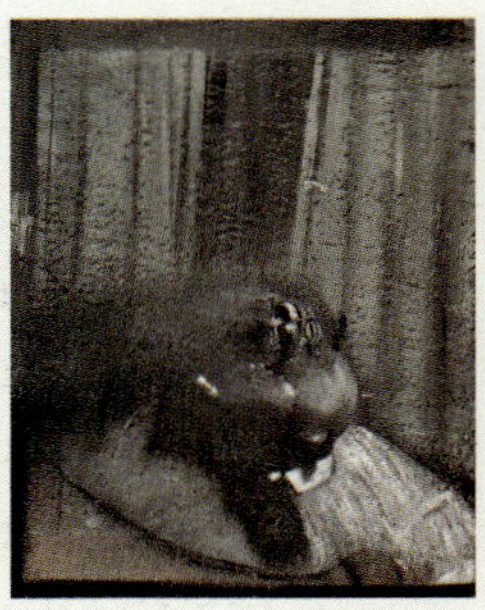
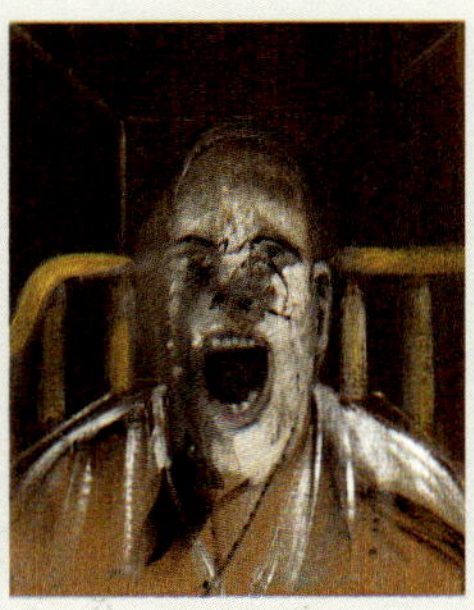
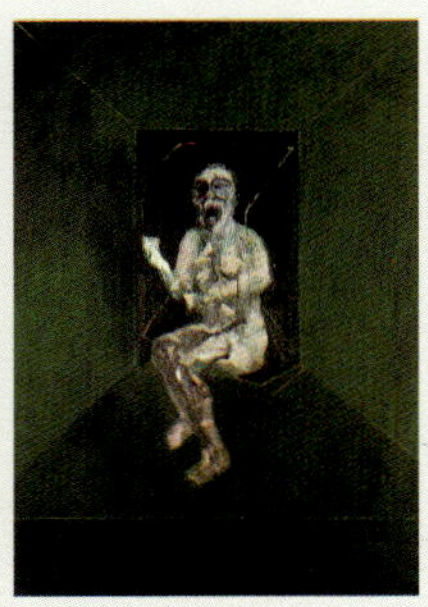
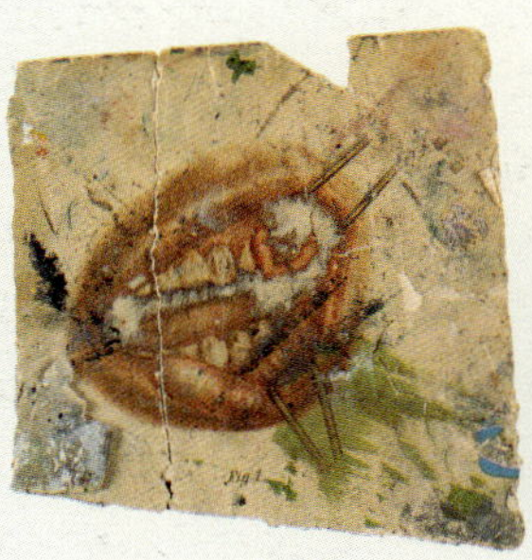
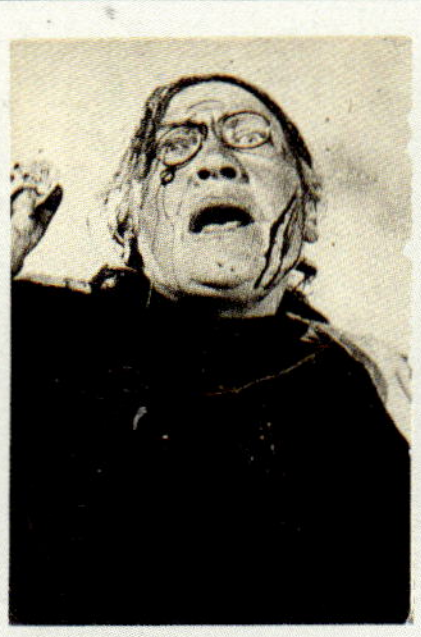
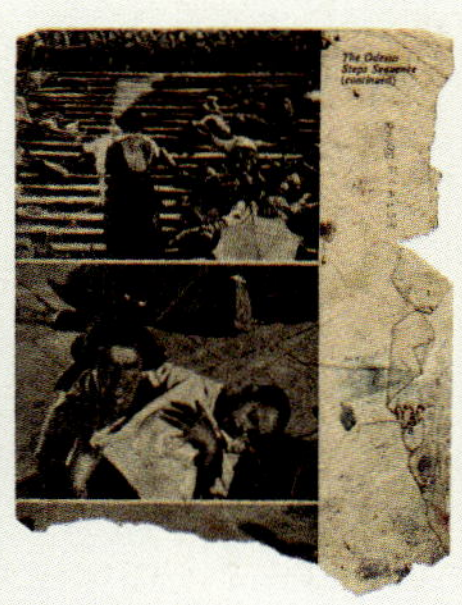
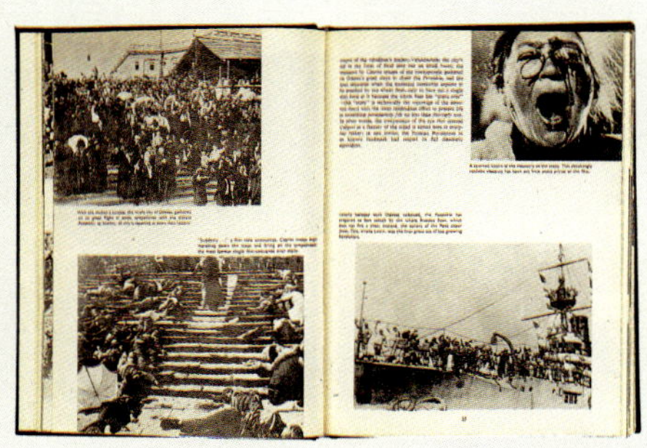
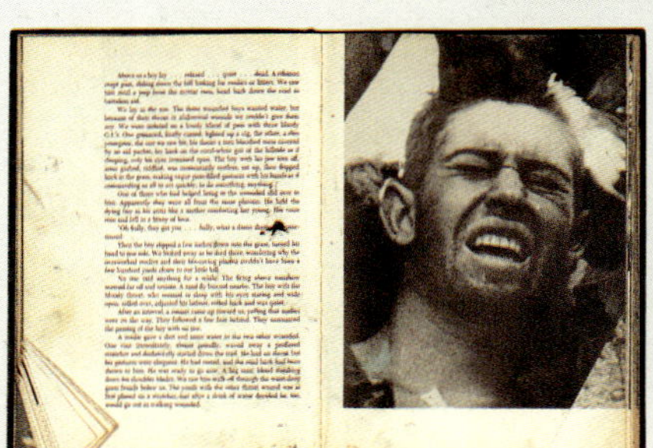
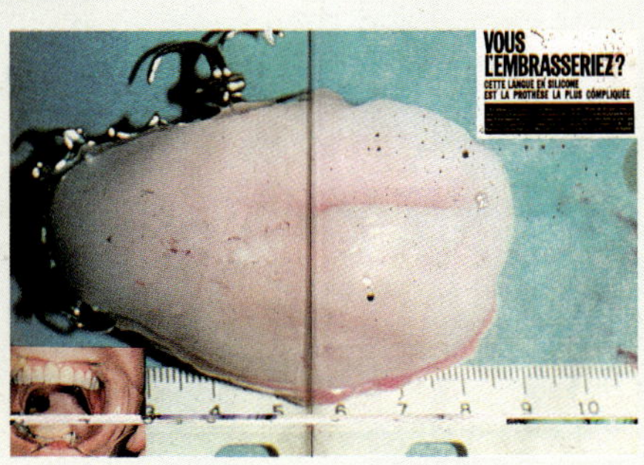
VOUS
L'EMBRASSERIEZ?
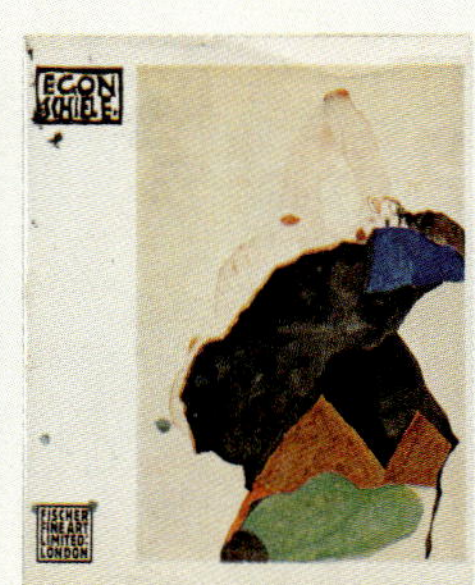
EGON SCHIELE
FISCHER FINE ART LIMITED LONDON
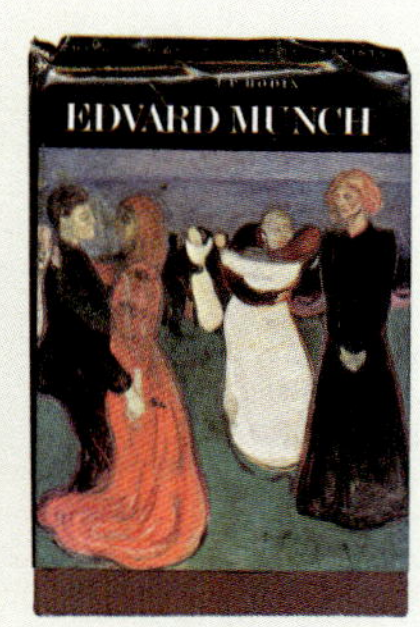
EDVARD MUNCH

Barbara Steffen

The Scream

Arthur Schopenhauer speaks in his *Treatise on the Aesthetics of the Plastic Arts* of the impossibility of depicting the scream in painting. He refers to Guido Reni, who in his version of *The Massacre of the Innocents* in the Pinacoteca Nazionale in Bologna portrays six people with mouths open wide: their screaming is not depicted by the suffering expression on their faces but still within an aesthetic ideal. Schopenhauer did not think that a scream could be portrayed in the plastic arts, and therefore does not occur in the *Laocoön*. The artist's task here was to suppress the expression of pain – the scream. Lessing also stresses that the portrayal of the scream is omitted in art in order not to distort the face in a repugnant manner. According to Schopenhauer, the sculptor of the *Laocoön* chose the time factor as a means of preventing the scream: "He solved this problem by portraying the snakebite neither as an already accomplished action nor as a threatened one, but rather as taking place at that very moment and in the victim's side: the lower body is contracted and screaming is thus made impossible."[1]

In Surrealism the scream is visualised as a symbol of experiencing mental and corporeal pain. An example is found in a photograph by Jacques-André Bouffard *(Plate 1)*, which depicts a mouth wide open wide in a scream as a dim cavern in which the dark-grey shadow of the tongue is hidden. Writing about this photograph, which was published in the French Surrealist magazine Documents 5, 1930, the author Georges Bataille spoke of the distortion and the characteristics of the screaming mouth. He wrote: "The terror and the atrocious suffering make the mouth the organ of a heart-rending scream."[2]

Francis Bacon attempted to visually capture the human scream in the very moment of terror. Bacon took a very early interest in film and photography and was a passionate devotee of motion pictures. He often said that he would have become a filmmaker if he had not become involved in painting. Sergej Eisenstein's film *Battleship Potemkin* of 1928, which Bacon saw for the first time in 1935, made a lasting impression on him. He used a still photograph of the scene of the nurse dying on the Odessa steps as the basis for his portrayal of the painful, suffering face of the Pope (cat. no. 35). The still photo depicts the nurse's face in close-up. She has been shot, and her broken glasses are hanging from her nose; blood is streaming from her right eye, and her mouth is wide open. The photograph is a depiction of agonised suffering and pain. Speaking to David Sylvester, Bacon confirmed his interest in *Battleship Potemkin:* "And then I saw – or perhaps I even knew by then – the *Potemkin* film, and I attempted to use the *Potemkin* still as a basis on which I could also use these marvellous illustrations of the human mouth. It never worked out, though."[3]

Later Bacon occasionally said that he actually regretted having painted the pictures of the Pope after Velázquez and *Potemkin;* he said they were distorted, silly records[4]. However, neither the Bacon experts nor he himself later agreed with this assessment. This series contains some of the most important portrayals of the tension that the artist himself harboured. But Bacon found distorted renditions of the mouth not only in the film *Battleship Potemkin* but also in a series of medical photos taken from books and magazines. They show close-up views of a disfigured mouth and teeth, or such obscure subjects as prosthetic tongues (cat. no. 40). In response to Sylvester's question of whether he always intended the open mouth as a symbol of the scream, the artist replied: "Most of them, but not all. You know how the mouth changes shape. I've always been very moved by the movements of the mouth and the shape of the mouth and the teeth. People say that these have all sorts of sexual implications, and I was always very obsessed by the actual appearance of the mouth and teeth, and perhaps I have lost that obsession now, but it was a very strong thing at that time."[5]

The mouth became Bacon's archetype, a metaphor for pain, suffering, greed and terror. His obsession of collecting books about oral diseases was not related to any particular medical or anatomical interest. It was rather a symbol of an analysis that had a depth-psychological dimension. Here one may refer to Freud, who described the mouth as a primarily libidinal zone: "The first organ to emerge as an erotogenic zone

Plate 1: J. A. Boiffard, "Terror and suffering make the mouth the organ of ear-splitting cries" (Translation from the French). C. 1930. Published in Documents 5, 1930.

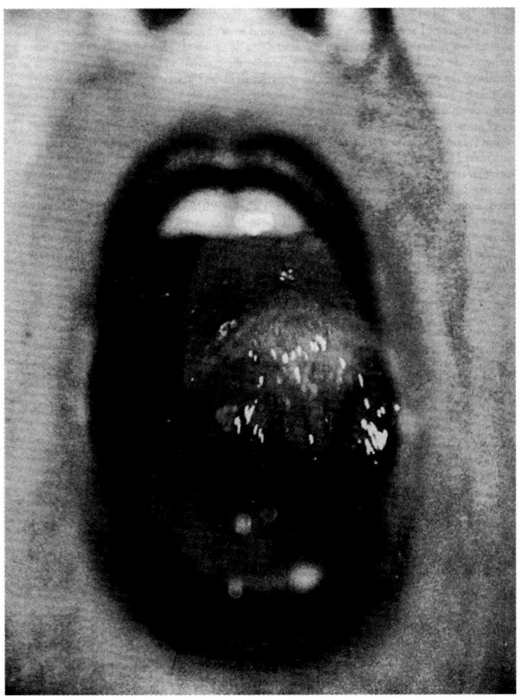

and to make libidinal demands on the mind is, from the time of birth onwards, the mouth. To begin with, all psychical activity is concentrated on providing satisfaction for the needs of that zone. [...] During this oral phase sadistic impulses already occur sporadically along with the appearance of the teeth."[6]

The open mouths are the most obvious characteristic of the series of heads and parts of heads that Bacon painted between 1948 and 1952. One of the paintings, using a still photograph from *Battleship Potemkin* as a source, is the *Study for the Head of a Screaming Pope* of 1952 (cat. no. 28). The figure is called the "Pope" but it could also be an image of a strong woman's face. As in the still photograph, the glasses are dangling in front of the left eye. The blood flowing from the right eye, down the right cheek and over the chin is depicted in Bacon's painting with smeared black and grey brushstrokes. The accentuation of the face is primarily in these shades as well in order to create a stronger contrast and to more sharply divide the two halves of the face between black and white. The Pope's mozzetta is suggested only by a number of short strokes and the lower part is seen only as a beige ground. The background depicts not the chair but rather a system of metal rods that resembles the head of a bed more than the back of a throne chair. The vertical lines of the metal framework could also be a reference to a bed in a psychiatric institution[7].

At the Hanover Gallery in November 1949, Bacon showed a series of six works entitled *Head I–VI*. The paintings, all of relatively small format (ca. 80 × 65 cm), are variations on the head theme. In *Head I* and *II* the artist concentrated on the screaming mouth and the teeth, which dominate the painting. *Head III* focuses on the eyes, glasses and mouth, while *Head IV* depicts a man seen from the rear with a monkey. In *Head V*, the most abstract painting in the series, the head and face are hardly recognisable beneath the blurred paint. *Head VI* is the first shoulder-length portrait to connect the screaming mouth of the nurse in Eisenstein's film with Velázquez's papal portrait. *Head II* (cat. no. 26) from the Ulster Museum in Belfast is the most densely painted portrait in the series; the open mouth dominates, leaving the question unanswered of whether the subject is a person or an animal. The upper part of the painting, which depicts grey curtains with a safety pin through the fabric, is painted in very thick brushstrokes, making it clear that Bacon repeatedly painted the shades of grey and black on top of one another until they gave the painting an abstract effect and made these shades the focus of attention. The open mouth that dominates the centre of the painting has been emphasised by the use of thick white paint that contrasts sharply with the black background. The white arrow, which is found again and again in Bacon's paintings to point out his visual symbolism, as well as the white teeth have been painted over so many times that these areas stand out from the surface as thick strata of paint, clearly revealing the intensity of Bacon's painterly hand. Bacon admitted to his biographer and friend David Sylvester that he worked on this painting for around four months, which for him was a very long time. The safety pin in Bacon's paintings is depicted in its actual function as a tool. When Bacon was sorting through the collection of reproductions and photos to prepare them for use as sources in his paintings, he often changed the shape and composition by folding the paper and fixing it with a safety pin. This is also an illustration of the fact that Bacon often not only used the subject of his source materials in his paintings but also their tangible character after he had prepared them (in this case, a folded piece of paper held together with a safety pin), including it in the painting. The open curtain is reminiscent of the photographs of occult trance sessions held by Baron Albert von Schrenck-Notzing (cat. no. 18).

The painting *Study for the Nurse from the Battleship Potemkin* from the Städel Museum (cat. no. 27) combines two themes that occupied Bacon during the 1950s and '60s. In this painting there is an evident blending of the screaming nurse from Eisenstein's film and a figure trapped in a cage, reminiscent of the papal portraits. Here the suffering person has been placed full-length in the cage. Blood is running from her eye, and the left lens of her glasses is about to fall out. Although the face is very clearly related to the nurse in Eisenstein's film, the body is not unambiguously feminine. It appears to be naked, wearing neither the black dress of the woman nor the papal garments found in Bacon's pictures of the Pope. The figure here is similar to a hermaphrodite, or perhaps Bacon deliberately left the sex of the subject unclear in order to focus more on the suffering being, the piteous creature.

The Portrayal of the Scream in the 20th Century

One depiction of a scream that has been important in the history of art is Nicolas Poussin's *Massacre of the Innocents* of 1630/31, which Bacon saw in Chantilly at the end of the 1920s. He said: "I think probably the best human cry in painting was made by Poussin."[8] Bacon speaks of a cry that conveys terror, although he was actually more interested in the scream itself than in the terror that triggered it.

One of the most famous portrayals of the scream in 20th-century painting is by the Scandinavian artist Edvard Munch, whose works are found in books and reproductions owned by Bacon. The Austrian artist Egon Schiele also depicts human suffering in his work at the turn of the century. The remarkable water-colour *Self-portrait with Distorted Facial Expression* of 1910 (cat. no. 32) depicts the artist with his mouth wide open, revealing a few isolated pointed teeth. In this portrait, which in the distinctive contours of the face twisted in pain and the gaunt body takes as its theme the exaggeration, excessiveness and pain of the artist, there is an obvious attempt at alienation. Bacon never explicitly named Schiele as a model for his painting, but he owned a large book with water-colours and paintings by the Austrian artist and used it to study the posture of Schiele's models (cat. no. 37). Munch, Schiele and Bacon – each in his own way – answered the question of how to make visible the invisible forces and negative energies that are at work within a person (suffering, pain, despair).

Bacon once described his interest in Picasso with the words, "At a certain time in my life I was influenced by Picasso. Perhaps 'influence' isn't quite the right word, I certainly don't think Picasso would have used it. [...] I admired Picasso greatly. For me, he was the genius of the century [...]"[9] At the same time Bacon was critical of certain works by Picasso. He repeatedly stressed that only those works by Picasso that had been influenced by Surrealism were interesting to him. These statements, however, like those about Giacometti, are full of contradictions. He found Picasso's variations on Velázquez's *Las Meninas* or *Guernica*, for example, by no means successful.

Even though Bacon apparently did not hold Picasso's *Guernica* in high esteem, there are many depictions among the preliminary studies for this painting that permit a comparison with certain works by Bacon. This suggests that Bacon was better informed about Picasso's work that would have resulted from a merely passing familiarity with his paintings. One example is found in the sketches Picasso's *Head of a Weeping Woman* of 1937 (cat. nos. 29 and 30), in which the theme of deformation is manifested in his work. The face is depicted in profile, the head inclined slightly to the rear. The mouth with its pointed tongue, rather resembling a knife or a blade, symbolises suffering and fear. In its power of representation and expression, this series of works, which took as its theme the horrors of war, is just as closely related to Bacon's screaming Popes as to his early head study *Head II* of 1949, in which the face consists mainly of a screaming mouth with pointed teeth. Both visualise human fear, the horror of death and violence. While Picasso with his Surrealistic and at the same time classicistic linear style evokes the unconscious, Bacon continued the Surrealistic beginnings that were inspired by Picasso and understood his work as "[...] a non-illustrational form [that] works first upon sensation and then slowly leaks back into the fact"[10].

[1] Schopenhauer 1996, p. 543.
[2] "La terreur et la souffrance atroce font de la bouche l'organe des cris déchirants." *Documents* 5, 1930. Reprinted by Jean-Michel Place, Paris 1991, p. 299.
[3] Sylvester 1999, p. 35.
[4] Sylvester 1999, p. 37.
[5] Sylvester 1999, pp. 48–50.
[6] Freud, 1998, p. 49–50.
[7] Exh. Cat. New Haven 1999, p. 72.
[8] Sylvester 1999, p. 34.
[9] Archimbaud 2000, p. 32.
[10] Sylvester 1999, p. 56.

Cat. no. 26
Francis Bacon
Head II
1949
Oil on canvas, 80 × 63,6 cm
Belfast, Ulster Museum, Gift of the Contemporary Art Society London, inv. no. 436

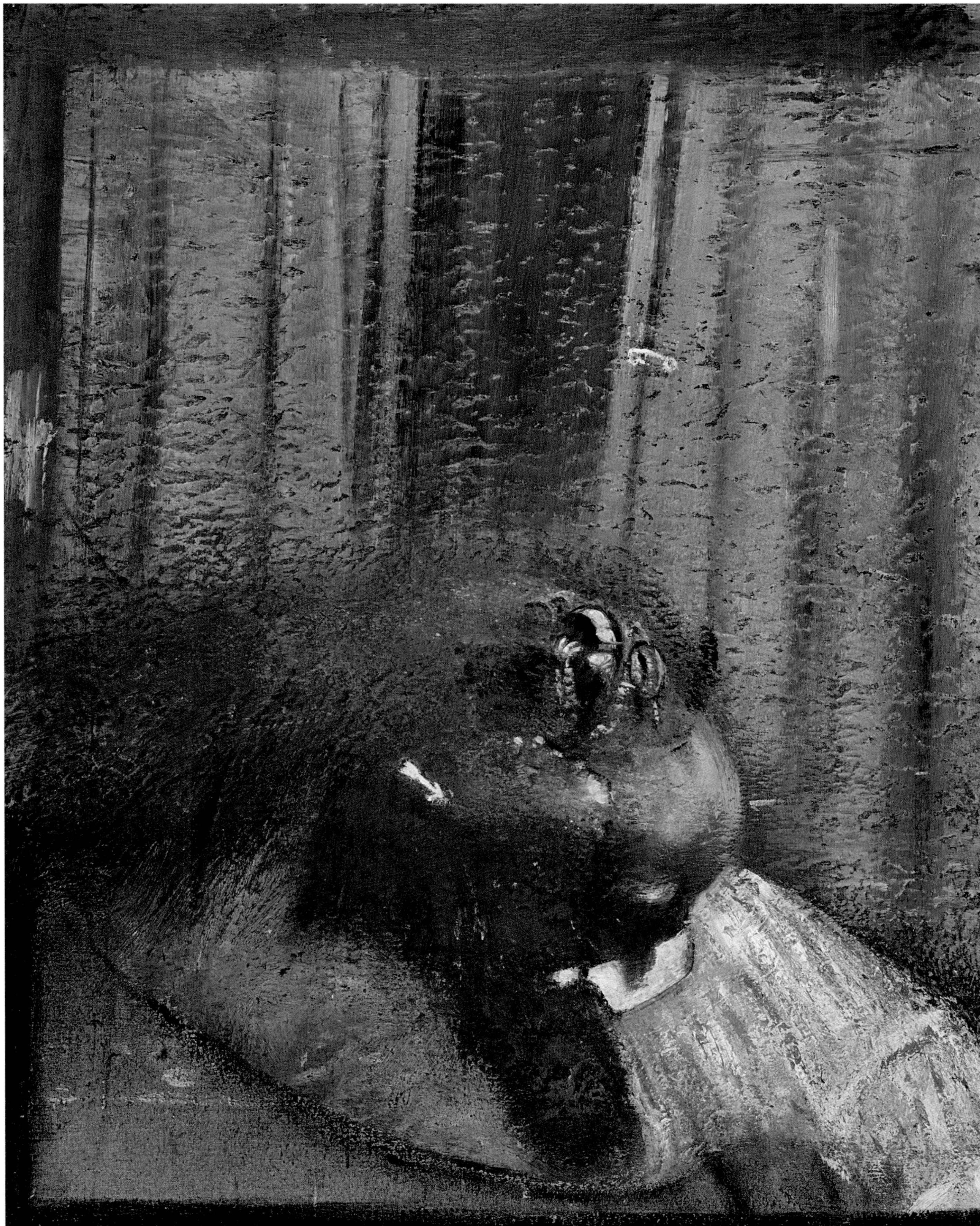

Cat. no. 26

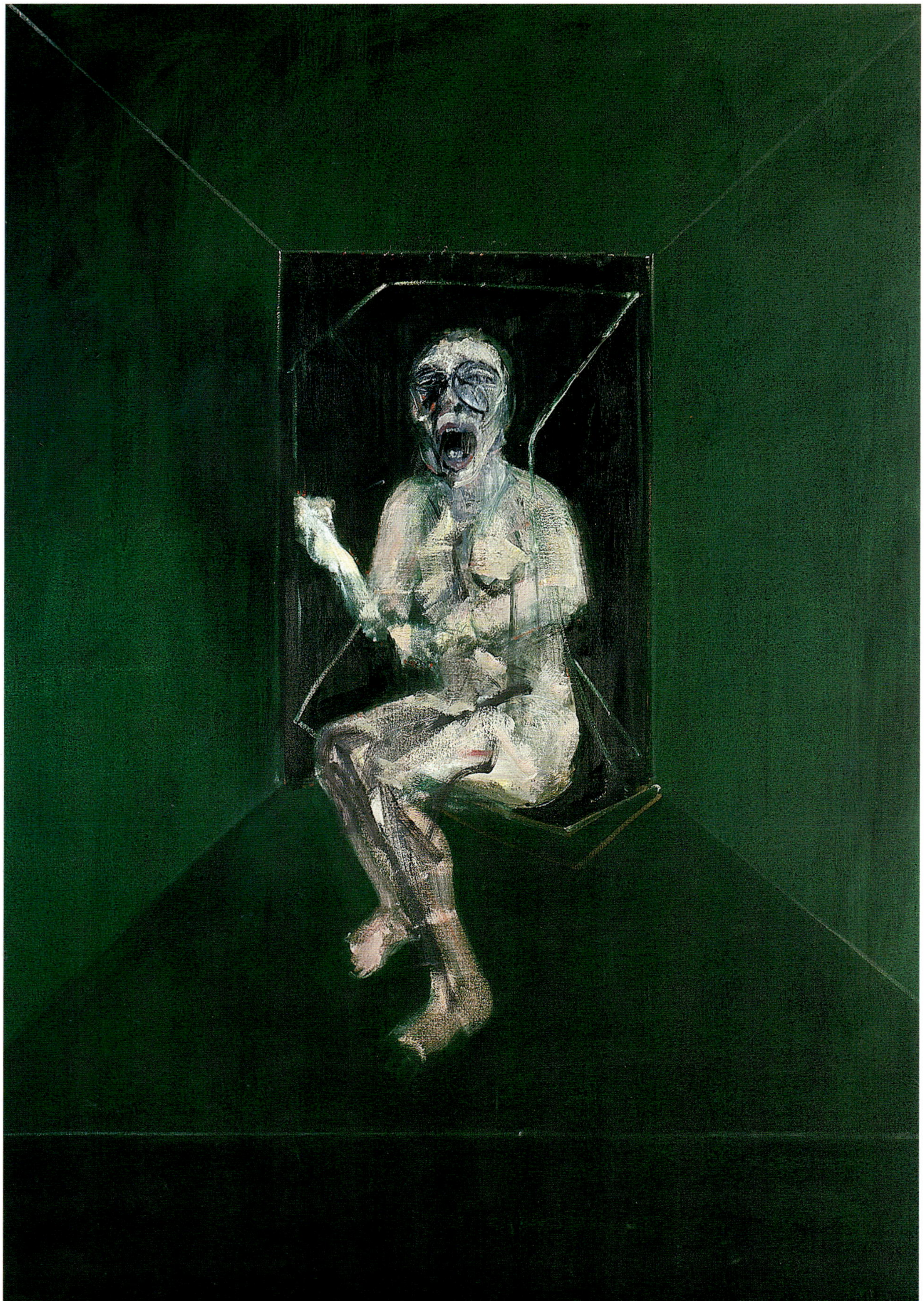

Cat. no. 27

Cat. no. 27
Francis Bacon
Study for the Nurse from
the Battleship Potemkin
1957
Oil on canvas, 198 × 142 cm
Frankfurt/Main, Städelsches
Kunstinstitut

Cat. no. 28
Francis Bacon
Study for the Head of a
Screaming Pope
1952
Oil on canvas, 49.5 × 39.3 cm
New Haven, Yale University
Art Gallery, Gift of Beekman C.
and Margaret H. Cannon

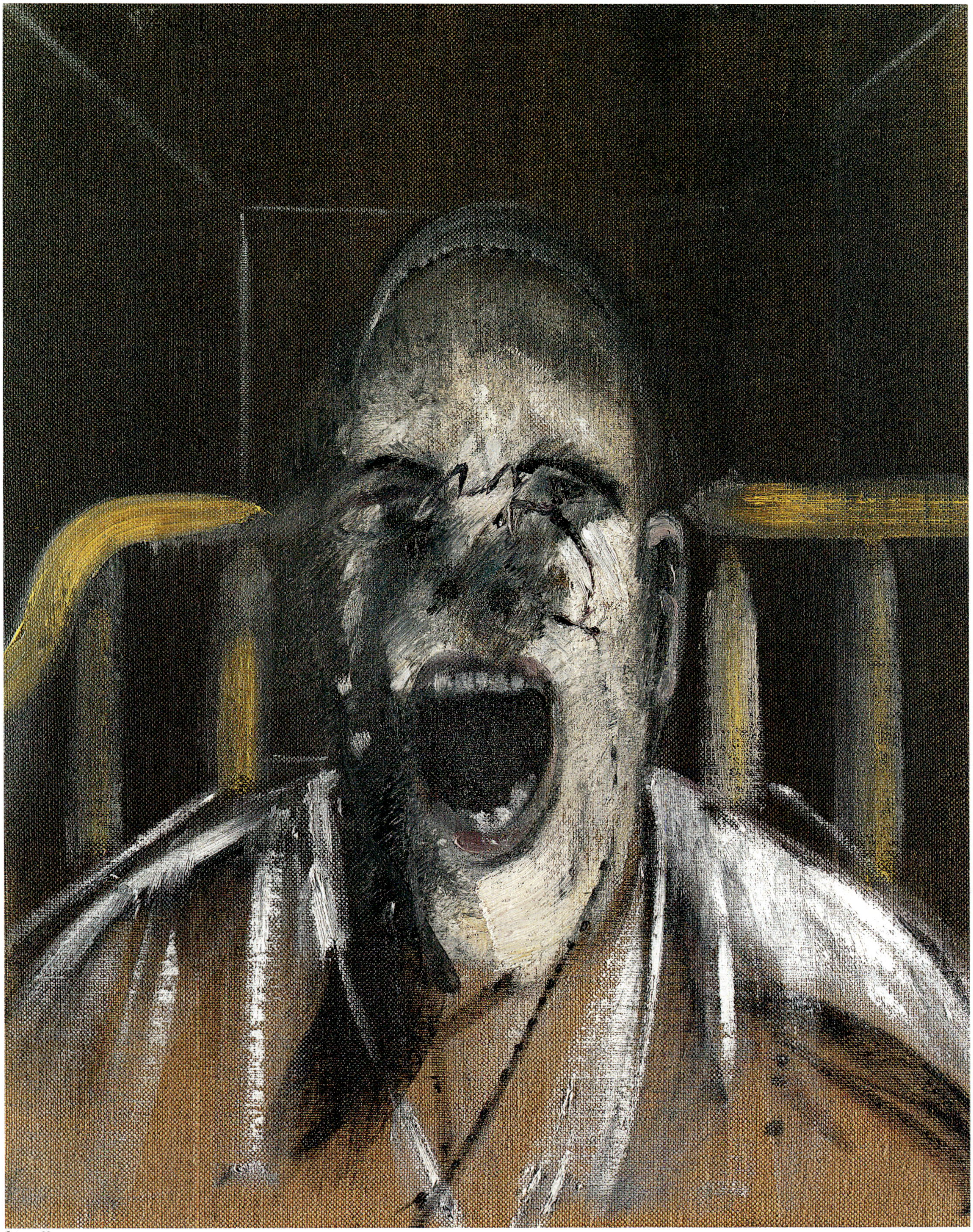

Cat. no. 28

Cat. no. 29
Pablo Picasso
Head of a Weeping Woman (I)
From the Guernica Sketchbook
1937
Pencil and gouache on paper,
292 × 231 mm
Madrid, Museo Nacional Centro de Arte Reina Sofia, inv. no. DE 00079

Cat. no. 30
Pablo Picasso
Head of a Weeping Woman (II)
From the Guernica Sketchbook
1937
Pencil and gouache on paper,
292 × 231 mm
Madrid, Museo Nacional Centro de Arte Reina Sofia, inv. no. DE 00080

Cat. no. 31
Pablo Picasso
Weeping Woman
1937
Dry point, aquatinta, etching and polished steel on copper,
692 × 495 mm, on paper:
770 × 570 mm
Riehen/Basel, Fondation Beyeler

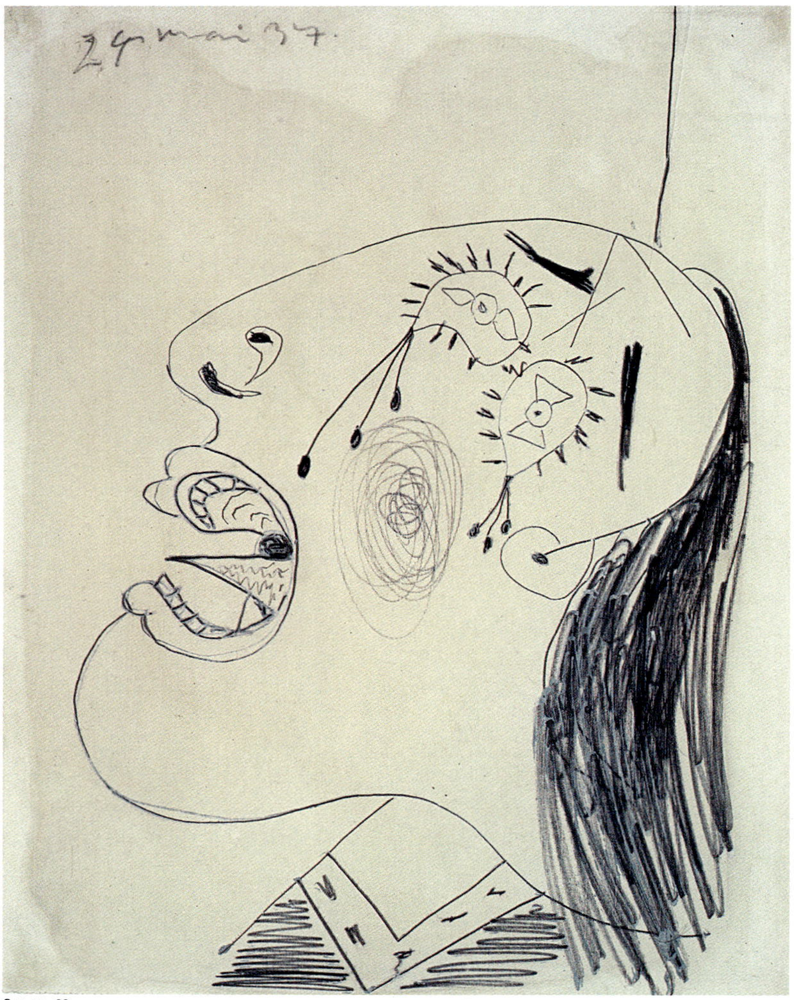

Cat. no. 29

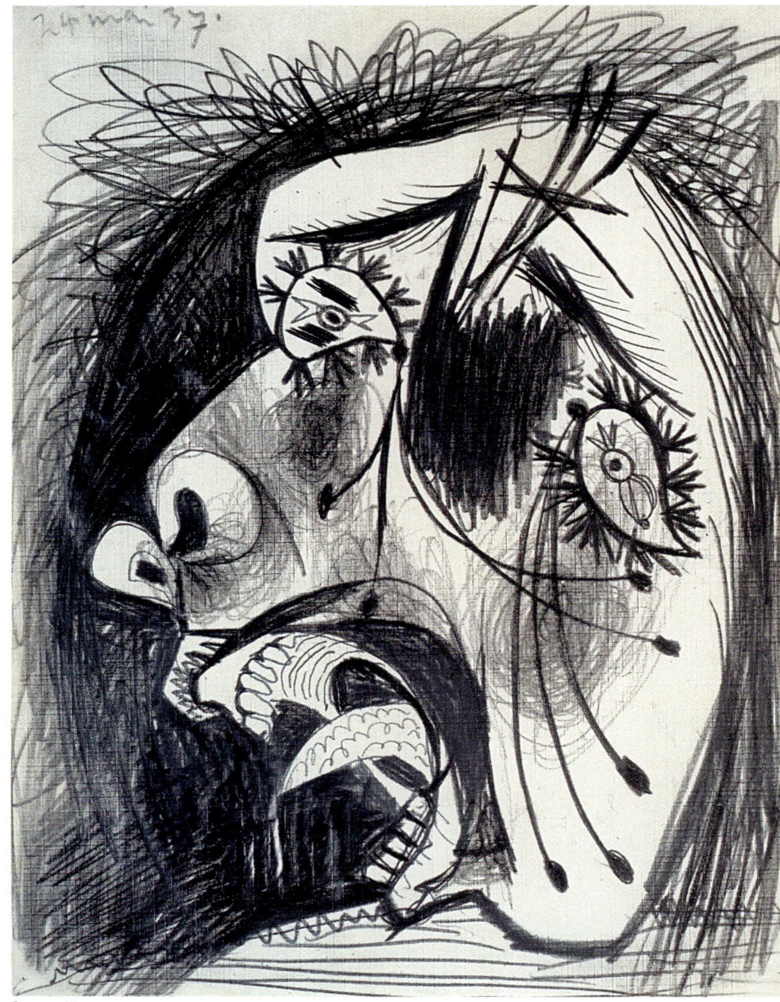

Cat. no. 30

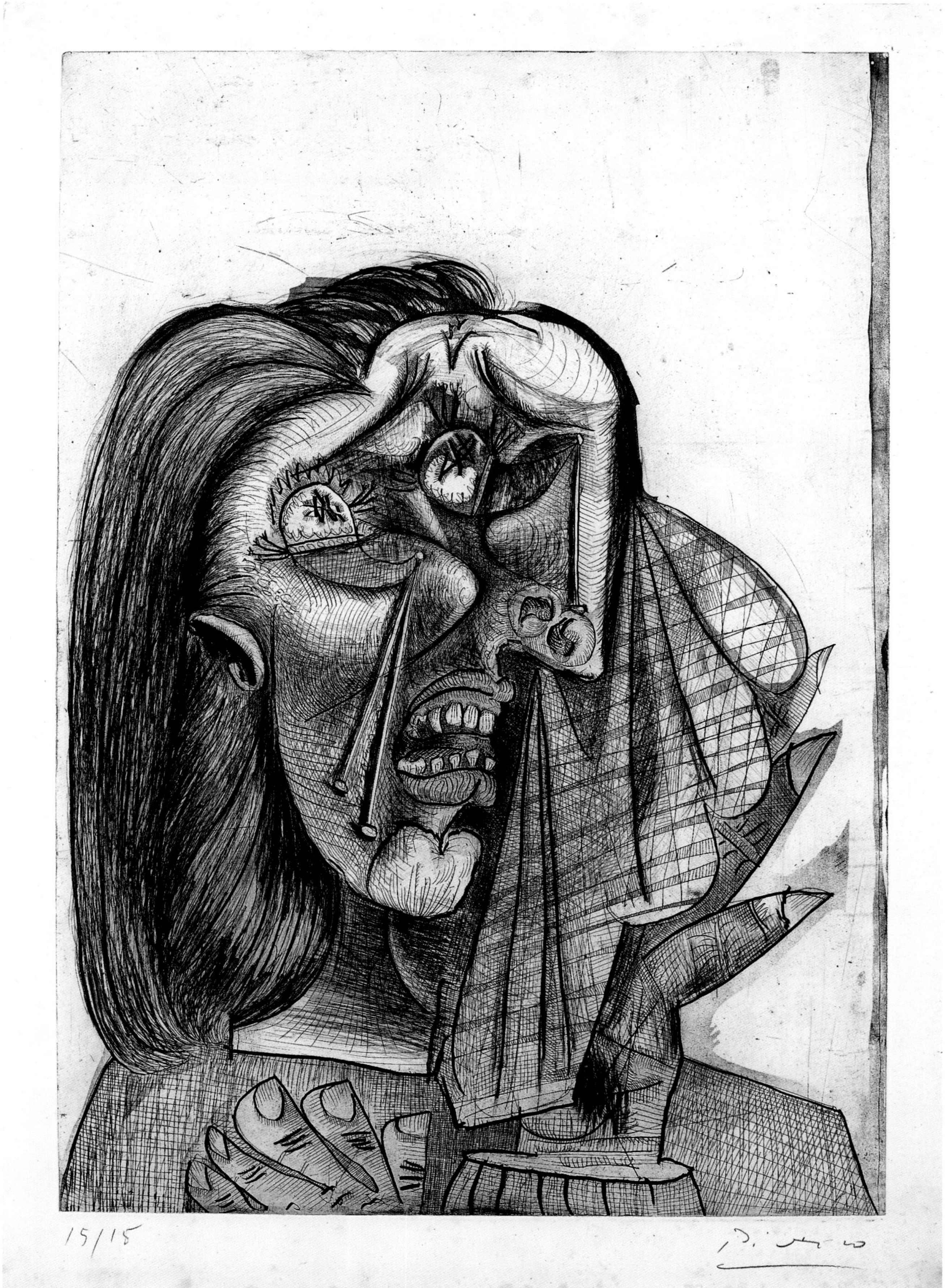

Cat. no. 31

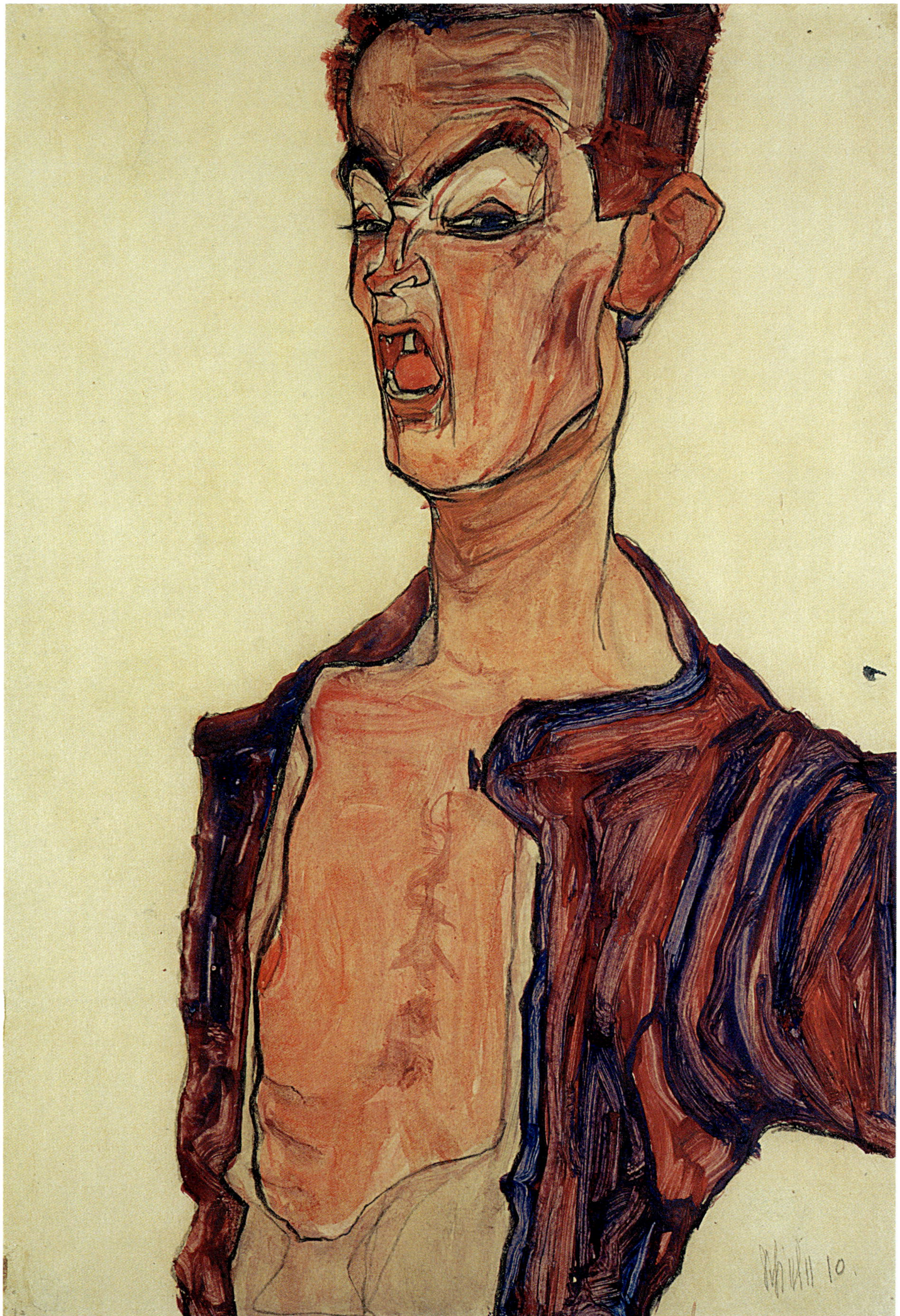

Cat. no. 32

Cat. no. 32
Egon Schiele
Self-portrait with a Distorted Expression
1910
Black chalk and poster paints on paper, 453 × 307 mm
Vienna, Leopold Museum – private donation, inv. no. 2312

Cat. no. 33
Exhibition catalogue, Egon Schiele, Fischer Fine Art Limited, London, November/December 1972.
252 × 196 × 5 mm
Dublin, Dublin City Gallery The Hugh Lane, F1:51

Cat. no. 34
Page with black-and-white illustration of The Scream, lithograph, 1895, by Edvard Munch
J. P. Hodin, Edvard Munch, London, 1972. 21.8 × 16 × 2.5 cm
Dublin, Dublin City Gallery The Hugh Lane, F93:3

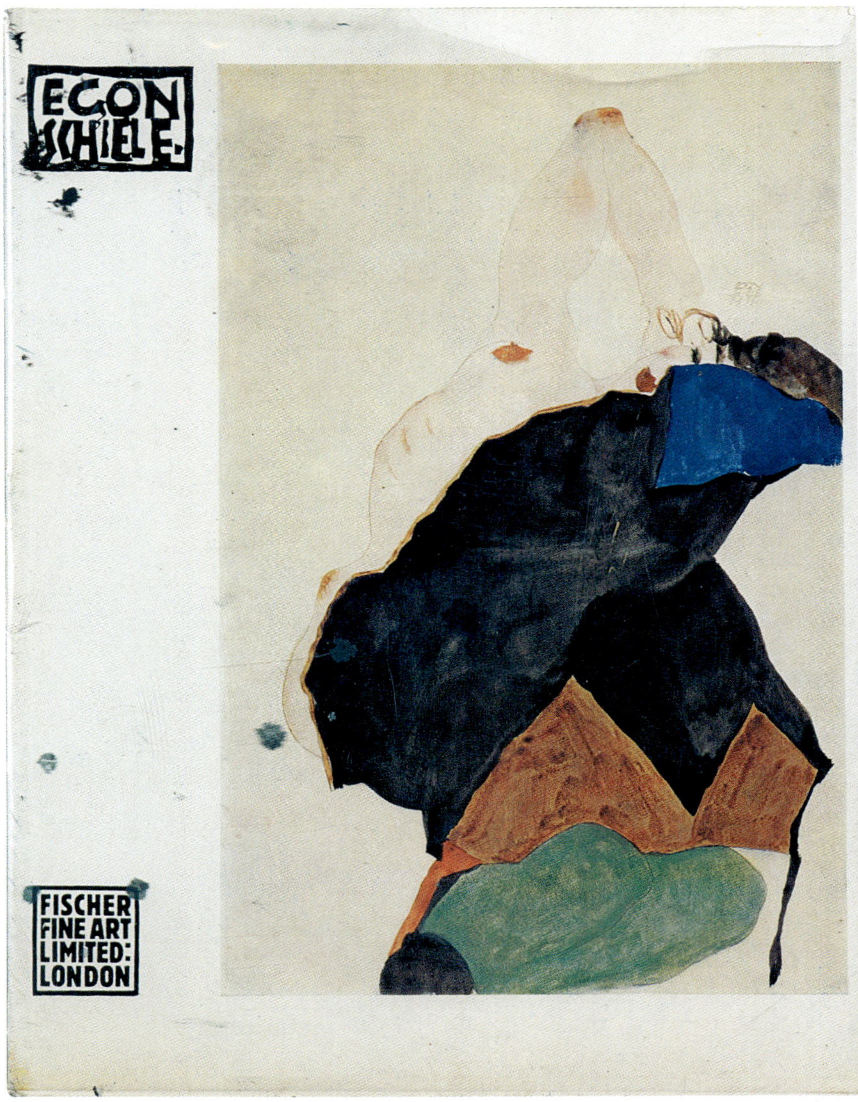

Cat. no. 33

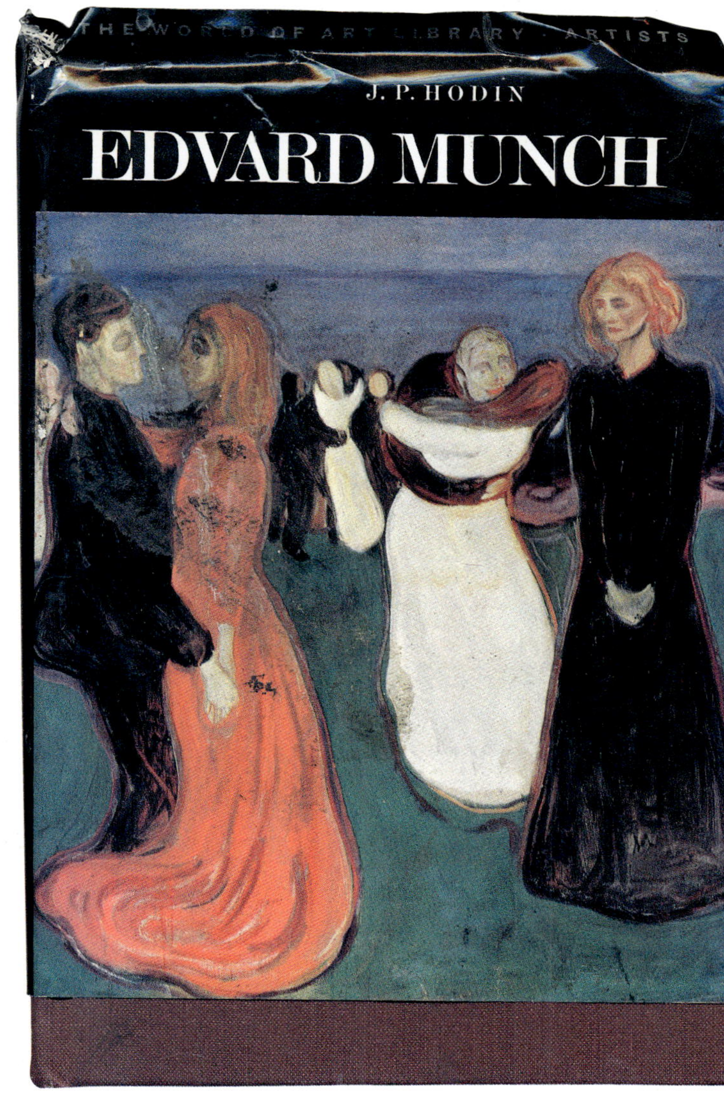

Cat. no. 34

Cat. no. 35
Film still of the nurse from the Odessa Steps sequence of Battleship Potemkin by Sergei Eisenstein.
Leaf from unidentified publication.
202 × 139 mm
Dublin, Dublin City Gallery The Hugh Lane, F105:144

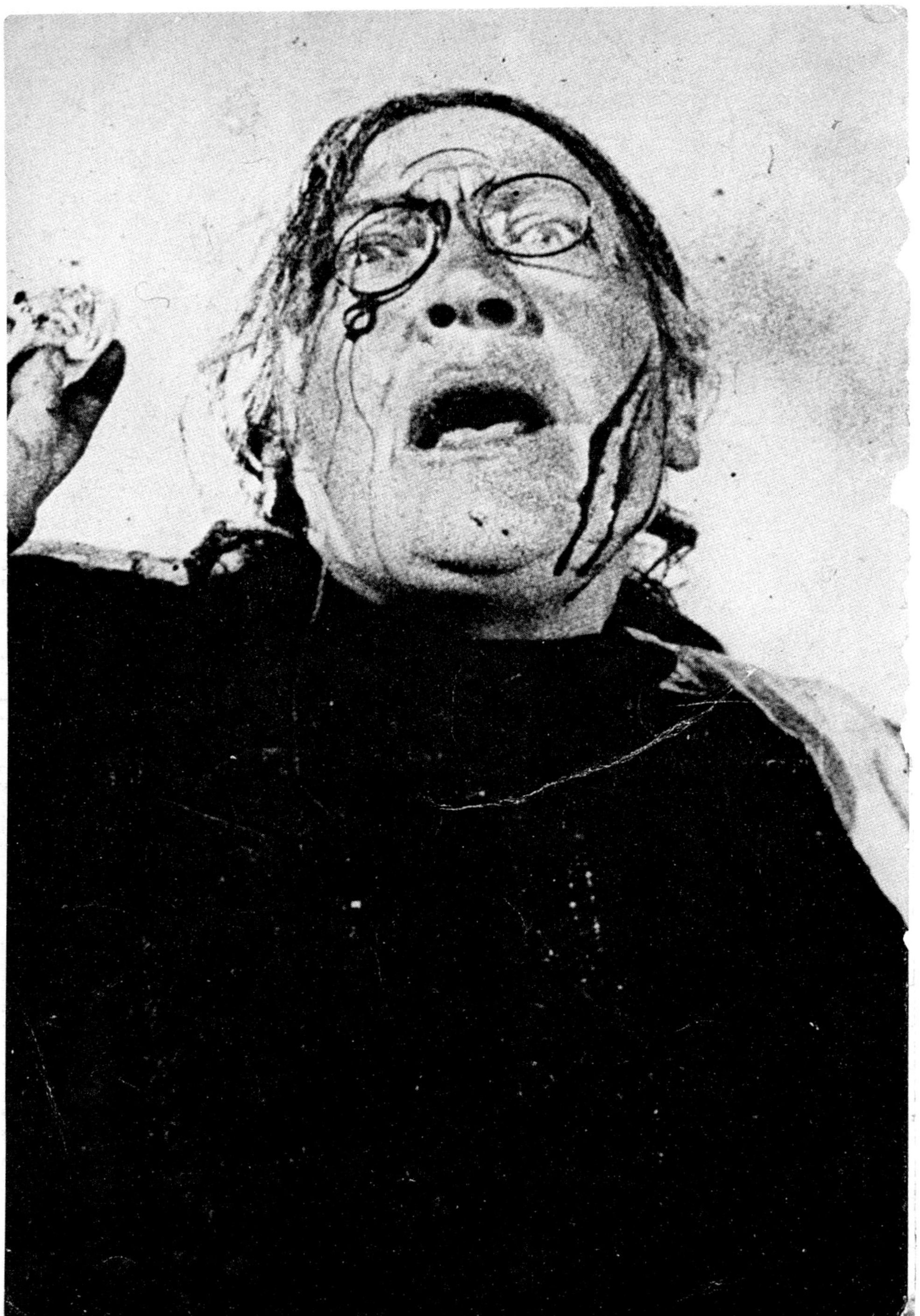

Cat. no. 35

Cat. no. 36
Standphotos aus der Szene auf der Treppe von Odessa aus dem Film Panzerkreuzer Potemkin von Sergej Eisenstein. Blatt aus einer nicht identifizierten Publikation
140 × 108 mm
Dublin, Dublin City Gallery
The Hugh Lane, F1A:39

Cat. no. 37
Standphotos (unter anderem mit der schreienden Amme) aus dem Film Panzerkreuzer Potemkin von Sergej Eisenstein. Parker Tyler, Classics of the Foreign Film: A Pictorial Treasury, London 1962
282 × 217 × 27 mm
Dublin, Dublin City Gallery
The Hugh Lane, F103:24

Cat. no. 38
Schwarz-Weiß-Illustration in Charles and Eugene Jones, The Face of War, New York 1951
270 × 202 × 20 mm
Dublin, Dublin City Gallery
The Hugh Lane, F136:14

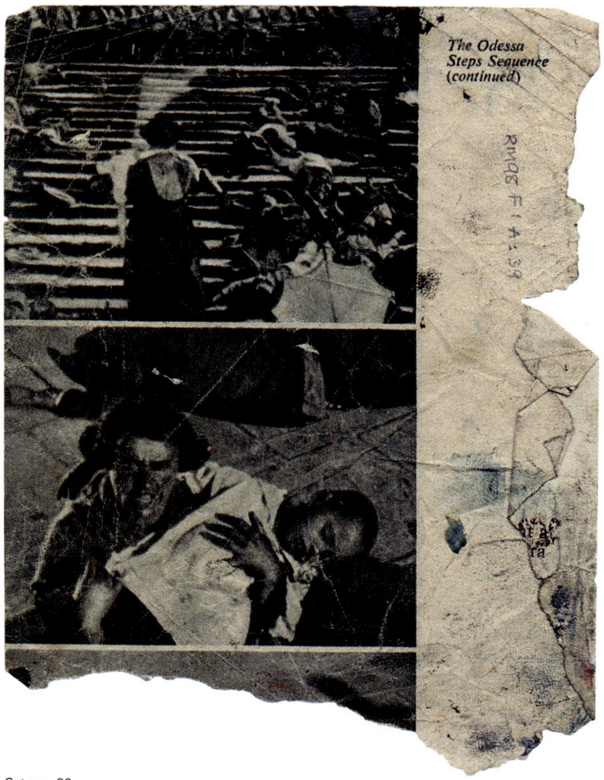

Cat. no. 36

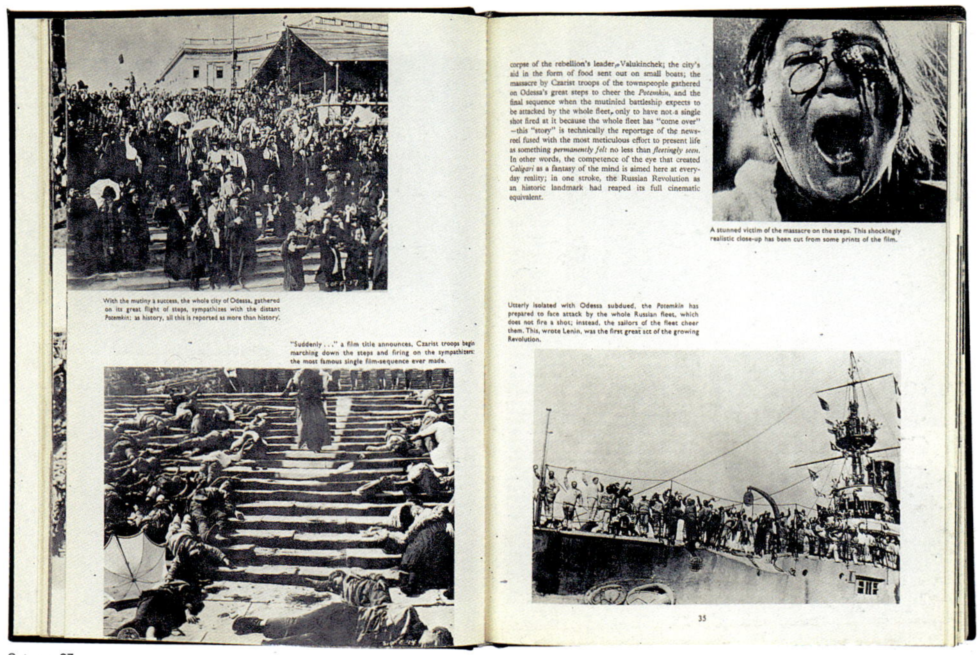
corpse of the rebellion's leader, Valukinchek; the city's aid in the form of food sent out on small boats; the massacre by Czarist troops of the townspeople gathered on Odessa's great steps to cheer the *Potemkin*, and the final sequence when the mutinied battleship expects to be attacked by the whole fleet, only to have not a single shot fired at it because the whole fleet has "come over" —this "story" is technically the reportage of the newsreel fused with the most meticulous effort to present life as something *permanently felt* no less than *fleetingly seen*. In other words, the competence of the eye that created *Caligari* as a fantasy of the mind is aimed here at everyday reality; in one stroke, the Russian Revolution as an historic landmark had reaped its full cinematic equivalent.

Cat. no. 37

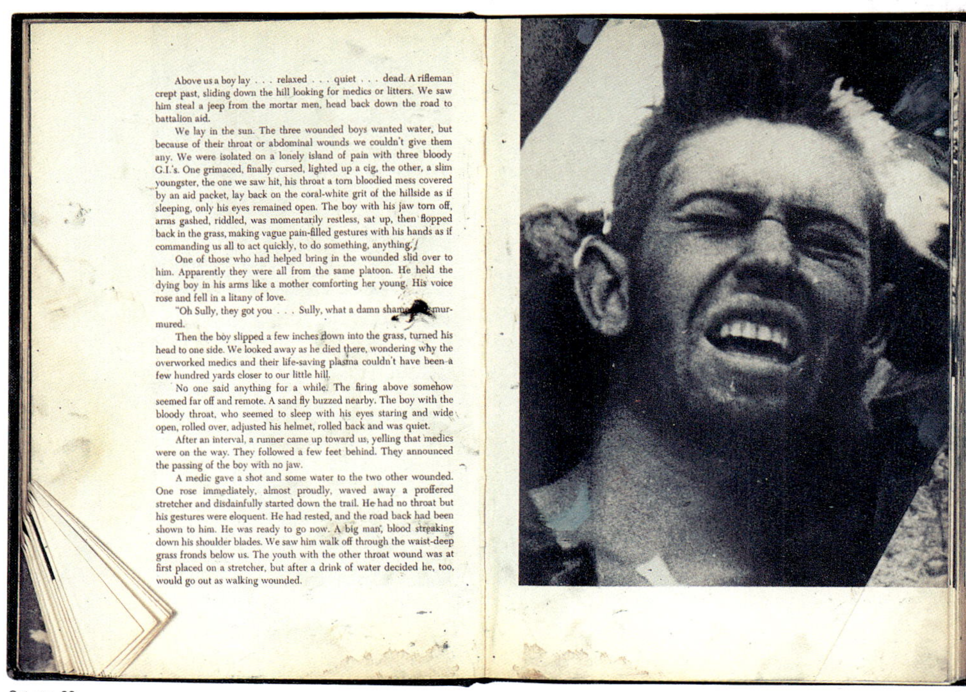
Above us a boy lay . . . relaxed . . . quiet . . . dead. A rifleman crept past, sliding down the hill looking for medics or litters. We saw him steal a jeep from the mortar men, head back down the road to battalion aid.

We lay in the sun. The three wounded boys wanted water, but because of their throat or abdominal wounds we couldn't give them any. We were isolated on a lonely island of pain with three bloody G.I.'s. One grimaced, finally cursed, lighted up a cig, the other, a slim youngster, the one we saw hit, his throat a torn bloodied mess covered by an aid packet, lay back on the coral-white grit of the hillside as if sleeping, only his eyes remained open. The boy with his jaw torn off, arms gashed, riddled, was momentarily restless, sat up, then flopped back in the grass, making vague pain-filled gestures with his hands as if commanding us all to act quickly, to do something, anything.

One of those who had helped bring in the wounded slid over to him. Apparently they were all from the same platoon. He held the dying boy in his arms like a mother comforting her young. His voice rose and fell in a litany of love.

"Oh Sully, they got you . . . Sully, what a damn sham[illegible]murmured.

Then the boy slipped a few inches down into the grass, turned his head to one side. We looked away as he died there, wondering why the overworked medics and their life-saving plasma couldn't have been a few hundred yards closer to our little hill.

No one said anything for a while. The firing above somehow seemed far off and remote. A sand fly buzzed nearby. The boy with the bloody throat, who seemed to sleep with his eyes staring and wide open, rolled over, adjusted his helmet, rolled back and was quiet.

After an interval, a runner came up toward us, yelling that medics were on the way. They followed a few feet behind. They announced the passing of the boy with no jaw.

A medic gave a shot and some water to the two other wounded. One rose immediately, almost proudly, waved away a proffered stretcher and disdainfully started down the trail. He had no throat but his gestures were eloquent. He had rested, and the road back had been shown to him. He was ready to go now. A big man, blood streaking down his shoulder blades. We saw him walk off through the waist-deep grass fronds below us. The youth with the other throat wound was at first placed on a stretcher, but after a drink of water decided he, too, would go out as walking wounded.

Cat. no. 38

Cat. no. 39
Two fragments of a leaf with coloured illustration of an open mouth held open by forceps and displaying an abscess. Publication uncertain but possibly from a book on diseases of the mouth which Bacon purchased while in Paris in the late 1920s.
110 / 92 × 75 / 30 mm
Dublin, Dublin City Gallery The Hugh Lane, F105:140

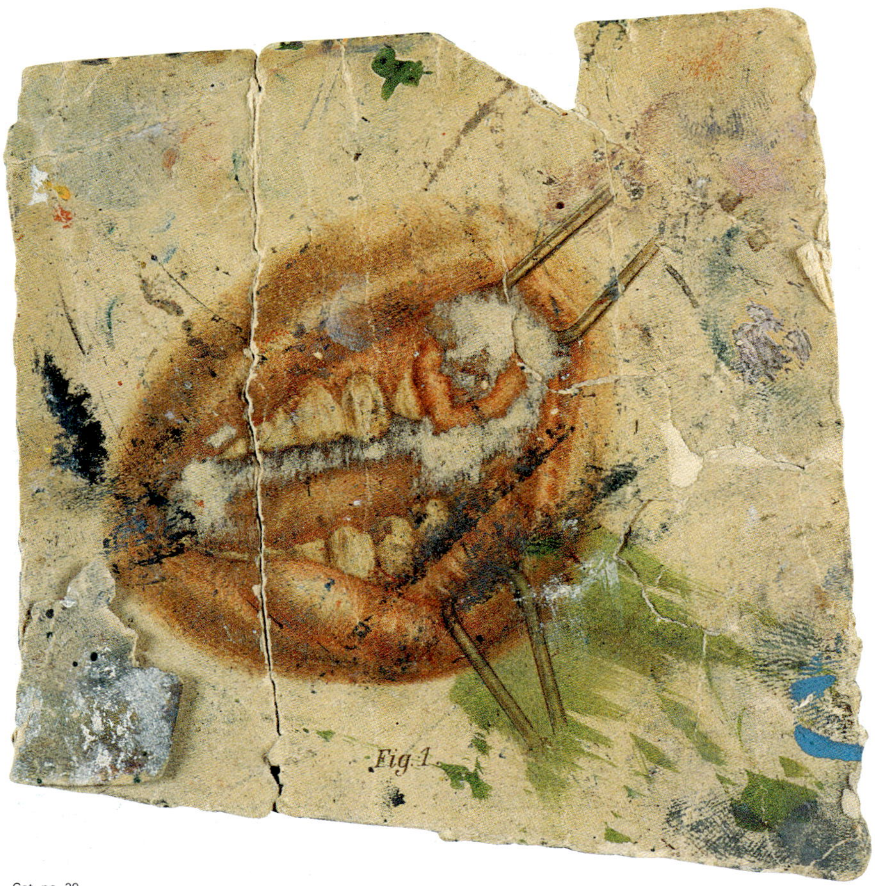

Cat. no. 39

Cat. no. 40
Colour illustration of an artificial tongue in Dernier Cri magazine, 1983 (title page and front pages missing)
301 × 235 mm
Dublin, Dublin City Gallery The Hugh Lane, F105:66

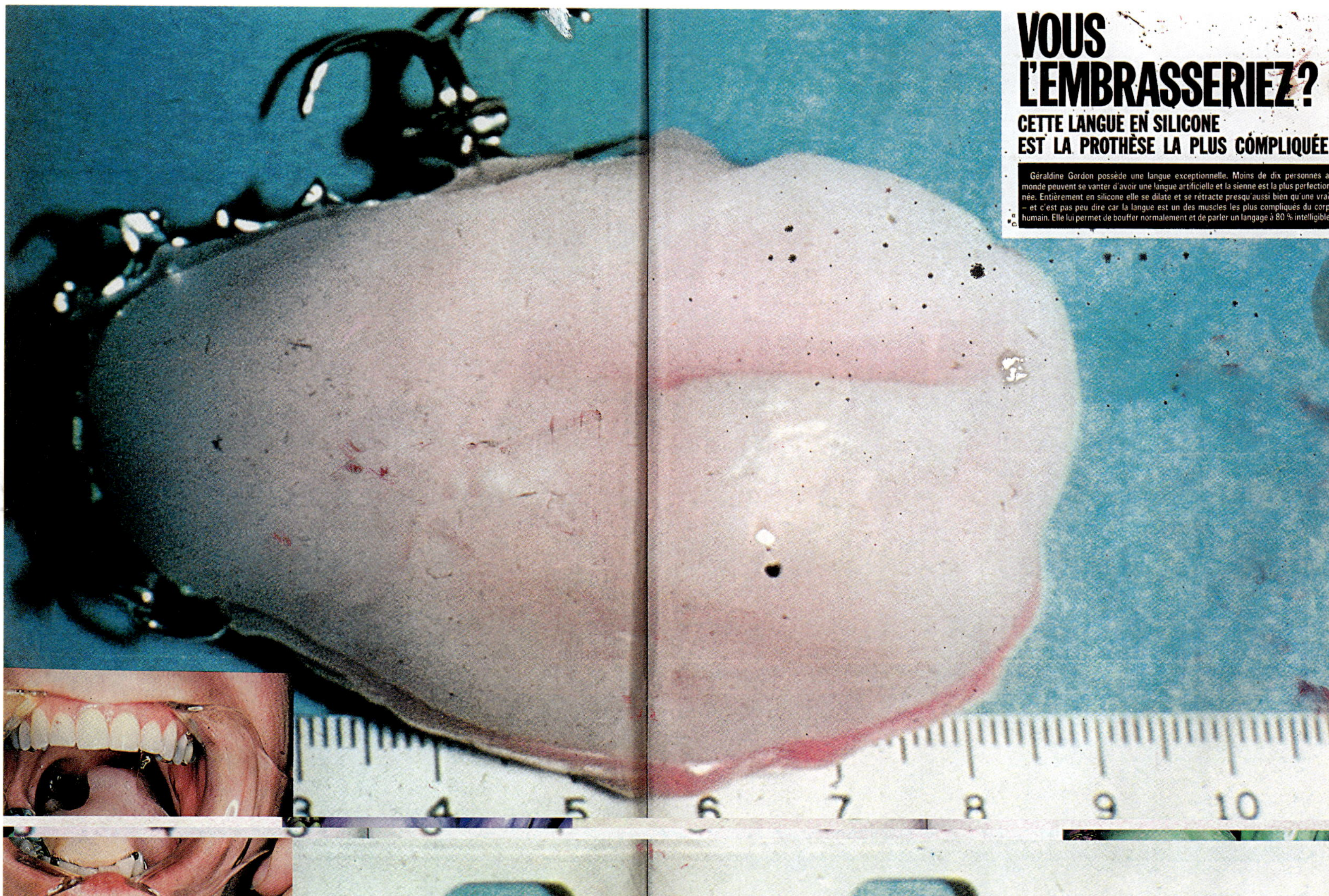

Cat. no. 40

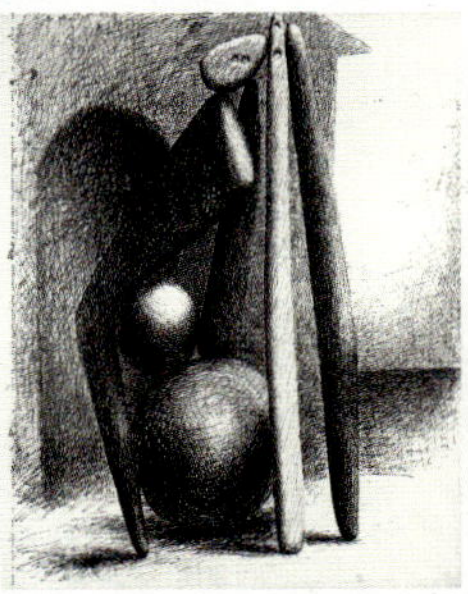

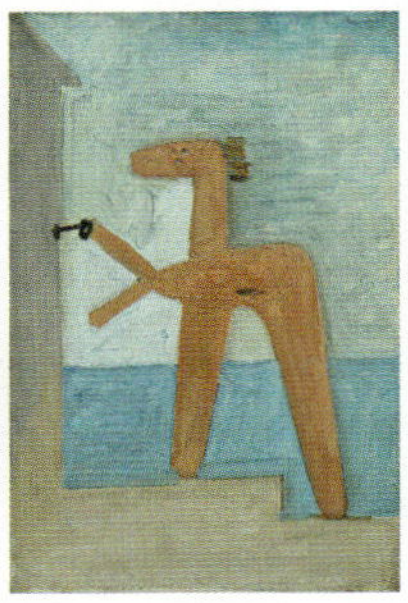

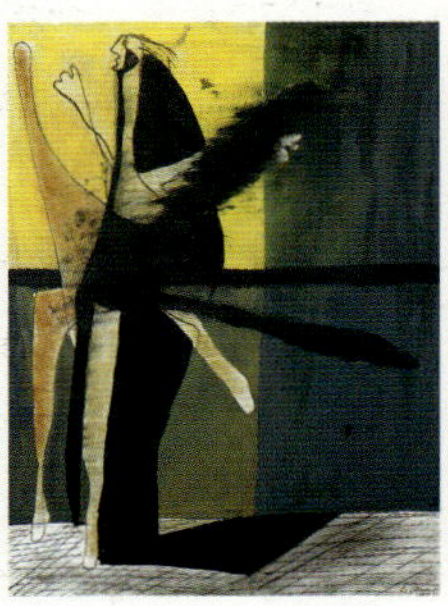

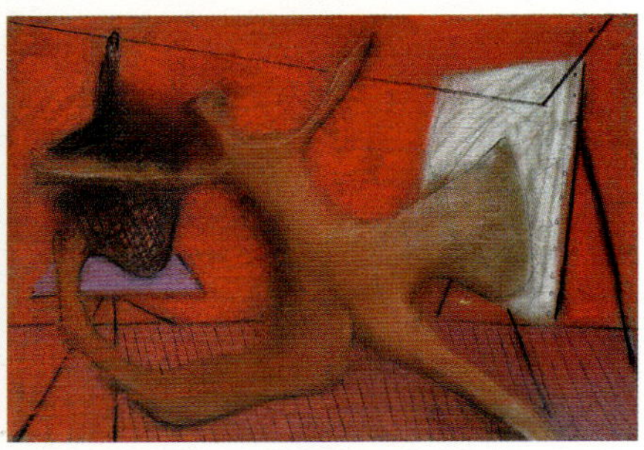

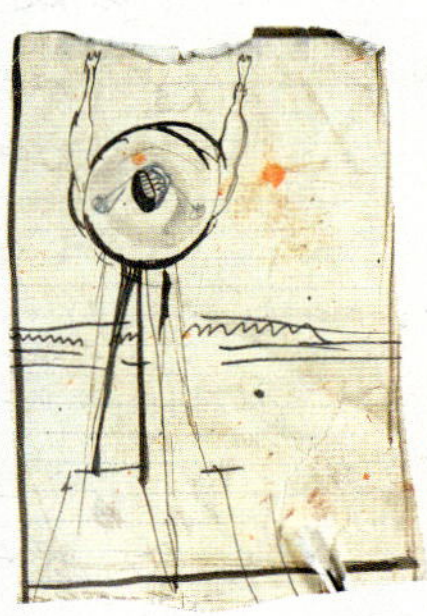

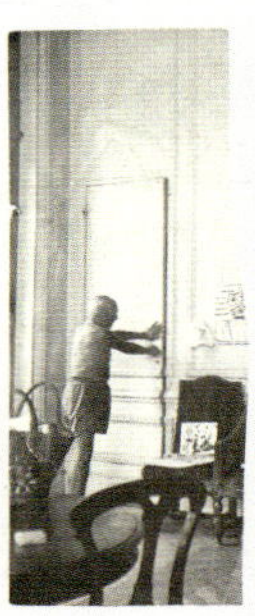

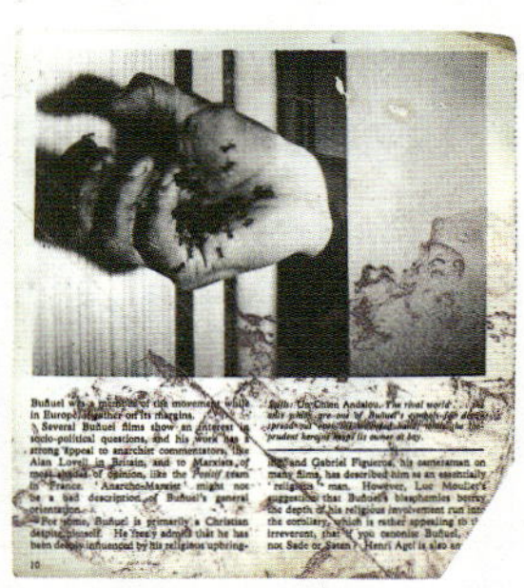

Buñuel was a member of the movement while in Europe, [illegible] on its margins.

Several Buñuel films show an interest in socio-political questions, and his work has a strong appeal to anarchist commentators, like Alan Lovell in Britain, and to Marxists of most shades of opinion, like the *Positif* team in France. 'Anarcho-Marxist' might not be a bad description of Buñuel's general orientation.

For some, Buñuel is primarily a Christian despite himself. He freely admits that he has been deeply influenced by his religious upbring-

Stills: Un Chien Andalou. *The rival world* [illegible] *prudent heroine keeps its owner at bay.*

[illegible] and Gabriel Figueroa, his cameraman on many films, has described him as an essentially 'religious' man. However, Luc Moullet's suggestion that Buñuel's blasphemies betray the depth of his religious involvement run into the corollary, which is rather appealing to the irreverent, that if you canonise Buñuel, why not Sade or Satan? Henri Agel is also an

10

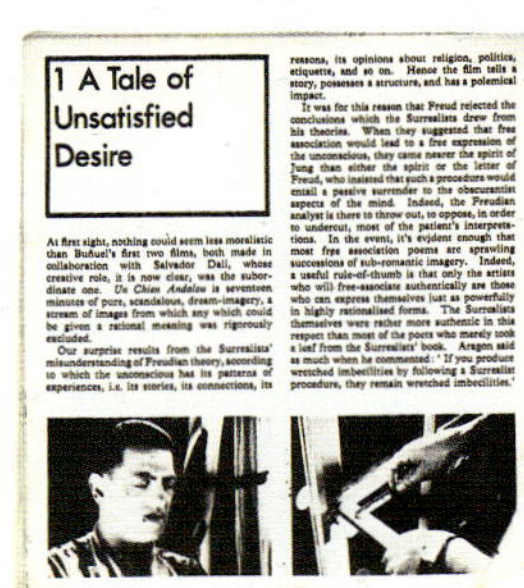

1 A Tale of Unsatisfied Desire

At first sight, nothing could seem less moralistic than Buñuel's first two films, both made in collaboration with Salvador Dali, whose creative role, it is now clear, was the subordinate one. *Un Chien Andalou* is seventeen minutes of pure, scandalous, dream-imagery, a stream of images from which any which could be given a rational meaning was rigorously excluded.

Our surprise results from the Surrealists' misunderstanding of Freudian theory, according to which the unconscious has its patterns of experiences, i.e. its stories, its connections, its reasons, its opinions about religion, politics, etiquette, and so on. Hence the film tells a story, possesses a structure, and has a polemical impact.

It was for this reason that Freud rejected the conclusions which the Surrealists drew from his theories. When they suggested that free association would lead to a free expression of the unconscious, they came nearer the spirit of Jung than either the spirit or the letter of Freud, who insisted that such a procedure would entail a passive surrender to the obscurantist aspects of the mind. Indeed, the Freudian analyst is there to throw out, to oppose, in order to undercut, most of the patient's interpretations. In the event, it's evident enough that most free association poems are sprawling successions of sub-romantic imagery. Indeed, a useful rule-of-thumb is that only the artists who will free-associate authentically are those who can express themselves just as powerfully in highly rationalised forms. The Surrealists themselves were rather more authentic in this respect than most of the poets who merely took a leaf from the Surrealists' book. Aragon said as much when he commented: 'If you produce wretched imbecilities by following a Surrealist procedure, they remain wretched imbecilities.'

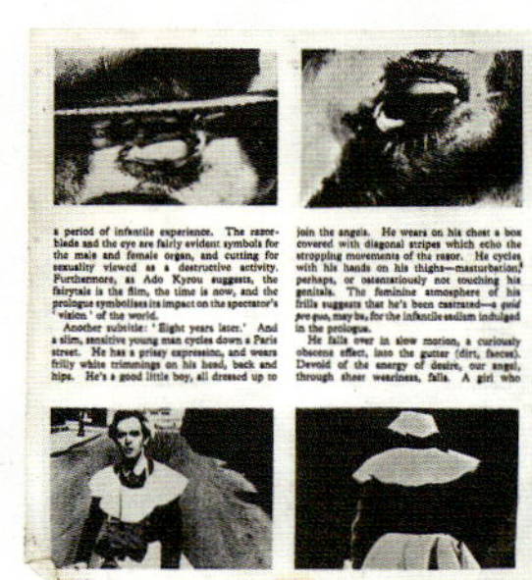

a period of infantile experience. The razor-blade and the eye are fairly evident symbols for the male and female organ, and cutting for sexuality viewed as a destructive activity. Furthermore, as Ado Kyrou suggests, the fairytale is the film, the time is now, and the prologue symbolises its impact on the spectator's 'vision' of the world.

Another subtitle: 'Eight years later.' And a slim, sensitive young man cycles down a Paris street. He has a prissy expression, and wears frilly white trimmings on his head, back and hips. He's a good little boy, all dressed up to join the angels. He wears on his chest a box covered with diagonal stripes which echo the stropping movements of the razor. He cycles with his hands on his thighs—masturbation, perhaps, or ostentatiously not touching his genitals. The feminine atmosphere of his frills suggests that he's been castrated—a *quid pro quo*, may be, for the infantile sadism indulged in the prologue.

He falls over in slow motion, a curiously obscene effect, into the gutter (dirt, faeces). Devoid of the energy of desire, our angel, through sheer weariness, falls. A girl who

Olivier Berggruen

Bacon, Picasso and Surrealism[1]

Picasso, although never officially part of the Surrealist movement, was heralded by both Bataille's magazine *Documents* and Breton's *Minotaure* as a forerunner to their ideas. Surrealism's emphasis on automatism, sexuality and the unconscious opened the door for Picasso to integrate the formal developments of Cubism within the terms of the body and the structuring of the self. The innovations that arose from Picasso's Surrealist works not only bolstered a whole artistic generation, but encouraged Francis Bacon to engage the workings of Surrealism in his thinking and imagery.

The series which most impressed Bacon is the set of Picasso's drawings and paintings created in Cannes and Dinard during the summers of 1927 and 1928. In these works, Picasso plays around notions of identity by showing that different parts of the body are interchangeable. In this sense, portrait painting does no longer seem to be removed from still-life painting. Picasso used the theme of bathers to elaborate his language of forms. If through the use of formal alliteration in Cubism, Picasso was able to equate and juxtapose parts of the body with elements of still life, in the Dinard drawings the bodies of the bathers become the site of transformation and fragmentation of the physical and psychological body.

In Picasso's 1928 painting *Bather Opening a Cabin* (cat. no. 45), the yellow form of a female body is framed by a spare horizon of sea and sky while holding a key opening a nearby cabin. The theme of the cabana – the symbol of the omnipresent darkness of death, while the outside space stands for the forces of life – has been elaborately commented upon.[2] The figure draws on the biomorphic forms elaborated by Picasso in drawings from the previous summer in Cannes. In these drawings, the basic contour of the female figure becomes a type of cartouche for the signs for the mouth, eyes, breasts, anus, and male and female sex, which become interchangeable in each of the body's permutations to create a corporeal language of sexual indeterminacy. Like the Cannes drawings, the body of the *Bather Opening a Cabin* is simplified into a soft, minimal form whose neck, arms and legs radiate from the oblong core of the body. With the reduction of the body's vocabulary, however, a new series of terms emerges. What would appear to be the navel of the figure also doubles as her sex, her neck is elongated into a phallic form, and her arms, which branch out from a breast-like protrusion in the centre of her body, could also be read as legs. To confuse matters further, the key brandished by the bather is obviously a phallic image. In an interview with Jean Clair, Bacon remarked on the influence *Bather Opening a Cabin* had for him, which can be read not only within the general terms of his own language of the body, but even more specifically within *Painting 1978 (Plate 1)* in which the body of a man whose foot holds a key is rotated horizontally and reaches across the space of a room to open a door. A picture from a catalogue in Bacon's London studio bears witness to an additional association between the figure of the bather and the image of Picasso himself (cat. no. 46). In the photograph, Picasso is in the process of opening a door, his arms directly mirroring the shape of those of the bather.

In another image, this time from Picasso's Dinard sketchbooks, the figure of a bather before a cabin takes on a new and more sculptural form (cat. no. 43). Conceived as preparatory sketches for a public sculpture project along the beach, the bathers in these images become more solid and stone-like in appearance, ossified descendants of the soft corporeal envelopes of the *Bather Opening a Cabin*. Here, Picasso's play with the multiple significations of the forms of the body breaks apart from a single contour into a number of different elements, at once cutting up and multiplying the body and its possibilities of meaning.

The breaking, cutting and cropping of the body was a matter of primary importance for the Surrealists both in terms of psychology and of fetishising sexuality. For Picasso and other artists working within a Surrealist mode, if the boundaries of the body were to be transgressed, the sanctity of the unitary self was no longer viable either.

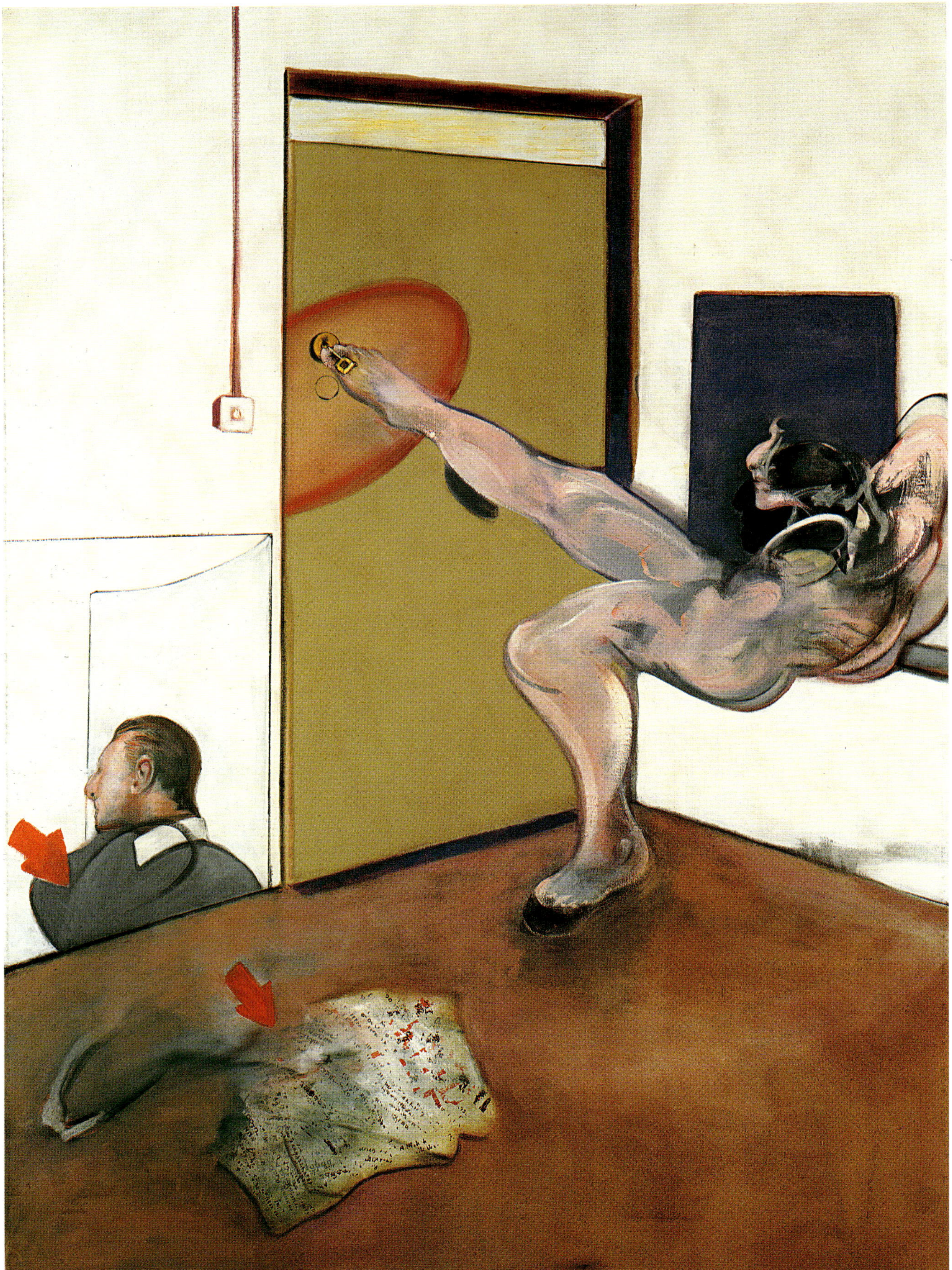

Plate 1: Francis Bacon, Painting 1978.
Oil on canvas, 198 × 147.5 cm.
Monaco, Private Collection.
(©: The Estate of Francis Bacon, VBK, Vienna, 2003, Photo: Marlborough Fine Art, London.)

Picasso's stretching of the body's outlines in the Cannes drawings and multiplication of associations between parts of the body in *Bather Opening a Cabin* stretch these limits until they break in this drawing from the Dinard sketchbook and in his later *Crucifixion* and *Anatomy* drawings published in *Minotaure* in 1933.[3] The body constructed from rounded geometrical shapes in the Dinard drawing suggests the transgression of the boundaries of the ego from a unified form into one which borders on dispersal and loss of subjectivity. Once again, each body part has the capability of representing another. The angled arm resembles a leg, the two spheres and post at the further side of the figure create a phallic form which is in turn echoed in the two upright posts which form the outline of a woman's sex.

That Bacon recognised the challenge of Picasso's art during the 1930s is apparent in his biomorphic drawing which could be interpreted as a bather (cat. no. 41). Even at first glance, the spare landscape described only by the four lines denoting the beach's horizon call to mind Picasso's own use of the austere beach setting to shift attention to the drama taking place within the body itself. Bacon's "bather" boasts small arms dangling in the air – an uncanny and emphatic upward gesture above the legs, which are strangely evocative of a tripod or an easel. Planted on an ill-defined shape resembling both a beach towel and a pedestal, the legs seem to transform the sculptural quality of Picasso's Dinard drawing into a reference to the idea of a sculpture itself. Framing the mouth of the „bather" squarely in the centre of the concentric circle of the head and body, Bacon creates a target with teeth at its focal point. The double image of the toothy mouth and the vagina dentata is a trope commonly used by Picasso and other artists of the Surrealist circle to denote the equivalence between various regions of the body, shifting the violently sexual image to the surface of the face. Of particular relevance to Bacon was the infamous scene from Dali and Bunuel's *Un Chien andalou* (cat. nos. 47–49) in which a razor blade cuts across the surface of an eye, a reference to the act of sex as well as that of castration through blinding. Indeed, Bacon's appreciation of Bunuel's films led him to keep a book on the director in his studio (cat. nos. 47–49). Adding to the aggression inherent in the image of the mouth as a vagina, Bacon's fixation on teeth endured throughout the period of his first studies for figures at the base of the Crucifixion to the excruciating screams of the papal portraits.

In Bacon's *Composition (Figure)* of 1933 (cat. no. 42), the relevance of Picasso's work to the younger artist is once more manifest. The figure appears to be a direct reference to Picasso's 1925 painting *The Dance (Plate 2),* in which three female bodies dance within the frame of two windows, casting shadows which seem to be just as solid as their own bodies. Anticipating Picasso's self-portraits as Harlequin of the late 1920s one of the dancer's shadows doubles as the profile of a man at the right edge of the picture. Just as he extended the form of the body beyond a single contour in the Dinard drawings, here the shadow performs the function of splitting the body into two personalities. Bacon takes up the strategy of division and multiplication of the body through light and shade in *Composition (Figure).* Against the outlined form of the figure, the limbs are multiplied by the black, slightly smudged form superimposed on her yellow body. This layer of black creates a shadow that simultaneously obscures and extends the body, taking on the weight of a figure in itself. One arm of the black figure resists the confines of line, disrupting the body's boundaries and partially disappearing into the obscure region to the right side of the picture. Michel Leiris observed with regard to shadow in Bacon's later paintings, "[...] a shadow taking the eminently material form of a pool or blot that seems to have been secreted by the figure, which thereby acquires greater weight; a reflection, like an appendage or a double with the same density as the original, so that the latter's reality is confirmed by repetition; the omission of part of the body under consideration or, conversely, its emphasizing through some addition."[4]

In *Composition (Figure),* Bacon can be seen using shadows as an extension and multiplication of the body. This procedure permeates the ego as well. Just as Freud

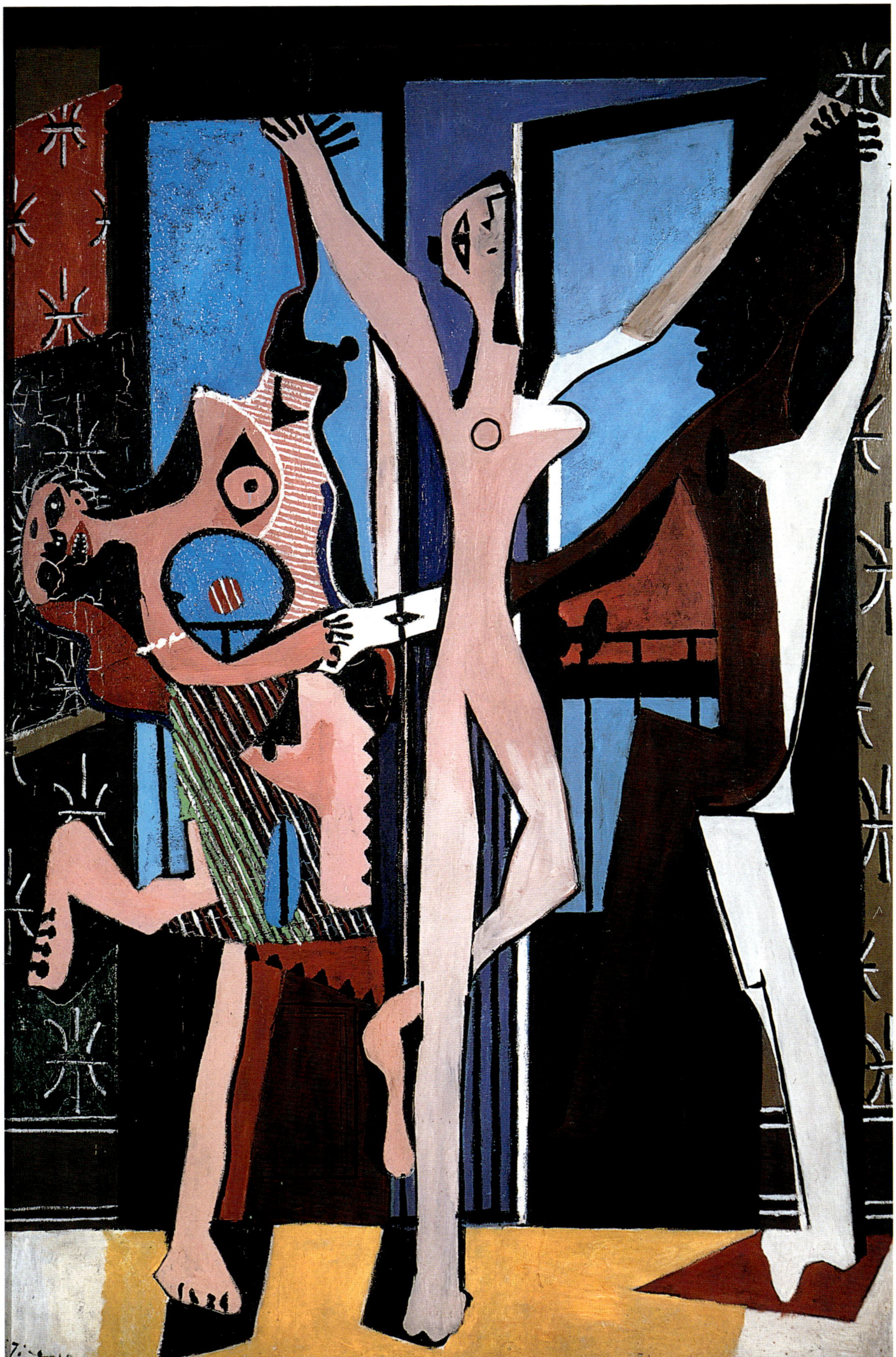

Plate 2: Pablo Picasso, The Dance, 1925. Oil on canvas, 215.3 × 142.2 cm. London, Tate Gallery. (©: Succession Picasso/VBK, Vienna, 2003.)

described the cleavage and deformation of the ego as a defence mechanism in order to avoid rupture, Bacon uses shadow to expand the body while clinging to its singular form.

A shadowy form recurs in Bacon's 1934 pastel *Studio Interior* (cat. no. 44) in the cross-hatched biomorphic shape sitting on a pedestal opposite a glaringly white canvas. Sprawled between the canvas and the pedestal, a figure, the same bright magenta as the studio's interior, connects the gap between the two objects. If Picasso used the theme of the studio to examine the interplay between artist, model and the artwork, Bacon's studio appears puzzling at first glance. A dark line – is it perhaps a cage? – reaches from the upper left side of the page to the surface of the white canvas to a space outside the frame of the image. It would seem that in this gesture, the confines of the cage which appear in Bacon's later work now open onto the space of the viewer, drawing him into the scene. Between the fairly solid form of the black shape and the representational space of the white canvas, the magenta figure blurs into the objects of the studio, only vaguely hanging on to its own boundaries. It is not the mere duplication of a biomorphic shape. This view into the studio acts as a window onto Bacon's own interiority where form, figure, representation and self all threaten to dissolve into the pink space of the room.

[1]I would like to acknowledge the assistance of Nicole Root in the research and drafting of this essay.

[2]See Gasman 1981, chapter V.

[3]*Minotaure – Revue artistique et littéraire,* Paris 1933, no. 1. This special issue included a whole section devoted to Picasso with an article by André Breton and some photographs of sculptures by Brassai.

[4]Leiris 1983, p. 35.

Cat. no. 41
Biomorphic drawing by Francis Bacon. 1930s. Black and blue ink on lined paper. 167 × 121 mm
Dublin, Dublin City Gallery The Hugh Lane, F1:37

Cat. no. 42
Francis Bacon
Composition (Figure)
1933
Gouache, pastel, pen and ink on paper, 535 × 400 mm
Vaduz, Marlborough International Fine Art

Cat. no. 43
Pablo Picasso
Carnet Dinard, page 4
1928
Ink and pencil on paper, 380 × 310 mm
New York, Private Collection

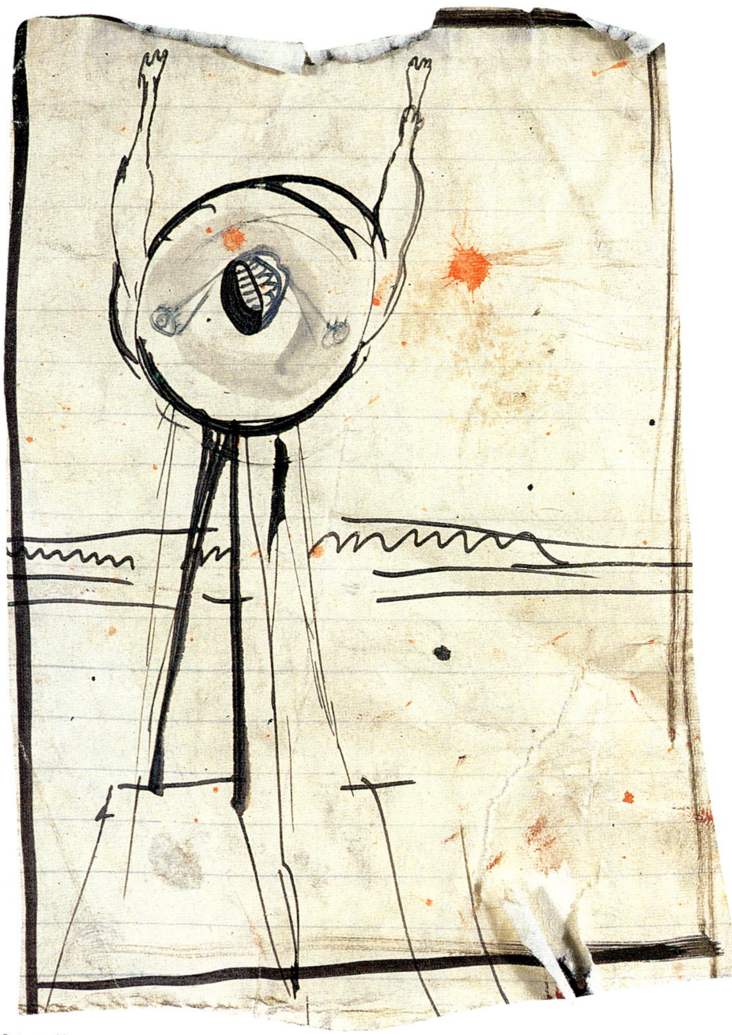

Cat. no. 41

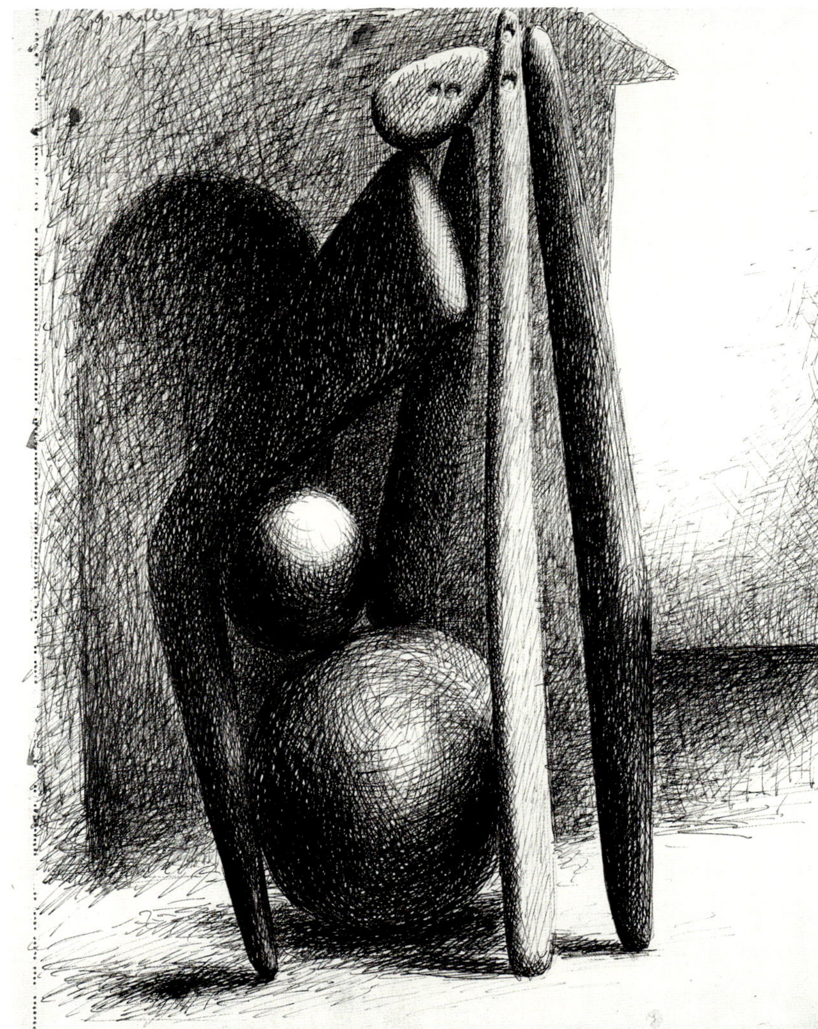

Cat. no. 43

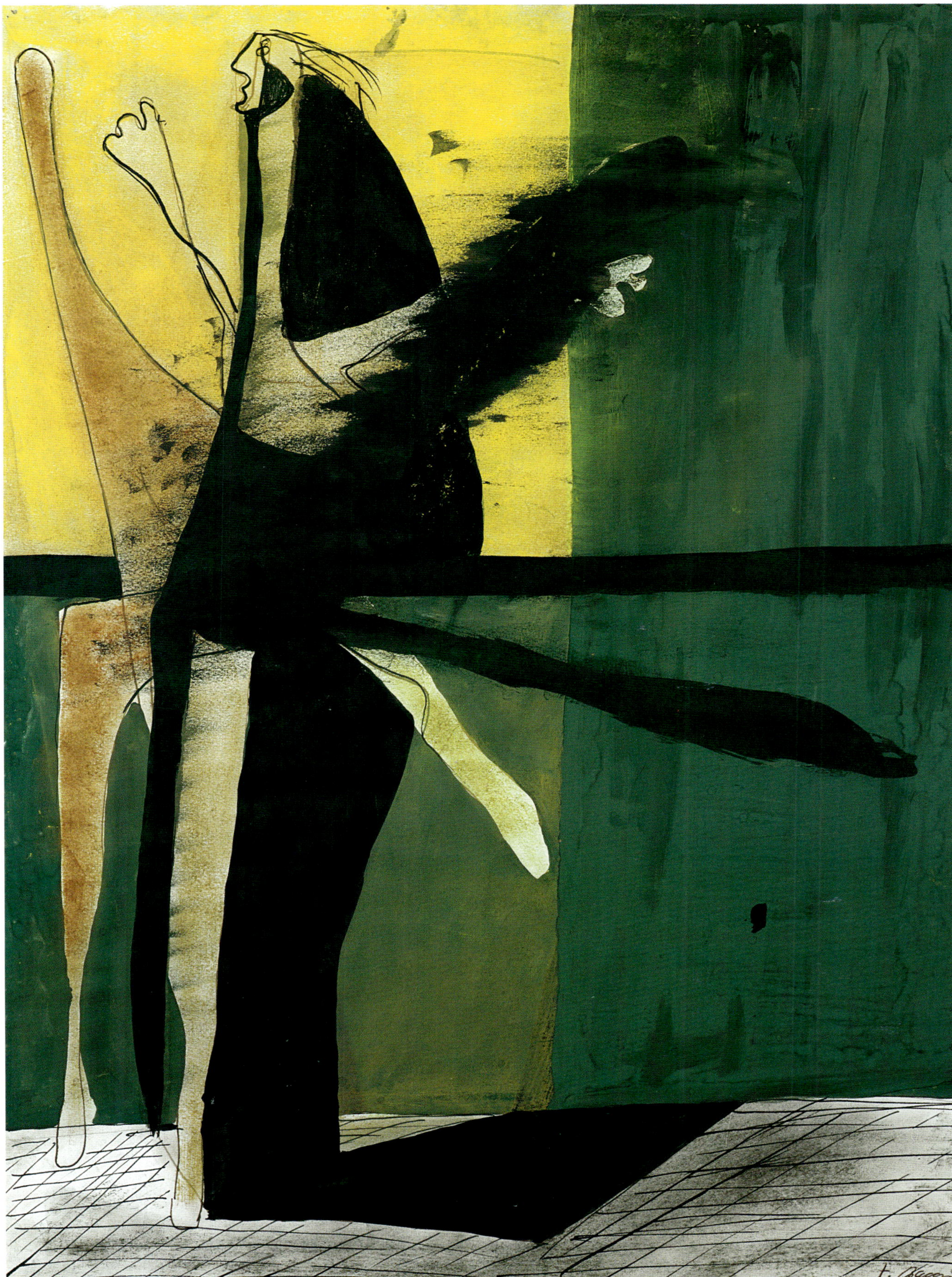

Cat. no. 42

Cat. no. 44
Francis Bacon
Studio Interior
C. 1934
Pastel on paper, 240 × 350 mm
Vaduz, Marlborough International
Fine Art

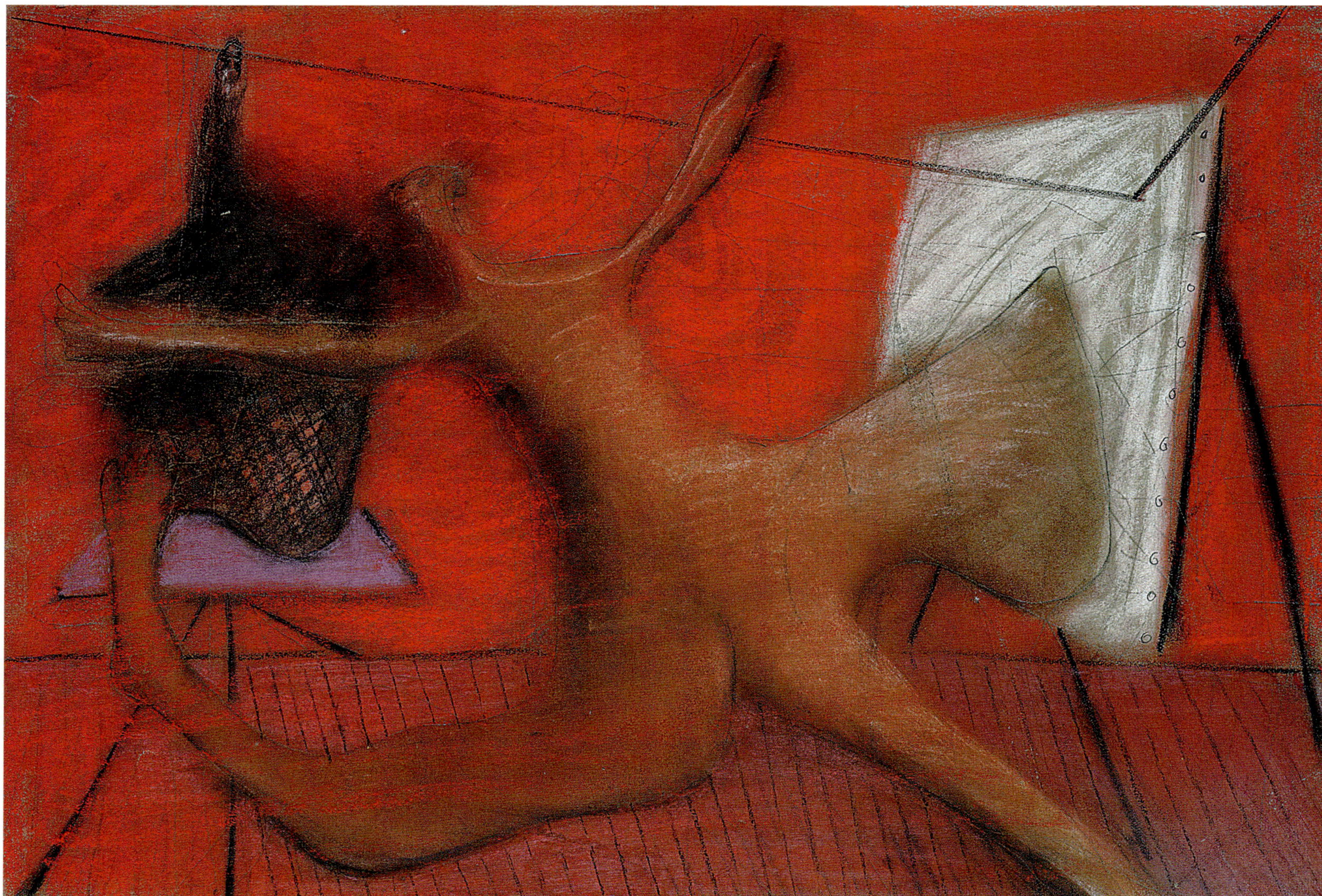

Cat. no. 44

Cat. no. 45
Pablo Picasso
Bather Opening a Cabin
1928, August 9th
Oil on canvas, 32,8 × 22 cm
Paris, Musée Picasso

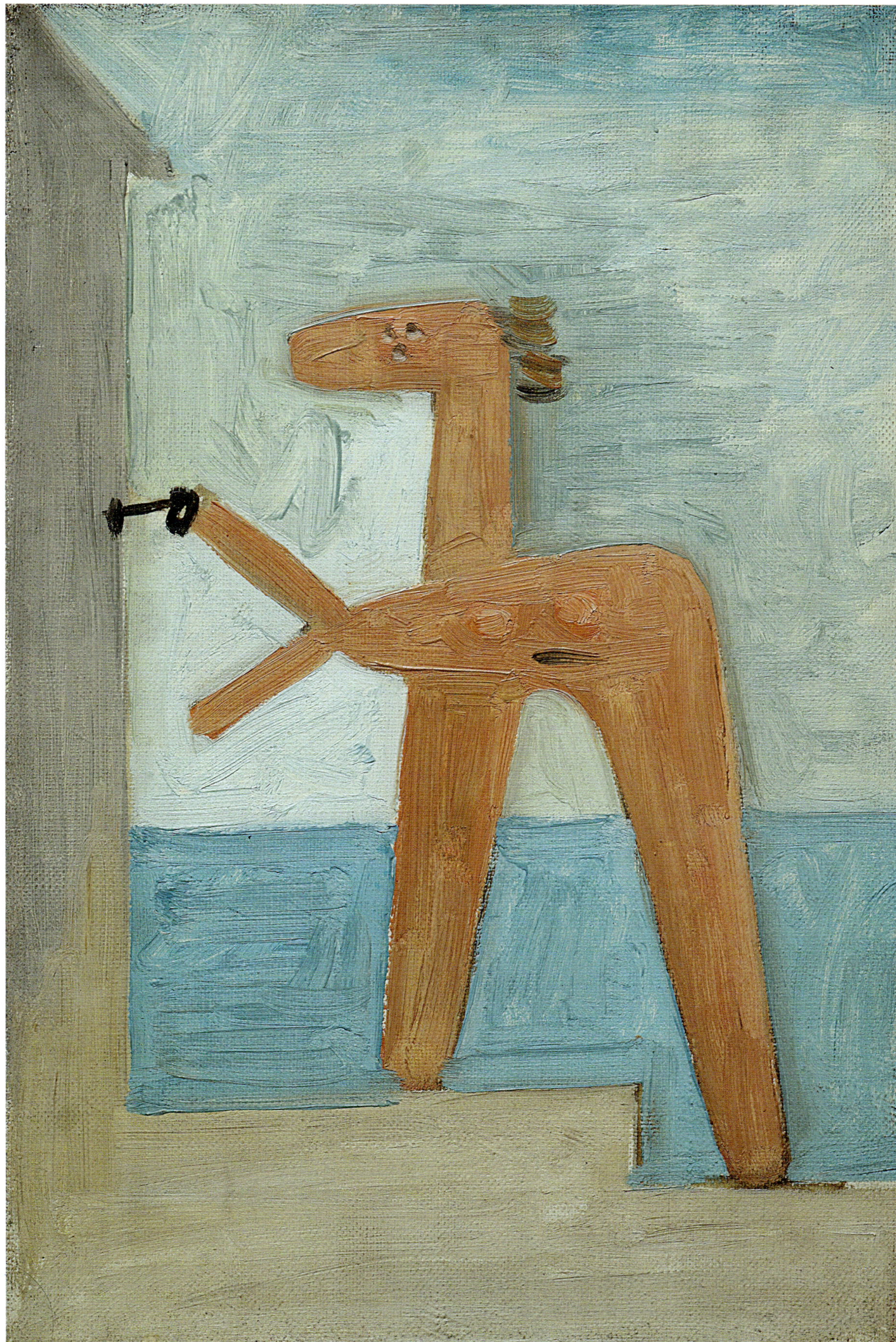
Cat. no. 45

Cat. no. 46
Cutting with black-and-white illustration of Pablo Picasso closing a concealed door. Unidentified publication. 262 × 110 mm
Dublin, Dublin City Gallery
The Hugh Lane, F106:15

Cat. no. 47
Film still from Un Chien Andalou by Luis Buñuel and Salvador Dali
Leaf from book, Raymond Durgnal, Buñuel, Studio Vista Ltd., 1967
165 × 150 mm
Dublin, Dublin City Gallery
The Hugh Lane, F16:85

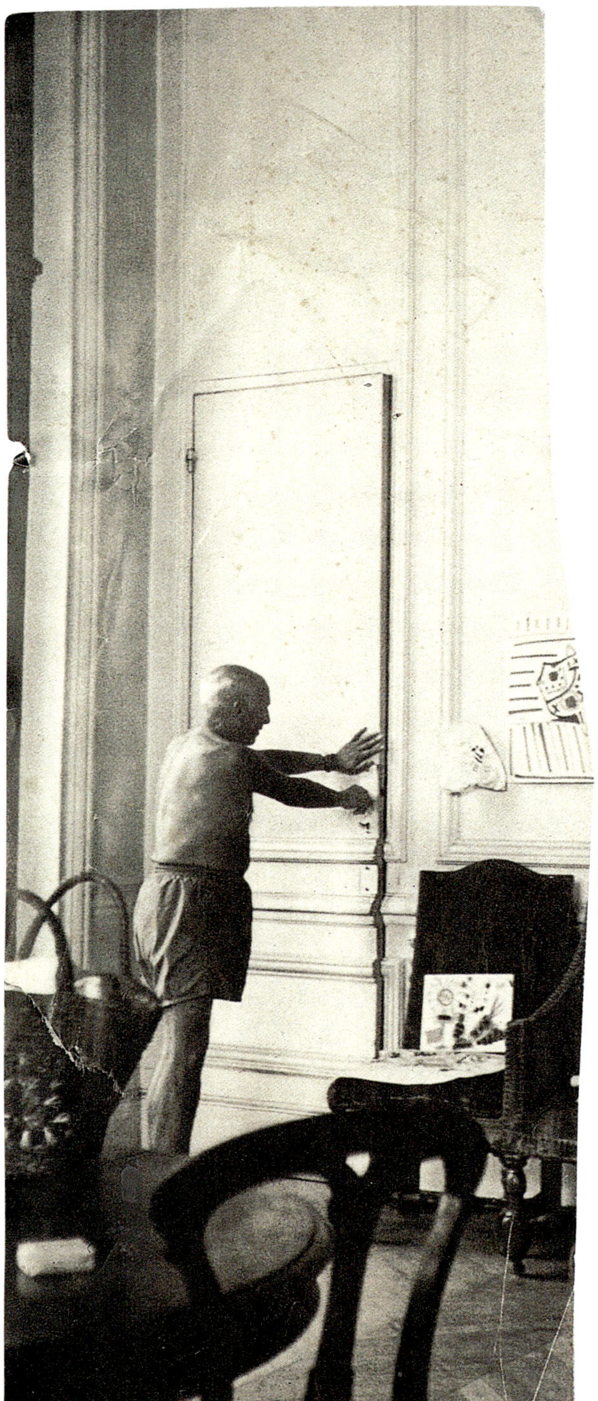

Cat. no. 46

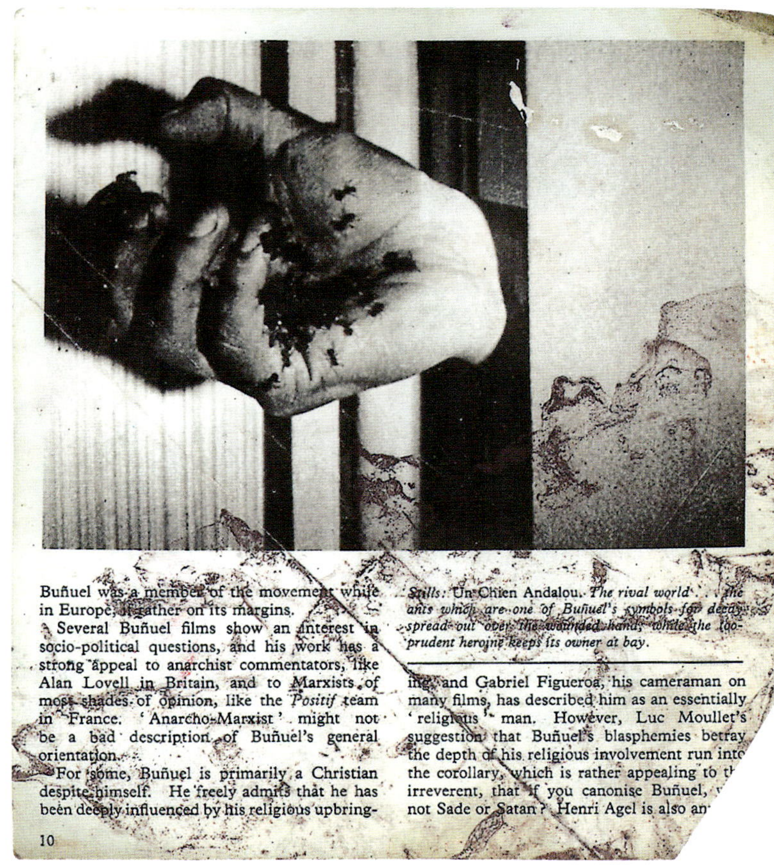

Buñuel was a member of the movement while in Europe, if rather on its margins.

Several Buñuel films show an interest in socio-political questions, and his work has a strong appeal to anarchist commentators, like Alan Lovell in Britain, and to Marxists of most shades of opinion, like the *Positif* team in France. 'Anarcho-Marxist' might not be a bad description of Buñuel's general orientation.

For some, Buñuel is primarily a Christian despite himself. He freely admits that he has been deeply influenced by his religious upbring-

Stills: Un Chien Andalou. *The rival world . . . the ants which are one of Buñuel's symbols for decay, spread out over the wounded hand, while the too-prudent heroine keeps its owner at bay.*

ing, and Gabriel Figueroa, his cameraman on many films, has described him as an essentially 'religious' man. However, Luc Moullet's suggestion that Buñuel's blasphemies betray the depth of his religious involvement run into the corollary, which is rather appealing to th irreverent, that if you canonise Buñuel, not Sade or Satan? Henri Agel is also an

10

Cat. no. 47

Cat. no. 48
Film stills from Un Chien Andalou
by Luis Buñuel and Salvador Dali
Leaf from book, Raymond Durgnal,
Buñuel, Studio Vista Ltd., 1967
165 × 150 mm
Dublin, Dublin City Gallery
The Hugh Lane, F23:50

Cat. no. 49
Film stills from Un Chien Andalou
by Luis Buñuel and Salvador Dali
Leaf from book, Raymond Durgnal,
Buñuel, Studio Vista Ltd., 1967
165 × 150 mm
Dublin, Dublin City Gallery
The Hugh Lane, F23:22

1 A Tale of Unsatisfied Desire

At first sight, nothing could seem less moralistic than Buñuel's first two films, both made in collaboration with Salvador Dali, whose creative role, it is now clear, was the subordinate one. *Un Chien Andalou* is seventeen minutes of pure, scandalous, dream-imagery, a stream of images from which any which could be given a rational meaning was rigorously excluded.

Our surprise results from the Surrealists' misunderstanding of Freudian theory, according to which the unconscious has its patterns of experiences, i.e. its stories, its connections, its reasons, its opinions about religion, politics, etiquette, and so on. Hence the film tells a story, possesses a structure, and has a polemical impact.

It was for this reason that Freud rejected the conclusions which the Surrealists drew from his theories. When they suggested that free association would lead to a free expression of the unconscious, they came nearer the spirit of Jung than either the spirit or the letter of Freud, who insisted that such a procedure would entail a passive surrender to the obscurantist aspects of the mind. Indeed, the Freudian analyst is there to throw out, to oppose, in order to undercut, most of the patient's interpretations. In the event, it's evident enough that most free association poems are sprawling successions of sub-romantic imagery. Indeed, a useful rule-of-thumb is that only the artists who will free-associate authentically are those who can express themselves just as powerfully in highly rationalised forms. The Surrealists themselves were rather more authentic in this respect than most of the poets who merely took a leaf from the Surrealists' book. Aragon said as much when he commented: ' If you produce wretched imbecilities by following a Surrealist procedure, they remain wretched imbecilities.'

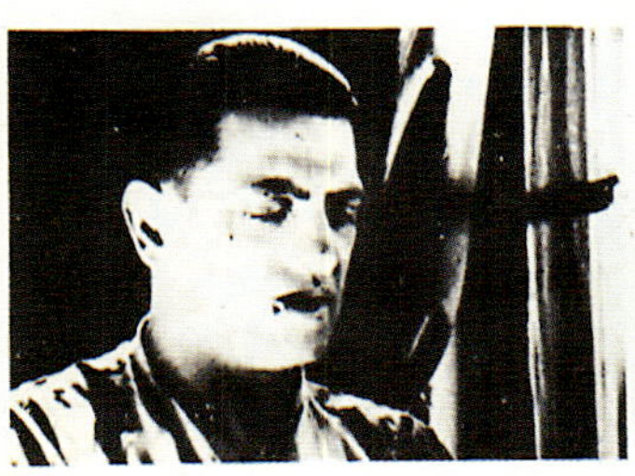

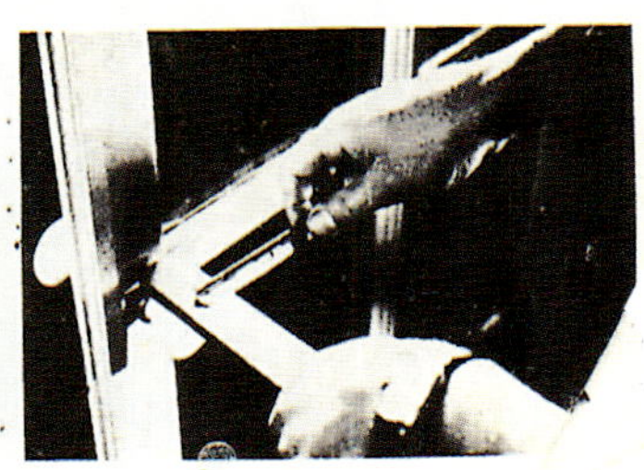

22

Cat. no. 48

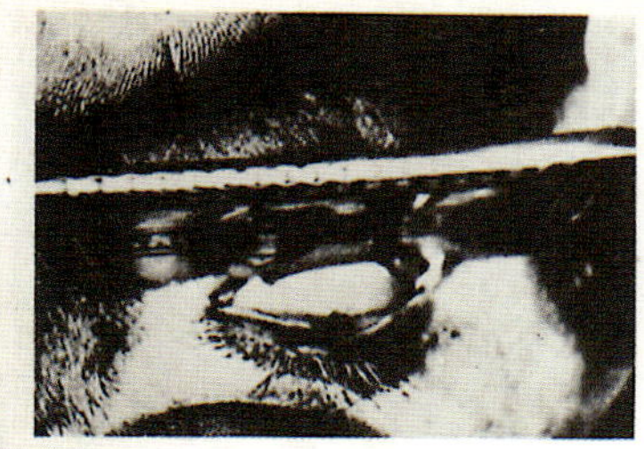

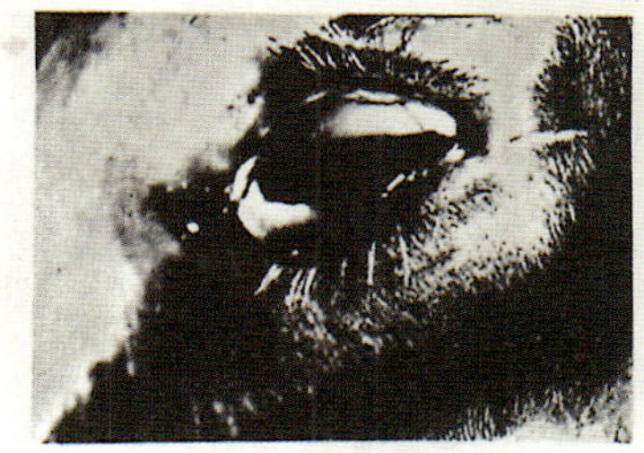

a period of infantile experience. The razor-blade and the eye are fairly evident symbols for the male and female organ, and cutting for sexuality viewed as a destructive activity. Furthermore, as Ado Kyrou suggests, the fairytale is the film, the time is now, and the prologue symbolises its impact on the spectator's ' vision ' of the world.

Another subtitle: ' Eight years later.' And a slim, sensitive young man cycles down a Paris street. He has a prissy expression, and wears frilly white trimmings on his head, back and hips. He's a good little boy, all dressed up to join the angels. He wears on his chest a box covered with diagonal stripes which echo the stropping movements of the razor. He cycles with his hands on his thighs—masturbation, perhaps, or ostentatiously not touching his genitals. The feminine atmosphere of his frills suggests that he's been castrated—a *quid pro quo*, may be, for the infantile sadism indulged in the prologue.

He falls over in slow motion, a curiously obscene effect, into the gutter (dirt, faeces). Devoid of the energy of desire, our angel, through sheer weariness, falls. A girl who

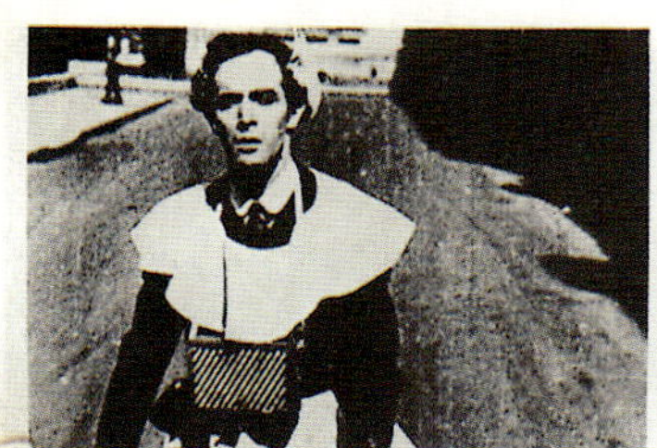

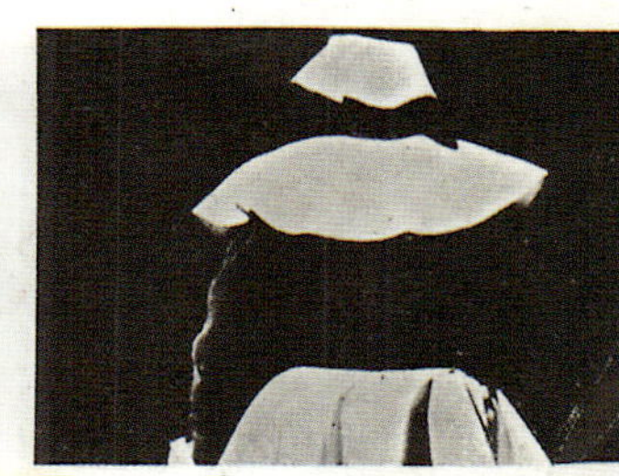

Cat. no. 49

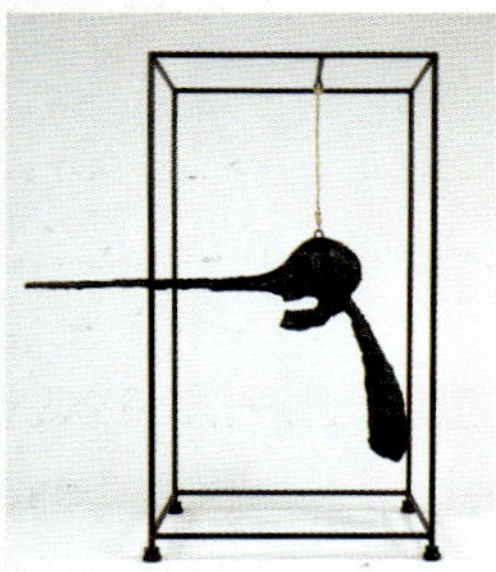

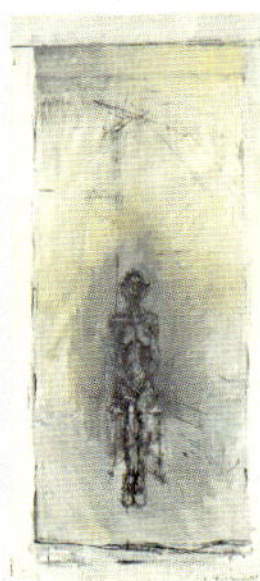

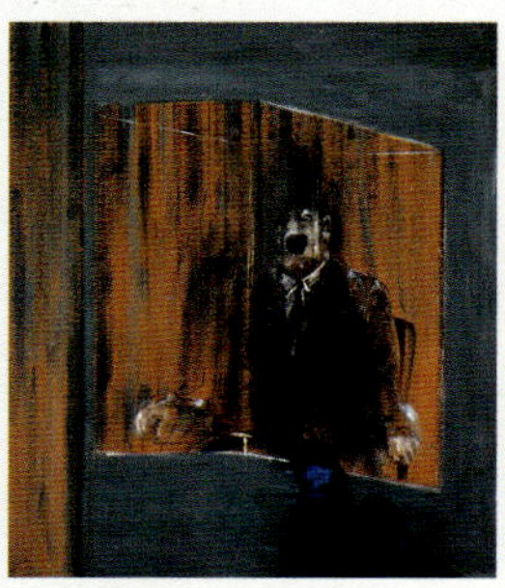

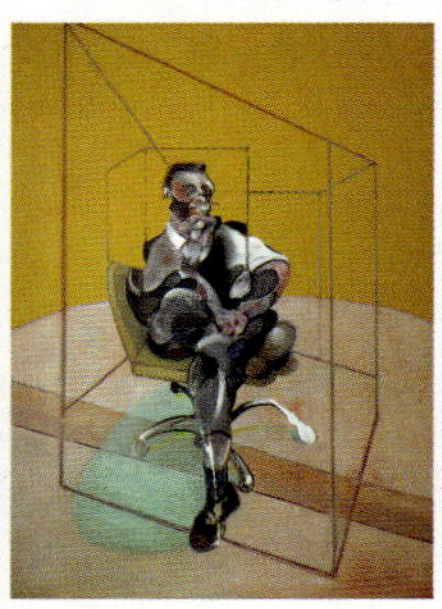

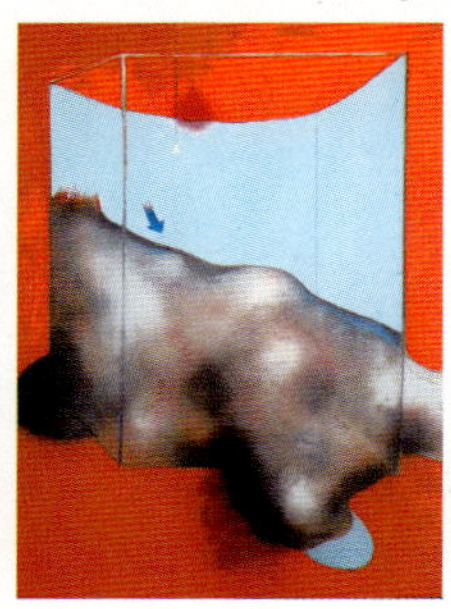

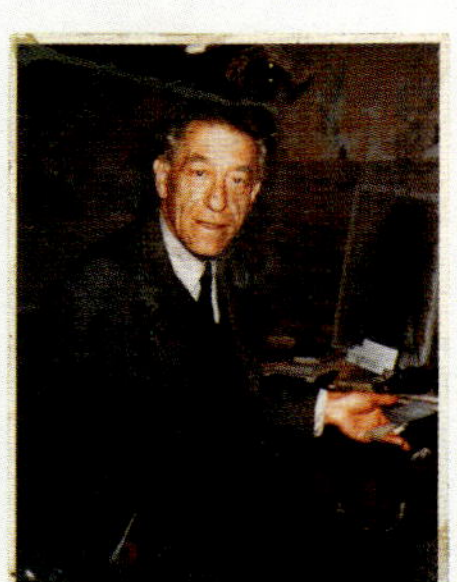

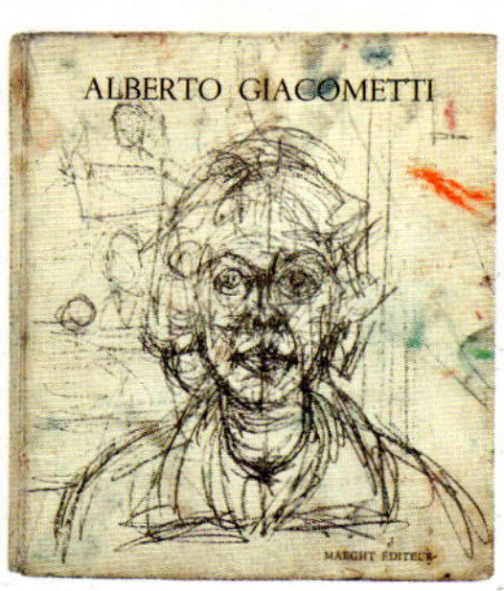
ALBERTO GIACOMETTI

Barbara Steffen

The Cage Motif

"[...] I cut down the scale of the canvas by drawing in the rectangles which concentrate the image down. Just to see it better. [...]"[1] This is how Francis Bacon describes the cube, which he was already using in his pictures during the 1950s. This "space-frame," as Sylvester calls it, developed within Bacon's oeuvre as an important compositional motif, which divides the canvas, emphasises and singles out the figures, and constructs many relationships of meaning in the artist's confrontation with the concept of space.

Head VI of 1949 is one of the first paintings featuring a frame or cage placed around the figure. Another picture from the same year, *Study for Portrait* (cat. no. 50), also defines both figure and space via a cube, a sort of co-ordinate system. In further paintings such as *Study for Portrait, July 1971* (cat. no. 52) and the late work *Sand Dune* of 1983 (cat. no. 54), Bacon continues to develop the cage motif: in the portrait of the sitting figure, the cage has grown to enclose almost the entire area of the picture, and in its interior, a second cube frames the head and shoulders of the figure being portrayed. Certainly, Bacon had already painted a similar upper body in one of his small-format triptychs with various head studies of his friends – specifically, the one he did for Isabel Rawsthorne. Here, however, he is once again concentrating on working out the face; the overlapping of the various layers of colour, the white spots in front of the mouth and the distortion of the ear and neck are familiar from many other works. The body is dynamically painted with round, grey brushstrokes; it seems compact and tense. The double framing steers the observer's gaze towards the body, whose concentrated, complexly painted tangibility powerfully accentuates the theme of the painting: namely the physical strength emanating from the figure and its flesh and blood. In *Sand Dune*, the figure is replaced by a sand dune from which individual grains seem to be trickling out of the glass box. In Bacon's studio, in which chaos always reigned supreme, the dust that had gathered over time was integrated into Bacon's painting technique. "I used dust from the studio in doing those paintings of the sand dunes that I saw in Brittany. It's an awful game getting all that dust up from the floor but there is plenty of it here, as you know, stuck to pictures and everything else. So I just took dust and a cloth and put it onto the wet paint and after it was dried I set it as one sets a pastel."[2] Bacon's working with various types of painting technique and his improvisation in this area are evident in both the pictures mentioned above. In place of the complexly painted body in *Study for Portrait, July 1971,* the dust picture simply features its mixture of colours and materials. Here, the cage is just a framing structure to give Bacon's painterly experiments a formal anchor.

The relevant literature speaks of glass boxes[3] when, in paintings such as *Study for Portrait*, the figure in the picture is enclosed by a cage-like structure. Bacon never referred explicitly to a glass box; rather he defined the cube as a frame or as a three-dimensional structure in which the figure sits. He did consider it important, however, that his pictures always be exhibited behind glass – which is not really the usual way oil paintings are presented. If one interprets the cube in his paintings as a glass box – which is to a certain extent justified – the intensity of isolation becomes more pronounced. The figure is trapped behind the glass and blocked off from its environment. It can look out of the glass box, but is separated from the outer areas of the picture and left to its own devices. In this regard, it bears mentioning that Bacon was repeatedly locked up by his father as a small child – an experience that certainly contributed to the fact that Bacon spent a large part of his life with the feeling of being a "self-committed [...] fugitive."[4] "Bacon himself is for much of his life a self-committed prisoner in a room, doubling as both jailer and prisoner, condemned man and prosecutor, hermit and fugitive."[5]

For Bacon, space is something that is "borrowed." Spaces where this is especially true are hotel rooms and bathrooms, shower stalls and train compartments. It is in such interior spaces that Bacon's emotional confrontation with other human beings plays out. Portraying them offered him additional opportunities to articulate human forms and configurations. "I want to make the interior so much there that the form will speak more eloquently,"[6] explained the artist. The cage motif, which Bacon employs in the form of a glass box or podium, as a shrine, as bedposts or simply as cordoned-off space, has several functions: it raises the attention with regard to the essential figure and creates a picture within the picture which focuses the gaze on the centrally placed motif. Furthermore, it isolates the portrayed figure, and in doing so underlines the distance between it and the viewer. This effect is also, in another way, caused by the displaying of the paintings behind glass which Bacon desired, since the resulting glare makes it that much more difficult for the observer to perceive details such as colour application, colour structure and the texture of the canvas. Bacon was very concerned with creating this distance with regard to space, as well as to content and to technical aspects. His figures are so loaded with emotionality, pain, existential fear and psychological depth that he has to construct around them a sort of protective space, a cage. In the representation of his figures, he seeks distance from that which is going on, in order to protect himself from his own feelings and to address his isolation.

Because of all this, it seems easy to understand that he did not let himself be limited by the materiality of the originals by Velázquez or Titian, but referred mainly to reproductions. Just as motifs such as ropes, cages, podiums, glass boxes, curtains or rondelles are used to isolate, the emphasis of the figures' contours also has a distancing effect. The continuous brushstroke, mostly white or black, separates internal from external space. The density of coloration as well as details in painting technique differ strongly between inner and outer space, and are set off even more by the prominent contours.

During the late 1960s Bacon went through a phase in which he considered becoming unfaithful to painting. "For several years, in fact, he made sculptures in his head. What he envisaged were sculptures of the human figure, a little below life-size. They were to be set in a simple, tubular steel framework, not unlike the ones which he has often used to isolate the human figure in his paintings, and each would be a unique cast. The intended material varied from month to month, but most often it was to be some kind of synthetic but not weightless substance which could take colour quite easily."[7] Russell describes how Bacon grappled with sculpture, and if one – according to Russell's descriptions – imagines Bacon's paintings as sculptures, one is reminded of Alberto Giacometti.

Bacon and Giacometti were close friends from the beginning of the 1960s until Giacometti's death in 1966. "I met him when he came to London for an exhibition of his work at the Tate Gallery. He was accompanied by his wife, Annette, as well as by Michel and Louise Leiris. He stayed at a hotel not far from here, and I remember that we spent a whole night talking to each other."[8] The two artists remained in close contact and discussed art frequently. Giacometti had seen Bacon's work – which he termed "expressionistic" – for the first time in 1955. Only several years later did it become clear to him that both he and Bacon were dealing with the same content. "What I want to do is to distort the thing far beyond the appearance, but in the distortion to bring it back to a recording of the appearance,"[9] is how Bacon put it.

Bacon did not hesitate to rave about Giacometti's work: "Giacometti was not only the greatest draughtsman of our time but among the greatest of all time"[10] Both artists had very high standards for themselves and therefore destroyed, while they were painting, a number of their own works. While Bacon, however, worked from photographs and other sources, Giacometti created – in particular his later – sculptures and paintings based on people who sat for him as models. Bacon and Giacometti were interested in a reduced formal language; while Bacon used similar motifs again and again in his work (portraits, male lovers, cages etc.), Giacometti concentrated in his late work on walking and standing figures as well as on busts. Both artists admired Picasso, especially the works from that artist's Surrealist phase during the late 1920s. Giacometti, who had his origins in Surrealism, was introduced by the artist André Masson to the art critic Michel Leiris, who was also to become an important champion and friend of Francis Bacon and, as a congenial interpreter, was to produce a number of important art-theoretical articles on him.

Giacometti's early work *Suspended Ball* of 1930, which was first exhibited at the Galerie Pierre in Paris, caused an instant sensation in the art world: Salvador Dalí called this prototype of Surrealist art an "object with a symbolic function."[11] This work is one of the first in which Giacometti created a sort of cage structure around the actual sculpture. In other works, such as *The Nose* of 1947 (cat. no. 51), he placed the sculpture in a metal frame – thereby relating its size and three-dimensionality to the surrounding frame. The fragmentary quality of this sculpture and the shifts in the proportions of individual body parts are similar to those in works later created by Bacon. In Giacometti's painting *Large Sitting Nude* of 1957 (cat. no. 53), the figure is emphasised through the vertical framing, which is characterised by separated black strokes, and the proportions of the figure in the context of the defined inner space become the actual theme of the painting.

The cage motif Bacon used in his paintings from the late 1940s onward can be seen as having been derived from the metal frames in Giacometti's sculptures. Bacon often thought of designing sculptures with similar frames: "Bacon had clearly borrowed certain formal devices from Giacometti, notably the cage-like structures the Swiss artist had used in early sculptures [...],"[12] writes Peppiatt in his monograph on Bacon. At the same time, however, Bacon had doubts about the quality of Giacometti's sculptures: "I do like some of his sculptures, but certainly not those from the Surrealist period, not the famous works such as The Nose or The Hand which don't work. I think there are some sculptures by Picasso which are much more important than many of Giacometti's sculptures, but I definitely prefer his drawings."[13] With this statement by Bacon in mind, one might ask whether his admiration of Giacometti was meant seriously and, in particular, which of Giacometti's sculptures he actually valued. It seems that Bacon was in general ambivalent in his attitude toward other artists and their work when the content of the latter got too close to that of his own paintings.

Bacon admired not only Giacometti's sculptures, but also the way in which the Swiss artist lived: reclusively, authentically, independent of financial success.

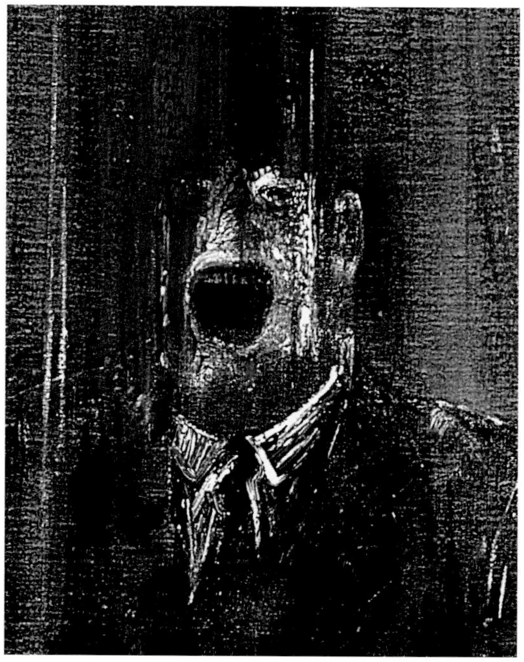

Cat. no. 50, detail.

Although Bacon, on the occasion of a Giacometti exhibition at the Galerie Bernard Haim in Paris, authored a catalogue text for his friend in which he praised the artist as being one of the most important of the 20th century, Peppiatt detects a fundamental ambivalence in Bacon's attitude toward his artistic colleague: "Despite the deep mutual admiration, that had existed between the two artists, Jacques Dupin, who was close to both men and knew their work well, considers that the compliments they exchanged on each other's artistic achievement were not altogether sincere."[14] As far as Giacometti's artistic work was concerned, Bacon ended up with a somewhat strained and reserved stance with regard to the work of his colleague. He distanced himself from the Swiss sculptor, who had been one of his few artist-friends, consciously walled himself off, and entered a self-imposed isolation reminiscent of that experienced by his caged-in figures.

[1] Sylvester 2000, p. 40.
[2] Sylvester 1999, pp. 191, 192.
[3] Ibid., p. 22. Sylvester refers to Eichmann, who was supposed to be portrayed in a glass box.
[4] Russell 1979, p. 73.
[5] Ibid., p. 73.
[6] Ibid., p. 75.
[7] Ibid., p. 101.
[8] Archimbaud 2000, p. 70.
[9] Sylvester 1999, p. 40.
[10] Sylvester 2000, p. 200.
[11] Exh. Cat. New York 2002, p. 85.
[12] Peppiatt 1996, p. 206.
[13] Archimbaud 2000, p. 71.
[14] Ibid., p. 282.

Cat. no. 50
Francis Bacon
Study for Portrait
1949
Oil on canvas, 147.5 × 131 cm
Chicago, Museum of
Contemporary Art

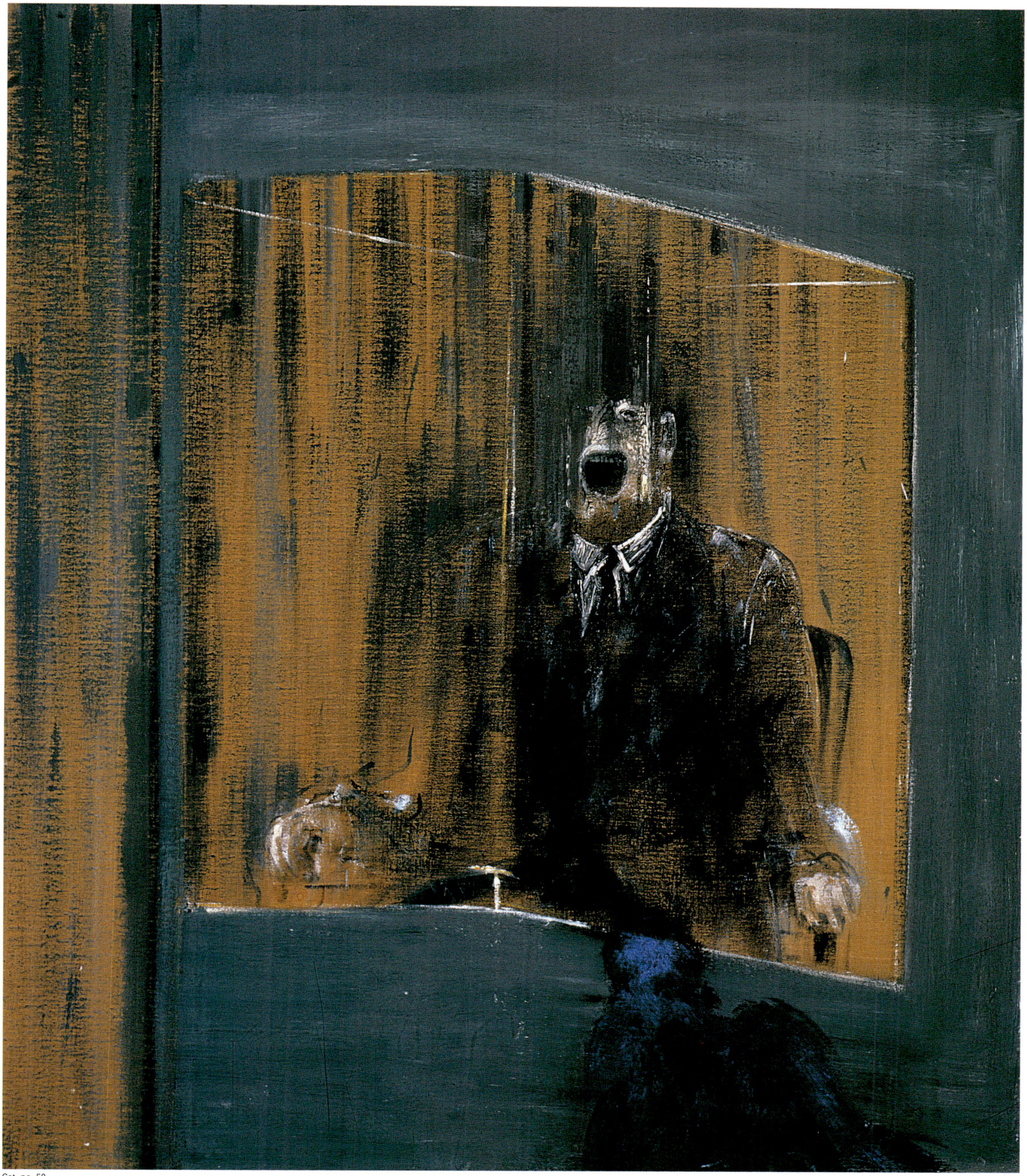

Cat. no. 50

Cat. no. 51
Alberto Giacometti
The Nose
1947
Bronze, wire, rope and steel,
81 × 97.5 × 39.4 cm
New York, Solomon R. Guggenheim
Museum

Cat. no. 52
Francis Bacon
Study for Portrait, July 1971
Oil on canvas, 198 × 147.5 cm
London, Private Collection

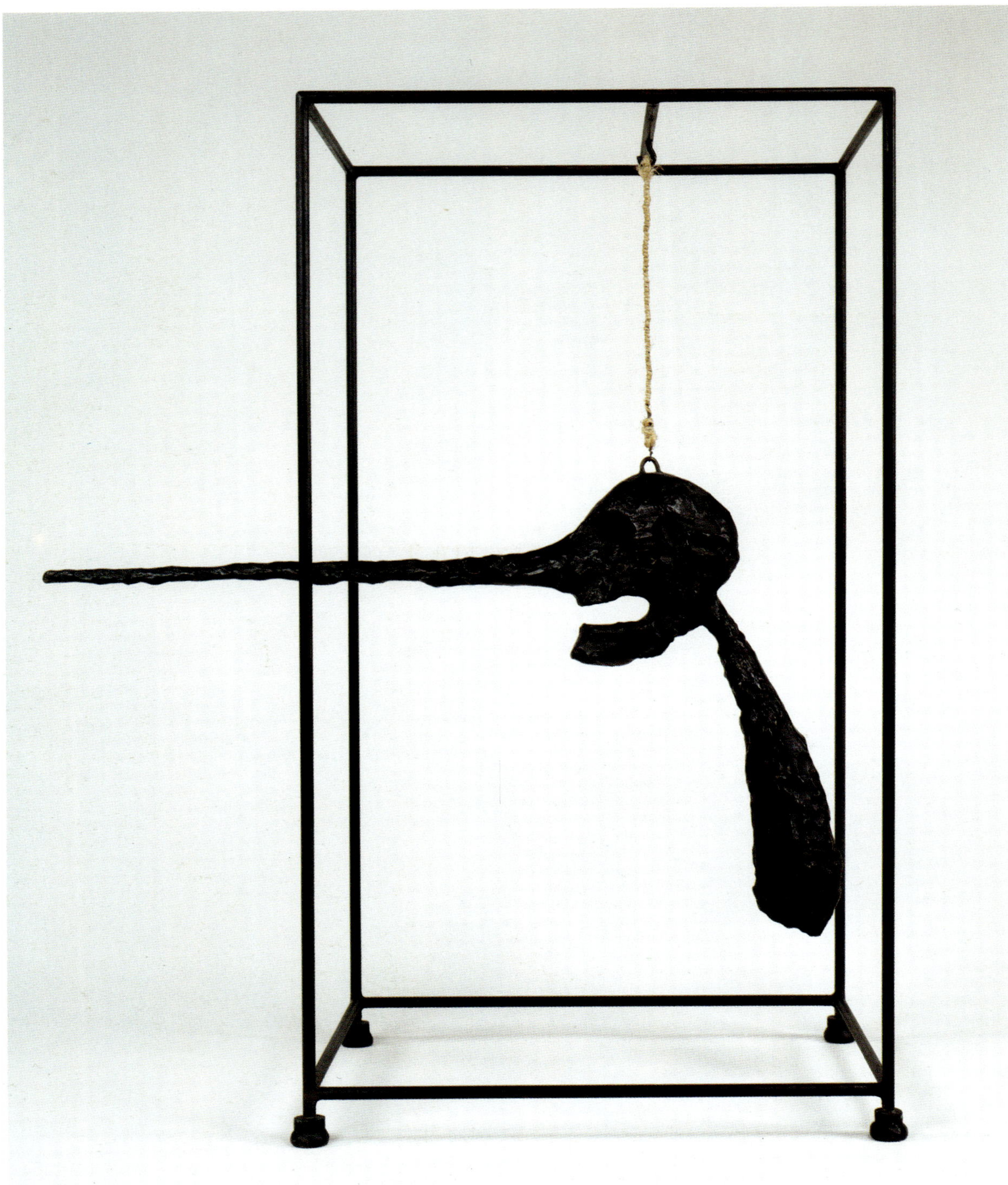

Cat. no. 51

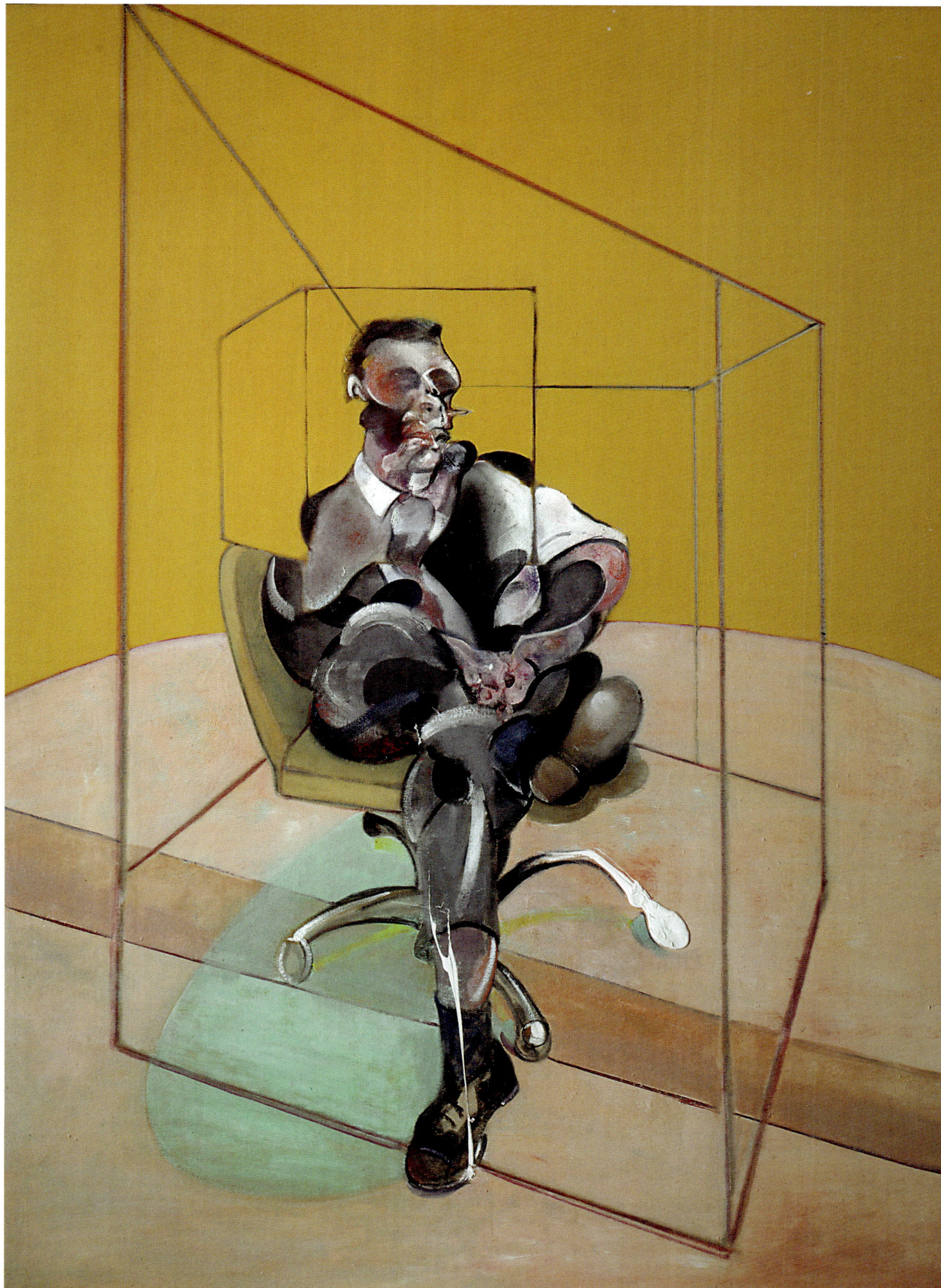

Cat. no. 52

Cat. no. 53
Alberto Giacometti
Large Seated Nude
1957
Oil on canvas, 154 × 59 cm
Frankfort, Städelsches Kunstinstitut

Cat. no. 54
Francis Bacon
Sand Dune
1983
Oil on canvas, 198 × 147,5 cm
Riehen/Basel, Fondation Beyeler

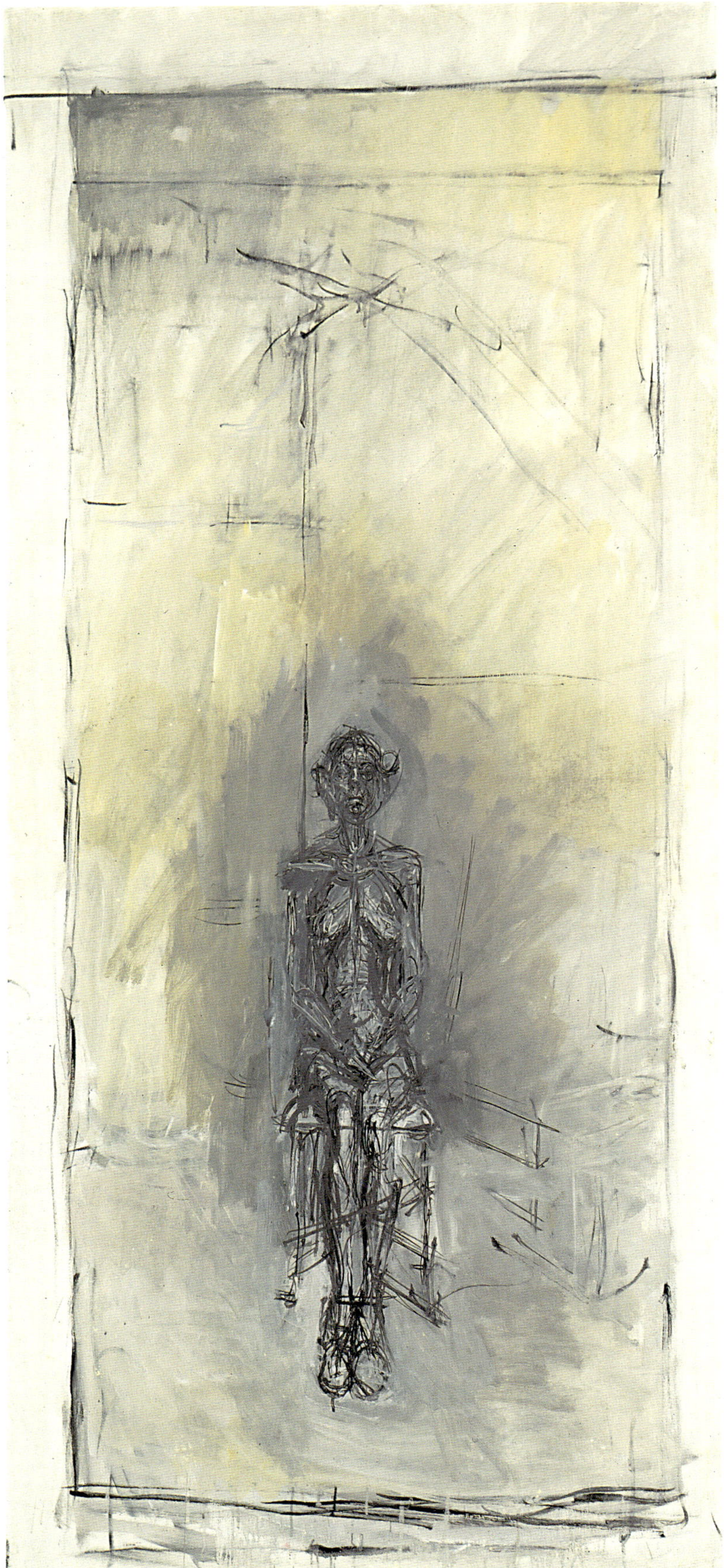

Cat. no. 53

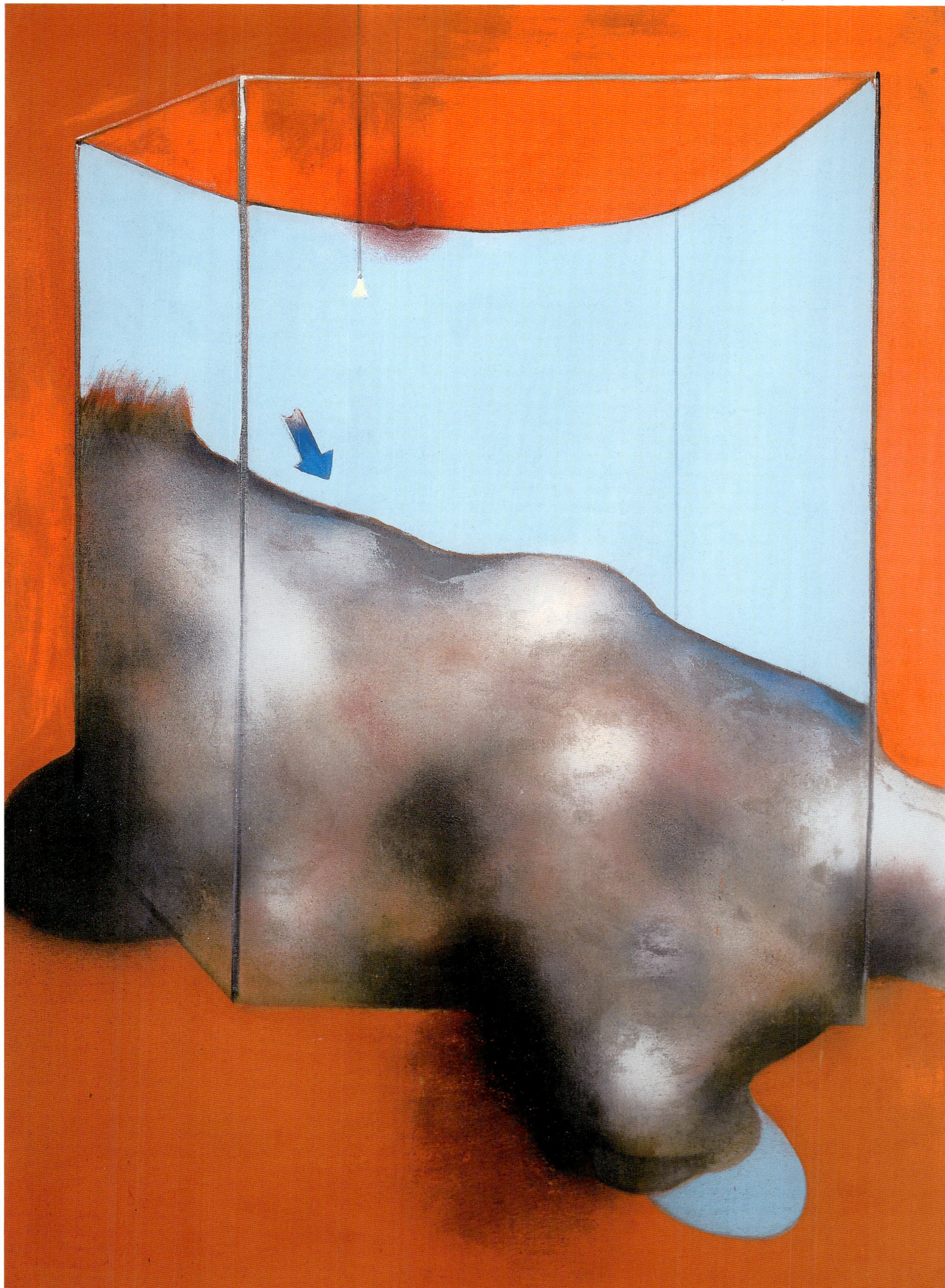

Cat. no. 54

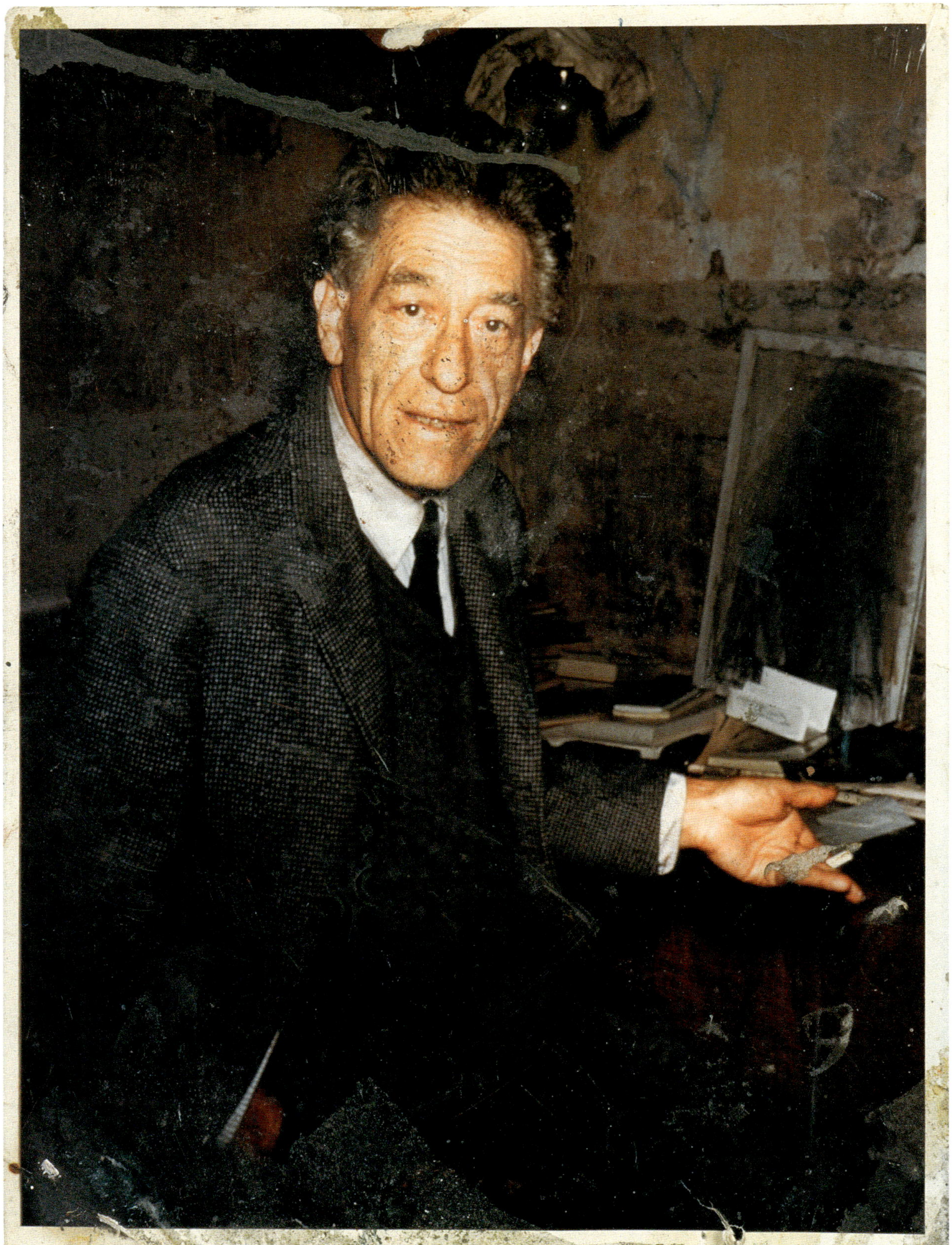

Cat. no. 55

Cat. no. 55
Colour photograph of Alberto Giacometti. Photographer and date unknown. 254 × 202 mm
Dublin, Dublin City Gallery The Hugh Lane, F8:5

Cat. no. 56
Jacques Dupin, Alberto Giacometti, Paris 1962
234 × 205 × 25 mm
Dublin, Dublin City Gallery The Hugh Lane, F114:84

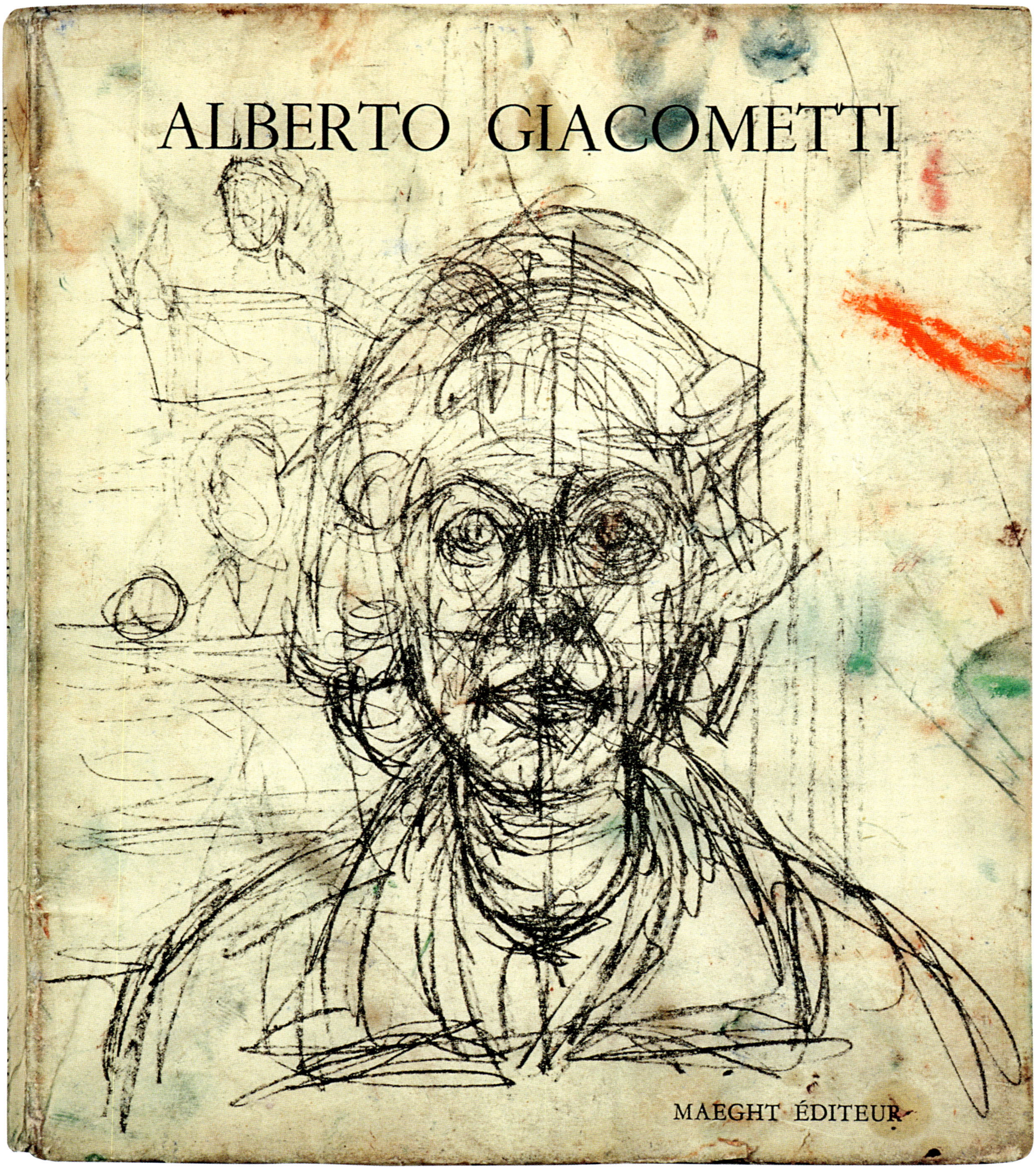

Cat. no. 56

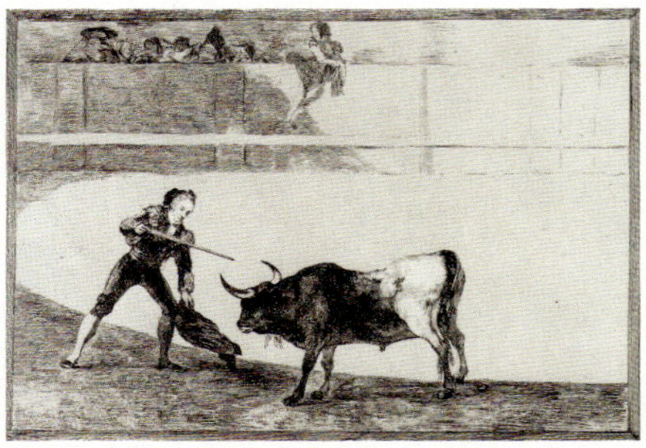
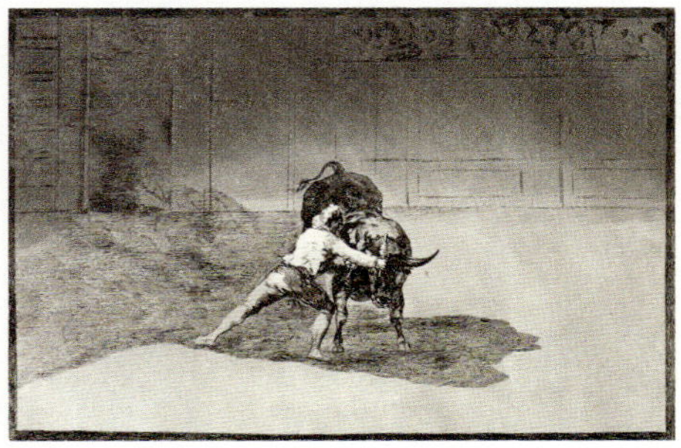
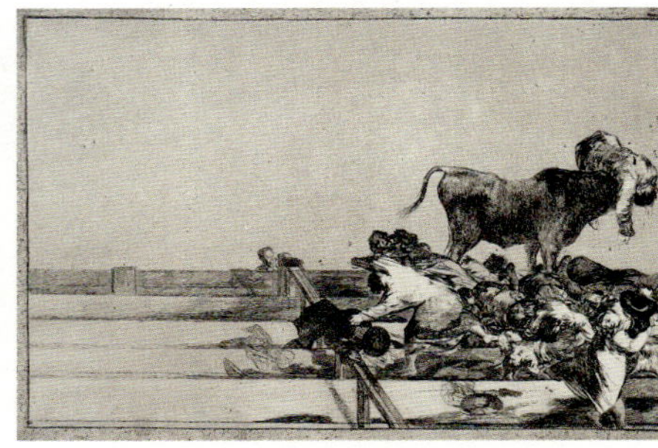

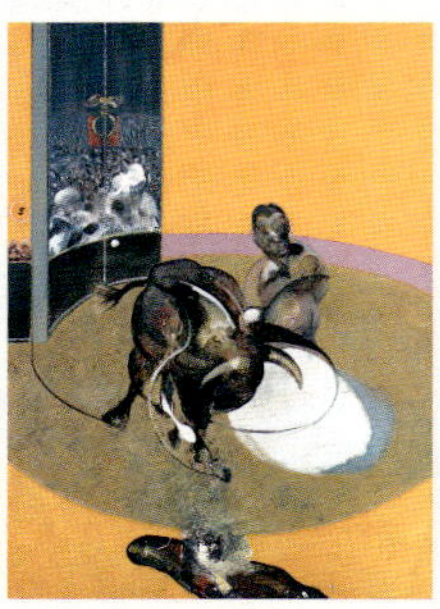
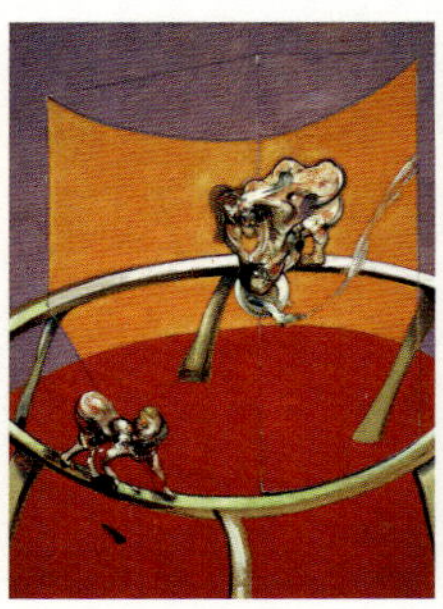
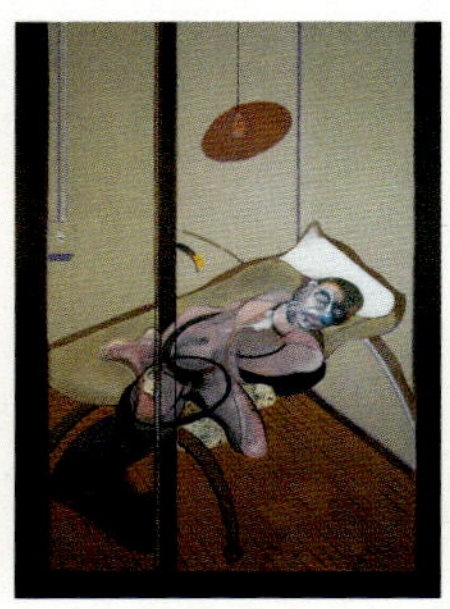
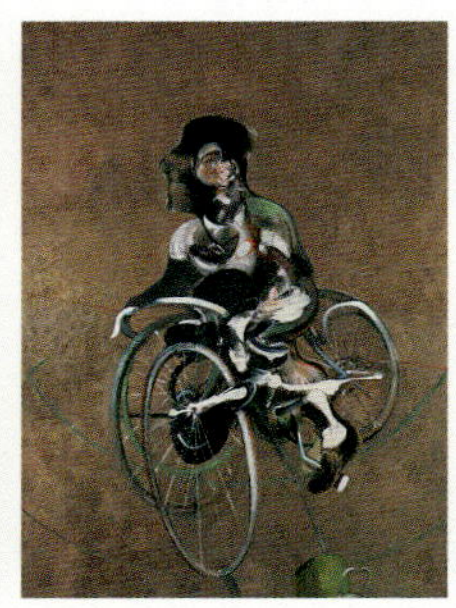
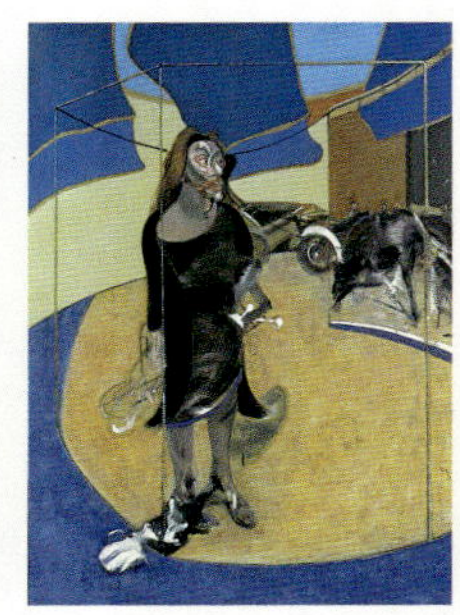
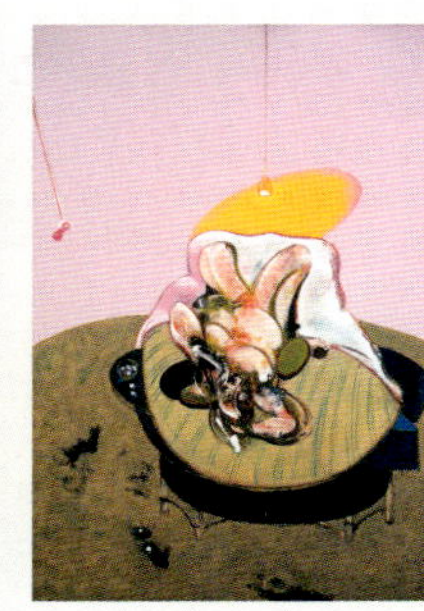

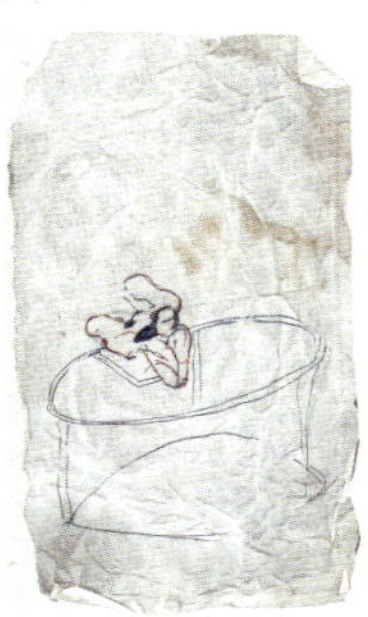
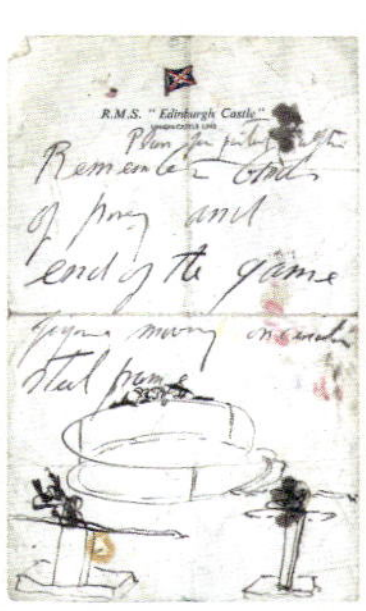
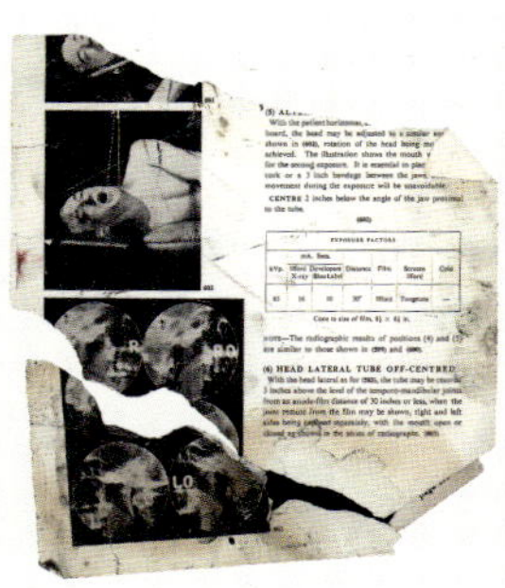
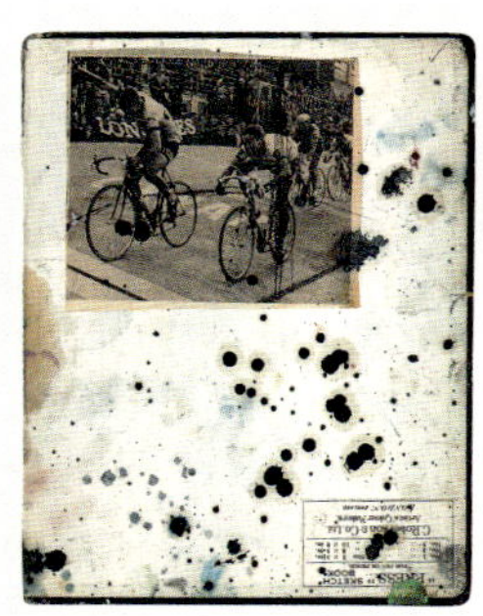
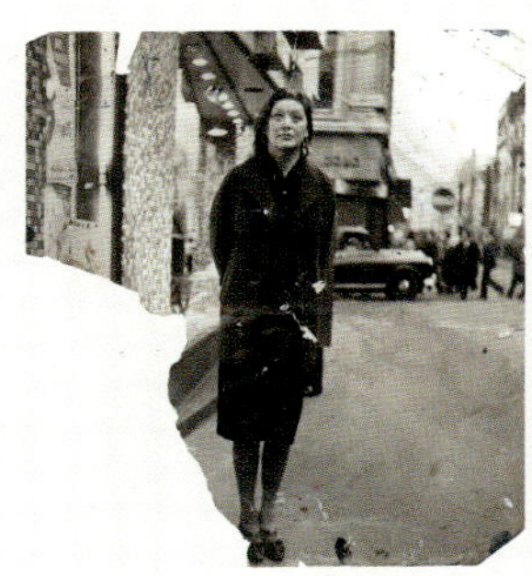
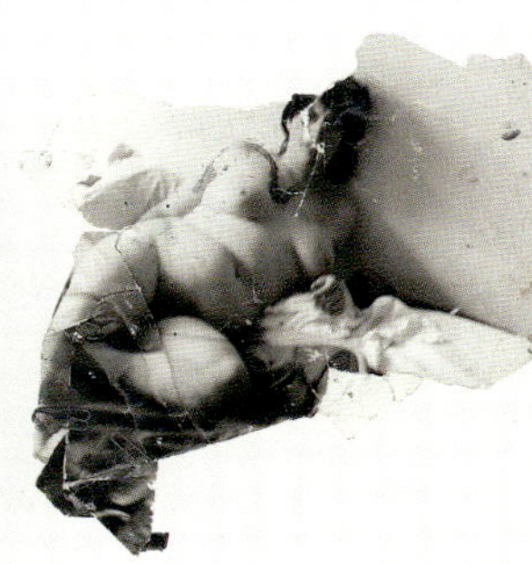

Margarita Cappock

The Round

Circles, ellipses and arcs are motifs that occur repeatedly in paintings by Francis Bacon. Curved devices serve a number of different purposes, the most important one being the delimitation and isolation of the space in which the figure is placed. Bacon also used rectilinear forms to achieve a comparable effect. Gilles Deleuze notes that Bacon's explanation for doing this "is to avoid the figurative, illustrative, and narrative character the Figure would necessarily have if it were not isolated."[1] Deleuze also points out that the figure and the surrounding areas of colour in a painting by Bacon coexist on a single plane with the ring or circle as "the common limit of the two, their contour."[2] Circles are echoed elsewhere in the canvas, such as in the furnishings of the space – beds, chairs and in the artist's use of circular segments to highlight particular areas of the image. The urge is also present in the interventions he made over photographs and photographic illustrations where the artist encircled areas of interest in paint or felt-tip pen. Sometimes the rest of the image was entirely painted so that nothing superfluous remained. The motif or detail might then be translated into paint where box-like structures and circles confine and bracket the protagonists within the painting. It also serves to heighten the effect of the movement of the figures. Bacon continually plundered K.C. Clark's publication, *Positioning in Radiography*, (1939) (cat. no. 68) with it's circular details of X-rays for the same reason.

There are a number of disparate origins for Bacon's use of the circle in his work. From early in his career, a curved line marks the boundary between floor and walls in several paintings by the artist. This device may be linked with a recollection he had of his maternal grandmother's house at Farmleigh, near Abbeyleix in Ireland. Bacon had a particular attachment to this house, where some of the rooms had curved walls. Later he was to say, "One never really knows, but the use I've made of curved backgrounds in some of my pictures may possibly be a recollection of those rooms."[3]

Another more definite source for the circular device is the modernist furniture that Bacon designed before he became established as an artist. On his return to London from Paris around 1928, Bacon worked as a furniture designer and interior decorator. Using materials such as glass, chrome-plated tubular steel and rubber, he produced furniture that was wholly modern in style. Very few examples of Bacon's furniture are still in existence, but photographs of his work indicate that he rapidly assimilated elements from the work of contemporary designers including Eileen Gray, Marcel Breuer and Le Corbusier. The large circular mirror, possibly the most singularly striking object in his Reece Mews studio, was probably designed by Bacon. A similar mirror appears in a photograph of his Queenberry Mews studio as early as 1932. While Bacon later dismissed this aspect of his career, he did concede that his work as a designer had some impact on his paintings, stating "The tubes do come from my own metal furniture, but fundamentally they are an attempt to lift the image outside its natural environment."[4]

When Bacon painted these tubular frames, he would usually place a human or animal form on or within the structure. Part of a circular steel structure first appears in *Figure in a Landscape,* 1945[5] and then more prominently in *Painting, 1946* but most often such objects occur in Bacon's paintings of the 1960s such as *From Muybridge: The Human Figure in Motion: Woman Emptying a Bowl of Water / Paralytic Child Walking on All Fours*, 1965 (cat. no. 57). Bacon's sources are clearly stated in the title of this work. He owned at least four copies of Muybridge's book, *The Human Figure in Motion* (1901). On this occasion, the artist has combined two separate sequences from Muybridge's sequential photographs. The geometric interiors, circular structures and planar surfaces are redeployed to create an artificial arena. The woman and child are precariously balanced on a circular ring, giving them the appearance of circus animals and the disorientating sense that the figures are going to end up where they started. Here Bacon's colour is as celebratory as his human figures are ghoulish. Around this time, the artist was thinking of

Plate 1: Francis Bacon, Study for Bullfight No. 1, 1969, Oil on canvas, 198 × 147.5 cm. Private Collection. (©: VBK, Vienna, 2003, Photo: Artothek, Joseph S. Martin.)

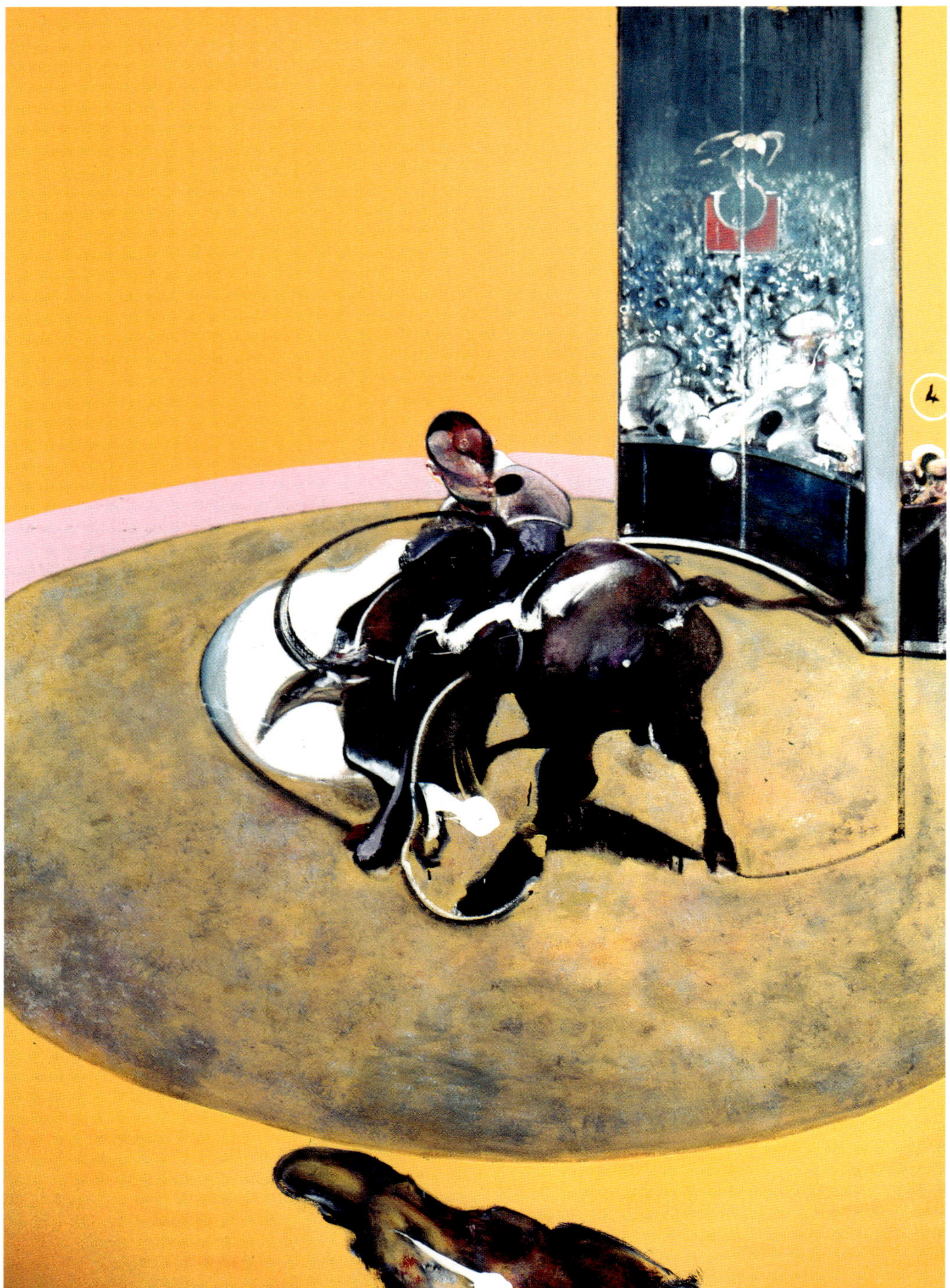

making sculpture. In relation to the possibility of producing sculptures based on this painting and other works, he commented, "I've thought of the rail in very highly-polished steel and that it would be slotted so that the image could be screwed into place in different positions."[6] He goes on to say that the figures would be cast in thin bronze to give them weight and then covered in flesh-coloured whitewash.[7] Two drawings from the 1960s found in the studio (cat. nos. 66, 67) can be related to this particular painting. In one, a single figure or possibly a pair are balanced at the edge of a circular tubular frame supported by three legs. It is executed in grey, blue and red felt-tip pens on paper. A piece of Sellotape along the right edge indicates that it may originally have been attached to a cardboard support.

The motif of the circular arena appears in *Study for Bullfight No. 1 (Plate 1)*, *Second version of Study for bullfight No. 1* and *Study for Bullfight No. 2* (cat. no. 61), all painted in 1969, and in a several other paintings from the 1980s, such as *Triptych, 1987*. The arena provided an environment where animals (bulls) were confined and exposed to the public gaze. Here Bacon's preference for a formal device was echoed in life. Bacon's interest in bullfighting developed during the 1960s on visits to the south of France and Spain, where he attended a number of bullfights. In a typically pithy remark, Bacon once said, "Bullfighting is like boxing – a marvellous apéritif to sex."[8] Bacon's close friend, the writer and intellectual Michel Leiris had written on the subject in his book *Miroir de la Tauromachie* (1938), a copy of which he sent to Bacon in 1969 and which may have influenced the artist. He had in his possession a considerable number of books, magazines and postcards on the subject of bullfighting.

Both Goya and Picasso had produced works on the subject of this quintessentially Spanish sport. A loose leaf from a book with three illustrations of works by Picasso on the subject of bullfighting was found in Bacon's studio. It is not clear whether Bacon had seen Goya's works on this theme but he certainly must have been aware of them. Bacon admired other works by Goya, in particular *La Junta*, which he described as "a very special painting because the figures seem to have been woven out of the air in such a mysterious way, as though the air actually entered into the being of each image of each person."[9] It is often thought that those works by Goya reflecting his bleak world-view and interest in the macabre would have attracted Bacon, but his admiration was in fact reserved for Goya's formal portraits.[10] In 1816 Goya published a series of 33 aquatint etchings of bullfight subjects (cat. nos. 63–65), now known as the *Tauromaquia,* published during his lifetime and under his supervision.[11] They are considered to be his most technically finished and stylistically coherent etchings. In *Pedro Romero matando a toro parado,* man and bull take centre stage in the circular arena. Within the *Tauromaquia* series he also turned to historical events from the past, particularly in *El famoso Martincho poniendo banderillas al quiebro* and *Desgracias acaecidas en el tendido de la plaza de Madrid, y muerte de alcalde de Torrejón*. In the latter illustration the action is taken out of the ring and into the spectators' stands. It re-enacts an event that took place on 15 June 1801, when a bull leaped over the barriers.

In one of the books found in Bacon's studio, entitled *The Swords of Spain*, Bacon wrote a note dated 14 July 1968, reads *Studies from the human body and The Bullfight,* indicating that as early as 1968, Bacon was considering painting bullfighting scenes. The three bullfighting paintings were made the following year. It would seem that originally Bacon planned a triptych on the theme of bullfighting but the works were then displayed as single paintings. Bacon's approach to the theme of the bullfight is much more explicit than in his other paintings. For this reason, David Sylvester faulted these works as looking like posters for the *corrida.*[12] A different opinion is expressed by the French intellectual Michel Leiris, who deemed these bullfighting scenes to be the most truthful representations of bullfighting yet painted, since the emphasis is placed on the bull, his weight, his force, his charge and on the horns with which he is armed.[13] John Russell points out that there are inherent difficulties in tackling a subject such as this; the bullfight is dramatic in a self-evident way, whereas Bacon strove to convey the emotional climate of the bullfight without resorting to illustration or picturesque description.[14] Apparently, Bacon never felt that the pictures were a complete success, although he refrained from destroying them.[15]

In both *Study for Bullfight No. 1 (Plate 1)* and *Study for Bullfight No. 2* (cat. no. 61), a section of a crowd from a Nazi rally is introduced. The circular arena is not simply the stage on which a deadly game between animals and men is played out, it is the context for a more sinister crowd spirit. The arena doubles as a place for mass rallies where violence on a broader scale can be fomented and encouraged. The arena concentrates and encloses the more aggressive instincts of man. In this way the formal device of the circle has been transformed into an abstracted yet recognisable space charged with a host of disturbing associations. The same section has been left blank in *Second Version of Study for Bullfight No. 1,* suggesting the artist was wary of pushing this theme too far.

Bulls make an appearance in Bacon's work on a small number of occasions and only rarely outside the context of the bullring. In the case of *Portrait of Isabel Rawsthorne Standing in a Street in Soho,* 1967 (cat. no. 59) a bull is incongruously shoehorned into a scene of metropolitan life. The environment in which Rawsthorne is placed is much more fully realised than in Bacon's paintings of the previous decade.[16] The alert, almost savage stance of Rawsthorne shows that the distance between human and animal life is only as wide as the artist chooses to make it. This painting was based on a number of photographs of Rawsthorne standing outside a plate-glass window in Dean Street in Soho, commissioned from John Deakin (cat. no. 70).[17] In the case of this painting, Rawsthorne is removed from the context of the photograph and placed on what resembles a sand-coloured circular arena, again possibly representing a bullring. The astonishing swirls of paint in this work achieve an exuberant and dynamic effect while also capturing Rawsthorne's personality.

Bacon's other great female model was Henrietta Moraes who, like Rawsthorne, was a key figure in post-war London's artistic and bohemian life.[18] Bacon asked Deakin to take some photographs of Moraes (cat. no. 71) and he used the resulting photos of a nude Moraes lying on a bed as the basis for a number of paintings. *Lying Figure,* 1969 (cat. no. 60) was one of these works. Bacon did at least three paintings of Moraes, the first one dating from 1963, in which she is seen with a hypodermic syringe piercing her arm. The choice of a detail that implies both medical intervention and addictive self-destruction is typical of Bacon's inventive use of loaded imagery. Its presence is all the more alarming in a figure whose pose and painterly texture are given over to such sensual abandon. The writhing figure of Moraes is placed upside down on a circular bed. The sense of movement is echoed in the rest of the painting, where one has the disconcerting sense that everything is swinging around.

A keen sense of motion is also evident in the work *Portrait of George Dyer Riding a Bicycle,* 1966 (cat. no. 58) where the figure of Dyer is given the appearance of a clown cycling around a circus ring. In this work, Bacon does not differentiate between wall and floor, which enhances the sensation of motion. Dyer, who is seen both in profile and full face, seems to be engaged in an endless activity of going around in a circle. Bacon may have been partly inspired by a newspaper or magazine cutting showing two cyclists which he mounted onto the back cover of a sketch book (cat. no. 69). Bacon has drawn lines in black ink on the ground which serve to enclose the cyclists. He has also drawn a number of vertical lines on the right of the illustration which bisect one of the cyclists. In the painting, Dyer is cycling on a similar racing bike and, like these cyclists, is portrayed wearing a white short-sleeved shirt.

In 1974, Bacon had an operation on his gall bladder and in the same year he painted *Sleeping Figure* (cat. no. 62). This self-portrait was painted from a photograph of the artist lying on a hospital bed after the operation.[19] The original photograph was not found amongst his Reece Mews studio contents. This would seem to be the only full-length portrait where the artist is seen nude, a reflection of his vulnerable post-operative state. Bacon's rendering of his own body in this painting has an almost transparent quality and creates a poignant sense of human frailty. The impression created is of Bacon seen behind glass doors or a window. The artist remarked, "I didn't in the first place intend to enclose it within those doors, and that came as an afterthought. I don't really think my pictures out, you know; I think of the disposition of the forms and then I watch the forms form themselves."[20] Although the painting is supposed to represent a hospital room, it is more reminiscent of his Reece Mews studio with its wooden floorboards, light fittings and bare bulbs, almost as if the artist were seeking the familiar in an unfamiliar place. Bacon loathed hospitals and found it difficult to visit friends who became ill, so clearly this experience was a traumatic one for him. The design of the hospital bed also recalls modernist furniture from the 1920s, and again the circular motif appears in the arcs of the legs of the bed, which serves as a counterpoint to the verticality of the window frame and light fittings. There is also a strong sense of motion in this work as the artist appears to be almost tumbling from the bed.

The round became such a ubiquitous presence in Bacon's works since it reflected the broad, cursive instincts of the artist's hand. Its implications, as we have seen, went much deeper. It could create a sense of enclosure, concentration and, indeed, movement. With the addition of a few elements it could suggest a bullring or the circus with its suggestions of the freakish and the strange. Both arenas imply a public spectacle and reflect the theme of voyeurism and observation so apparent in Bacon's works.

[1] Deleuze 2003, p. 2.
[2] Deleuze 2003, p. 6.
[3] Sylvester 2000, p. 108.
[4] Henry Geldzahler, Francis Bacon "recent paintings 1968–1974", in: Exh. Cat. New York 1975, p. 12.
[5] Bacon used rectilinear elements in earlier paintings and there is the possibility that circular elements may have been used in unrecorded lost or destroyed works.
[6] Sylvester 1999, p. 110.
[7] Sylvester 1999, p. 112.
[8] Russell 1993, p. 143.
[9] Sylvester 2000, p. 239.
[10] Russell 1993, p. 41.
[11] Tomlinson 1994, p. 222.
[12] Carter Ratcliff, "Francis Bacon: 'The Violence of Reality'," in Exh. Cat. New York 2002, p. 10.
[13] Jacques Dupin, "Notes sur les dernières peintures," in *Francis Bacon, Peintures Récentes*, repères cahiers d'art contemporain no. 39, Paris, Galerie Lelong, 1987. Dupin paraphrases the words of Michel Leiris, p. 14.
[14] Russell 1993, p. 143.
[15] Ibid.
[16] Isabel Rawsthorne (1912–1992), an artist and set designer, was one of Bacons closest female friends and the subject of a number of his paintings. Her unconventional beauty captured Bacons imagination and along with Henrietta Moraes she became one of his favourite models.
[17] Rawsthorne is seen full face and in profile and the shots include full length and head and shoulders.
[18] Henrietta Moraes began as a model in art schools. Determined to meet Francis Bacon and Lucian Freud, she frequented bars such as the French House, and became part of the Soho set which included Daniel Farson, Jeffrey Bernard, Brendan Behan, John Deakin and others.
[19] Michael Peppiatt, "Les rêves décomposés de Francis Bacon," in Connaissance des Arts, no. 351, p. 56.
[20] Sylvester 1999, p. 136.

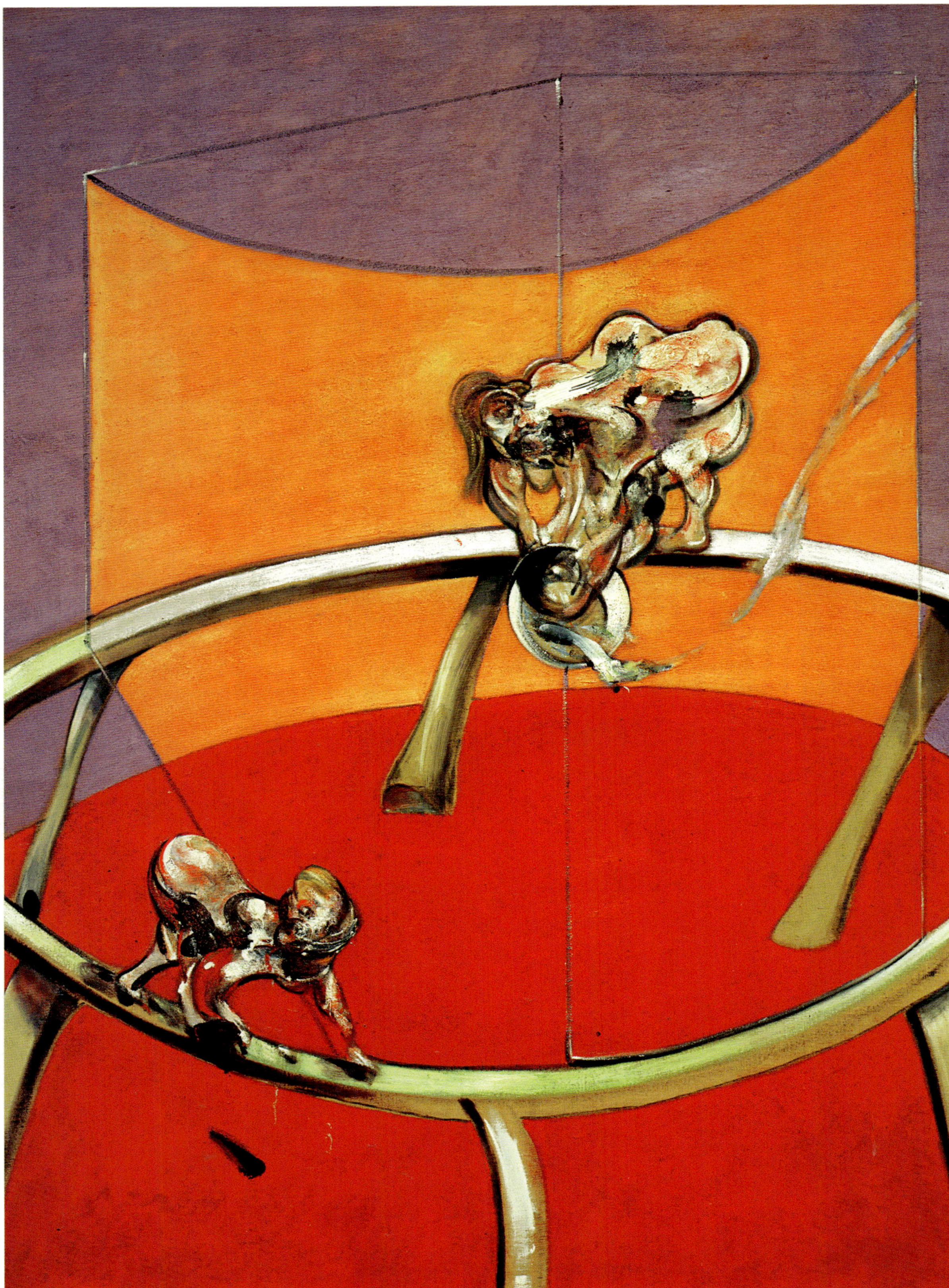

Cat. no. 57

Cat. no. 57
Francis Bacon
From Muybridge: The Human Figure in Motion: Woman Emptying a Bowl of Water/Paralytic Child Walking on all Fours
1965
Oil on canvas, 198 × 147,5 cm
Amsterdam, Stedelijk Museum,
inv. no. A 37611

Cat. no. 58
Francis Bacon
Portrait of George Dyer Riding a Bicycle
1966
Oil on canvas, 198 × 147,5 cm
Riehen/Basel, Fondation Beyeler

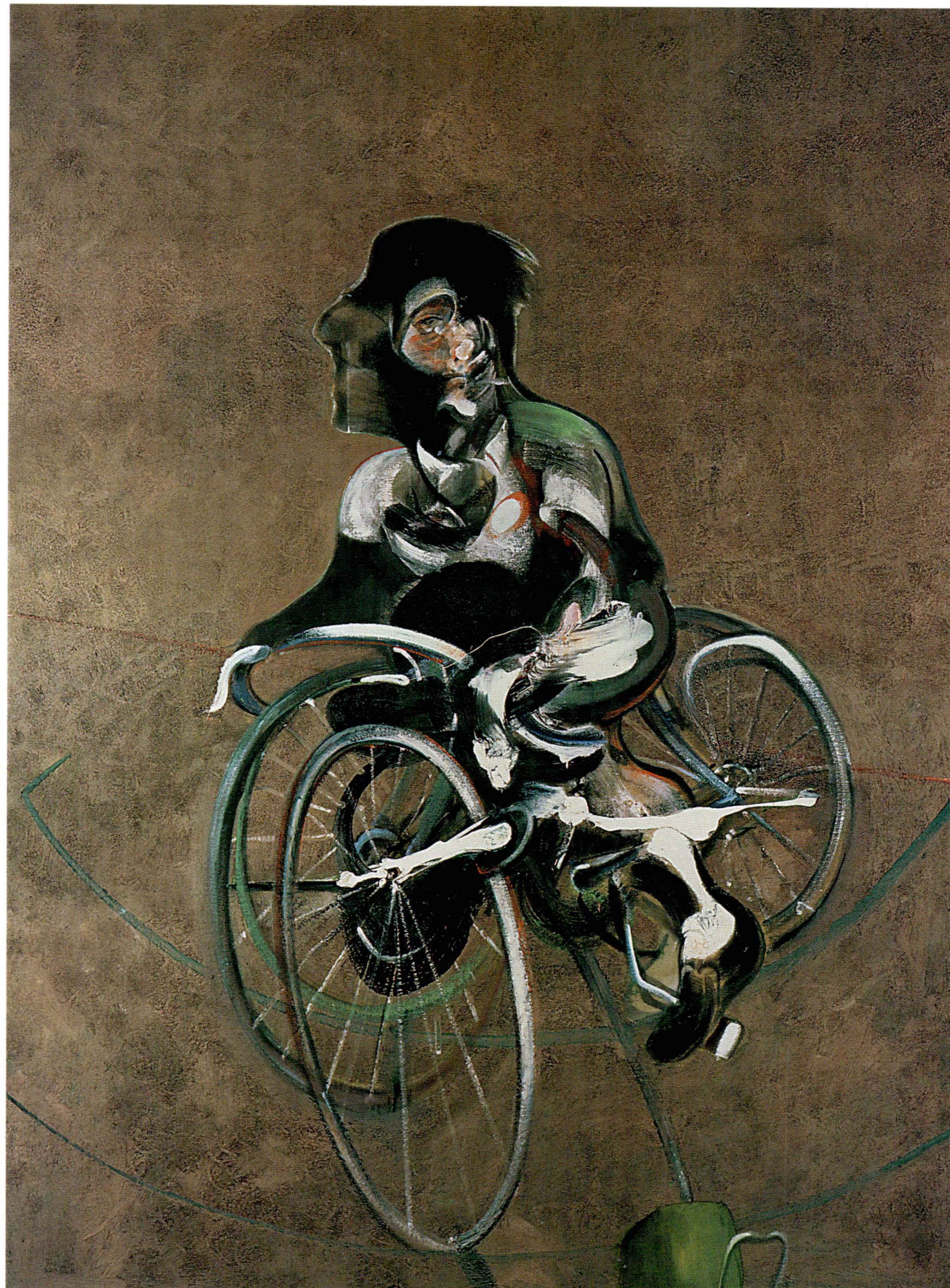

Cat. no. 58

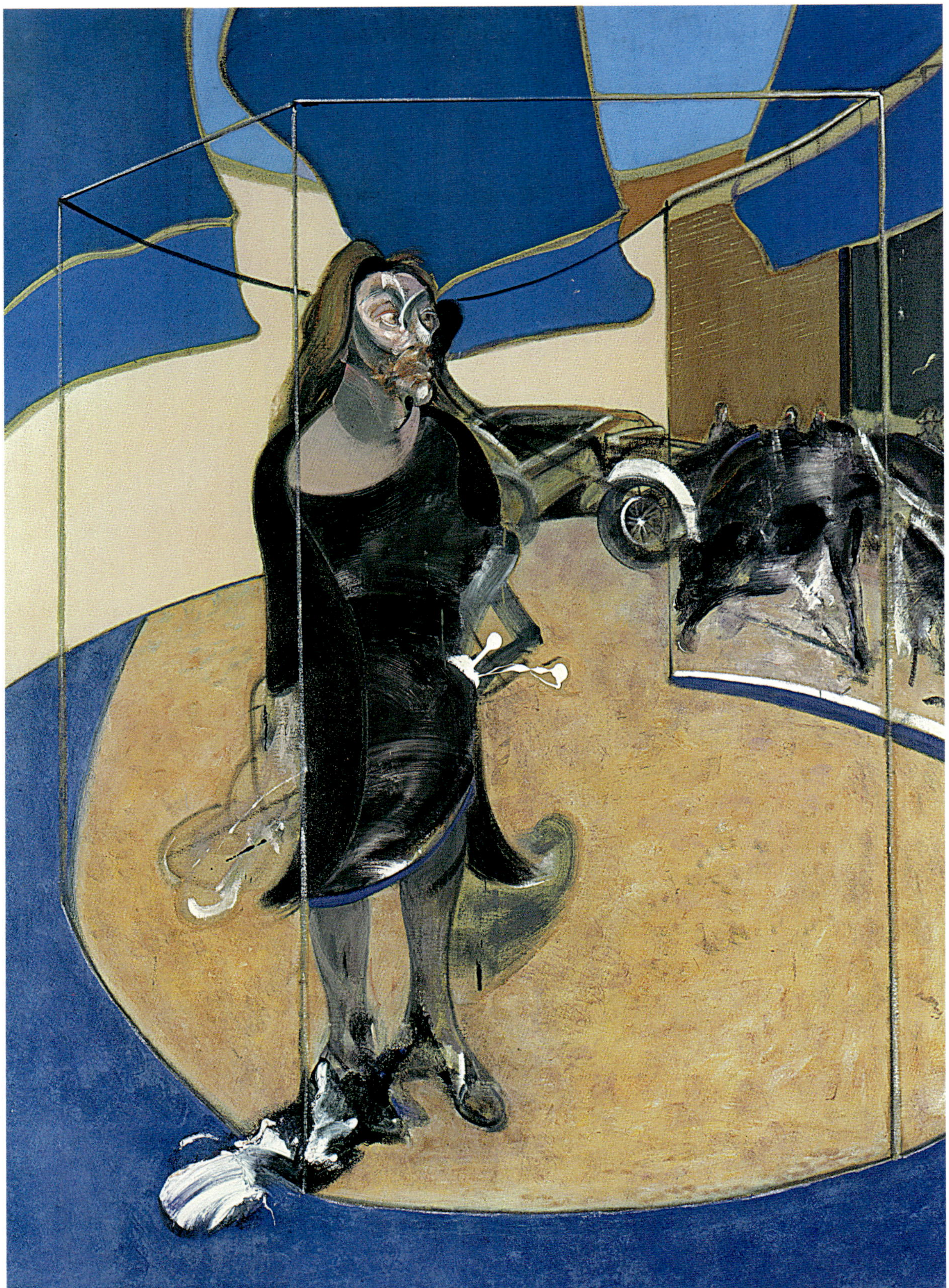

Cat. no. 59

Cat. no. 59
Francis Bacon
Portrait of Isabel Rawsthorne
Standing in a Street in Soho
1967
Oil on canvas, 198 × 147,5 cm
Berlin, Staatliche Museen zu Berlin,
Neue Nationalgalerie,
inv. no. B 897

Cat. no. 60
Francis Bacon
Lying Figure
1969
Oil on canvas, 198 × 147.5 cm
Riehen/Basel, Fondation Beyeler

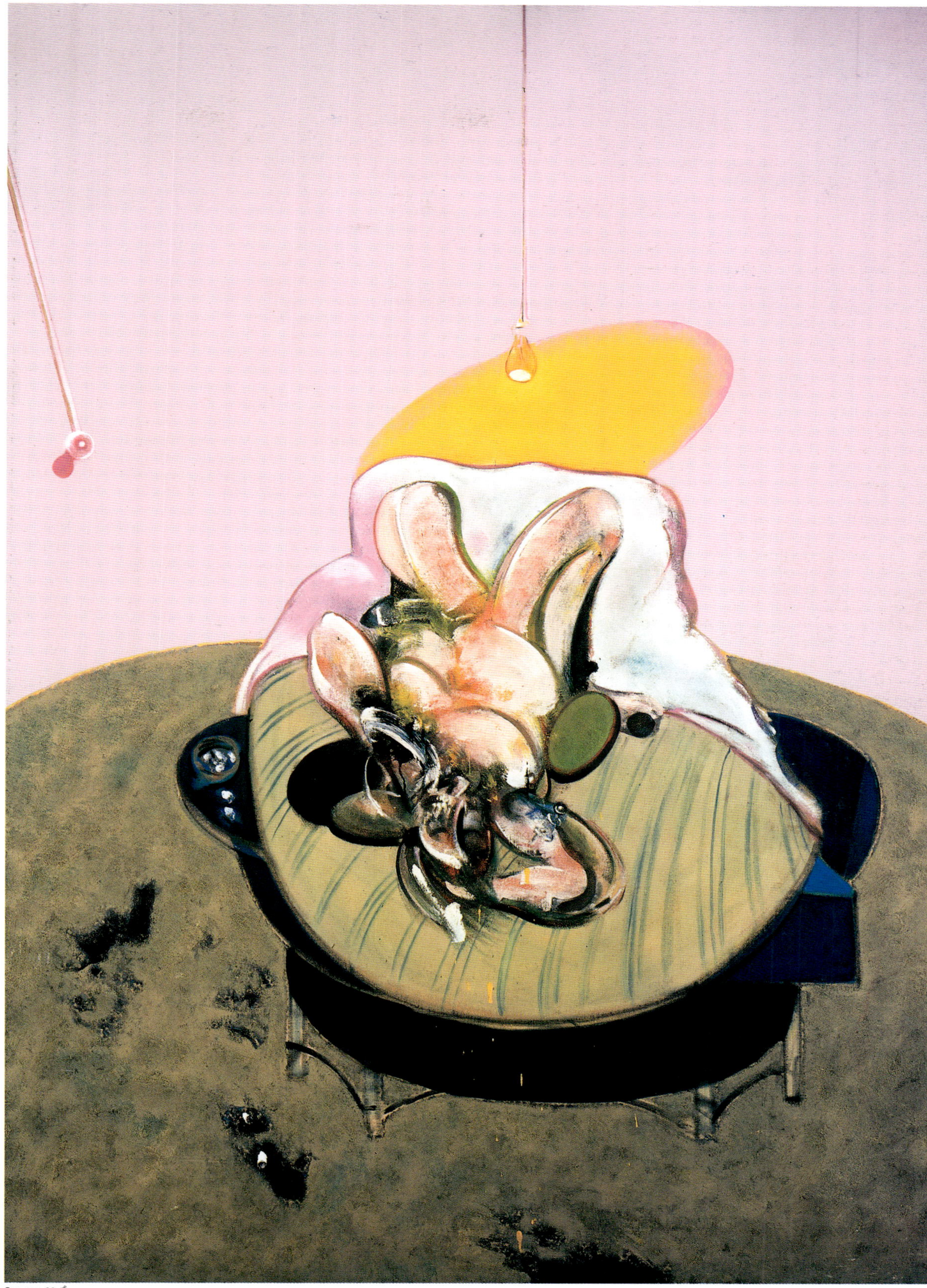

Cat. no. 60

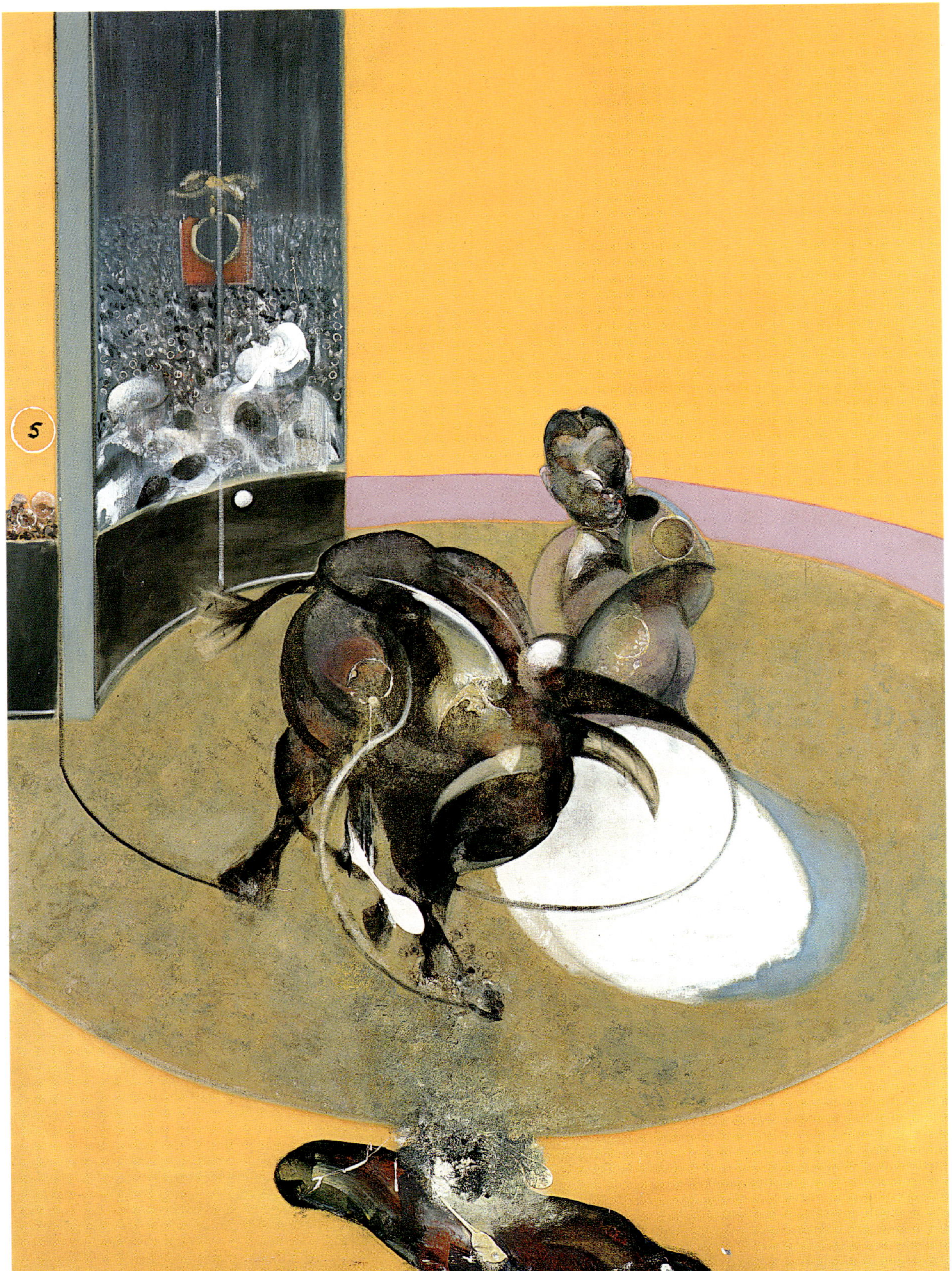

Cat. no. 61

Cat. no. 61
Francis Bacon
Study for Bullfight no. 2
1969
Oil on canvas, 198 × 147.5 cm
Lyon, Musée des Beaux-Arts
de Lyon, inv. no. 1997–20

Cat. no. 62
Francis Bacon
Sleeping Figure
1974
Oil on canvas, 198 × 147.5 cm
New York, Private Collection

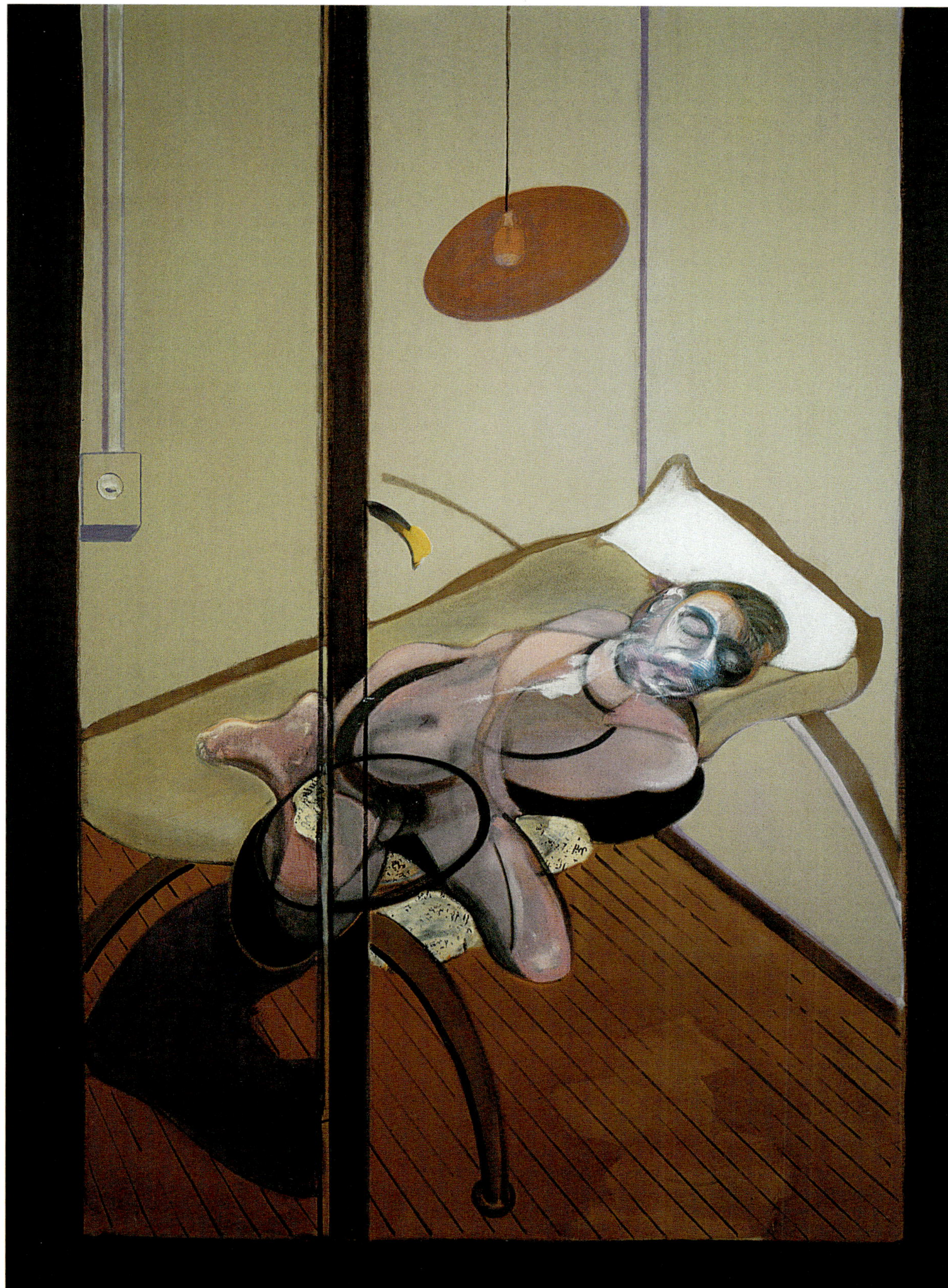

Cat. no. 62

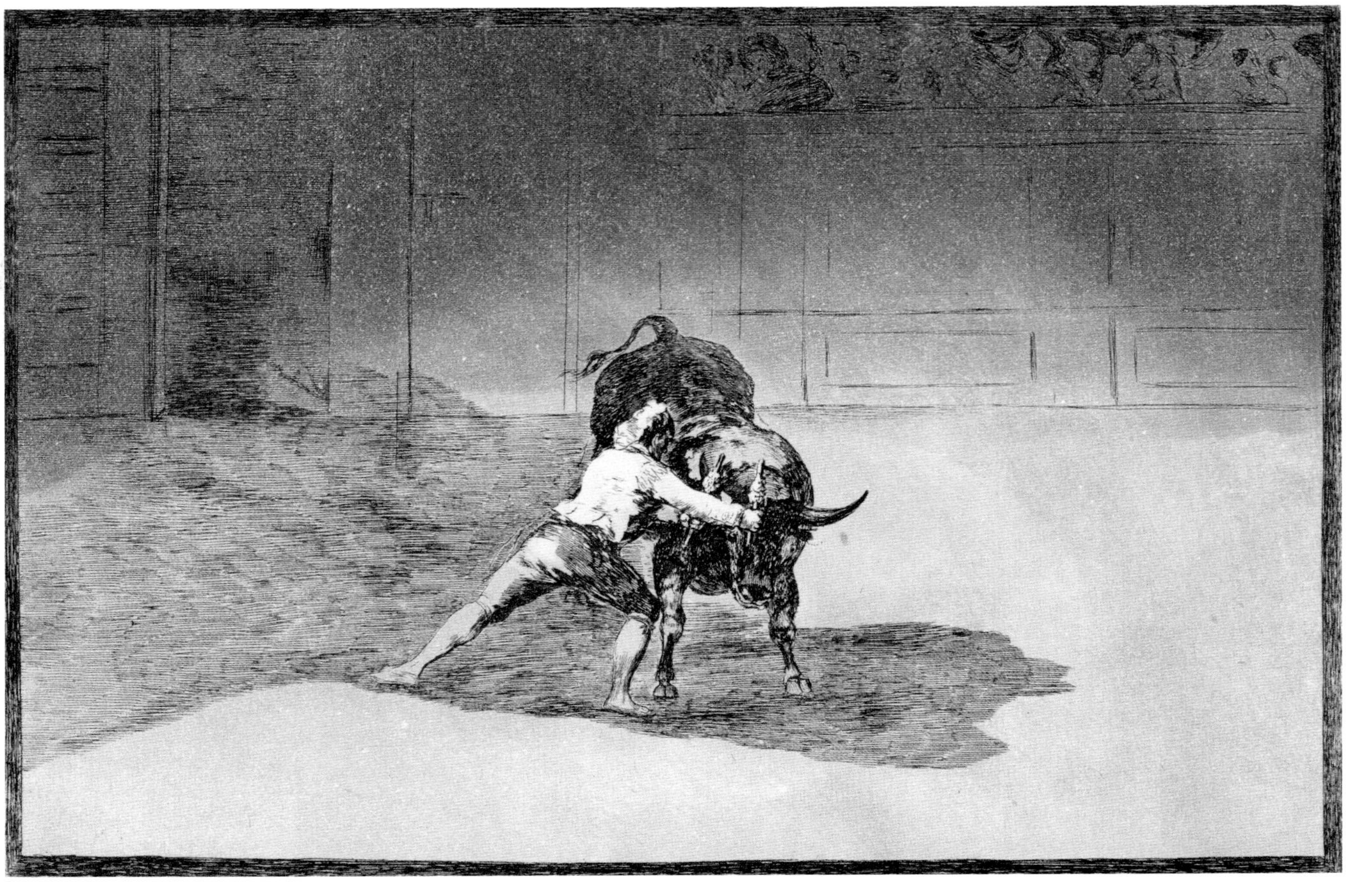

Cat. no. 63

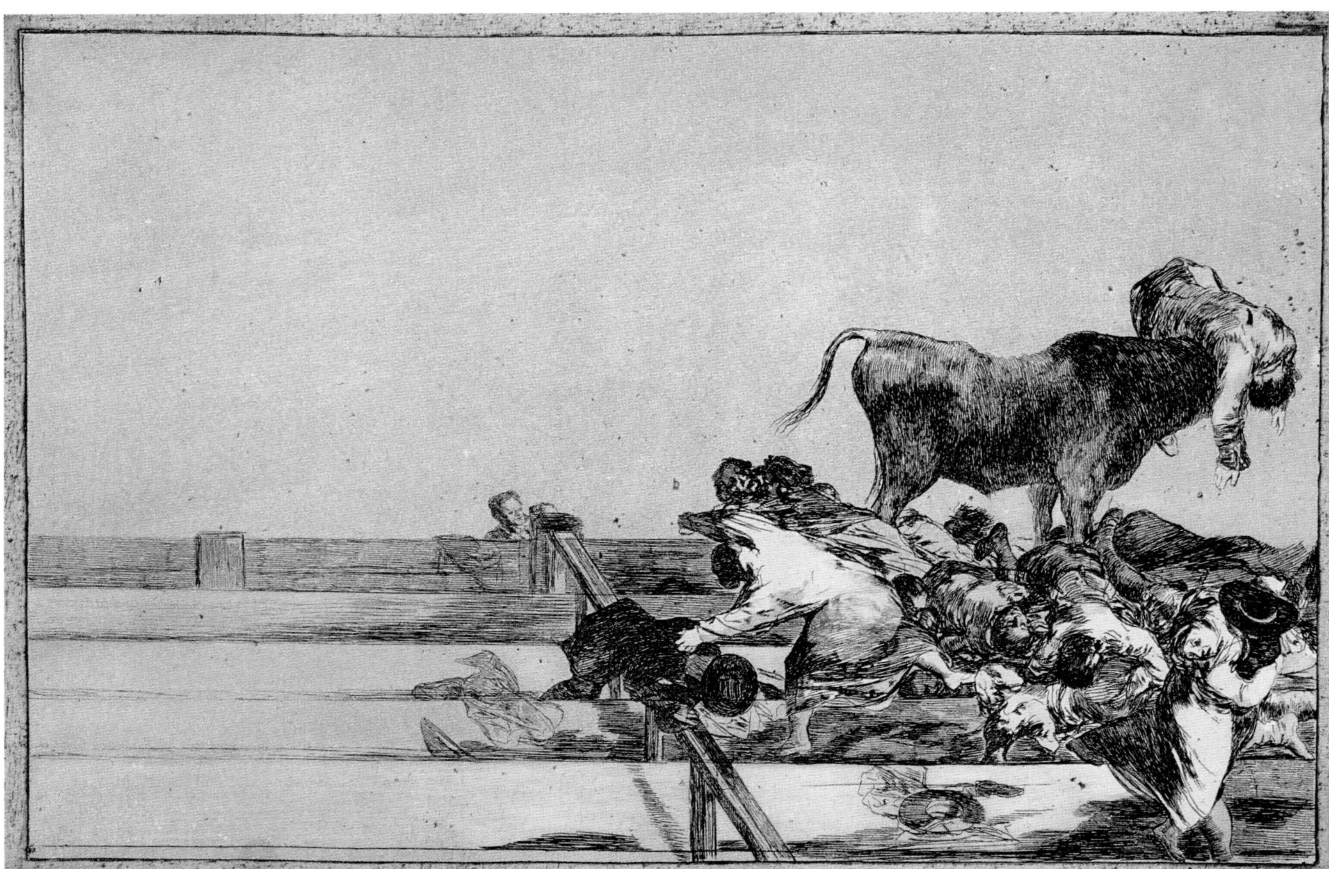

Cat. no. 64

Cat. no. 63
Francisco José de Goya y Lucientes
The famous Martincho places the banderillas as he turns his body
Aquatinta, 315 × 445 mm
Vienna, Albertina,
inv. no. DG 1924/625

Cat. no. 64
Francisco José de Goya y Lucientes
An unfortunate accident in the stalls of the arena at Madrid and the death of the Alkalde of Torrejon
Aquatinta, 315 × 435 mm
Vienna, Albertina,
inv. no. DG 1924/631

Cat. no. 65
Francisco José de Goya y Lucientes
Pedro Romero kills the standing bull
Aquatinta, 316 × 437 mm
Vienna, Albertina, inv. no. 1924/640

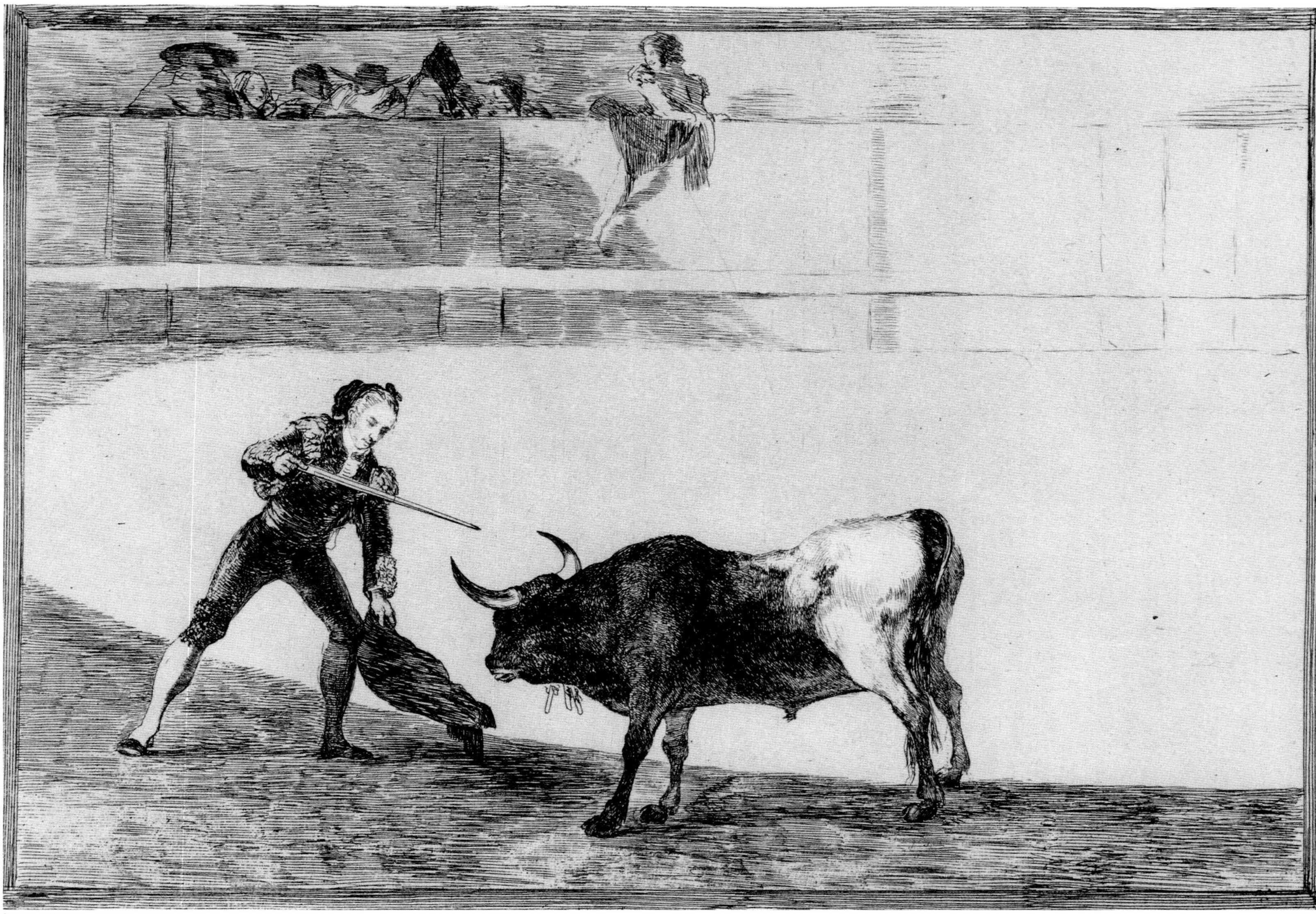

Cat. no. 65

Cat. no. 66
Figures on a rail by Francis Bacon.
c. 1960s. Grey, blue and red felt-tip
pen on paper, 392 × 233 mm
Dublin, Dublin City Gallery
The Hugh Lane, F102:13

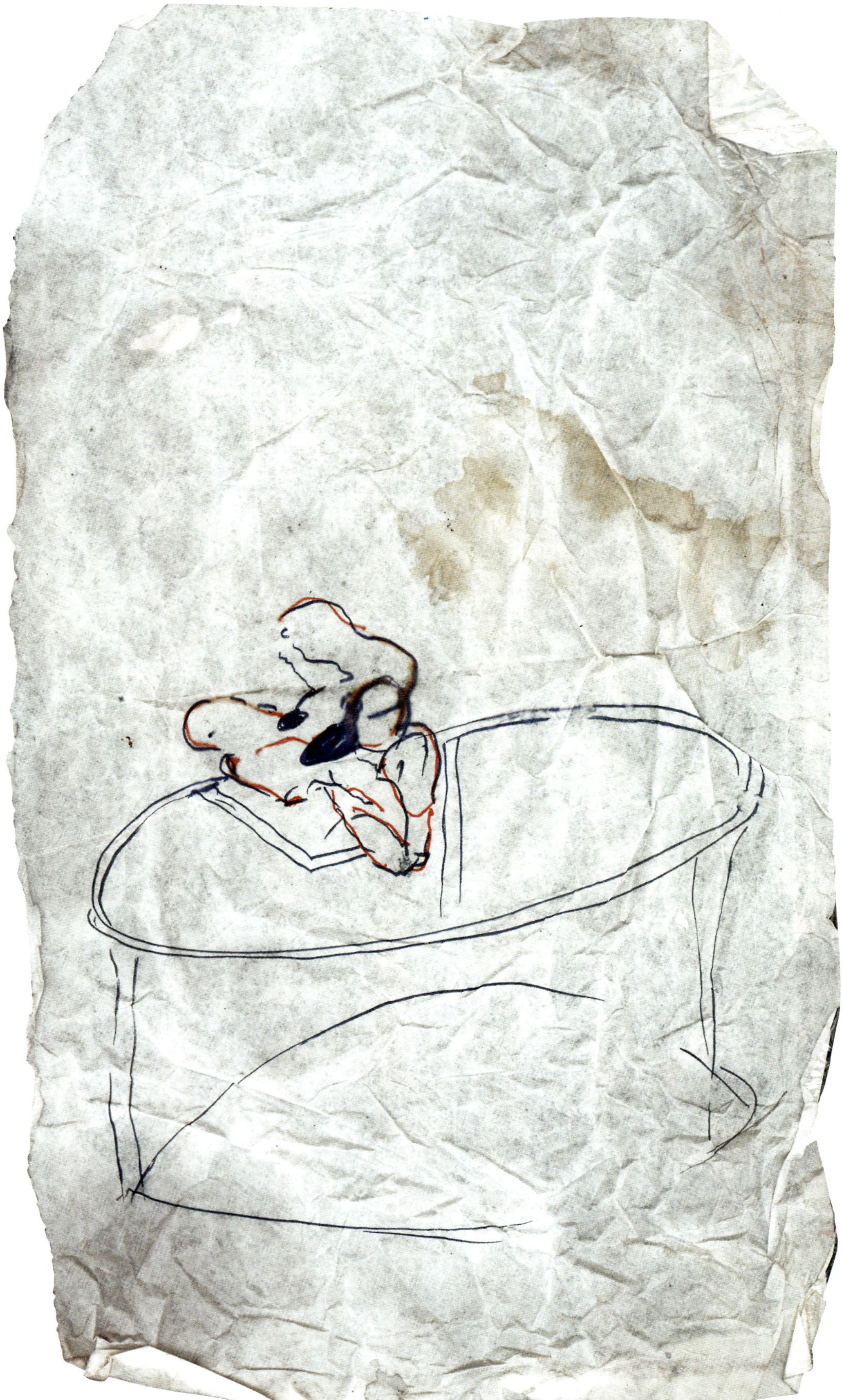

Cat. no. 66

Cat. no. 67
RMS 'Edinburgh Castle' sketch by Francis Bacon. Late 1960s. Black ink on headed notepaper, 202 × 127 mm
Sketch found inserted in book, Alistair Graham and Peter Beard, Eyelids of Morning The Mingled Destinies of Crocodiles and Men being a description of the Origins, History and Prospects of Lake Rudolph , New York, 1973
202 × 127 mm
Dublin, Dublin City Gallery The Hugh Lane, F137:3

Cat. no. 68
Torn leaf from K.C. Clark, Positioning in Radiography, London, 1939 (or later edition)
234 × 228 mm
Dublin, Dublin City Gallery The Hugh Lane, NF91

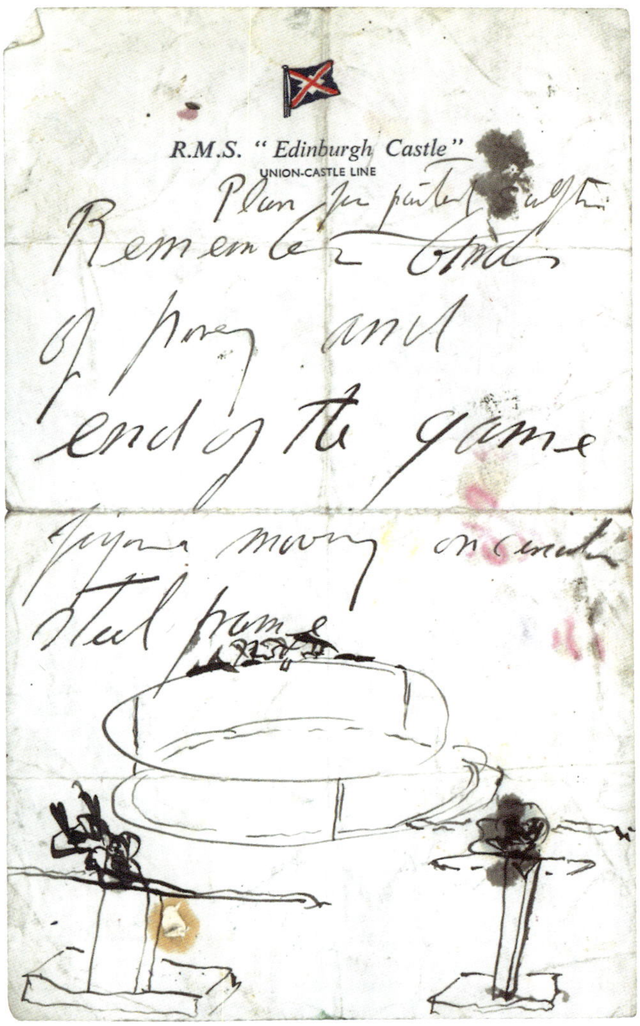

Cat. no. 67

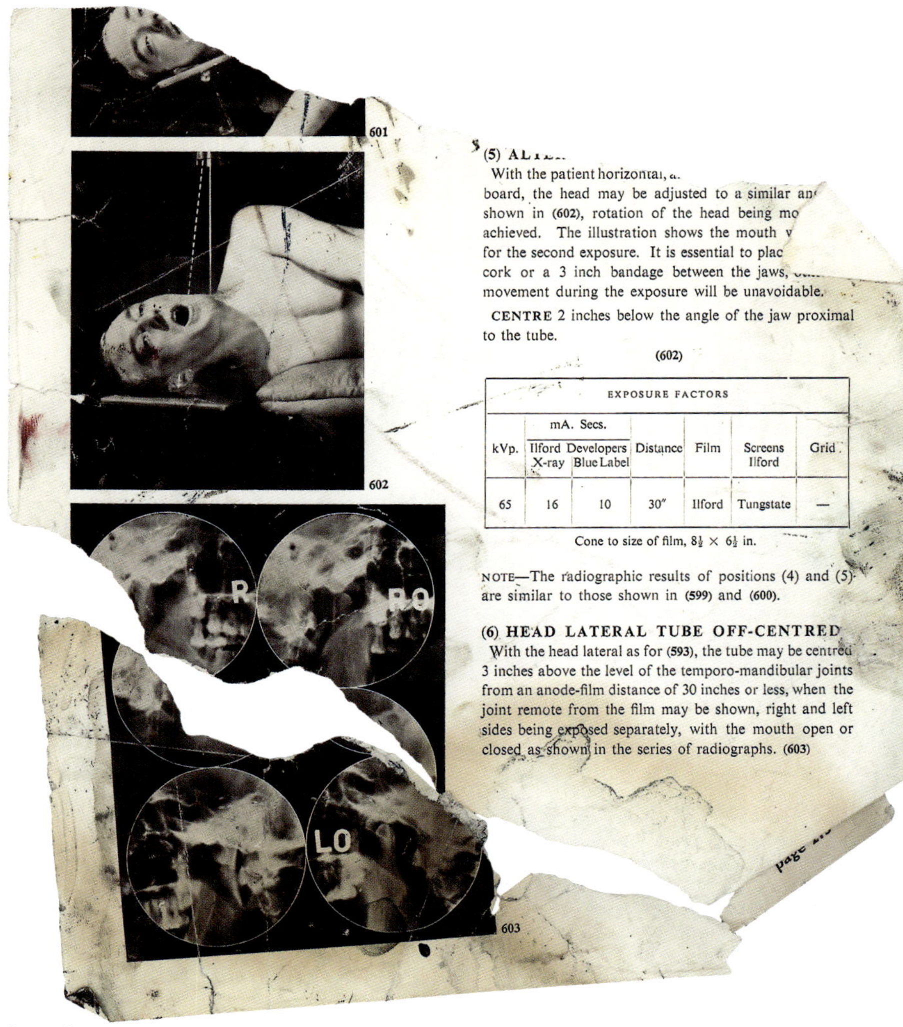

(5) AL...
With the patient horizontal, ... board, the head may be adjusted to a similar an... shown in (602), rotation of the head being mo... achieved. The illustration shows the mouth ... for the second exposure. It is essential to plac... cork or a 3 inch bandage between the jaws, ... movement during the exposure will be unavoidable.

CENTRE 2 inches below the angle of the jaw proximal to the tube.

(602)

EXPOSURE FACTORS						
	mA. Secs.					
kVp.	Ilford X-ray	Developers Blue Label	Distance	Film	Screens Ilford	Grid
65	16	10	30"	Ilford	Tungstate	—

Cone to size of film, $8\frac{1}{2} \times 6\frac{1}{2}$ in.

NOTE—The radiographic results of positions (4) and (5) are similar to those shown in (599) and (600).

(6) HEAD LATERAL TUBE OFF-CENTRED
With the head lateral as for (593), the tube may be centred 3 inches above the level of the temporo-mandibular joints from an anode-film distance of 30 inches or less, when the joint remote from the film may be shown, right and left sides being exposed separately, with the mouth open or closed as shown in the series of radiographs. (603)

Cat. no. 68

Cat. no. 69
Intervention by Francis Bacon in black ink on a cutting of a black-and-white illustration of two cyclists in a race. Date unknown. Cutting mounted on the back cover of a Roberson & Co. sketch book
260 × 207 mm
Dublin, Dublin City Gallery
The Hugh Lane, BC1

Cat. no. 70
Black-and-white photograph of Isabel Rawsthorne, taken by John Deakin. Early/mid 1960s. 306 × 303 mm
Dublin, Dublin City Gallery
The Hugh Lane, F16:9

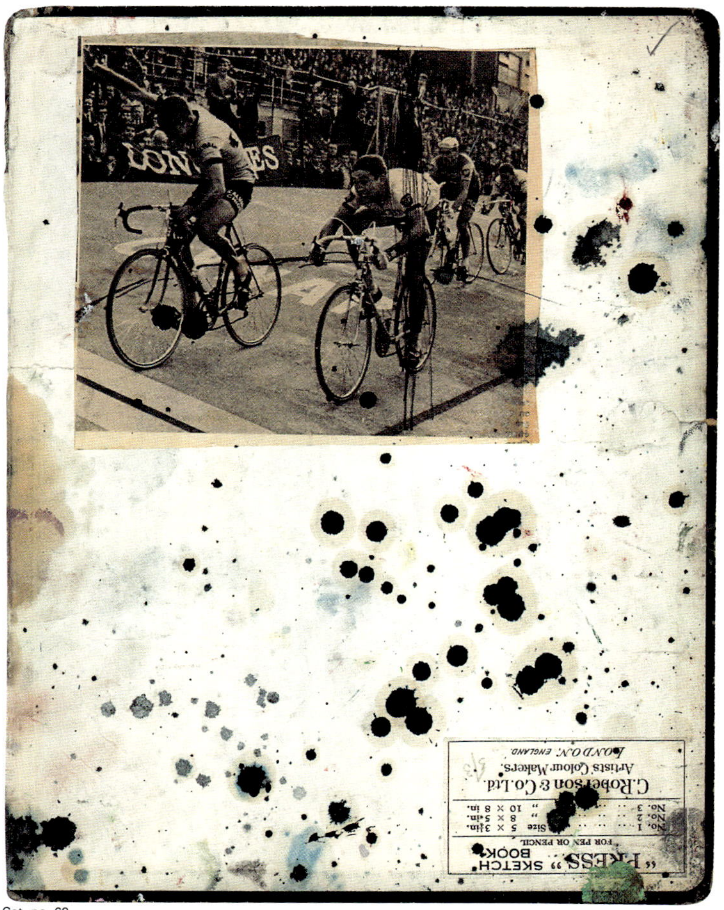

Cat. no. 69

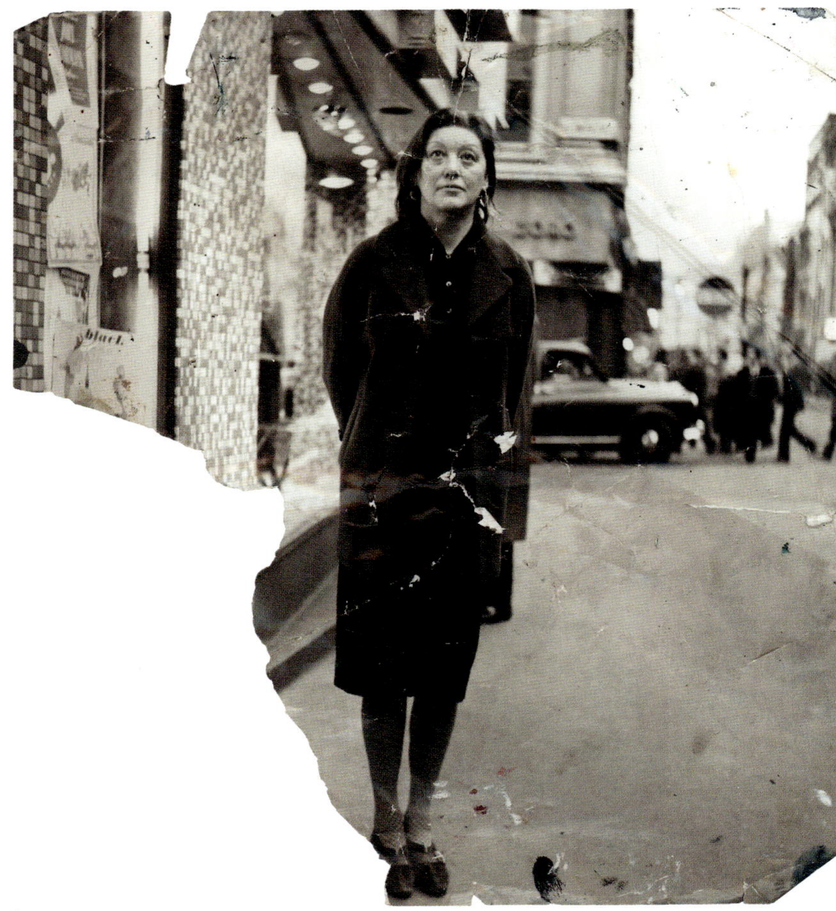

Cat. no. 70

Cat. no. 71
Fragment of black-and-white photograph of Henrietta Moraes, taken by John Deakin. Early 1960s.
207 × 249 mm
Dublin, Dublin City Gallery The Hugh Lane, F17:124

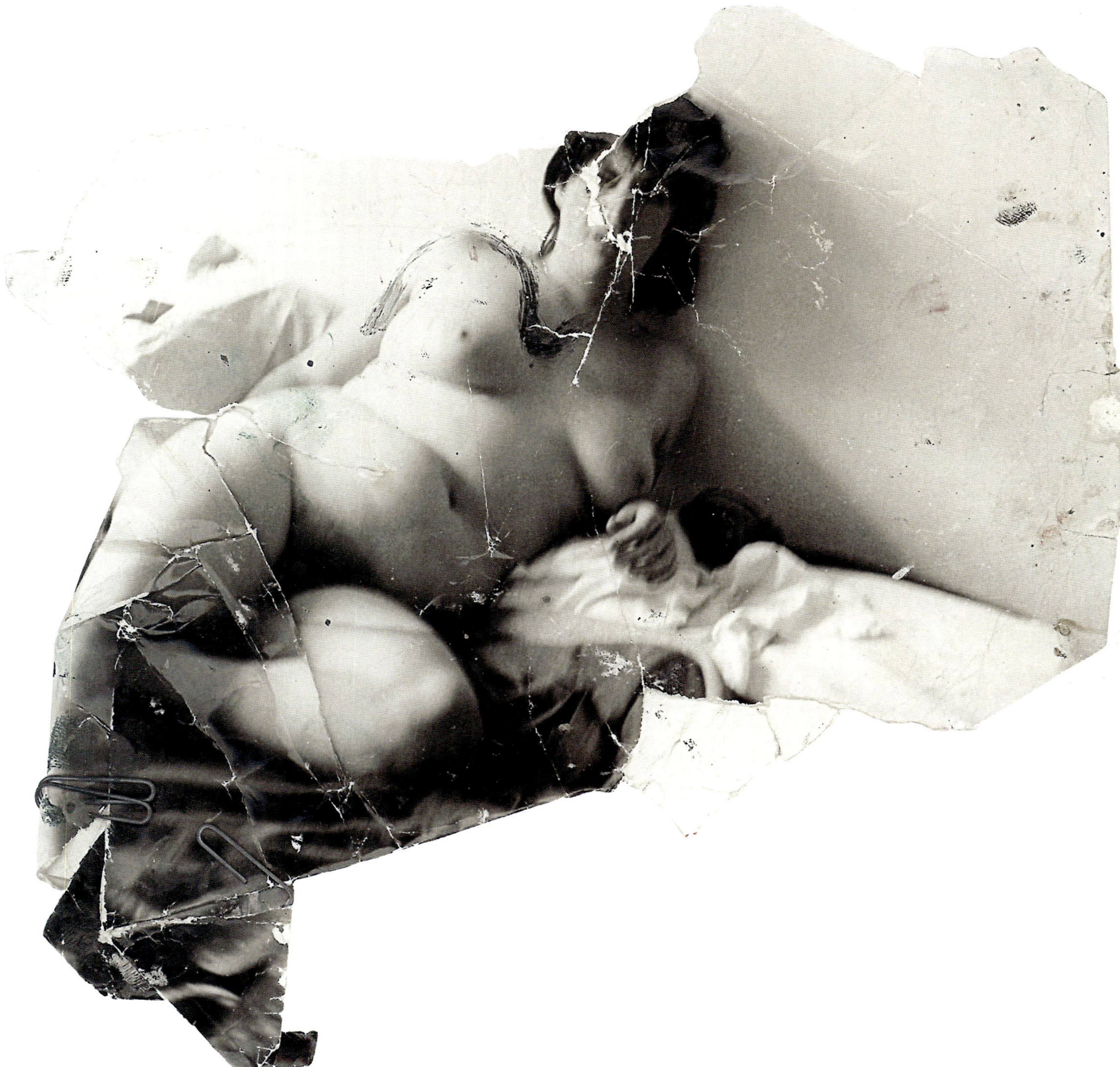

Cat. no. 71

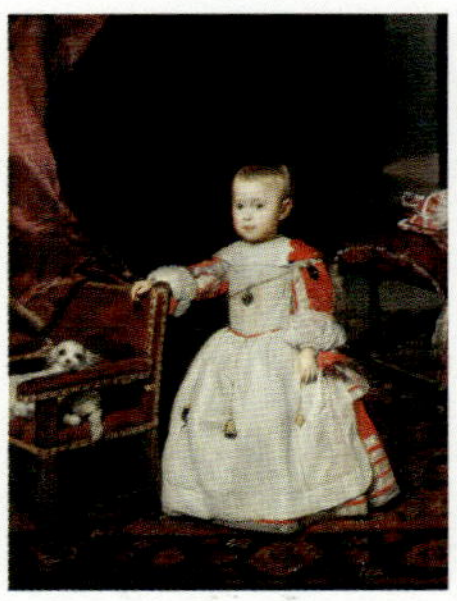
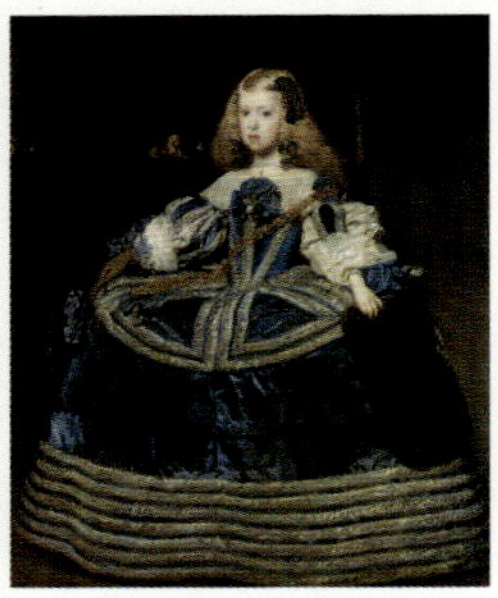
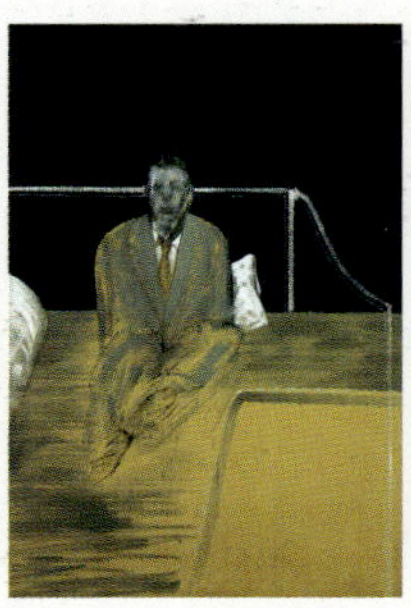
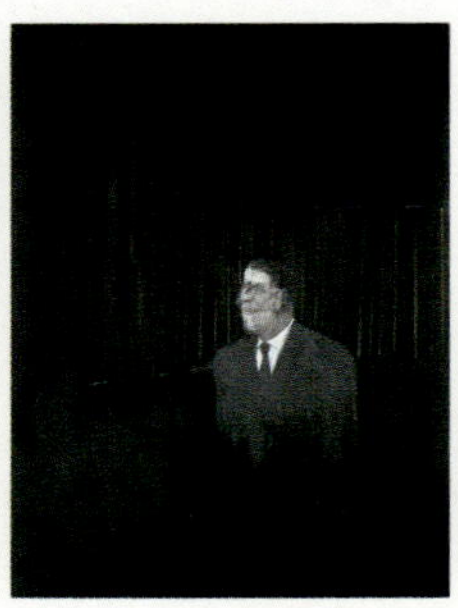
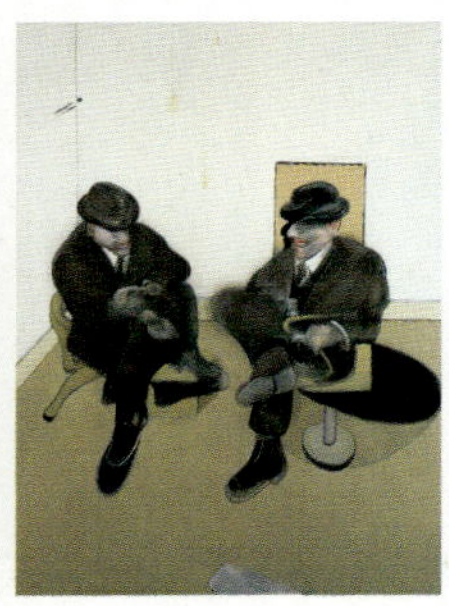
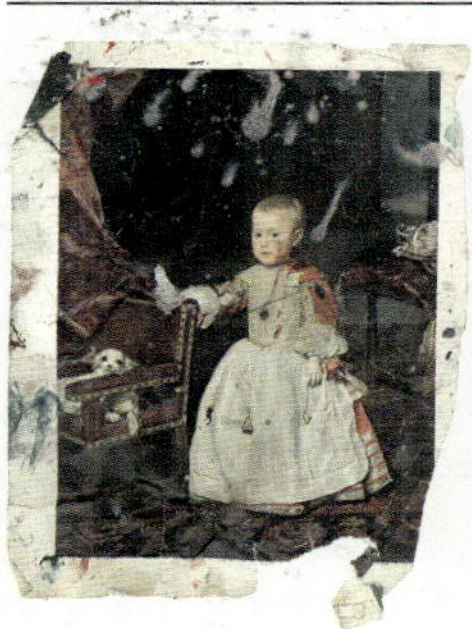
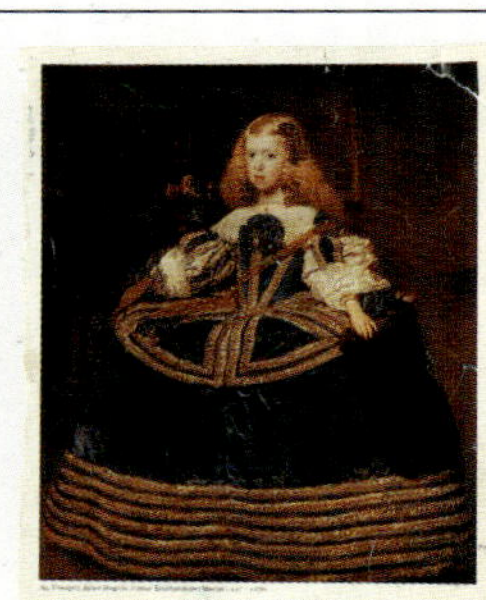
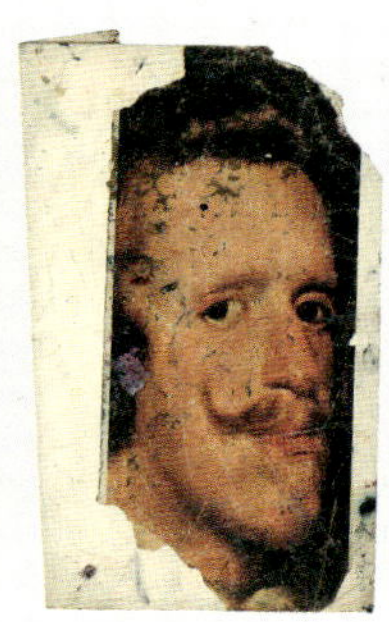

Barbara Steffen

The Representation of the Body: Velázquez – Bacon

"[...] which makes him such an amazing painter. Because one really does believe that Velasquez recorded the court at that time and when one looks at his pictures, one is possibly looking at something which is very, very near to how things looked."[1] (Francis Bacon on Diego Velázquez.)

One is struck by the fact that Bacon painted portraits mainly of male figures and that the pairs of lovers he portrayed were almost exclusively male. In the 1953 series *Man in Blue I–VI*, he painted a man with whom he had made passing acquaintance at the Imperial Hotel in Henley-on-Thames and who agreed to model for him. The figure is "masked"[2] as a businessman, and his masculine wardrobe is of special significance. Bacon selects an appearance that, through clothing, demonstrates the construct of masculinity and power. One immediately notices, however, that all men portrayed in this series have an empty facial expression, their masculine attributes rendering them a mere shell of themselves, devoid of any significant identity. The reason for this could be that Bacon usually only painted portraits of close and intimate friends, and that he had no close relationship with this model. A letter written by Bacon to his dealer Erica Brausen indicates that, at this point, he was supposed to quickly paint a series of pictures for an exhibition planned during the coming year – for which he requested more time, since he was neither psychologically nor financially in good shape.[3]

Man in Blue II of 1954 (cat. no. 75) and *Study for Figure II*, 1953–55 (cat. no. 74) have several things in common: while the first picture has the figure leaning on a sort of bar, the second picture's figure sits on a bed; in both pictures, however, the background – marked by vertical and horizontal stripes, respectively – serves to frame the figure and is part of a construction reminiscent of a closed-off space or a cage. In *Man in Blue II* (cat. no. 75) one is struck by the painting of the face, which is overlaid by white lines, while in *Study for Figure II* (cat. no. 74) the horizontal bed-frame forms a compositional contrast to the head of the person portrayed. Here, Bacon concentrates on the contours of the black or beige tie and the collar of the shirt. One might think he was concerned primarily with creating the greatest possible contrast between light and dark, as well as with the colour details of the tie, while the rest of both pictures tends to be rather generously and superficially painted. In *Study for Figure II* one also notices the horizontal division of the picture between light and dark, as well as between a sketch-like and a more finely finished style. The upper part of the picture is related to both the *Man in Blue* series and the Pope paintings. The figure here may not be a Pope – being, after all, characterised as a businessman – but he has an open, screaming mouth very much like the Pope, and sits turned toward the viewer on the bed. Without arms and feet, the upper body seems flat and exhausted, and the figure seems to have lost its lower body, because one sees only the drawn-up legs and knees. While the upper body with its grey suit is done in colour, the lower body is only implied; the legs are hatched in black and grey tones. The lower and larger part of the picture is sketched in loose brushstrokes, and the lower right-hand side of the picture remains unfinished, allowing the light colour of the canvas to have its effect. Here, too, the protagonist seems anonymous in a way similar to the *Man in Blue* series; the only details emphasised by means of painting technique are the tie and the white shirt. The man seems helpless, weakened and unmoving. In contrast, *Man in Blue II* is a traditional portrait. The figure is portrayed in profile; even through the white spots his facial features are still recognisable. Again, the figure here is depicted without arms or lower body. Bacon's objective is not so much to represent masculine identity as it is to point out that masculinity is a construct, a stereotype which he fights by making his figures appear weak and unstable by virtue of their positions and the technique used to paint them.[4] Neither does their gaze meet the eyes of the viewer, nor is it defined by the way their eyes are painted.

A similar phenomenon can be seen in the 1979 painting *Two Seated Figures* (cat. no. 76), which shows two men dressed in suits and hats, sitting together but seemingly unrelated one another. Their faces are only implied by noses and mouths. Again, they are very dark figures in a limited space; they sit on what appear to be swivel chairs or barstools, and the head of the right-hand figure is noticeably emphasised by a frame painted in the background. In this, Bacon removes this head from the context of the entire picture, creating a painting within a painting, a portrait within the picture, which intensifies the masculine attributes portrayed (man with a dark hat, a large nose, an aggressive jaw-line, his head in a diagonal profile) and, as Van Alphen notes, almost becomes a kind of satire of the masculine image.[5] This becomes even clearer through the doubling of the seated persons and the mirror-effect it creates.

Bacons admiration for Velázquez, the great Spanish master of the 17th century, is evident in his interest not only in the painting *Pope Innocent X.*, but also in works such as the portraits *Infanta Margarita in a Blue Dress* and *Infante Philip Prosper*, both from 1659 and in the collection of the Kunsthistorisches Museum (cat. nos. 72 and 73). As we know, Bacon owned not only several colour and black-and-white reproductions of the papal portrait, but also books on Velázquez's oeuvre and dozens of reproductions of his paintings, such as the torn-out catalogue reproductions of the two works (cat. nos. 73 and 72).

Over the course of his 17th-century career, Velázquez took the art of portraiture – which had only become important in Spain in the 1640s – to exceptional heights. His portrait of the *Infanta Margarita in a Blue Dress* was cut into an oval form in order to be hung in Vienna's Stallburg during the 18th century. After having been lost for a long period of time, the picture was rediscovered in 1923 in the vaults of the Kunsthistorisches Museum in Vienna, and cut into a new rectangular, but smaller, form. Velázquez had painted this picture, which is exemplary of the quality of his late portraits, together with the picture of Philip Prosper for Leopold I and sent it to Vienna from Madrid.

The infanta faces the viewer with her arms angled somewhat diagonally and away from her body and resting on her large hoop skirt, angled somewhat diagonally and away from her body. She holds a sort of fur muff in her left hand. In keeping with fashion at the Madrid court, the dark-blue dress is made of a shining, thick silk or silk organza; it is richly decorated, embroidered with gold edging and ornamented with white lace at the collar and on the sleeves. The infanta seems serious and, by virtue of her upright, representative posture, she does justice to her noble birth despite her young age. Her melancholy, innocent child's gaze suggests sweetness and fragility, even though she does her best to look a self-assured infanta in her official clothing. Velázquez does without a dominating spatial setting and pictures the Infanta with only a few attributes. Her head is emphasised by a golden frame which suggests an oil painting hanging in the background, resulting in a sort of picture-within-a-picture. One can find a similar such picture in Bacon's painting *Two Seated Figures* (cat. no. 76).

In a further Velázquez portrait, *Infanta Maria Teresa* of 1652/53, the artist does largely without background detail. Here the infanta, dressed in white and pink, is depicted in front of a dark space with which the colours of her bright clothing create a strong contrast. Like Velázquez, Bacon, too, was fascinated by the difference between light and dark – one need only think of his contrast-rich paintings of the 1950s.

Velázquez's way of depicting figures in their individuality – even though the official form of representation and the stiff clothing were meant to suppress all personality and characterisation – is the most striking thing about his portraits for the Spanish court. He succeeds in depicting feelings and psychological states in spite of the conventions of official representation. Despite their white-powdered faces, Velázquez turned the members of the royal family into living beings who seem human and vital in their official robes, even if they often look weak, stupid or even ugly. Bacon recognised this characteristic of Velázquez's paintings and, three centuries later, created works in which his protagonists may have appeared masculine, powerful and influential in terms of their outward appearances (Popes), but in which their inner state – their psychological condition – takes on another, deeper meaning beyond their superficial appearances because of screams, disembodiment and deformation.

Philip Prosper was the son of Philip V and Queen Maria Anna and died in his fifth year of life. His portrait was sent in 1659 to the emperor in Vienna. The young prince is pictured full-length in a red-and-white, long dress; his similarly red-and-white hat lies on a footstool behind him and to the right. The prince's face is very finely painted; the glow of his eyes and the red shimmer on his cheeks give the impression of gentle freshness. With his right hand, he supports himself on the scarlet-red back of a chair which stands next to him and upon which a small white dog lies. The portrayal of the infante, as well as the colourful vitality of the chair and the red-brown curtain, remind one of the portrait of Pope Innocent X. Bacon especially admired the presence and honesty that emanated from Velázquez's figures. This is not so much an indication of any direct influence of Velázquez on Bacon as it is a reflection of the fact that the portraits of both artists communicate a world of feelings, the presence of the figures and the aura that surrounds them.

[1] Sylvester 1999, p. 29.

[2] Ernst van Alphen, *Die Dekonstruktion der Männlichkeit – Zur Körpersprache im Werk Francis Bacons,* in: Exh. Cat. Munich 1996, p. 37.

[3] Ibid., p. 124.

[4] Van Alphen 1998, p. 169. Van Alphen gives a survey of masculinity as a construct and, in his book, refers first and foremost to the deconstruction of masculinity and the stereotypical discourse that Bacon's oeuvre provokes.

[5] Ibid., p. 137.

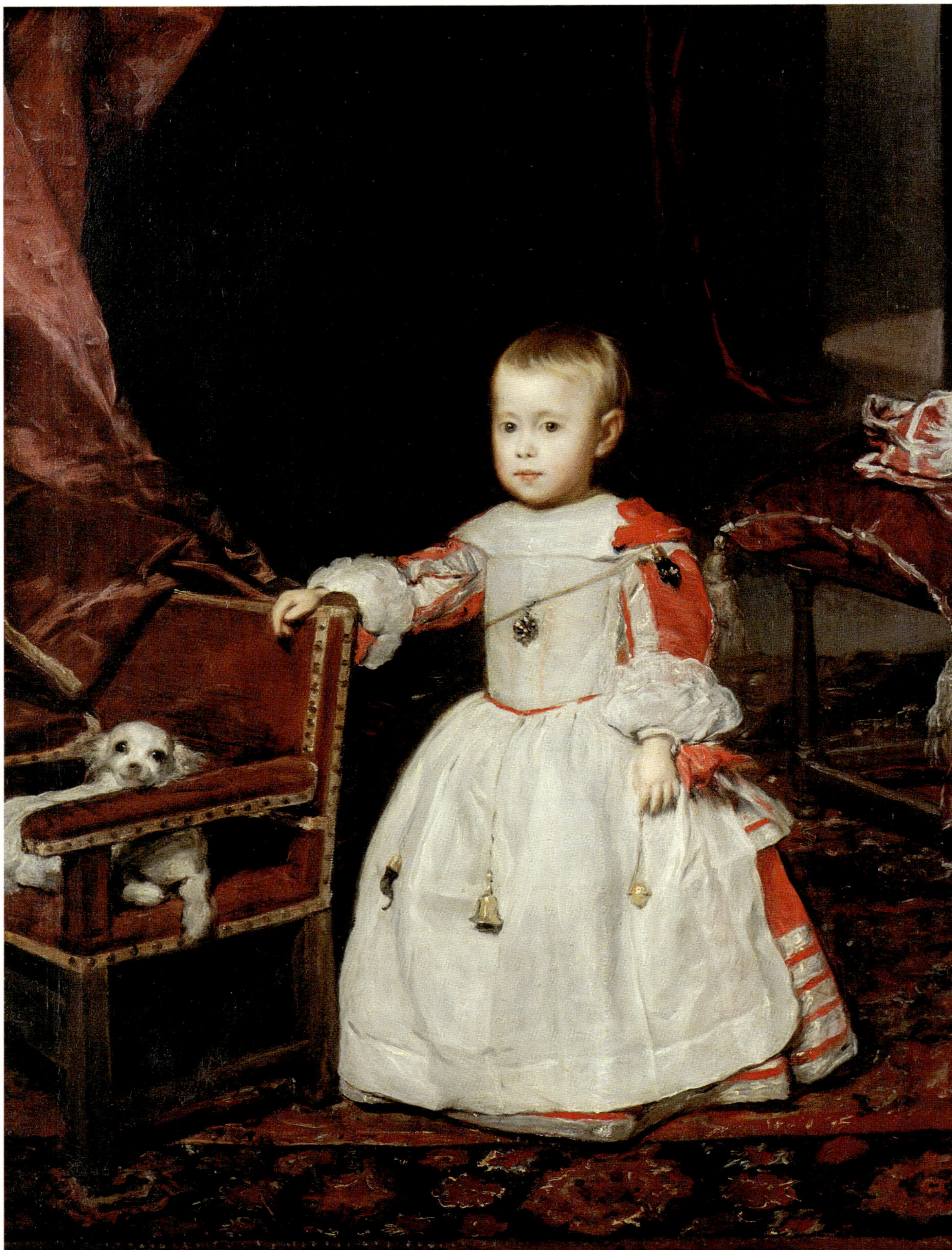
Cat. no. 72

Cat. no. 72
Diego de Silva y Velázquez
Infant Philipp Prosper
1659
Oil on canvas, 128.5 × 99.5 cm
Vienna, Kunsthistorisches Museum, Picture Gallery, inv. no. 319

Cat. no. 73
Diego de Silva y Velázquez
Infanta Margareta Teresa in a Blue Dress
1659
Oil on canvas, 127 × 197 cm
Vienna, Kunsthistorisches Museum, Picture Gallery, inv. no. 2130

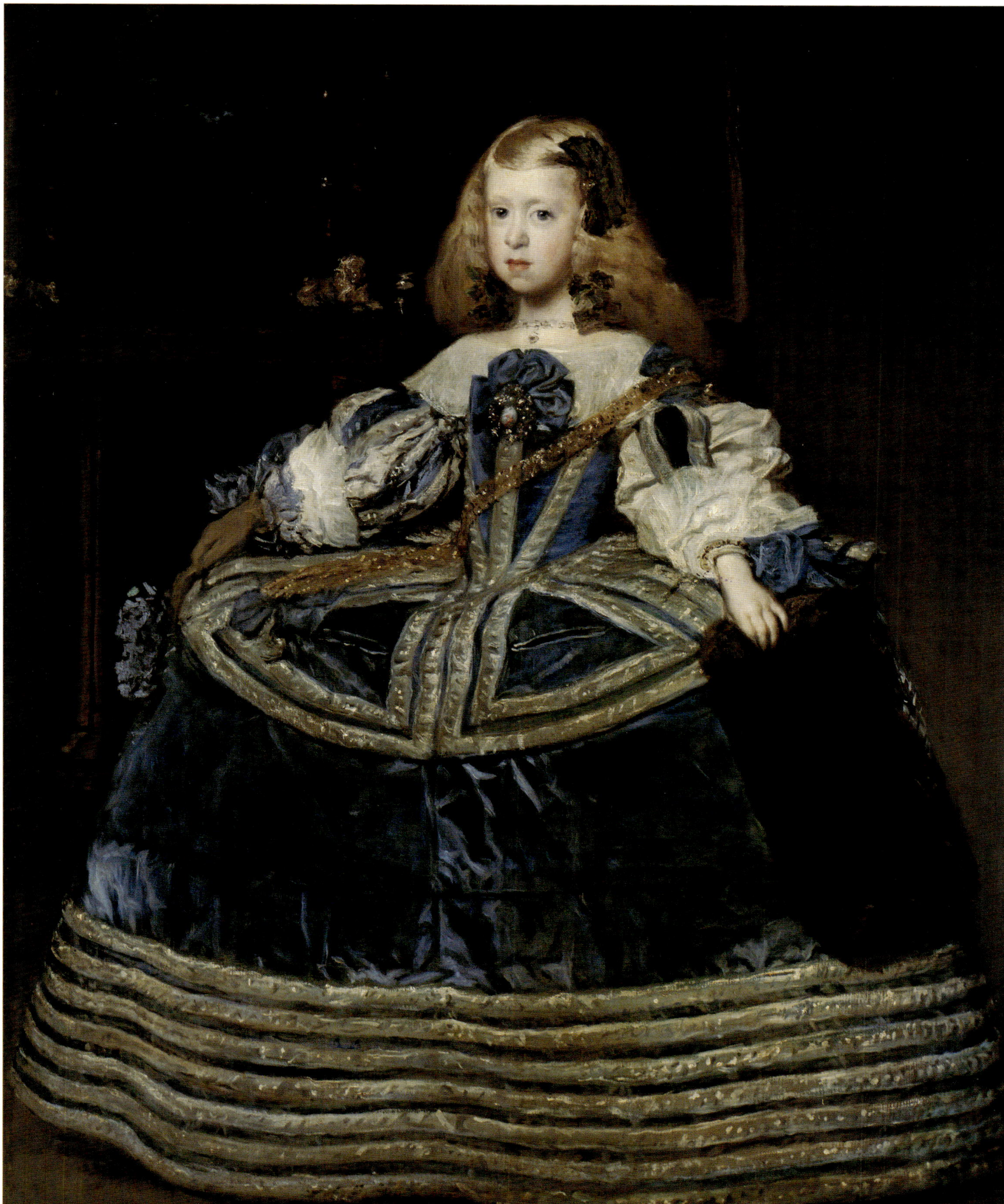

Cat. no. 73

Cat. no. 74
Francis Bacon
Study for Figure II
1953/55
Oil on canvas, 198 × 137 cm
New York, The Collection
of Mr. and Mrs. J. Tomilson Hill

Cat. no. 75
Francis Bacon
Man in Blue II
Oil on canvas, 152 × 117 cm
Basel, Coll. Galerie Beyeler

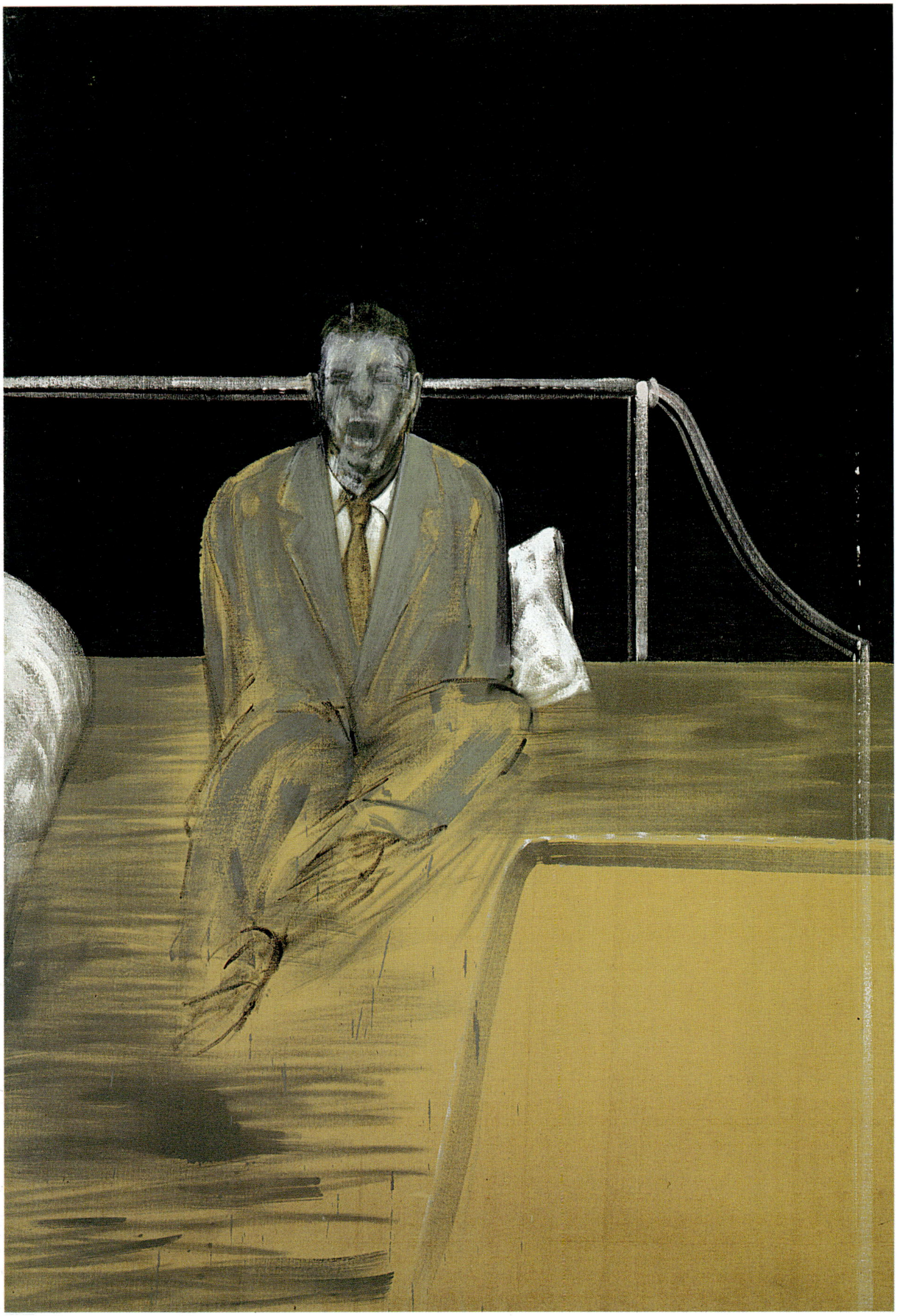

Cat. no. 74

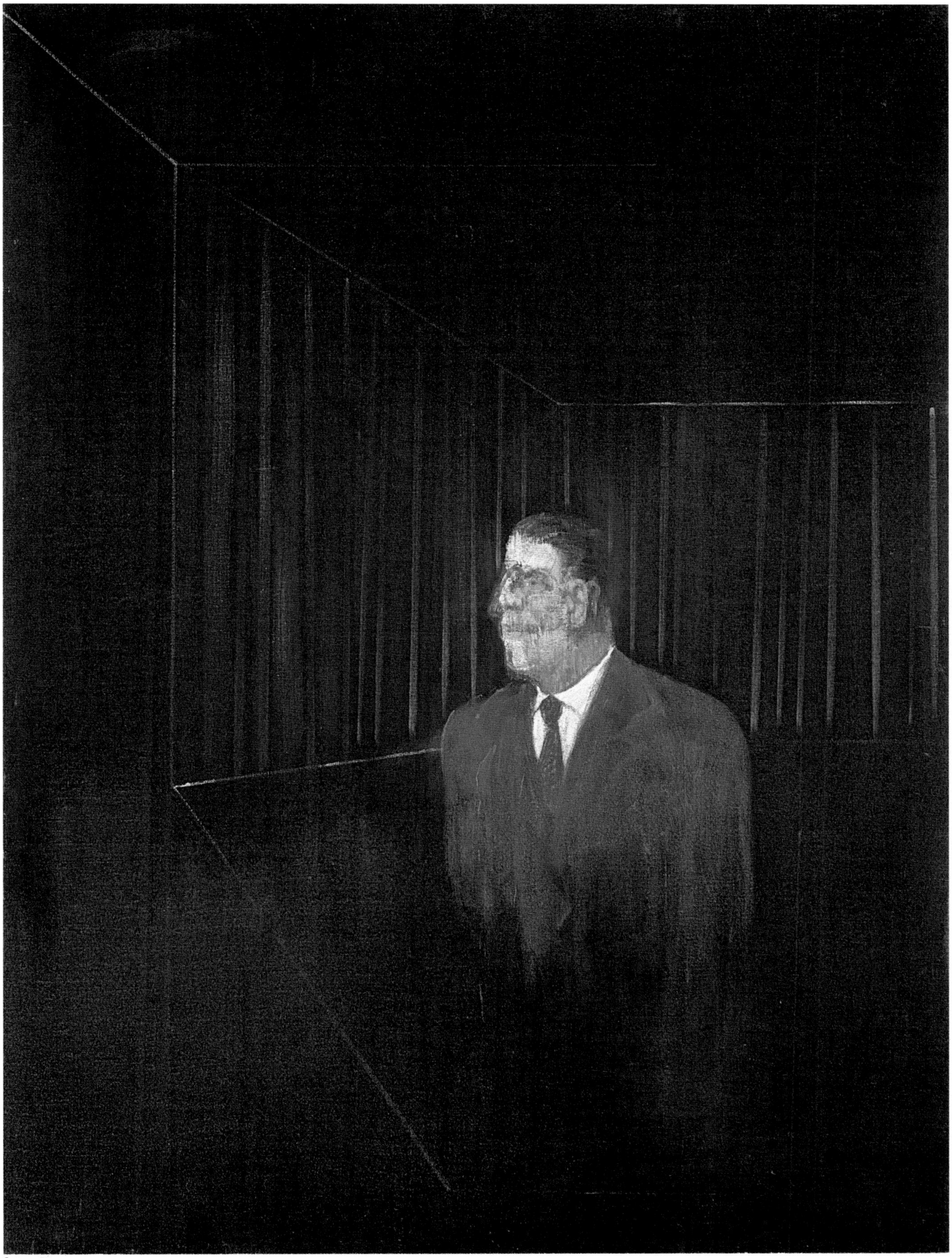

Cat. no. 75

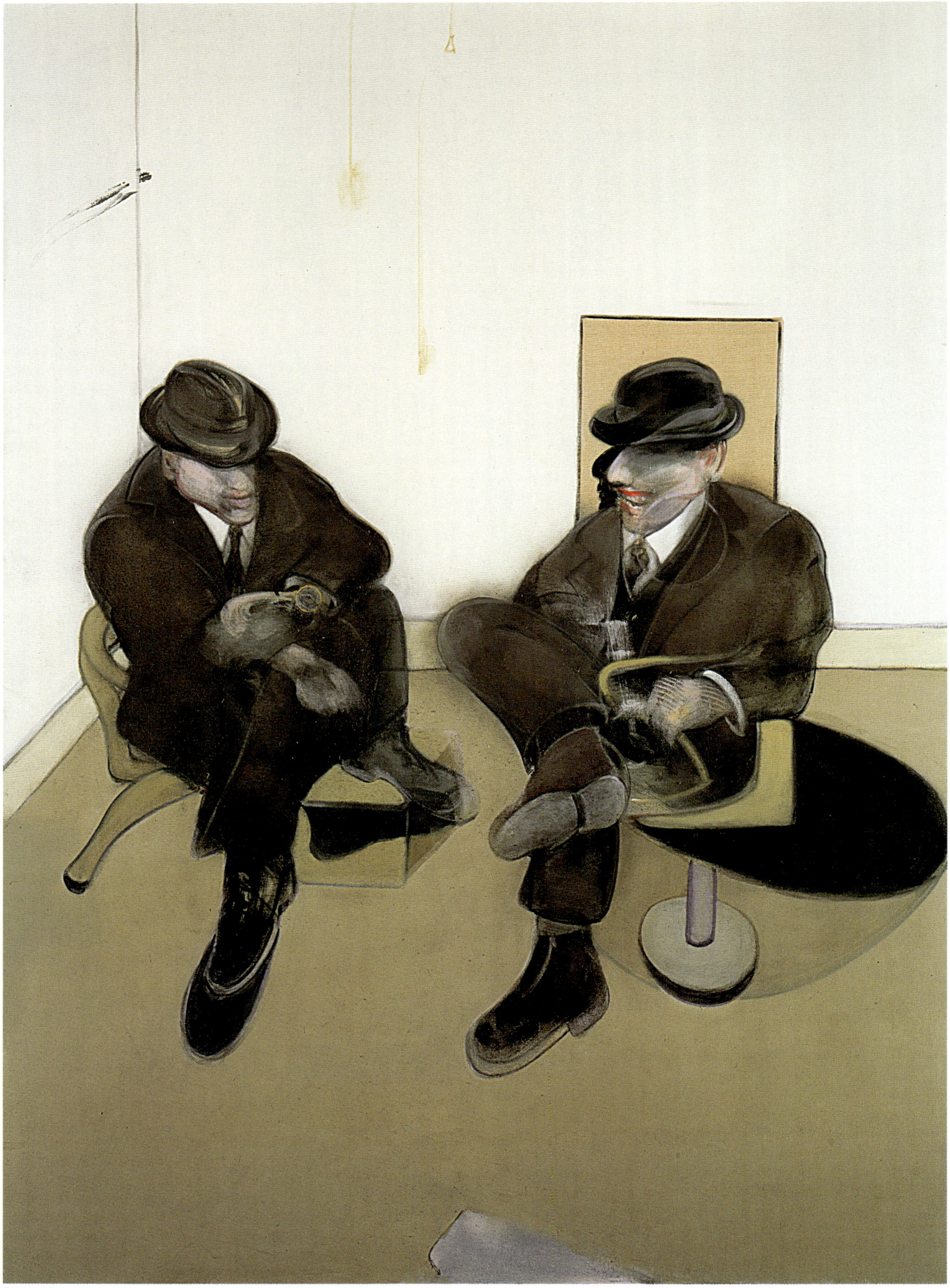

Cat. no. 76

Cat. no. 76
Francis Bacon
Two seated Figures
1979
Oil on canvas, 198 × 147.5 cm
Switzerland, Private Collection

Cat. no. 77
Colour plate of a portrait of Prince Felipe Próspero, 1659 by Diego Velázquez (Vienna, Kunsthistorisches Museum). Leaf from unidentified book, 282 × 232 mm
Dublin, Dublin City Gallery The Hugh Lane, F112:39

Cat. no. 78
Colour plate of Infanta Margarita, 1659 by Diego Velázquez (Vienna, Kunsthistorisches Museum). Leaf from unidentified book, 323 × 257 mm
Dublin, Dublin City Gallery The Hugh Lane, F17:29

Cat. no. 79
Fragment of a colour illustration of a portrait of King Philipp IV by Diego Velázquez, mounted on an A4 envelope, 303 × 253 mm
Dublin, Dublin City Gallery The Hugh Lane, F1:41

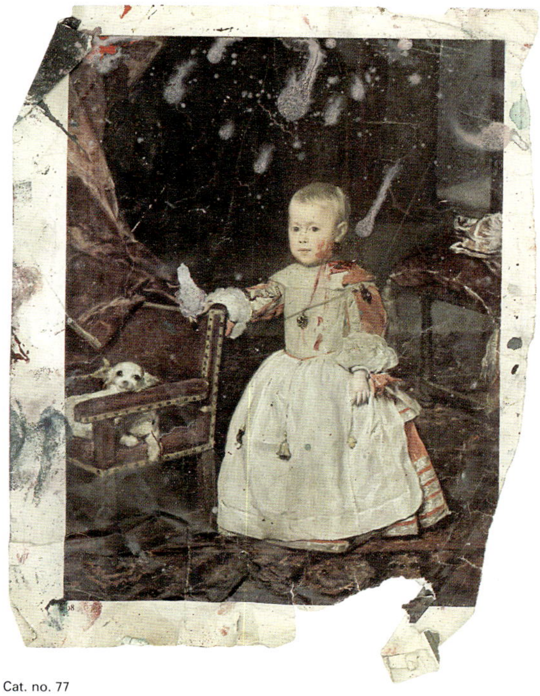

Cat. no. 77

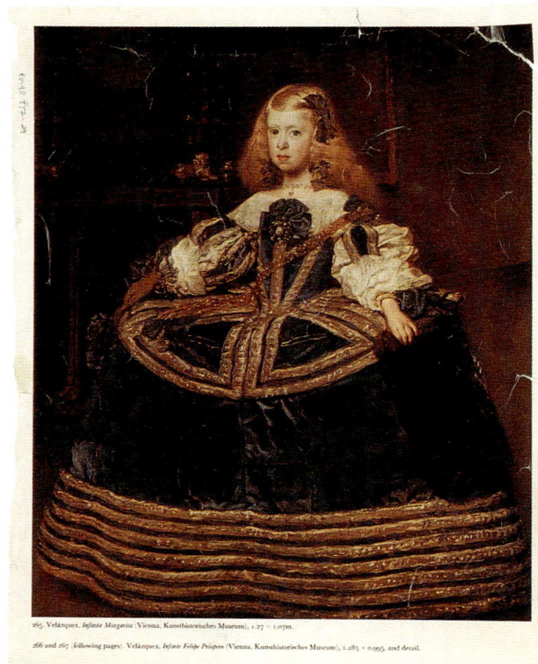

Cat. no. 78

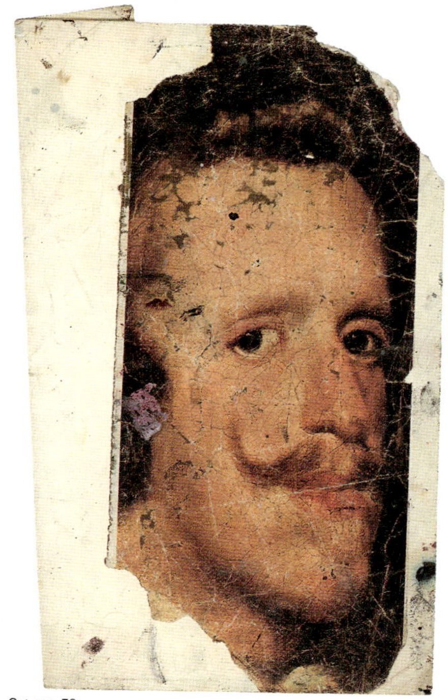

Cat. no. 79

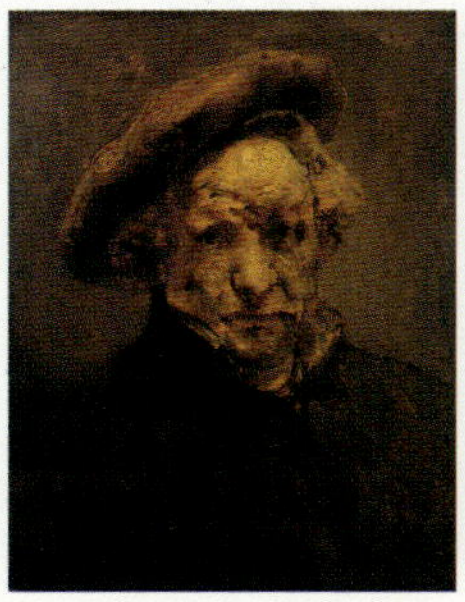
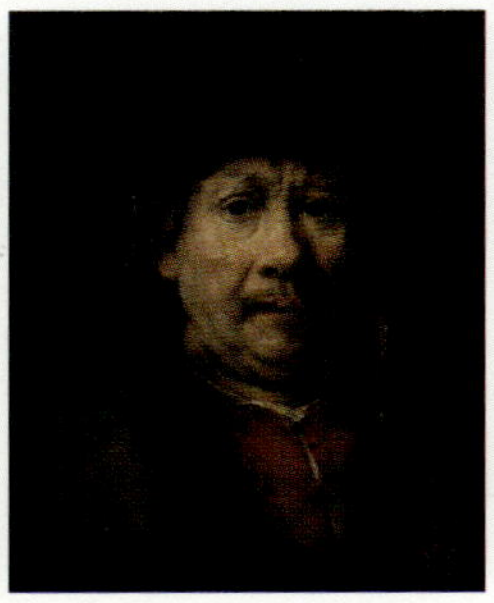
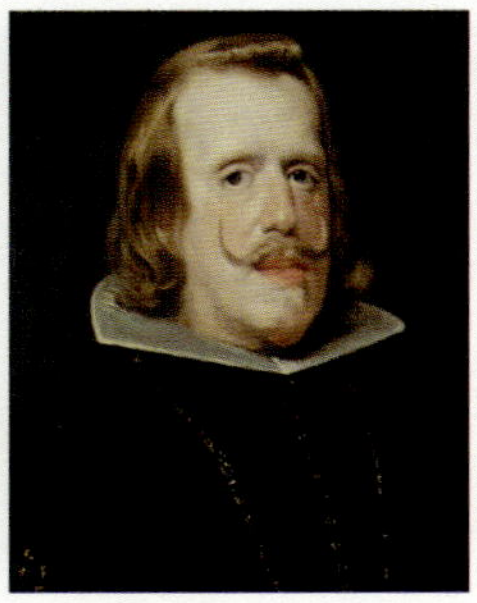
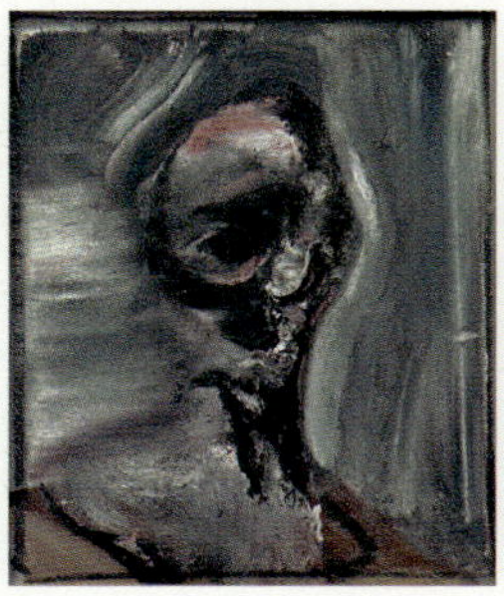
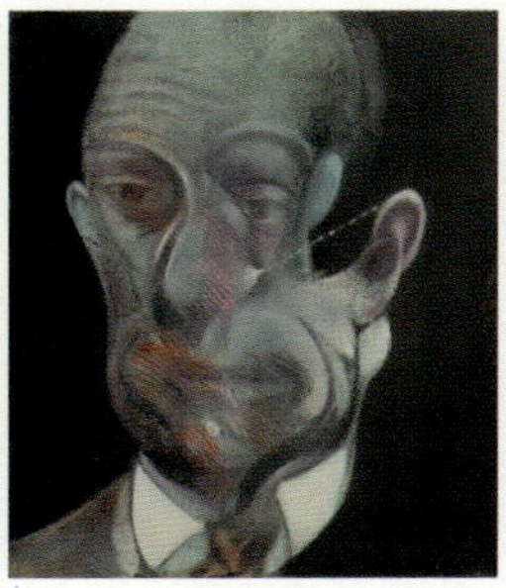
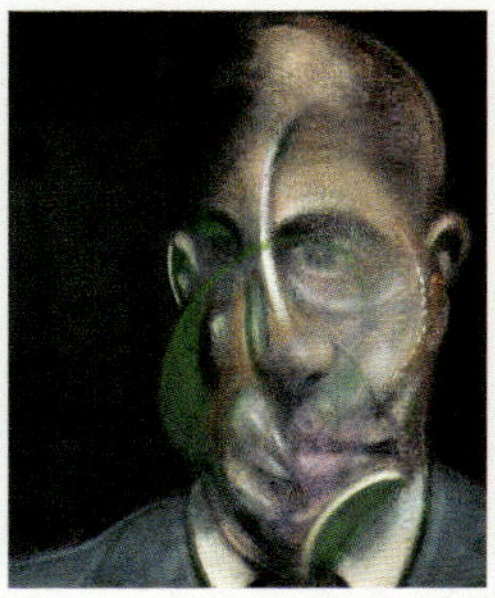
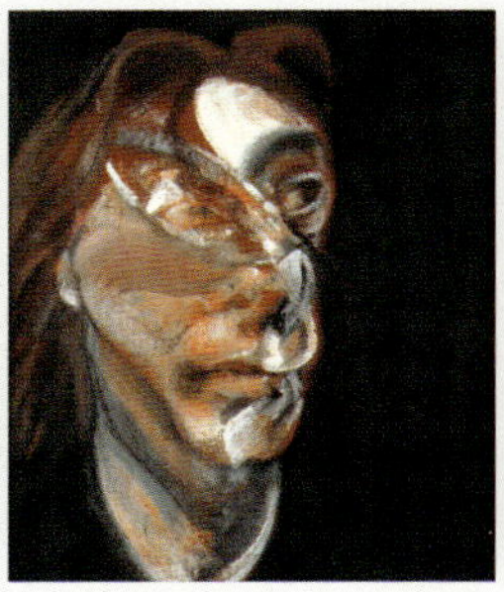
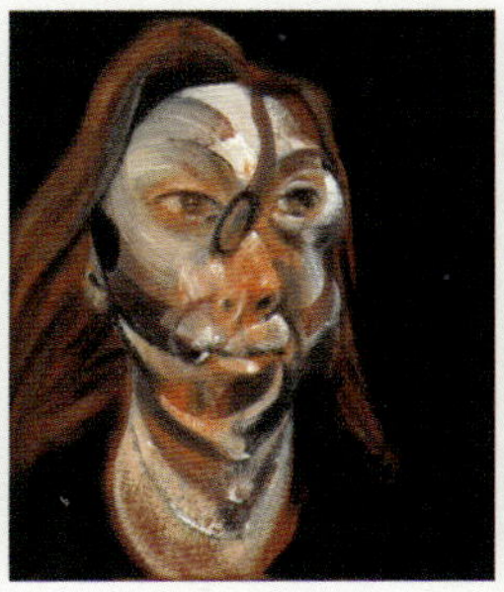
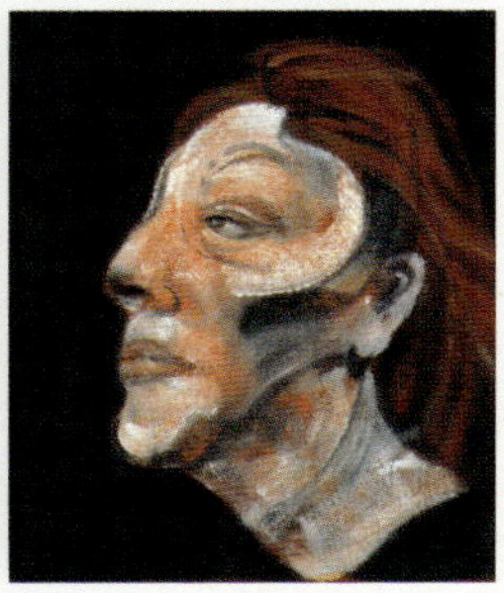
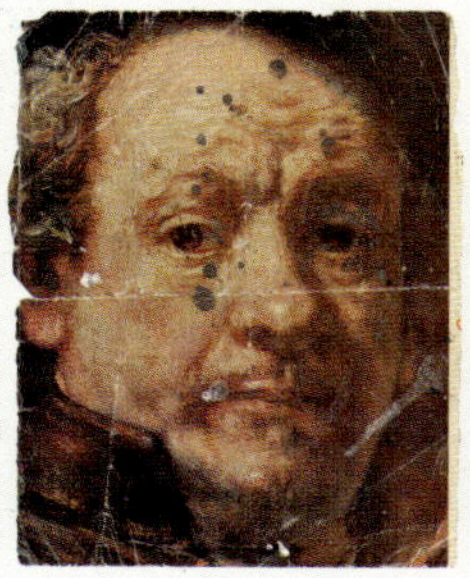
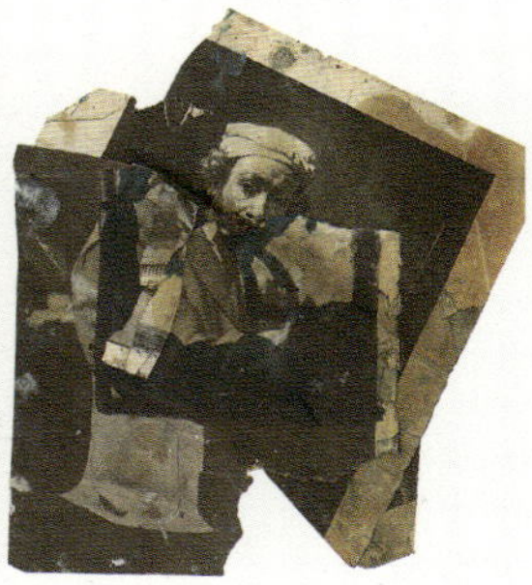
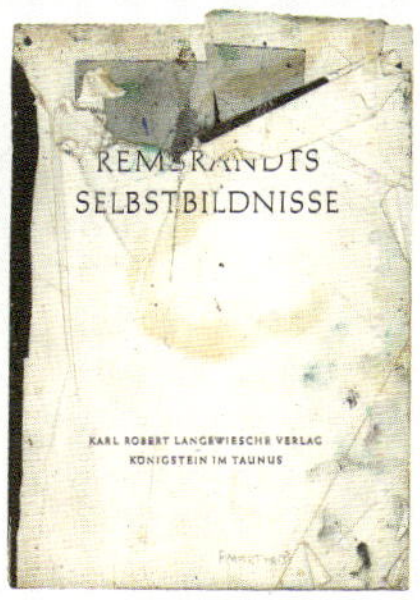
REMBRANDTS
SELBSTBILDNISSE
KARL ROBERT LANGEWIESCHE VERLAG
KÖNIGSTEIN IM TAUNUS

Alexandra Hennig

Francis Bacon: Portraiture after Representation

"Because one wants to do this thing of just walking along the edge of the precipice, and in Velázquez it's a very, very extraordinary thing that he has been able to keep it so near to what we call illustration and at the same time so deeply unlock the greatest and deepest things that man can feel."[1]

In this remark about Velázquez and in countless statements concerning Rembrandt's self-portraits, which were no less fascinating to him, Francis Bacon quite simply describes the dilemma of portraiture: namely, depicting a person, whether oneself or another, and capturing not only what distinguishes the subject as an individual but also what makes him or her alive, without forfeiting the true likeness. Liveliness and transitoriness, life and death, the fact that each day when one views oneself in the mirror, one sees death at work.[2] This is what Bacon attempts to depict in his portraits and what ultimately gives them a strange brutality and an inalienable liveliness. In addition, Bacon succeeded in his portraits in portraying his contemporary, crisis-ridden subjects in full consciousness of their vulnerability and transitoriness. "People seem to feel in looking at your figures that they are seen in moments of crisis, moments of acute awareness of their mortality, moments of acute awareness of their animal nature – moments of recognition of what might be called elemental truths about themselves."[3]

Throughout his life Rembrandt tried to capture this "elemental truth about oneself" in countless self-portraits. It is remarkable that instead of discovering an all-illuminating truth about himself, he discovered various facets of his ego, which are made manifest in the late self-portraits that Francis Bacon so admired, in an enormous variety of variations on one and the same subject, namely Rembrandt's face. Like no other artist, Rembrandt reinvented himself with brush and paint in each of his self-portraits. "I think that's probably what is so haunting about that small German book where they have put all of Rembrandt's self-portraits together, from a young man to the very end of his life. [...] On the other hand, there are painters who find a subject and just go on doing the same thing, which is not at all the same as somebody who is reinventing the methods by which the subject can be recorded."[4]

A remarkable example of Rembrandt's late self-portraits is the so-called *Small Self-Portrait* (cat. no. 80A) painted around 1657, which depicts the artist in a broad-brimmed hat. The portrait is appealing in its informal character, not only with regard to the free-flowing brushwork, in which impasto alternates with smooth brushstrokes, but also in its depiction of the artist in everyday attire.[5] The rough surface of the master's face is marked by the process of ageing and reminiscent in its bumps and dents of a mountain landscape. Conspicuous in this self-portrait is the contrast between the steady gaze, reflecting strength of will, and the lively, fleshy facial features. The ruthlessness with which Rembrandt depicted his facial features deformed by age reaches a peak in the *Small Self-Portrait* in the Musée Granet in Aix-en-Provence (cat. no. 80B),[6] a work that is the subject of controversy among experts. The bold sketchiness of this work made a lasting impression on Bacon. As we know from his conversations with David Sylvester, what particularly fascinated Bacon about this painting was the mystery of how Rembrandt succeeded in producing from an accumulation of completely non-illustrational marks a painting that was capable of reproducing a recognisable reality: "Well, if you think of the great Rembrandt self-portrait in Aix-en-Provence, for instance, and if you analyze it, you will see that there are hardly any sockets to the eyes, that it is almost completely anti-illustrational. I think that the mystery of fact is conveyed by an image being made out of non-rational marks."[7]

Bacon's admiration of this individualistic late work by Rembrandt is based on its ability to capture reality within the opposition of abstract marks and figurative depiction. Rembrandt's self-portrait conveys in a double sense an image of the destruction of the artist's face. On the one hand, it is an image of destruction to which the face has been subjected by the natural process of ageing; on the other hand, it is a violation of the likeness through the brutal use of brush and paint. Rembrandt's head appears, in a manner similar to the *Small Self-Portrait* in Vienna, as a lively, fleshy mass; the skin is pale and slack, and yet behind the crumbling façade, the severe frontality and the decisiveness in the facial expression of the subject convey his unconditional presence, standing firm against the assaults of life and the brutal treatment of the canvas that represents them. This self-portrait reminds one of Bacon's pronouncement concerning the "brutality of facts." The manner in which Rembrandt in this painting unsparingly depicts the marks of life on his face with the help of an unbelievably free application of paint touches the viewer with the kind of power that Bacon is also striving to achieve in his paintings.

A small study painted around 1959 is a portrait in which the traces of the brush left behind while ploughing across the canvas are particularly clear. It is entitled *Portrait Head* (cat. no. 81), and the title is just as confusing as it is enlightening[8]. *Portrait Head* depicts a head that is not further defined. When the title of a painting contains the word "portrait," the viewer usually expects to learn the identity of the subject, the possibly well-known personality who has been portrayed. *Portrait Head* subverts this expectation of the genre – which in the traditional sense is understood as being a mimetic (imitative) portrayal – by depicting an almost faceless head. The small portrait conveys the impression that Bacon went behind the sometimes deceptive façade of the face and exposed the head to view with its raw flesh and naked skull, with the "brutal gesture of the painter" – as Milan Kundera calls it in his poetic essay about Bacon: "The view of the painter descends like a brutal hand on the face and attempts to take possession of its character, of this diamond, which is hidden within its deepest interior."[9]

The face here is only outlined. The left half appears to be encrusted beneath the impasto paint, while the contours of the head on the right side appear to be dissolving, wiped towards the edge of the painting. The red-bluish, fleshy coloration that predominates in Bacon's small painting additionally intensifies the impression of the loss of the face, which in the absence of any closer identification of the subject in the title becomes virulent. Even today, Rembrandt's late self-portrait can provoke an unease similar to that caused by Bacon's small portrait study. By attacking the face, the human countenance, the two portraits are examples of violating an ethical boundary, of breaking a taboo: "The deformation in the portraits provokes immediate sympathy on the part of the viewer, because from an ethical point of view the face as countenance is considered to be the quintessentially inviolable aspect of human appearance."[10] It seems as though Bacon wanted to get away from a conventional depiction of the face here. The deformation of it functions as an act of liberation that makes it possible for the artist to "tear away the veil" and push forward to Kundera's "diamond;" in Bacon's case this diamond is the immediate, living appearance of a person.

If there was a painter who seemed to Bacon more capable than any other of "walking along the edge of the precipice" in his portraits, it was Velázquez, who according to Sylvester was Bacon's favourite painter.[11] Even more than by Rembrandt's self-portraits, Bacon was fascinated by Velázquez's portraits of members of the Spanish royal family, of which several outstanding examples are in the Picture Gallery of the Kunsthistorisches Museum in Vienna. These include portraits of the Infante Philip Prosper (cat. no. 72) and the Infanta Margarita Teresa (cat. no. 73) as well as the portrait of King Philip IV of Spain from the period around 1652/53 (cat. no. 82), a high-quality studio replica. This small portrait is closely related to Velázquez's most famous late portrayals of the monarch in the Prado Museum in Madrid and the National Gallery in London. Bacon was familiar with the portrait in the National Gallery, which he included in his exhibition there, *Francis Bacon: The Artist's Eye*, a subjective selection of his favourite masterpieces from the museum's collection. Velázquez painted portraits of Philip IV over a period of almost a quarter of a century and was hardly more gentle with the face of his king than Rembrandt was with his own visage.

A closer look at Philip IV in the Vienna painting reveals behind the long, pale countenance with its high forehead, strange beard, thick lips and strikingly deformed chin a large number of indications of feelings and character traits that could not be more ambivalent. It is this ambivalence, in which the conflict of extremely varied feelings in the king's nature comes to the surface, that makes this portrait so lively. While the eyes appear sad and serious, the lower part of the face seems unbelievably lively, almost impertinent, with a beard that curves upward like the horns of a bull, thick red lips and, not least, a misshapen chin. In an eloquent remark about Velázquez, Bacon expressed the element that connects him with Rembrandt and Velázquez across the centuries: the fact that every successful portrait contains a reminder of death: "You feel the shadow of life passing all the time"[12] or: "[...] the greatest art always returns you to the vulnerability of the human situation."[13] What Bacon stressed about Rembrandt and Velázquez was their ability to work at the limits of representation by not concealing the natural state of the paint, by not being afraid to use irrational signs, as in the case of Velázquez's *Portrait of King Philip IV* (cat. no. 82) or Rembrandt's *Self-Portrait* in the Musée Granet. An example of this is the peculiar deformation on the chin of the monarch, which leaves the viewer in doubt of whether it is a swelling or a kind of fault in the representation, an indexical sign, a reference to the medium and the act of painting.

In his deformation of the face Bacon goes substantially further than the painters who inspired him. With this disfigurement he violates one of the last great taboos, thus making a theme of the existential contingency and purposelessness of the individual. Bacon's profound examination of the meaning of human existence links him to the Paris intelligentsia of the post-war period in general and to the French writer and ethnologist Michel Leiris in particular. Bacon and Leiris are united in their emphatic interest in the human being in his greatness and meaninglessness, in his presence which already implies his inevitable future absence. Within this field of tension are the two portraits of Michel Leiris that Bacon painted in the years 1976 and 1978 (cat. nos. 83 and 84). David Sylvester believes that the first one, which the artist himself also preferred,[14] is among the triumphal moments of Bacon's career. He called it "[...] in my opinion one of the most beautiful portrait heads he ever painted on a small canvas [...]."[15] In this small portrait Bacon depicted the head of the writer powerfully and at the same time sensitively, but without trying to create an unscathed likeness of the face. On the contrary, he undoes its symmetry, creating in a rhythmic structure of curves an emotional and highly subjective portrait of his friend. The unusually lengthened head of Leiris, turned slightly towards the right edge of the painting, emerges from a deep-black background. As in *Portrait Head* (cat. no. 81) the entire concentration is focused on one half of the face, Leiris's left side. His right side, oddly neglected and drastically shortened, appears to have been absorbed by the dark background and is bounded by the upper half of the ear. The irritating and at the same time captivating aspect in this portrait of Michel Leiris is its asymmetry, culminating in the fact that only one eye of the subject is depicted. The two halves of the face are separated by a distinctly curved line, which rises from the skull of the scholar like a protruding artery on his high forehead and makes its way between the arched eyebrows to the lump that is the end of his nose. The nose is inclined to the right, directed by the white curve that forms a highlight along the ridge. Two other curves – a broken line that provides a border between the face and Leiris's left ear and a sharp white curve along the lower edge of the left side of his chin – respond to this movement and provide balance to the painting. In this portrait Bacon portrayed in a masterly manner, comparable to Velázquez's portrait of Philip IV, the writer's intellect and introspection, not at the price of similarity, but yet based on his physical appearance. In keeping with the philosophical trends of his time, Bacon frees himself from the traditional Cartesian model of the dualism of the soul and body, of the internal and external, and portrays in this portrait of his friend his inner constitution in an appropriate external form.

The *Portrait of Michel Leiris* of 1978 (cat. no. 84), which was painted two years later, bears a closer resemblance to him in the more rounded shape of the head and the characteristic wrinkles on the forehead, but does not succeed in depicting to the same degree the special charisma that he must have exuded. Here Leiris is not depicted frontally, as in the earlier portrait, but turned slightly to the left. Conspicuous details in this portrait are the incision in his face in the right half of the painting and the thin, white broken line that runs across the black crater in Leiris's face from the left side of his nose to his left ear. Elements such as the broken line and the pink hatching, which obscure the facial features in both portraits, tie the otherwise extremely sculptural heads to the surface of the canvas and remind one of the material reality of the painting.

Although Bacon was convinced that it was impossible to ever completely unravel the mystery of a person, he became an almost fanatical observer of his friends in his efforts to discover the secret of their appearance, their living energy, the triggering factor in their immediate presence. To this end, like Velázquez and Rembrandt before him, he was prepared to walk "along the edge of the precipice" and expose the energy of his subjects along with their vulnerability and mortality. Michel Leiris's skull in *Study for Portrait (Michel Leiris)* of 1978 (cat. no. 84) is reminiscent of another precise form of recording the body, which quasi disembodies the subject and views it as a skeleton: namely, medical examination with the help of X-ray photographs: "The skull-like depiction of Leiris's cranium at right, the broken white line that links Leiris's nose and ear, and the black ground against which the head is viewed offer compelling evidence that as Bacon considered the face of his friend, he remembered as well the photograph and X-ray images of K. C. Clark's book *Positioning in Radiography* (1929) which had long intrigued him."[16] The gesture which points to the inevitability of death in *Portrait of Michel Leiris* may seem brutal, but it exposes Bacon's deeply-felt affection for one of his closest friends.

An important role in Bacon's life as well as in his paintings of the time was played by Isabel Rawsthorne, one of his closest female friends, who can be seen in two important portraits from the 1960s in the exhibition: namely, the small triptych *Three Studies for Portrait of Isabel Rawsthorne,* 1965 (cat. no. 85) and *Portrait of Isabel Rawsthorne Standing in a Street in Soho* of 1967 (cat. no. 59). The triptych form with the dimensions of 35.5 × 30.5 cm is typical of Bacon's portraits of this time, which consciously imitated police photographs of criminals in depicting the subject in three small individual portraits frontally and from both sides. Bacon is less interested in the serial effect than he is in the simultaneous perception of three different views, which in contrast to Picasso's female portraits (see: *Bust of Woman with a Hat, Dora,* 1939, cat. no. 93) he does not combine in a single painting but displays side by side in triptych format. The arrangement of the three heads is more or less symmetrical and thus creates an effect of surrounding the viewer – or in the words of Leiris, a "stereoscopic" effect.[17] Bacon repeatedly stressed that his portraits were based on photographs made for the purpose because he felt inhibited by the presence of the model when he was painting portraits – as was almost always the case – of his closest friends. The small triptychs in the format of a bathroom mirror demand that the viewer precisely study the facial features as well as the dynamically applied paint in its flow and interruptions. The individual views of Isabel Rawsthorne's head are severely distorted in part and are reminiscent of the condition of the photographs that lay about on the floor of Bacon's studio. The left painting, in particular, is markedly deformed. The subject's right eye, which is turned towards the viewer, is smeared almost to the point of being unrecognisable, and the nose is completely misshapen. One has the impression that the flesh has taken on a life of its own,

Plate 1: Francis Bacon, Three Studies for Self-Portrait, 1974. Oil on canvas, triptych, each panel 35.5 × 30.5 cm. New York, Private Collection.

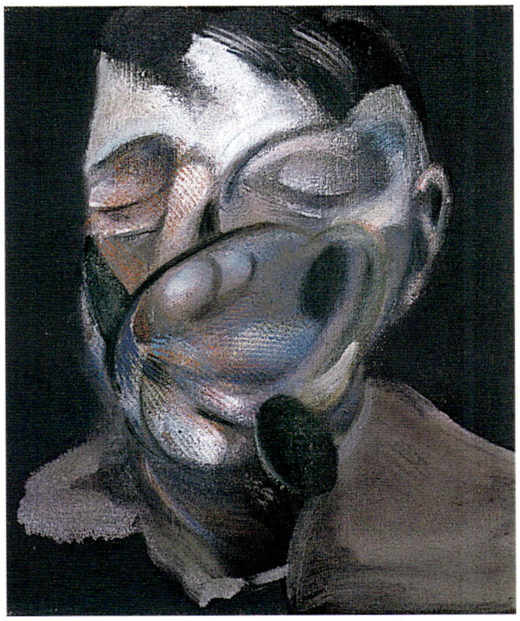

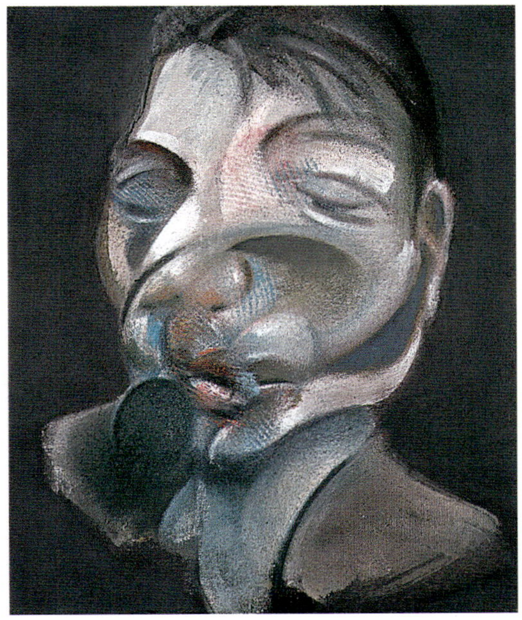

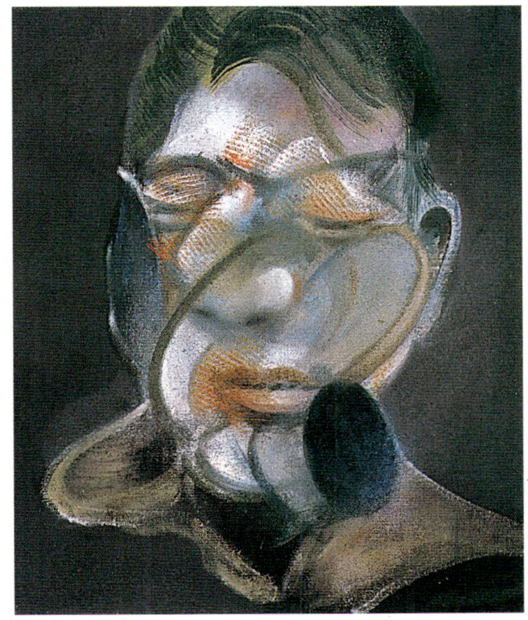

refusing to subordinate itself to the smooth surface of the face, as through inner, more profound emotional zones were pushing outwards, breaking through the façade of the face. One has the impression of being able to grasp Isabel Rawsthorne's pulsating physical energy, and this unshakeable vitality must have been entirely to the artist's liking.

In later years Bacon also painted self-portraits with increasing frequency. In conversation with David Sylvester, however, he emphasised that the reason for this was not narcissism or egocentricity but rather a dearth of models: "I've done a lot of self-portraits, really because people have been dying around me like flies and I've had nobody else left to paint but myself."[18]

An appropriate example of a late self-portrait is *Three Studies of Self-Portrait*, 1974 *(Plate 1)*. The format of this triple self-portrait is similar to that of Isabel Rawsthorne. But in all three canvases Bacon depicts himself in a frontal view and, remarkably, always with his eyes closed. In contrast to the *Three Studies for Portrait of Isabel Rawsthorne* (cat. no. 85), which was painted almost ten years earlier, the brushwork in the self-portraits is more sweeping and unified, comparable to the portraits of Michel Leiris from the second half of the 1970s. The three portrait studies depict a taciturn, passive Bacon, who appears to be helpless against the forces working against him; devoid of energy, weakened by his ceaseless examination of the dialectic of life and death, frustrated by the fact that his fellow-travellers have been dying around him "like flies."

The quality that unites Rembrandt, Velázquez and Bacon across several centuries as great masters of portraiture is their willingness to go to the limits, to walk "along the edge of the precipice" and, if necessary, to break all the rules and to destroy the face in order to get as close as possible to their subject and his or her true appearance. While Rembrandt and Velázquez were exploring the possibilities and boundaries of portraiture, centuries later Bacon had to cross those boundaries in order to find his way back to the face and capture the living energy of his subject, at a time when portraiture was being displaced by photography and the concept of a unified subject identical with itself had become obsolete. In this sense we may join Gilles Deleuze in emphatically proclaiming: "Yes, the face has a great future, but only if it is destroyed, dismantled."[19]

[1] Sylvester 1999, p. 28.
[2] Sylvester 1999, p. 133: "One of the nicest things that Cocteau said was: 'Each day in the mirror I watch death at work.' This was what one does oneself."
[3] Sylvester 1999, p. 80.
[4] Sylvester 2000, p. 242. The small German book mentioned by Bacon in this quote is the first publication on Rembrandt's self-portraits: Wilhelm Pinder, *Rembrandts Selbstbildnisse*, Königstein im Taunus (Karl Robert Langewiesche Verlag) 1943 (cat. no. 88). Bacon's battered and well-worn copy in his Reece Mews studio testifies to his often-cited admiration for Rembrandt's self-portraits. Other leaves found in Bacon's studio are a single page from an unidentified book with a detail from one of Rembrandt's late self-portraits (cat. no. 86) and a kind of collage with dark-blue spots of paint. It consists of a fragmented depiction of a pianist attached to a torn and creased leaf from a Rembrandt book (cat. no. 87).
[5] Cf. White 1999/2000, p. 195.
[6] In the text that follows, the painting will be attributed to Rembrandt in keeping with Bacon's assertion.
[7] Sylvester 1999, p. 58.
[8] At this point it must be pointed out that the question of Bacon's titles cannot be clearly answered. He preferred not to assign titles to his paintings and often did so only to please his gallery-owners. But no matter who gave the small study its title, it was the kind that Bacon himself would have used: short and to the point.
[9] Kundera 1996, p. 9.
[10] Nicola Suthor, "Francis Bacon: Life hurts (1962)," in: Preimesberger – Baader – Suthor 1999, p. 450.
[11] Cf. David Sylvester, *Stationen eines Lebenswerkes,* in: Exh. Cat. Munich 1996, p. 17.
[12] Sylvester 1999, p. 81.
[13] Sylvester 1999, p. 199.
[14] Sylvester 1999, p. 146: "I think that [...] the one I did which is less literally like him is in fact more poignantly like him."
[15] David Sylvester, *Stationen eines Lebenswerkes,* in: Exh. Cat. Munich 1996, p. 30.
[16] Davies – Yard 1986, p. 78, 79.
[17] Cf. Michel Leiris, *Francis Bacon heute* (1971), in: Leiris 1989, p. 22.
[18] Sylvester 1999, p. 129.
[19] Cf. Gilles Deleuze – Félix Guattari, *Die Erschaffung des Gesichts,* in: idem., *Tausend Plateaus,* Berlin 1992, p. 233–235, quoted from: Nicola Suthor, *Gilles Deleuze und Félix Guattari: Das Gesicht ist Politik* (1980), in: Preimesberger – Baader – Suthor 1999, p. 466.

Cat. no. 80A
Rembrandt Harmensz. van Rijn
Small self-portrait
C. 1657
Oil on wood, 48.8 × 40.6 cm
Vienna, Kunsthistorisches Museum,
Picture Gallery, inv. no. 414

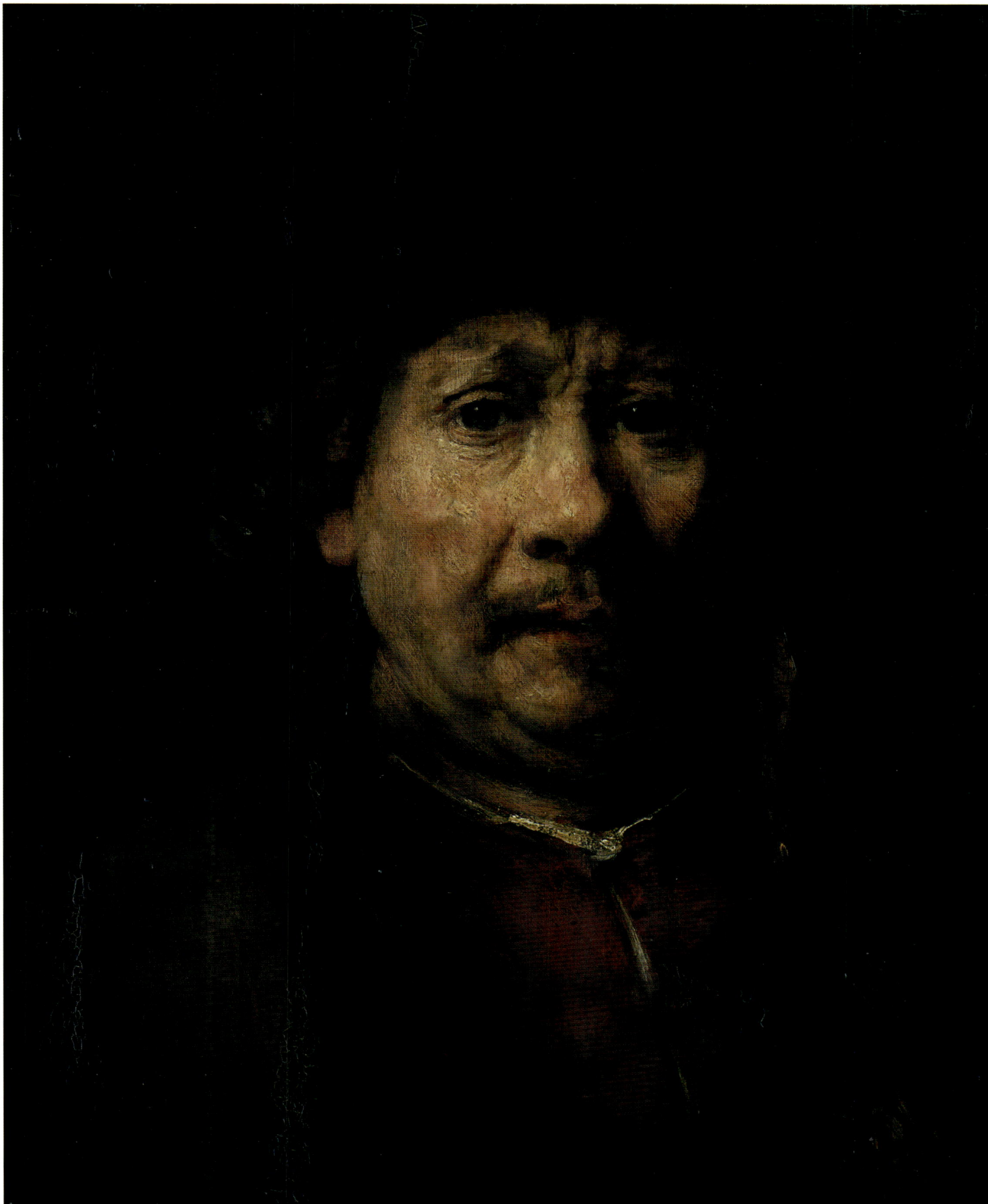

Cat. no. 80A

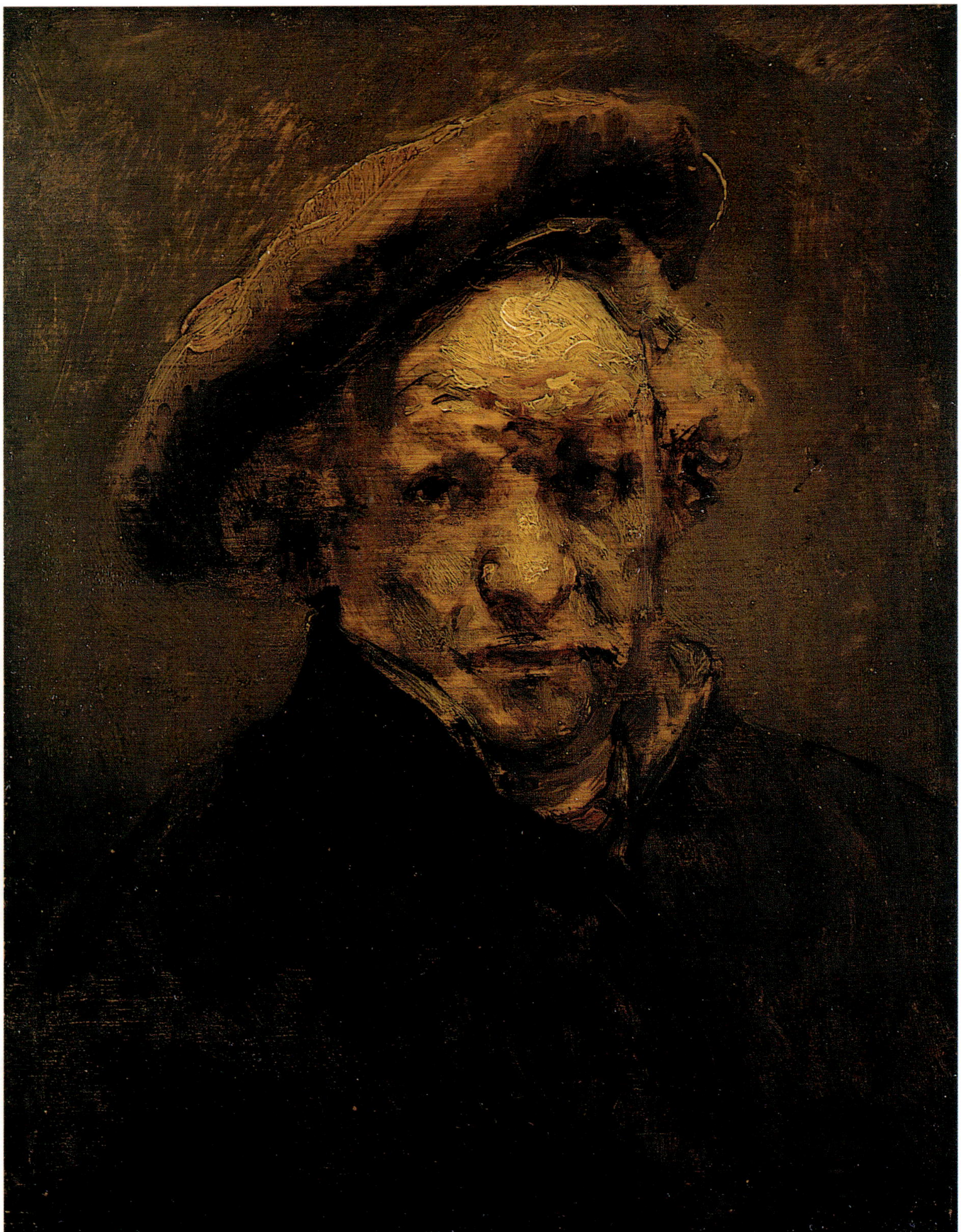

Cat. no. 80B

Cat. no. 80B
Rembrandt Harmensz. van Rijn, Self Portrait. Oil on canvas, 30 × 24 cm. Aix-en-Provence, Musée Granet

Cat. no. 81
Francis Bacon
Portrait Head
1959
Oil on canvas, 38.1 × 31.7 cm
New York, Collection Franklin and Susanne Konigsberg

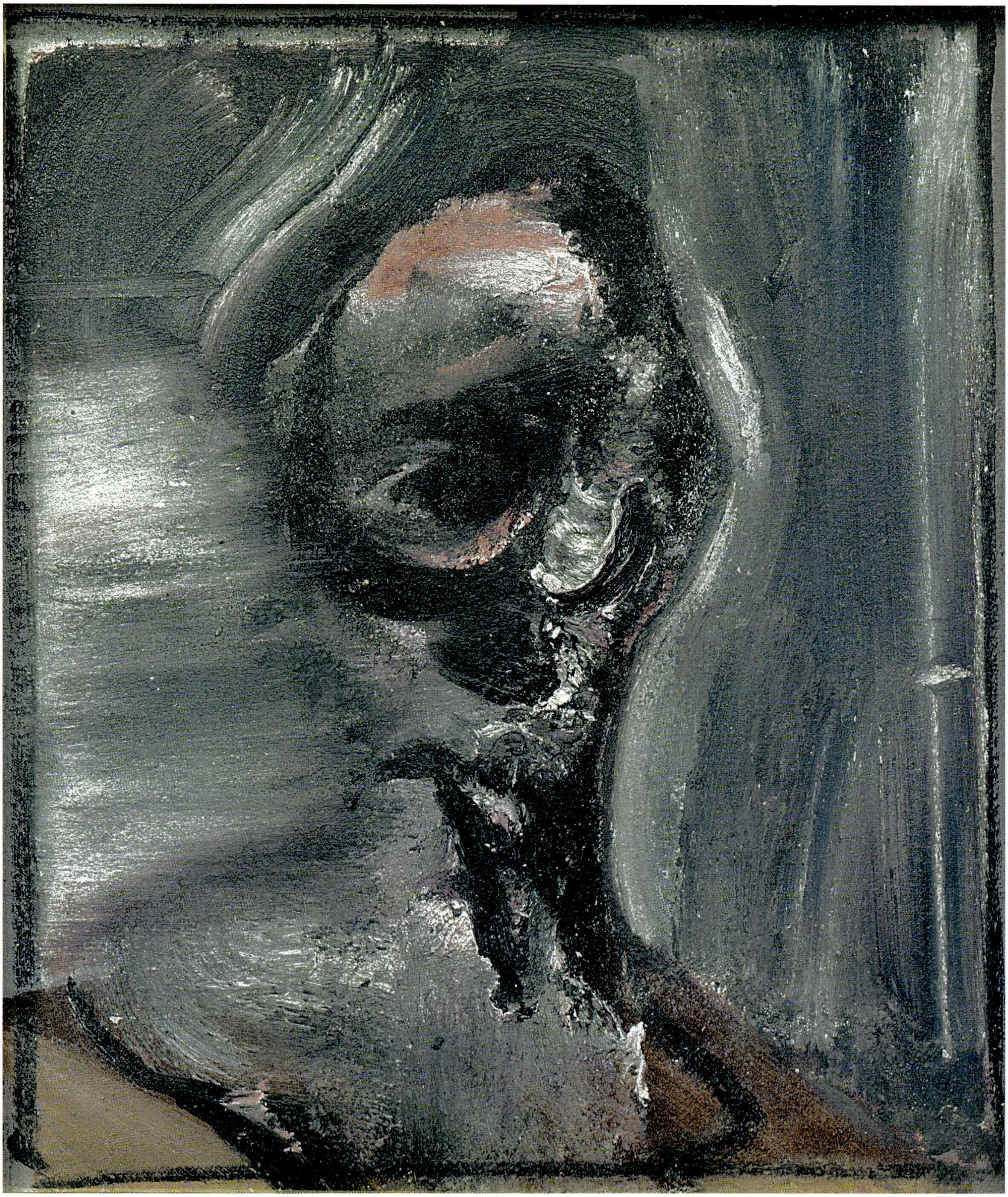

Cat. no. 81

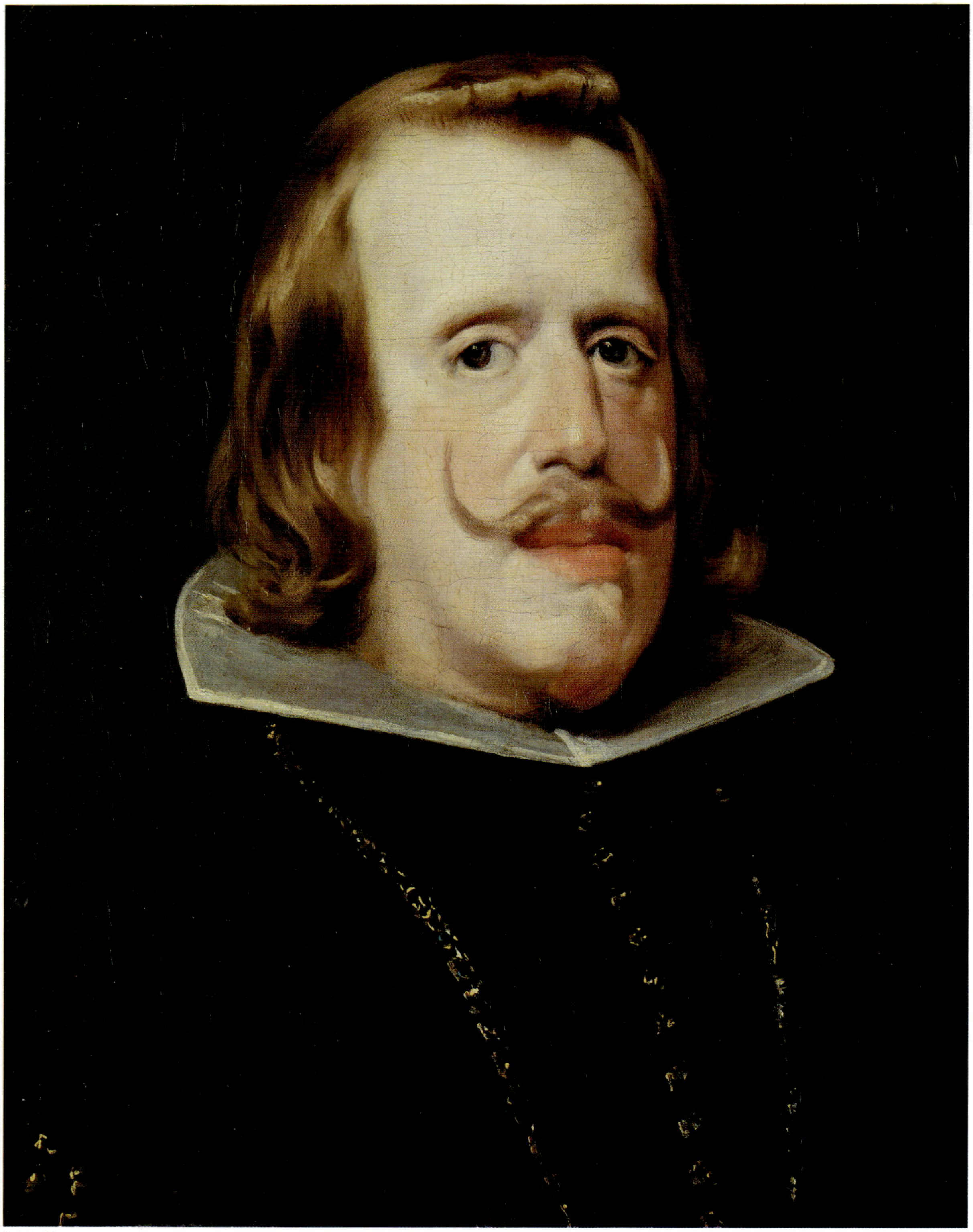

Cat. no. 82

Cat. no. 82
Velázquez' studio
King Philipp IV of Spain
C. 1652/53
Oil on canvas, 47 × 37.5 cm
Vienna, Kunsthistorisches Museum, Picture Gallery, inv. no. 324

Cat. no. 83
Francis Bacon
Portrait of Michel Leiris
1976
Oil on canvas, 34 × 29 cm
Paris, Musée National d'Art Moderne, Centre de création industrielle Centre Georges Pompidou, AM 1948-487, Gift of Louise und Michel Leiris, 1984

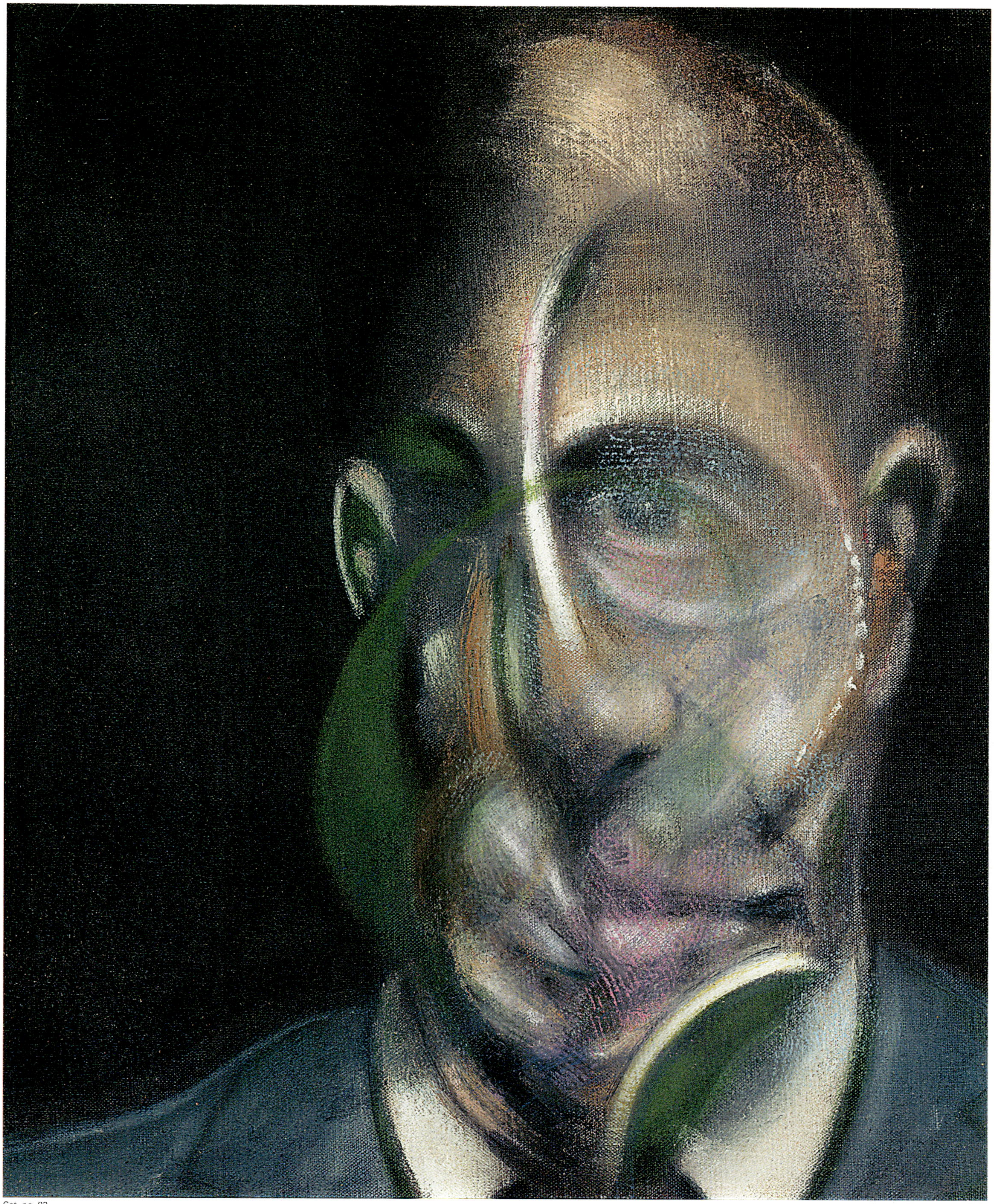

Cat. no. 83

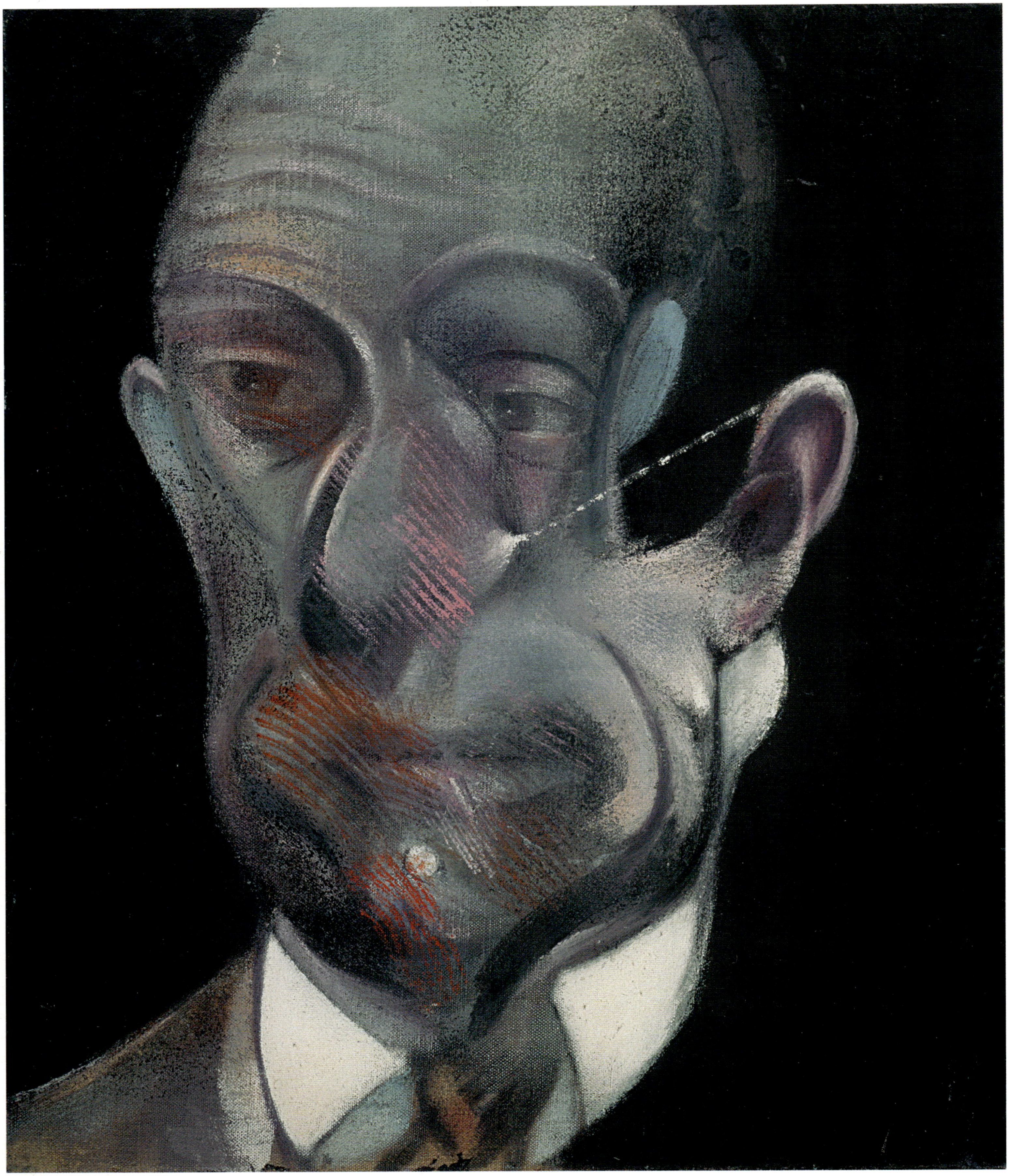

Cat. no. 84

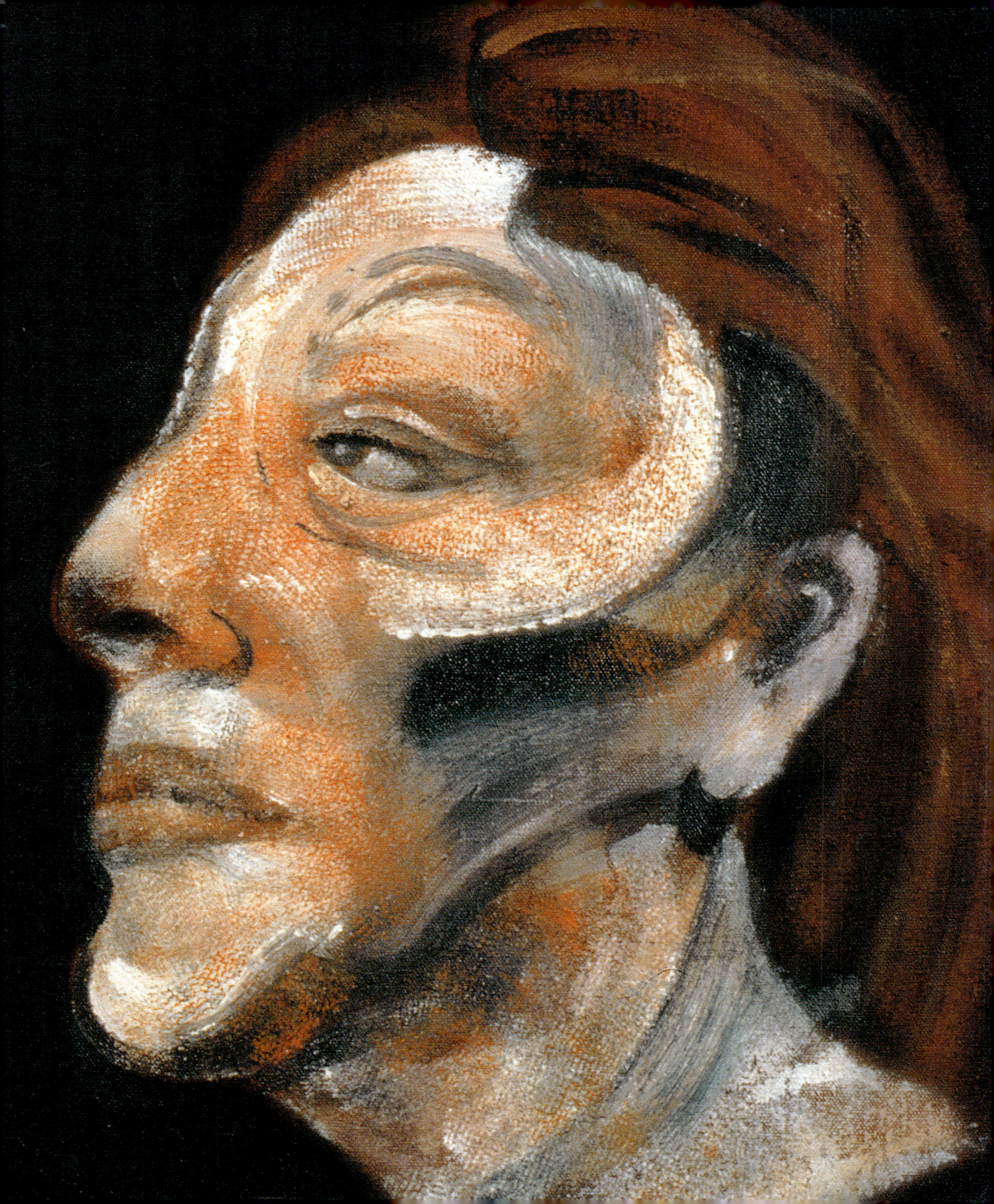

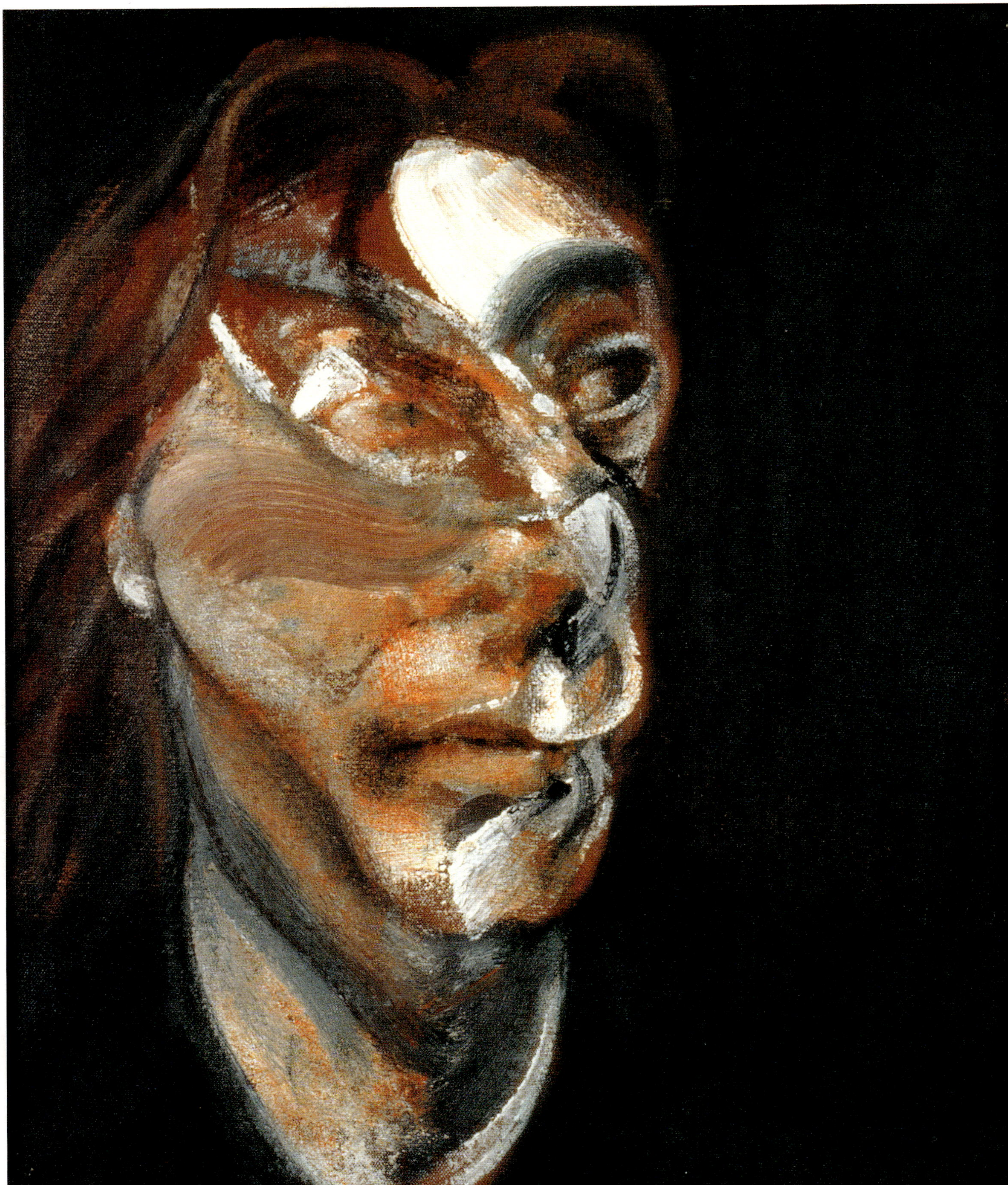

Cat. no. 85

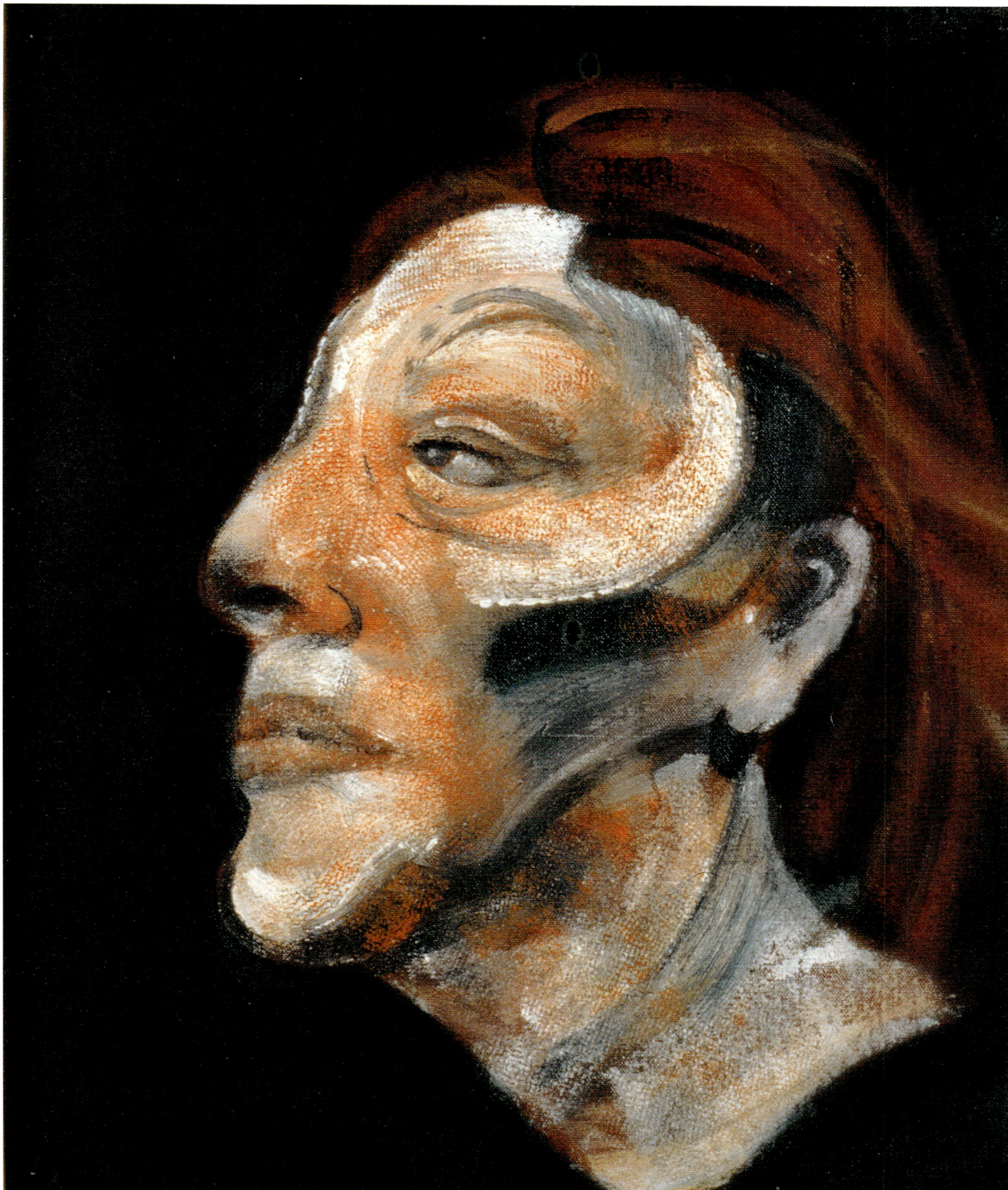

Cat. no. 85

On p. 226: Cat. no. 84
Francis Bacon
Study for Portrait (Michel Leiris)
1978
Oil on canvas, 35.5 × 30.5 cm
Paris, Musée National d'Art Moderne, Centre de création industrielle Centre Georges Pompidou, AM 1948–488, Gift of Louise und Michel Leiris, 1984

On p. 227: Cat. no. 85, detail

Cat. no. 85
Francis Bacon
Three Studies for Portrait of Isabel Rawsthorne
1965
Oil on canvas, triptych, each panel 35.5 × 30.5 cm
Norwich, University of East Anglia, Sainsbury Centre of Visual Arts, Collection Robert und Lisa Sainsbury, purchased 1965, UEA 37

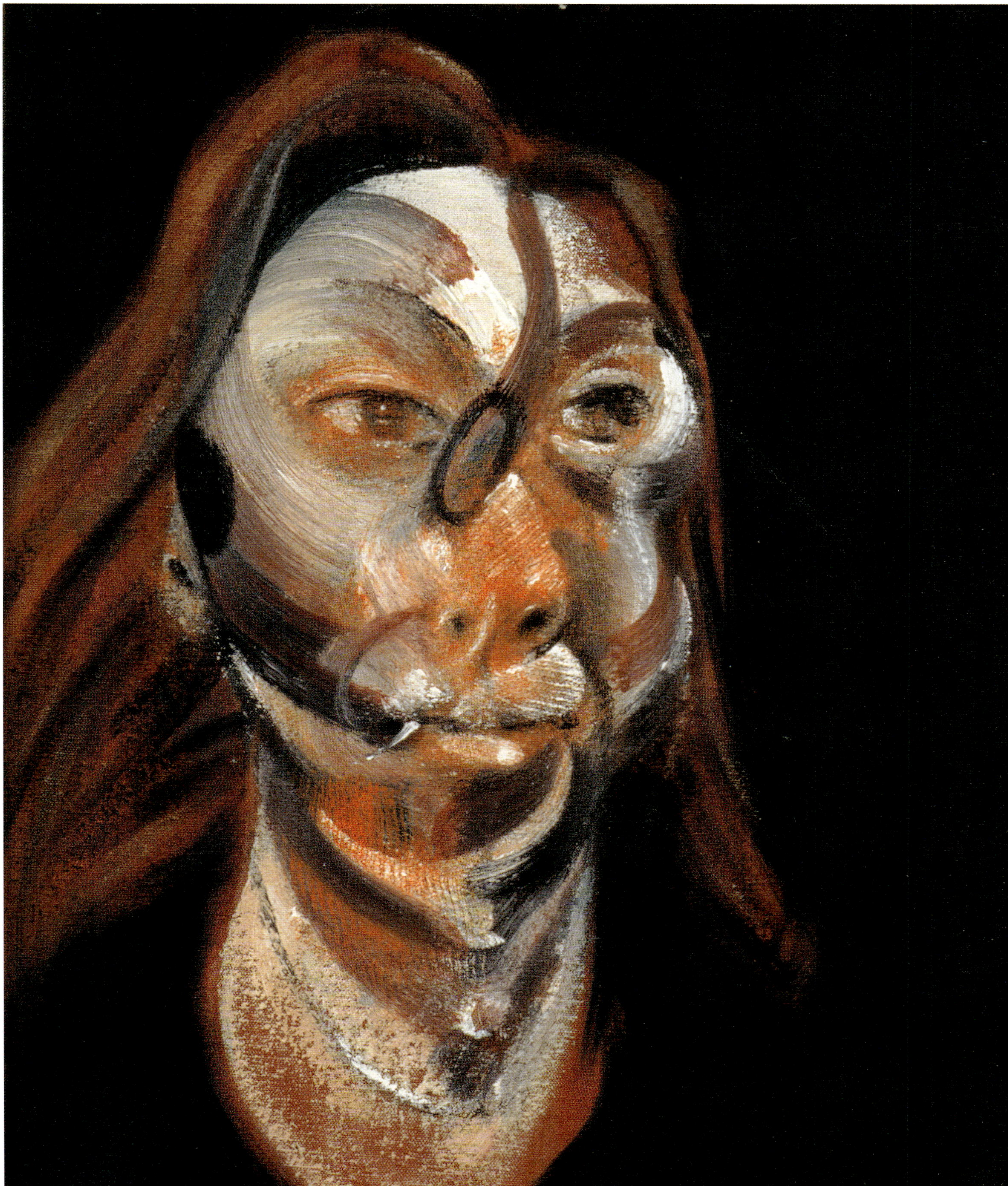

Cat. no. 85

Cat. no. 86
Leaf with colour plate of a self-portrait by Rembrandt (detail) from unidentified book, 23.6 × 19.5 cm
Dublin, Dublin City Gallery The Hugh Lane, F1A:79

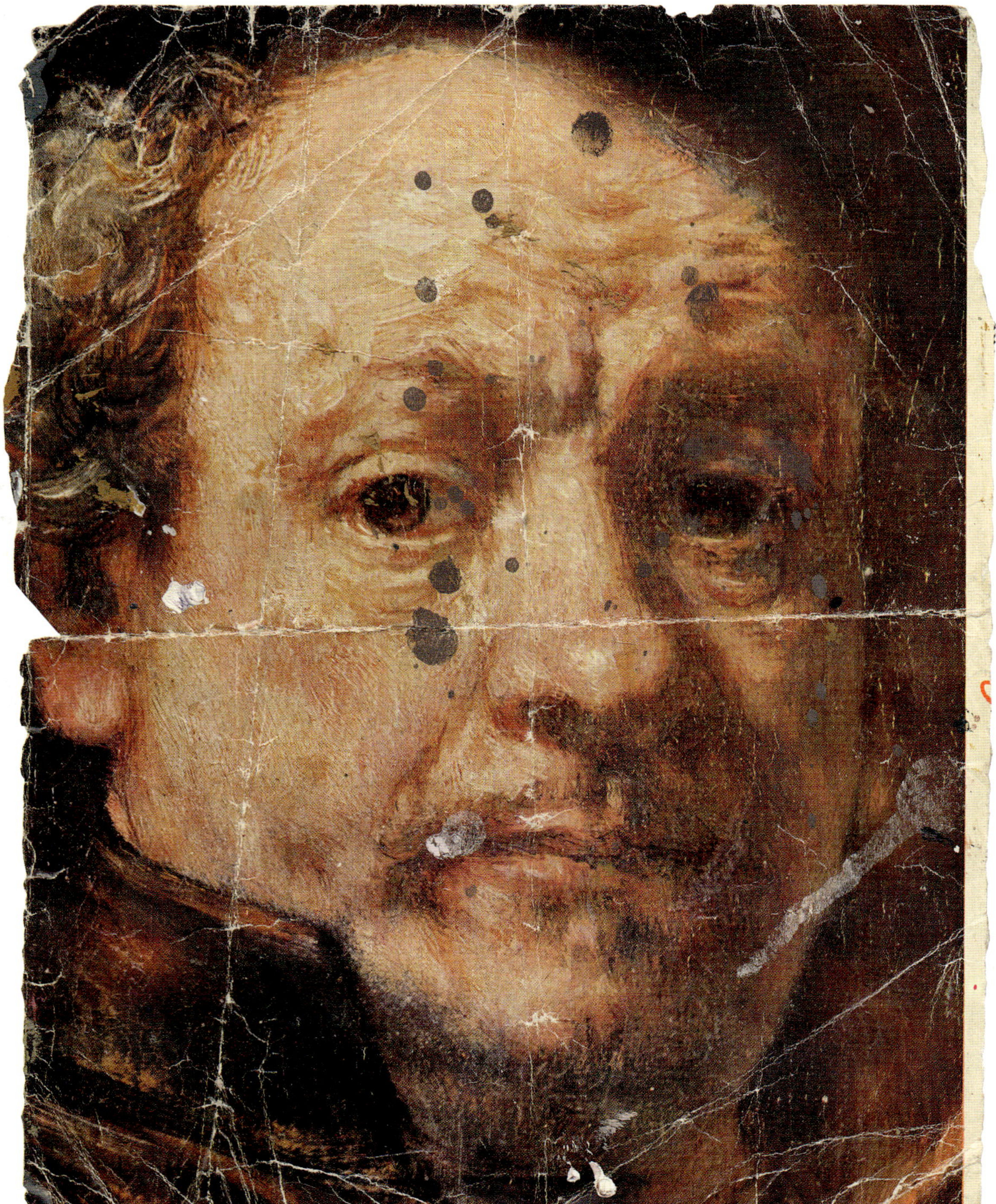

Cat. no. 86

Cat. no. 87
Intervention by Francis Bacon in dark blue paint on leaf with black-and-white illustration of a pianist. This leaf is held with a pin to another leaf with black-and-white illustrations of paintings by Rembrandt. 263 × 222 × 30 mm
Dublin, Dublin City Gallery The Hugh Lane, F129:50

Cat. no. 88
Rembrandts Selbstbildnisse, Karl Robert Langewiesche Verlag (no publication date).
266 × 188 × 14 mm
Dublin, Dublin City Gallery The Hugh Lane, F108:33

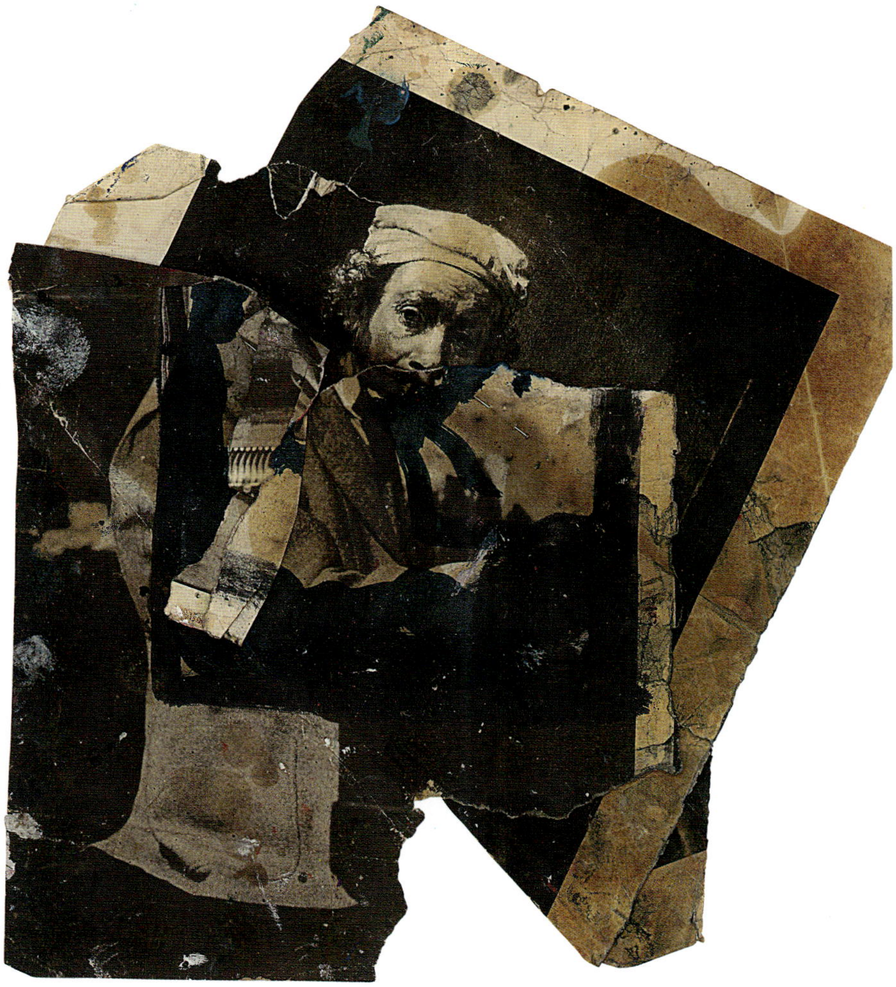

Cat. no. 87

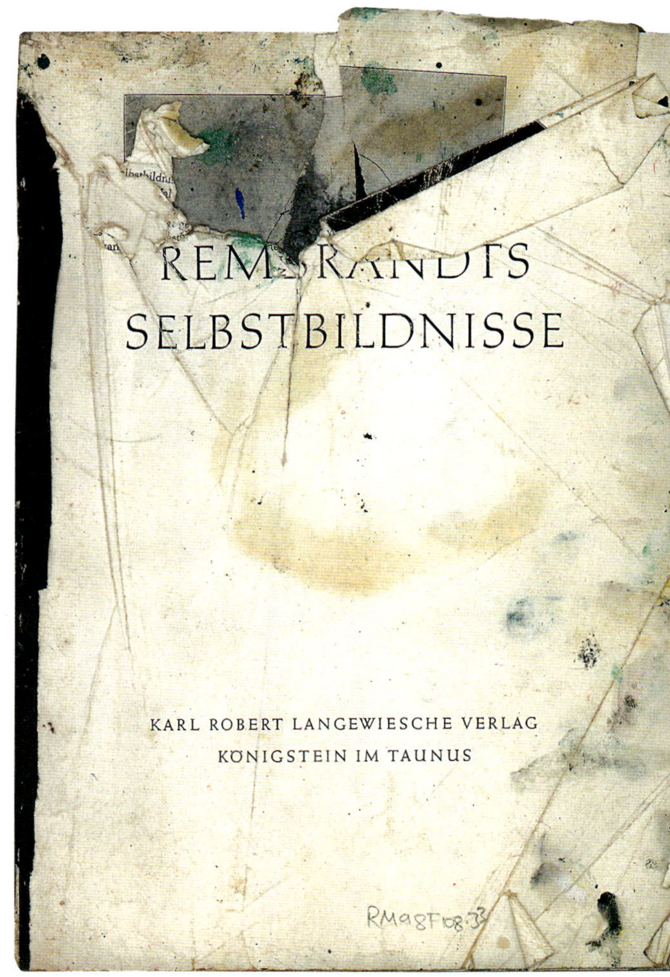

Cat. no. 88

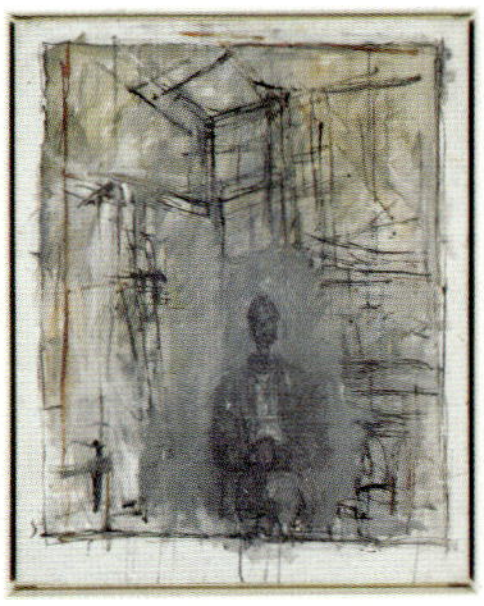

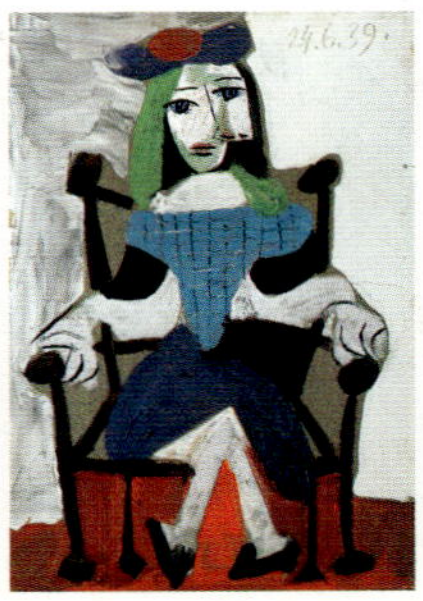

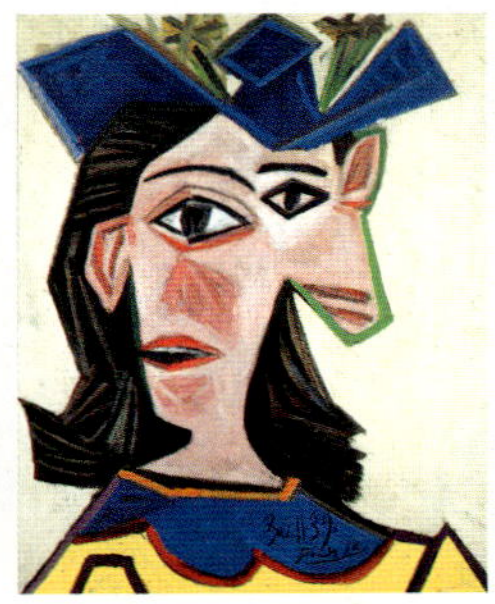

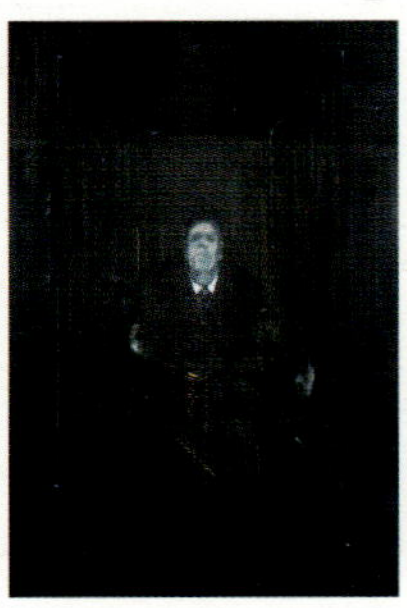

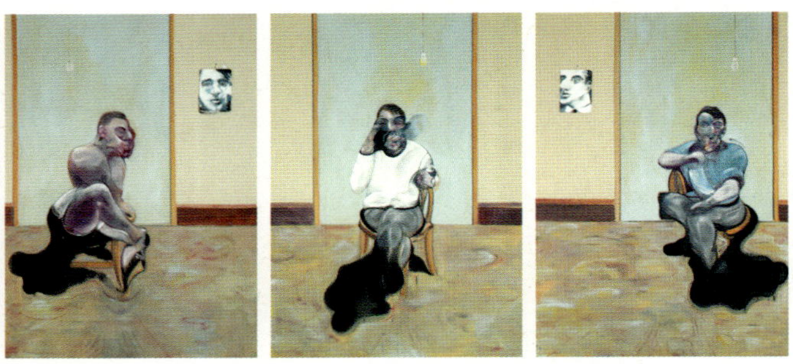

Michel Leiris
Bacon Picasso Masson

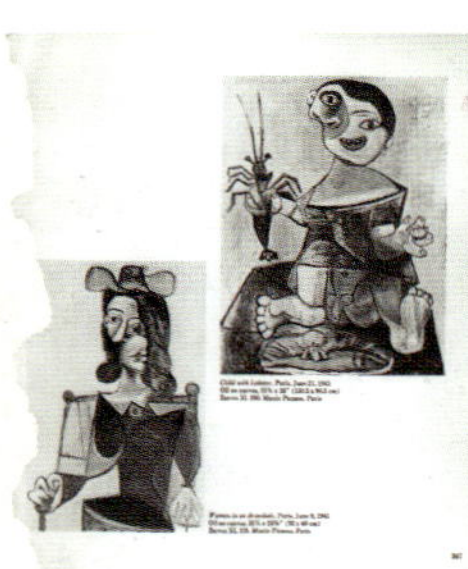

Olivier Berggruen

The Representative Portrait[1]

"I would like my pictures to look as if a human being had passed between them, like a snail, leaving a trail of the human presence and memory trace of past events, as the snail leaves its slime."
Francis Bacon, 1955[2]

It is appropriate that Bacon drew on the idea of a trace when speaking about the intended effect of his paintings. Like a photograph, the canvas was to capture the essence of the sitter. But dismissing any of the supposed serene objectivity of the camera, Bacon's grotesque simile of slime to paint is much more apt to describe the messiness of the artist's encounter with portraiture. Indeed, Bacon did use photographs as a starting point for most of his portraits, using them to take care of the requisite task of verisimilitude while allowing the artist to paint what exists on the periphery of the mechanically recorded image. Having rejected the opposite paths of abstraction and illustration, Bacon expands the idea of realism to encompass his own subjectivity.

Bacon's portraiture displays a strategy of distortion and erasure that will no doubt recall the examples of Picasso and Bacon. More striking, however, are the parallels between each artist in terms of processes and conception of the art of portraiture. It may be no surprise that Bacon, Picasso as well as Giacometti devoted multiple series of paintings to lovers, relatives and friends. This may be linked to the modern artist's need to create empathy through the act of painting. The compulsion to repeat the process of portraiture speaks to something which exists outside of the painted surface, the performative act of the portrait. For Picasso, this act took place with his lovers, most notably Marie-Thérèse Walter and Dora Maar, whose images reflect not only the changing moods of the sitter, but the shifting intensities and desires of the artist himself. For Giacometti, the act of painting had to do with the act of seeing his subject, capturing what David Sylvester has called the "residue of vision."[3] In general terms, we can characterise this process as one of sustained vision and engagement with the sitter. Beyond reproducing the mere appearance of the sitter, the artists attempt to register a trace of the always fleeting exchange between the painter and his subject.

That Bacon was aware of Picasso's portraits of Dora Maar from the late 1930s is attested by the presence of a ripped-out page found in the Reece Mews studio (cat. no. 94). Torn from the catalogue of Picasso's retrospective at the Museum of Modern Art in New York,[4] the page contains two images, one of a child holding a lobster and another of the seated Dora Maar wearing a hat. Like the other reproductions that Bacon kept in his studio, the twisting and dislocations of Dora Maar's face and body as shown in this page must have provided fertile ground for Bacon's own innovations in the portrayal of his subjects. (It is interesting to note that Bacon tore up this page in the last decade of his life, as the Picasso retrospective took place in 1980.) Perhaps these images reminded him of his own involvement with portraiture. Obviously he was keen to be reacquainted with Picasso's paintings. In *Female Head with Hat,* 1939 (cat. no. 93), Dora Maar's head is closely framed within the white ground of the picture. One large eye stares out from the centre of Dora's face, its diamond shape echoed in her other eye, in the blush of her cheek and in her two ears. The formal alliteration of the diamond shape ties together a face that would seem to be falling apart into a number of different directions. The central eye consolidates her gaze into a single stare, like that of a cyclops. The face of Dora Maar is typically subject to an infinite number of permutations given the mood of the sitter and the artist's attitude towards her, always varying the degree of her own personal presence within the picture in relation to Picasso's treatment of her. In *Female Head with Hat,* we sense a greater distance between Picasso and Dora. What he sees appears in his emphasis on her central eye, open mouth, the outlines of her hat and dress, yet only superficially penetrates into the sitter's psyche. The tight handling of paint within the geometric shapes of the head conveys the impression that the painting is more of an image of Picasso's own vision than Dora's involvement.

In contrast, Picasso's *Woman Seated in an Armchair,* 1939 (cat. no. 92) draws on the sitter's participation with greater depth. Although her face is doubled into the frontal and profile views which recur throughout Picasso's portraits, both of her eyes have a single focus, size and expression. Quick dashes of green and white lie beneath the black lines of her features, adding an air of melancholy to the sickly green of her hair. Dora's own body becomes a loosely contained white shape, described in broad, relaxed brushstrokes. Letting the green ground of the canvas show through, the vigorous white brushstrokes of the background blend with black paint, revealing a dramatic haste in execution, while the red area beneath Dora's chair adds a touch of sensuality to her otherwise forlorn image. In *Woman Seated in an Armchair,* the entire figure is contained within the picture's surface, allowing for Dora's gaze to be directed towards the viewer. The blue of each eye spills out of its black boundary, giving her gaze a watery intensity and unsettling Picasso's ability to confine her face and body within a neatly defined form.

Perhaps most relevant to the discussion of the performativity of portraiture is the presence of Giacometti within Bacon's arsenal of images.[5] From the accounts of David Sylvester and others, Giacometti was notorious for his relentless, prolonged portrait sessions. Sitters such as Yanihara were forced to rearrange their travel plans in order to satisfy Giacometti's demand for multiple sittings. Not surprisingly, the familiar faces of his wife Annette and his brother Diego served as the ideal subjects of Giacometti's series of portraits; personal closeness and physical proximity were ideal prerequisites. Given that Giacometti worked both from life and memory, he gained much from using such familiar faces and features. When describing what would seem to be the simple task of "copying" a glass on a table, Giacometti notes that, "You never copy the glass on the table; you copy the residue of a vision."[6] This vision therefore equates memory with perception, both of which are in constant flux. For Giacometti then, the process of looking defines his project of portraiture in the same manner as his still life, except that in portraiture, the subject is very explicitly looking back. The performative aspect of Giacometti's paintings reveals a power struggle between the artist who attempts to use his gaze to engulf and stabilise the sitter within his surroundings and the sitter who constantly eludes the artist's gaze. What seems to be at risk here is the loss of subjective control.

In his 1953 portrait *Diego* (cat. no. 91), Giacometti returns to the familiar presence of his brother sitting within his studio. Diego's features are heavily worked over in series through a process of additions and erasures of the paint. While the features of the face are delineated by the relative clarity of thin black lines, the edges of Diego's shoulders risk being lost within the aura of grey that surrounds his body. Giacometti's eye and hand can only see one part of the figure at a time, unable to reconcile the face and torso of Diego with the ground of his immediate surroundings. Although the grey accumulation of erasures that surround Diego tend to isolate his figure, the wiry geometry of the lines of the studio walls attempt to frame and stabilise the image of the sitter, concentrating the gaze much like the linear cages of Giacometti's Surrealist period. Beyond the walls of the studio, Giacometti has also painted a frame within the original frame of the canvas, always trying to define and secure the space of the sitter and his setting within his painted field of vision. That each line of *Diego* exists only through its effacement is a testimony to the impossibility underlying Giacometti's agenda of vision and representation.

Giacometti's use of the cage to solidify the presence of his subjects reappears in Bacon's paintings, but with a different purpose. When he embarked on his papal series, the cage became the device for isolating the figures. In Bacon's *Study for a Portrait,* 1953 (cat. no. 89), the sitter rests within a cage-like frame. The barely visible outlines of the room create a frame within the frame of the canvas, opening a zone for the viewer to peer into the close space of

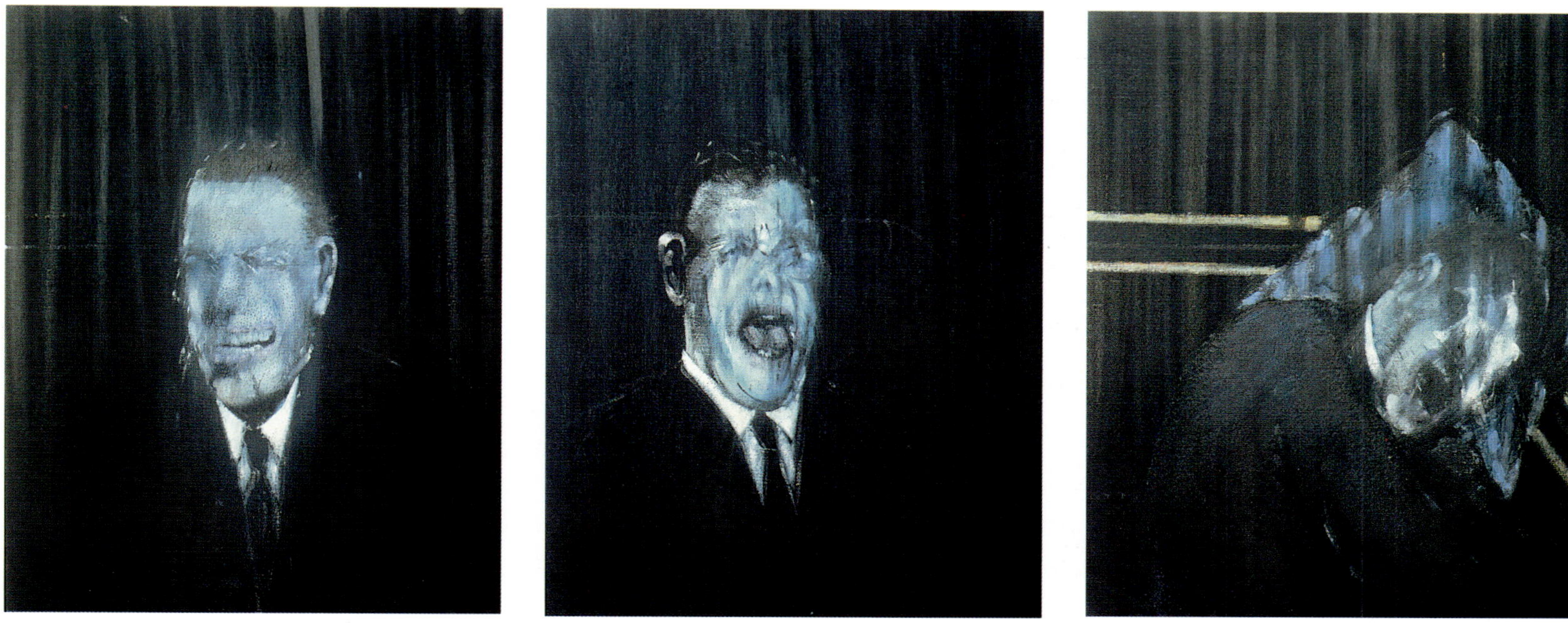

Plate 1: Francis Bacon, Three Studies for the Human Head, 1953. Oil on canvas, triptych, each panel 61 × 51 cm. Private Collection. (©: The Estate of Francis Bacon/ VBK, Vienna, 2003, Photo: Marlborough Fine Art, London.)

the sitter. The chair, a secularised version of the papal throne, reiterates the geometry of the room, pressing the tight boundaries of visual space even closer around the figure. *Study for a Portrait* falls within the period when Bacon was painting pictures of men in dark suits – alluding to the power of the dominant order. In *Study for a Portrait,* however, the figure shows none of the angst that we usually associate with Bacon's portraits, such as *Three Studies of the Human Head,* 1953 *(Plate 1).* The face of the sitter in *Study for a Portrait* shows a remarkable likeness atypical of Bacon's usual distortions. He gazes upward with his mouth shut, closing off any possibility of expression. His eyes stare out from behind his very particular style of glasses without any hint of angst or pain. Even the vertical streaks, which appear in other Bacon pictures at the time, only barely efface the sitter's visage, leaving something close to the idea of a true likeness intact.

In his later portraits, Bacon strays from the idea of illustrational likeness, using photographs to launch the series of transformations that end in the snail's trace of the sitter's portrait. Yet in his 1973 triptych, *Three Portraits; Posthumous Portrait of George Dyer, Self-Portrait, and Portrait of Lucian Freud* (cat. no. 90), Bacon inserts the idea of photography within the painting. Posted to the walls behind Dyer and Freud, black-and-white paintings of photographs create an opposition between the truth of the photographic image and that of the painted one, all within the space of the painting. The black-and-white snapshot of reality is juxtaposed with the contorted flesh of the sitters themselves. Each figure is framed within a glaring light-blue plane which closes off the space of a room, evoking a feeling of frightening isolation reminiscent of Beckett's *Lost Ones*. In contrast to another triptych of the same period showing Dyer bent over a bathroom sink (cat. no. 131), *Three Portraits* unites the separate surroundings of each sitter into a single space. The bare light bulbs and reflective backgrounds which appear in each panel seem unconnected to the weight of the black shadows that flow onto the floor as an extension of the body. Rather, the shadows, when seen together, all seem to emanate from a single light source outside of the triptych, uniting the image through the supposed position of the painter himself. What Bacon creates in *Three Portraits* is the space of the mind. Using the idea of the objective glance of the photograph as a supplement to the subjective and real trace of the sitter's body and history, Bacon subsumes the look within the vision of his own psyche. It is also notable that Bacon's self-portrait at the centre of the triptych does not contain the image of a painted photograph. Rather, a black shape obscures the left eye of Bacon's face, extending over to the right side of his nose. It is possible that this is a reference to the lens of a camera, whose shutter is activated by the remote switch of the shutter held in the image of Bacon's other hand. This allusion to photography would then equate the space of the triptych with the space of Bacon's own inner vision, conflating the objective with the subjective.

If Giacometti's work bears the marks of a struggle with his subject, Bacon eliminates the possibility of exchange between sitter and painter only to create a new space of interaction with the viewer. In effect, the figures in *Three Portraits* look out at us, demanding a new relationship between subject and object that extends beyond the boundaries of the canvas.

[1] I am indebted to Nicole Root for her assistance in the preparation of this essay.

[2] Sylvester 2000, p. 33. The quotation is from an interview in 1955. It was originally published in *The New Decade: 22 European Painters and Sculptors*. New York, Museum of Modern Art, 1955, p. 63.

[3] Sylvester 1999, p. 22. "Residue of a vision" is also used in Giacometti's own description, p. 36.

[4] Exh. Cat. New York 1980, p. 367.

[5] Although Bacon first saw Giacometti in a Parisian café, it was Isabel Rawsthorne who brought them together at the time of Giacometti's retrospective at the Tate Gallery in 1965. See Peppiatt 1997, pp. 205–206.

[6] Sylvester 1994, p. 36.

Cat. no. 89
Francis Bacon
Study for a Portrait
1953
Oil on canvas, 197 × 137 cm
Napa (California), Bern,
Hess Collection

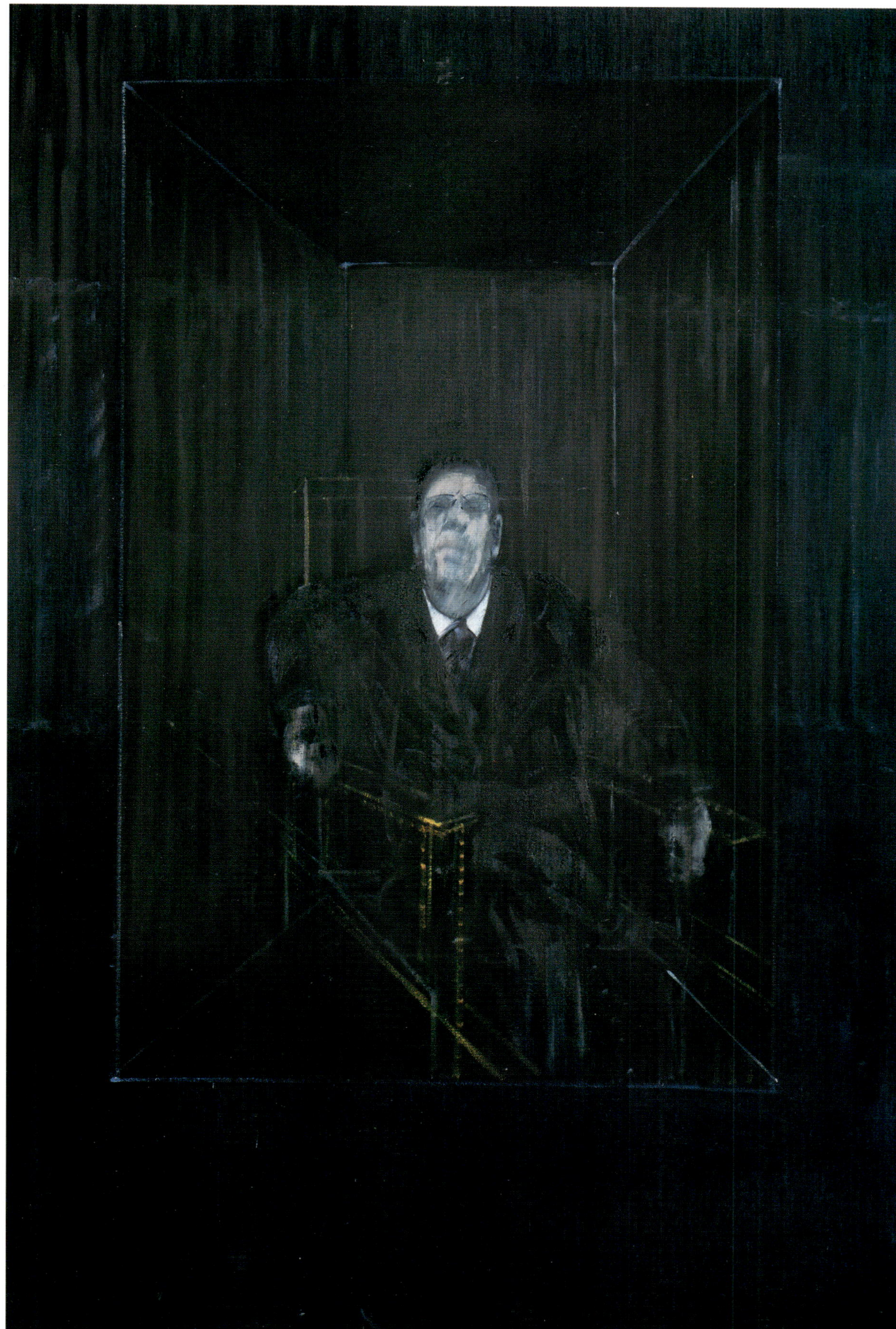

Cat. no. 89

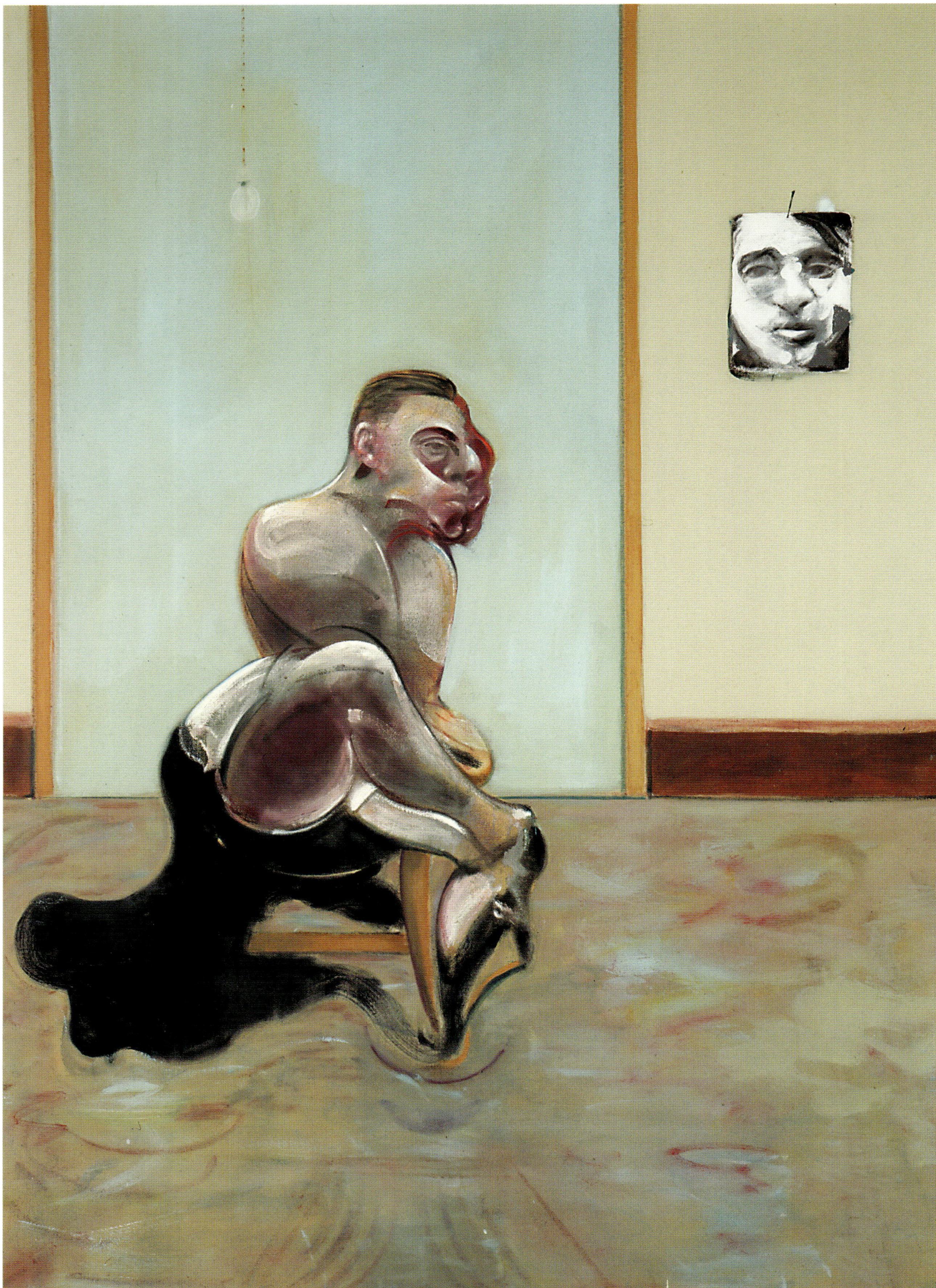

Cat. no. 90

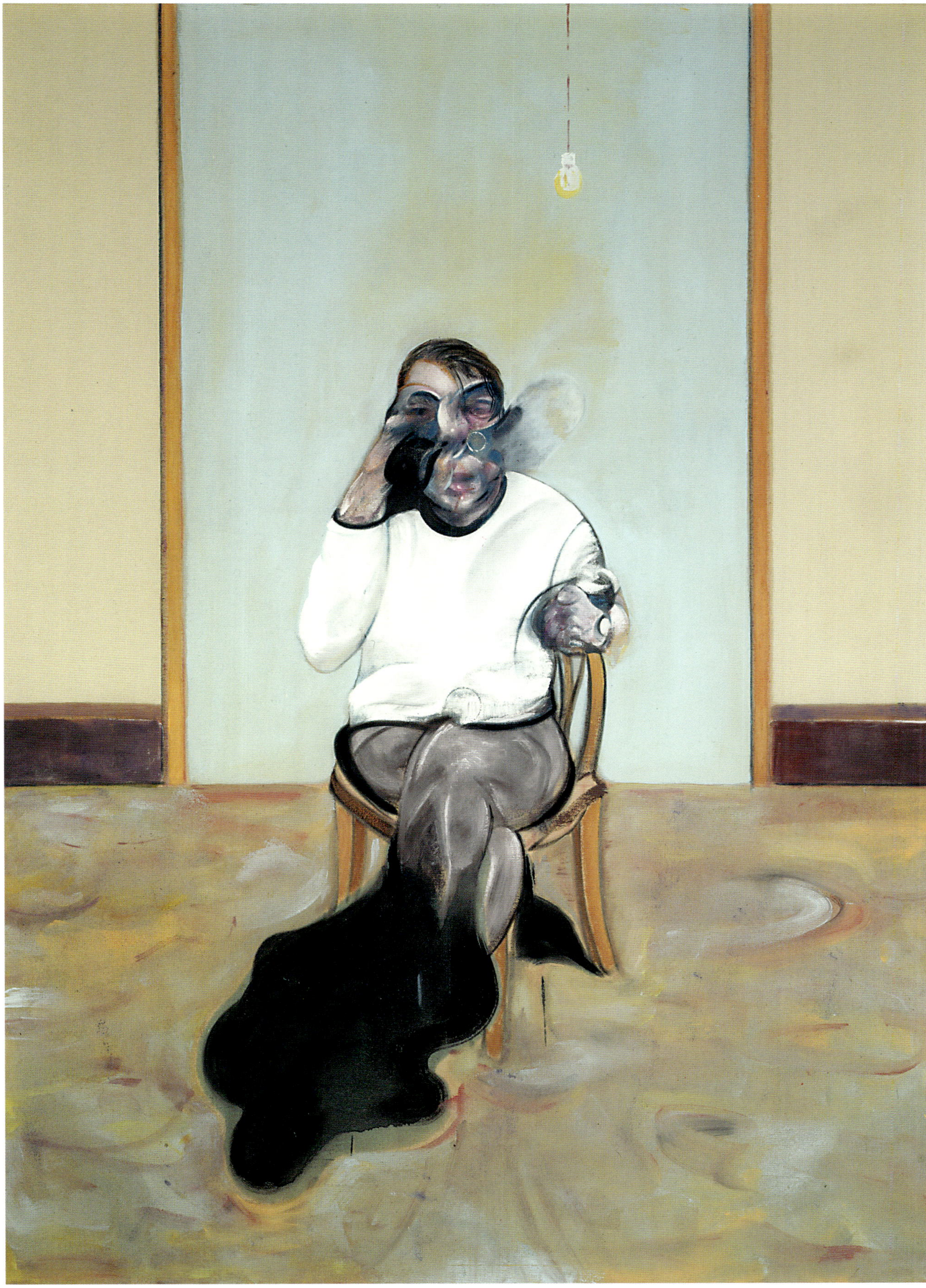

Cat. no. 90

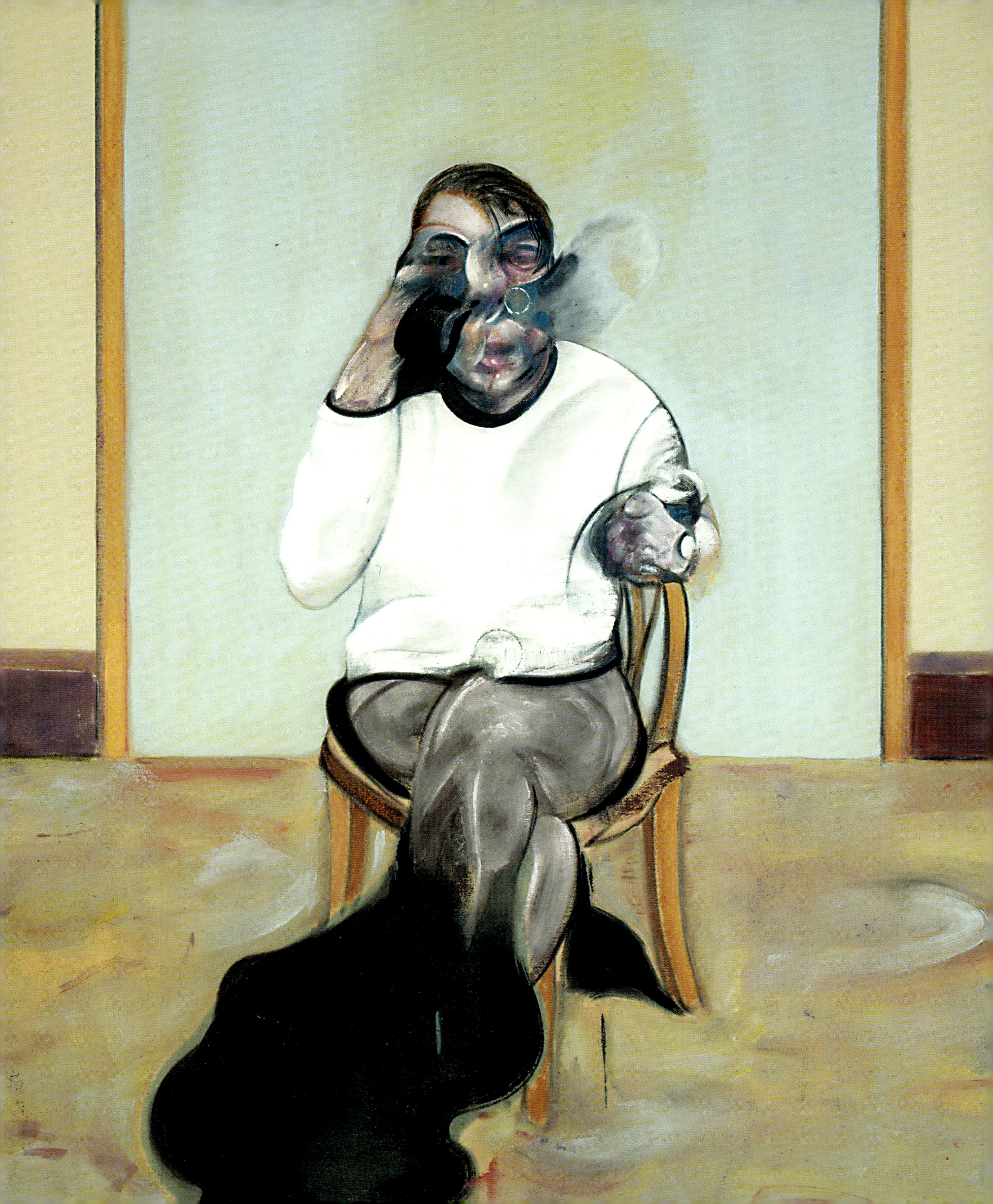

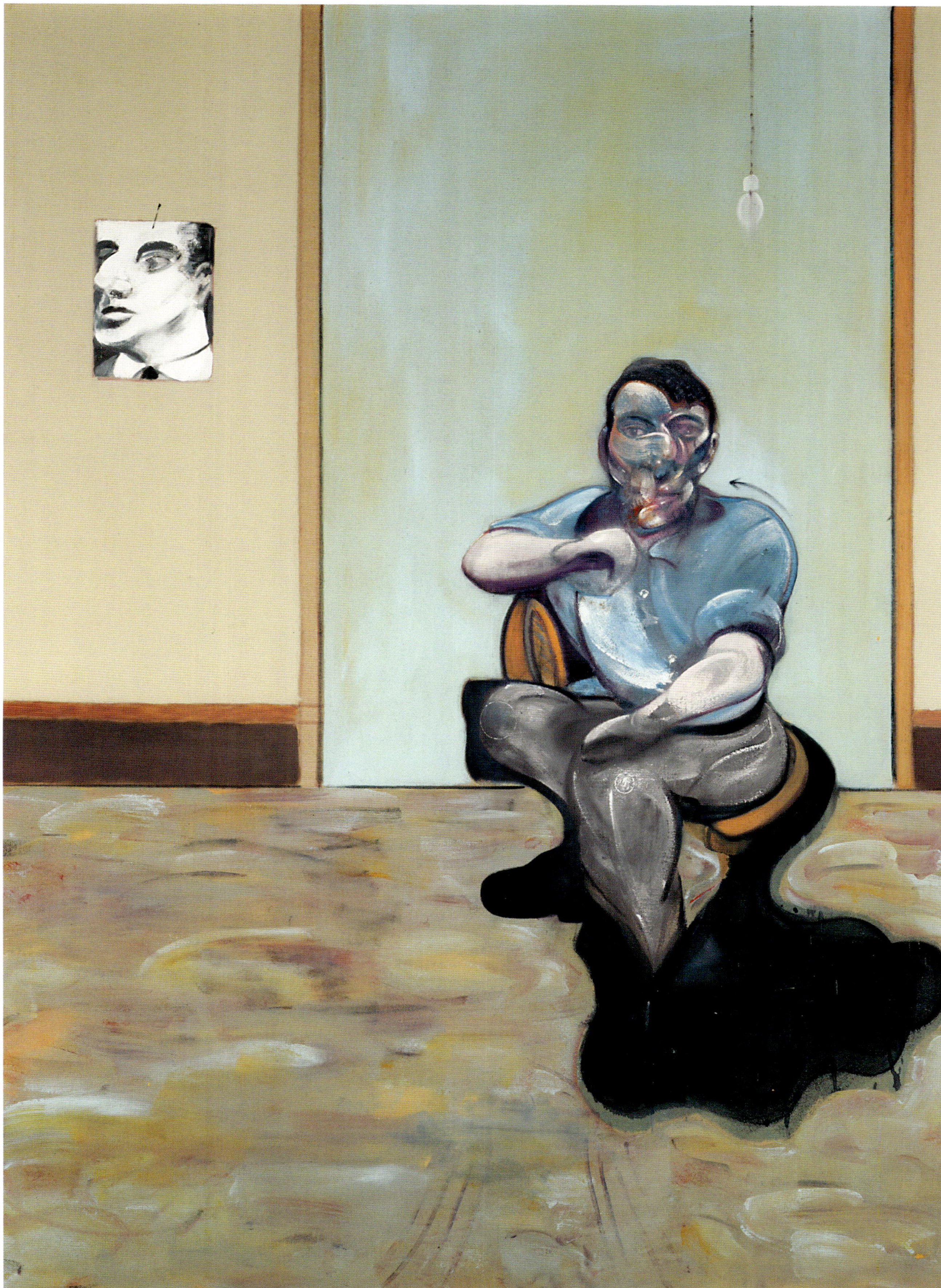
Cat. no. 90

Cat. no. 90
Francis Bacon
Three Portraits: Posthumous Portrait of George Dyer, Self-Portrait, Portrait of Lucian Freud
1973
Oil on canvas, triptych, each panel 198 × 147.5 cm
Switzerland, Private Collection

On p. 240: Cat. no. 90, detail

On p. 241: Cat. no. 91
Alberto Giacometti
Diego
1953
Oil on canvas, 100.5 × 80.5 cm
New York, Solomon R. Guggenheim Museum

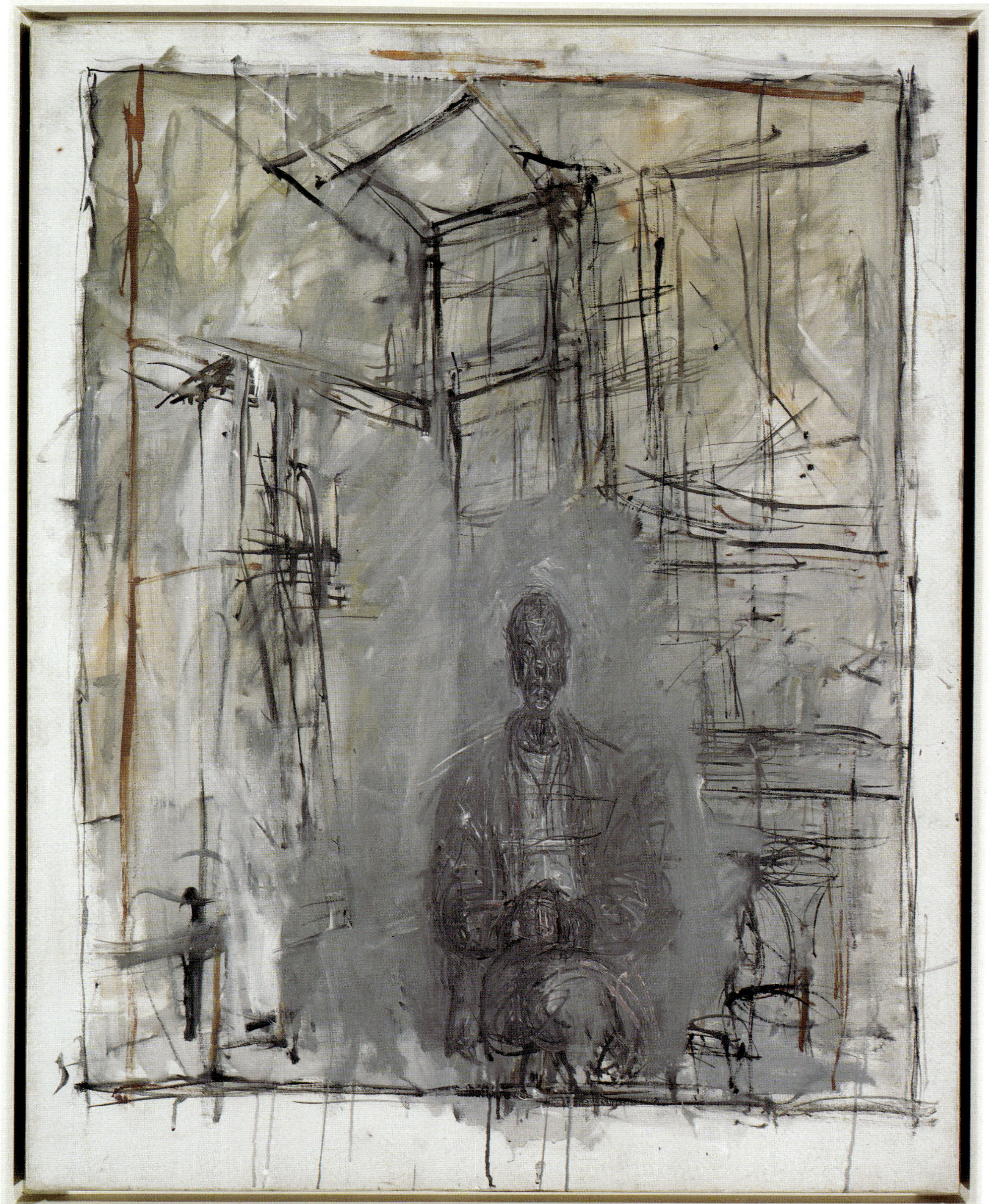

Cat. no. 91

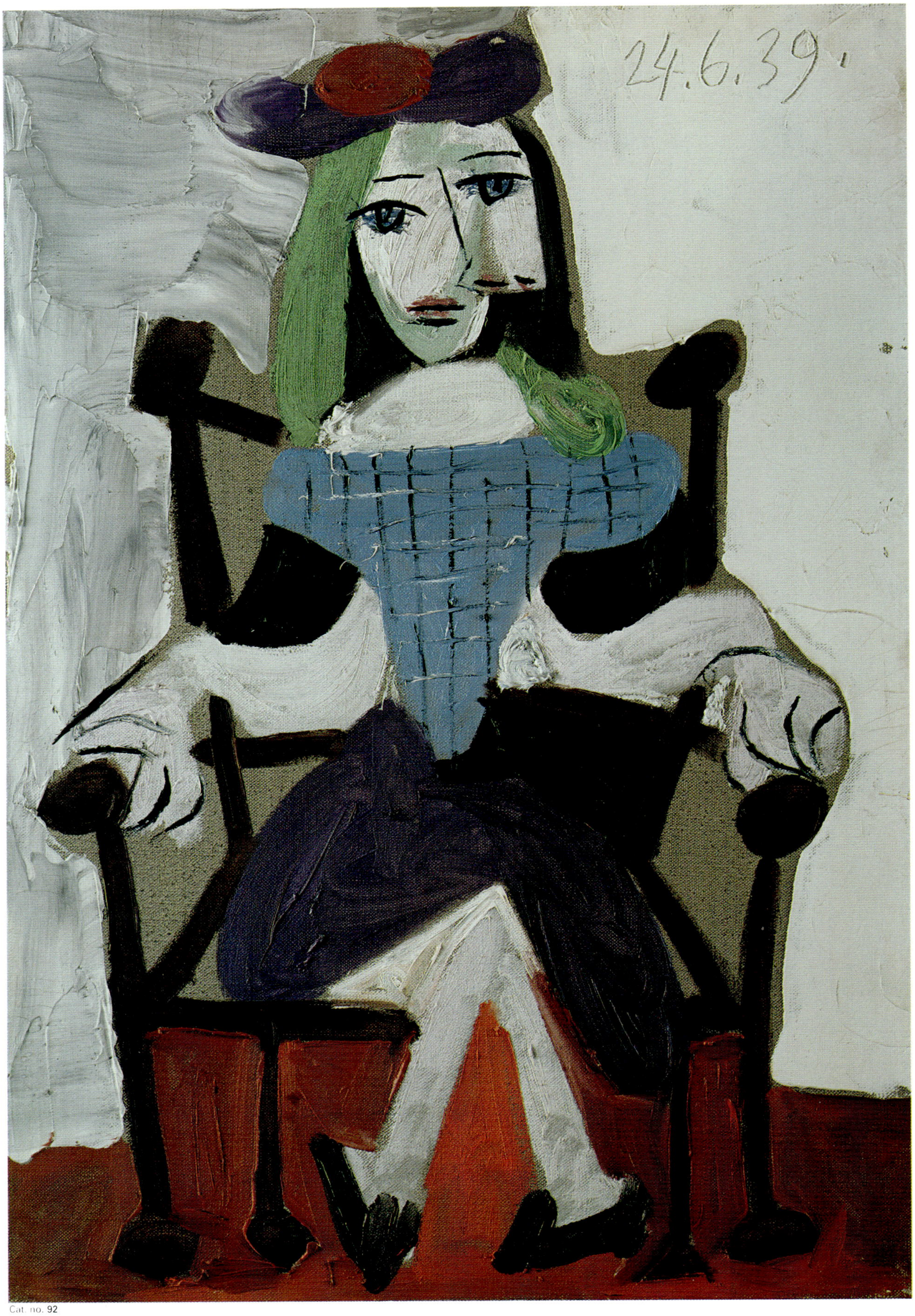

Cat. no. 92

Cat. no. 92
Pablo Picasso
Woman Seated in an Armchair
1939
Oil on canvas, 46 × 33 cm
Berlin, Staatliche Museen
zu Berlin, Nationalgalerie,
Collection Berggruen

Cat. no. 93
Pablo Picasso
Female Head with Hat (Dora)
1939
Oil on canvas, 55 × 46.5 cm
Riehen/Basel, Fondation Beyeler

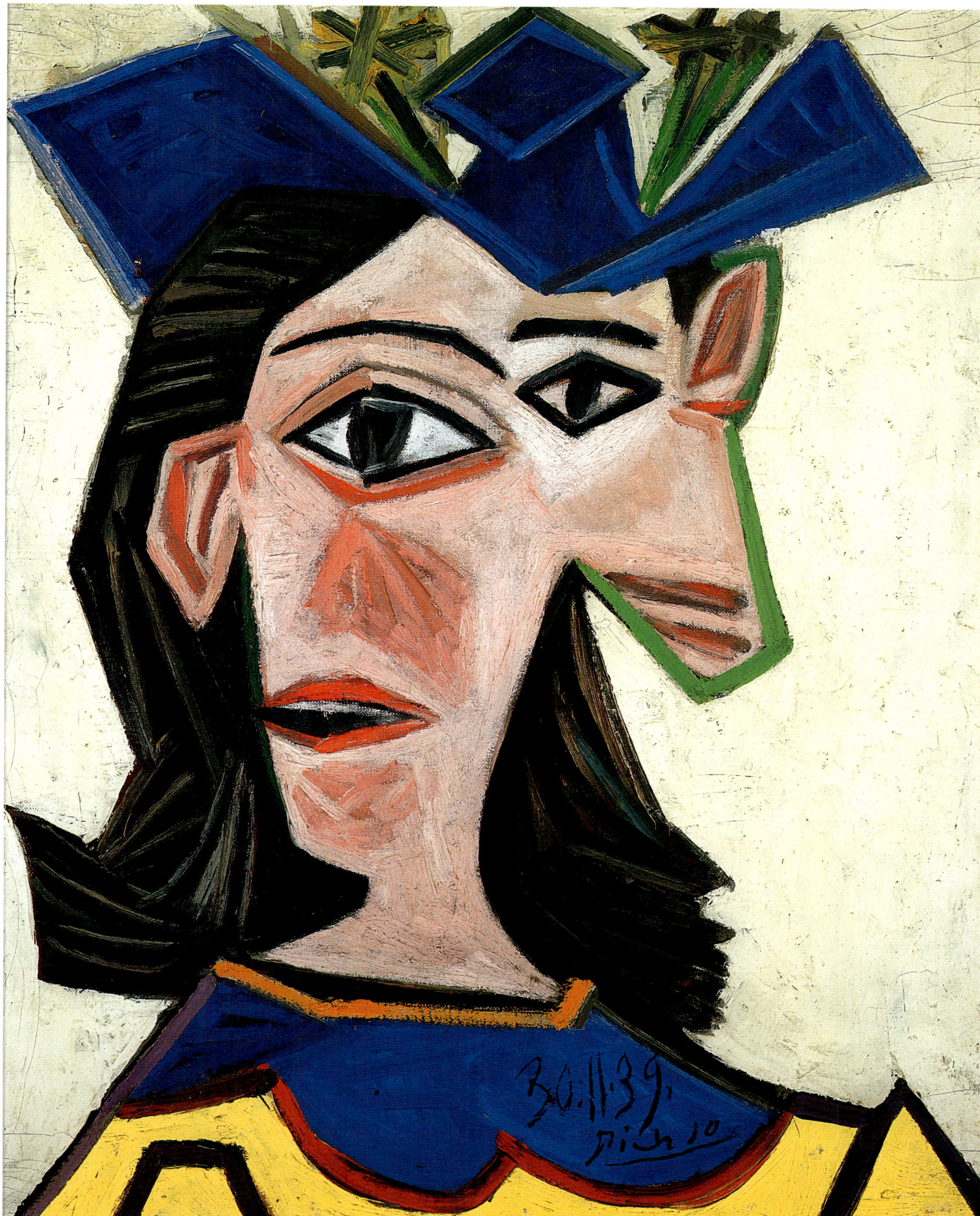

Cat. no. 93

Cat. no. 94
Leaf with black-and-white illustrations of painting by Pablo Picasso, torn from unidentified book, 276 × 226 mm
Dublin, Dublin City Gallery The Hugh Lane, F16:169

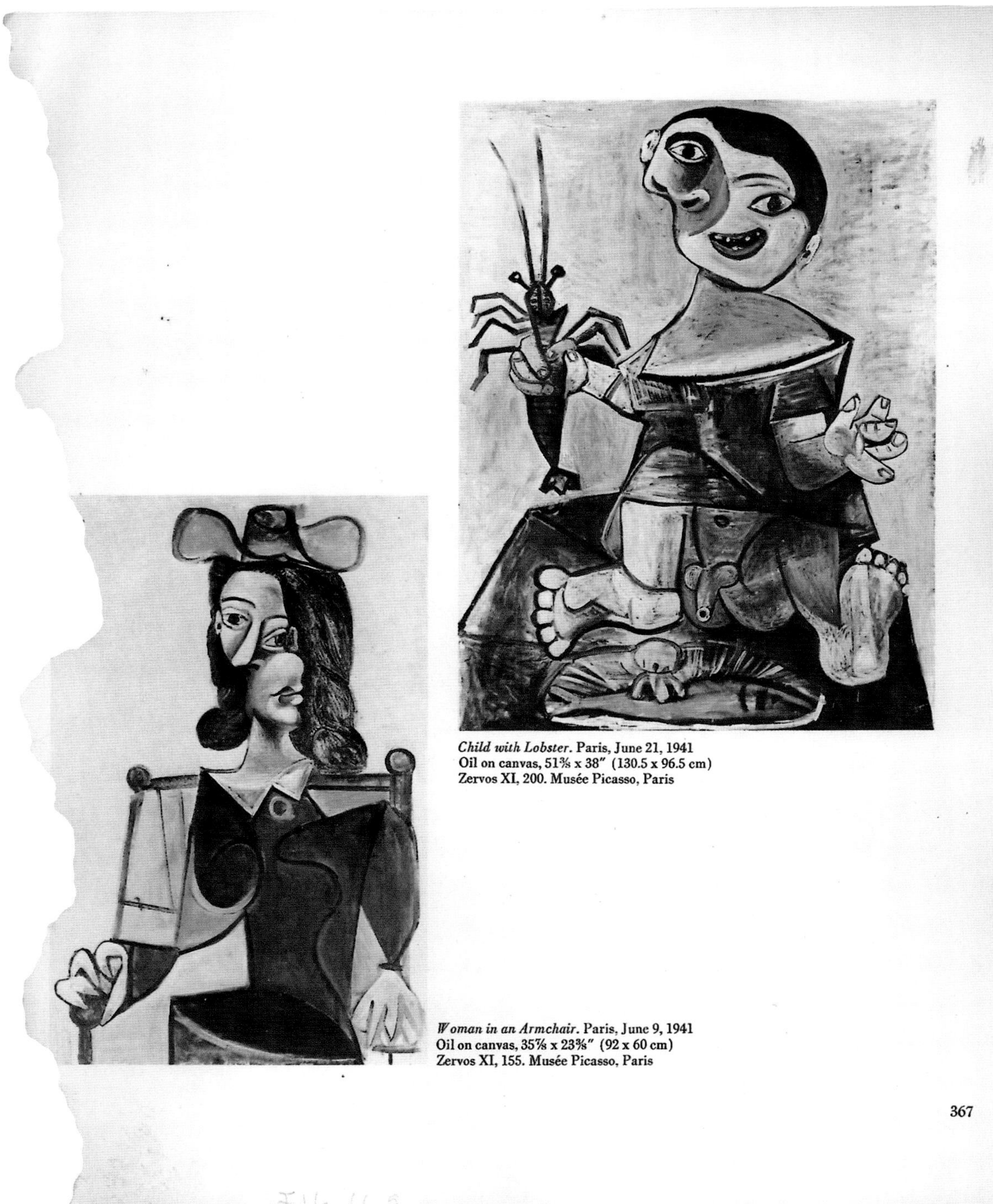

Child with Lobster. Paris, June 21, 1941
Oil on canvas, 51⅜ x 38" (130.5 x 96.5 cm)
Zervos XI, 200. Musée Picasso, Paris

Woman in an Armchair. Paris, June 9, 1941
Oil on canvas, 35⅞ x 23⅝" (92 x 60 cm)
Zervos XI, 155. Musée Picasso, Paris

367

Cat. no. 94

Cat. no. 95
Michel Leiris, Bacon, Picasso, Masson, with articles by George Limbour, and George Bataille, Portrait 8, 1982
208 × 127 × 8 mm
Dublin, Dublin City Gallery The Hugh Lane, F228:21

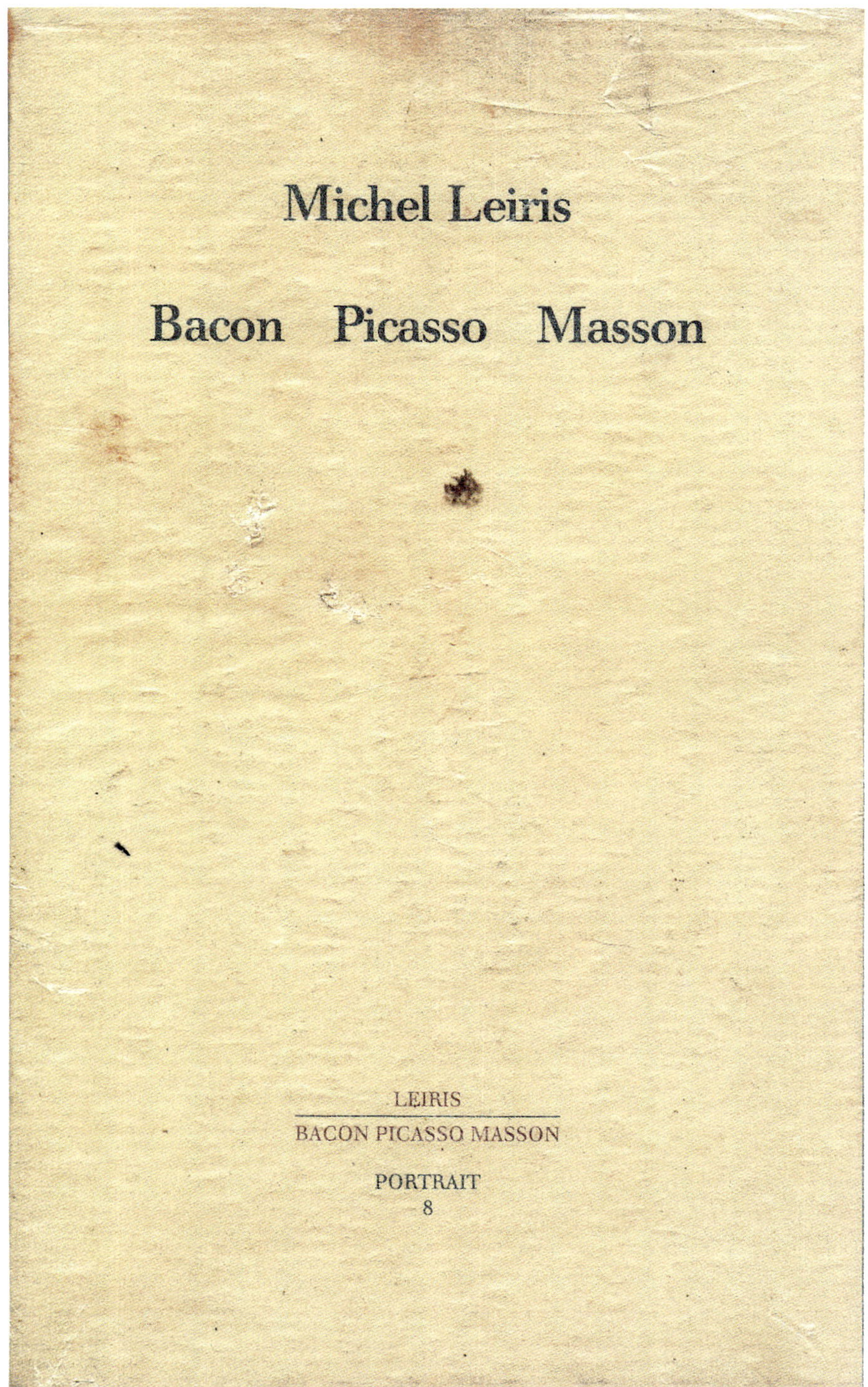

Cat. no. 95

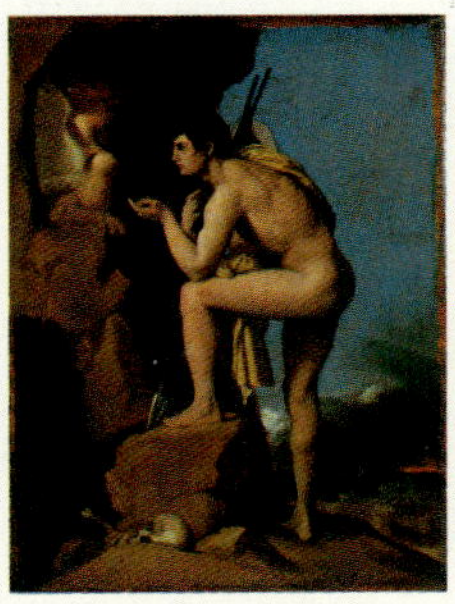
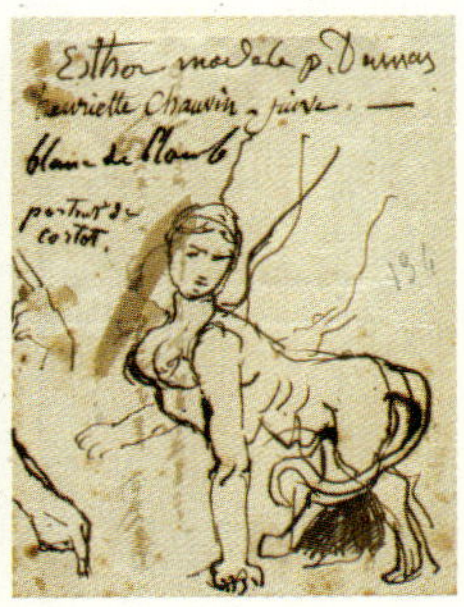
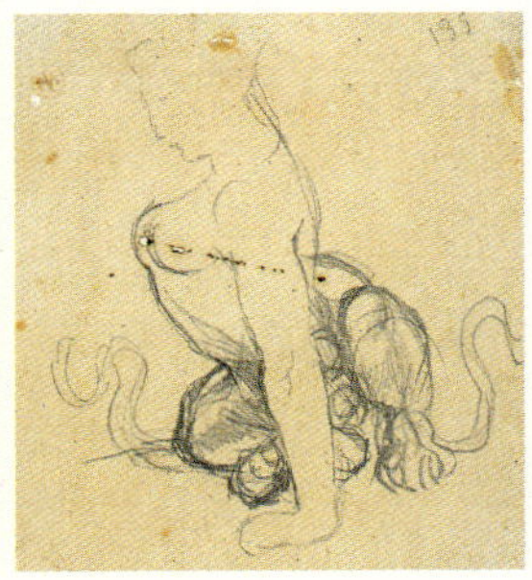
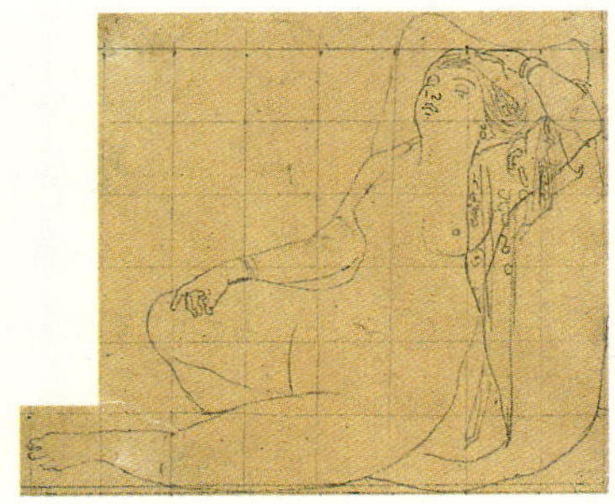
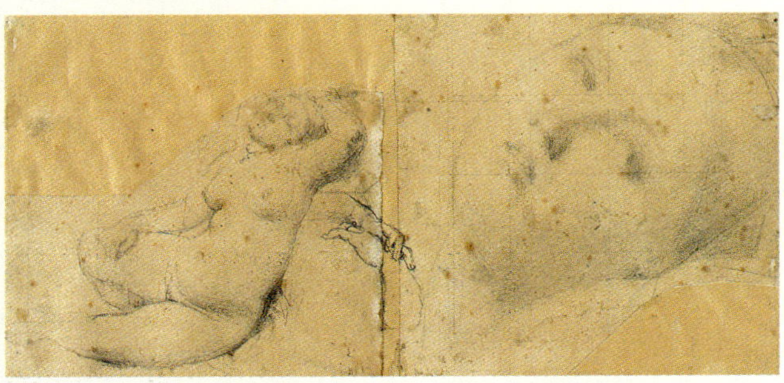
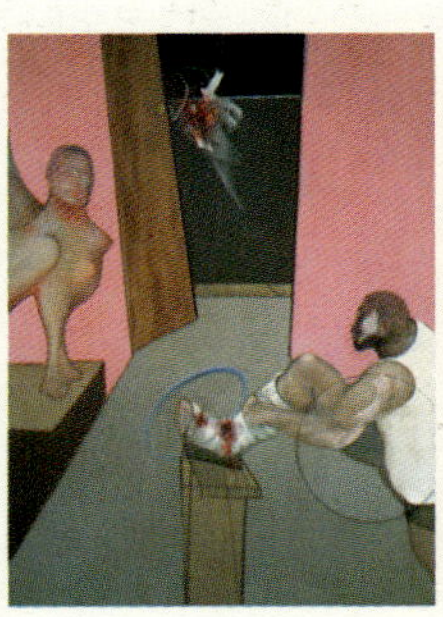
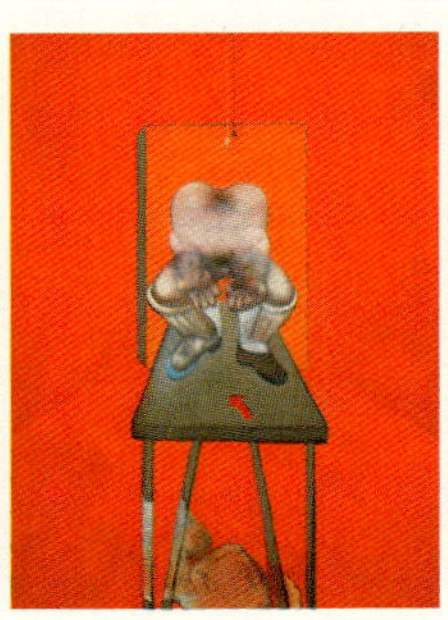
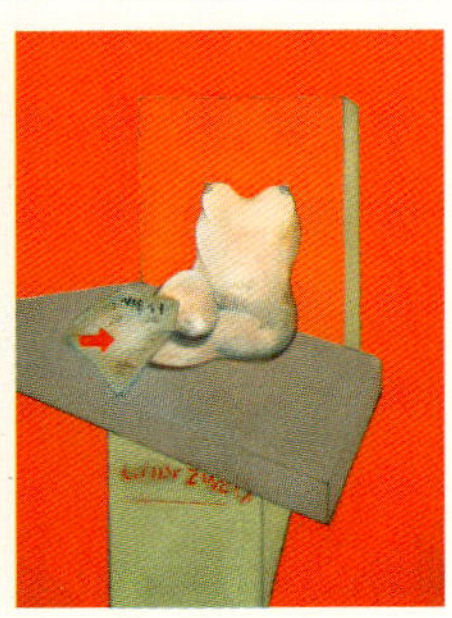
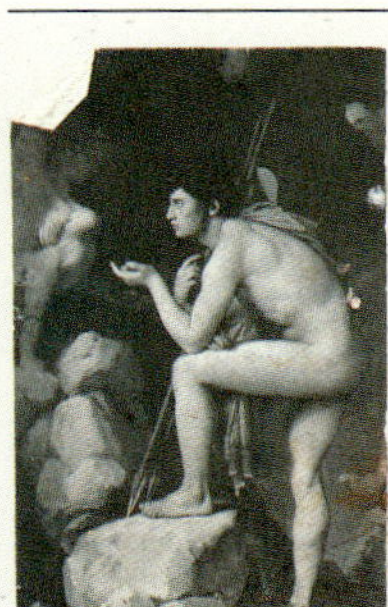
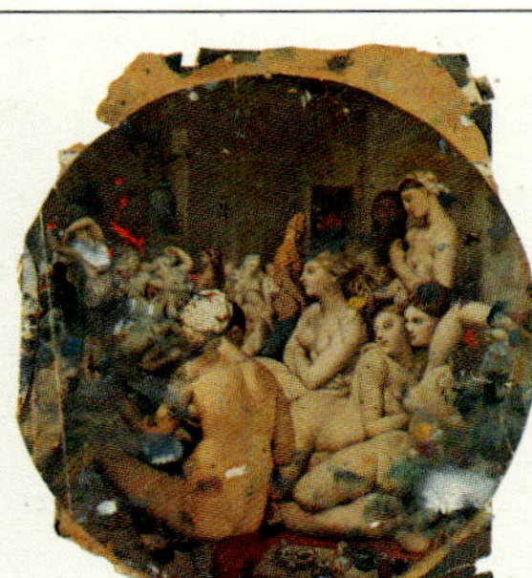
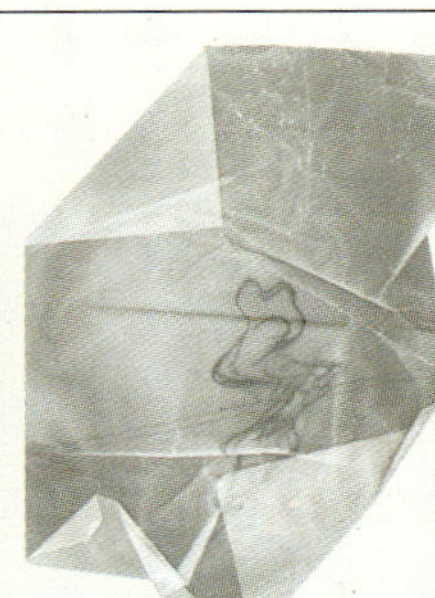
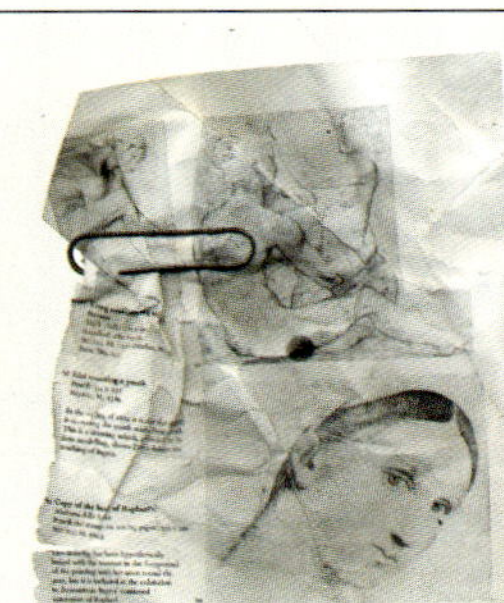
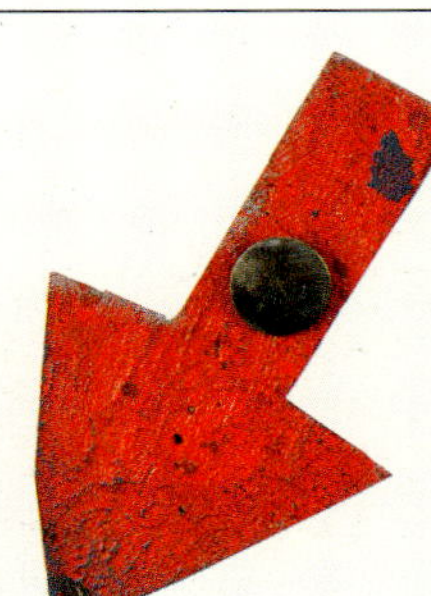

Margarita Cappock

Bacon and Ingres

Francis Bacon greatly admired the work of the French artist Jean-Auguste-Dominique Ingres. In 1967, he and fellow artist Lucian Freud travelled together to Paris to see an Ingres exhibition.[1] However, the depth of Bacon's interest in the Neoclassical master only became apparent in his later years when his own painting underwent a general simplification and distillation of expression. At first glance, Ingres's cool, enamel-like paintings and his needle-sharp drawings seem unlikely sources of inspiration for Bacon. The smooth perfection of Ingres's work is in stark contrast with the textured surface of Bacon's paintings. Yet during the 19th century Ingres's paintings were not only noted for their classicism, they were by turns admired and derided for their anatomical licence. His manipulations of the human body were graceful rather than abrupt. The languor of his female nudes, though, could be subtly disquieting. A number of Bacon's paintings are variations on works by Ingres, including *Diptych: Study from the Human Body; Study of the Human Body, From a Drawing by Ingres*, 1982–84 (cat. no. 102) and *Oedipus and the Sphinx after Ingres*, 1983 (cat. no. 97).

A distinction must be made between the degree of influence that the work of Ingres exerted on Bacon compared with that of Velázquez and Van Gogh. Whereas with those artists Bacon focused on a single painting with intense commitment, in the case of Ingres his attention was divided between several works. Notwithstanding his high regard for the artist, Bacon did not flinch from criticism and once remarked, "I'm very fond of certain portraits by Ingres and I also like the Turkish Bath, but I don't see any value at all in history painting."[2] As John Russell explains, "He admires Ingres, very much, for instance; but he nevertheless detects in Ingres a certain meanness of spirit or defensive tightness which puts him just below the very first rank."[3] Nevertheless, when Bacon made a selection of paintings for *The Artist's Eye* exhibition at the National Gallery, London in 1985, he included *Madame Moitessier Seated*, one of Ingres's finest female portraits.[4]

Both Bacon and Ingres admired the heroic art of classical antiquity, each gravitating towards Greek art. Bacon was fascinated above all by Greek sculpture. He visited mainland Greece and Crete in 1965 and a photograph found in his studio shows him posing in front of the Erectheum of the Acropolis in Athens. He was also attracted to ancient Greek literature and his paintings make explicit and implicit reference to classical Greek tragedies such as *The Oresteia* by the Greek poetic dramatist, Aeschylus.

Among the myths enacted on the classical stage, that of Oedipus was pre-eminent and became a touchstone for Bacon. The legend of Oedipus solving the riddle of the Sphinx also appealed to Ingres who saw it as the triumph of human intelligence over a terrible adversary.[5] It was a subject that Ingres painted, with variations, until the end of his life.[6] His first version was painted in Rome in 1808, a work that now resides in the Louvre in Paris. The painting was included in the annual exhibition of the Académie de France in Rome along with the *Bather of Valpinçon,* and when they were sent on to Paris, both paintings received criticism for inconsistencies of drawing, lighting and for insufficient idealisation.[7] The director of the Académie des Beaux-Arts in Paris commented, "One would wish that he had been more imbued with the beautiful character of antiquity and with the grand and noble style, which the beautiful productions of the great masters during the finest days of the Roman school should inspire."[8]

Ingres enlarged and reworked the Louvre picture in 1826/27, and the National Gallery painting exhibited here (cat. no. 96) is a smaller variant that may be a study, made about 1826, in connection with changes to the Louvre composition. The technical assurance of Ingres and his mastery in the rendering of forms, even when working on a very small scale, are much in evidence in the figure of Oedipus. Fragments of a skeleton in the lower foreground suggest the deadly power of the Sphinx. Oedipus, by contrast, is a majestic, athletic figure who calmly confronts the monster. The bowed head of the Sphinx lends her a wary and submissive air. A book leaf with a black-and-white reproduction of the Louvre painting was found in Bacon's studio (cat. no. 107). There are also drawings by Ingres on the same subject in the exhibition (cat. nos. 98 and 99).

In Bacon's *Oedipus and the Sphinx after Ingres,* 1983 the roles are reversed and the Sphinx has been made dominant with Oedipus placed in a more submissive position. This is reflected in the composition of the painting, with Oedipus occupying the lower right corner of the foreground while the Sphinx, standing on a platform, stares directly out at the viewer. As Sylvester notes, "Bacon turns a winner into a loser."[9] The facial features of both the Sphinx and Oedipus are intriguing. The face of the Sphinx seems to be an amalgamation of that of John Edwards and Muriel Belcher, whereas the profile of Oedipus has definite similarities with that of George Dyer. In *Oedipus and the Sphinx,* 1979, Bacon's first known version of this subject, the figure of Oedipus also has the features of George Dyer. In this earlier work, the figure is completely naked and the Sphinx is absent from the painting. The canvas had, in fact, been originally paired with *Sphinx – Portrait of Muriel Belcher,* 1979. It is possible that this now-separated diptych was the first of Bacon's extant works to owe a thematic, if not a visual, debt to Ingres. If so, it may be viewed as a precursor to *Oedipus and the Sphinx after Ingres,* 1983.

In *Oedipus and the Sphinx after Ingres,* 1983 the figure of Oedipus wears a singlet and shorts, lending him a contemporary appearance. His attire is similar to that worn by the figure in the left panel of *Triptych in Memory of George Dyer*, 1971 (cat. no. 121) and similar to some of the images of boxers found in the books in the artist's studio. Bacon takes licence with the legend of Oedipus by placing Oedipus's large bloodied, bandaged foot prominently in the composition.[10] Emphasis is placed on this wound by a white directional arrow, encircled by blue paint. The inclusion of the detail of the wound is clearly anachronistic since the injury occurred while Oedipus was still an infant. Oedipus also seems more preoccupied with his bound foot than with the Sphinx. The position of the bandaged leg of this figure is also unusual and gives the impression that the left leg is actually where the right should be. A winged creature hovers in the open doorway behind Oedipus. This being is derived from the Furies, agents of divine vengeance in *The Oresteia* by Aeschylus.

Two hand-written notes by Bacon found in the Reece Mews studio are revealing in relation to Ingres and provide evidence that the artist's original intention may have been to produce a triptych on the theme of Oedipus and the Sphinx. The notes read as follows: *"Oedipus & the Sphinx 1983/wn*ce central Panel/***/anel c**** ****/Third Panel/finish Tryptih/25th." "Oedipus & the Sphinx/1st panel as in F./2" panel " " "/with blood/against the door/~~Th~~/3" panel Oedipus consults the sphinx."*

Bacon's work *Diptych: – Study from the Human Body; Study of the Human Body, From a Drawing by Ingres*, 1982–84 pays homage to Ingres's draughtsmanship. He originally wanted the right panel of this diptych to be linked to a painting, *Study from the Human Body,* 1982, which the Centre Georges Pompidou had acquired in 1983. When this could not be arranged, he painted another panel, *Study from the Human Body, 1982–84* which was a variant on the Pompidou painting.[11] Both panels of this diptych display headless figures, one male, one female. The left-hand panel contains a strong sexual element in the way the headless figure's open hands serve to concentrate the viewer's attention on the male's genitalia. Numerous illustrated histories of cricket were found in the studio and Bacon consulted these and assimilated elements into his paintings during the 1980s.

While the figure is male, there is a suggestion of femininity in the rounded breast-like forms, without nipples, on the top of the torso. Its contours are reminiscent of the curvaceous forms of Ingres's female nudes. There is a strong sculptural quality in this diptych with both the figures presented on raised pedestals against a searing orange background. The fragmentary nature of ancient classical sculpture, which

Bacon so admired, finds clear expression in these late paintings where the pictorial language is simplified and pared down to its essentials. The human body has been abbreviated to mere stumps.

Drawings by Ingres for *Le Bain Turc* provided Bacon with the inspiration for the female figure in the right-hand panel of this diptych (cat. nos. 100 and 101). Ingres, a supreme draughtsman, preached a severe doctrine on the discipline of line in art, believing that if something were well drawn it would be well painted. Many reproductions of drawings by Ingres were found in the studio, in particular reproductions of pencil studies for *Le Bain turc*, 1859–63, where the fluency of Ingres's draughtsmanship is formidable. However, it is notable that the work Bacon devoted most attention to, and the one on which the right-hand panel of this diptych is based, was a painted sketch entitled *Nude Woman Sitting on the Ground*. As a study, it was unusually painterly for Ingres.

A crumpled black-and-white reproduction of this drawing was found in the studio. Bacon attached a paper clip to hold one of its creases in place and created a deliberate distortion so that part of the figure's face is obscured. While admiring the more characteristic drawings of Ingres, it was this atypical one, with its additional arm, that prompted Bacon's variations such as *Kneeling Figure*, c. 1981, a headless figure with breasts in place of arms.[12] Indeed, it may have been the alternate position of the right arm in Ingres's study that suggested to Bacon that limbs themselves were dispensable. If this is accepted, Ingres's role in the formation of Bacon's late works is much further reaching than previously allowed. Bacon also admired the completed painting, *Le Bain turc* (cat. no. 104) itself, and a colour illustration of this work was found attached to a piece of card in the studio.[13]

In the right-hand panel of the diptych Bacon seems to have been influenced by another leaf from a book found in the studio on female anthropometry. It is one of the few leaves in the studio that deals with the female form. One photograph in particular shows a nude photographed from the knees up with her head tilted back, and Bacon may have borrowed the upper section of this female figure and combined it with the lower section of the drawing by Ingres.

During his lifetime, Bacon professed great admiration for the drawings of Michelangelo, Degas, Picasso and Giacometti, often rating their graphic work as amongst the best things they did. Simultaneously, he persistently denied throughout his life that he ever made preliminary sketches for his paintings and preferred that people believed his work on canvas was spontaneous. Bacon's own preliminary drawings do not compare favourably with the work of the artists he so admired and this may have led to a sense of insecurity about his own lack of graphic prowess. Very likely it inspired an admiration, bordering on envy, of the talents of true masters such as Ingres and Michelangelo. Ingres represented the quintessence of that very discipline which Bacon so manifestly lacked. The singular concentrated nature of his drawings posed a challenge to the unschooled and painterly artist. Since Bacon's death, a number of drawings, both by and attributed to him, have surfaced. With the emergence of these different bodies of work, the notion that Bacon did not produce preparatory drawings has finally been dismissed.

More than 70 works on paper were found in Bacon's Reece Mews studio and at least five of these drawings, all made in pencil on tracing paper, can be related to *Diptych: Study from the Human Body; Study of the Human Body, From a Drawing by Ingres*, 1982–84. That so many of the drawings found in the studio are executed on tracing paper is noteworthy and suggests that behind his choice of materials there lay a method and a practice.[14] Bacon kept many of his own exhibition catalogues in the studio and he often painted over plates of his own work, almost as if he were still experimenting with the completed painting. It is possible that he also traced over these plates and that this particular drawing came about in this way. Certain figures repeatedly surface in Bacon's oeuvre and this may have been a simple way of borrowing a figurative motif from one painting and using it as a basis for another. This theory is further strengthened by the fol-

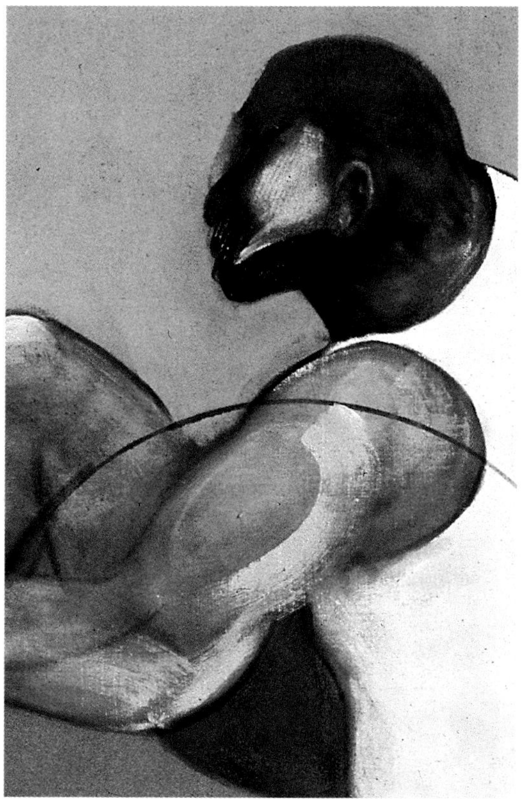

Cat. no. 97, detail

lowing comment by John Edwards on Bacon's work practices, "He would sometimes draw on tracing paper, slowly mirroring images underneath."[15]

The drawings that relate to this particular diptych depict a headless kneeling figure with breasts and nipples, all relating to the right-hand panel of this painting. The figure is perched on two parallel lines which tilt downward towards the left-hand side of the sheet. A short near-vertical pencil line leads from the lower of the two parallel lines to the right hand-edge of the sheet. A stain-like shadow is cast from the two feet and roughly reflects the form of the kneeling figure. In all five sheets, the figure is similar in form and size. The feet of the figure are placed on two lines descending towards the left side of the sheet. Each drawing is a variation on the other. In this series of sketches one sees evidence of Bacon becoming committed to resolving a figure by stages before attempting it on canvas. That very discipline is redolent of Ingres's own continual urge to refine his figural motives, and throughout their careers both artists practised variations on existing paintings.

The work of Ingres provoked and fascinated Bacon on a number of levels. Through his interest in antiquity, Bacon was drawn to Ingres's authoritative and iconic treatment of the resonant theme of Oedipus and the Sphinx. Ingres's supreme draughtsmanship suggested to Bacon another way of handling the female figure as well as feminising the male. His rounded and closed forms offered an antithesis to Bacon's fragmented and twisted bodies, and his sensual distortions a way of eroticising the lone figure. Bacon's later work charts a development away from the breaking up of the figure to a more defined and condensed treatment. The nudes of Ingres's *Le Bain turc* suggested a way of reconceiving the body as a compressed bulbous form with an emphasis on the torso. It was an approach Bacon found he could adopt for both male and female figures. The static and polished character of Ingres's art is certainly in marked contrast to the high experimentation and risk-taking of Bacon's oeuvre. Yet is it this aloof perfection that may have made the later painter curious about an artist so temperamentally different from himself but so driven to produce original variations on the human form. Bacon's statements from the latter part of his life indicate a wish to refine and distil his art. Ingres, who could scarcely have imagined or welcomed it, provided a model for this evolution as Bacon directed his painting towards more sculptural ends.

[1] Hughes 1988, p. 17.
[2] Archimbaud 1993, p. 40.
[3] Russell 1993, p. 50.
[4] Lucian Freud also included this painting in his *Artist's Eye* exhibition, which took place at the National Gallery, London in the summer of 1987.
[5] Oedipus was the son of Laius, King of Thebes and his wife Jocasta. When he was a child, the oracle prophesised that Oedipus would eventually kill his father and marry his mother. In an attempt to circumvent this prophecy, a spike was driven though his foot and the young Oedipus was left to die (the literal meaning of the name is "swell foot"). A shepherd rescued the infant from a hillside and brought him up. Oedipus later went to Delphi to establish the identity of his parents but on his way to Thebes he quarrelled with, and killed an old man, who unbeknownst to him was his father. Oedipus solved the riddle of the Sphinx, a monster who destroyed those who could not solve a riddle she asked, and by doing so he gained the kingdom of Thebes. In ignorance Oedipus married his mother, Jocasta. Having discovered what he had done, he blinded himself and went into exile.
[6] Rosenblum 1990, p. 68.
[7] Exh. Cat. New York – Washington, D.C., – London 1999, p. 101 and p. 546.
[8] As quoted in Exh. Cat. New York – Washington, D.C. – London 1999, p. 101.
[9] Sylvester 2000, p. 164.
[10] Bacon frequently included bandaged limbs in his paintings, such as *Three Studies from the Human Body,* 1967, where the figure with a bandaged leg on a splint is closely based on an illustration in K.C. Clark's book, *Positioning in Radiography* (1939). A book on Orthopaedic Surgery published in 1971 was also found in the studio and contains many diagrams of feet and legs bound in bandages. These have close parallels with Bacon's work of the late 1970s and 1980s.
[11] In 1983 the single painting was purchased by the Centre Pompidou after Michel Leiris had spoken on its behalf to the Acquisitions Commission at the invitation of its Chairman, Dominique Bozo, who felt that Leiris's formidable authority was needed to make the acquisition acceptable. See Sylvester 2000, p. 162.
[12] Ratcliff 2002, p. 9.
[13] On the back of the card is a black- and-white reproduction of the portrait of *Pope Innocent X,* by Velázquez.
[14] Thirteen drawings by Bacon executed on tracing paper were found in the Reece Mews studio.
[15] Ogden 2001, p. 13.

Cat. no. 96
Jean-Auguste-Dominique Ingres
Oedipus and the Sphinx
C. 1826
Oil on canvas, 18.8 × 14.8 cm
London, The National Gallery

Cat. no. 97
Francis Bacon
Oedipus and the Sphinx after Ingres
1983
Oil on canvas, 198 × 147.5 cm
Lisbon, The Berardo Collection –
Sintra Museum of Modern Art

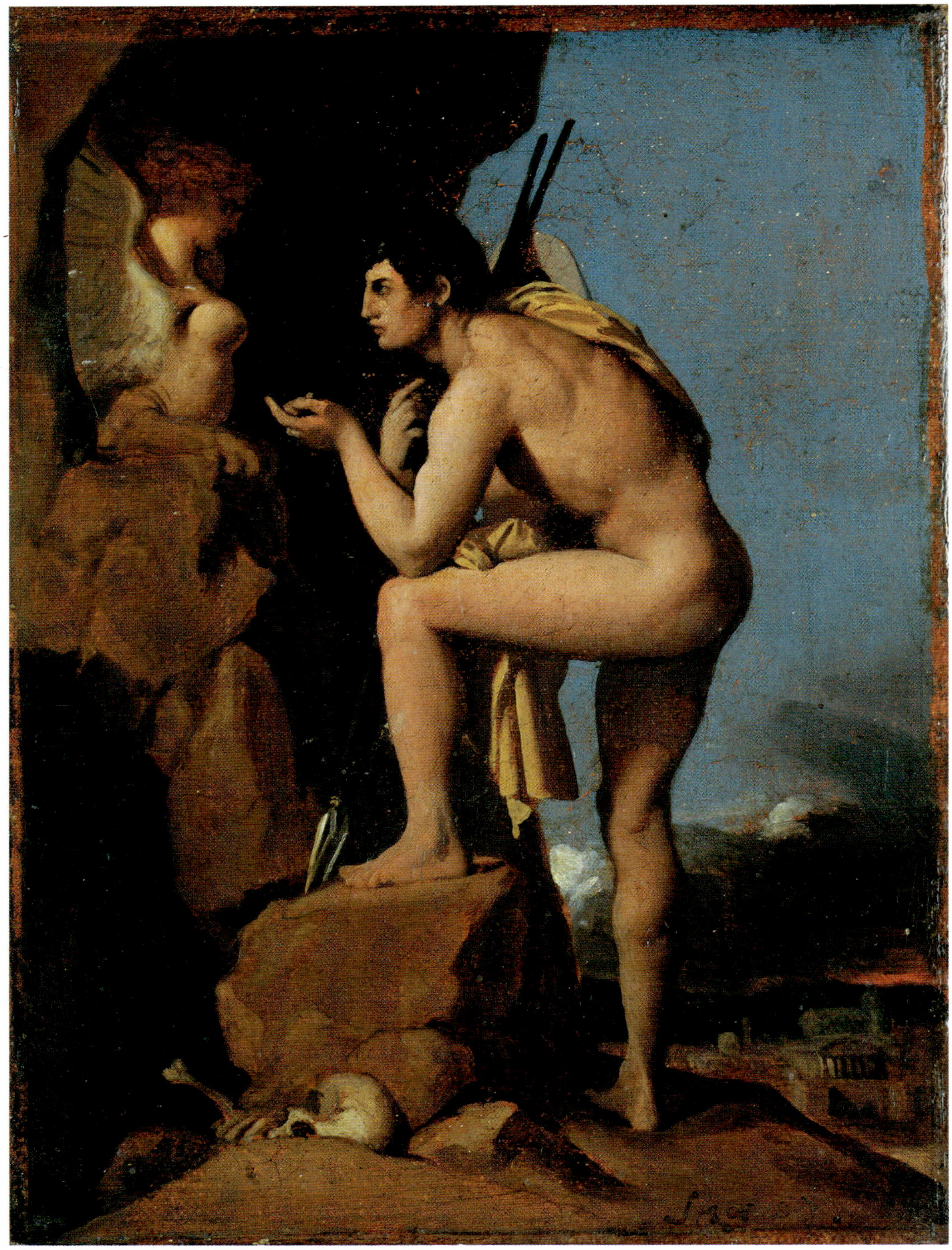

Cat. no. 96

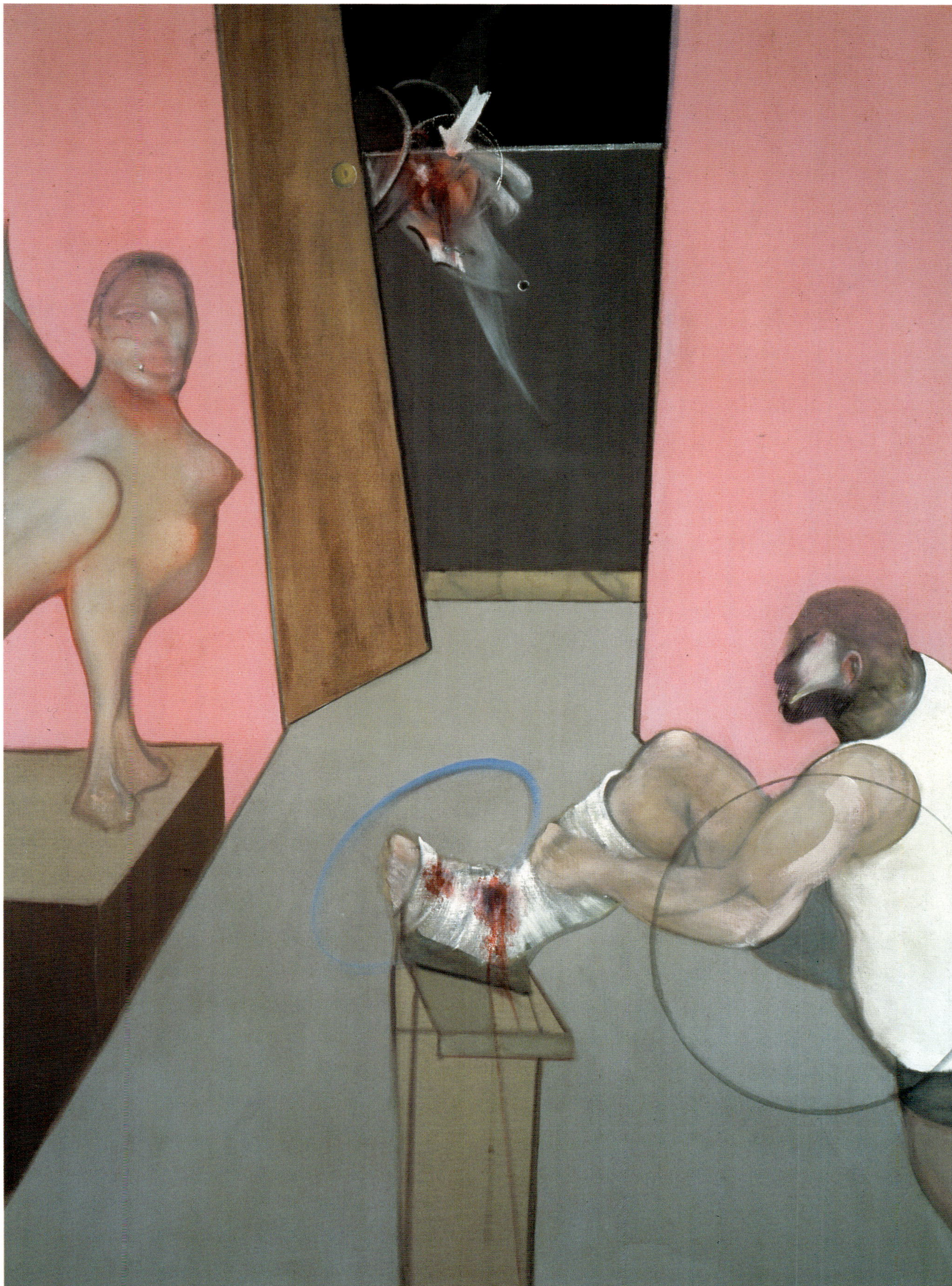
Cat. no. 97

Cat. no. 98
Jean-Auguste-Dominique Ingres
Sketch for the Sphinx
Pen on paper, 132 × 102 mm
Montauban, Musée Ingres,
MI.867.2044

Cat. no. 99
Jean-Auguste-Dominique Ingres
Sphinx (turned to the right)
Pencil on tracing paper,
146 × 123 mm
Montauban, Musée Ingres,
MI.867.2045

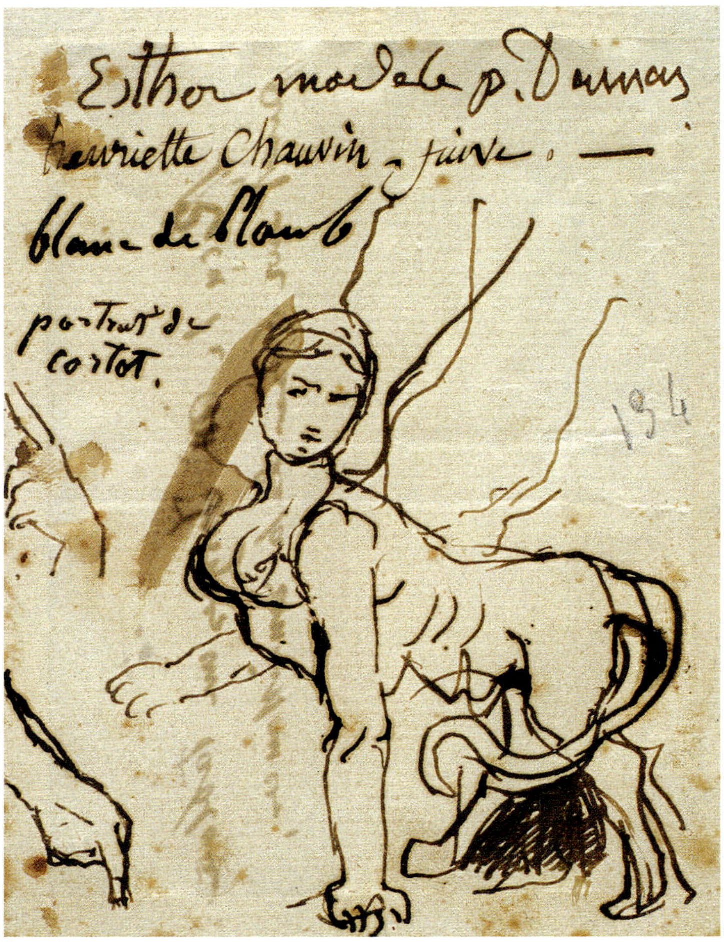

Cat. no. 98

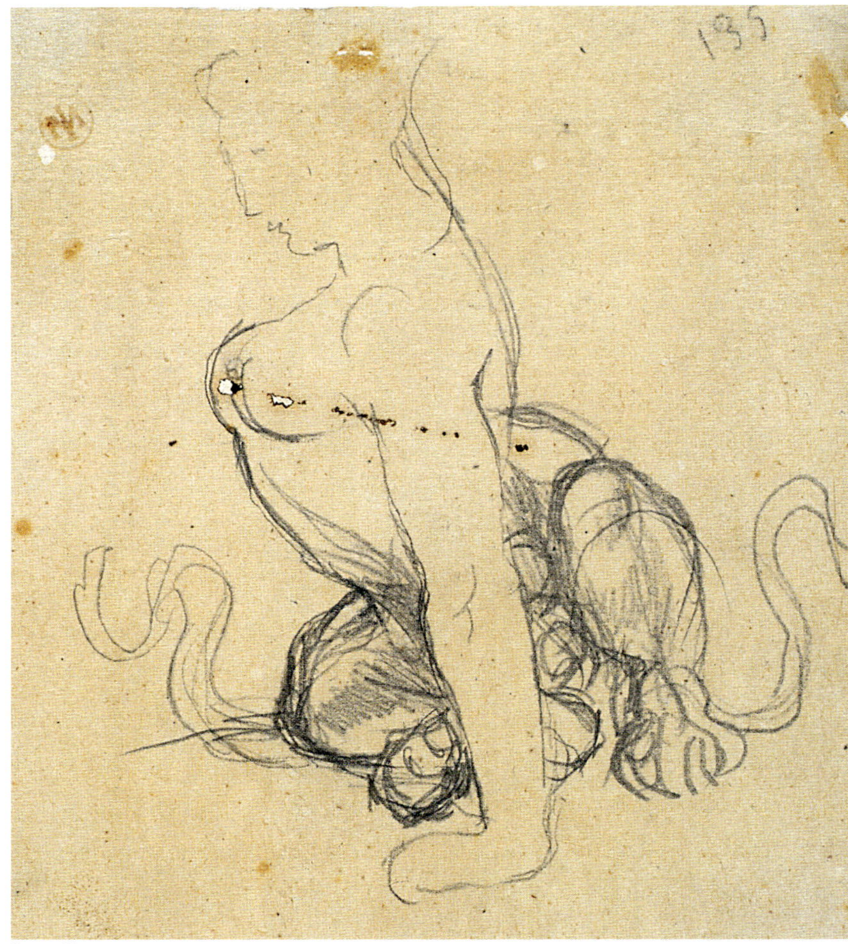

Cat. no. 99

Cat. no. 100
Jean-Auguste-Dominique Ingres
The Woman with the three Arms (with a detail of the head and the two joined hands)
Charcoal on paper, 184 × 385 mm
Montauban, Musée Ingres, MI.867.1216 and 1217

Cat. no. 101
Jean-Auguste-Dominique Ingres
Turkish Women on a Sofa
Pencil on tracing paper, 149 × 181 mm
Montauban, Musée Ingres, MI.867.1202

On p. 256–257: Cat. no. 102
Francis Bacon
Diptych; Study form the Human Body; Study of the Human Body – From a Drawing by Ingres
1982–1984
Oil and transfer type on linen, diptych, panel A: 198.5 × 148 cm, panel B: 195.5 × 147.6 cm
Washington D.C., Hirshhorn Museum and Sculpture Garden, Smithsonian Institution, HMSG 89.21.A–B, Gift of Marlborough International Fine Art and the Joseph H. Hirshhorn Foundation, by exchange, 1989

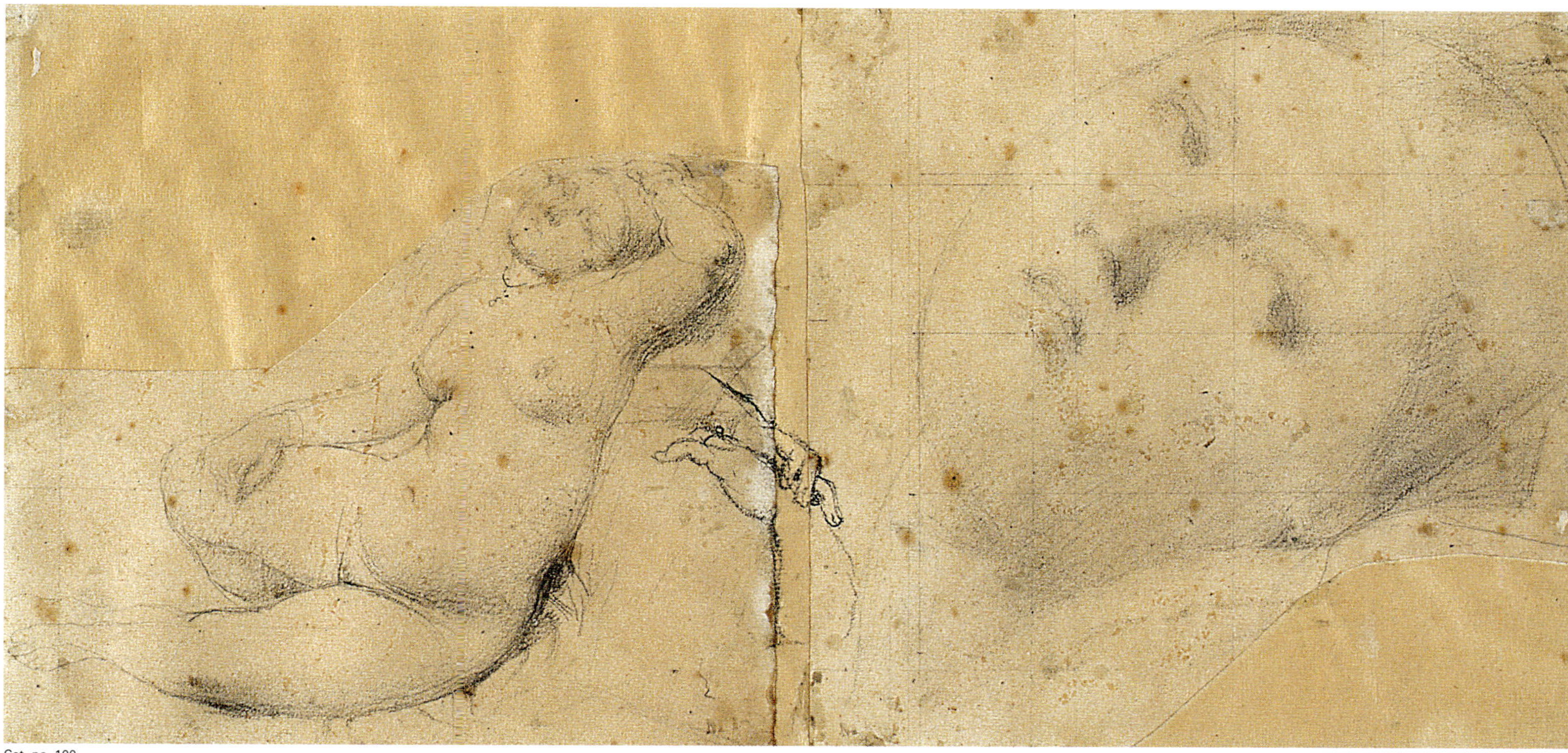

Cat. no. 100

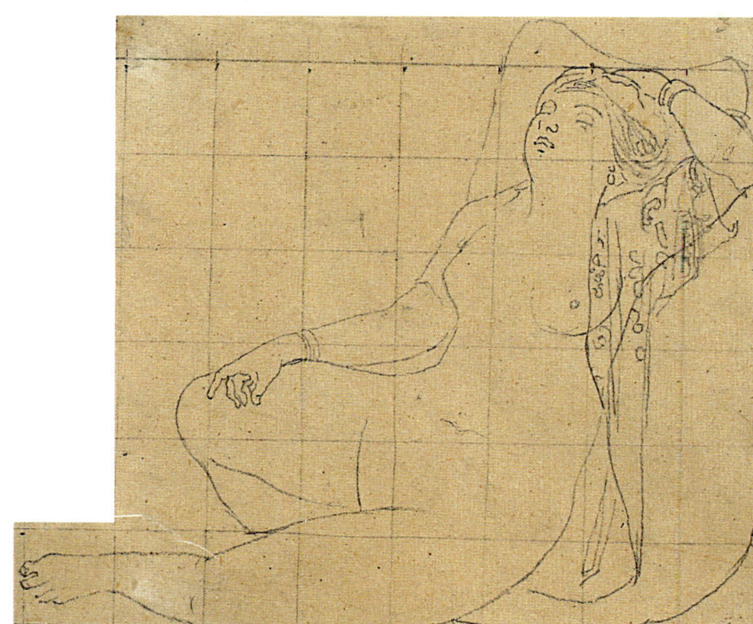

Cat. no. 101

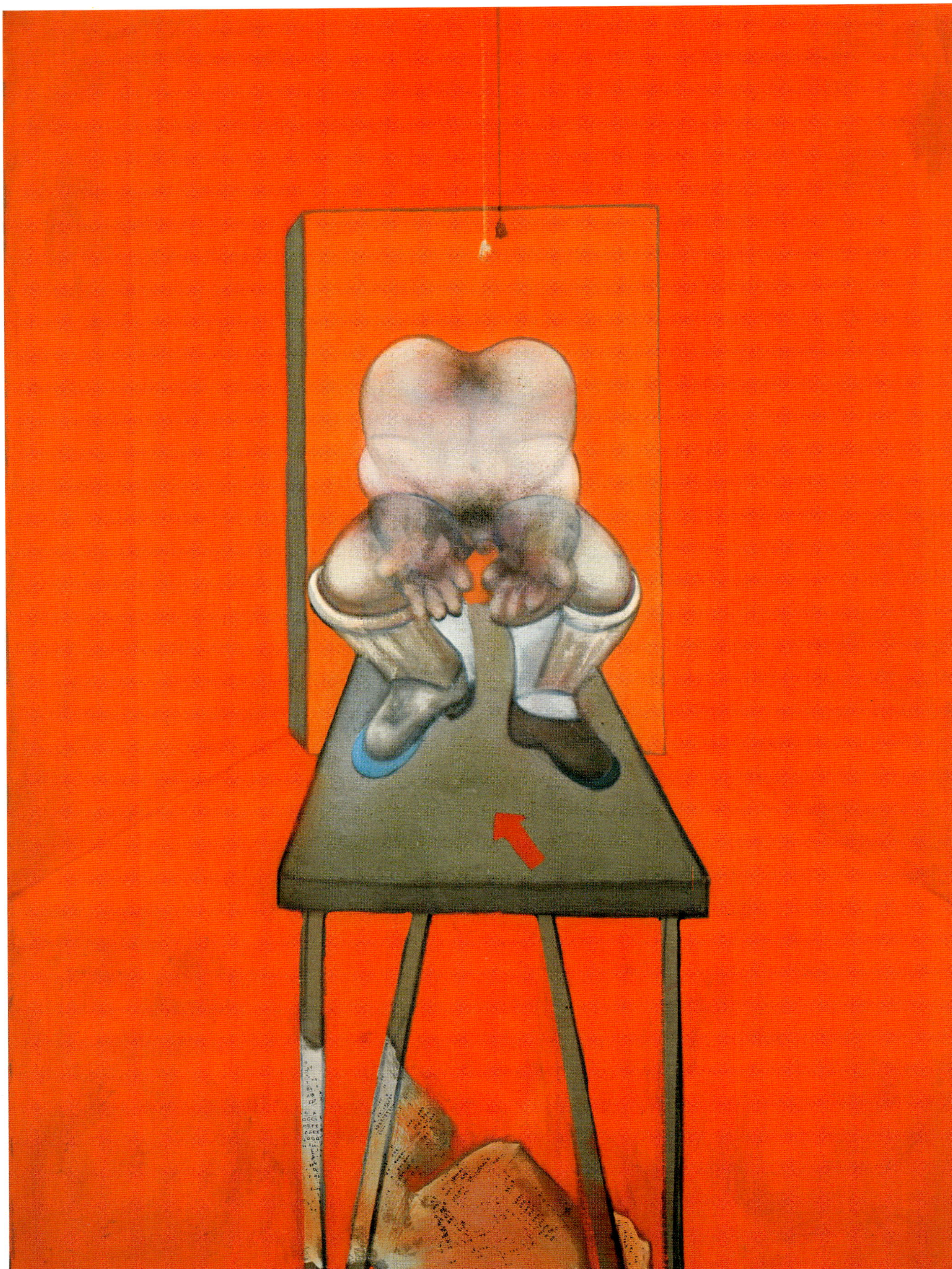

Cat. no. 102

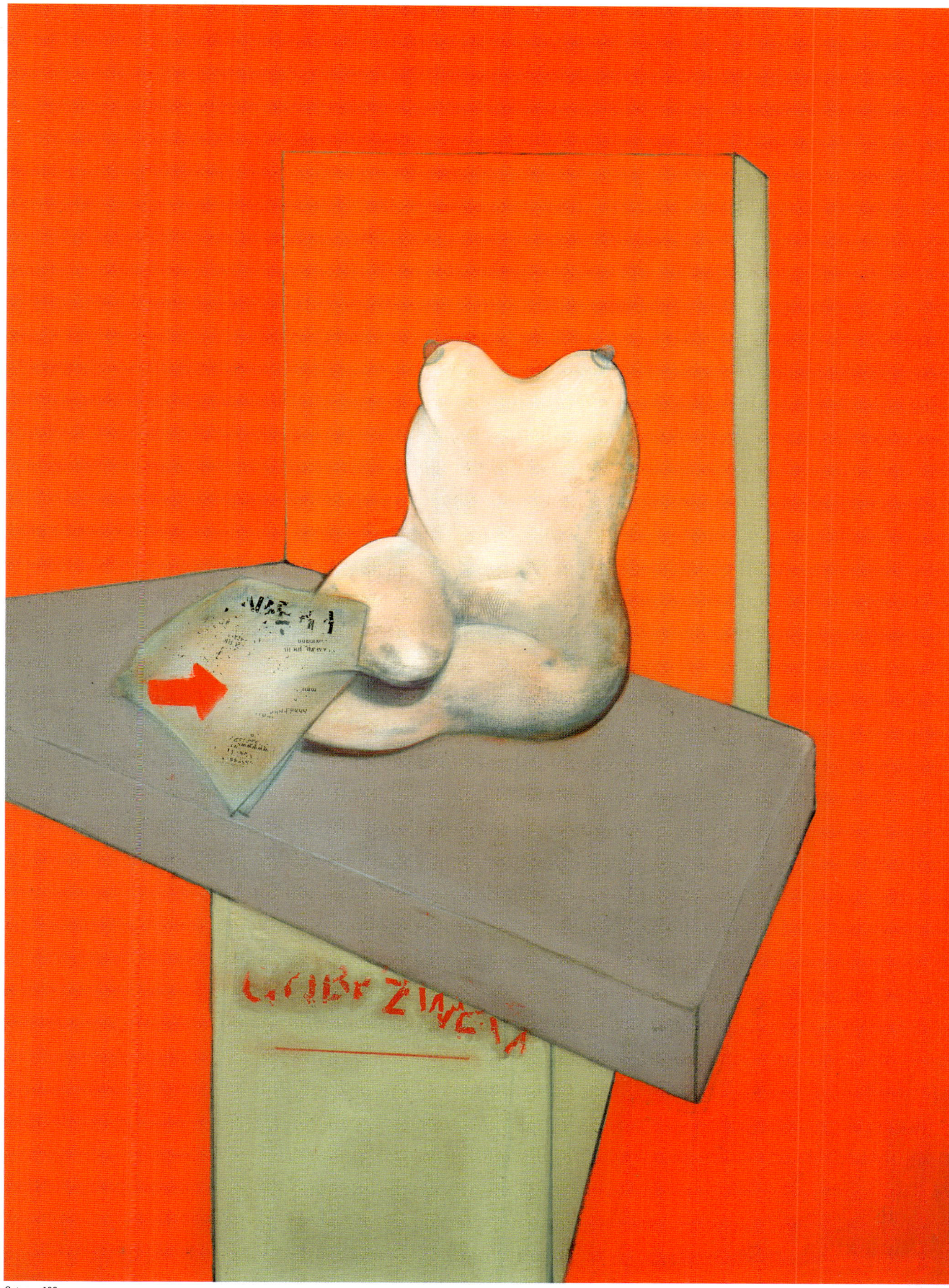

Cat. no. 102

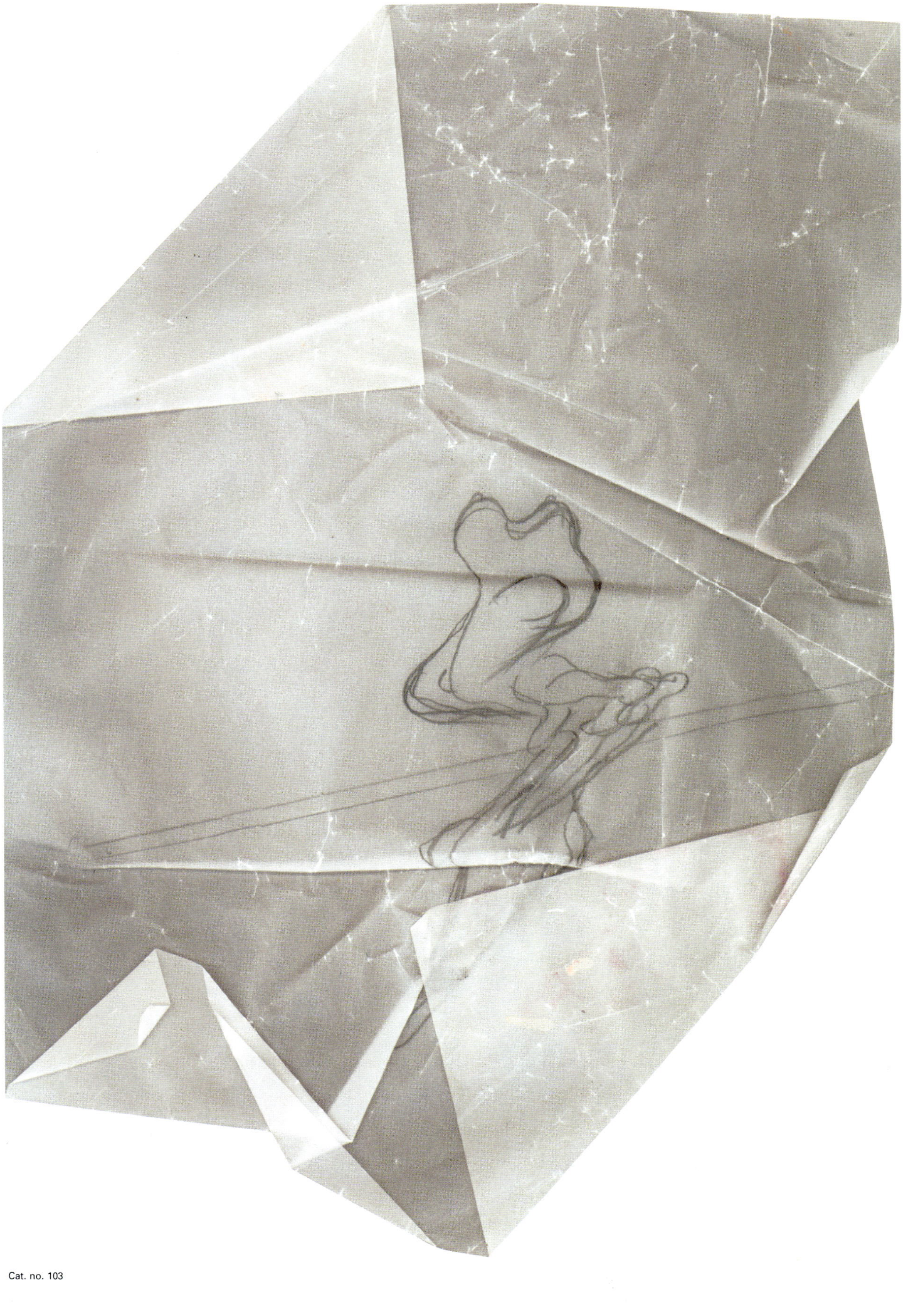

Cat. no. 103

Cat. no. 103
Drawing by Francis Bacon
C. late 1970s/early 1980s
Pencil on heavy grade tracing paper,
399 × 294 mm (folded)
Dublin, Dublin City Gallery
The Hugh Lane, F1A:118

Cat. no. 104
Colour plate of Le Bain Turc,
1859–63, by J.A.D. Ingres mounted
on card. Black-and-white plate of
Pope Innocent X, 1650, by Diego
Velázquez mounted on verso
219 × 230 mm
Dublin, Dublin City Gallery
The Hugh Lane, F232:1

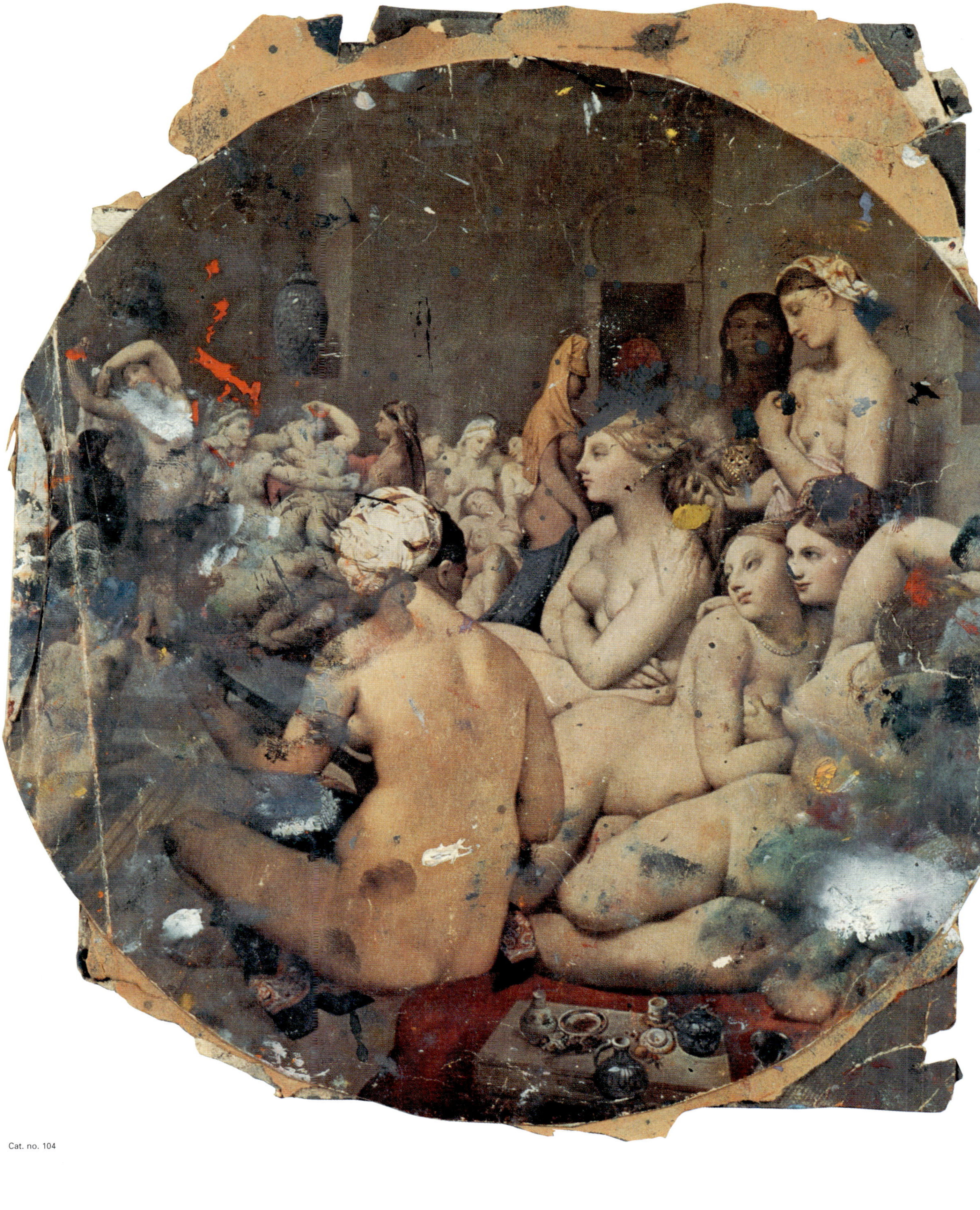

Cat. no. 104

Cat. no. 105
Leaf with illustrations of studies for Le Bain Turc, 1859–63, by J.A.D. Ingres. Paper clip applied to fold by Francis Bacon
243 × 213 mm
Dublin, Dublin City Gallery The Hugh Lane, F114:24A

Cat. no. 106
Cut-out card arrow with brass tack. Red paint covers one side of cut-out with numerous pin holes through body of arrow
81 × 51 mm
Dublin, Dublin City Gallery The Hugh Lane, F8:151

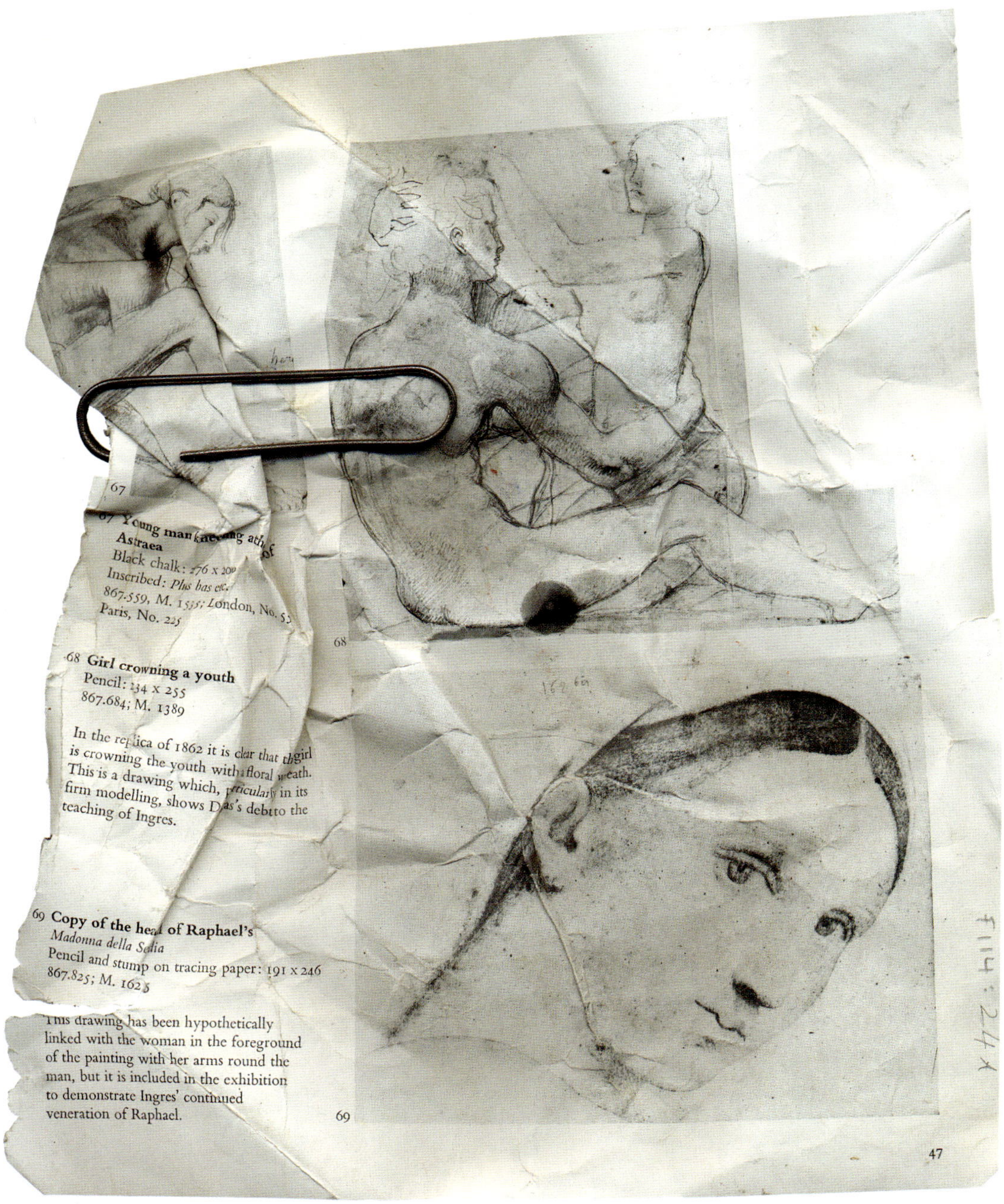

Cat. no. 105

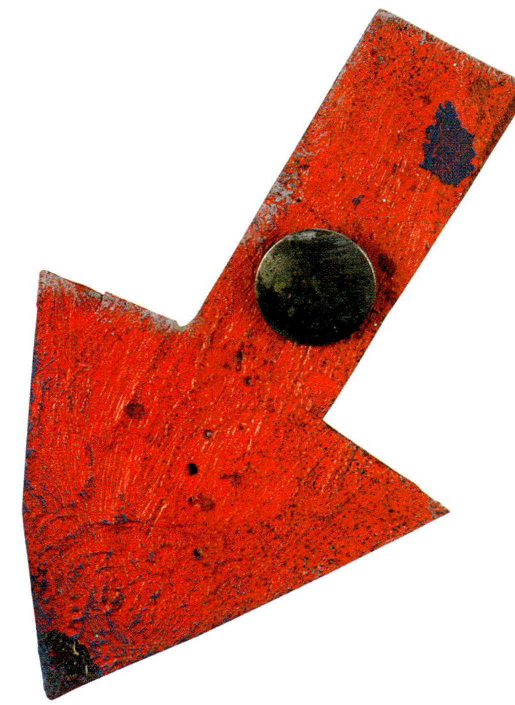

Cat. no. 106

Cat. no. 107
Leaf with illustration of Oedipus and the Sphinx, 1808, by J.A.D. Ingres.
Unidentified French publication
248 × 152 mm
Dublin, Dublin City Gallery
The Hugh Lane, F17:149

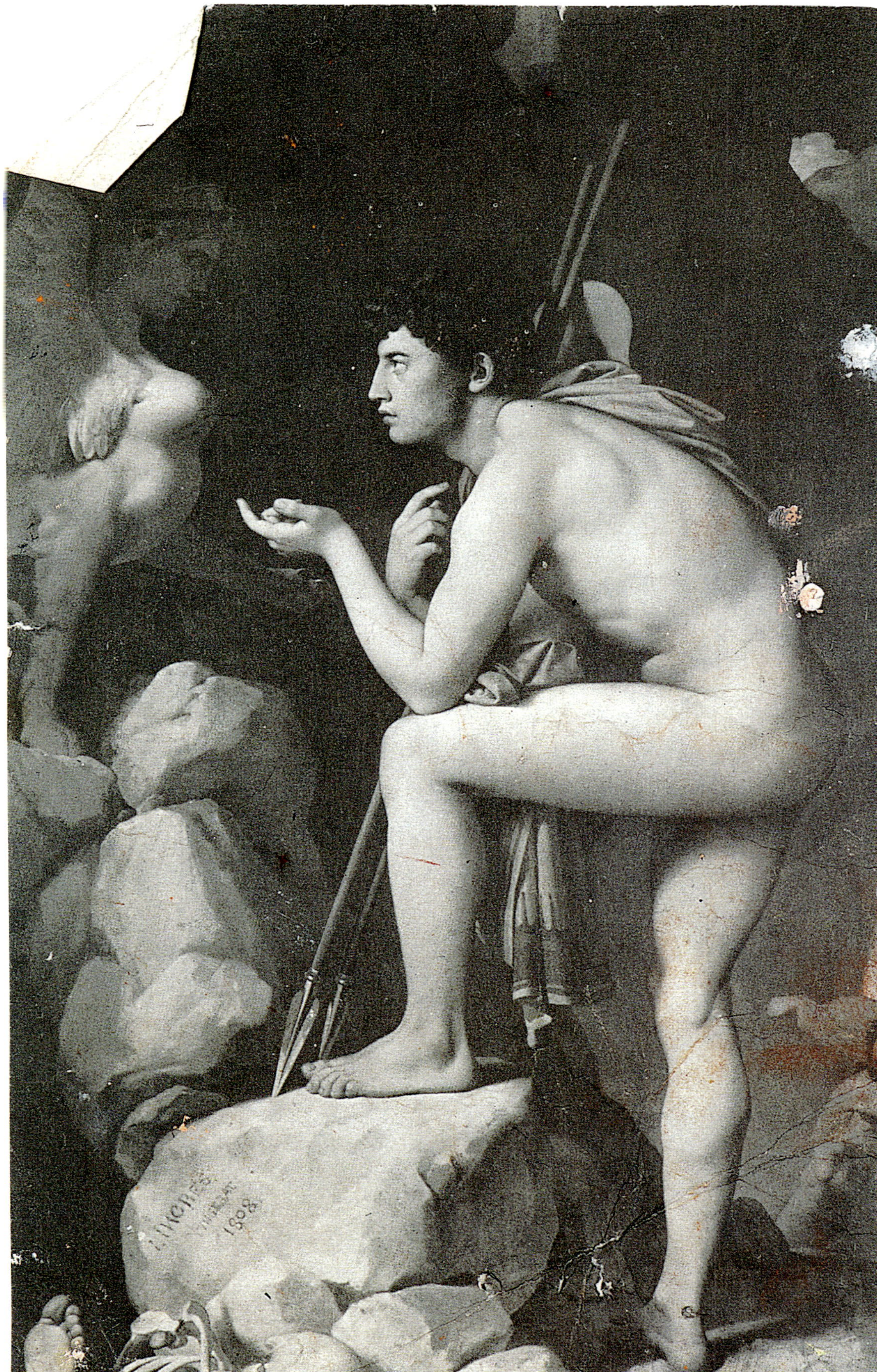

Cat. no. 107

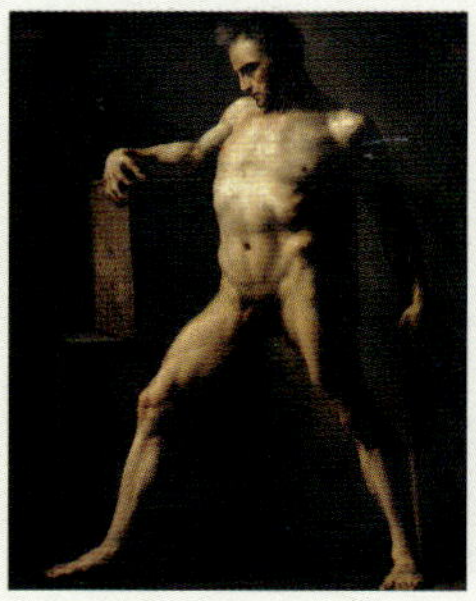
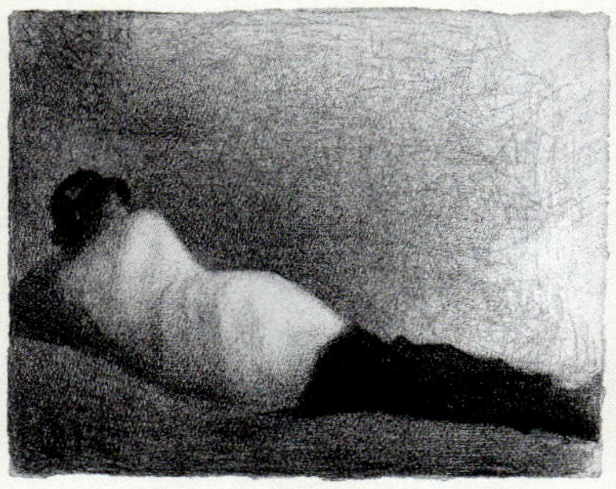
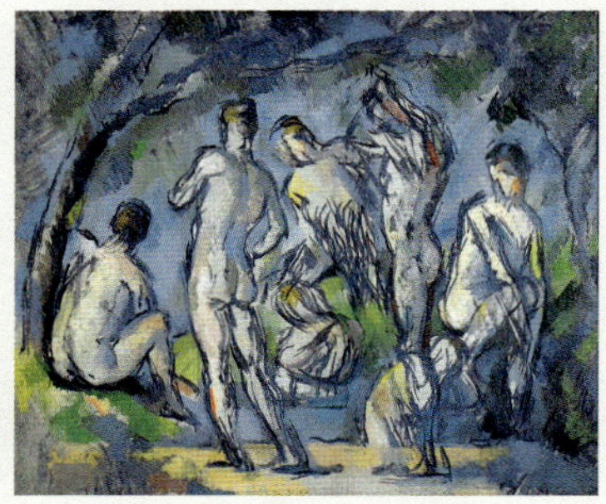

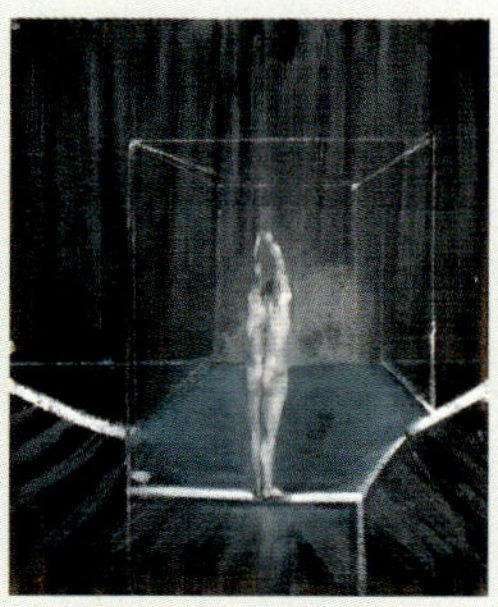

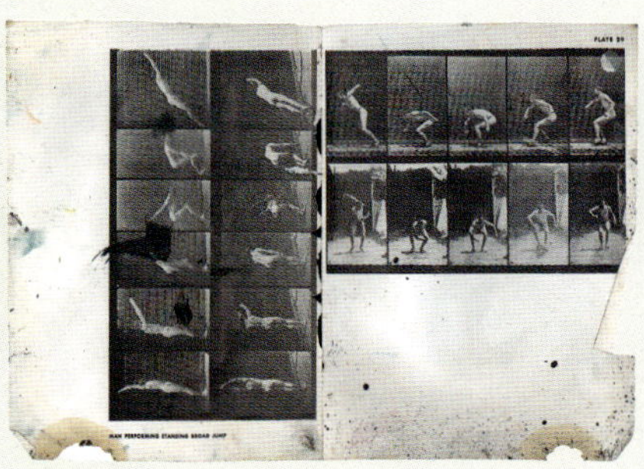
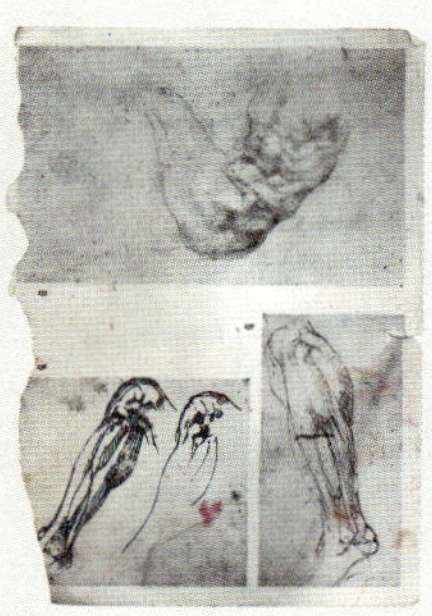
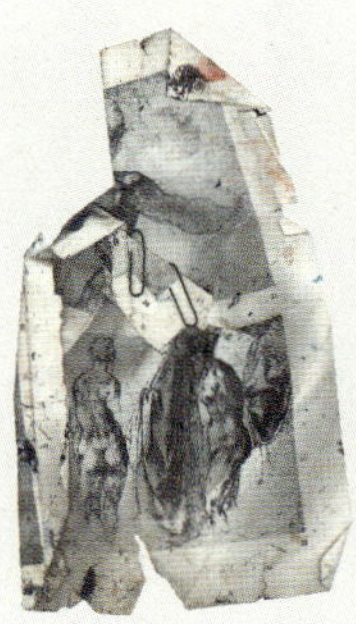
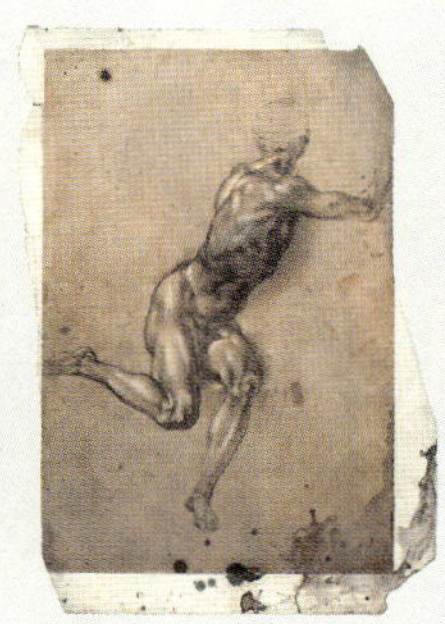
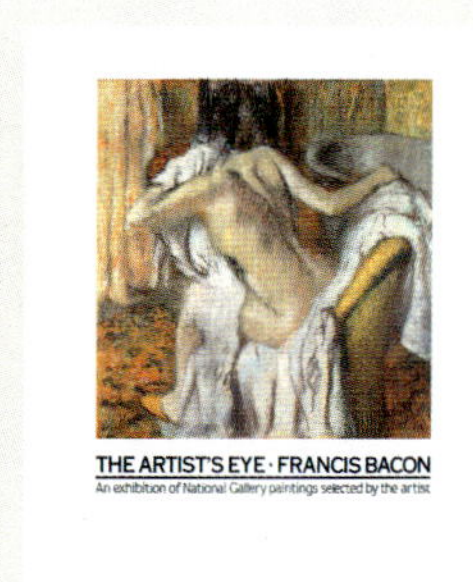
THE ARTIST'S EYE · FRANCIS BACON
An exhibition of National Gallery paintings selected by the artist
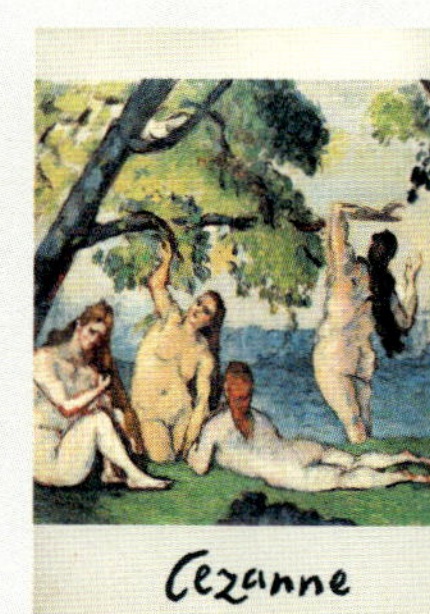
Cezanne

Felicitas Kunth

Representations of Nudes According to Traditional Models

In any attempt to describe Francis Bacon's oeuvre, it soon becomes apparent that his motifs are primary concerned with the human body: "I think art is an obsession with life and after all, as we are human beings, our greatest obsession is with ourselves."[1] Within the field of figurative representation, Bacon directed his view towards the male body in particular, and his exploration of the masculine figure followed more his own personal preferences and ideas than any tradition of Western painting. Even so, he does resort to the pioneers of art since the 16th century in light of this fact, works by Michelangelo, Géricault, Seurat and Cézanne are being shown here as triggers of inspiration.[2]

Bacon's *Study of a Nude* (cat. no. 109) of 1952/53[3] shows a naked male figure surrounded by a cage structure; he is standing with tensed muscles and outstretched arms on a narrow white ridge, ready at any moment to submerge himself in the blue of the area lying before him.[4] It seems that the figure is being represented during a moment of greatest possible tension. The grey-black background is defined as a flat wall by means of vertical lines, supported through a narrow, blue line running horizontally from left to right somewhat below the middle of the painting. Beneath this line, fan-like extensions, painted with a wide brush, extend to the outer sides and to the lower edge of the painting and remind one of the scenic framing in the Pope image of 1951.[5] The nude stands on a narrow ridge before a blue surface, deconstructed by way of perspective distortion, the contours of which are emphasised in white on two sides. From this construction, rough white lines on each side lead one diagonally outward from the image's composition, as if the structure were hung up by them on an invisible point. The surface is enclosed by a cage or baldachin structure which, however, leaves at least one side open and, in its materiality, is less enclosing than it is defining and linking. At the same time, the figure's latitude of movement is determined and limited through this spatial construct, around which Bacon organises the space in his image. "I think that the very great artists were not trying to express themselves. They were trying to trap the fact, because after all, artists are obsessed by life and by certain things that obsess them that they want to record. And they've tried to find systems and construct the cages in which these things can be caught."[6]

Thus Bacon creates his glass boxes, cages and baldachins for the purpose of enclosing the subject of the work at hand, namely the human figure. "I use that frame to see the image [...] I cut down the scale of the canvas by drawing in the rectangles which concentrate the image down. Just to see it better."[7]

Describing spatial situations in Bacon's paintings is so difficult because he has often not imbued these situations with identity; the environments in which his figures exist cannot be precisely categorised; consequently, it is also impossible to make a statement about the human subjects based on their environment. In the opinion of many authors, the neutral representation of space gives the subjects an expression of isolation and loneliness; alienation between human beings and the world is suggested, isolation being an illustration of this loneliness. However, it must be noted that, precisely due to this supposed isolation, the figure has the opportunity to express itself more intensively and lend its whole concentration to the momentary activity. Here is the man, his back turned to us, his head lowered, arms and legs stretched out, upright and ready to perform a movement the next instant. The source of the figure's position is a photograph by Eadweard Muybridge, *Man performing standing broad jump,* of 1887 (cat. no. 115). Francis Bacon kept in his studio many pages of the American photographic pioneer's movement studies. Bacon characterises Muybridges' photos as a "dictionary"[8] for the positions of the human body, and they offered him – fascinated as he was by the illustration of the male body in the traditional discourse – the opportunity to study photographs of athletes, wrestlers, boxers and cyclists in action. While Bacon usually "processed" these sources in his own manner before he,

Plate 1: Francis Bacon, Study from the Human Body , 1949 (cat. no. 15).

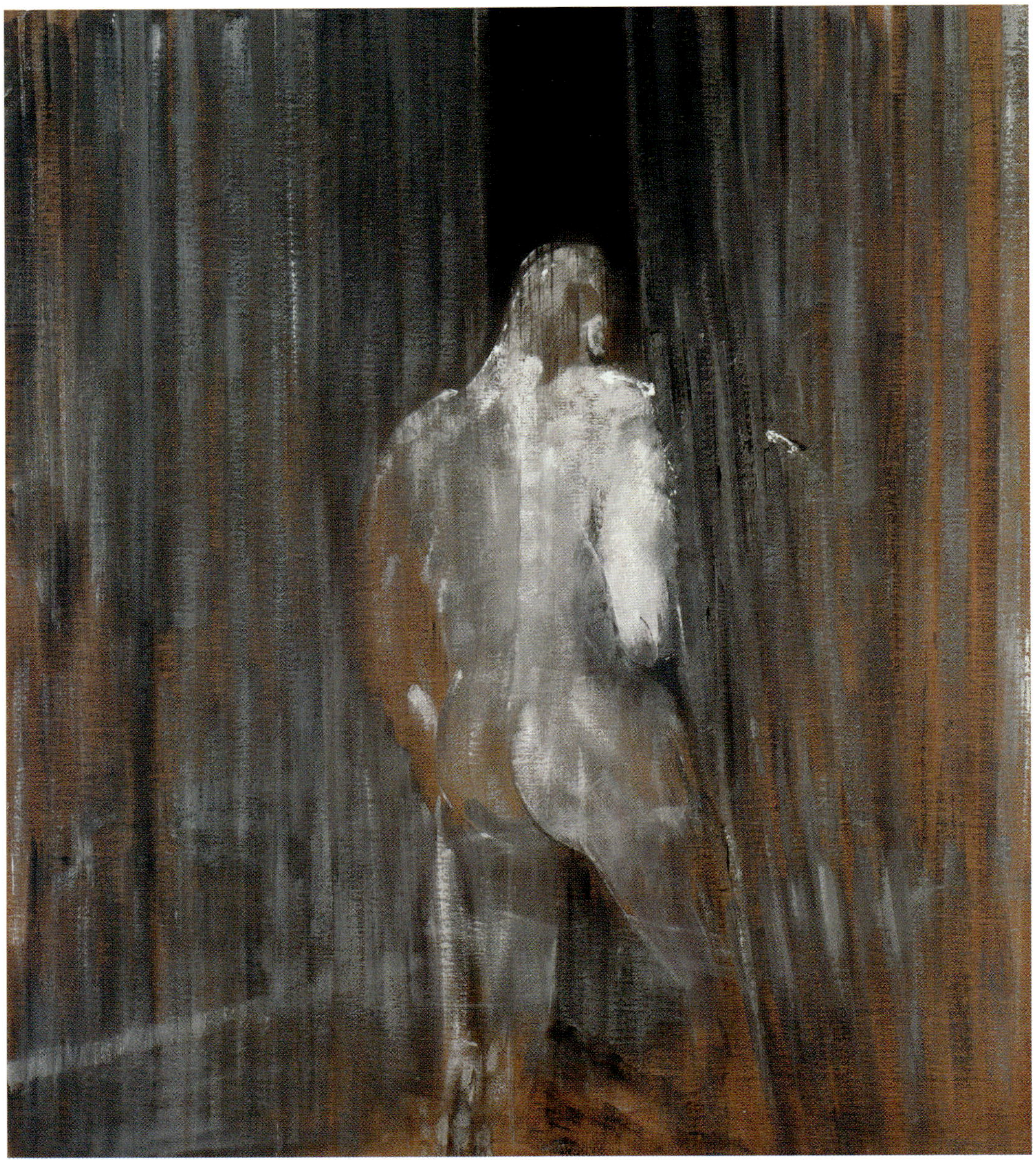

one way or another, integrated them into the concepts of his images, he made an exception in this case, transposing a study by Muybridge directly into a work of his own: the first image in the second row of the Muybridge movement study in question shows a figure in a position identical to that of the male figure in Bacon's oil painting.

Study from the Human Body of 1949 (*Plate 1*) once again shows a male nude from behind; portrayed in the foremost level of the picture from the knees upward, he is in the process of making a stepping movement with his right leg. The figure is framed by a curtain or veil[9] falling from the upper to the lower edge of the picture, with only a narrow opening in the centre allowing a glimpse of an undefined, black background. The interaction between the veil and the nude is a source of vexation; it remains unclear whether the figure is coming out from behind the veil, or moving from the foreground into the space beyond. The stepping movement almost seems not to be an action of propulsion; the standing figure might simply want to push the curtain aside with his bent right arm and leg. This veil, which distances the subject from the observer, contributes to the confusion inhabiting the structure of the image – a confusion which is lent additional support by the puzzling vanishing line at the lower left. A possible inspiration for Bacon's nude from the rear can be found in Michelangelo's sketches for the

Battle of Cascina of 1504. The Florentine Republic had commissioned this fresco – today lost – in order to commemorate Florence's 1364 victory over Pisa. The fresco portrayed the moment in which the soldiers, after bathing in the Arno and taking a rest on its banks, got back into their uniforms to do battle against the troops of Pisa; the men, eager for the next battle, exude strength and intensity.

Bacon possessed a reproduction of Michelangelo's *Study for the Battle of Cascina* from the British Museum in London in the form of a coloured page which he had torn out of a book (cat. no. 114). Here, the Florentine artist shows a male nude who, sitting on a parapet, turns the lower part of his torso towards the viewer while his upper body is turned to the left – a movement which the figure's unfinished head follows completely. It was long a matter of debate whether this work was actually created by Michelangelo since, in the eyes of the sceptics, it was far too complete.[10] The master had, in fact, produced this difficult body position with the greatest attention to detail, defining anatomical nuances by using a mixed technique and by heightening in white. The Renaissance painter paid close attention to the movement and gestures of the human body. Michelangelo criticised his great predecessor Dürer, saying, "To tell the truth, Dürer deals only with the measurements and differences of bodies [...] He says nothing about the much more important subject of human movements and gestures."[11] Bacon tore a reproduction of just such a sketch by Michelangelo concerned with movement, a torso and a male lower leg, out of a book and kept it in his studio (cat. no. 112). But the direct inspiration for his work *Study from the Human Body* was probably a study of a back by Michelangelo now at the Albertina in Vienna, *Male Torso, Back View*[12] *(Plate 2).* In Bacon's studio was a reproduction of this drawing (cat. no. 113), which the artist had, in a way typical of him, creased, torn and transformed by bending away parts of the book's page and fixing with paper clips the change he thus achieved. The artist often included such "devices" – which he had used to modify the images – in his oil paintings, causing irritation among viewers who were not familiar with the modified source the artist had used. In *Study from the Human Body*, there is a safety pin stuck through the right-hand veil that attracts the gaze and for which the viewer seeks an explanation. Such safety pins are often found in Bacon's work; they can be traced back to his occupation with Picasso and Duchamp, and correspond to his idea of the destruction of pictorial illusions through the use of an element foreign to the context.[13]

As has been noted, Michelangelo was essential to Bacon's portrayals of the male body: "[...] Michelangelo, he's always been deeply important in my way of thinking about form. But although I have this profound admiration for all his work, the work that I like most of all is the drawings. For me he is one of the greatest draughtsmen, if not the greatest. [...] as most of my figures are taken from the male nude, I am sure that I have been influenced by the fact that Michelangelo made the most voluptuous male nudes in plastic art."[14] In addition to the erotic masculinity of Michelangelo's figures, other pioneering artists of European figurative painting – in whose tradition Francis Bacon saw himself – also played a role with respect to the figure for *Study from the Human Body*. The man's broad lower back catches one's eye immediately. Bacon's genius is revealed in the way he brings across the strong and athletic back without modelling the individual muscles. He rather uses just a few colour tones[15] for emphasis and, following Degas, emphasises bone structure and flesh simultaneously.[16] In the composition of the left half of the nude's body, which is covered by the veil, Bacon also referred to Degas: "I always think that the interesting thing about Degas is the way he made lines through the body, in a way, shuttered the image and then he put an enormous amount of colour through these lines. And having shuttered the form, he created intensity by putting this colour through the flesh."[17]

The directional ambiguity of the man's movement in Bacon's painting has already been mentioned, as well as the question as

Plate 2: Michelangelo Buonarroti, Male Nude, seen from the rear. C. 1504. Black chalk highlighted in white, 194 × 266 mm. Vienna, Albertina. (©: Albertina.)

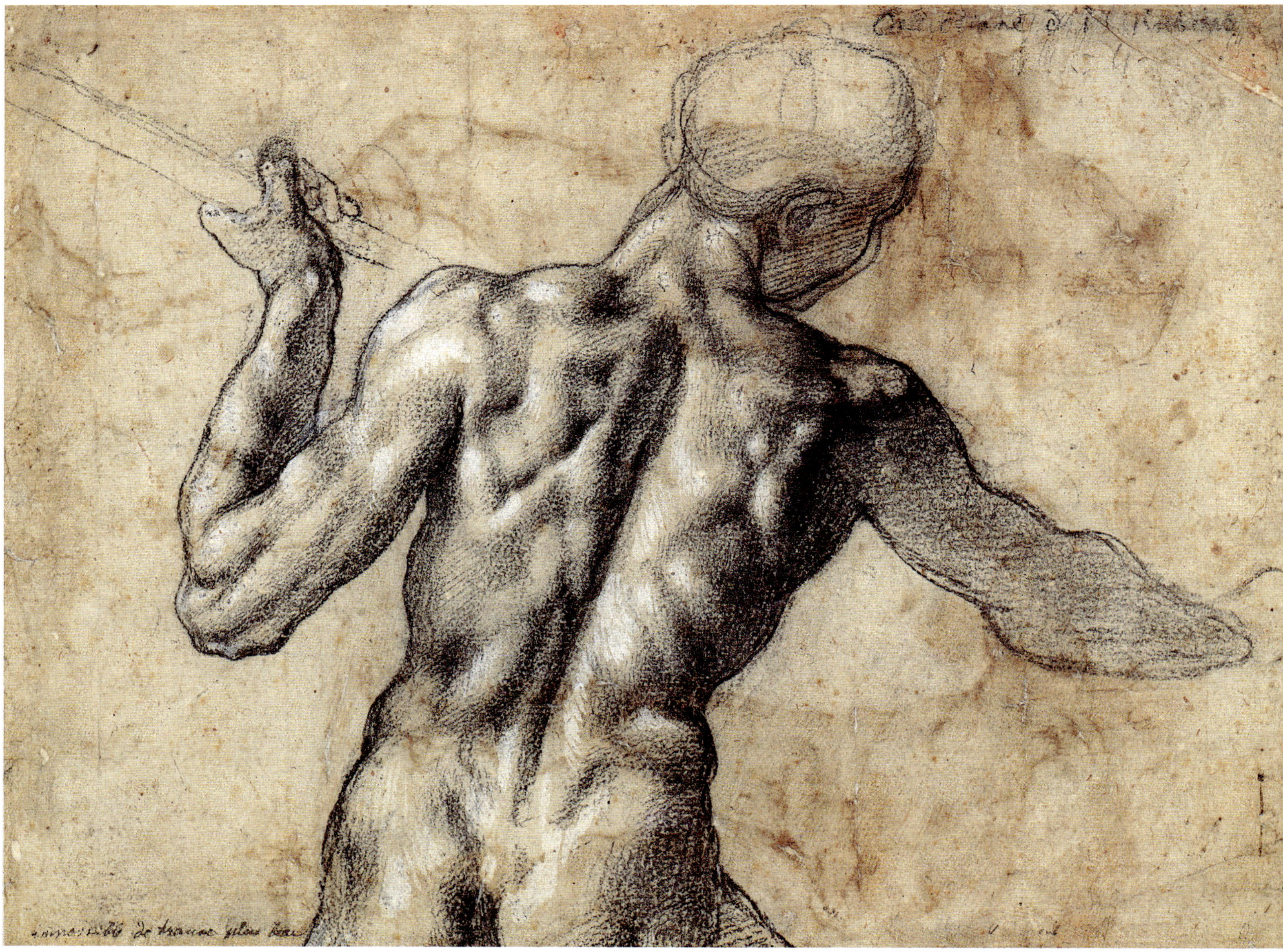

to whether the figure is actually in motion. Francis Bacon, who acknowledged that he absorbed like a sponge the works, ideas and means of artistic execution of painters he admired,[18] was thinking of Géricault here, attempting to implement the other painter's idea of movement in his own work: "The impressive thing about Géricault is the sense of movement in everything. [...] But when I talk about movement, I don't mean the representation of speed, that's not what it's all about. Géricault somehow had movement pinned to the body [...]."[19] Théodore Géricault's *Académie d'homme debout de trois quarts à gauche* (cat. no. 108) shows a naked man standing with his legs apart, his body pointed slightly to the right, his head cocked all the way on its side and turned forward; in his left hand he holds a stick, the ends of which rest on his upper arm and his heel, while the right arm is bent and lies on the higher of two wooden blocks. The light entering from the left side of the picture leaves the left part of the man's body in the dark.[20] Both Géricault and Bacon greatly admired Michelangelo; it is said of the French master that he "trembled" before works by the Italian artist.[21] Even so, neither artist copied directly from his predecessors, each preferring rather to incorporate their achievements into his own respective style. In the works at hand, both Géricault's and Bacon's portrayals of the male body pay tribute to the image of the *corps glorieux*, the muscular, magnificent, potent body as glorified by Michelangelo. But while in Géricault's work Michelangelo-like affection, hard contours and bulging muscles dominate, this impression of the powerful, magnificent body is not entirely uniform with Bacon. While Bacon adopted the physicality of Michelangelo's nudes so typical of the Renaissance, whose "magnificence of form and appearance"[22] he admired, he simultaneously denied his nudes anatomic exactitude and linear completeness in their contours, thereby dampening their heroic, powerful, energetic outward appearance.[23] The masculine energy radiating from the figure is also disrupted by the fragmentation of individual body areas in the pictures, of the legs below the knee, of the right arm below the elbow, as well as by the discoloration of the left arm.

Francis Bacon was an admirer of Seurat, particularly of his drawings,[24] and the French artist shared with Bacon a belief that the human being was the most important subject of artistic expression. Alongside Ingres and Degas, Georges Seurat was the 19th-century artist who placed the most value on the drawing as an independent form. Correspondingly, he worked out the final forms for the *Bathers at Asnières* more through drawings of individual figures and parts of the picture than he did through oil studies. Precisely this oil painting was the object of Francis Bacon's special interest[25] – he included it in the exhibition *The Artist's Eye*, of which he was the curator. For this reason, the present exhibition includes a study for this work, *Man Lying Down* (cat. no. 110). Seurat drew as if he were painting in oil: he created a harmony of the conflicting values of light and dark, alternated these rhythmically and distanced himself from the isolated black line of his contemporaries.[26] No painter before him had brought the light-dark contrast as close to the brink of abstraction as Seurat did. The male figure lying on his side is noticeably "modulated" from shaded areas; at the same time, it indicates a further characteristic of Seurat's style: the prominence of surfaces. Every illusion of the three-dimensional is denied, flat surfaces are pieced together, the peaceful, immovable appearance is simplified as far as possible, and, like its environment, barely defined. In removing people from their usual environments (the people who frequented his Asnières bathing area were solidly working-class) and denying them individual characteristics, Seurat monumentalised them and elevated them to the level of universal significance[27].

The lonely and sad mood that enshrouds the better part of his drawings was also evoked by the authors of naturalism: "From the waning heavens falls imperceptibly this grey veil which, in the still existing day, brings uncertainty to the appearance of things [...], and drowns the forms and contours of nature, slowly going to sleep as twilight thickens: this sad and gentle and barely perceptible agony of the life of daylight."[28] It was the air of the mysterious that Bacon loved so much in the drawings of Seurat,[29] and in his own work *Study from the Human Body,* he succeeded in transposing this mysteriousness, fleetingness and instability into a strong and – itself very present – body. The subtle way in which Bacon used grisaille painting in order to give the muscular back-figure this fragility and fleetingness was the manifestation of his fascination with newspaper reproductions of photographs, after which the surface structure of the picture is modelled.

In the figural work of Francis Bacon, it is noticeable that he usually limits his portrayals of the human being to one single individual – as in our examples –, to a couple or, at the most, to three figures; larger groups of people do not appear. One of the reasons for this will have been Bacon's fear of his own inability to place several figures on the same canvas while still avoiding that they tell a story. "I always hope to be able to make a great number of figures without a narrative," Bacon admitted once to David Sylvester;[30] "I don't want to avoid telling a story, but I want very, very much to do the thing Valéry said – to give the sensation without the boredom of its conveyance. And the moment the story enters, the boredom comes up."[31] The painter who was able to portray groups of people in a picture without falling into the boredom of narration was, in Bacon's eyes, Cézanne: although he admitted finding Cézanne's landscapes better, the artist's representations of figures – particularly the ones with the "bathers" – appealed to him more,[32] and he subjected this thematic area to thorough scrutiny,[33] as is shown by study material from his studio.[34] The theme of the bathers spanned 45 years of Cézanne's oeuvre; he dedicated an equal number of studies and paintings to female and male bathers, but never handled the sexes together in a single picture. The work *Seven Bathers* of 1896–97 (cat. no. 111) shows the painter's preferred frieze-like grouping of seven male bathers, in which figures standing, squatting on the banks or submerged in the water alternate. One is struck by the sketch-like handling of the strokes, the explanation for which surely lies in the fact that it is a preparatory work for a lithograph of the so-called *Small Bathers,* which the art dealer Ambroise Vollard had commissioned and which appeared in 1897 in Vollard's second album of *Peintres Graveurs.*[35] It is precisely the sketch-like quality of this painting, however, that Bacon was taken by: "[...] I only like the works from the end of his life. [...] It's the period when there is almost nothing on the canvas, when the subjects have almost completely disappeared, are hardly there any more, when one has the impression that they have barely been sketched and that they're about to disappear."[36] The figures in the landscape, surrounded by grass and trees whose branches extend toward each other in "Gothic arches," communicate no contents intelligible to the viewer, but rather reflect "oblivious togetherness"[37] and, in doing so, fulfil Bacon's credo of a multi-figural portrayal that tells no story and, therefore, does not overpower the painting itself.[38]

The two works by Francis Bacon discussed here – *Study of a Nude* (cat. no. 109) and *Study from the Human Body* (cat. no. 17) – do not yet correspond to the male representations typically found in his work. If, in the first picture, the male body takes on an almost phallic symbolism, the large nude from the back is – despite all the resolutions within the colour structure – first and foremost powerful. While many artists aim to portray controlled strength in their representations of the male body, most of Bacon's works fail to show precisely this characteristic. Although Bacon was interested in illustrations of men involved in athletics, where the men display mastery of their bodies, in his works he indicates that masculinity is, above all, a social construct and must be revealed as such.[39] His method is that of deconstruction and of the obvious masquerading of masculinity; the aim is to wage battle against the stereotypical discourse on masculinity. The nude portrayals by Francis Bacon discussed here do not yet enter these philosophical reaches; they much rather follow classical ideas and bear witness to the magnificent gift of the male body, which the artist so loved.

[1] Sylvester 1999, p. 63.

[2] Here I would like to thank Alexandra Hennig very much for her research on this topic.

[3] The small format of the picture is striking: while over the course of his career, Bacon painted almost exclusively on canvasses measuring 200 x 150 cm, the nude pictured here is only 1/8 of its natural size.

[4] With this work, Bacon for the first time used the – still very dark – colour blue in a monochrome painting.

[5] *Pope I,* 1951. Oil on canvas, 198 x 137 cm. Aberdeen, Scotland, Aberdeen City Art Gallery and Museums.

[6] Sylvester 2000, p. 248.

[7] Sylvester 1999, pp. 22, 23.

[8] Ibid., p. 30: "dictionary."

[9] No opinion is being expressed here on the theme of the veil in this work. For a discussion of this motif – which assumed a role of growing importance in Bacon's work beginning in the late 1940s, see the essay by Barbara Steffen in this catalogue.

[10] For more on the authenticity debate, see Goldschneider 1966, p. 33, Gould 1966, p. 3, and Wilde 1953, pp. 15, 16.

[11] Quoted in Goldschneider 1966, p. 12.

[12] See note 7.

[13] See Exh. Cat. Munich 1996, p. 97.

[14] Sylvester 1999, p. 114.

[15] The colours of the work itself, the white, ochre and black tones, may be a reference to Cubism; see Vanel in the Exh. Cat. Munich 1996, p. 97.

[16] Bacon on *After the Bath* (National Gallery, London) by Edgar Degas: "And you will find at the very top of the spine that the spine almost comes out of the skin altogether. And this gives it such a grip and a twist that you're more conscious of the vulnerability of the rest of the body than if he had drawn the spine naturally up to the neck. He breaks it so that this thing seems to protrude from the flesh. Now, whether Degas did this purposely or not, it makes it a much greater picture, because you're suddenly conscious of the spine as well as the flesh, which he usually just painted covering the bones." Sylvester 1999, pp. 46, 47.

[17] Sylvester 1999, p. 176.

[18] See Archimbaud 1993, pp. 31, 32.

[19] Ibid., p. 41.

[20] For more on Géricault's nude representations, see also *Academic Study of the Nude,* ca. 1816. Oil on canvas. Bayonne, Musée Bonnat, in: Eitner 1983, p. 91.

[21] See Lebel 1961, p. 10.

[22] Archimbaud 1993, p. 37: "grandeur of form and grandeur of image."

[23] See also Michelangelo's *Male Nude, Back View,* ca. 1504, from the Casa Buonarroti in Florence (no. 21 in Goldschneider 1966) and his *Male Torso, Back View* ca. 1504, at the Albertina in Vienna (no. 24 in Goldschneider 1966). Both works are study sketches for Michelangelo's commissioned work *The Battle of Cascina.*

[24] See Archimbaud 1993, p. 44.

[25] See note 21.

[26] Herbert 1962, p. 103.

[27] Rich 1958, p. 25.

[28] Goncourt, *Les frères Zemganno,* quoted in Rich 1958, p. 25.

[29] Sylvester 2000, p. 243.

[30] Sylvester 1999, p. 63.

[31] Ibid., p. 65.

[32] Ibid., p. 63.

[33] Among the works exhibited, the theme of the bathers deserves special notice, since the figure in Bacon's *Study of a Nude* (cat. no. 91) is captured in the act of jumping into water, since Michelangelo's soldiers in the *Battle of Cascina* also represent nudes after bathing, since Seurat's *Bathers at Asnières* are pursuing the same activity, and since, in Cézanne's *Bathers*, the theme is implied by the very title.

[34] See Exh. Cat. Basel 1983, cat. no. 99.

[35] Adriani 1993, pp. 235, 236.

[36] Archimbaud 1993, p. 42.

[37] Adriani 1993, p. 236.

[38] Sylvester 1999, pp. 22, 63.

[39] See Van Alphen in Exh. Cat. Munich 1996, pp. 37–41.

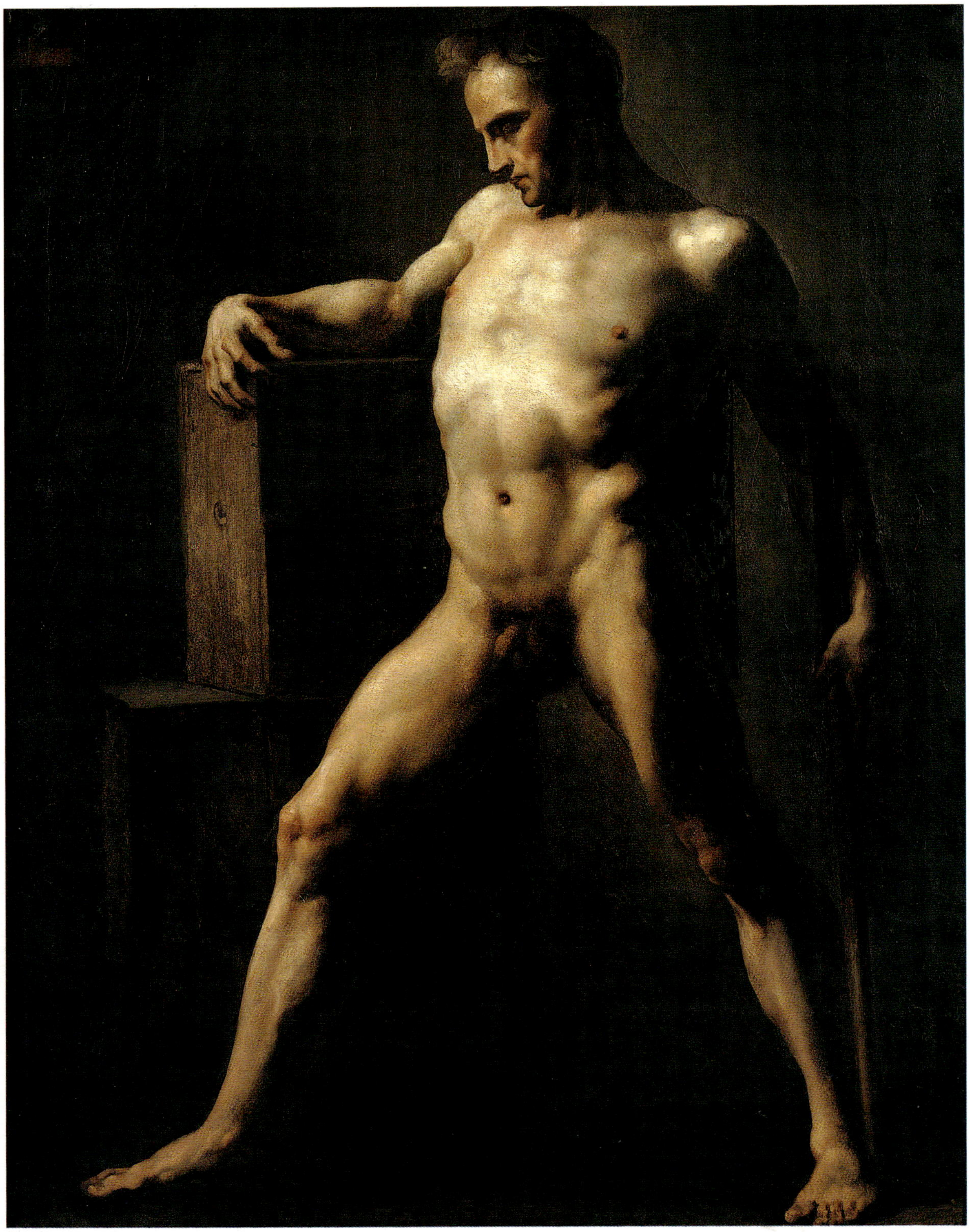

Cat. no. 108

Cat. no. 108
Théodore Géricault
Standing Male Nude, three-quarter profile, turning to the left
C. 1816
Oil on canvas, 79 × 61 cm
Rouen, Musée des Beaux-Arts, inv. no. 876–7

Cat. no. 109
Francis Bacon
Study of a Nude
1952/53
Oil on canvas, 61 × 51 cm
Norwich, University of East Anglia, Sainsbury Centre for Visual Arts, Collection Robert und Lisa Sainsbury, purchased 1953, UEA 29

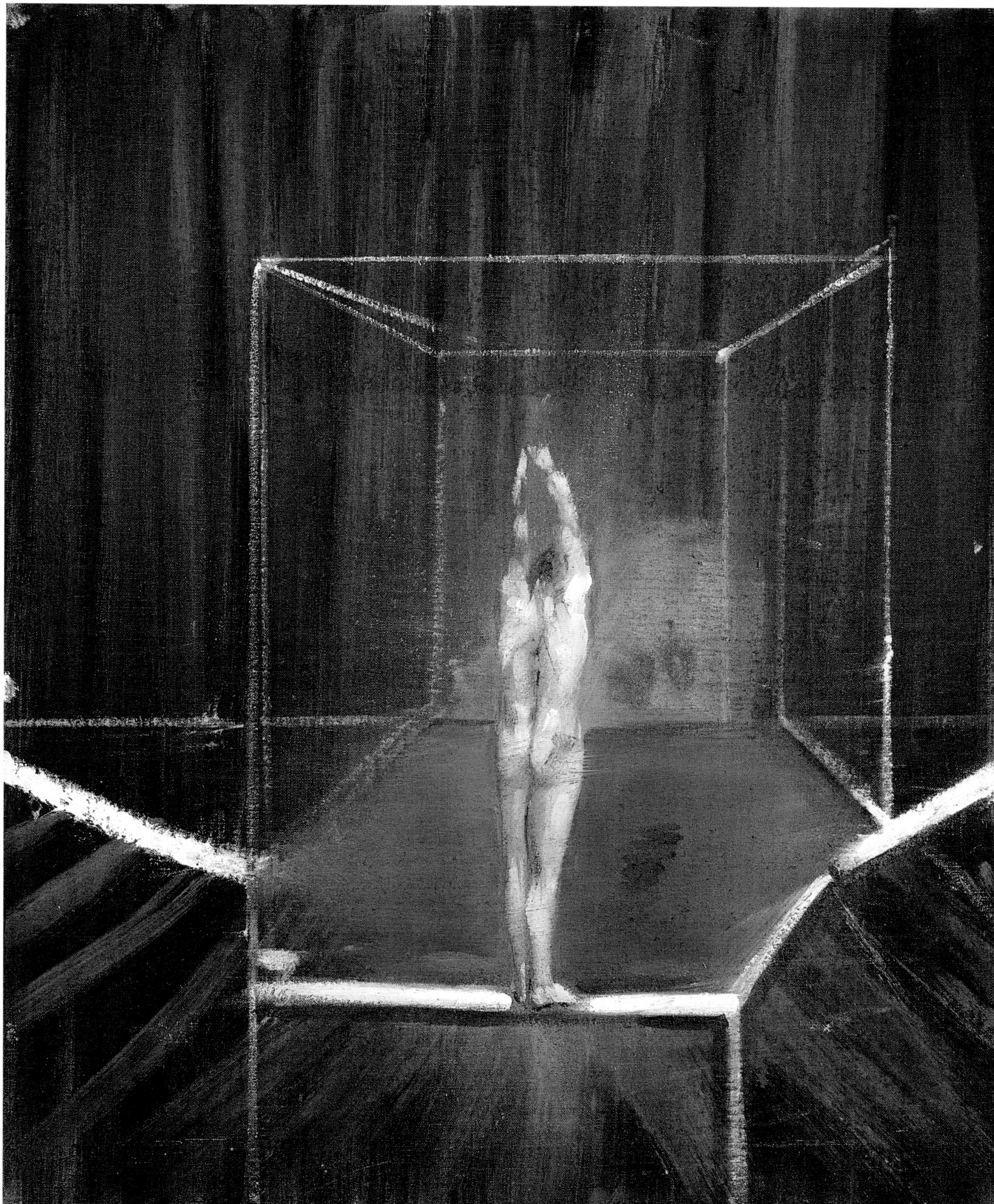

Cat. no. 109

Cat. no. 110
Georges Seurat
Lying Man (Study for Bathing Place near Asnières)
1883/84
Conté chalk on Ingres-paper,
240 × 310 mm
Riehen/Basel, Fondation Beyeler

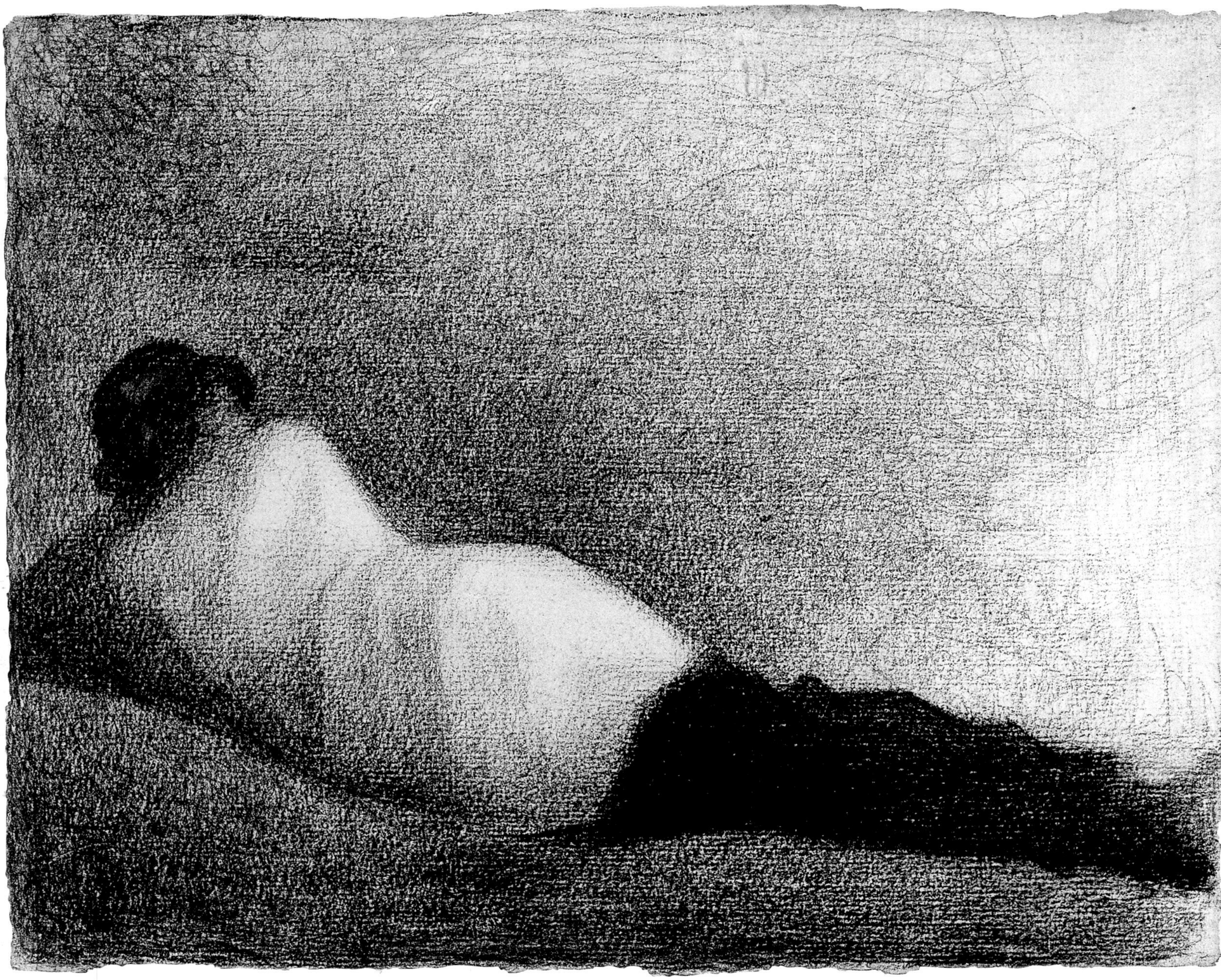

Cat. no. 110

Cat. no. 111
Paul Cézanne
Seven Bathers
C. 1900
Oil on canvas, 38 × 46 cm
Riehen/Basel, Fondation Beyeler

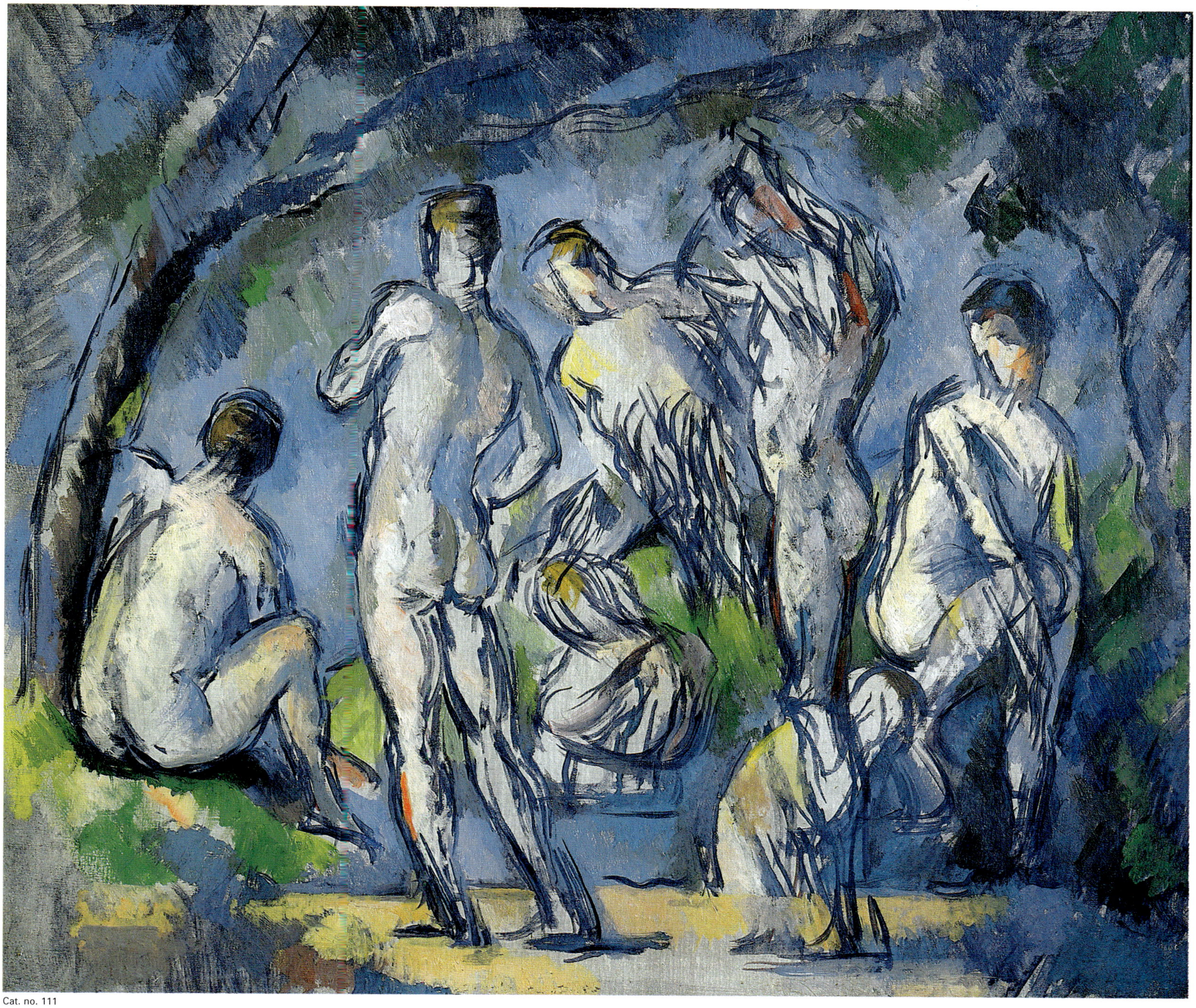

Cat. no. 111

Cat. no. 112
Leaf with black-and-white illustrations of studies by Michelangelo, torn from unidentified book
317 × 230 mm
Dublin, Dublin City Gallery The Hugh Lane, F114:58

Cat. no. 113
Leaf with black-and-white illustrations of studies by Michelangelo, torn from unidentified book. Two metal paper clips attached by Francis Bacon to a fold
293 × 200 mm
Dublin, Dublin City Gallery The Hugh Lane, F24:25

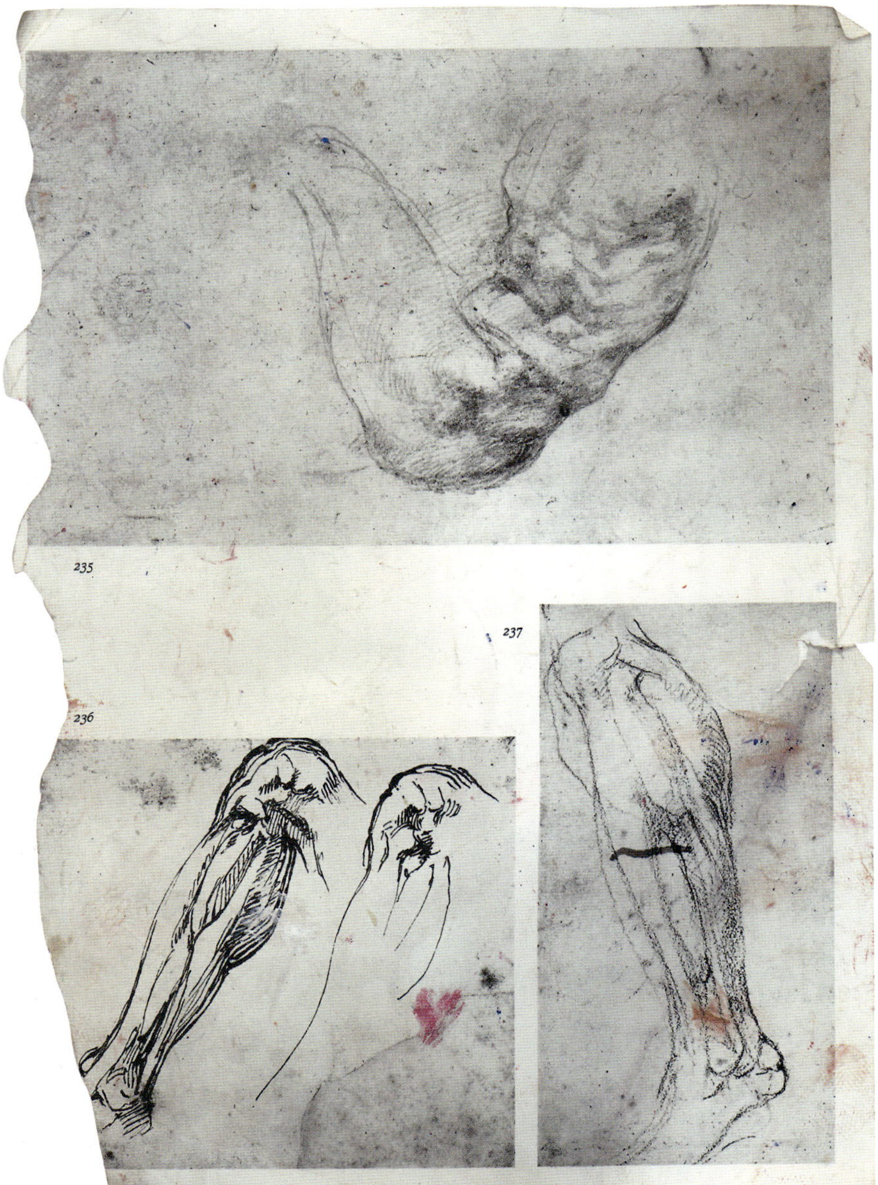

Cat. no. 112

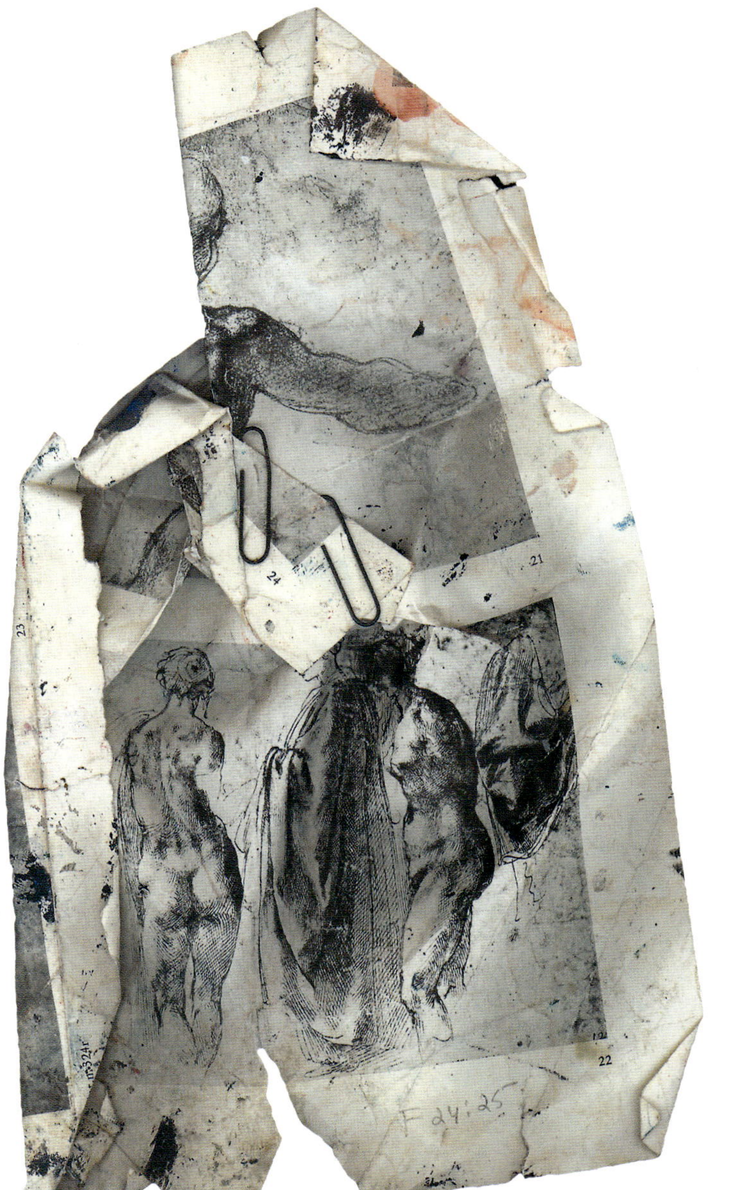

Cat. no. 113

Barbara Steffen

Mirrors and Reflections

The mirror has always served mankind as a symbol of self-knowledge; the youth Narcissus in Greek mythology fell in love with his own reflection on the surface of the water. In painting, the first mirrors to be depicted were round and convex; later mirrors were depicted as flat, but for a long time they retained their round shape. The mirror was used in biblical and mythological scenes and was a symbol of vanity in *vanitas* paintings. In 15th-century Netherlandish painting, the mirror was an integral part of domestic interior scenes, as found, for example, in the double portrait *The Marriage of Giovanni Arnolfini and Giovanna Cenami* of 1432, by Jan van Eyck. Artists such as Michelangelo, Caravaggio, Tintoretto and Vermeer used the mirror as a voyeuristic and psychological symbol in their paintings. Since the Netherlandish painting of the 17th century, the motif of the mirror has been increasingly integrated into paintings.

Hans von Aachen's oil painting *Joking Couple* of 1596, which is in the Picture Gallery of the Kunsthistorisches Museum in Vienna (cat. no. 119), depicts a pair of lovers in an erotic game: the man is holding a hand-mirror up to the face of his lover, and she peers into it in a jocular and coquettish manner, seeing her own face reflected. Thus three faces can be seen: the face of the man, his lover next to him, and her reflection in the mirror, which is also turned towards the viewer.

The artist Girolamo Francesco Mazzola, who was born in Parma in 1503 and became known under the name Parmigianino, was influenced especially by Correggio but also by the Venetian artist Pordenone. Between 1523 and 1527 Parmigianino was in Rome, where he was under the influence of Raphael and of Mannerism, making it a period of great importance to the artist. At the age of 21 he painted his *Self-portrait in a Convex Mirror* (cat. no. 118). In this painting Parmigianino is holding his right hand at the edge of a round mirror, making the hand appear larger, longer, distorted and disproportionate to the face in the portrait. Thus the viewer concentrates less on the artist, dressed attractively in fur, and focuses more on the view of the hand enlarged in the mirror. This distortion of the body is a theme that Francis Bacon dealt with in his paintings four centuries later.

When Bacon returned to London from Berlin and Paris at the end of the 1920s, he moved into a studio in South Kensington, where he began working as a furniture designer. Bacon designed furniture and carpets in Bauhaus style. The magazine *The Studio* published an article entitled *The 1930's Look in British Decoration* on Bacon's tables, chairs, carpets and mirrors. At the beginning of the 1930s Bacon gave up his work as a designer and painted his first oil studies. He was influenced by the Australian-born painter Roy de Maistre (1894–1968), who for several years was an important mentor to Bacon, in his twenties at the time. While much of the furniture Bacon designed has not been preserved, a mirror remained hanging in his studio in Reece Mews until his death. It was hung above a medium-high shelf on which the artist kept his paint-pots and brushes as well as pictures and newspaper cuttings that he used as sources for his work. On the opposite wall stood Bacon's easel, so that the artist could see himself and his pictures reflected in the mirror while he was painting. The mirror became an instrument in his work and a metaphor for what he was seeing, allowing him to check the composition and the effect of the painting. This is in keeping with Bacon's approach to the works of art history, whose themes he adopted from reproductions he found in books on art. With works created in or after 1961, when Bacon moved into the new studio in Reece Mews, the reflected images of his paintings need to be analysed as well in order to provide new and more accurate readings of the works.

A photograph that the photographer Michael Pergolani took in Bacon's studio shows the artist with his brushes and paint-pots reflected in the mirror (cat. no. 151). The photograph depicts a youthful Bacon, with the dark spots from the old mirror reflected in his face. The material condition of the mirror alters the reflected image, creating an irritation similar to that of a distorting mirror.

The mirror plays an important role in Bacon's paintings: it creates self-reflection, distortion and change in the depicted figures as well as a doubling of the image. One normally trusts a mirror to reflect a likeness of reality as we know it from our sensory organs. But the reflection in a distorting or convex mirror is distorted. When one studies those works by Bacon in which he depicts a figure reflected in a mirror, it is obvious that the reflection makes the face of the subject appear distorted, alienated or divided. The reflected image appears to be enlarged and deformed, as in *Study of George Dyer in a Mirror* (cat. no. 120). Here Dyer's face has been alienated by dividing it into two parts. In this work, painted in 1968, the background of the reflected image has been altered to light-blue. It depicts George Dyer in profile, but it is divided into two halves at his left eye. Dyer is sitting on a swivel chair, with the left half of his body turned towards the viewer but his head turned to the right. The right half of his body is not only painted in lighter colours than the left and with a free brush-stroke; its proportions have also been altered. The right shoulder begins at the corner of the left eye, while the right half of the face appears to have disappeared into the mirror. A broken white line, which could have been caused by a marking on or an alternation to the paper of photograph, divides the two different halves of the body.

"Bacon's mirrors can be anything, but not a reflected surface [...]. The figure is not just the isolated body but also the deformed body that is escaping," is the way Deleuze explains the change that takes place in the reflected image[1]. In the triptych *In Memory of George Dyer,* 1971 (cat. no. 121), many motifs can be recognised that are characteristic of Bacon's work. The left panel depicts Dyer on a dark red-and-green beam as a boxer in a fighting posture that at the same time appears tired. As his source Bacon used one of his photographs of boxing matches. The shadow of the boxer runs in two directions: in a light-grey shade towards the upper half of the picture and in a skin-tone towards the bottom. The composition of the centre panel of the triptych is especially complex. It shows Dyer opening a door that leads to a stairway reminiscent of the narrow stairway leading to Bacon's studio in Reece Mews. Opening the door with a key is reminiscent of a motif in Picasso's early works, such as *Bather Opening a Cabin* (cat. no. 45). The right panel depicts George Dyer in a rectangular frame, also positioned on an arched beam. A table-top functions as a mirror in which Dyer is reflected in profile, pointing to the left, while his face in the painting points to the right. By using this irritating reversal, Bacon increases the tension in the painting. Dyer's upper body positively flows into his reflected image. The difference between the two depictions in profile is that the face turned to the right has a white, semicircular spot of colour at the cheekbone, giving the face movement and dynamism. Umberto Eco calls the mirror a "prothesis" and compares it with a magnifying glass. He says it is an "absolutely neutral prothesis" that makes it possible to see the reflection in the same size but also to depict images that our eye otherwise could not see[2]. Bacon changes the reflected image, giving the subject a new, altered intensity and aura. Bacon says: "What I want to do is to distort the thing far beyond the appearance, but in the distortion to bring it back to a recording of the appearance."[3]

The source for Bacon's portrait of George Dyer was a black-and-white photograph showing him in profile and taken by the photographer John Deakin (cat. no. 122). Bacon altered the photograph by exactly cutting around the contours of the face, in order to further elaborate the lines of the distinctive profile. The photograph is badly torn, and Bacon stained the paper with paint, as he did many other photographs. The rips in the paper correspond with abstract traces of paint and lines in the oil painting. At the point of the neck, the photographic paper has a crease that points vertically to Dyer's ear. This "incision" in the material can be seen in the oil painting as a white stripe on the left side of the neck. Unlike the rip in the photograph, however, it does not point diagonally to

Plate 1: Sergej Eisenstein, Still from the film "Battleship Potemkin". 1925.

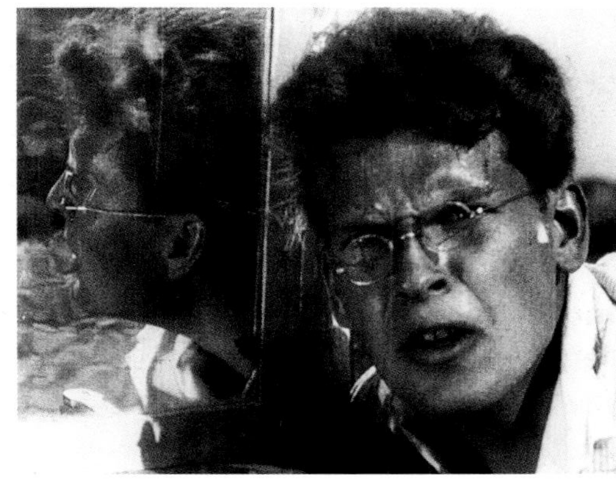

the ear but runs vertically to the middle of the neck, parallel to the shirt-collar. Thus the material texture of the photographic paper becomes the real theme of the painting. Bacon worked with the motif of the mirror in order to distort, double and underscore the identity of the figure. The reflected image was not just a reflection but also depicted new identities, making, so to speak, the unconscious conscious and the invisible visible.

There is also an interesting scene with a mirror in Eisenstein's film *Battleship Potemkin (Plate 1):* In the scene of massacre and conquest on the steps of Odessa, a young man, whose reflection is shown, witnesses the battle on the steps. It is not clear from the scene where the mirror could have been mounted outdoors on the steps, but it is interesting that during the massacre scene the director presents a fearful portrait of this young man reflected in a mirror. The man, who looks as though he might be an artist or writer and is a critical observer of the events, creates a link to the viewer by looking into the camera. His reflected image, in which he is seen in profile, appears to be parallel to the screen, while his horrified gaze at the audience draws them into the dreadful situation of the massacre, making it appear for a moment to be frightfully real.

A reproduction of a photograph entitled *Reflexions and Mirroring* was found in Bacon's studio. In it, sunlight falls on a white wall with a striped pattern and is reflected on the glass of an open top-hung window. This visual interplay of real image and illusion in a reflected image explains the complicated perceptive experience that the artist used in order to integrate various levels of seeing in a painting and draw the viewer into his world of expanded vision.

[1] Deleuze 1995, p. 18.
[2] Eco 1988, p. 35.
[3] Sylvester 1997, p. 41. Cf. Sylvester 1999, p. 40.

Cat. no. 118
Francesco Mazzola, called Parmigianino
Self-portrait seen in a convex mirror
1523/24
Oil on a wooden cup, diameter 24.4 cm
Vienna, Kunsthistorisches Museum, Picture Gallery, inv. no. 286

Cat. no. 119
Hans von Aachen
Joking Couple With a Mirror
C. 1596
Oil on copper, 25 × 20 cm
Vienna, Kunsthistorisches Museum, Picture Gallery, inv. no. 1155

Cat. no. 120
Francis Bacon
Study of George Dyer in a Mirror
1968
Oil on canvas, 198 × 147.5 cm
Madrid, Fundación Collección Thyssen-Bornemisza

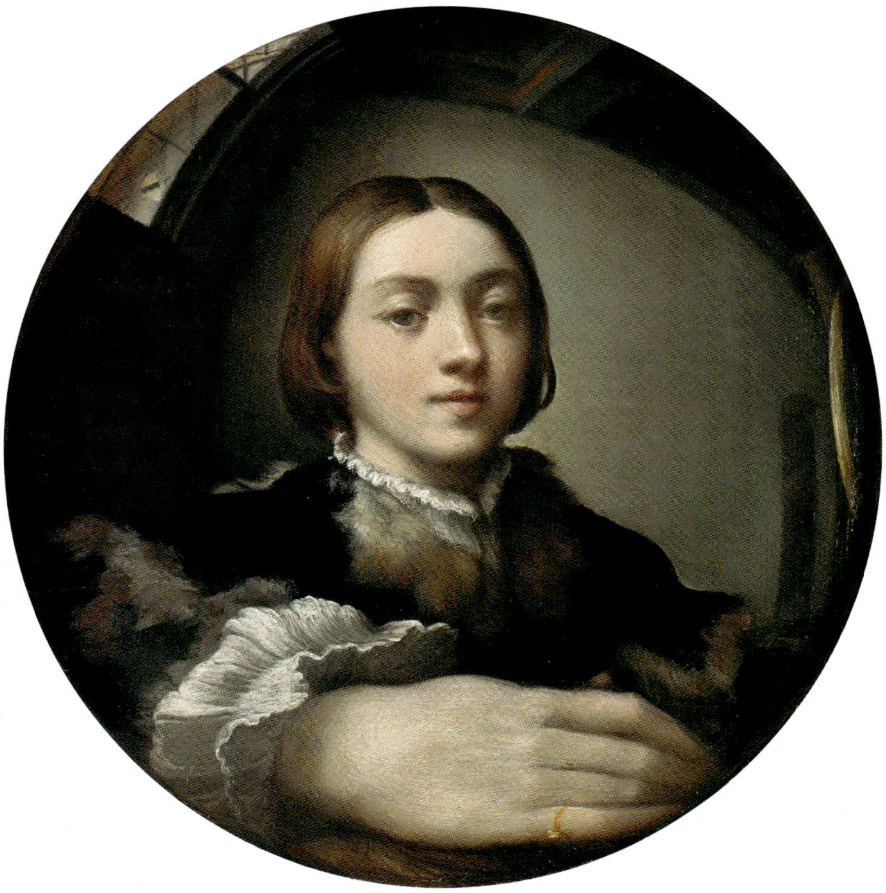

Cat. no. 118

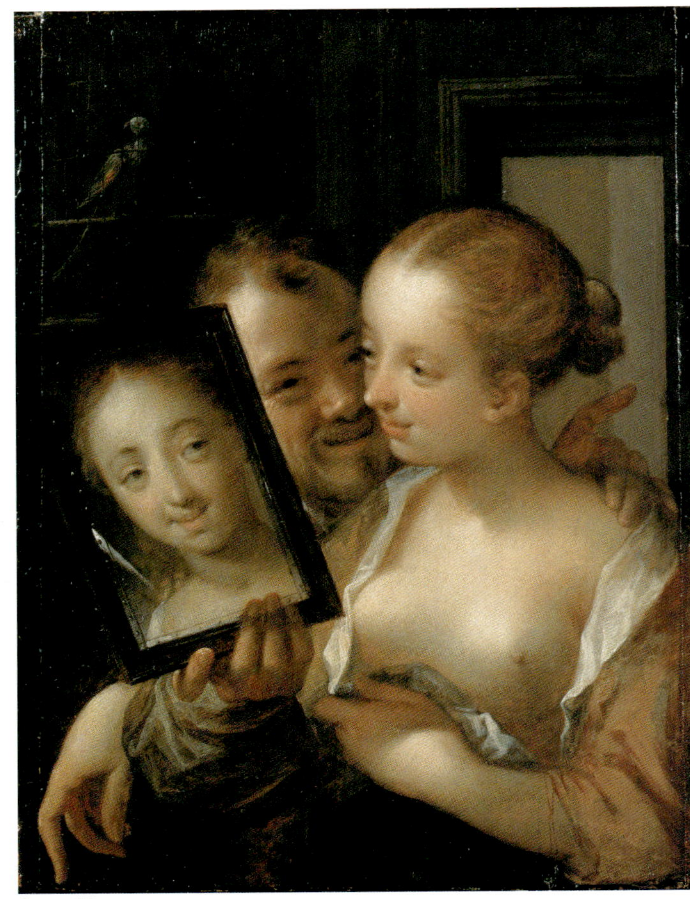

Cat. no. 119

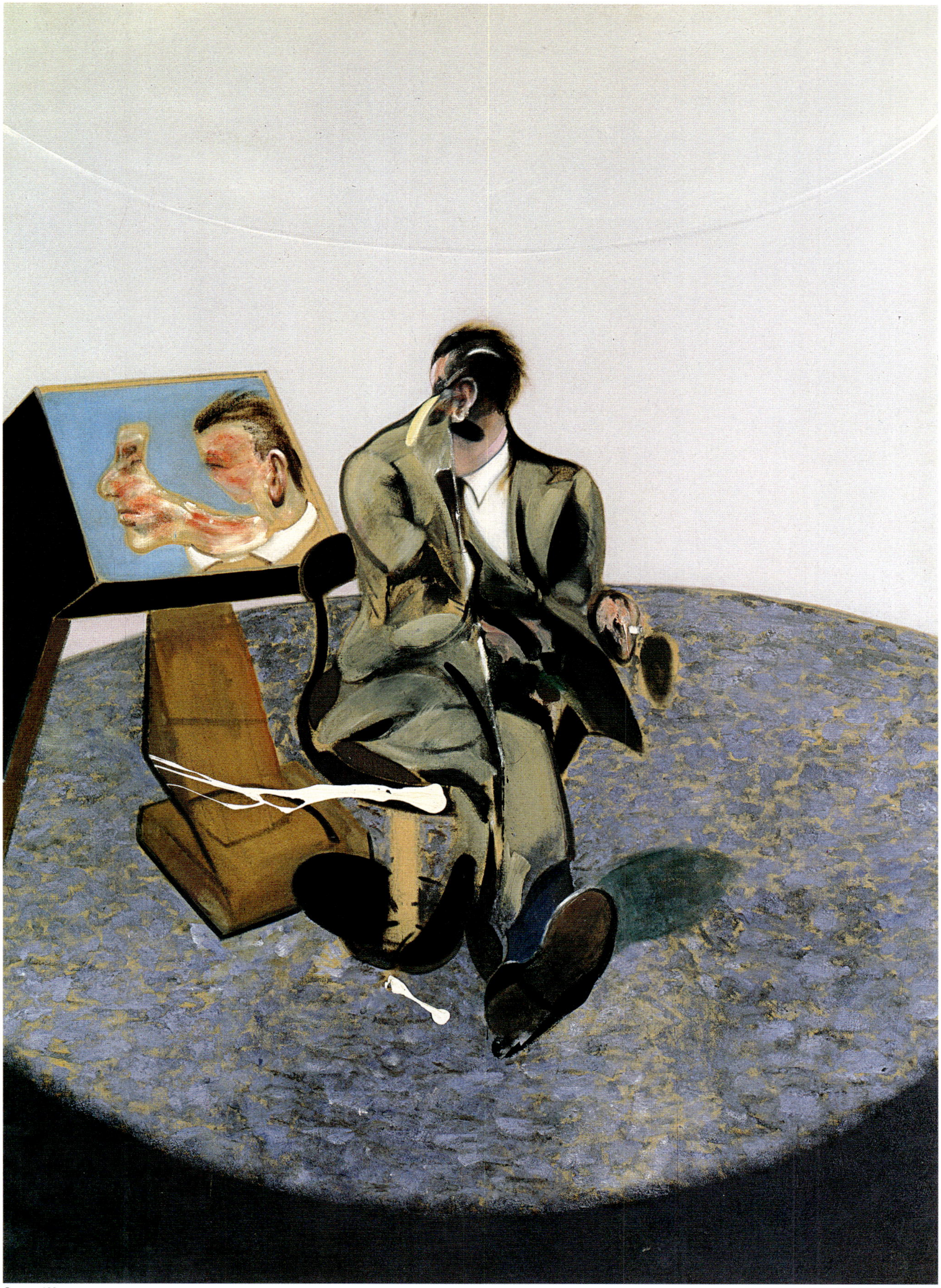

Cat. no. 120

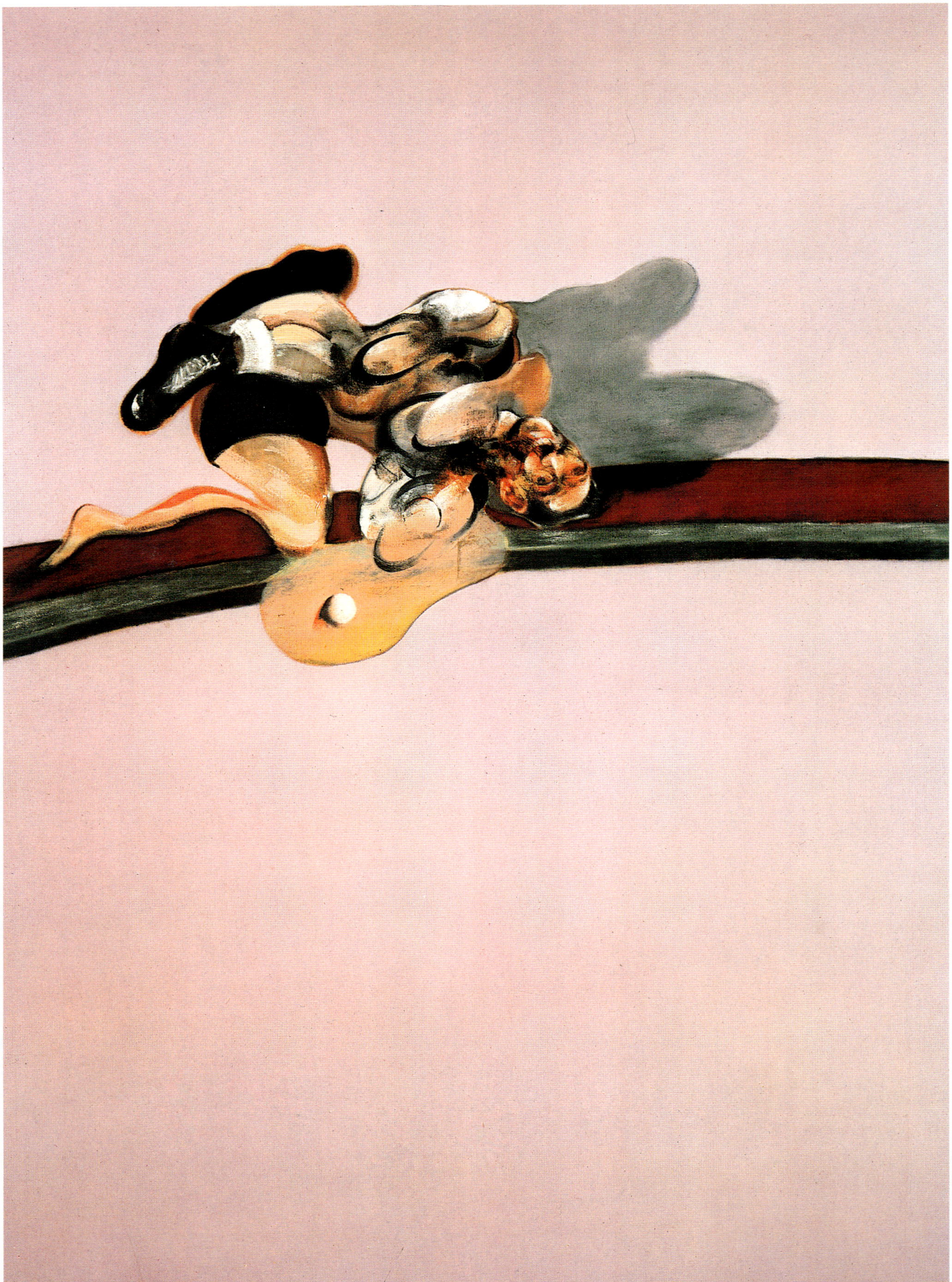

Cat. no. 121

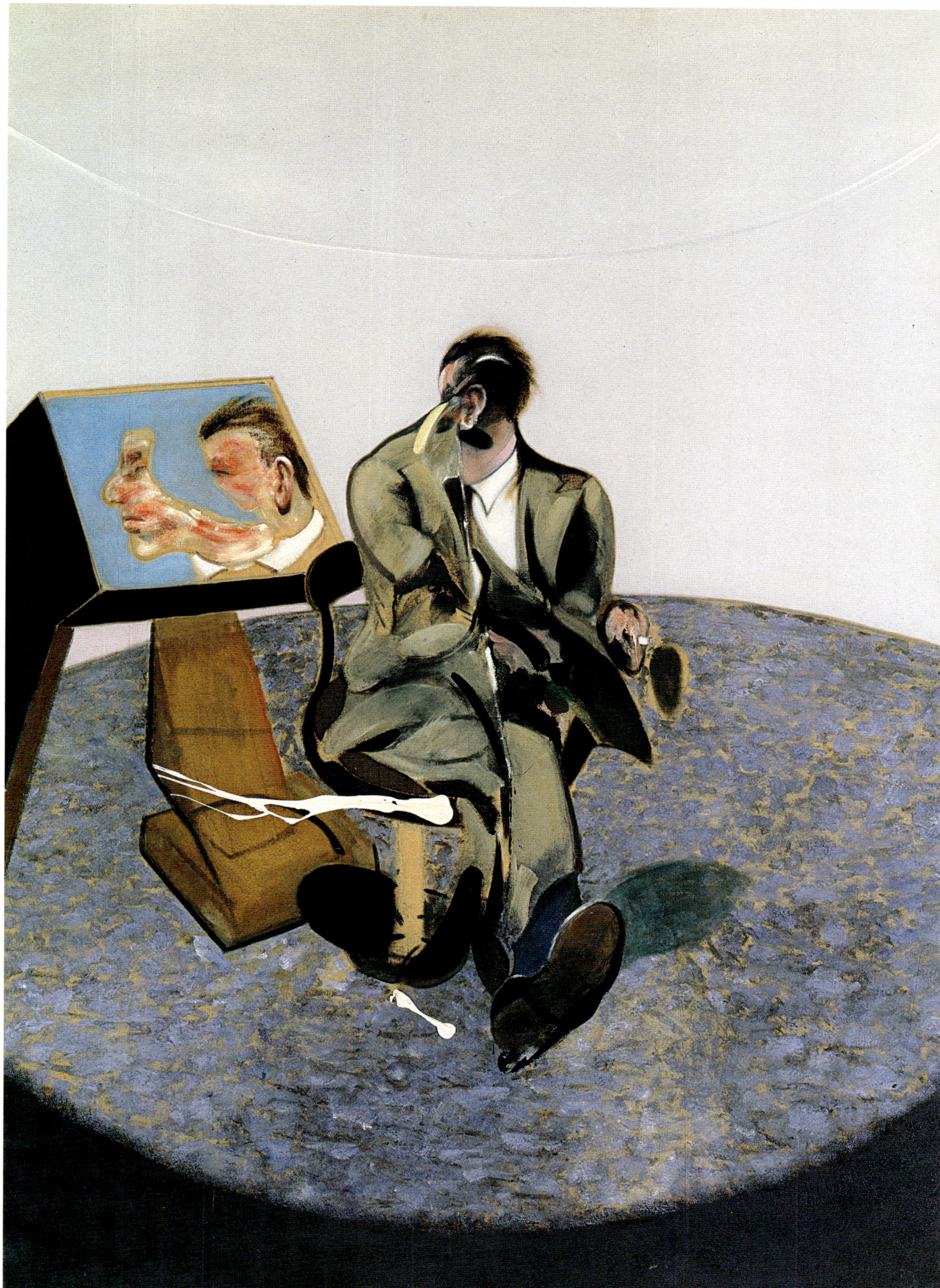

Cat. no. 120

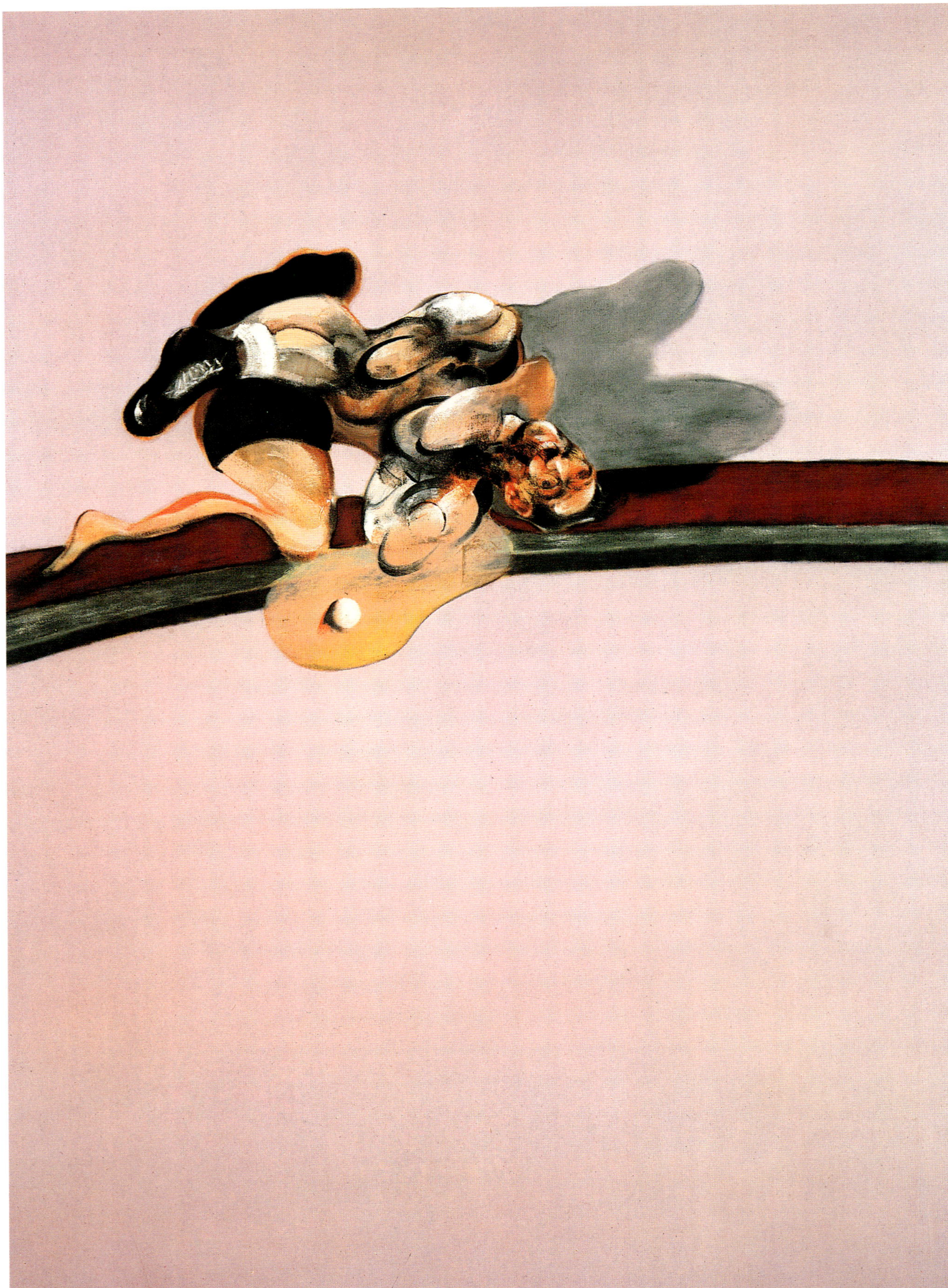

Cat. no. 121

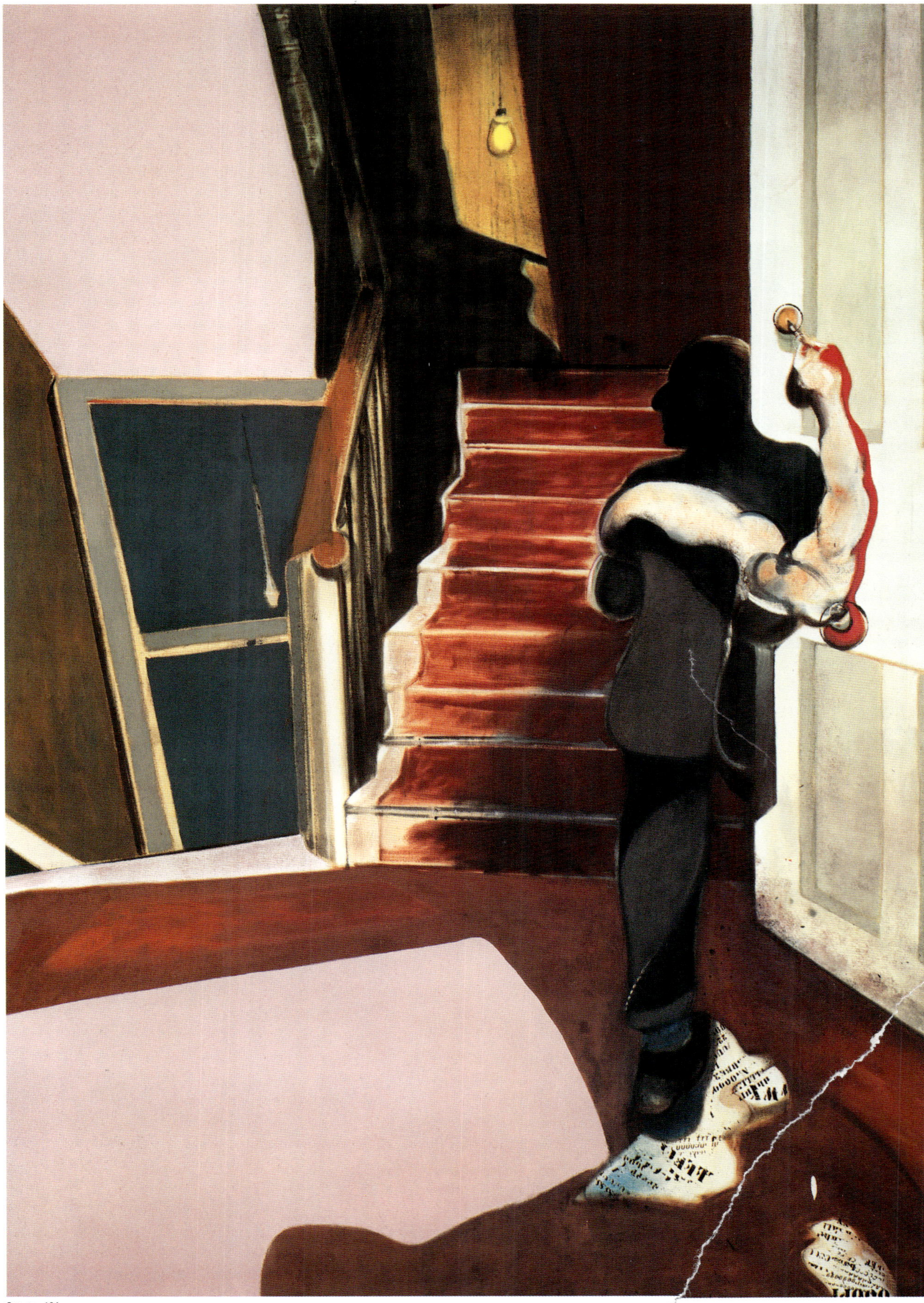

Cat. no. 121

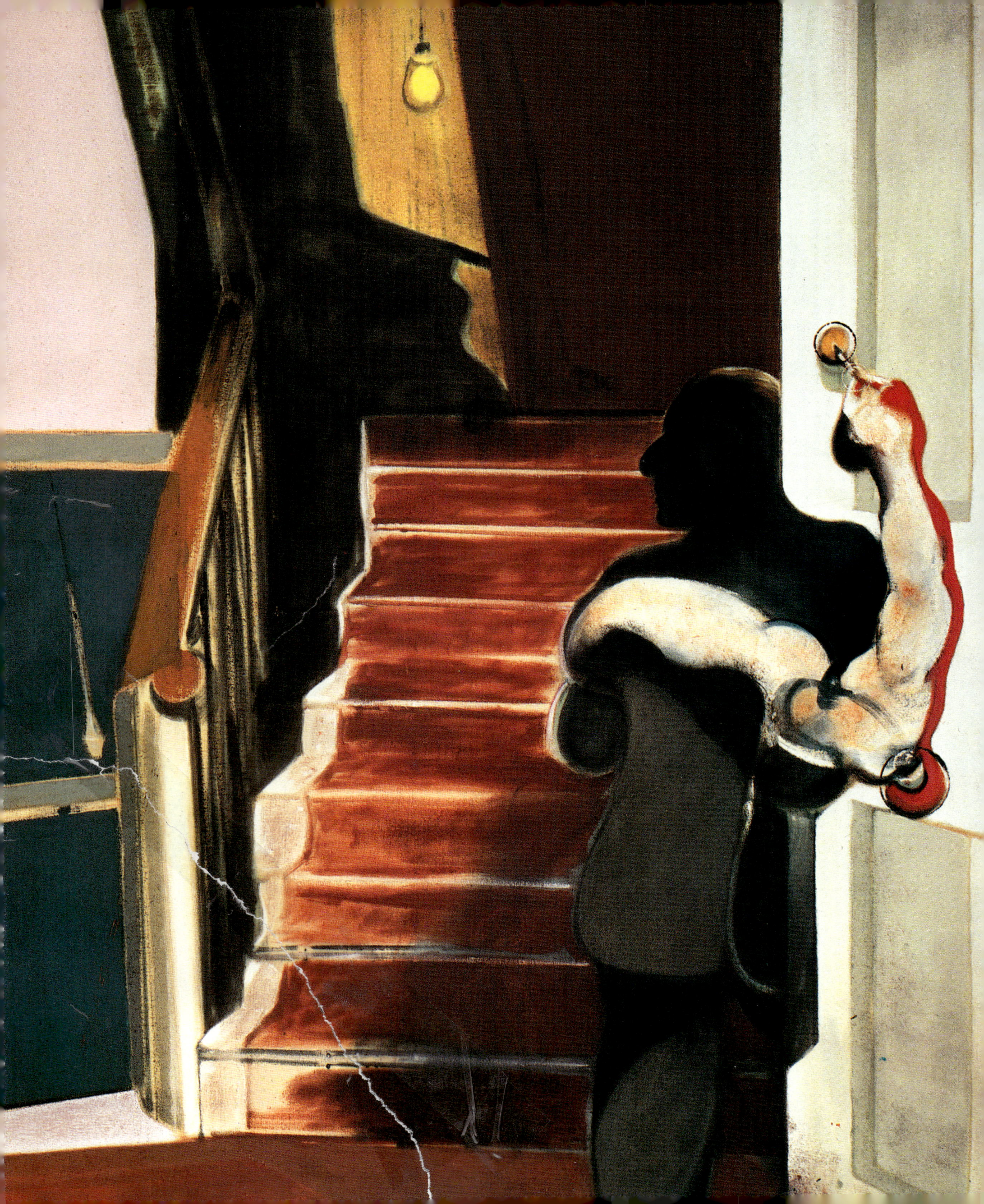

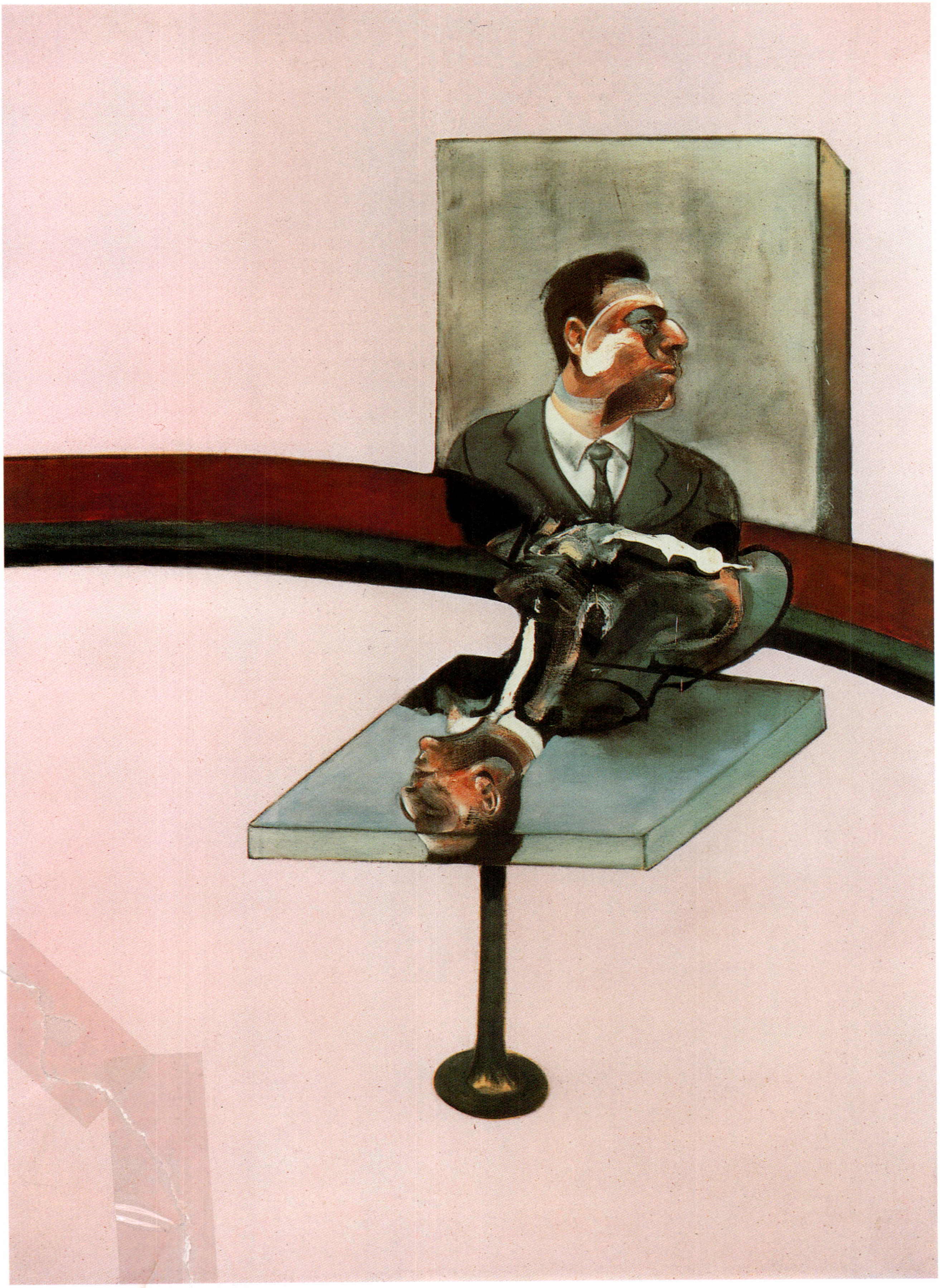

Cat. no. 121

Cat. no. 121
Francis Bacon
Triptych – In Memory of George Dyer
1971
Oil on canvas, triptych, each panel
198 × 147.5 cm
Riehen/Basel, Fondation Beyeler

Front page: Cat. no. 121, detail

Cat. no. 122
Cut-out head of black-and-white photograph of George Dyer, taken by John Deakin Mid 1960s
227 × 152 mm
Dublin, Dublin City Gallery The Hugh Lane, F130:82

Cat. no. 123
Black-and-white photograph of George Dyer, taken by John Deakin 1960s
298 × 250 mm
Dublin, Dublin City Gallery The Hugh Lane, F1A:104

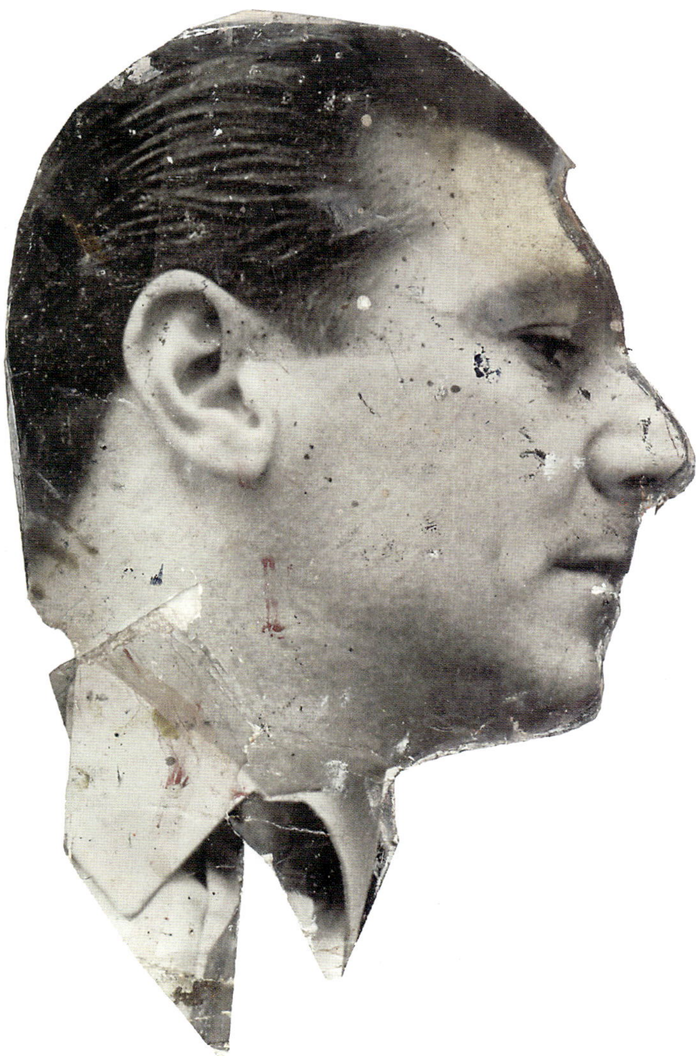

Cat. no. 122

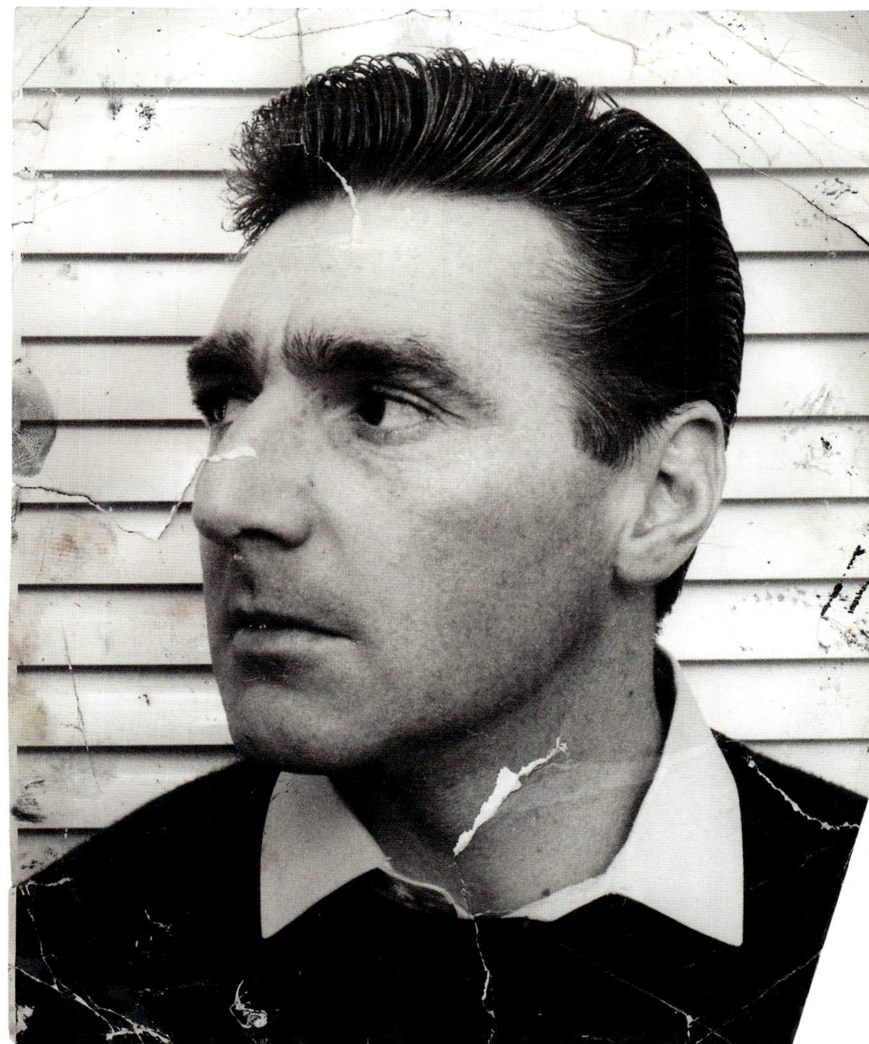

Cat. no. 123

Cat. no. 124
Torn black-and-white photograph of George Dyer in Francis Bacon's 7 Reece Mews studio, taken by John Deakin
C. 1964
299 × 294 mm
Dublin, Dublin City Gallery The Hugh Lane, F1A:164

Cat. no. 125
Black-and-white photograph of Lucian Freud, taken by John Deakin
Early/mid 1960s
298 × 295 mm
Dublin, Dublin City Gallery The Hugh Lane, F24:65

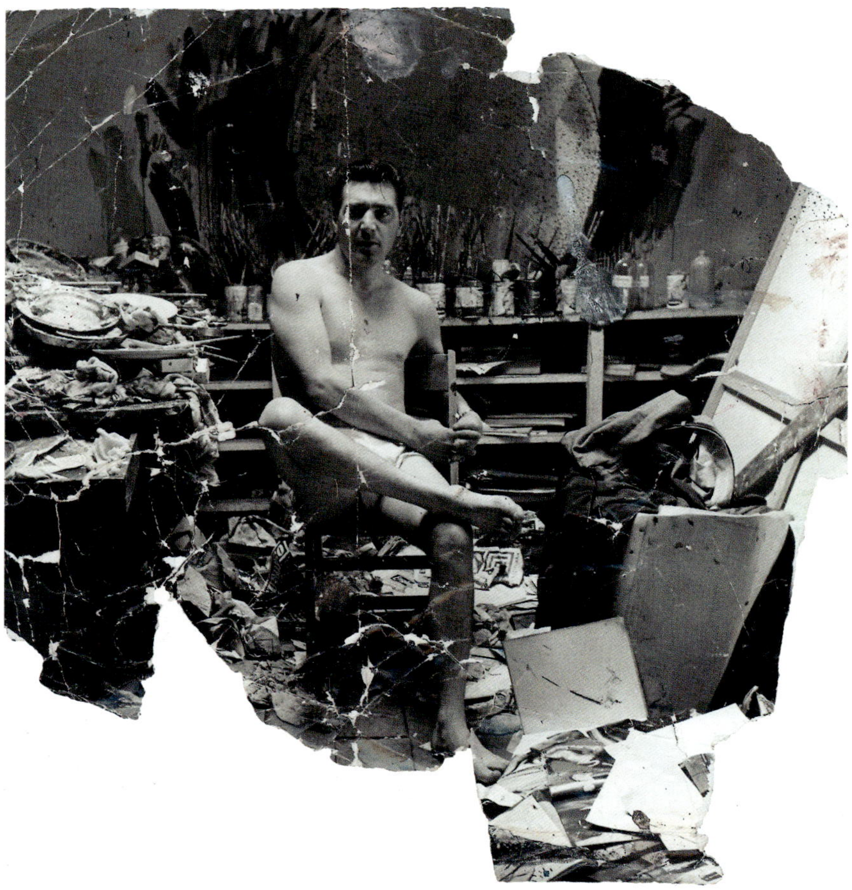

Cat. no. 124

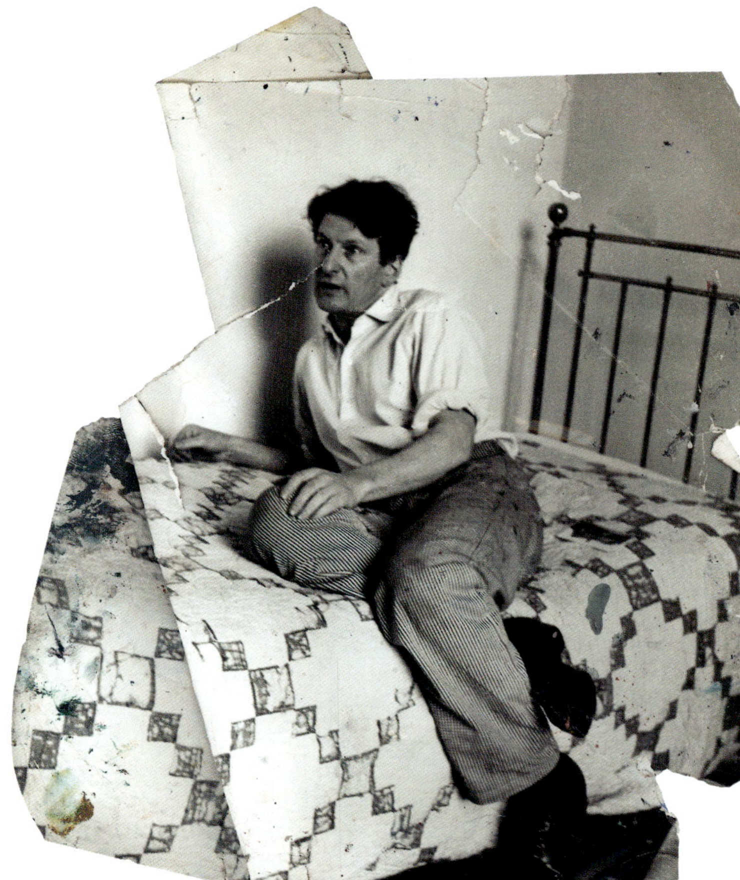

Cat. no. 125

Cat. no. 126
Black-and-white illustration of open windows and reflections by O. William Keck, 1939. Leaf from unidentified book
277 × 215 mm
Dublin, Dublin City Gallery The Hugh Lane, F1A:52

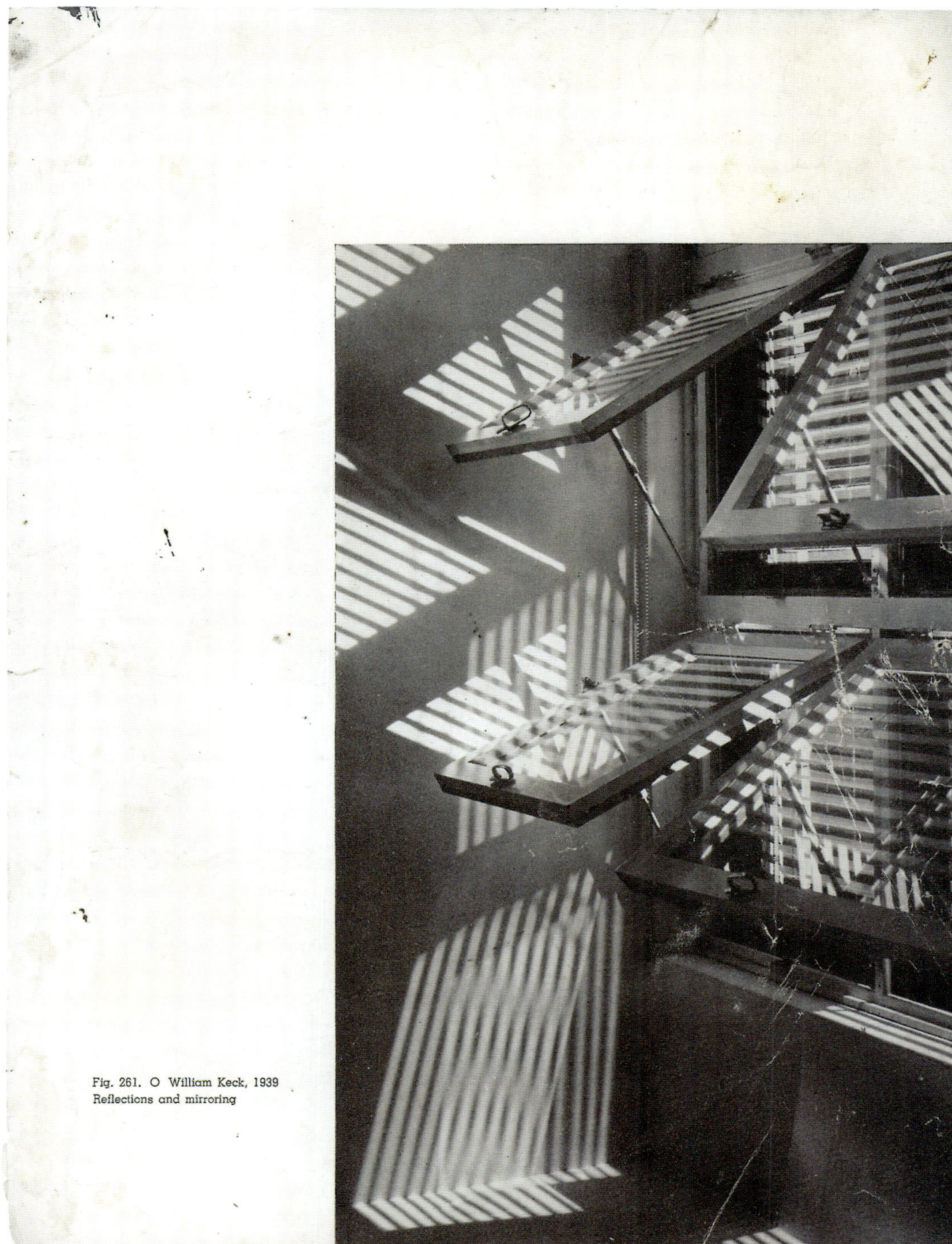

Cat. no. 126

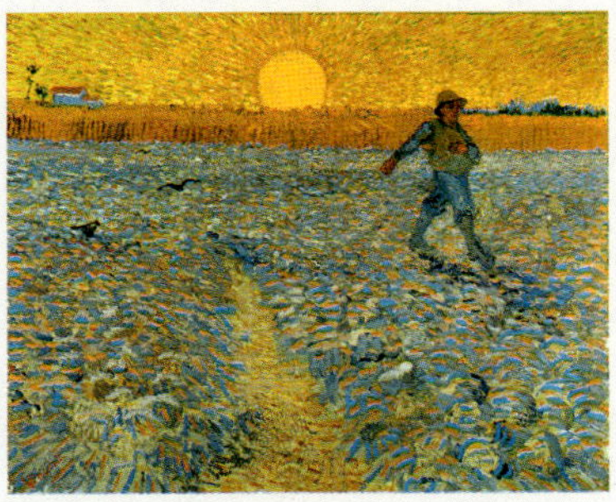

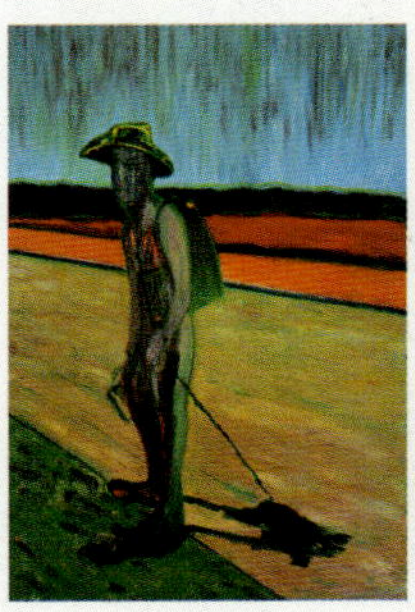

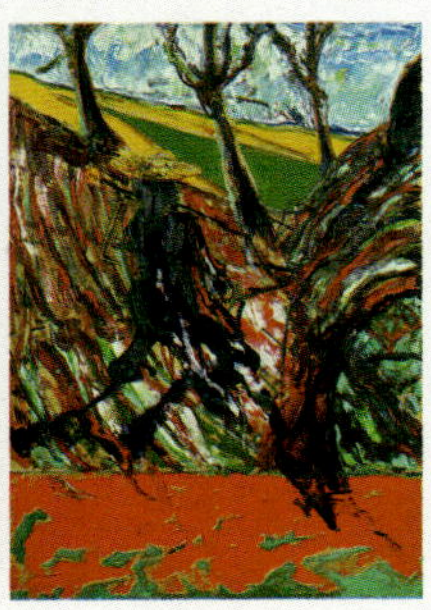

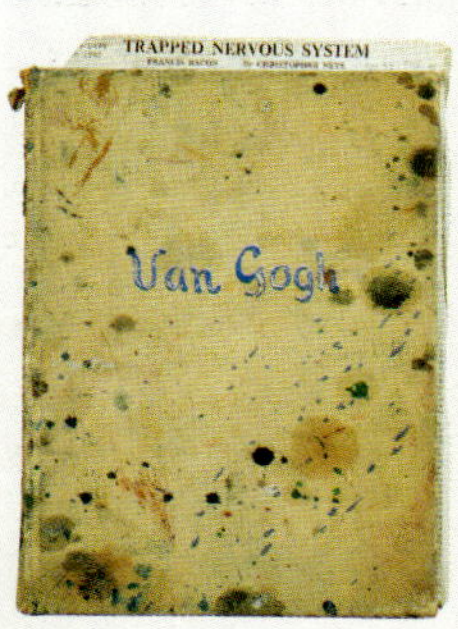
TRAPPED NERVOUS SYSTEM
Van Gogh

Verena Gamper

Bacon's Realism after Van Gogh

Following his intensive study of Velázquez' *Portrait of Pope Innocent X* at the beginning of the 1950s, Francis Bacon turned his attention a short time later to a paradigmatic work by an artist. For an exhibition planned for March – April 1957 by the Hanover Gallery in London, Bacon took as his theme variations on a painting by Vincent van Gogh.

Only one year earlier, Bacon had made a first Van Gogh portrait study that was stimulated by an oil painting that had been destroyed, *The Painter on the Road to Tarascon,* 1888 (formerly Magdeburg, Kaiser-Friedrich-Museum) *(Plate 1).* For the Hanover Gallery exhibition he picked up the thread from this first experience and created within a very short period the *Studies for Portrait of Van Gogh II–VI.* The model from which he worked was available only as a colour illustration taken from a monograph on the artist. (In his studio was found a Van Gogh monograph by René Huyghe, where this self-portrait of the artist is also reproduced in colour, cat. no. 130.) The destruction of the original work in 1945 in the wake of the war had left behind a "phantom" image in the form of a colour photograph. However, this unbridgeable distance that separates the recipient from the painting, has its benefits. This created the only situation in which he could devote himself – liberated from any sense of responsibility towards the original – to the work of another artist. It allowed him to emotionally charge the motif with the full spectrum of meanings that it held for him.

Speaking to John Russell, Bacon had the following to say about Van Gogh's painting: "I'd always loved that picture – the one that was burnt in Germany during the war – and as nothing else had gone right I thought I'd try to do something with it. Actually I've always liked early Van Gogh best, but that haunted figure on the road seemed just right at that time – like a phantom of the road, you could say."[1]

In this self-portrait Van Gogh portrays himself as an archetypal artist, in the same tradition in which Bacon once set off on his journey to the south. Loaded up with easel, canvas, brush and palette and attired in a straw hat and working clothes, the *peintre ouvrier* is searching for the next motif that can quench his creative thirst. He trails a shapeless shadow behind him that follows him everywhere like an irksome demon, urging him to work.

Bacon was fascinated by the Dutch artist's drawings and paintings of cultivated and ploughed land, whose portrayals of farm work are among the most impressive works of his œuvre. In the case of *Sower with Setting Sun,* 1888 (cat. no. 127) a single small figure is set against the expanse of the countryside, and yet his act of sowing has the greatness of a gesture of creation. Van Gogh has incorporated into this picture everything that preoccupied and moved him during his first months in the south: the fantastic light, his exploratory walks in the surrounding area and his interest in the daily life of the working people. The artist began to identify with the population that lived in and with nature: like the sower, the artist tramps across the fields and performs his daily work. While on the motific level Van Gogh remains trapped in the period before Arles and thus in his homeland – the figure of the sower, for example, is a concrete reference taken from an earlier sketch after François Millet –, his use of colour is completely revolutionary. Van Gogh now tends to give things their inherent luminosity, increasingly banning every external sources of light from the picture. While such a source is still present in *Sower with Setting Sun,* the powerful solar disc does not radiate its rich yellow across the landscape; the soil asserts itself in a complementary contrast. The sky and earth have exchanged their colour roles; the sky glows yellow, while the tilled field takes on the violet blue of the sky. This is a vivid example of the autonomy of colour that Van Gogh continued to develop forcefully in these years.

In the course of Bacon's intensive study of Van Gogh, which continued even after the opening of his exhibition in the Hanover Gallery and led him to add two additional oil paintings to it before they were even dry, his colour palette lightens visibly. After years of gloomy tones in the series of the

Plate 1: Vincent van Gogh, The Painter on the Road to Tarascon. 1888. Oil on canvas, 48 × 44 cm. Destroyed, formerly Magdeburg, Kaiser Friedrich Museum.

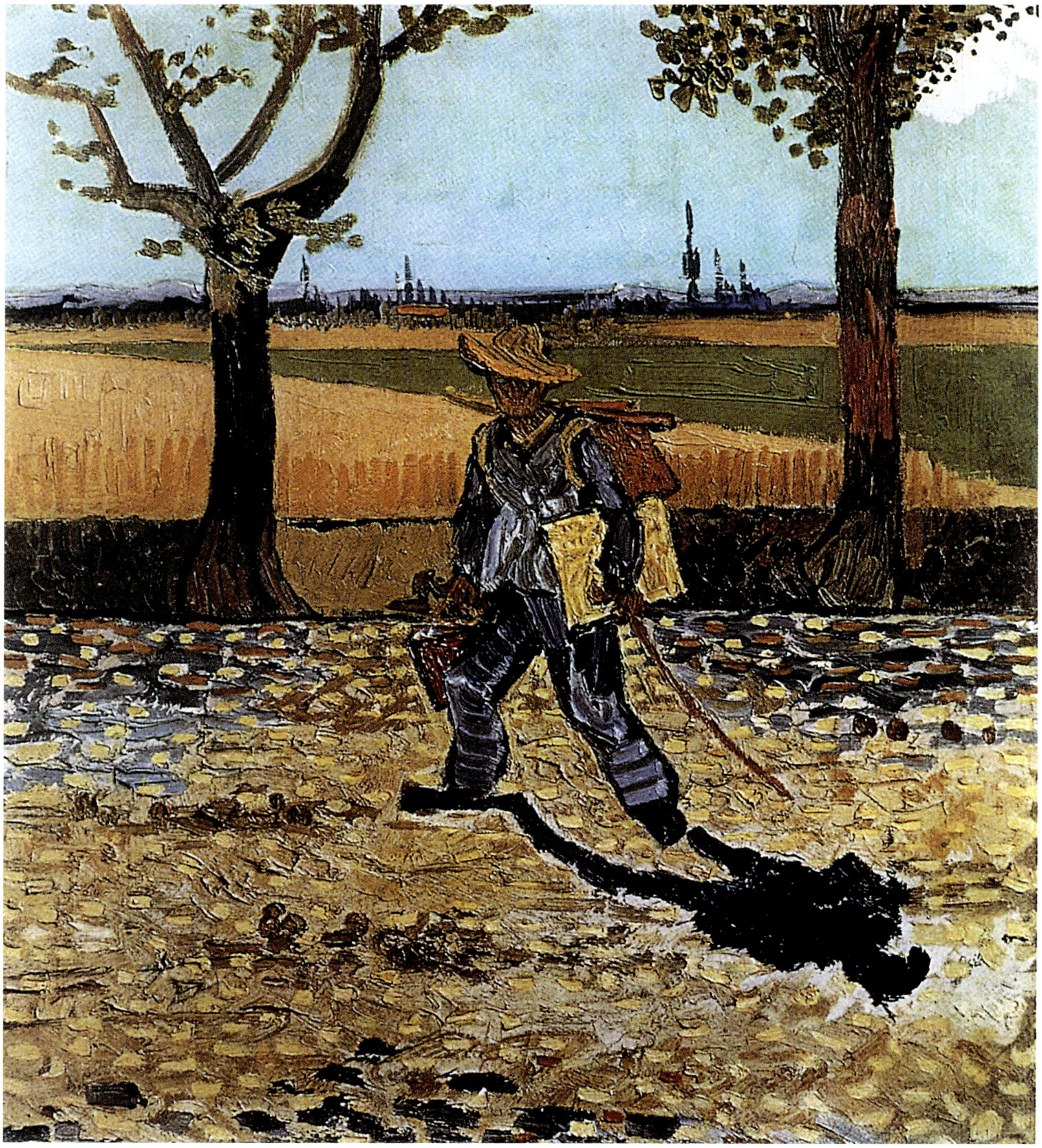

Popes and *Men in Blue,* he adopts Van Gogh's motif together with his expressive colours.

Study for a Portrait of Van Gogh V, 1957 (cat. no. 128) is one of the paintings that were still wet when shown at the exhibition. In contrast to the earlier variations on the theme, the decidedly calm composition is conspicuous here. The clearly delineated areas of colour are in strong, luminous hues and appear to be monochrome despite the cloudy intrusion of other colours. The fields of colour are separated from one another, cloisonné-like, by black or green lines. In the foreground the gaunt, vertical figure of the walker extends across all the fields of colour; the only pieces of his characteristic equipment that can be seen clearly are his straw hat and walking-stick. The shimmering flesh and skin tones make his body appear three-dimensional and distinguish it clearly from the surrounding landscape. It is possible to perceive the features of a landscape with a path vanishing to the left as it is depicted in the original painting and in other works from Bacon's Van Gogh series, but Bacon has removed the natural vegetal elements from the picture. The green triangular field of colour is reminiscent of a meadow and the adjoining wide yellow surface is reminiscent of the path, and yet the following orange and red bands of colour are a departure from the actual model. Here, too, in a manner similar to Bacon's later backgrounds composed of monochromatic fields of colour, an unambiguous reading of the scene as a space – in this case as a landscape – has been made as difficult as possible.

The harsh shadow thrown to the right by the figure of the artist deserves closer examination. Only in the second variation in this series, *Study for Portrait of Van Gogh II*, 1957, is the shadow found as prominently as here. In *The Painter on the Road to Tarascon* Van Gogh portrayed himself accompanied by his blue-black shadow. This functions as a metaphor for the dark side of the artist's psyche, which is as much a part of him as his shadow. This must have been one of Bacon's points of reference in his strong identification with Van Gogh.

The image of the suffering, restless artist who is being destroyed by his excessive lifestyle leads us to interpret the black mark on the back of the figure's hand as a stigma. In Bacon's version of the wandering artist, the figure merges with its shadow. In the stigmatised hand the walker holds his stick, which has a vividness and texture that give it the same degree of reality as the shadow to which it provides a transition. The figure forfeits corporeality to the extent that the shadow gains it. In addition, the shadow proves to be a valve through which the figure and the surroundings can communicate with one another.

Study for Portrait of Van Gogh VI, 1957 (cat. no. 129) was the second picture that was added to the Hanover Gallery exhibition after it had been opened, together with *Study for Portrait of Van Gogh V* the two works could hardly be more different. Here Bacon again finds his language in the style of large gestures; he crosses the entire canvas with rough brushstrokes. The gestural manner in this work is frequently attributed to the American Abstract Expressionism gained in England, but it is likely that Chaim Soutine was the artist who had the greatest influence on Bacon at the time.

The lowest band is separated from the rest of the picture by a hard horizontal line and is painted in unbridled, luminous red and green. Bacon uses the same colours to paint the path lying above it, but this time he uses lines of thick, flowing brushstrokes. The right field of the picture is dominated by a motif generated from a tree, which binds together the three horizontal bands of the picture. The restless coloured striae of the road cross into this field and, in a continuation of this movement, are swept in a high arch out of the picture. Next to this tree motif, the figure of the walker appears almost illegible; in striking contrast to the surrounding opulent frenzy of colour, he is lacking in colour in the sense of value and material. While his straw hat is depicted with relative precision, the yellow field that lies behind it offers almost no contrast and absorbs it. The colour appears to have been scraped off the black smudge of the figure. Particularly dreadful is the split that has been torn through the centre

Plate 2: Cat. no. 129, detail

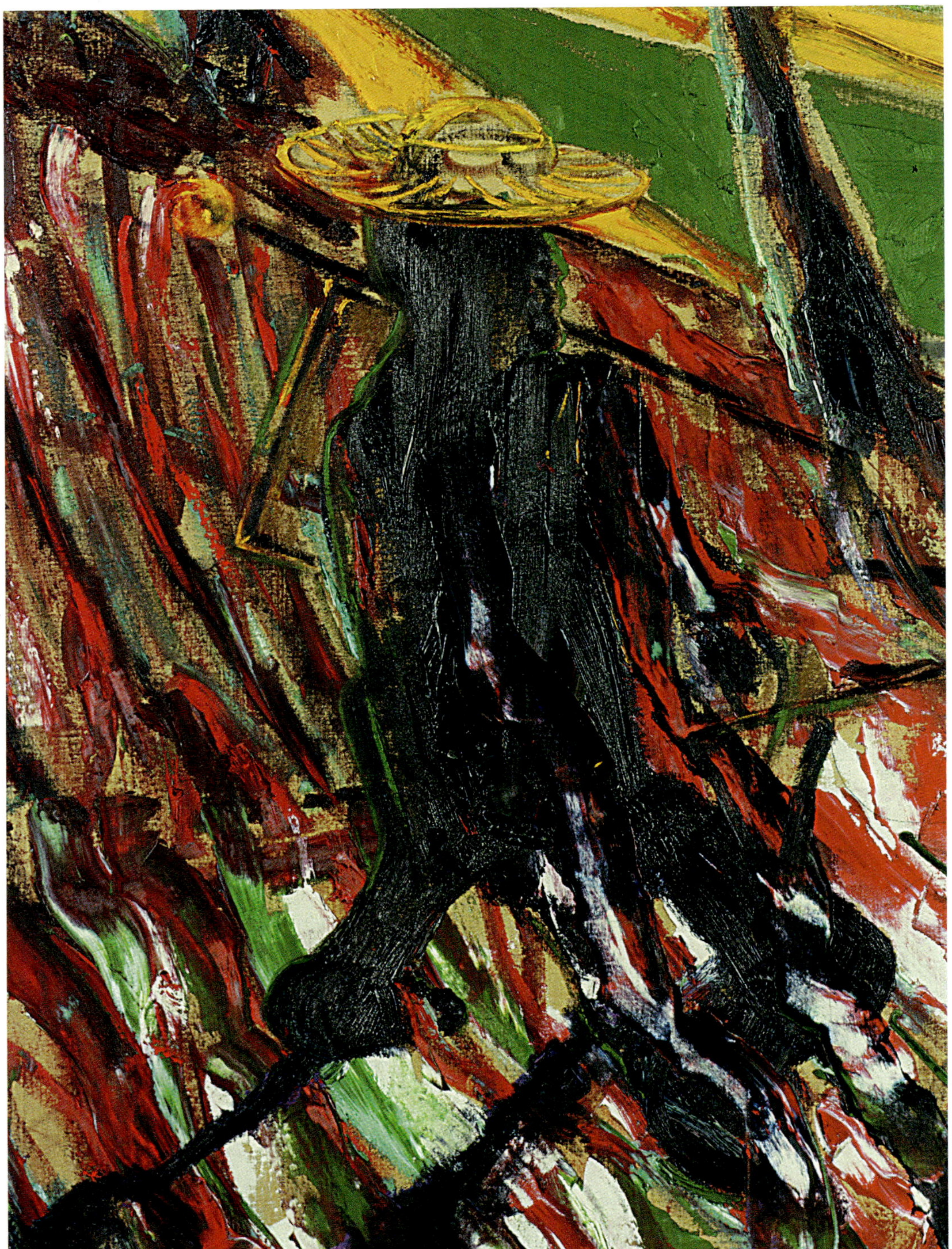

of the figure, where the colour has been removed down to the base itself, revealing its corporeal colouring. Revealingly, this break runs parallel to the brushstrokes of the ground. Thus the figure draws its consistency, or inconsistency, from the surrounding space and surface.

The urgency of *Study for Portrait of Van Gogh V* and *VI* results from the intensification of an aspect that is already present in Van Gogh's work. In Bacon's variations, howerer, it is filtered and becomes a central theme: the lonely artist is portrayed, driven by the search for inspiration, which he seeks to suck in from in the outside world like a sponge. Bacon's walkers appear passive, overcome, lost in the excessive frenzy of colour that surrounds them. The shadow, however, gives them a connection to the outside world; it allows them to express their presence in the world. The role of the shadow is, however, double-edged: parallel to its function as a means of connecting with the environment and of anchoring the figure there, it also means a loss of corporeality. The motif of the shadow expresses a double movement: on the one hand the flow of inspiration from the outside world to the artist, and on the other hand the loss of status as an isolated figure by the imprint of the artist in the world.

In a conversation with David Sylvester, Bacon made a very revealing remark about what he considered to be the purpose and validity of painting: "I believe that realism has to be re-invented. It has to be continuously re-invented. In one of his letters Van Gogh speaks of the need to make changes in reality, which become lies that are truer than the literal truth. This is the only possible way the painter can bring back the intensity of the reality which he is trying to capture. I believe that reality in art is something profoundly artificial and that it has to be recreated. Otherwise it will be just an illustration of something – which will be second-hand."[2]

Here Bacon is trying to express what art is all about for him. He has to try to make truth accessible through his art, but he cannot do this by simply imitatively reproducing what he sees. The highest goal is the revelation of a truth that surpasses reality in its truthfulness. This is what Bacon means with his statement about the artificial lie of art that in comparison reveals itself as "truer than the literal truth". And here he finds a great predecessor in Van Gogh. It is not the passive, retinal orgies of colours of the Impressionists that touch him – and thus the real importance of his Van Gogh variations does not lie in his rediscovery of vivid colour but in Van Gogh's active approach to reality; it is his heretical alienation of the same through his arbitrary choice of colours. This is the only way for the artist to abandon the field of illustrative art and find its genuine responsibility: to create a new reality. In a conversation with Michel Archimbaud, Bacon stated the following about Van Gogh: "His way of treating the material is quite different from the technique of the Impressionists. You know, his use of that very thick paint, that very thick material. His manner was unique. He is one of the great geniuses of painting. For me Van Gogh is the greatest. He really did find a new way of depicting reality, even for the simplest things, and that method wasn't realist, but was much more powerful than simple realism. It was really a work of re-creating reality."[3]

The goal for Van Gogh, as it was for Bacon, is to find again reality in all its intensity. In this endeavour to recreate reality beyond the simple reproduction of it, both artists prove, indeed, to be realistic painters.

[1] Russell 1993, 51.
[2] Sylvester 1999, 172.
[3] Archimbaud 1993, 42.

Cat. no. 127
Vincent van Gogh
The Sower
1888
Oil on canvas, 64.1 × 80.1 cm
Otterlo, Collection Kröller-Müller
Museum, KM 106.399

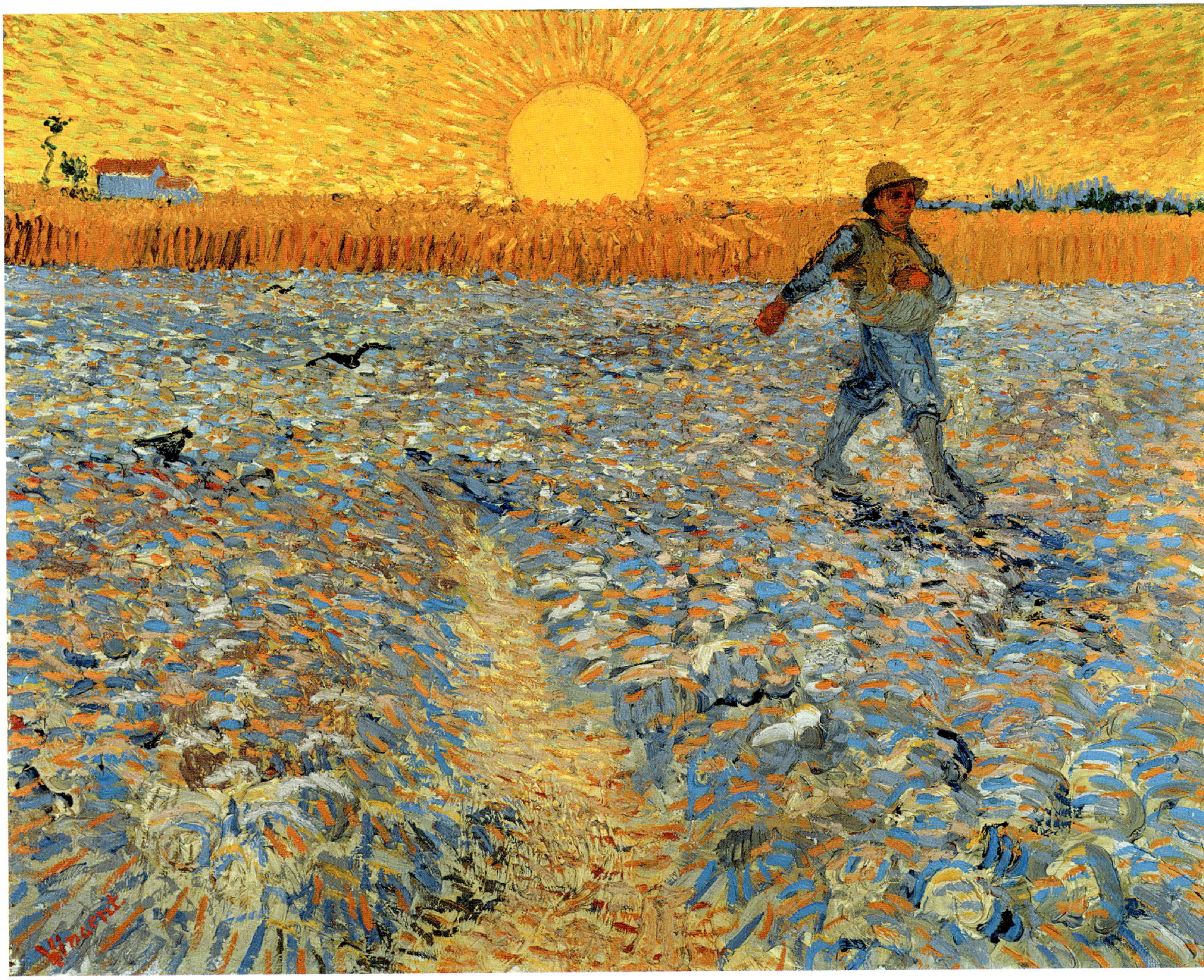

Cat. no. 127

Cat. no. 128
Francis Bacon
Study for Portrait of Van Gogh V
1957
Oil and sand on canvas,
198 × 142 cm
Washington D.C., Hirshhorn
Museum and Sculpture Garden,
Smithsonian Institution, Gift
of the Joseph H. Hirshhorn
Foundation, 1966,
HMSG 66.187

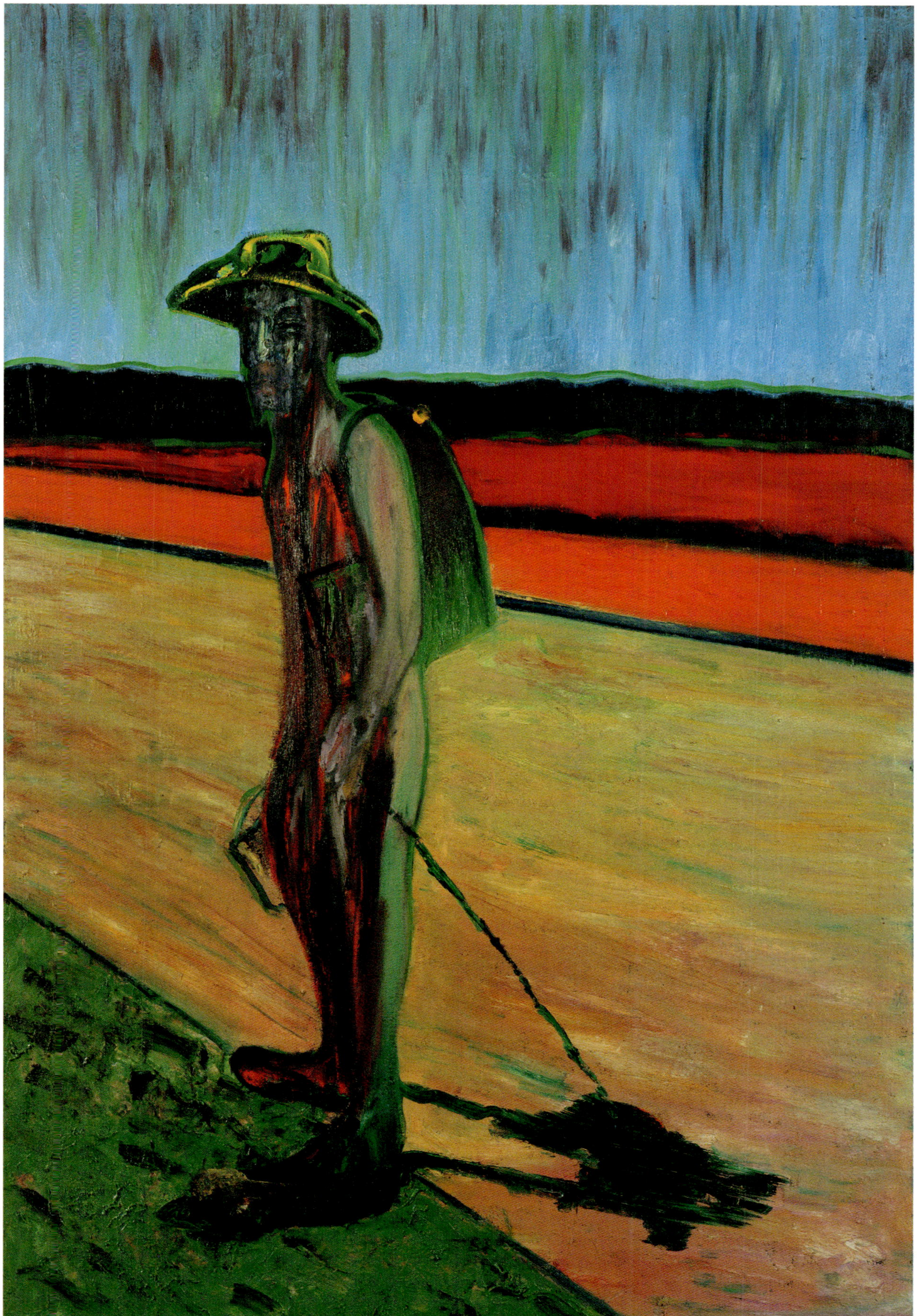

Cat. no. 128

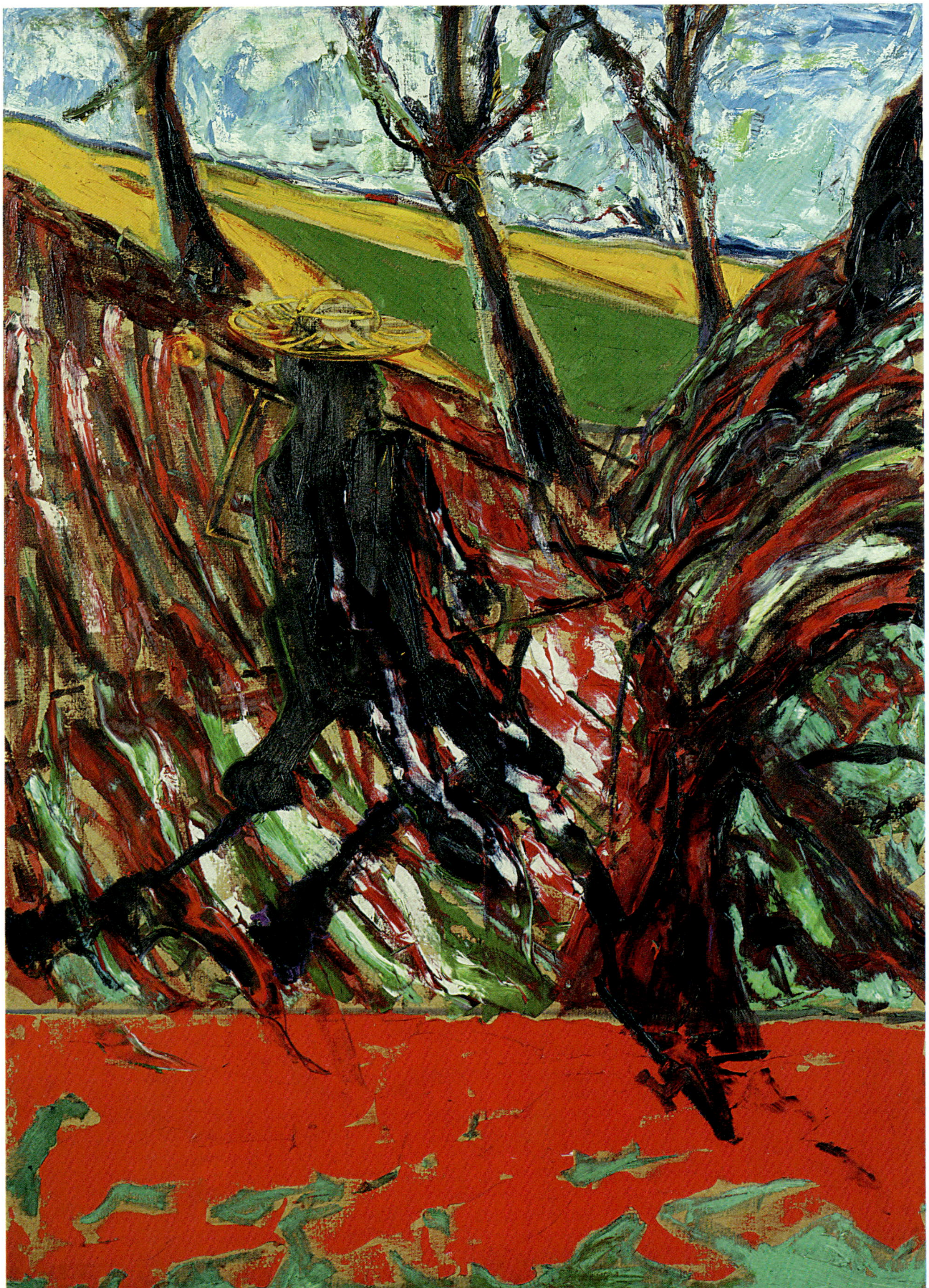
Cat. no. 129

Cat. no. 129
Francis Bacon
Study for Portrait of Van Gogh VI
1957
Oil on canvas, 198.1 × 142.2 cm
London, Arts Council Collection
and Hayward Gallery

Cat. no. 130
René Huyghe, Van Gogh, Milan
(no publication date). Insert visible
of photocopied article on Francis
Bacon by Christopher Neve
in Country Life, 13 June 1985
285 × 215 × 16 mm
Dublin, Dublin City Gallery
The Hugh Lane, F100:4

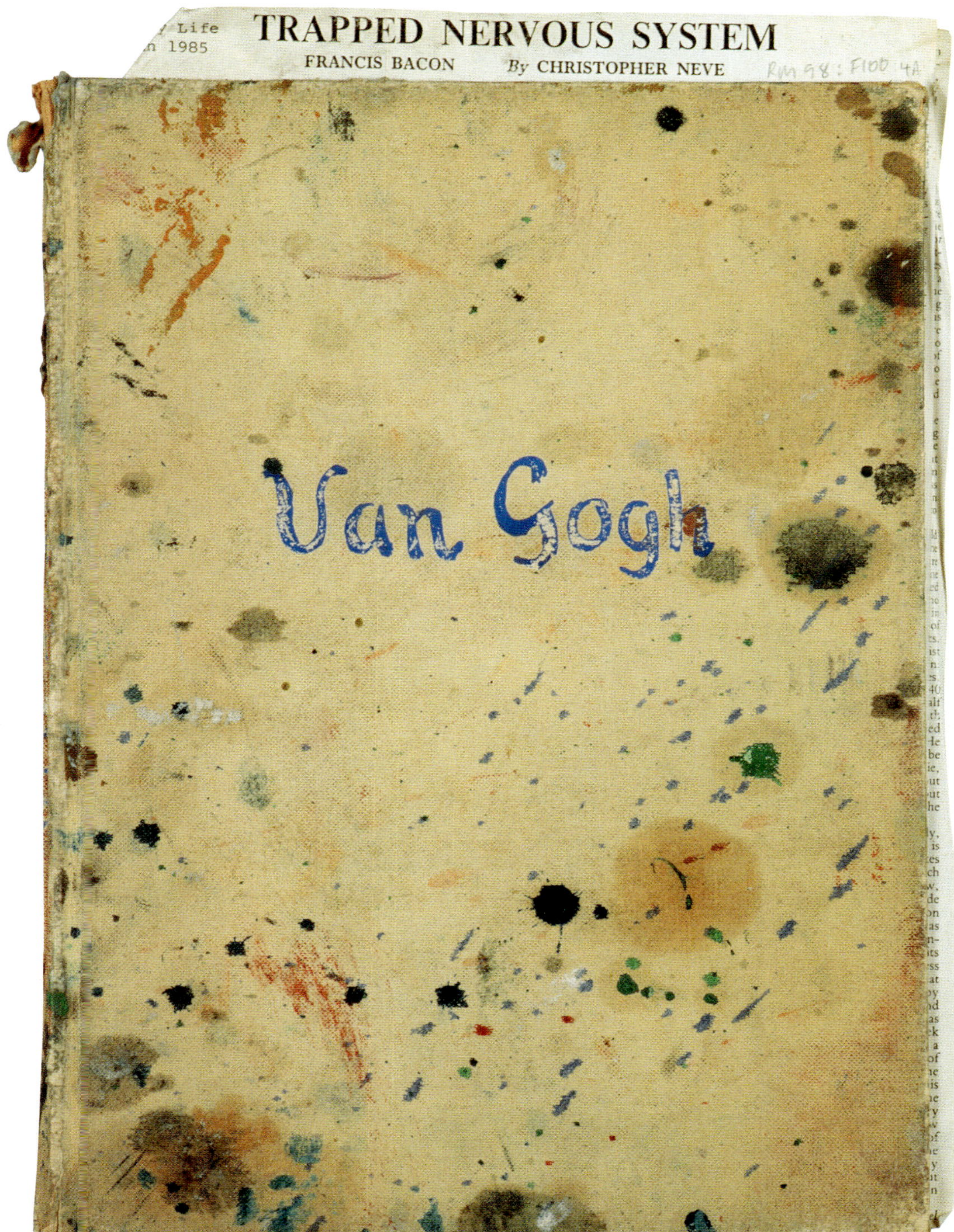

Cat. no. 130

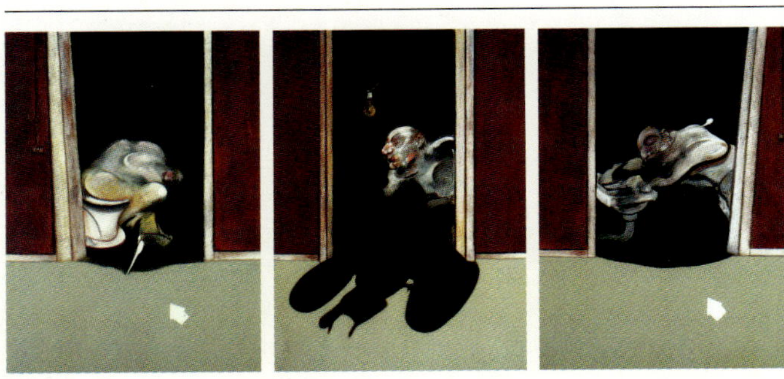

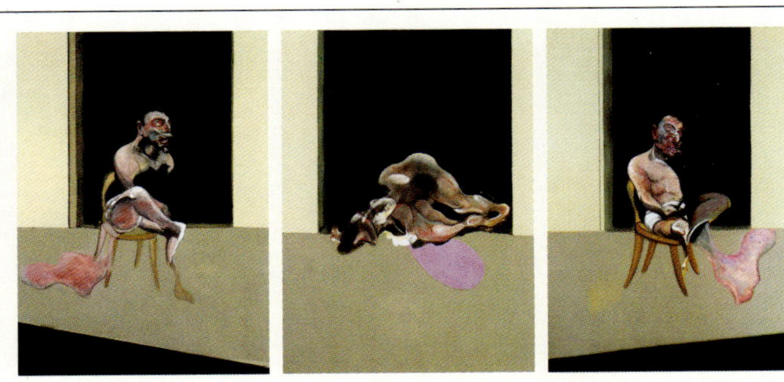

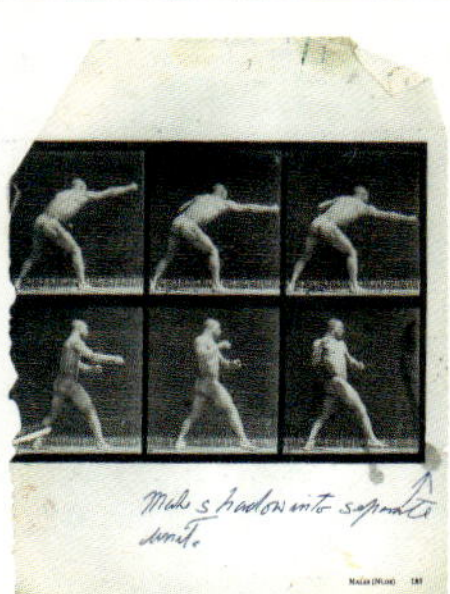
Make shadow into separate
unit.

Verena Gamper

The Ambivalent Function of the Shadow

Cages and platforms, intimated vanishing lines and curved surface areas reminiscent of arenas are among the motifs in Bacon's repertoire that assign a position to the figures on the canvas. The persistence with which he uses these devices time and time again, combining them in a variety of ways, is astonishing. No single indicator of space appears able to hold the figure; it requires the combination of several of these devices to make it legible within the space. The artist's motive for taking this approach can be found in his treatment of the figure itself, which never creates an impression of unity and sovereignty but rather appears to be worn, unstable and waning,[1] almost demanding that its presence be externally emphasised and confirmed. In addition to the pictorial elements already mentioned, shadow also performs the function of an indicator of space. Although the artist in most cases depicts an individual figure on the surface of the canvas, it would be incorrect to assert that it is depicted alone: it is usually accompanied by a shadow, which connects the figure to the space, gives it a habitat, and testifies to its presence. The shadow anchors the figure within the space.

In *Triptych May – June 1973* (cat. no. 131), the shadow is seen in its most distinctive form in the centre panel; shaped like a bat, it dominates the ochre-coloured lower section of the painting. The figure, which is seen within a door-frame, has the characteristic facial features of Bacon's companion George Dyer. The background behind the figure is black, "which projects the background colour to the front, affirming or no longer negating the shallow depth, but filling it in an appropriate manner."[2] The black of the surrounding area gnaws away at the figure's extremities, visibly groping its way towards the head, which is reddened with pain. While the figure appears to be slowly dissolving, the shadow maintains an intact contour. In contrast to Bacon's bodies, which are frequently distorted, the silhouettes of the shadow correct any deformation, providing an intact image of the body's original state. This gives the viewer the impression of seeing the body itself in its shadow. This reveals the ambivalent role that the shadow plays in Bacon's paintings: on the one hand it serves to anchor the figure, to support it in its precarious position between surface and space. The shadow provides the instability of the spatial structure with a strong, spatial counter-argument because it is taken from the real world. On the other hand, the shadow also embodies an attack on the figure. Its intactness, which is so obvious in comparison with the disabled body, additionally weakens the latter. In a reversal of the traditional attribution of roles, the shadow becomes the actual figure, while the body is degraded to an illusion.

The material status of the shadow in *Triptych May – June 1973* cannot be clearly established: on the one hand, it appears to be born uninterruptedly of the black mass threatening the body, giving it sensory qualities for the viewer – note, for example, the way it undercuts the lower edge of the door-frame – while on the other hand its silhouette-like form seems to be a non-spatial extension of the surface. The question arises of whether Bacon's shapes are actually shadows at all. A shadow in a picture always demands the existence of a light-source. In keeping with this traditional principle, the centre panel of the triptych depicts a lightbulb hanging from the ceiling, allowing the figure that is crouched in the door-frame to cast a shadow. A classical analysis of the painting would fault the inconsistency of the way the scene is illuminated; the effective light-source and shadow are not consistent with one another. But the figure and its shadow cannot be reconciled, regardless of the source of illumination. Even allowing for distortion of the shadow, the shapes are not congruent. Thus this shadow is not an iconic sign in the conventional manner, bearing within it a relationship to the viewer. An exciting insight can be gained, however, by reading this unscathed image as a kind of reconstruction: in this reading, Bacon's shadow figures are a projection of a past, undamaged condition, a relic of a time when the body was still intact. The figure always carries within it its archetype, marked by unity and entirety, underlining its own precarious corporeality.

An excursion into the history of the origins of *Triptych May – June 1973* can be helpful in a closer examination of the role of the shadow in Bacon's work. Along with *Triptych August*, 1972 (cat. no. 132) and *Triptych – In Memory of George Dyer*, 1971 (cat. no. 121), this work is one of the so-called "black triptychs."[3] They were painted in the years following the death of Bacon's companion George Dyer.[4] In the centre panel of the triptych, the coming event already casts its shadow. The subsequent throes of death are indicated in the two flanking panels by arrows, and the figures have lost their shadow. Or to quote Dante, they have already, like Virgil, become shadow. The shadow of the body becomes, metaphorically, the shadow of approaching death. In this reading of the triptych, the shadow can be seen as a symbolic sign, in addition to the indexical and iconic functions mentioned above.

With regard to the substantiality of the shadow, *Triptych August 1972* (cat. no. 132) features another remarkable aspect. In the centre panel of the triptych, we find the copulating bodies familiar to us from other works by Bacon and prompted by Muybridge's studies of wrestlers (cat. no. 144). In an extremely confined space they are writhing on the threshold of a door. The fact that this very sparse architecture can be read as a room at all is due less to the figures themselves than to the mauve-coloured oval shape that extends to the right from beneath the bodies. In its form and position it is reminiscent of part of the shadow figure of *Triptych May – June 1973* (cat. no. 131), but apart from that, an interpretation of this shape as a shadow suggests itself, despite the arbitrary coloration. In addition, the rounded shape, which serves in many other paintings to provide order to the figure being presented, occurs here as part of the scenery. In this hybrid of shadow and rounded shape, we see once again how necessary this device is to Bacon's figures: it assigns a place to the sculptural tangle of bodies by performing the function of an anchor for the pair of figures, which otherwise appear to be rolling off the surface of the painting.

A further development of the conventional shadow is found in the side panels of this triptych. Here the mauve-coloured oval of the centre panel has degenerated to a dirty-pink puddle, which no longer anchors the body; it is no longer read as an external element but rather as part of the body itself. Here the conventional shadow in the form of an immaterial imprint takes on the consistency of flesh. Like an emanation, the body pours into the space of the painting, creating a concrete connection with it. With regard to Bacon's shadow, John Russell once spoke of melting candles that flow into their own wax.[5] The shadow becomes a corporeal appendix of the figure; its connecting function becomes particularly clear in these flesh-coloured shadows. The body leaves its body through an opening and degenerates into deformity, creating its own connection with the surrounding space; it becomes its own anchor, as though all the spatial indicators were unable to offer the figure sufficient anchoring. It is evident here that the shadow belongs to the body, because it has taken on the consistency of flesh. Body and shadow merge into oneness, and the traditional boundary between the figure and its double becomes an indiscernible zone. Each shows characteristics of the other; a clear attribution is impossible.

Freud pointed out that repetition of the same thing, such as shadow as the double of the body, is among the most important factors that induce an uncanny feeling.[6] In contrast to that assertion, Otto Rank affirms that the double originally offered protection against the destruction of the ego as "an energetic denial of the power of death."[7] This ambivalent role of the shadow, which on the one hand threatens the body but at the same time protects it, substantiates the impression of a double movement in the relationship between figure and shadow in Bacon's work. Shadow is no longer the "illusional enemy" as defined by the first dictionary of the French language[8] but rather testifies as an indexical sign to the presence of the figure and, in addition, attributes to it the status of a creator, namely of the shadow itself. The wretched figure thus draws from its shadow a power that the artist has denied it.

A document from Bacon's Studio deserves closer examination. A note by Bacon about shadow can be found on a page of Muybridge's *The Human Figure in Motion* (cat. no. 133). Beneath the six photographs of a shadow boxer, Bacon wrote: "make shadow into separate unit." The meaning of this phrase is made clear by the arrow corresponding to the comment. It ends exactly at the edge of a spot of paint that most likely occurred by chance. It is tempting to consider that here, as in other cases in which "studio accidents" occurred in the form of soiling and creasing of the collected material, the idea of creating an opponent for the boxer was provoked by the dark spot. Because of its rounded upper edge, it has an unmistakably anthropomorphic quality; in addition, the posture of the boxer is consistent with this interpretation in the way he recoils from the shadow figure. Here the boxer literally becomes a s h a d o w b o x e r. Muybridge's motion studies freeze the individual segments of a sequence of photographs. In this study of a boxer, however, the flowing course of the event has been relatively sharply interrupted in comparison with other photographic sequences by the artist; it comes to a halt and visibly forfeits its logical consistency. The shadow figure, which has crept into the last of the six images, actively opposes this process of decomposition; it regains control of the sequence of individual images and retrospectively makes them into a story again. It was Bacon's intention, however, to make the shadow figure an autonomous unit and thus prevent this movement. This may be related to the artist's constant effort to prevent any stories that the viewer might be able to imagine in his constellations of figures. Wieland Schmied rightly says of Francis Bacon that he was not a story-teller but rather a story-destroyer.[9] The story that had crept by chance into the existing source material had to be destroyed in order to prevent the figures from entering into a narrative relationship with one another.

In Bacon's paintings the figures of the body and shadow become a single figure, avoiding the danger of narration. The action does not take place between two autonomous figures but rather occurs in the form of a double movement within the "shadow-figure." This happens because the shadow performs an ambivalent function: on the one hand, it supports the figure and creates a place for it, but at the same time it weakens it by virtue of its own intact appearance.

[1] An exception is the right panel of *Three Studies for a Portrait of Isabel Rawsthorne,* 1965 (cat. no. 85), which depicts the head of the subject in an unscathed profile view. But this intactness is undermined in the triptych's other two panels, in which the head is deformed in the usual manner.

[2] Deleuze 1995, p. 91.

[3] Davies 1975, pp. 62–68.

[4] George Dyer committed suicide in 1971. On the evening before the opening of his large retrospective at the Grand Palais in Paris, Bacon found him slumped in the foetal position on the toilet.

[5] Russell 1998, p. XXX.

[6] Quoted by Stoichita 1999, p. 131.

[7] Ibid., p. 137.

[8] Ibid., p. 137: "SHADOW, chimerical enemy. Should we do battle with our *shadow*? Which means, with our suspicions and thoughts?"

[9] Schmied 1996, p. 84.

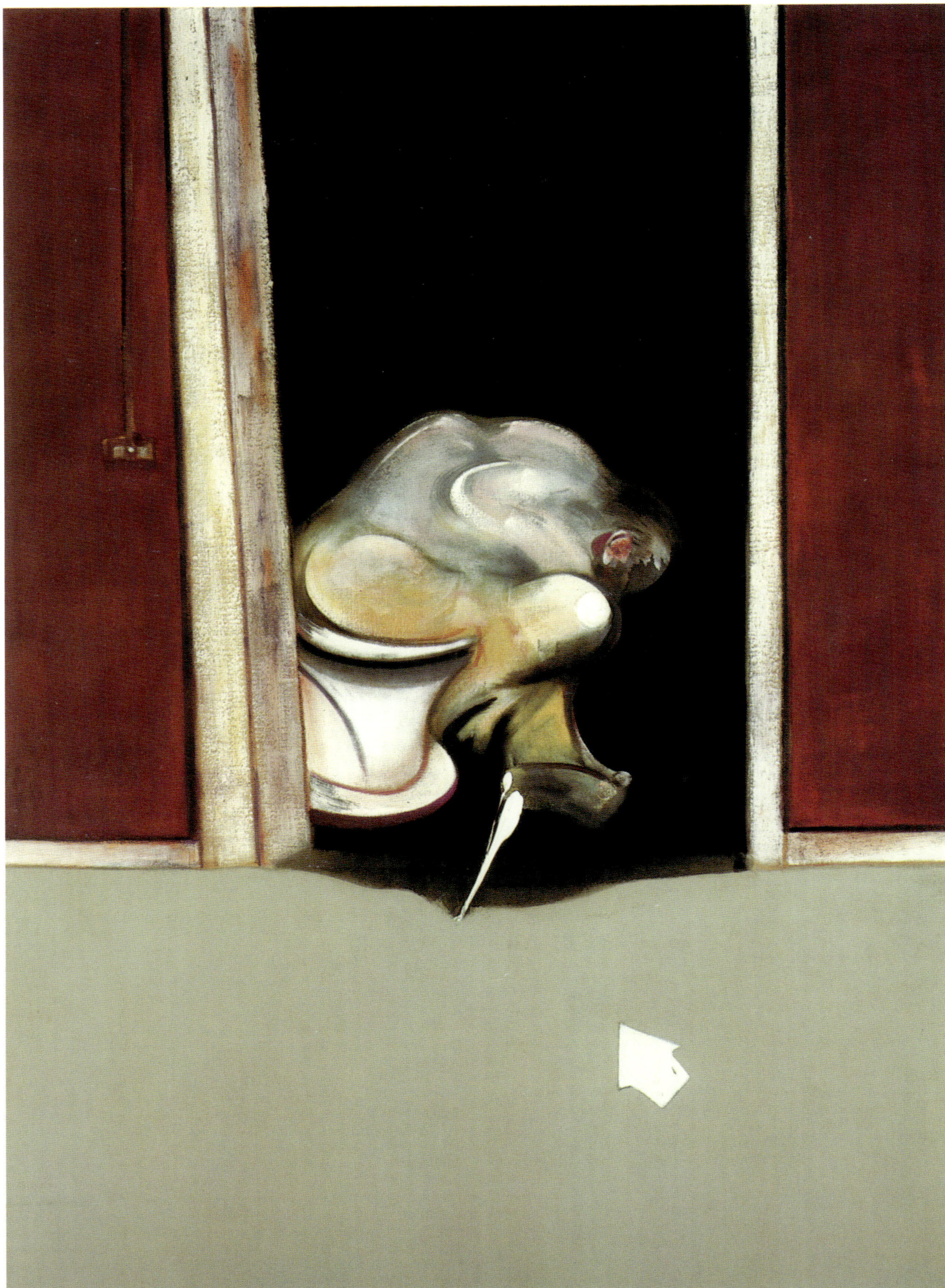

Cat. no. 131

Cat. no. 131
Francis Bacon
Triptych, May – June 1973
Oil on canvas, triptych, each panel
198 × 174.5 cm
Switzerland, Private collection

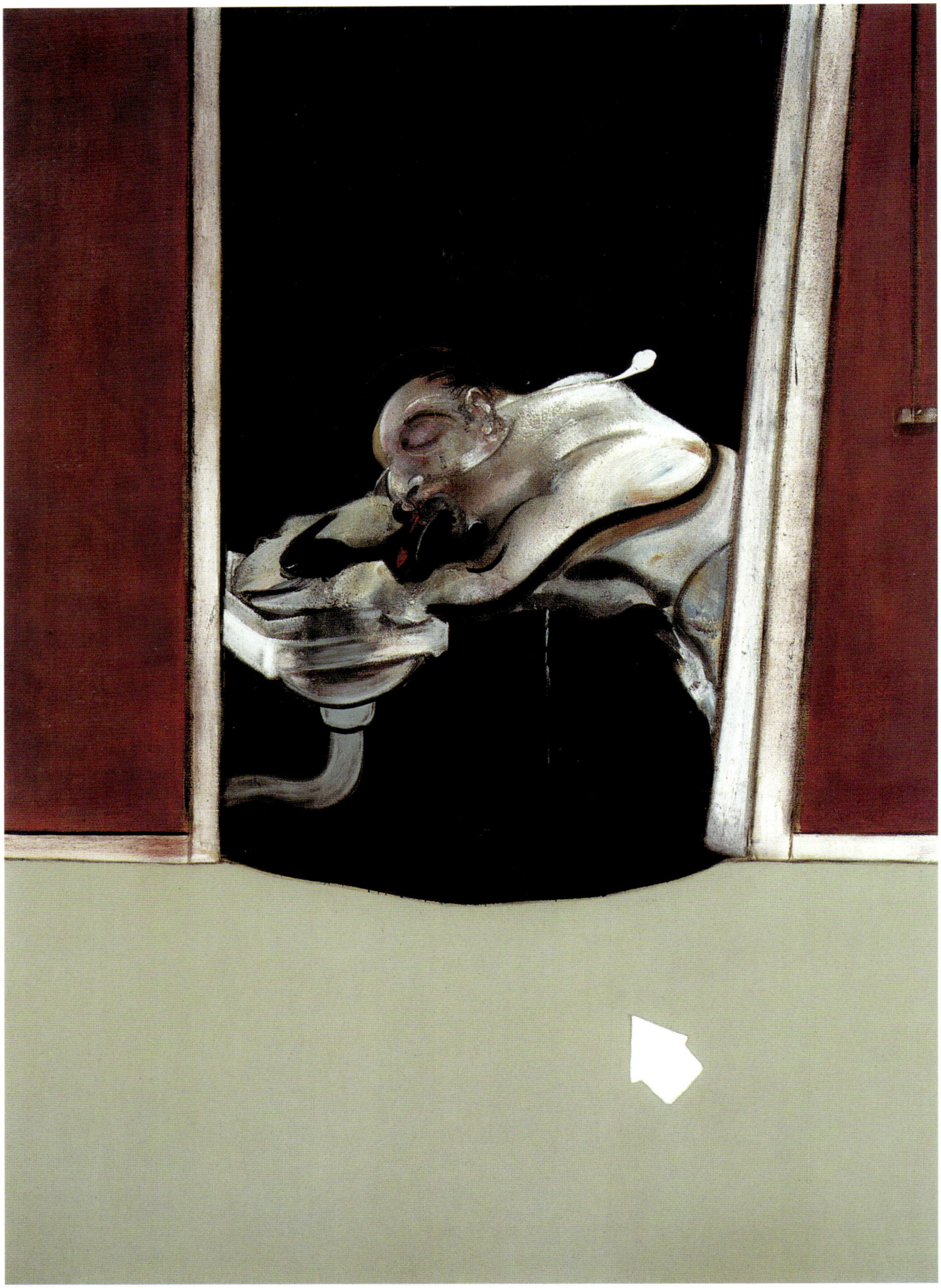

Cat. no. 131

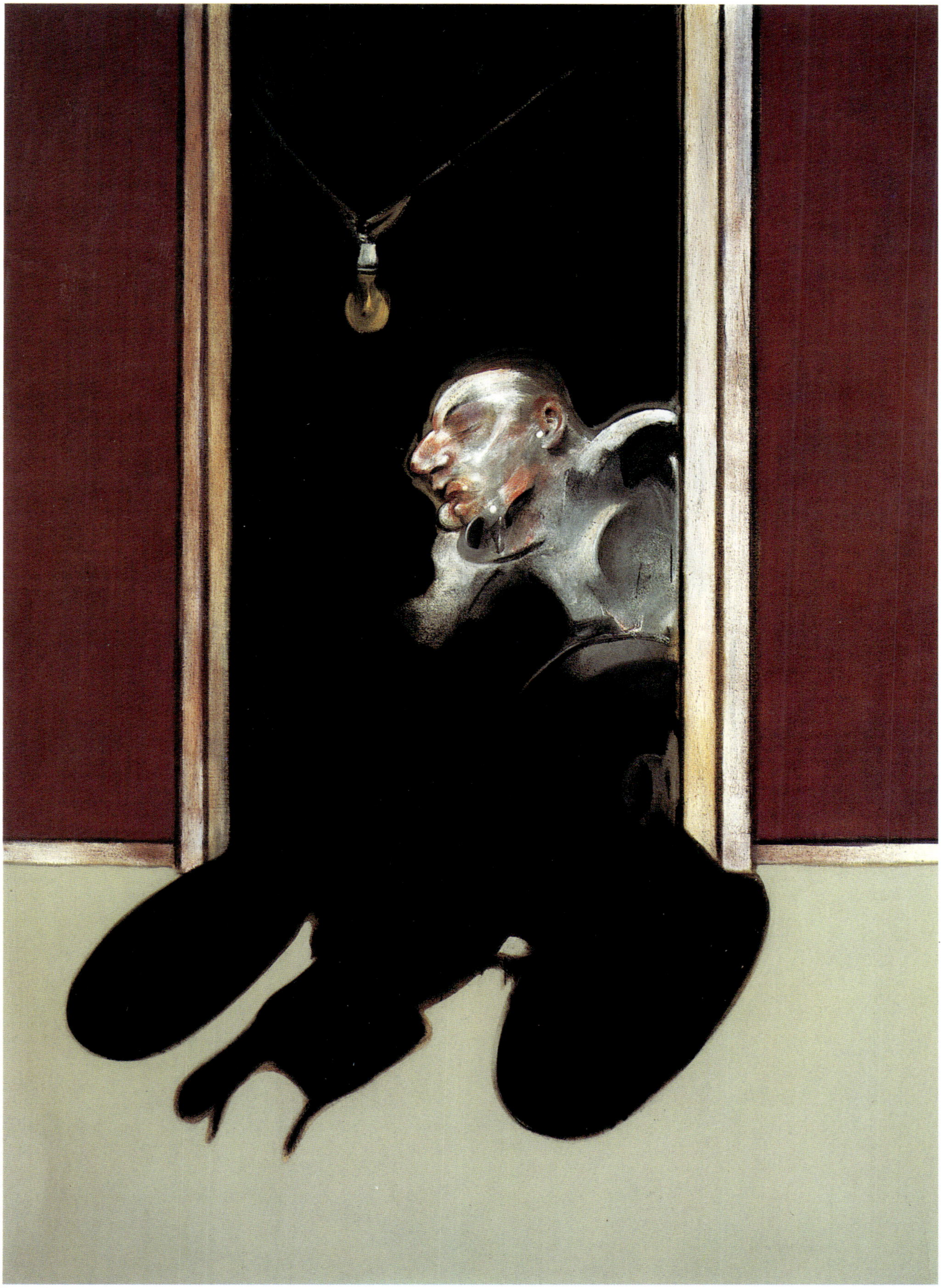

Cat. no. 131

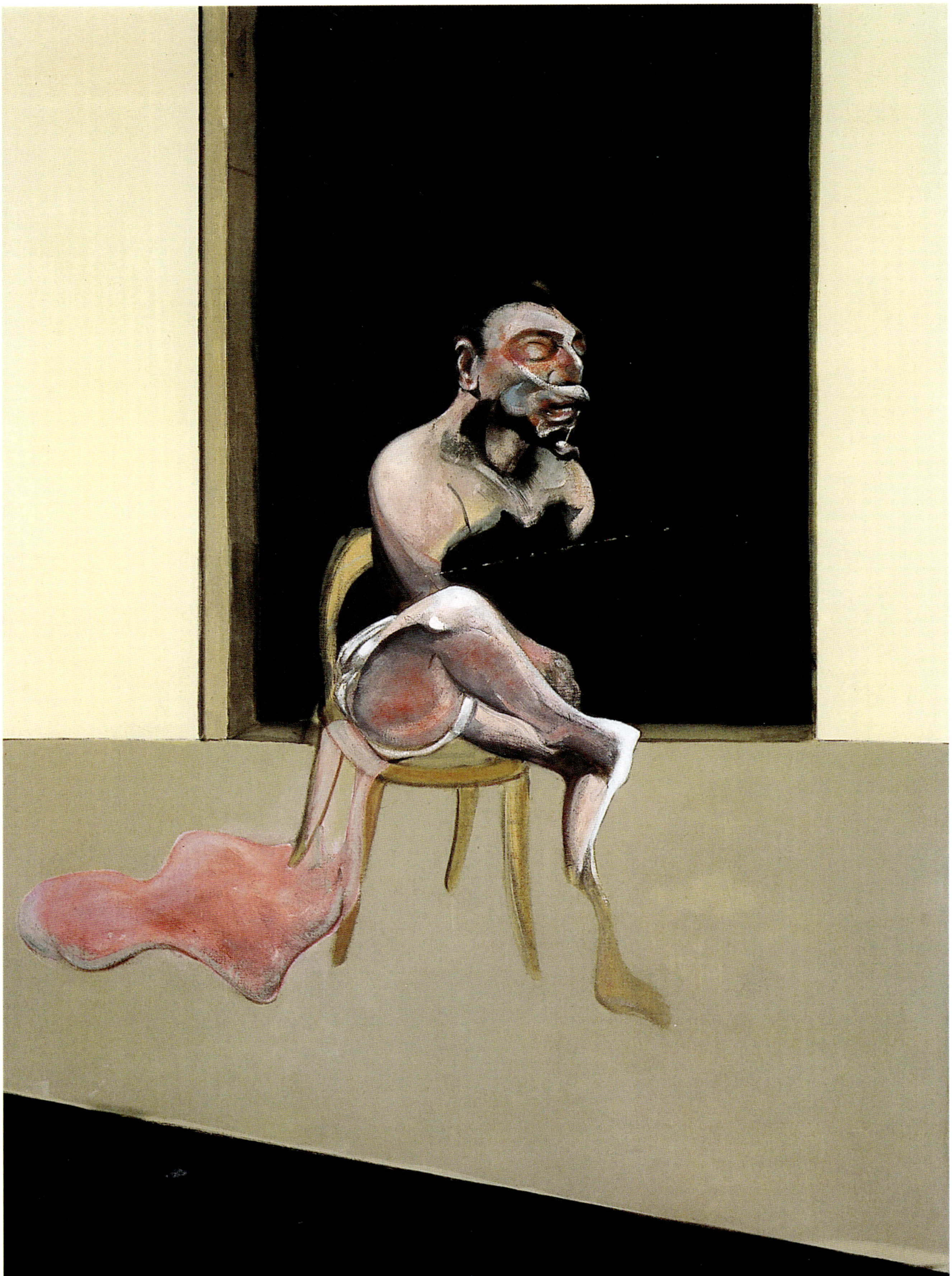

Cat. no. 132

Cat. no. 132
Francis Bacon
Triptych, August 1972
Oil on canvas, triptych, each panel
198 × 147.5 cm
London, Tate Gallery, purchased
1980

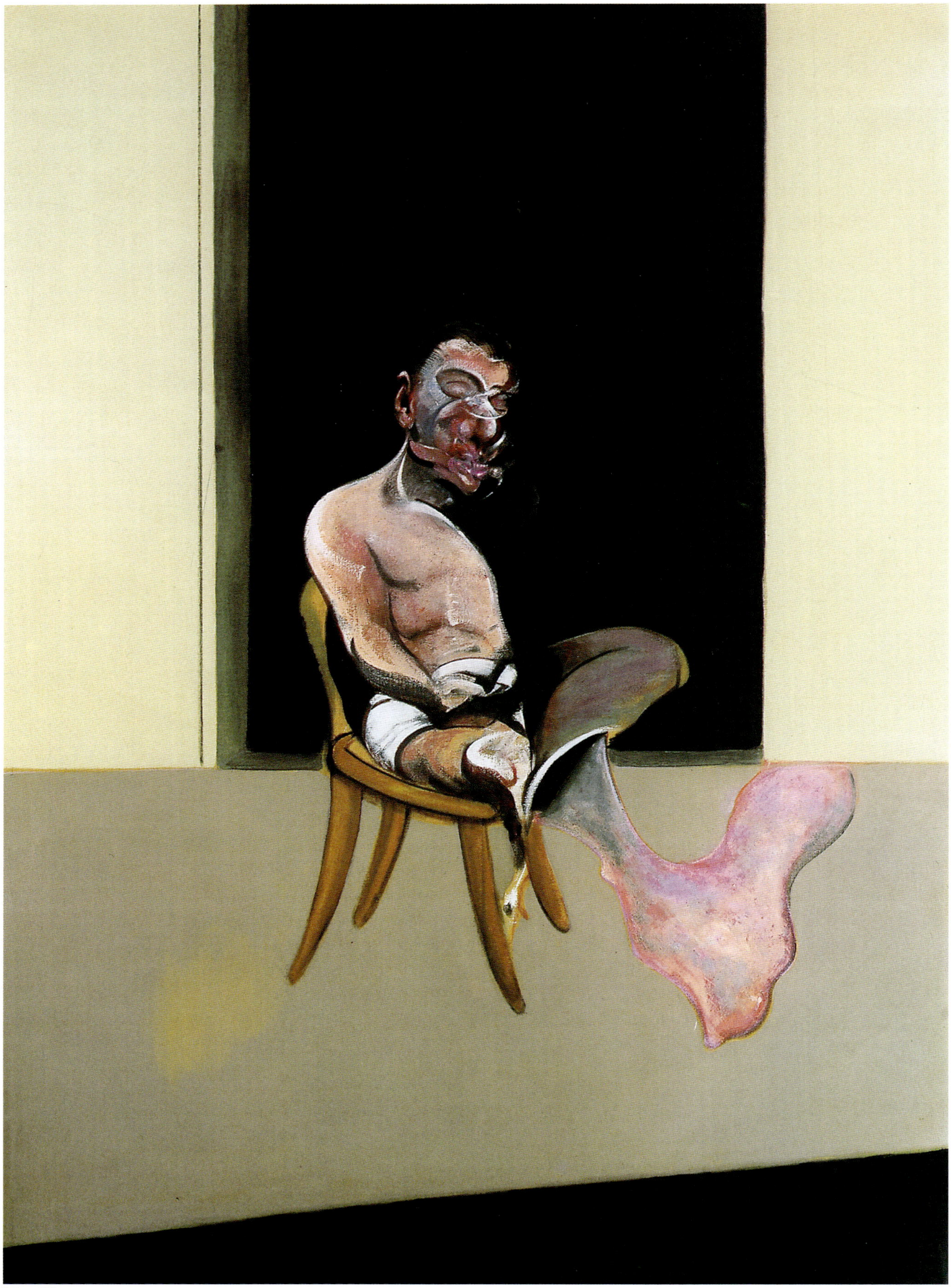

Cat. no. 132

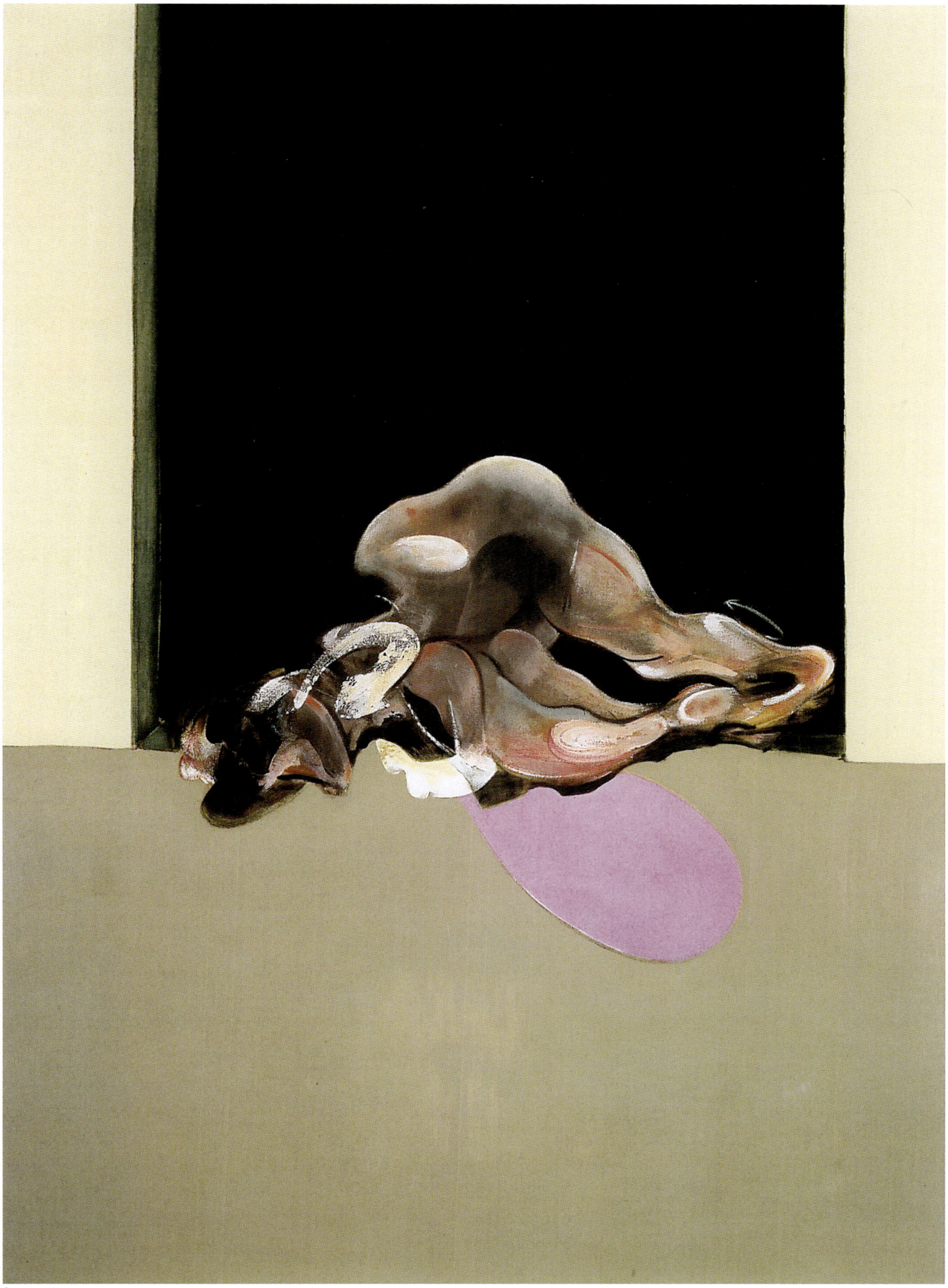

Cat. no. 132

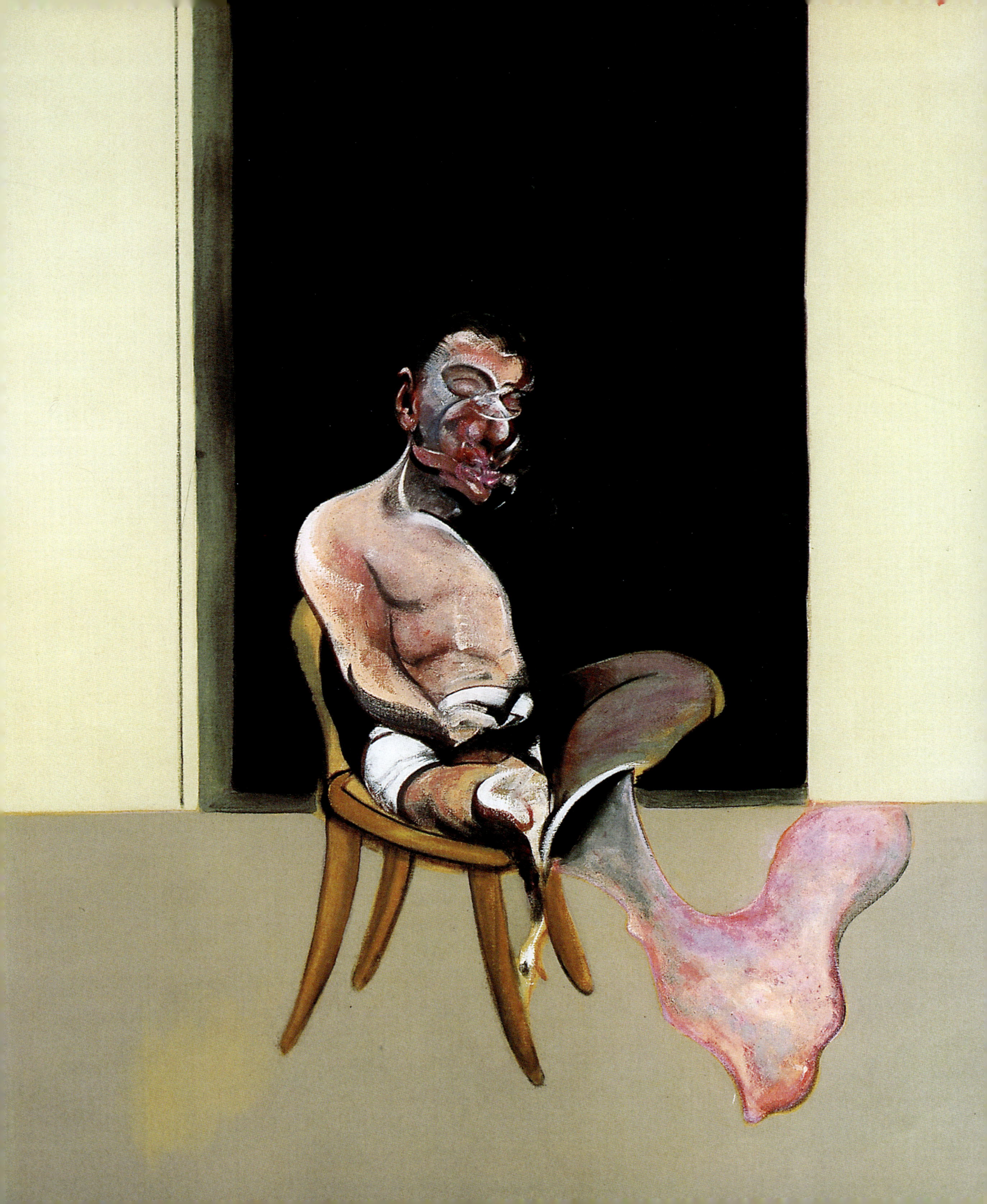

Front page: Cat. no. 132, detail

Cat. no. 133
Hand-written note by Francis Bacon in blue ball-point pen on leaf from Eadweard Muybridge's The Human Figure in Motion, Philadelphia, 1887, London, 1901 (later edition)
310 × 235 mm. Note undated
Dublin, Dublin City Gallery
The Hugh Lane, F1:59

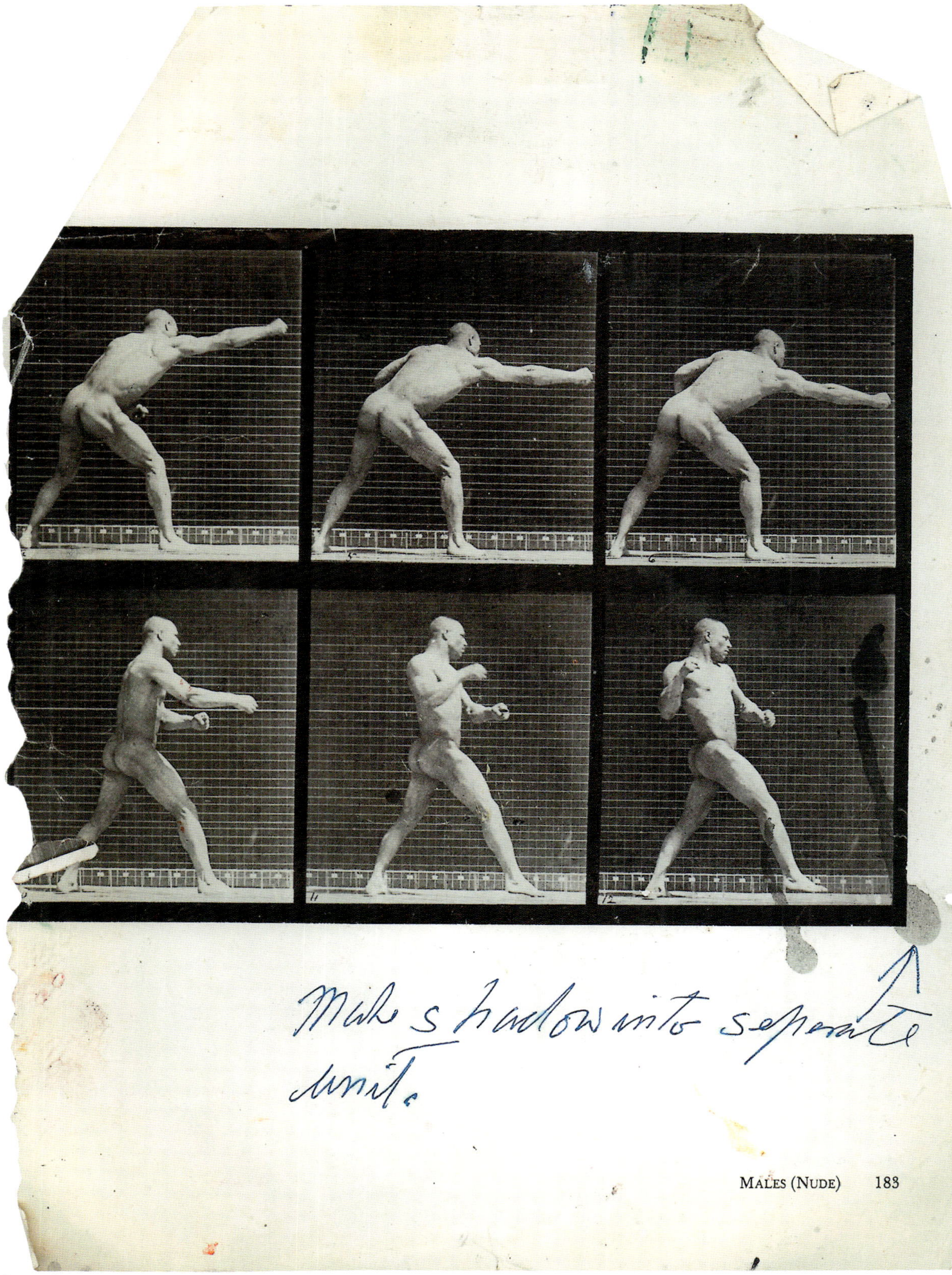

Cat. no. 133

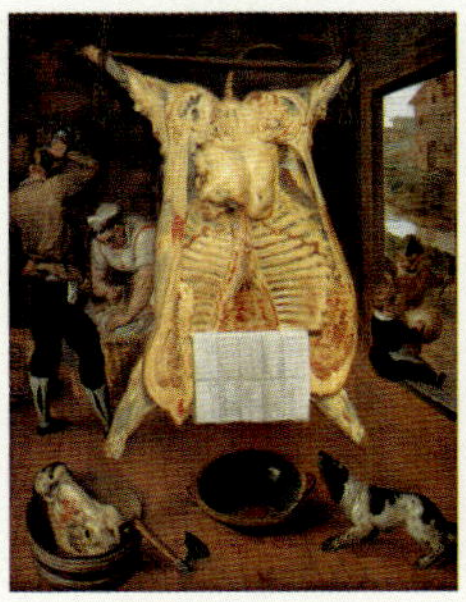
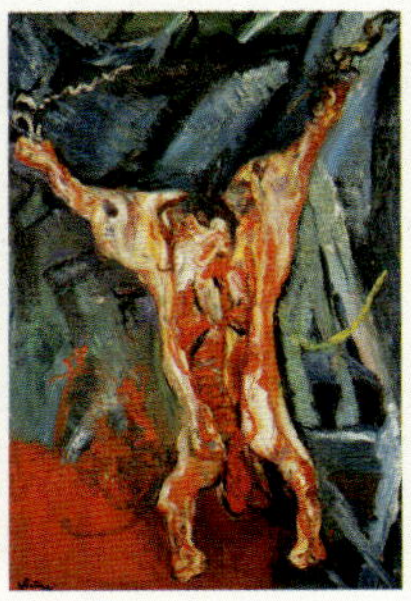

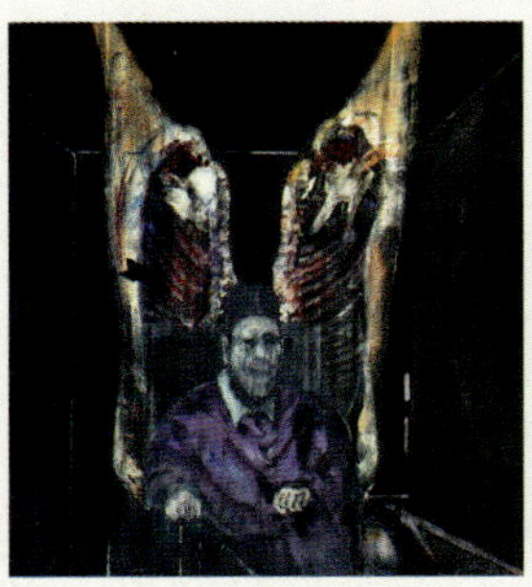
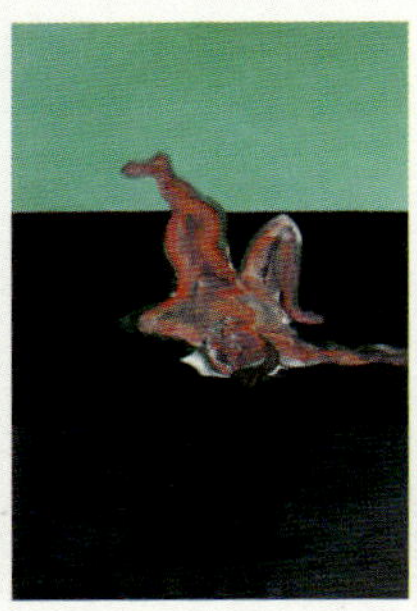
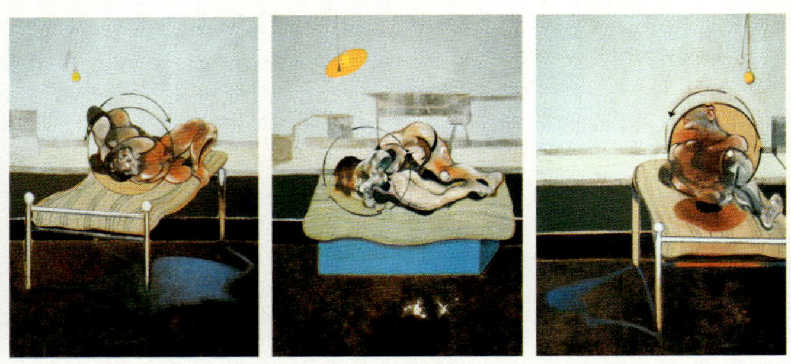

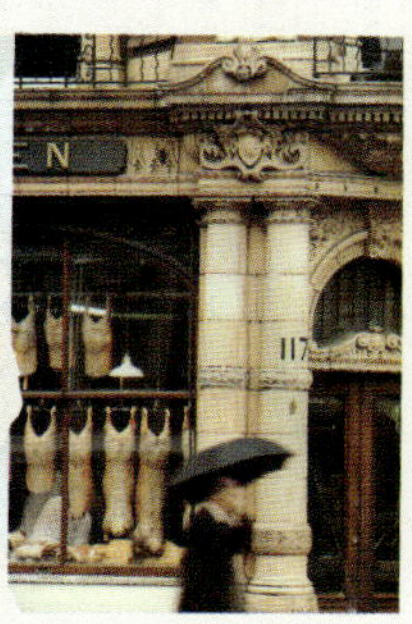
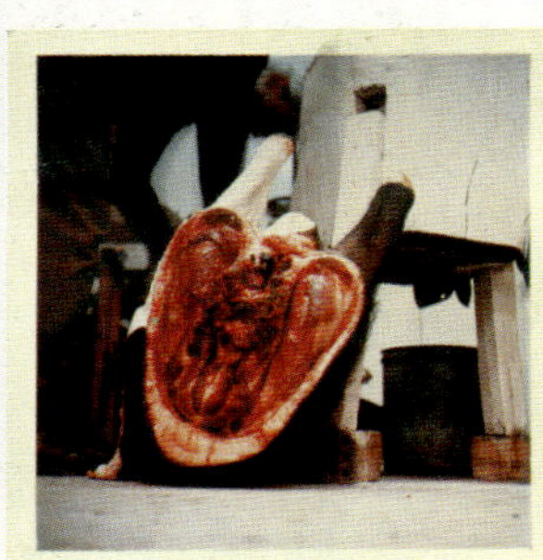
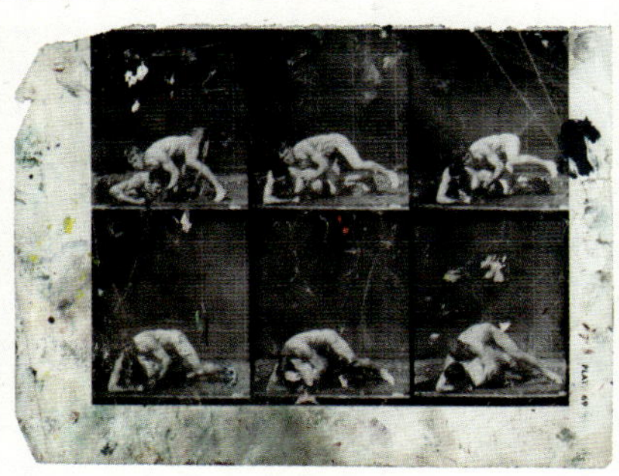
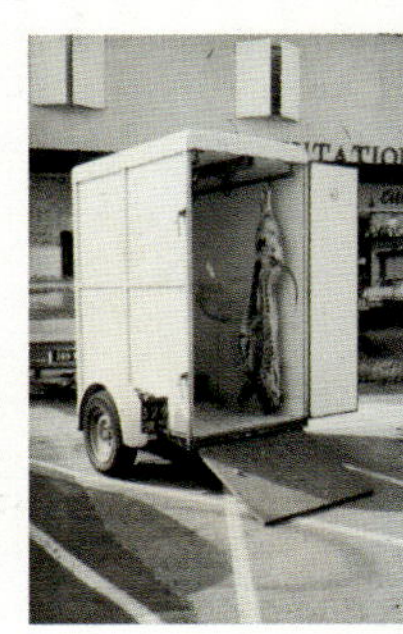
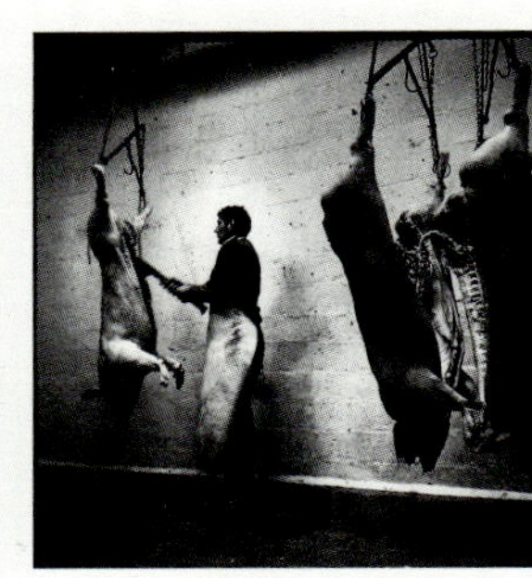

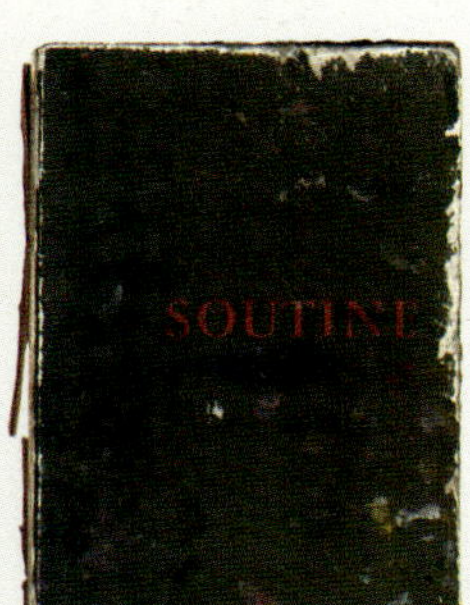
SOUTINE

Margarita Cappock

The Motif of Meat and Flesh

In conversation with David Sylvester in December 1962, Bacon explained, "I've always been very moved by pictures of slaughterhouses and meat, and to me they belong very much to the whole thing of the Crucifixion."[1] The Crucifixion, one of the central themes of Western art, had an altogether unchristian significance for Bacon, a professed atheist. It was devoid of any religious meaning and instead epitomised mutilation of the flesh, pain, butchery, and ultimately, death in a horrific manner. The Crucifixion rendered the human form into nothing more than a splayed slab of meat, yet one that possessed a strange kind of beauty. As an artist, Bacon was attracted to the vividness of the colours of raw meat but it also reminded him of his own mortality. In a somewhat humorous vein he commented, "Well, of course, we are meat, we are potential carcasses. If I go into a butcher's shop I always think it's surprising that I wasn't there instead of the animal."[2]

A friend from his early years in Ireland recalls how Bacon was mesmerised by the local butchers' shops in Sallins, County Kildare, near where he lived with his parents in the 1920s. He persuaded her to go in and closely view the hanging meat with him.[3]

The imagery of the slaughterhouse informed many of Bacon's paintings. From early in his artistic career, Bacon's experience of meat was mediated through photography. He was attracted to photographs of abattoirs, such as the striking images of La Villette abattoir in France, published in the European magazine *Documents,* edited by Georges Bataille between 1929 and 1930. While this particular magazine was not found in the Reece Mews studio, other items confirm Bacon's interest in meat (cat. nos. 139–142). They range from reproductions of other artists' depictions of meat, such as those of Rembrandt and Chaim Soutine, to more mundane images of joints of beef and mutton. A black-and-white photograph, taken in France, of an animal carcass hanging in a van has similarities with the painting *Carcass of Meat and Bird of Prey,* 1980. One of a series of colour photographs of a cross-section of an animal carcass and dated September 1966 calls to mind the heap of bloody clothes in the central panel of *Triptych Inspired by T.S. Eliot's "Sweeney Agonistes,"* painted the following year. Like several of the artist's other areas of interest, an obsession with meat stayed with Bacon his entire life.

A split carcass appears in *Painting, 1946 (Plate 1),* a work that began as an attempt to paint a bird alighting on a field and ended as an assemblage of meat carcasses and a mutilated, almost headless man beneath an umbrella. The manner in which the carcass is portrayed calls to mind a crucified figure with outstretched arms. Bacon's fascination with meat is also reflected in portrait photographs of the artist. An arresting photograph of Bacon, taken by John Deakin, appeared in Vogue magazine in 1952. Bacon was seen with his chest bare, holding two sides of a split carcass. A later painting, *Figure with Meat,* 1954 (cat. no. 136) featured a seated Pope flanked by two sides of beef. It is likely that the Deakin photograph provided a model for this work, although a Pope now takes the place of the artist. This is the only papal portrait in which Bacon includes a reference to the Crucifixion, now taking the form of a carcass.

Three Studies for a Crucifixion, 1962 (cat. no. 147) is a further development of the Crucifixion and meat theme. It also marks a change in Bacon's approach to the painting of flesh. In the late 1940s and up until the mid-1950s, his rendering of flesh is largely monochromatic. In the 1962 triptych, his handling of flesh becomes more visceral, more direct and even more sensuous. The use of vibrant reds and pinks in the rendering of meat and skin makes it much more graphic than in previous paintings. Bacon started this work in February 1962 shortly after he moved into 7, Reece Mews, South Kensington. It was included, along with 90 other works, in his first retrospective exhibition, which opened at Tate Gallery, London on 24 May 1962 and confirmed his pre-eminence among contemporary British artists. The hot, intense palette of reds and oranges recalls the vibrant orange background of *Three Studies for Figures at the Base of a Crucifixion,*

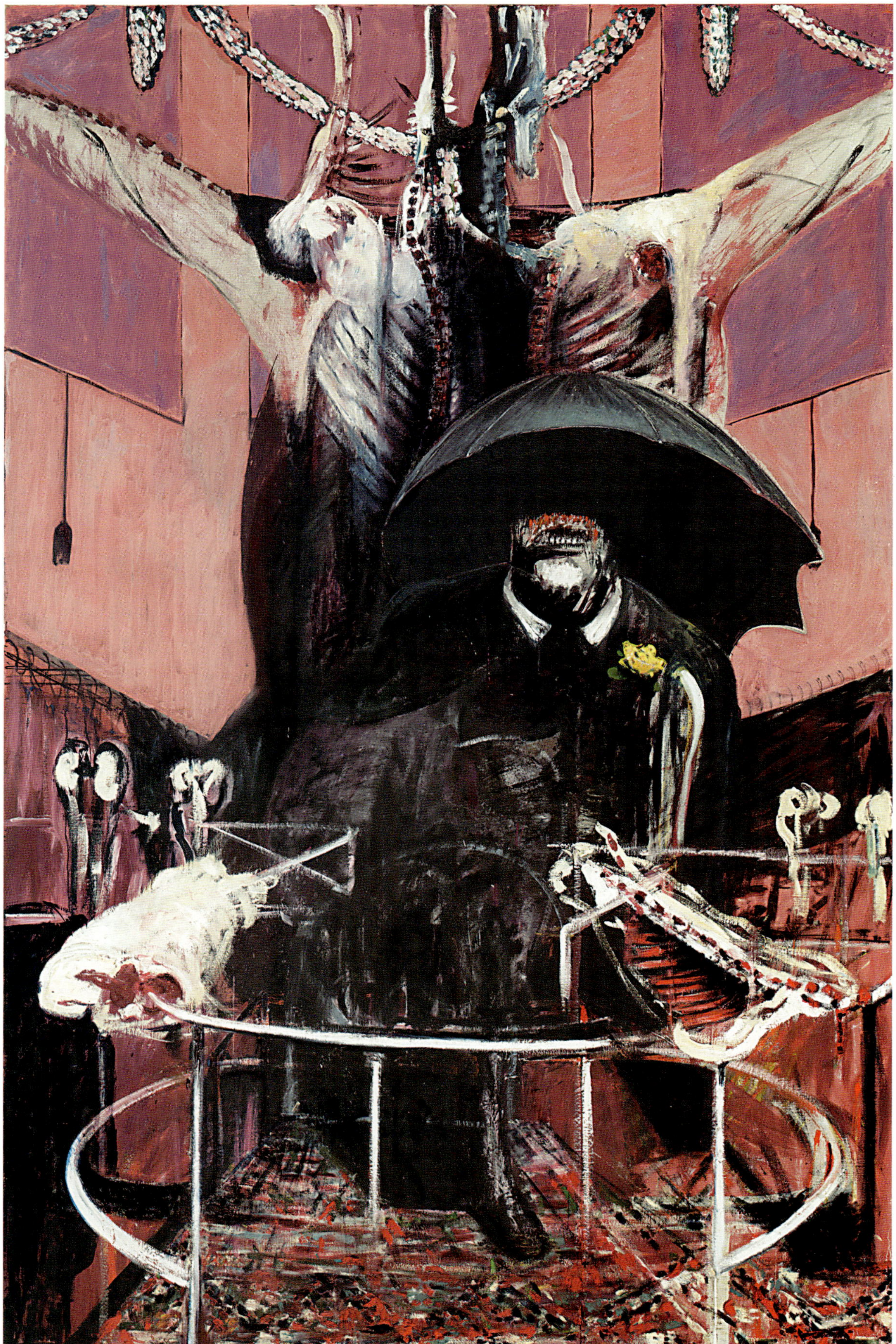

Plate 1: Francis Bacon, Painting 1946. Oil and pastel on canvas, 197.8 × 132.1 cm. New York, The Museum of Modern Art. (©: VBK, Wien, 2003.)

1944. The 1962 triptych was painted in an alcohol-fuelled fortnight, one of the few works he was able to make under the influence of drink. On this occasion, he felt alcohol had a liberating effect on him. Initially, he worked on the canvases separately and then, when nearing completion, brought them together.[4] After the work was finished and photographed, Bacon took it back and repainted part of the left-hand panel.

A split carcass appears in the lower left foreground of the left-hand panel and there is no ambiguity regarding its animal nature. In the central panel, the figure is most definitely human whereas in the right-hand panel it is an amalgamation of human and animal.

In the central panel, raw flesh is exposed and blood is spattered around the figure. The foot seems to be pierced by a white-topped nail, which is repeated on the pillow and above it, so that they also resemble bullet-holes. The spots of blood on the black blind behind the bed also give the impression that the figure has been shot. There is a marked contrast between the treatment of the figure in the central panel whose form is huddled and compressed with that of the figure in the right-hand panel who is stretched up and opened out. The result is equally horrific. Sylvester notes that this triptych marks a change in Bacon's treatment of the human body. While he had shown opened carcasses before, this was the first time that he had opened up the human body, which he does in the right-hand panel.[5] In numerous paintings, Bacon entirely collapsed the distinction between human and animal, and this figure retains vestiges of both. The fangs in the open mouth resemble those of primates and Bacon may well have consulted his copy of Václav Jan Stanek's book *Introducing Monkeys* (London, c. 1957) for ideas. The exposed ribs call to mind photographs of carcasses in a slaughterhouse, the main difference being that the grimace of this creature suggests that it is something living.

The influence of the Russian-born French painter Chaim Soutine, whom Bacon held in high esteem, is crucial in this triptych and most pronounced in the right-hand panel. Several parallels can be drawn between the work of Bacon and Soutine; both were untrained and valued spontaneity in painting. In terms of subject matter, their work features exaggeratedly distorted human figures and both artists had a keen interest in carcasses. Furthermore, both cited the work of Rembrandt as an important influence. An encounter with Rembrandt's *Slaughtered Ox*, 1655 in the Louvre had prompted Soutine to produce a number of still lifes of animal carcasses, beginning around 1922. While Bacon greatly admired Rembrandt's self-portraits, he was less impressed with his *Slaughtered Ox*, which he described as looking like "a lump of wax hanging there."[6]

The motif of the slaughtered animal featured in 16th-century Dutch genre paintings such as *The Slaughtered Ox*, 1566 (cat. no. 134), by the Antwerp-born artist Marten van Cleve. However, it was usually as an additional feature to the main theme such as a marriage scene, a painting of the seasons or a genre scene. By contrast, in Rembrandt's painting the focus is entirely on the dead animal and the painting can be read as a metaphor for death and suffering. In van Cleve's work the detail of the carcass is studiously observed, but despite this display of death, the lively scene going on in the background is light-hearted with the figures almost oblivious to the presence of the carcass. A child, seated in the doorway, inflates the animal's bladder. These genre elements serve to enliven the scene. Van Cleve's carcass differs also from those in Bacon and Soutine's works in that the beast represented is emphatically dead. The brushstrokes do not bring it to life. With the carcasses of Rembrandt and Soutine, there is almost a human quality to the animals. Bacon's treatment is, to an extent, the reverse in that he raises the suggestion of the human only to dehumanise it and make it more animal-like. This is achieved by subjecting the figure to unseen acts of startling and unaccountable violence. It would appear that Bacon enhances the sense of ambiguity between carcass and living flesh so that he can convey pain, the most direct vehicle of sensation in art as well as life.

On occasion Soutine's works may also have

provided a source for Bacon. A copy of the catalogue for Soutine's exhibition at the Museum of Modern Art, New York in 1950 was found in Bacon's studio (cat. no. 143). It is covered with smudges and fingerprints of paint, indicating extensive use. It also contains two monochromatic sketches in black paint, which Bacon made on the front and back end-papers. Around 1953 Bacon took David Sylvester to the Redfern Gallery in London to see a small number of paintings by Soutine who, along with Bonnard and Picasso, was one of the few 20th-century artists admired by Bacon. The works on display included two or three landscapes which Soutine did when he stayed at Céret, in the French Pyrenees, between 1919 and 1923. In 1957 Bacon completed a series of works after a reproduction of van Gogh's painting *The Painter on the Road to Tarascon*. However, rather than employing van Gogh's striated brushstrokes, Bacon adopted a free-flowing expressive style more reminiscent of Soutine's Céret landscapes.[7] Soutine's influence became even more apparent in the 1962 triptych. He must have been aware of Soutine's *Side of Beef*, c. 1922–23 (reproduced in black and white in the Soutine catalogue) as the corkscrew effect in the right-hand panel of his triptych has strong echoes of this work.

Apart from inciting an element of spontaneity, Soutine's method of working differed significantly from that of Bacon. While Bacon collected photographs of slaughterhouses and carcasses, Soutine preferred to work from life. He practised painting real pieces of meat, which he had procured from friends who worked in a slaughterhouse. In 1925, Soutine obtained the carcass of an entire steer, which he brought to his studio in the rue du Mont St. Gothard. He did a number of paintings and sketches of this, and as the steer decomposed, it is alleged that Soutine paid someone to fan away the flies, which were obscuring its beautiful colours.[8] He also got a bucket of blood from a butcher in order to freshen up the meat as it dried out. *Carcass of Beef*, 1925 (cat. no. 135) is one of the resulting paintings. The vitality of this work, the vibrancy of the colours and the frenzied energy of the brushstrokes almost belie the fact that it is a painting of a dead animal. After the series of carcasses, Soutine moved on to a series of plucked or half-plucked fowl. Bacon also produced a small number of paintings on this subject.[9] Bacon was not alone in his admiration for Soutine and his handling of flesh. The Dutch-American artist Willem de Kooning cited Soutine as his favourite painter. Like Bacon, he admired the spontaneity of gesture and emotional resonance in Soutine's painting. De Kooning was also an admirer of Bacon's work and was particularly struck by *Painting*, 1946, acquired by the Museum of Modern Art in New York in October 1948. Bacon was less generous about de Kooning's paintings and referred to his women series as "playing-cards".[10] De Kooning once said, "You can't always tell a man from a woman in my painting. Those women are perhaps the feminine side of me – but with big shoulders. I'm not so big, but I'm very masculine and this masculinity mixed with femininity comes out on the canvas."[11] This statement is interesting in the context of Bacon's series of paintings of lying figures to which *Lying Figure #2,* 1959 (cat. no. 137) belongs. There are six works – four paintings and two drawings – which show a figure lying on a sofa. The body of the figure in each of these works is androgynous and only one of them, *Reclining Woman,* 1961, actually specifies the gender of the figure. Sylvester suggests that the bodies of these figures may have been based on the artist's own, although Bacon denied this.[12] *Lying Figure #2,* 1959 was done in St. Ives, a coastal town in Cornwall, where Bacon was based from late September 1959 until the middle of January 1960. Again there is a clear differentiation between the figure and the flat bands of colour on which it is placed.

The motif of a figure lying on a bed is more fully developed in his painting *Three Studies for Figures on Beds,* 1972 (cat. no. 138). The central panel of this triptych is a variation on *Two Figures,* 1953, though the later painting pays homage to Bacon's former lover George Dyer. In the 1950s, Bacon had begun to tackle the male nude in a more forthright manner, and *Two Figures,* 1953 is the most notable example of this tendency. The poses of the coupling male figures in both paintings were based on Eadweard Muybridge's sequential images of wrestlers in *The Human Figure in Motion* (1901) (cat. no. 144) but manipulated to more personal and sexual ends. In 1953, Bacon was involved in an emotionally turbulent and sadomasochistic relationship with Peter Lacy, and the facial features of the two figures are unquestionably those of Lacy and Bacon. As Bacon once said, "I very often think of people's bodies that I've known, I think of the contours of those bodies that have particularly affected me, but then they're grafted very often onto Muybridge bodies."[13]

In Bacon's mind, meat, flesh and sex were intrinsically linked and nowhere is this more apparent than in *Three Studies for Figures on Beds,* 1972. In a late interview, Bacon discussed meat and sex in the same breath. He did so in order to underline what he saw as our animal natures and impulses, and to stress our mortality. "All the inhabitants of this planet are made of meat. And most of them are carnivores. And when you fuck, it's a piece of meat penetrating another piece of meat."[14] This triptych is one of Bacon's most sexually explicit works. In the left-hand and central panels of the triptych, flesh is depicted as a malleable substance almost without bone. The legs of the figures in the central panel undulate and their flesh merges together in the upper section of their bodies as they become seemingly indistinguishable from one another. In the central panel, Bacon exposes the constituents of flesh as the head of the figure dissolves into blood that seeps out onto the mattress. This is further emphasised in the right-hand panel where the central area of the figure becomes a pool of blood and viscera without the protective membrane of skin. This red area contrasts markedly with the greyness of the figure's head and leg, whose pallor is that of decomposing flesh. Two broken white lines give the impression of partially visible bone.

Lorenza Trucchi notes that *Three Studies for Figures on Beds,* 1972 differs from other triptychs by Bacon because, "[...] the sexual battle explodes simultaneously in all three parts of the paintings. In dramatic contrast to the foreground of bodies quivering in orgasm, their frenzy pointed up by concentric arrows, the setting is calm and luminous, possibly a gymnasium with a few essential pieces of equipment."[15] The presence of repeated motifs, such as the circles and directional arrows, can be directly linked to K.C. Clark's publication, *Positioning in Radiography* (1939), a medical textbook which contained over 2,500 black-and-white photographic illustrations, diagrams and text on X-ray techniques. The rotary motion suggested by the circles and arrows has also been likened to the halting movement of the waterwheel and chocolate grinder in Marcel Duchamp's image of frustrated love, *La mariée mise à nu par ses célibataires, même (The Large Glass)*, 1915–1923.[16] Bacon was drawn to the diagrammatic aids in illustrated books and magazines on sport, such as judo and karate, of which he had a large collection. Arrows and other devices lend an objectified and even scientific detachment to the presentation of the body. The contorted and damaged figures counter this strategy. They involve us through their movement, grimaces and palpable life.

Bacon's treatment of flesh in his work changed quite considerably during the course of his life. In early works, the artist's style of painting flesh reflects an emphasis on its thickness and textural density, rather than its colour. In conversation with David Sylvester, Bacon remarked that "[...] the texture of, for instance of rhinoceros skin would help me think about the texture of human skin"[17] and this is apparent in the clogged surfaces of works such as *Painting,* 1946 and *Head II,* 1949 (cat. no. 26). The flesh depicted in these works from the late 1940s is of a pallid nature, drained of its life-giving qualities but evocative in substance. In the 1960s, his handling of flesh became much bolder and more painterly. It is pushed towards the vulgar and excessive but rescued by an enhanced fluency and a mastery of suggestion. In later works from the 1980s he used spray paints to achieve a finer, more granular finish. On occasion, there is a sense of ambiguity, as flesh becomes indistinguishable from shadow and liberates itself from the body. Bacon addressed this notion in one of his handwritten notes where he refers to a "flesh coloured shadow." It is a fuller reflection of the artist's comment that "Appearance is like a continually floating thing."[18] In several late works, the fragility of human flesh is emphasised and the open wound appears in stark contrast to the smooth, lightly bruised skin. There is a greater precision of effect in these paintings, bordering on the clinical, and indicative of a more medical outlook on flesh and an awareness of his own physical decline.

In a letter to the Irish artist Louis le Brocquy, dated 20 March 1992, Bacon wrote that his lungs were "pulverised by asthma," a typically forceful description of his condition. The same letter provides evidence that at the end of his life (he was to die the following month), his interest in meat had endured. He wrote, "At the Saatchi collection there is a very interesting installation by a young man called Damien Hirst called 'A Thousand Years' it is of a cows head in one compartment and in the second part they breed the flies which swarm around the cows head it really works." For Bacon, meat served as a reminder of the cycle of life and death, a central theme of the work described. Bacon could not have missed the paradox that as his own flesh failed him, another artist, young and determined, was prepared to look at the motif of meat and flesh with renewed vigour and ambition.

[1] Sylvester 1999, p. 23.
[2] Sylvester 1999, p. 46.
[3] Molony 1977, p. 9.
[4] Sylvester 1999, p. 13. As Bacon's studio became increasingly cluttered, it would have become extremely difficult, if not impossible, to have such an assemblage of panels across the room.
[5] Sylvester 2000, p. 108.
[6] Sylvester 2000, p. 241.
[7] Sylvester 2000, p. 88.
[8] Exh. Cat. New York 1950, p. 68.
[9] *Triptych,* 1981–82 (Left Panel) shows a bird hanging upside down.
[10] Peppiatt 1996, p. 182.
[11] Ibid.
[12] Sylvester 1999.
[13] Sylvester 2000, p. 72.
[14] "Francis Bacon: I painted to be loved", Interview with Francis Giacobetti, *The Art Newspaper,* No. 137, June 2003, p. 29.
[15] Trucchi 1976, p. 17.
[16] Davies – Yard 1986, p. 83.
[17] Sylvester 1999, p. 32.
[18] Sylvester 1999, p. 118.

Cat. no. 134
Maerten van Cleve
Gutted
1566
Oil on wood, 68 × 53.5 cm
Vienna, Kunsthistorisches Museum,
Picture Gallery, inv. no. 1970

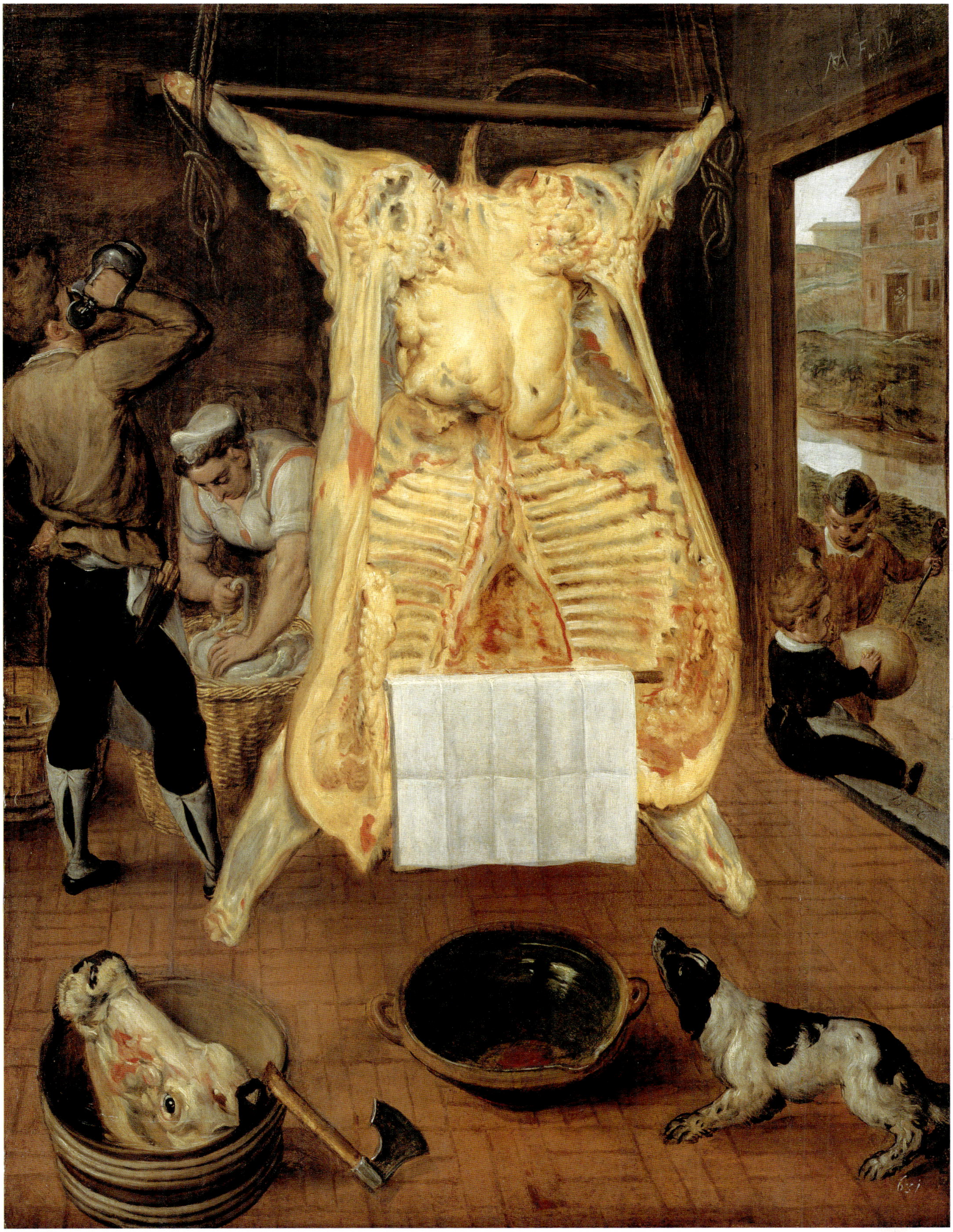

Cat. no. 134

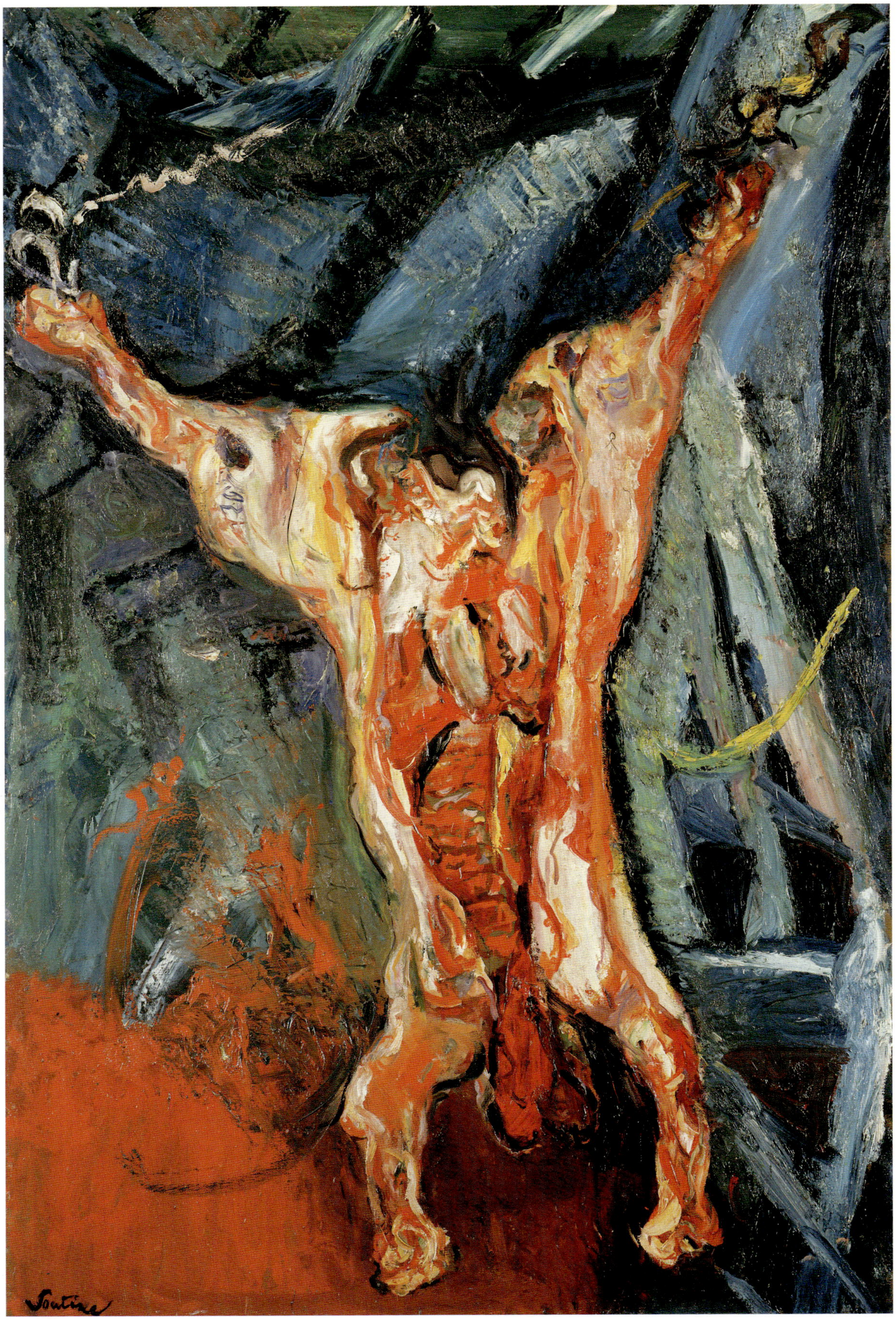
Cat. no. 135

Cat. no. 135
Chaim Soutine
Carcass of Beef
1925
Oil on canvas, 116.21 × 80.65 cm
Minneapolis, Minneapolis Institute of Arts, Gift of Mr. And Mrs. Donald Winston and an anonymous donor

Cat. no. 136
Francis Bacon
Figure with Meat
1954
Oil on canvas, 129.9 × 121.9 cm
Chicago, Art Institute of Chicago, Harriott A. Fox Fund 1956.1201

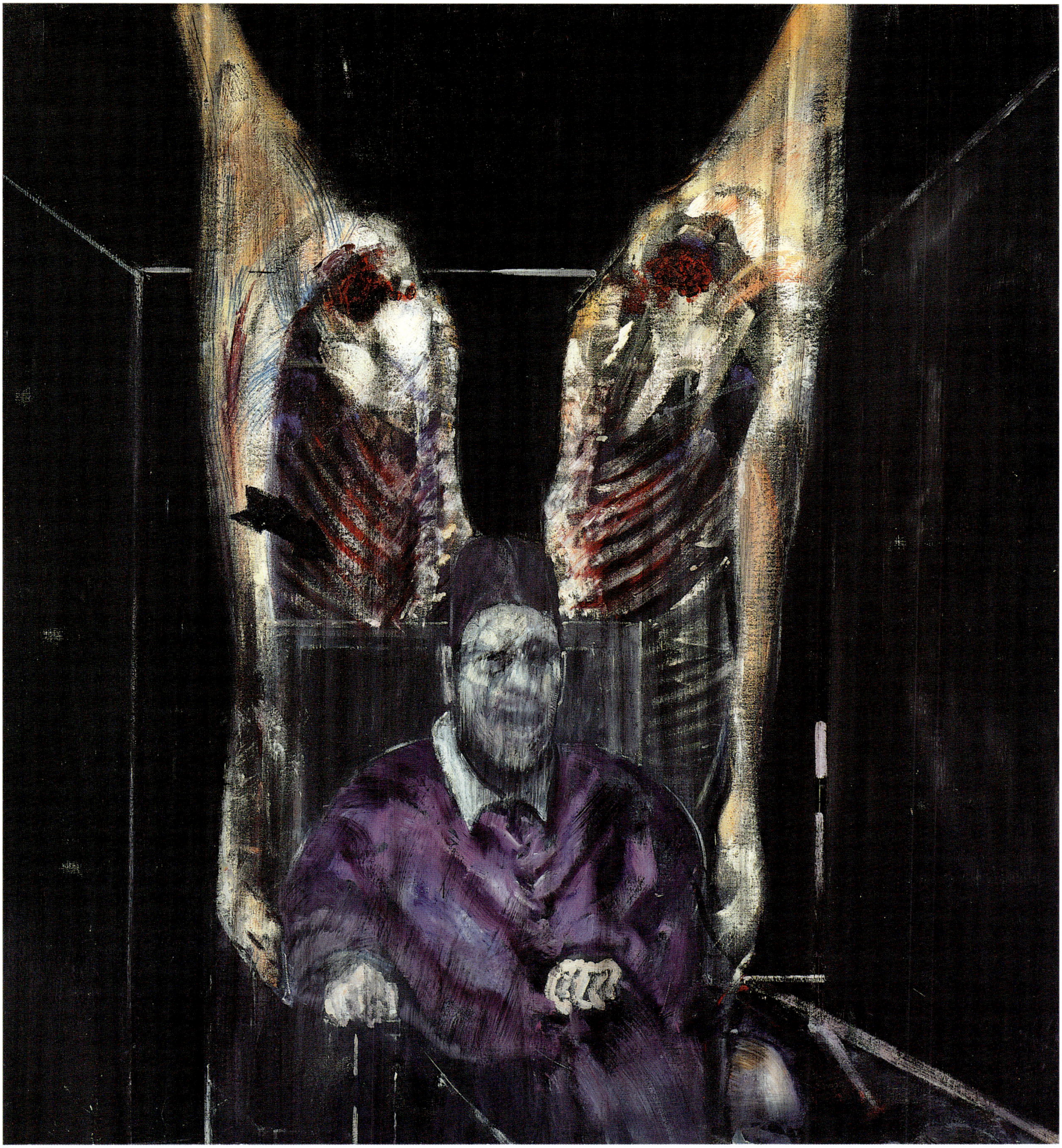

Cat. no. 136

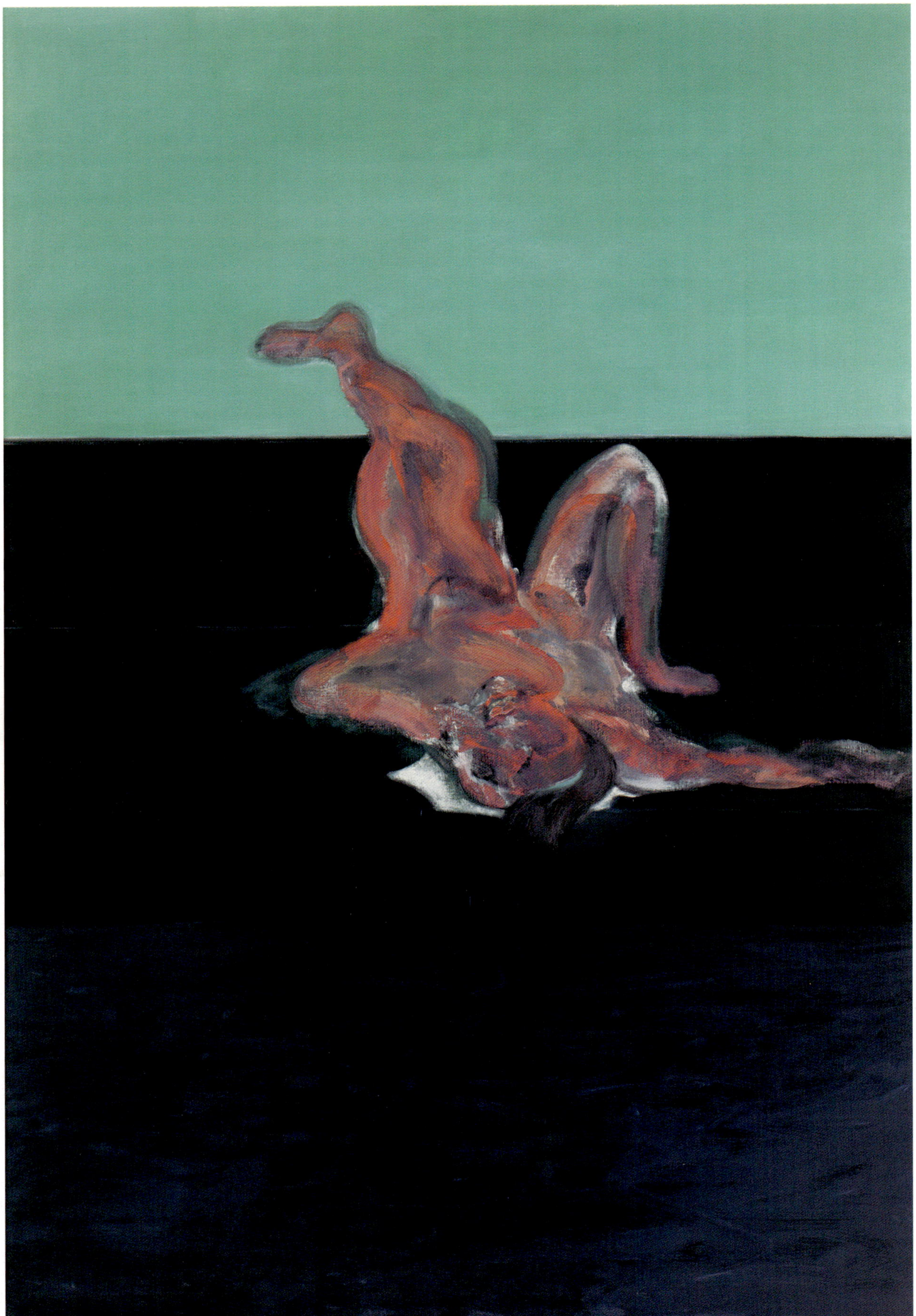
Cat. no. 137

Cat. no. 137
Francis Bacon
Lying Figure #2
1959
Oil on canvas, 185.4 × 147.3 cm
New York, Collection Franklin
and Susanne Konigsberg

On p. 321: Cat. no. 138, detail

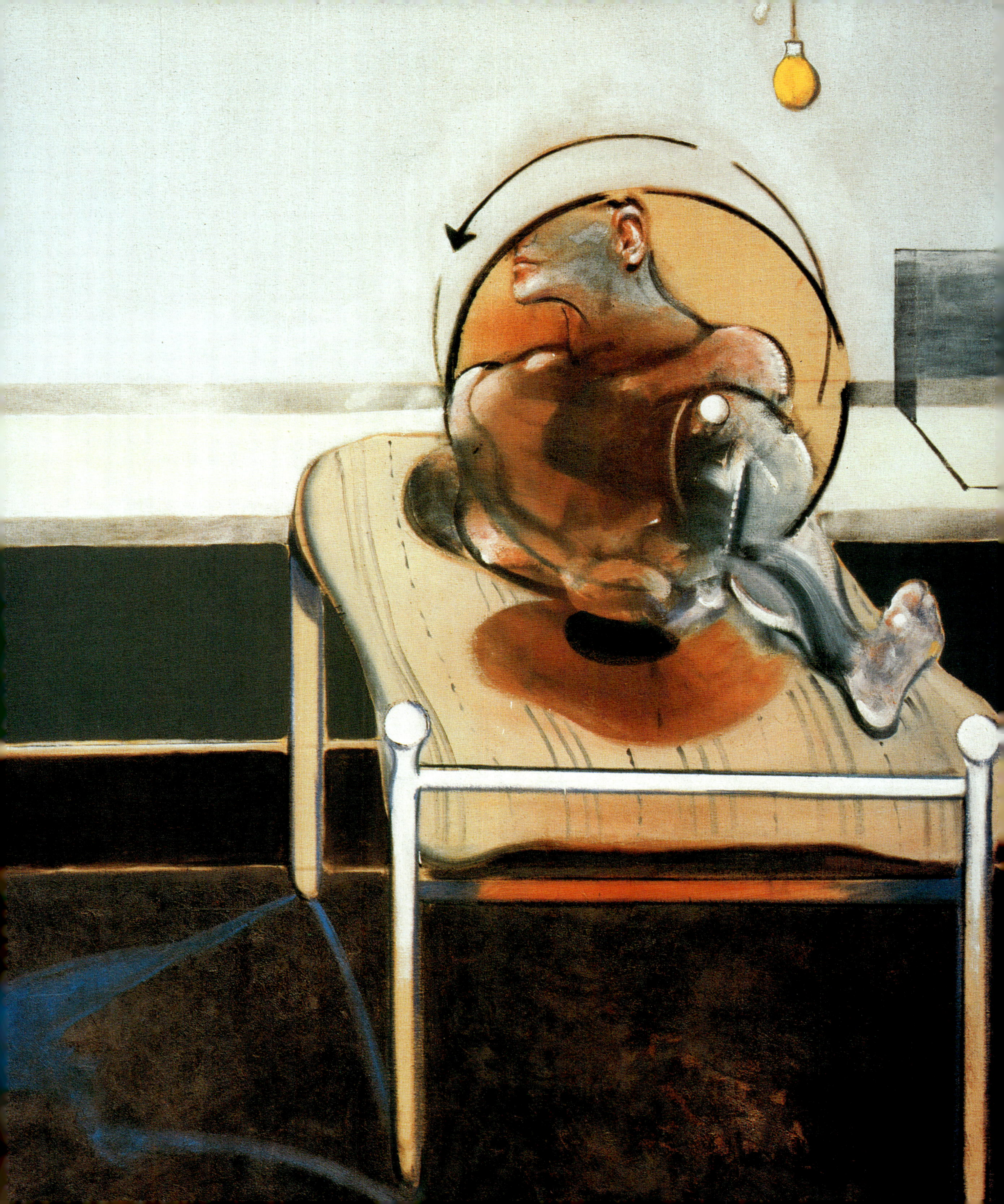

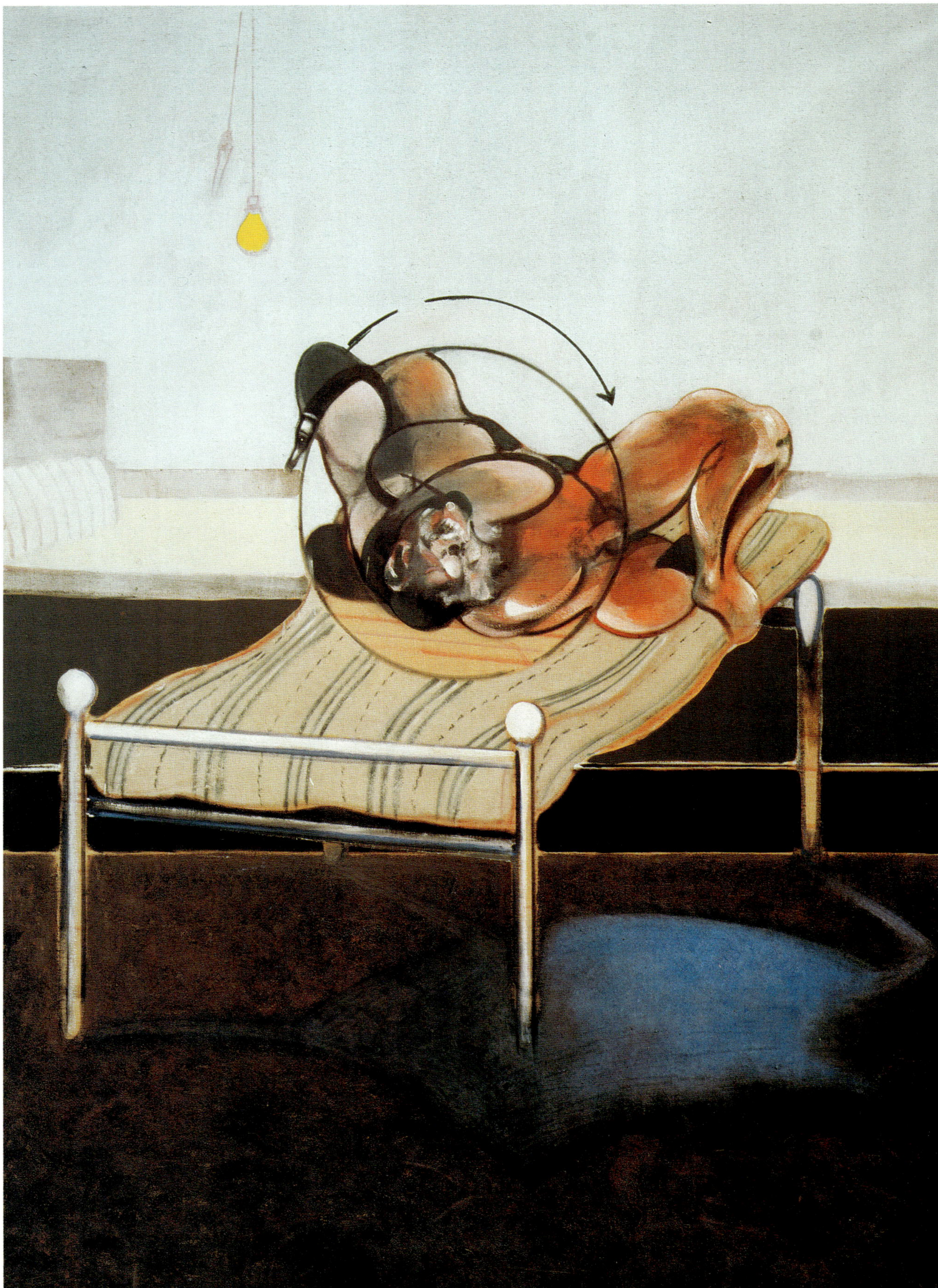

Cat. no. 138

Cat. no. 138
Francis Bacon
Three Studies of Figures on Beds
1972
Oil and pastel on canvas, triptych,
each panel 198 × 147.5 cm
Switzerland, Private Collection

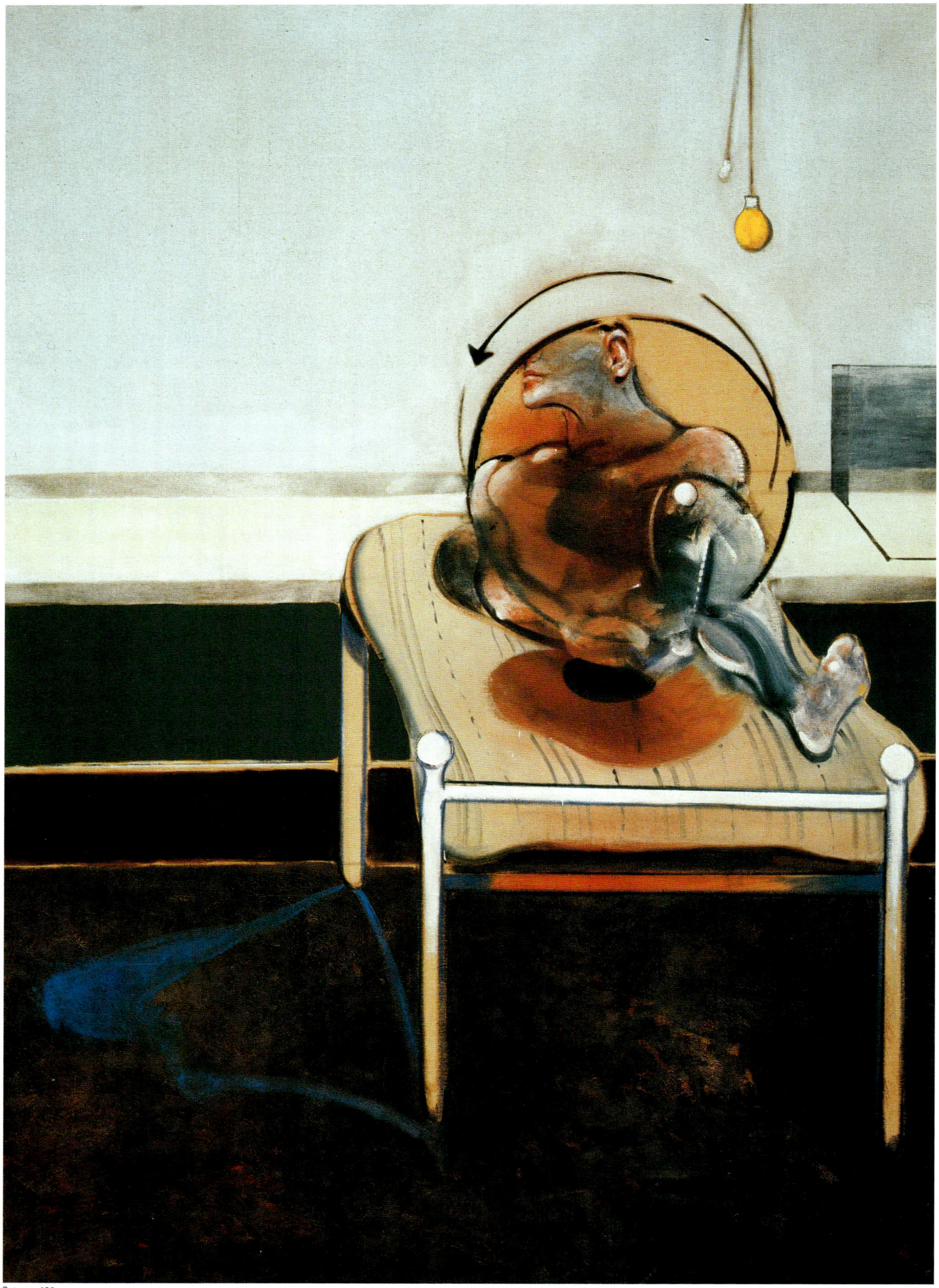

Cat. no. 138

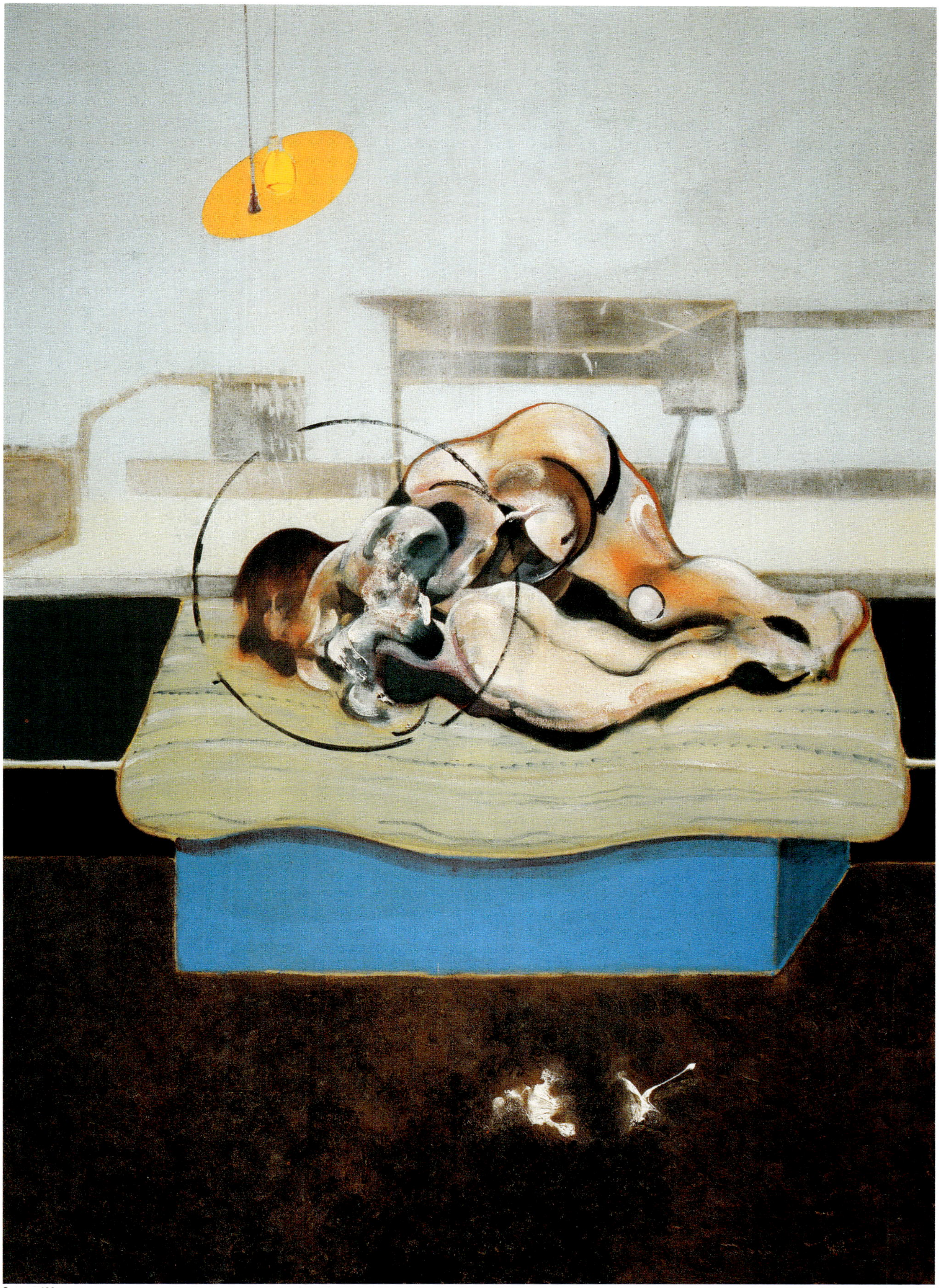

Cat. no. 138

Cat. no. 139
Leaf with colour illustration of animal carcasses hanging in a butcher's window, from unidentified French magazine
284 × 203 mm
Dublin, Dublin City Gallery The Hugh Lane, F112:63

Cat. no. 140
Colour photograph of a cross-section of an animal carcass. Stamp on verso, "Sept. 1966"
89 × 89 mm
Dublin, Dublin City Gallery The Hugh Lane, F15:80

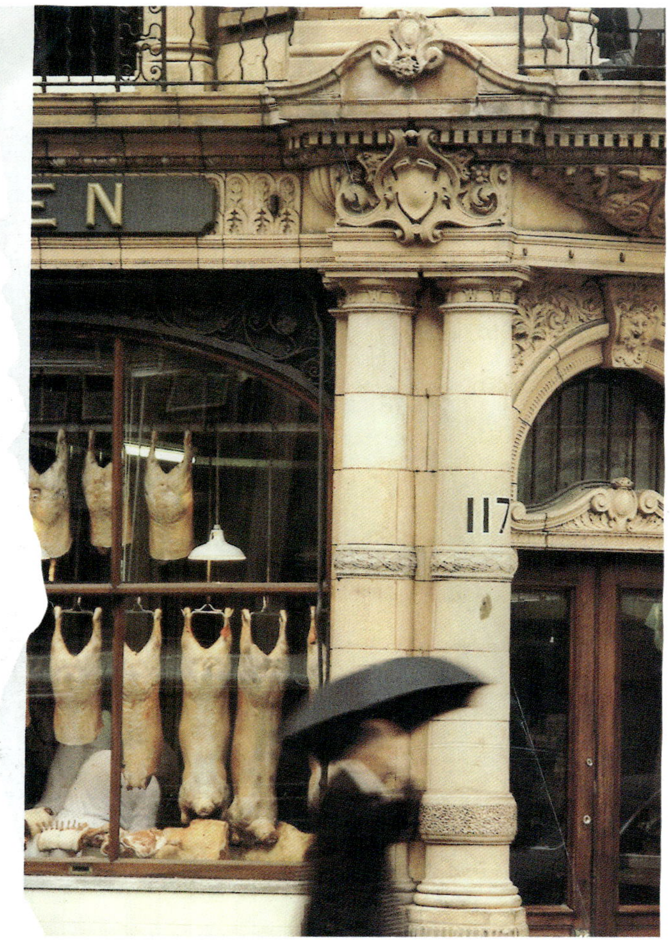

Cat. no. 139

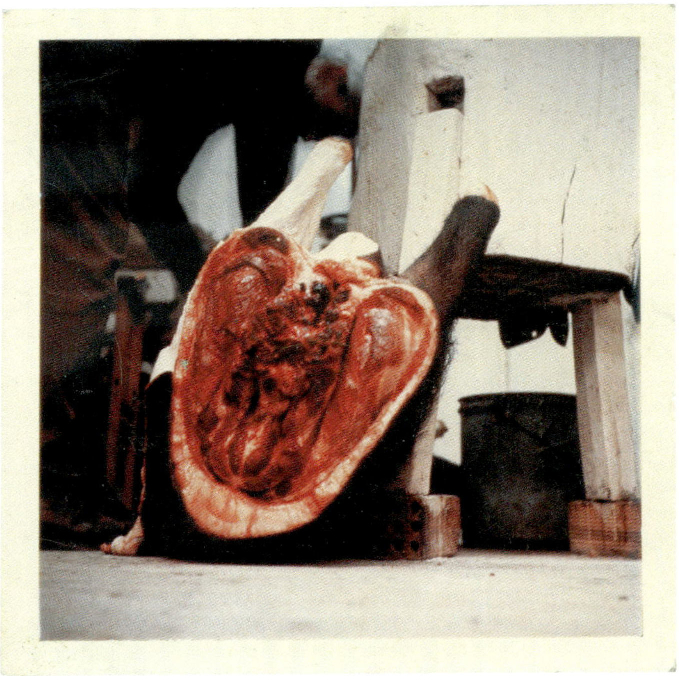

Cat. no. 140

Cat. no. 141
Black-and-white photograph of animal carcasses hanging in a trailer. Photograph taken in France and undated
127 × 86 mm
Dublin, Dublin City Gallery The Hugh Lane, F23:12

Cat. no. 142
Black-and-white photograph of a butcher cutting open a pig carcass in an abattoir. Photograph undated
238 × 240 mm
Dublin, Dublin City Gallery The Hugh Lane, F108:71

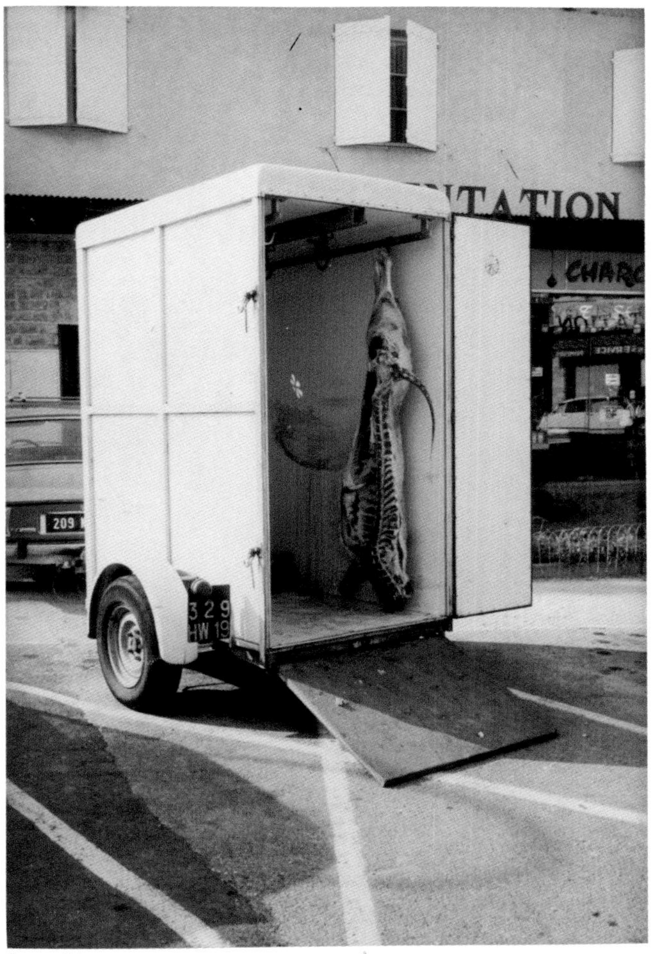

Cat. no. 141

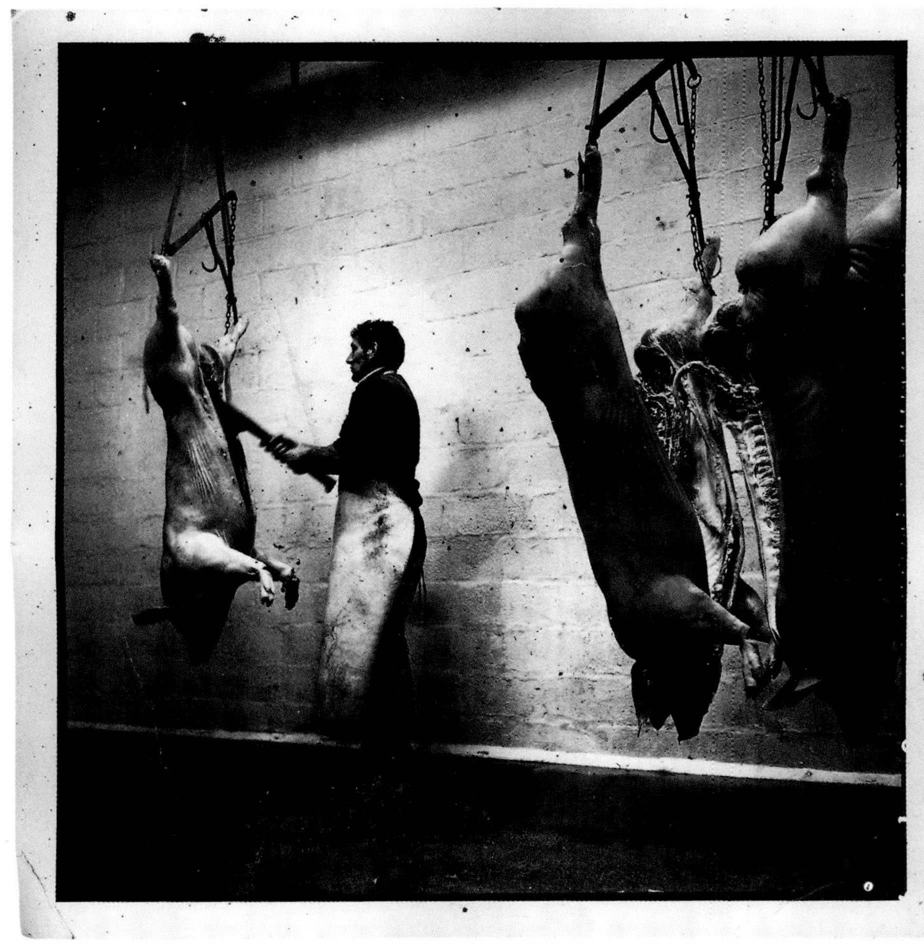

Cat. no. 142

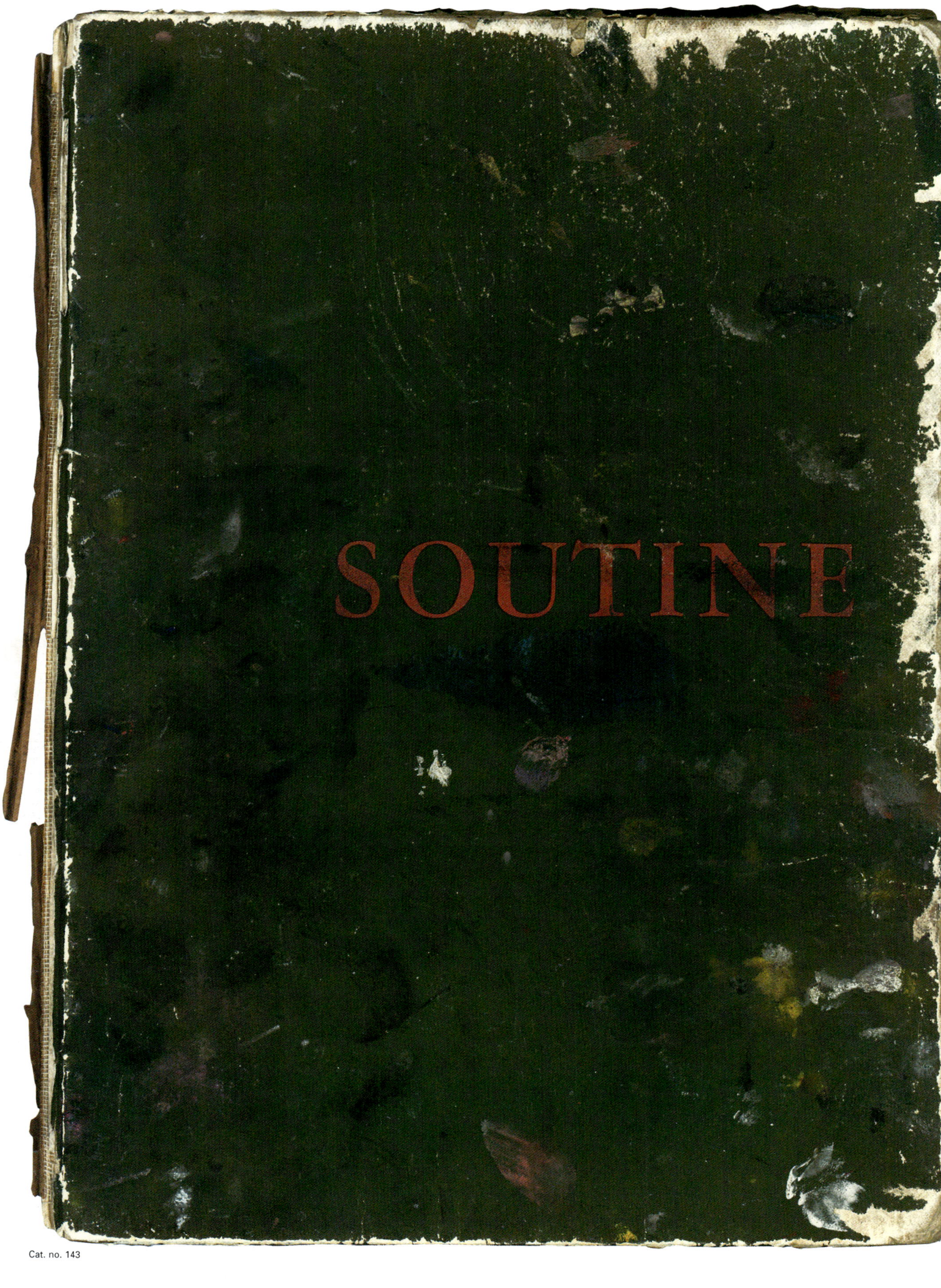

Cat. no. 143

Cat. no. 143
Drawing by Francis Bacon in black paint on front end-papers of the Chaim Soutine exhibition catalogue, Museum of Modern Art, New York, 1950
258 × 190 × 14 mm
Dublin, Dublin City Gallery
The Hugh Lane, F1A:149

Cat. no. 144
Black-and-white images of two wrestlers. Leaf from book, Eadweard Muybridge, The Human Figure in Motion, Philadelphia, 1887, London, 1901 (later edition)
273 × 197 mm
Dublin, Dublin City Gallery
The Hugh Lane, F1A:27

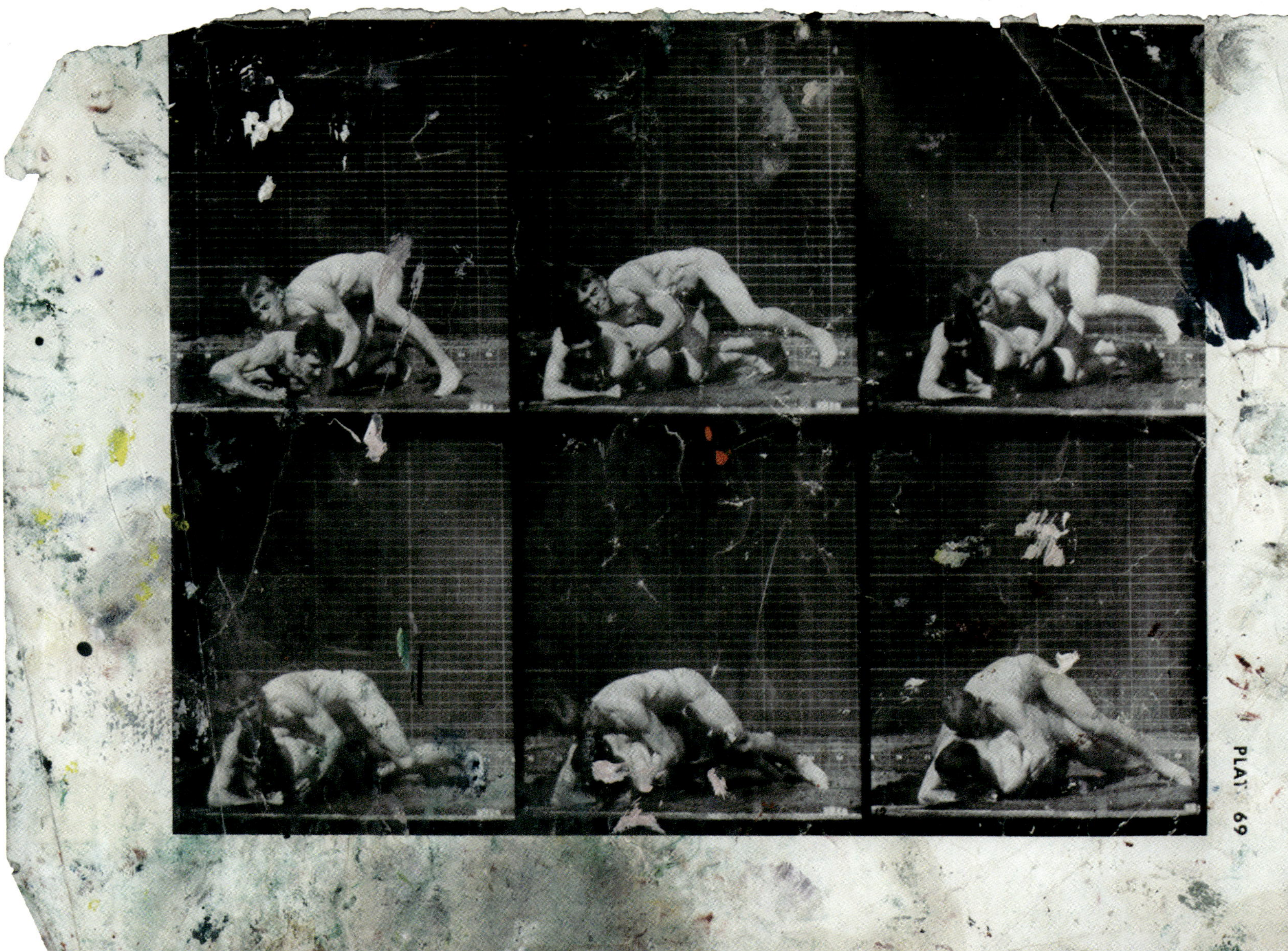

Cat. no. 144

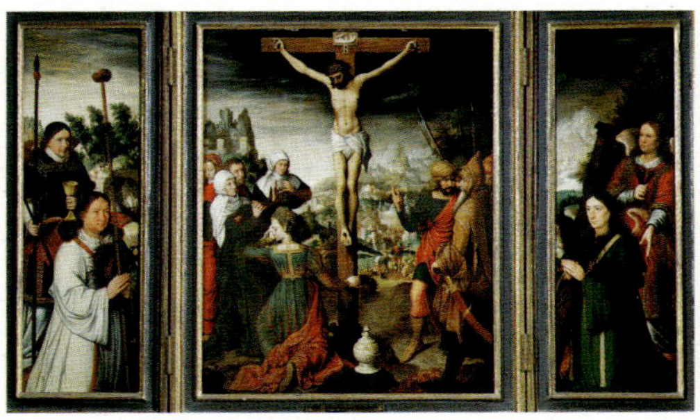

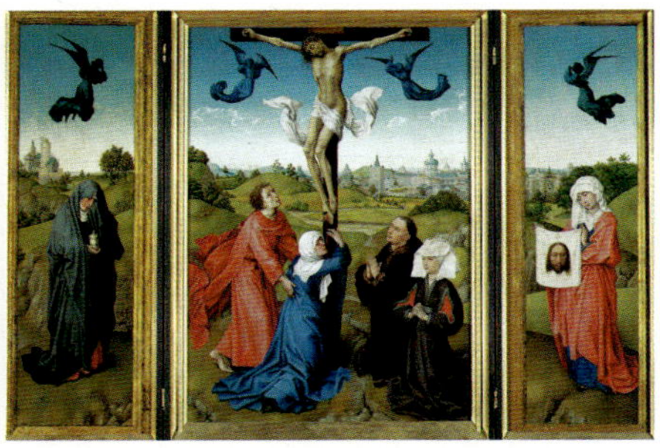

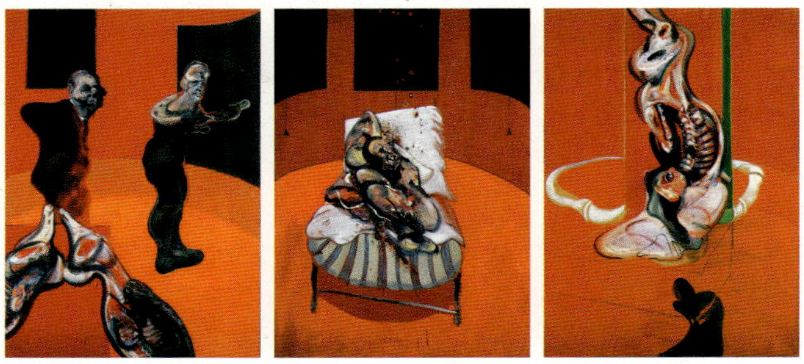

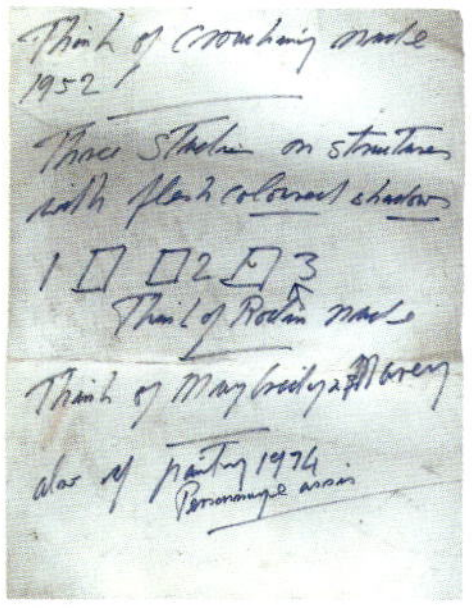
Think of crouching nude
1952
Three studies on structures
with flesh coloured shadow
1 ☐ ☐ 2 ☐ 3
Think of Rodin nude
Think of Muybridge & Marey
of painting 1974
Personnage assis

Verena Gamper

The Motif of the Crucifixion in Triptych Format

A theme that fascinated Bacon as a painter and that he returned to repeatedly over the decades was the Crucifixion. With it he made a public appearance in 1933 in a publication of Herbert Read,[1] and he turned to it for a final time in 1965. After that, while Bacon no longer considered the Crucifixion to be a valid motif, the format of the triptych – which is closely related to the Crucifixion in his work – still remained a pictorial form he frequently used, especially in the final decades of his creative life.

According to Bacon's stated view, the Crucifixion, like the motif of the Pope, was not tied to the Christian faith: "There have been so many great pictures in European art of the Crucifixion that it's a magnificent armature on which you can hang all types of feeling and sensation. You may say it's a curious thing for a non-religious person to take the Crucifixion, but I don't think that that has anything to do with it. The great Crucifixions that one knows of – one doesnot know whether they were painted by men who had religious beliefs."[2] To the question of whether the theme of the Crucifixion demands a special approach on the part of the artist, Bacon responded: "Well, of course, you're working then on your own feelings and sensations, really. You might say it's almost nearer to a self-portrait. You are working on all sorts of very private feelings about behaviour and about the way life is."[3] These statements testify to the meaning of the Crucifixion theme to Bacon: he was no longer interested in the suggested promise of salvation made by a Christ who had died for mankind, but rather in the Crucifixion as a basic purpose for man in the world. The Crucifixion was a motif that was already present, thoroughly formulated but – for him – free of any baggage, and it offered a good "skin" for the material that he wanted to put on the canvas. The special position of Francis Bacon within this 20th-century pictorial tradition is also based on the fact that he not only adopted the motif of the Crucifixion but did so in a pictorial form that had established itself in Christian art as a classic Crucifixion format.

Like every pictorial form, the triptych also possesses a certain type of expressivity. The symmetrical composition expresses a very high degree of dignity and grandeur, but also of hierarchy and subordination. This pictorial formula manifested itself in the ceremony and art of the emperor's cult in late antiquity. The already heightened emotional content of the three-part picture was further intensified in Christian use. For Klaus Lankheit, the Christian triptych – which possesses this special religious effect, power of feeling, and charisma – becomes a "pathos formula."[4]

The definition of the triptych derived from the history of liturgical painting limits the term to a picture in three panels in which the two flanking panels are subordinate to the central one. In the case of the *Crucifixion Triptych* of ca. 1560[5] (cat. no. 145), attributed to Pieter Claeissens, we have a triptych of the classic type, whose central panel dominates the work in form and content. It depicts the crucified Christ flanked by soldiers and mourners, with the city of Jerusalem behind them in the middle distance. The figure of Mary Magdalene to some extent breaks up the otherwise strictly symmetrical composition. The landscape which provides the background to the scene extends over all three panels, but with certain obvious discrepancies in the transitions to the side panels. The figures of the patrons represented there are on a wholly different scale. They are noticeably larger than the figures on the central panel, which suggests that they may have been added later on. This inconsistency of scale has an ambivalent effect: on the one hand, the patrons are identified and isolated as not being participants in this biblical happening. On the other hand, this "zoom-in" effect with relation to the viewer raises the status of the secondary scenes on the side panels in relation to that of the dominant central panel. The independence of their respective levels of reality is underlined.

Rogier van der Weyden's *Crucifixion Triptych*, of around or after 1440 (cat. no. 146), depicts the Crucifixion of Christ with Mary, St. John and the patrons on the middle panel, as well as Saints Mary Magdalene and Veronica on the wings. It is an abbreviated representation of the Passion, focusing only on the central points with past events represented by Veronica with the sudarium, the future by Mary Magdalene with the ampulla. A greatly reduced landscape done in a bright green extends over the three panels of the triptych, creating a hard break with the azure sky above. Even if Rogier had not developed anything totally new by standardising the picture space, he certainly did perfect it in this work. The eye-catching dichromatic background serves as the "missing link" between the individual, chronologically distant events of the Passion of Christ. Instead of the architectural frame, this triptych is supposed to have originally possessed a painted-on, golden inner frame.[6] Even so, the scenery appears as if being viewed through three different windows. This effect is interesting with regard to Bacon's pictorial spaces: in the triptych *Three Studies for a Crucifixion* of 1962 (cat. no. 147), the repeatedly curved lower edge makes the space in the pictures seem to fold around the viewer, which causes the different subjects of the individual panels to be viewed as being in the same space. The viewer, then, is no longer faced with three separate pictorial fields, but three aspects of the same space.

It is of course tempting to venture a comparison based solely on the composition between Rogier van der Weyden's Crucifixion and several of Bacon's triptychs based solely on composition. There is a striking similarity in the way the artists weighted the pictorial space, exemplified by clearness of the colours and motifs as well as by the overall reserve. If one were to exaggerate the comparison a bit, one could say that Rogier's figures were backed up Bacon-style by flat colour surfaces which weaken the space in favour of the figures while also serving to undermine the hierarchic scheme of the triptych.

In his Crucifixion, then, Rogier van der Weyden took an important step towards departure from the hierarchy upon which the triptych form was based. Through the "democratisation" of the individual panels, reinforced on the formal level, this pictorial format loses something of its sacred aura. Bacon goes even a step further by making panels of uniform dimensions. In doing so, he reaches the point where he can claim for his work both the designation of the "series"[7] and that of the "triptych." The connotations connected to these two terms are all present in his triptychs, and form the basis for the impression of complexity which they make upon the viewer.

But the triptych in its definition as a three-part picture can, as exemplified above, also represent the principle of the triad, which is based on the equality of the individual notes. Francis Bacon spoke out repeatedly against the linking of his triptychs with the Christian pictorial tradition: "Actually I don't know if one should talk about a triptych in my case. Of course, there are three canvases, and you can link that to a long-standing tradition. The primitives often used the triptych format, but as far as my work is concerned, a triptych corresponds more to the idea of a succession of images on film. There are frequently three canvases, but there is no reason why I couldn't continue and add more."[8] Here Bacon expressly emphasises the serial principle of the pictorial s e r i e s as a formula for his triptychs. It is relatively difficult, however, to imagine his triptychs as having been extended by one or more additional panels. In a conversation with David Sylvester he once said: "I see images in series. And I suppose I could go on long beyond the triptych and do five or six together, but I find the triptych is a more balanced unit."[9] Bacon's style calls for a heroic, emotive pictorial format, of which the triptych is probably the purest form. Hence, his formulation does not represent a complete break with the classic weighting, but is probably best viewed as a hybrid which observes both the hierarchic/traditional and the democratic/serial principles.

In *Three Studies for a Crucifixion* of 1962, Francis Bacon combines for the first time a depiction of the Crucifixion with the triptych format. A monumental Crucifixion was originally planned in connection with the *Three Studies of Figures at the Base of a Crucifixion* of 1944 *(Plate 1)*, but it was never executed. Thus while this triptych bears "Crucifixion" in the title, the only relatively strong reference in the picture itself is the white cloth that one of the figures wears as a blindfold and which points to Christ's loincloth.[10]

In the Guggenheim triptych, the crucified

Plate 1: Francis Bacon, Three Studies for Figures at the Base of a Crucifixion. Oil and pastel on hardboard, triptych, each panel 95 × 73.5 cm. London, Tate Gallery. (©: London, Tate Gallery.)

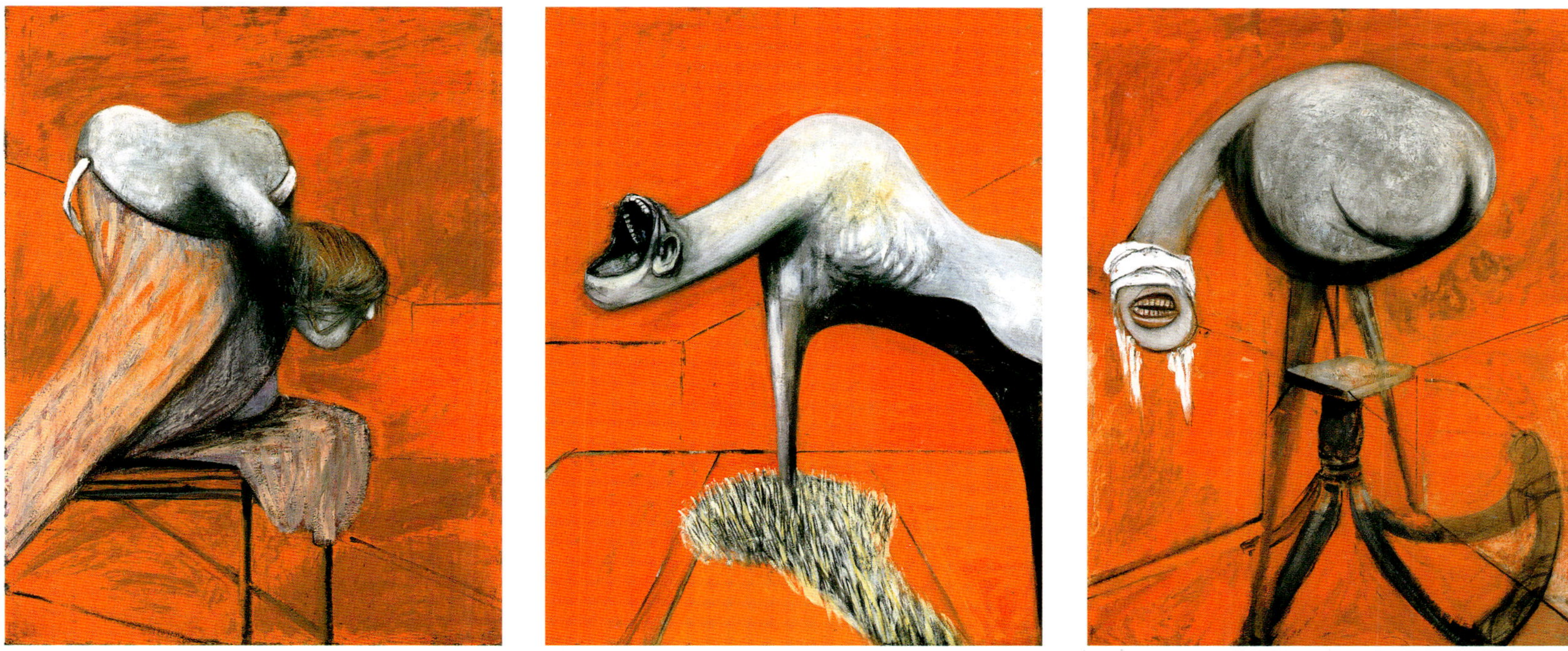

Christ has been displaced from the central panel. Instead, the right panel is occupied by a figure reminiscent in its raw carnality of a slaughtered animal. It writhes headfirst down a vertical supporting framework that merges into a base, the form of which is only suggested. In a continuation of the exposed spine, a small skull with its mouth wide open protrudes from the mass of flesh. The background scenery is provided by a ring that seems to be made of bones joined together. Speaking of this figure on the Cross in a conversation with David Sylvester, Bacon said: "The figure on the right is something which I have wanted to do for a long time. You know the great Cimabue *Crucifixion*? I always think of that as an image – as a worm crawling down the cross. I did try to make something of the feeling which I've sometimes had from that picture of this image just moving, undulating down the cross."[11] Two similar pieces of flesh are found on the left panel of the triptych. They are familiar from earlier works such as *Painting 1946 (Plate 2)* and *Figure with Meat,* 1954 (cat. no. 136), in which the slaughtered animal carcass in its positioning in the painting points more directly to the crucified Christ. Two ghoul-like figures, which inevitably make one think of their origin in the classic patron portraits on the wings of triptychs, point to the central panel. Formally, this does not represent any further intensification with regard to the side panels. The aggressive orange-red background is found in all three panels, as is the curvature of the space. The black curtains of the left panel occur in the central panel in the form of a triptych *en miniature,* which underscores the central position of this panel. Instead of a Crucifixion scene we find a completely shattered figure lying on a bed in frontal view. It almost seems as though the chunk of meat from the centre black surface had slid directly onto the bed. Thus the curtain becomes the foot of the Cross where the tortured body that has been taken down from the Cross now rests. From notes found in his studio, we know that Francis Bacon definitely planned his three-panel pictures to be exactly that (cat. no. 152). The following remark by Bacon illustrates just how important it was to him that the distance between them remain intact. "Well, there was something very unsatisfactory, for instance, when I had the show in Paris and the Guggenheim lent their Crucifixion triptych and the canvases were all together in one frame. It absolutely ruined the whole picture. I wrote and told them that if I'd wanted them all to be together I would have put them together. I wanted them to be in separate frames. It ruins the balance putting them together, because, if I'd wanted to do that, I would have painted them a different way."[12]

Bacon's fear of destroying the balance mentioned here is closely related to his fear of the stories that his triptychs might tell. For Bacon as a figural painter, and as one who, in addition, made use of the triptych format, this meant a constant balancing act between his figural painting, which was committed to sensation,[13] and the tendency to drift off into the realm of the illustrative and narrative. In the rigorous separation of the individual panels by a golden frame, he saw an additional opportunity to halt the flow of a narrative that inevitably imposes itself and, in this way, to prevent the viewer from r e a d i n g the picture.

[1] In 1933 in his *Art Now: An Introduction to the Theory of Modern Painting and Sculpture*, Herbert Read compared it with a 1929 "Bather" by Picasso.
[2] Sylvester 1999, p. 44.
[3] Ibid., p. 46.
[4] Cf. Lankheit 1959, p. 13.
[5] The old attribution to Pieter Claeissens (around 1500 – 1576) by Ludwig Scheibler (1887) was recently confirmed by Paul Huvenne (orally, 1991).
[6] Cf. Davies 1972, p. 18.
[7] To allow for a better distinction when speaking of the three-part picture, I use the terms "series" (serial principle) and "triptych" (hierarchic principle).
[8] Archimbaud 1993, p. 165.
[9] Sylvester 1999, p. 84.
[10] On this aspect cf. Heck 1992, p. 95.
[11] Sylvester 1999, p. 14.
[12] Ibid. 1999, p. 86.
[13] Cf. Deleuze 1995.

Cat. no. 145
Pieter Claeissens (attributed)
Crucifixion
C. 1560
Oil on oak, central panel:
51 × 41 cm, wings each 51 × 18 cm
Vienna, Kunsthistorisches Museum,
Picture Gallery, inv. no. 878

Cat. no. 146
Rogier van der Weyden
Crucifixion
C. 1440
Oil on oak, central panel:
96 × 69 cm, wings each 101 × 35 cm
Vienna, Kunsthistorisches Museum,
Picture Gallery, inv. no. 901

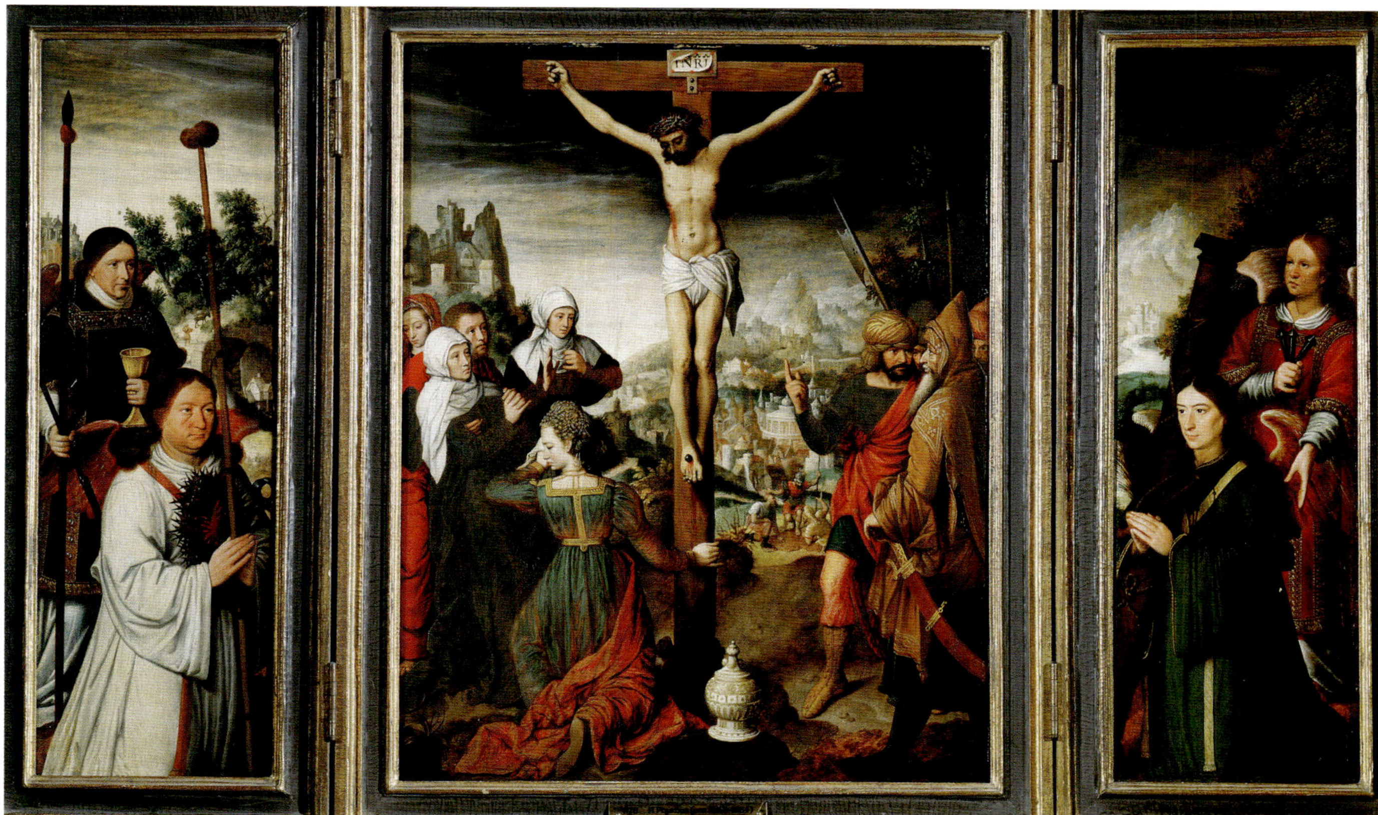

Cat. no. 145

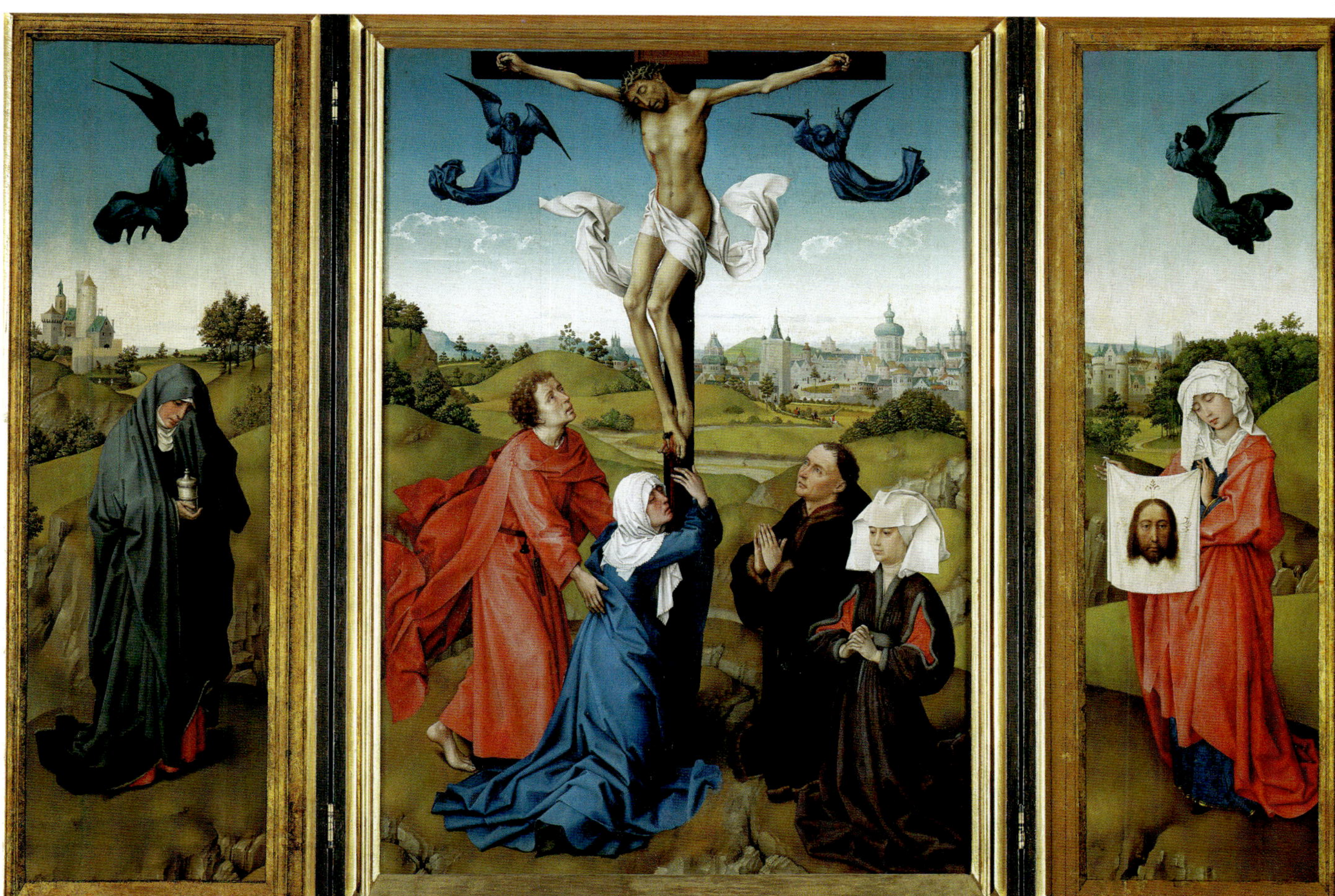

Cat. no. 146

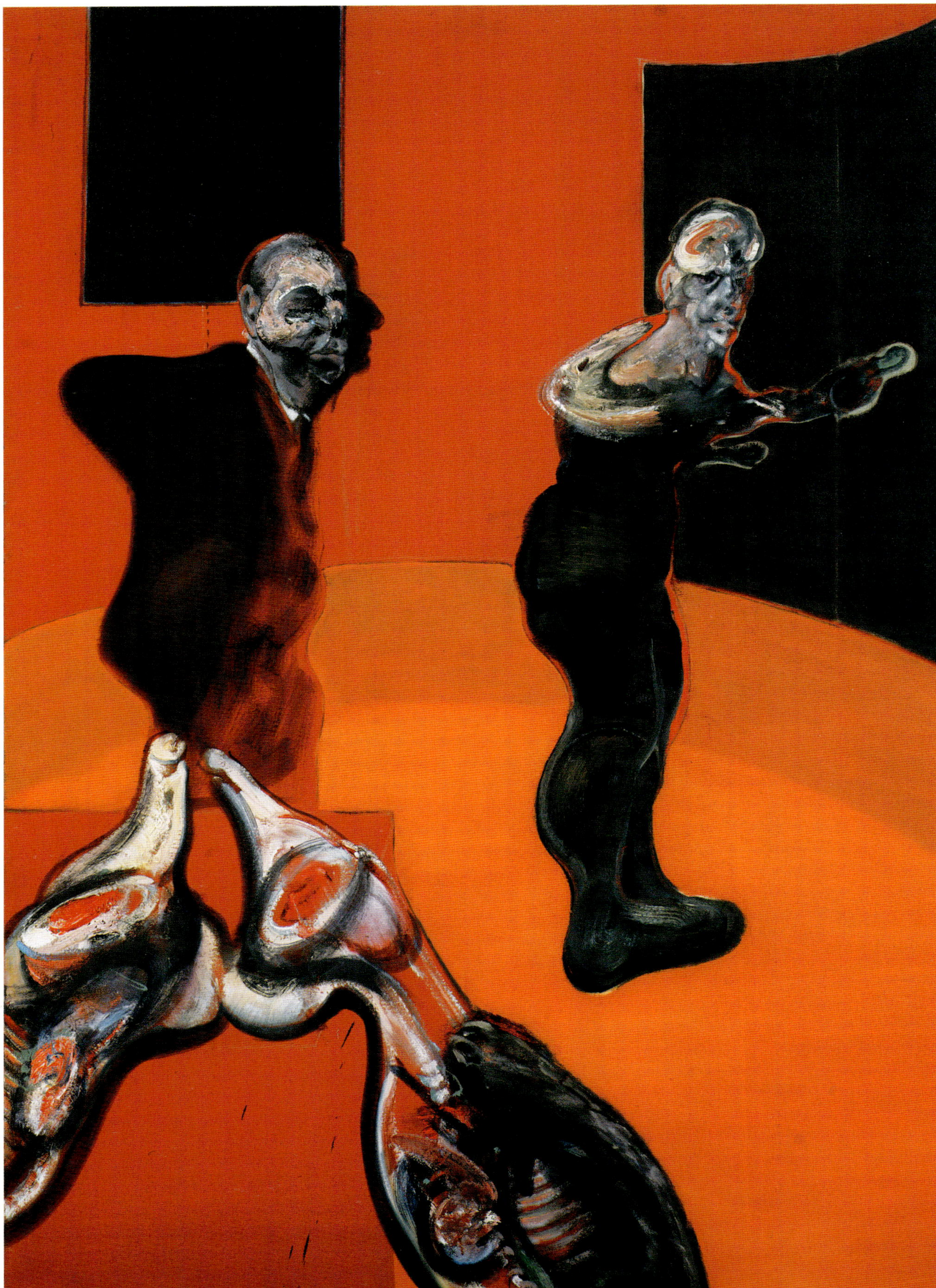

Cat. no. 147

Cat. no. 147
Francis Bacon
Three Studies for a Crucifixion
1962
Oil and sand on canvas, triptych,
each panel 198.2 × 144.8 cm
New York, The Solomon
R. Guggenheim Museum

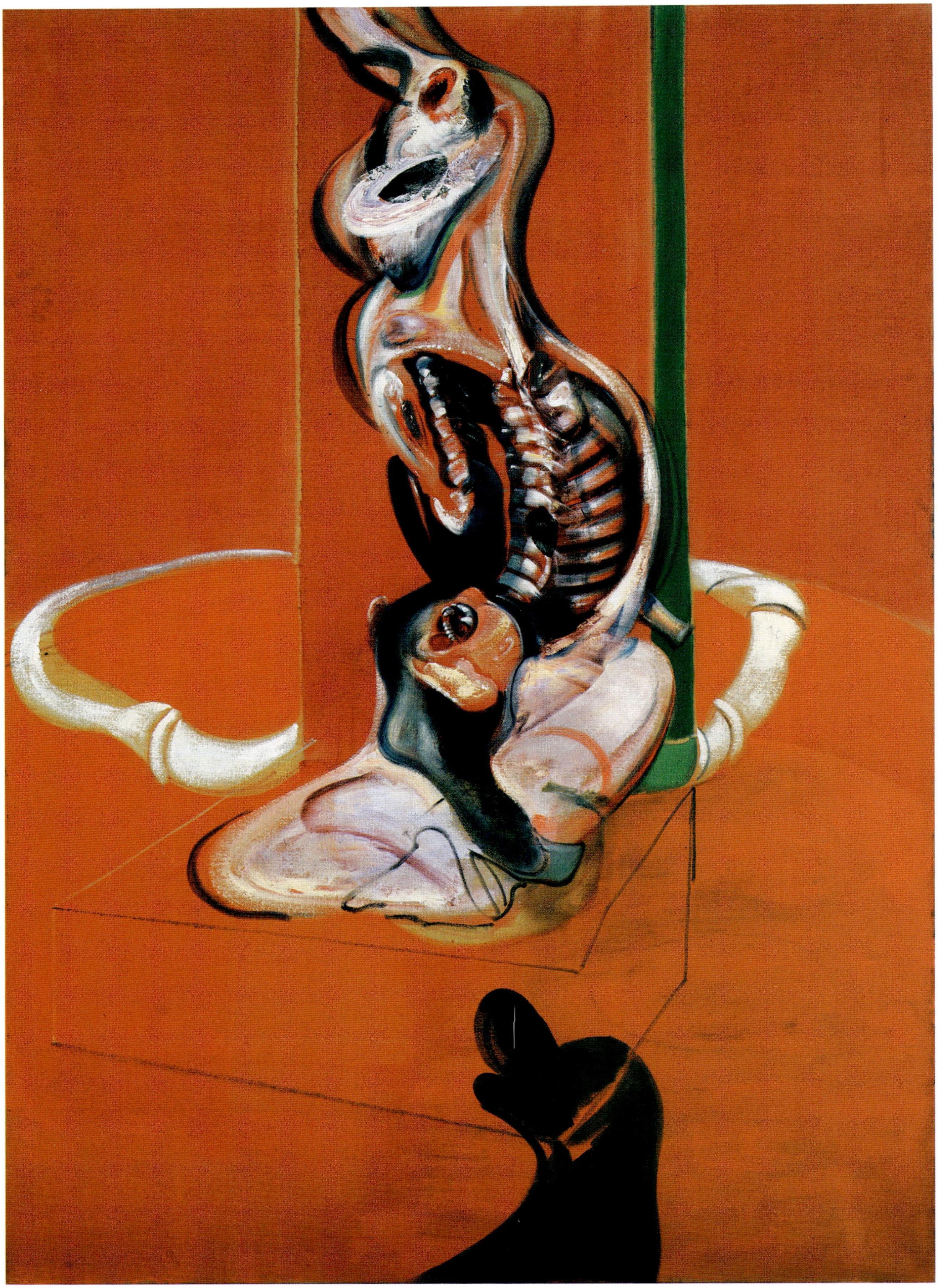

Cat. no. 147

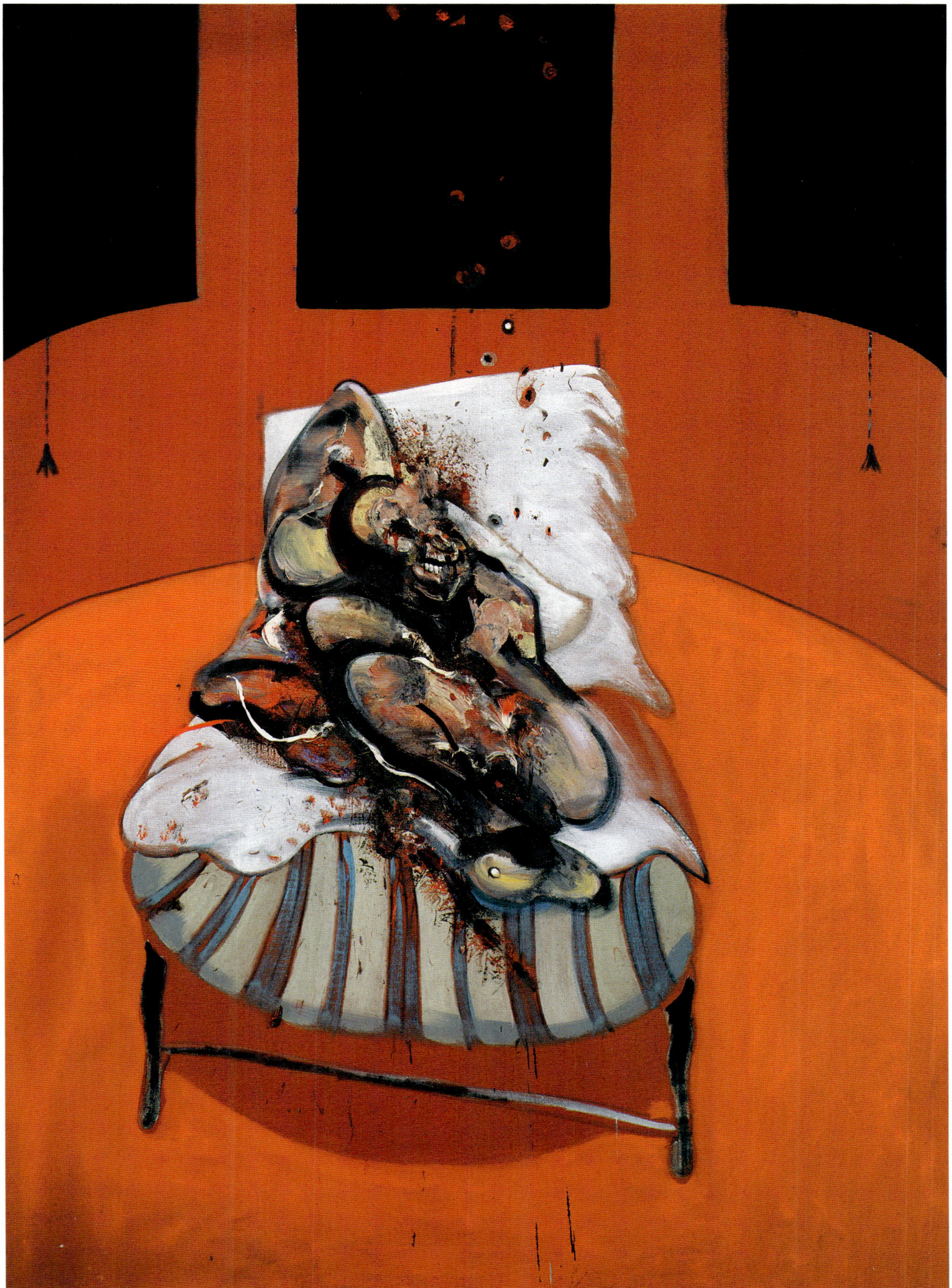

Cat. no. 147

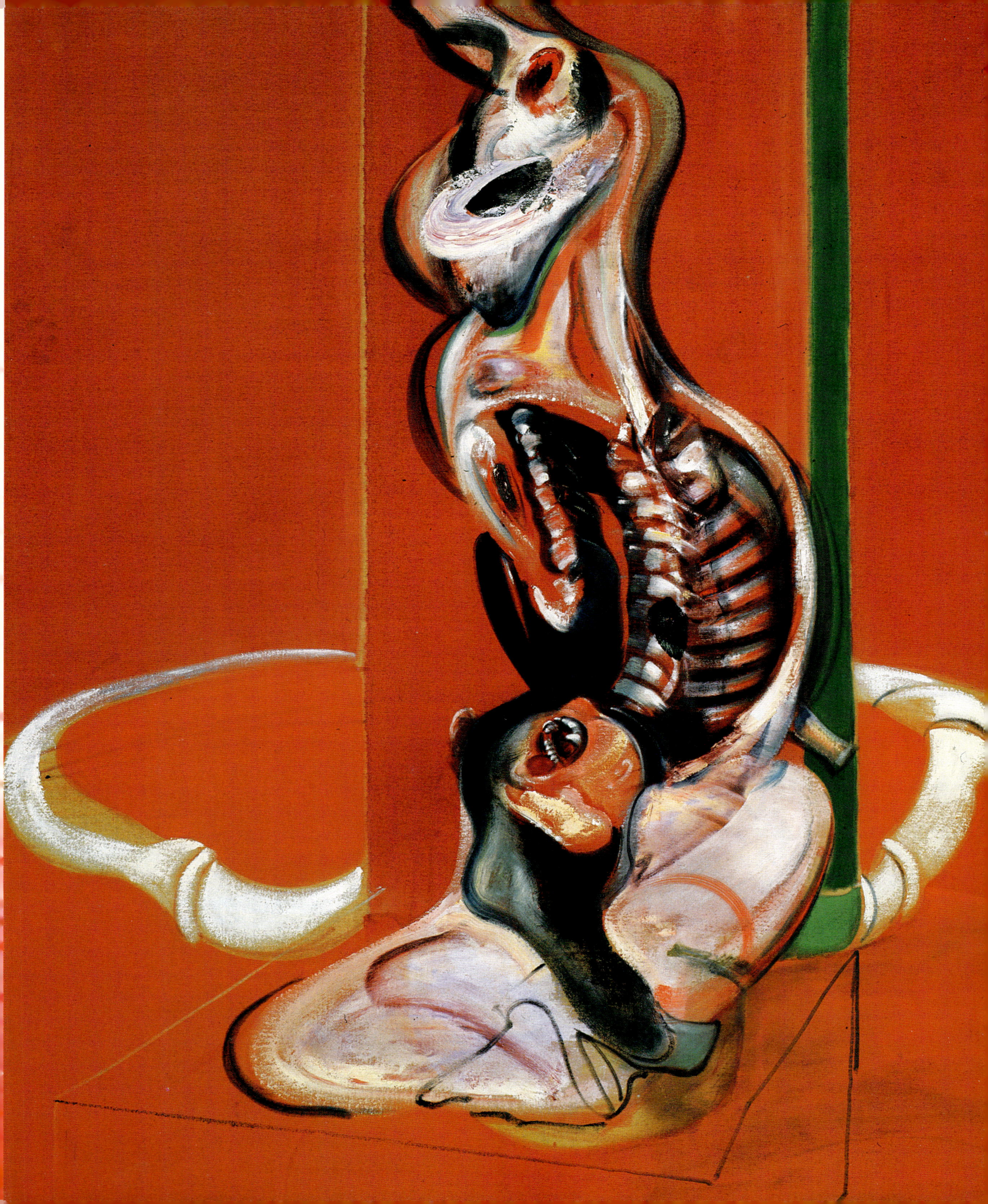

Front page: Cat. no. 147, detail

Cat. no. 148
Hand-written notes by Francis Bacon in blue felt-tip pen on blank sheet of paper. Post-1974
228 × 177 mm
Dublin, Dublin City Gallery The Hugh Lane, F107:9

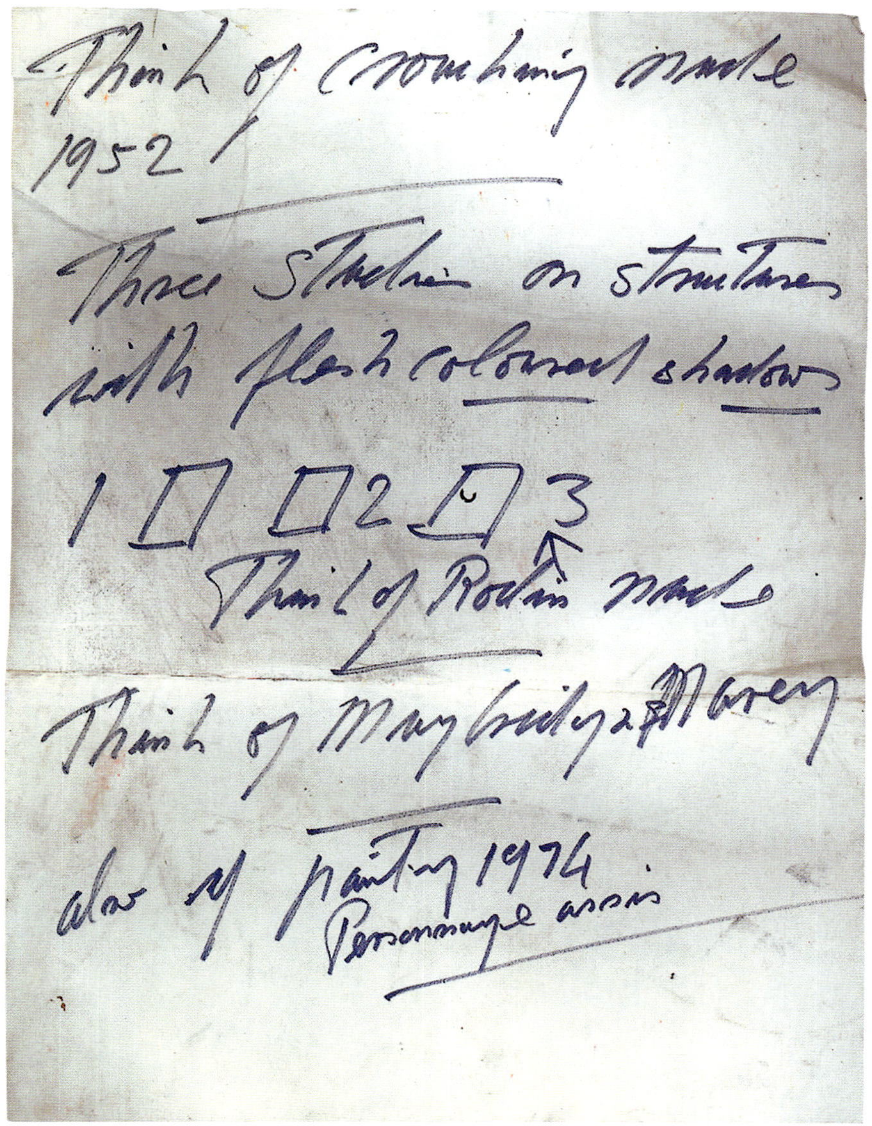
Think of crouching nude
1952

Three studies on structures
with flesh coloured shadow

1 2 3
Think of Rodin nude

Think of Muybridge & Marey

also of painting 1974
Personnage assis

Cat. no. 148

Photographs of Francis Bacon

Cat. no. 149
Black-and-white photograph of
Francis Bacon in 7 Reece Mews,
taken by Peter Stark
Early 1970s
252 × 202 mm
Dublin, Dublin City Gallery
The Hugh Lane, F22:5

Cat. no. 150
Black-and-white photograph of
Francis Bacon in 7 Reece Mews,
taken by Peter Stark
Early 1970s
252 × 203 mm
Dublin, Dublin City Gallery
The Hugh Lane, F112:1

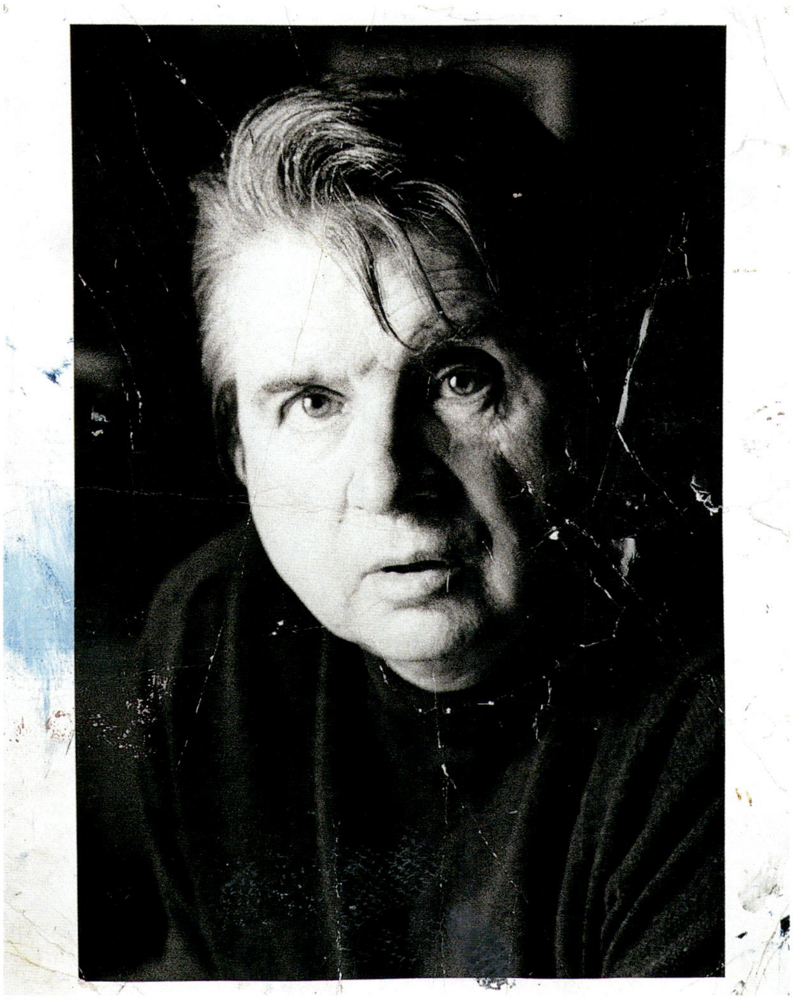

Cat. no. 149

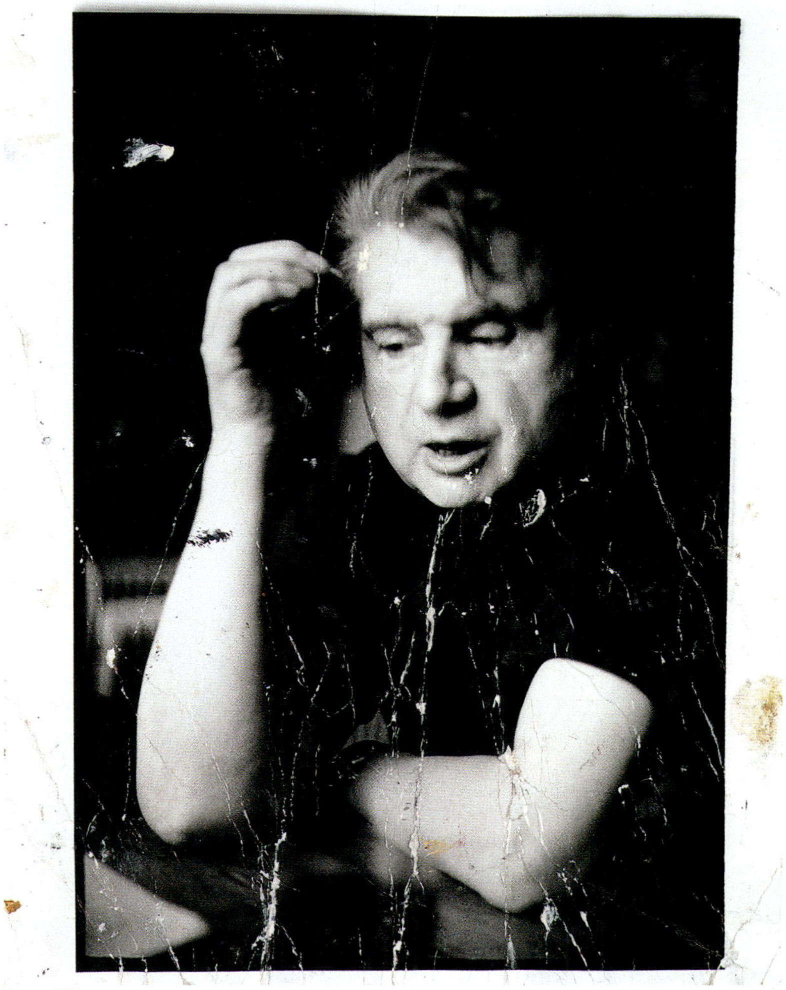

Cat. no. 150

Cat. no. 151
Black-and-white photograph of Francis Bacon reflected in the circular mirror in the 7 Reece Mew studio, taken by Jorge Lewinski
1966
371 × 283 mm
Dublin, Dublin City Gallery The Hugh Lane, F1A:176

Cat. no. 152
Colour photograph of Francis Bacon in the 7 Reece Mews studio, taken by Michael Pergolani
May 1970
192 × 239 mm
Dublin, Dublin City Gallery The Hugh Lane, F105:143

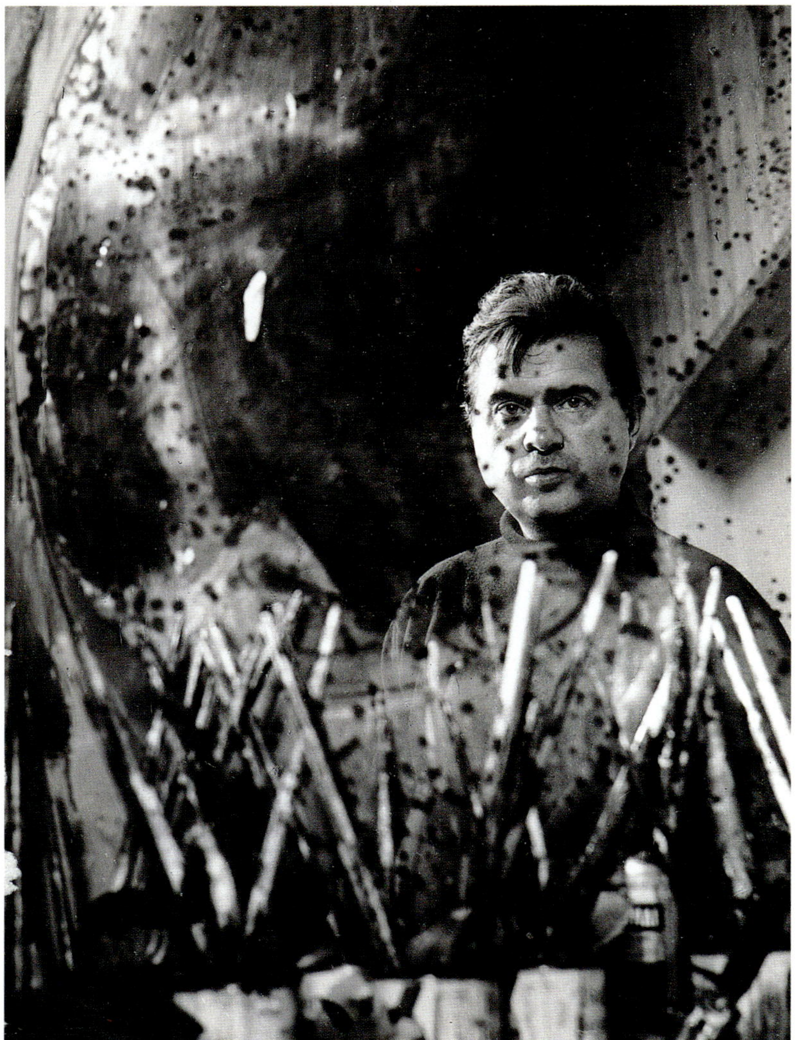

Cat. no. 151

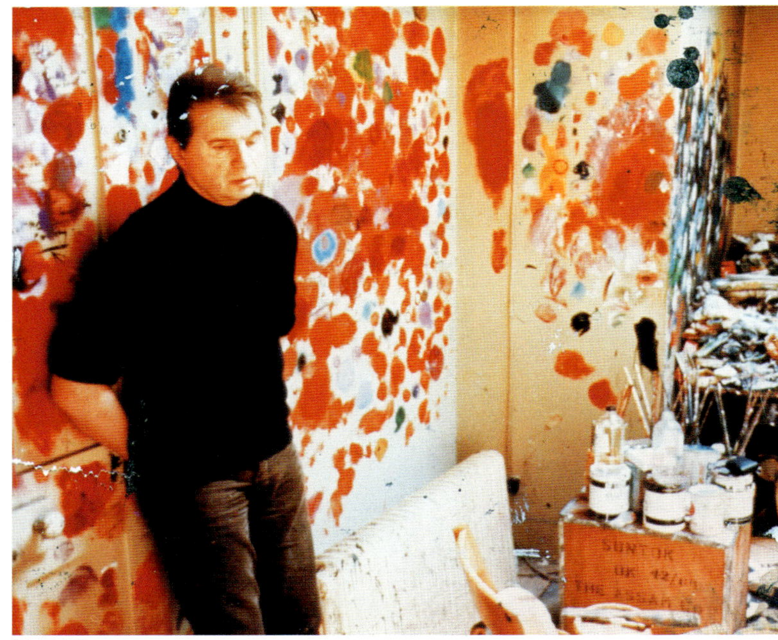

Cat. no. 152

Cat. no. 153
Black-and-white photograph of Francis Bacon and George Dyer on the Orient Express train on their way to Greece, taken by John Deakin
1965
203 × 202 mm
Dublin, Dublin City Gallery The Hugh Lane, F149:33L

Cat. no. 154
Colour photograph of Francis Bacon in the dining car of a train (possibly the Orient Express), taken by John Deakin
1965; photograph printed in September 1966
89 × 89 mm
Dublin, Dublin City Gallery The Hugh Lane, F149:45B

Cat. no. 155
Colour photograph of Francis Bacon and George Dyer in the dining car of a train (possibly the Orient Express), taken by John Deakin
1965
122 × 121 mm
Dublin, Dublin City Gallery The Hugh Lane, F105:98

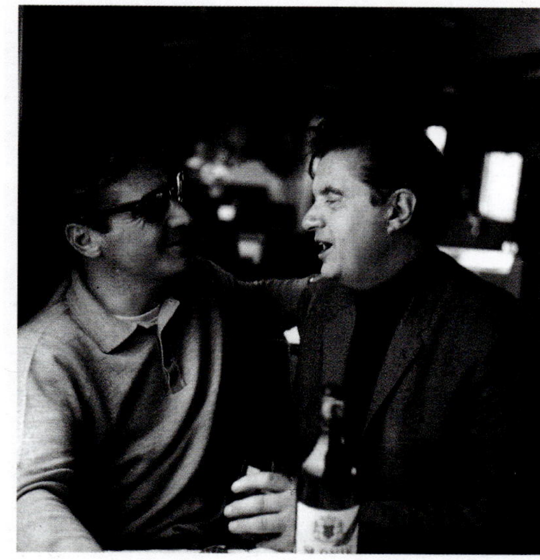

Cat. no. 153

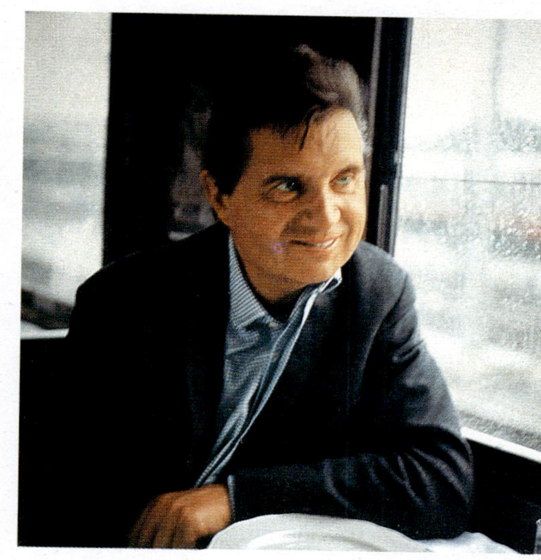

Cat. no. 154

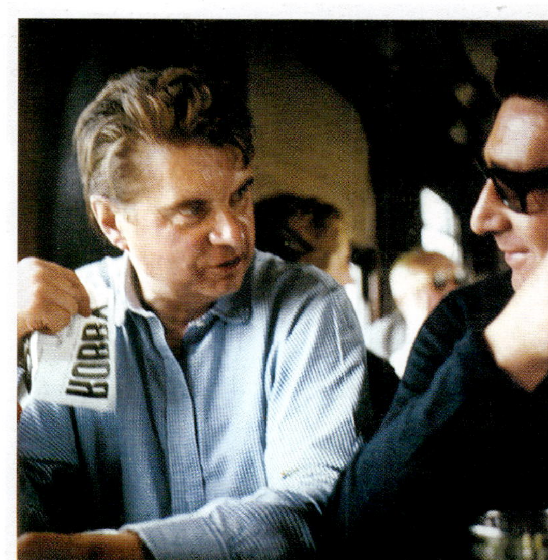

Cat. no. 155

Appendix

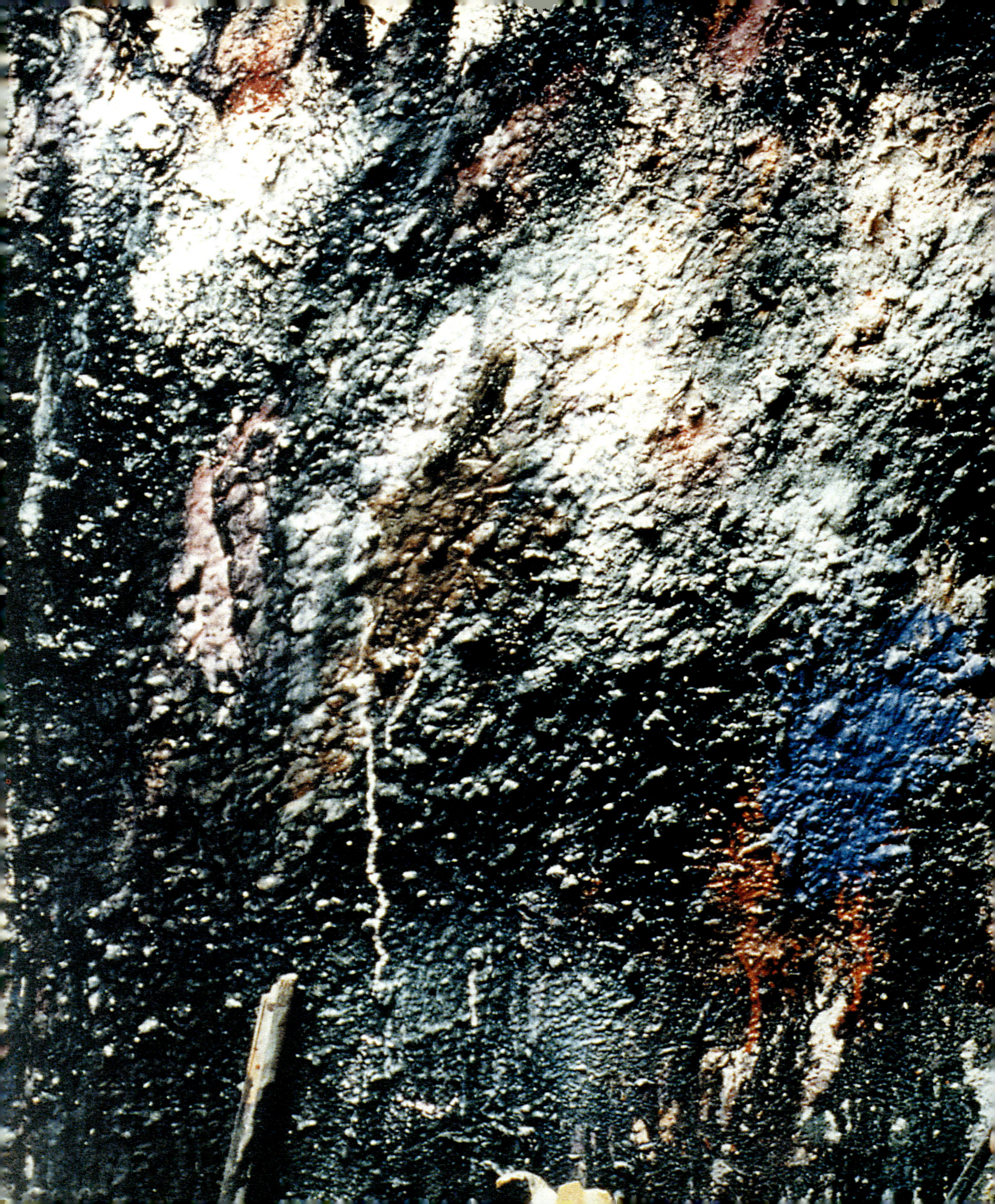

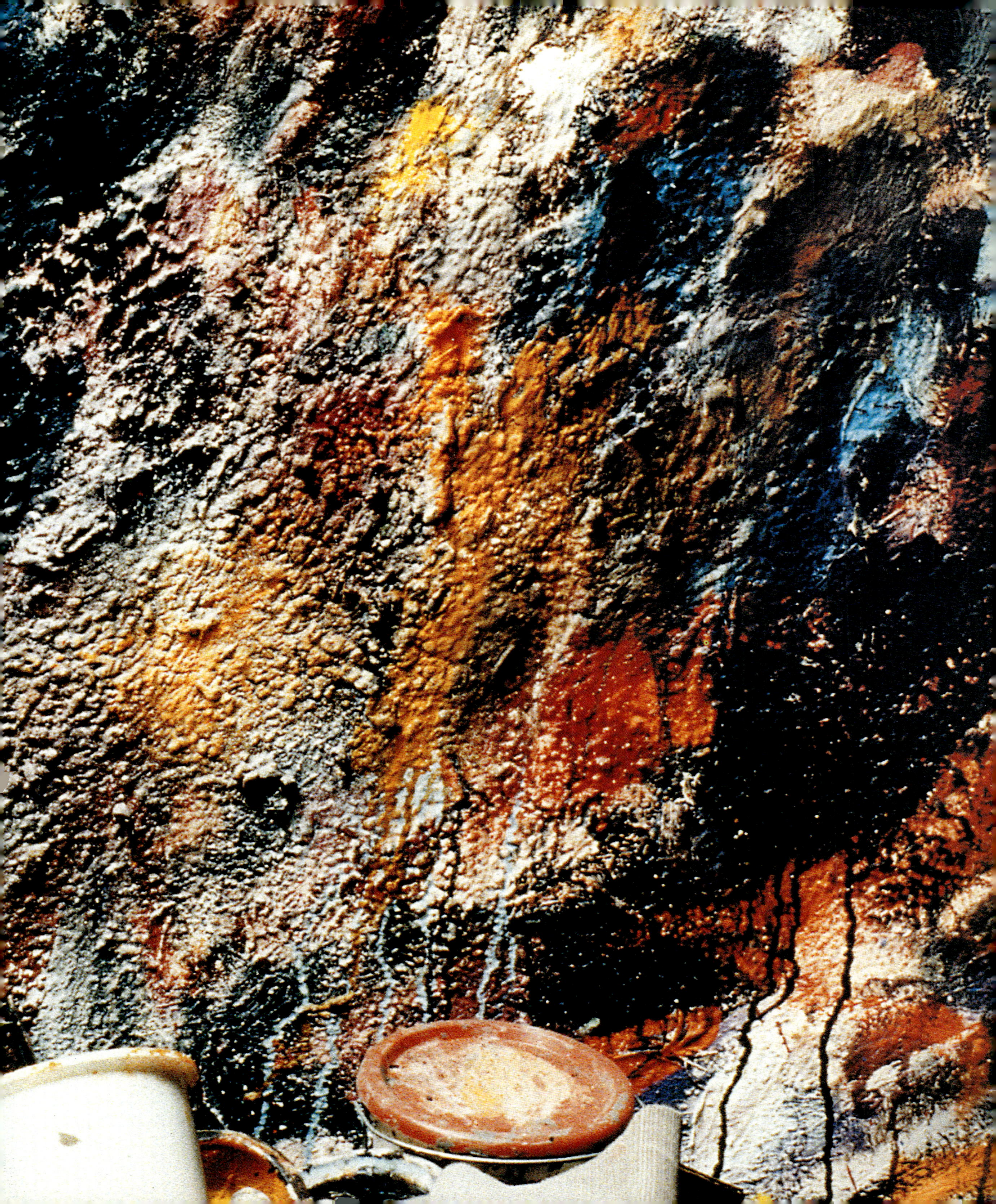

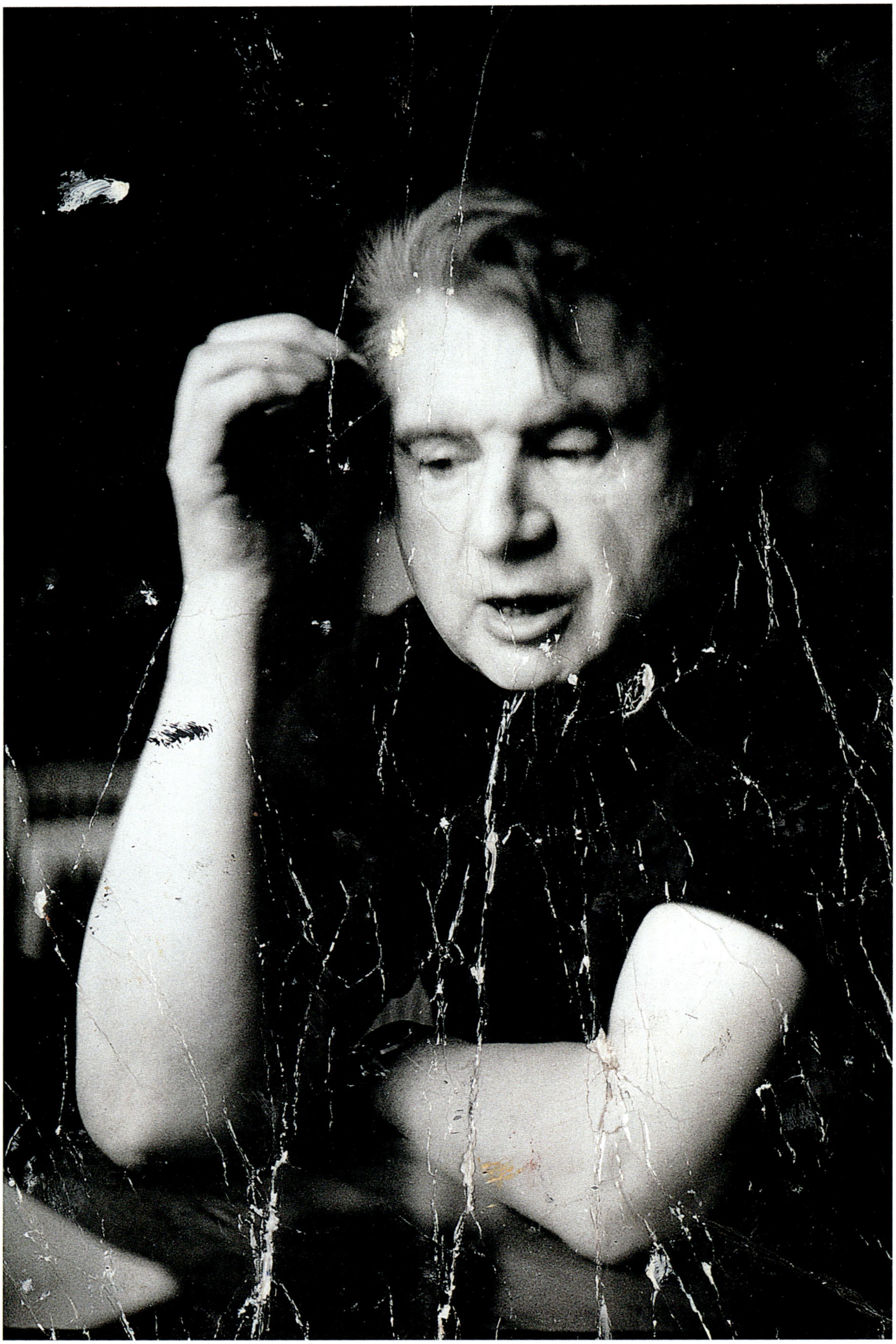

Interviews with Francis Bacon by David Sylvester and Michel Archimbaud

David Sylvester, *Interviews with Francis Bacon*, enlarged edition, Thames and Hudson, London 1999.

1. Francis Bacon on Diego Rodriguez de Silva y Velázquez:

FB: In the Popes it doesn't come from anything to do with religion; it comes from an obsession with the photographs that I know of Velázquez's *Pope Innocent X.*
DS: *But why was it you chose the Pope?*
FB: Because I think it is one of the greatest portraits that have ever been made, and I became obsessed by it. I buy book after book with this illustration in it of the Velázquez Pope, because it haunts me, and it opens up all sorts of feelings and areas of – I was going to say – imagination, even, in me.
DS: *But aren't there other equally great portraits by Velázquez which you might have become obsessed by? Are you sure there's nothing special for you in the fact of its being a Pope?*
FB: I think it's the magnificent colour of it.
DS: *But you've also done two or three paintings of a modern Pope, Pius XII, based on photographs, as if the interest in the Velázquez had become transferred onto the Pope himself as a sort of heroic figure.*
FB: In those magnificent professional photographs when he was being carried through St. Peter's. It is true, of course, the Pope is unique. He's put in a unique position by being the Pope, and therefore, like in certain great tragedies, he's as though raised onto a dais on which the grandeur of the image can be displayed to the world.
(P. 24–26.)

FB: You want to open up so many levels of feeling if possible, which can't be done ... It's wrong to say it can't be done in pure illustration, in purely figurative terms, because of course it has been done. It has been done in Velázquez. That is, of course, where Velázquez is so different to Rembrandt, because, oddly enough, if you take the great late self-portrait of Rembrandt, you will find that the whole contour of the face changes time after time; it's a totally different face, although it has what is called a look of Rembrandt, and by this difference it involves you in different areas of feeling. But with Velázquez it's more controlled and, of course, I believe, more miraculous. Because one wants to do this thing of just walking along the edge of the precipice, and in Velázquez it's a very, very miraculous thing that he has been able to keep it so near to what we call illustration and at the same time so deeply unlock the greatest and deepest things that man can feel. Which makes him such an amazingly mysterious painter. Because one really does believe that Velázquez recorded the court at that time and, when one looks at his pictures, one is possibly looking at something which is very, very near to how things looked.
(P. 28.)

DS: *You've used the Eisenstein image as a constant basis and you've done the same with the Velázquez Innocent X, and entirely through photographs and reproductions of it. And you've worked from reproductions of other old master paintings. Is there a great deal difference between working from a photograph of a painting and from a photograph of reality?*
FB: Well, with a painting it's an easier thing to do, because the problem's already been solved. The problem that you're setting up, of course, is another problem. I don't think that any of these paintings I've done from other paintings actually have ever worked.
DS: *Not even any versions of the Velázquez Pope?*
FB: I've always thought that this was one of the greatest paintings in the world, and I've used it through obsession. And I've tried very, very unsuccessfully to do certain records of it – distorted records. I regret them, because I think they're very silly.
DS: *You regret them?*
FB: Well, I do, because I think that this thing was an absolute thing that was done and nothing more can be done about it.
(P. 37.)

DS: *Yet, when you finally went to Rome, though you stayed a couple of months, I think, you didn't take the opportunity to see the Innocent X.*
FB: I didn't. No. It's true to say that at that time I was extremely unhappy emotionally. And, though I loathe churches, I spent most of my time in St. Peter's, just wandering around. But I think another thing was probably a fear of seeing the reality of the Velázquez after my tampering with it, seeing this marvellous painting and thinking of the stupid things one had done with it.
(P. 38.)

DS: *When you say you didn't have a subject, are you saying it from hindsight or were you aware of it at the time?*
FB: No, I say it through hindsight. But I always thought of those paintings from Velázquez as a failure, and that was perhaps one of the first subjects that I had. I became obsessed by this painting and I bought photo-

graph after photograph of it. I think really it was my first subject.
(P. 71.)

DS*: Well, of course, there's not all that number who are painting the figure today. But I think it does more. And people seem to feel in looking at your figures that they are seen in moments of crisis, moments of acute awareness of their mortality, moments of acute awareness of their animal nature – moments of recognition of what might be called elemental truths about themselves. [...]*
FB: [...] One is particularly aware of it in Velázquez, of course. I don't know whether it's because of Velázquez's tremendous sophistication. Obviously, he was a profoundly sophisticated man living in the society of the Court, and he was probably the only really sophisticated being existing around the Court at the time; that was the reason the King insisted on keeping him near him, because he was the only man that at least enlivened for a moment his day. But one feels in all his paintings the whole poignancy that Velázquez must have felt – even in those beautiful things where the figures have this wonderful structure and yet at the same time have the colouring of a Monet. You feel the shadow of life passing all the time.
(P. 80–81.)

2. Francis Bacon on Sergej Eisenstein's films:

DS*: But it's interesting that the photographic image you've worked from most of all isn't a scientific or a journalistic one but a very deliberate and famous work of art – the still of the screaming nanny from* Potemkin.
FB: It was a film I saw almost before I started to paint, and it deeply impressed me – I mean the whole film as well as the Odessa Steps sequence and this shot. I did hope at one time to make – it hasn't got any special psychological significance – I did hope one day to make the best painting of the human cry. I was not able to do it and it's much better in the Eisenstein and there it is.
(P. 34.)

FB: I was certainly, when I was much younger, influenced by the films of Eisenstein, and then after that I was also very influenced by the films of Buñuel, especially the early ones, because I think that he too had a remarkable precision of imagery. I can't say how they directly affected me but they certainly have affected my whole attitude to visual things – by showing the acuteness of the visual image that you have got to make.
(P. 199.)

3. Francis Bacon on the scream:

FB: I think probably the best human cry in painting was made by Poussin.
DS*: In* The Massacre of the Innocents*?*
FB: Yes, which is at Chantilly. And I remember I was once with a family for about three months living very near there, trying to learn French, and I went a great deal to Chantilly and I remember this picture always made a terrific impression on me. Another thing that made me think about the human cry was a book that I bought when I was very young from a bookshop in Paris, a second-hand book which had beautiful hand-coloured plates of diseases of the mouth, beautiful plates of the mouth open and of the examination of the inside of the mouth; and they fascinated me, and I was obsessed by them. And then I saw – or perhaps I even knew by then – the *Potemkin* film, and I attempted to use the *Potemkin* still as a basis on which I could also use these marvellous illustrations of the human mouth. It never worked out, though.
(P. 34–35.)

FB: You could say that a scream is a horrific image; in fact, I wanted to paint the scream more than the horror. I think if I had really thought about what causes somebody to scream, it would have made the scream that I tried to paint more successful. Because I should in a sense have been more conscious of the horror that produced the scream: In fact they were too abstract.
DS*: They were too purely visual?*
FB: I think so. Yes.
DS*: The open mouths – are they always meant to be a scream?*
FB: Most of them, but not all. You know how the mouth changes shape. I've always been very moved by the movements of the mouth and the shape of the mouth and the teeth. People say that these have all sorts of sexual implications and I was always very obsessed by the actual appearance of the mouth and teeth, and perhaps I have lost that obsession now, but it was a very strong thing at one time. I like, you may say, the glitter and colour that comes from the mouth, and I've always hoped in a sense to be able to paint the mouth like Monet painted a sunset.
DS*: So you might well have been interested in painting open mouths and teeth even if you hadn't been painting the scream?*
FB: I think I might. And I've always wanted and never succeeded in painting the smile.
(P. 48–50.)

4. Francis Bacon on Edgar Degas:

FB: [...] we are constantly seeing images of the human body through X-ray photographs and that obviously does alter the ways by which one can use the body. You must know the beautiful Degas pastel in the National Gallery of a woman sponging her back. And you will find at the very top of the spine that the spine almost comes out of the skin altogether. And this gives it such a grip and a twist that you're more conscious of the vulnerability of the rest of the body than if he had drawn the spine naturally up to the neck. He breaks it so that this thing seems to protrude from the flesh: Now, whether Degas did this purposely or not, it makes it a much greater picture, because you're suddenly conscious of the spine as well as the flesh, which he usually just painted covering the bones. In my case, these things have certainly been influenced by X-ray photographs.
(P. 46–47.)

DS*: But why does one have to distort as freely as modern artists like yourself do, rather than simply achieve that kind of abbreviation which somebody like Degas achieved?*
FB: Yes, but photography hadn't been developed as far in Degas's time as it has now. Another thing is, when you talk of Degas, the very great Degas are the pastels, and don't forget that in his pastels he always striates the form with these lines which are drawn through the image and in a certain sense both intensify and diversify its reality. I always think that the interesting thing about Degas is the way he made lines through the body: you could say that he shuttered the body, in a way, shuttered the image and then he put

an enormous amount of colour through these lines. And having shuttered the form, he created intensity by putting this colour through the flesh.
(P. 176.)

5. Francis Bacon on Luis Buñuel:

FB: I was certainly, when I was much younger, influenced by the films of Eisenstein, and then after that I was also very influenced by the films of Buñuel, especially the early ones, because I think that he too had a remarkable precision of imagery. I can't say how they directly affected me but they certainly have affected my whole attitude to visual things – by showing the acuteness of the visual image that you have got to make.
DS: *Have you come across a remark of André Bazin's that Buñuel's cruelty was a means to rediscover humanity in all its grandeur?*
FB: Is it real cruelty in Buñuel? Anything in art seems cruel because reality is cruel. Perhaps that's why so many people like abstraction in art, because you can't be cruel in abstraction.
(P. 199–200.)

6. Francis Bacon on Rembrandt Harmenszoon van Rijn:

FB: Well, if you think of the great Rembrandt self-portrait in Aix-en-Provence, for instance, and if you analyze it, you will see that there are hardly any sockets to the eyes, that it is almost completely anti-illustrational. I think that the mystery of fact is conveyed by an image being made out of non-rational marks. [...] But what can happen sometimes, as it happened in this Rembrandt self-portrait, is that there is a coagulation of non-representational marks which have led to making up this very great image. [...]
Behind all that is Rembrandt's profound sensibility, which was able to hold onto one irrational mark rather than onto another. And abstract expressionism has all been done in Rembrandt's marks. But in Rembrandt it has been done with the added thing that it was an attempt to record a fact and to me therefore must be much more exciting and much more profound.
(P. 58.)

FB: You want to open up so many levels of feeling if possible, which can't be done in. ... It's wrong to say it can't be done in pure illustration, in purely figurative terms, because of course it has been done. It has been done in Velázquez. That is, of course, where Velázquez is so different to Rembrandt, because, oddly enough, if you take the great late self-portraits of Rembrandt, you will find that the whole contour of the face changes time after time; it's a totally different face, although it has what is called a look of Rembrandt, and by this difference it involves you in different areas of feeling.
(P. 28.)

FB: Well, oddly enough, I even like Rembrandts under glass. And it's true to say in many ways they're more difficult to see, but you con still look into them.
(P. 87.)

FB: I use anything. I use scrubbing brushes and sweeping brushes and any of those things that I think painters have used. They've always used everything. I don't know, but I'm certain Rembrandt used an enormous amount of things. (P. 90.)

7. Francis Bacon on Alberto Giacometti

DS: *Perhaps the tendency to interpret your work as saying something comes from the fact that people like to try and find a story in art and are rather starved of stories in the art of our time, so that, when they find an art like yours, it's a great temptation to weave stories.*
FB: Yes, I'm sure it is.
DS: *Something similar has happened with Giacometti – the tendency to interpret his figures as Existential Man.*
FB: And how did he feel about it?
DS: *He thought it was rather crass. He said he was only trying to copy what he saw.*
FB: Exactly.
(P. 82.)

8. Francis Bacon on Pablo Picasso:

FB: I've had a desire to do forms, as when I originally did three forms at the base of the Crucifixion. They were influenced by the Picasso things which were done at the end of the 'twenties. And I think there's a whole area there suggested by Picasso, which in a way has been unexplored, of organic form that relates to the human image but is a complete distortion of it.
(P. 8.)

FB: [...] much of Picasso I don't like, but nevertheless I've never felt for one second that he was ever short of images. And I suppose I'm lucky in that images just drop in as if they were handed down to me. Really, I think of myself as a maker of images.
(P. 166.)

FB: I think that our sense of realism has been changed to some extent since Surrealism – well, really, since Freud – because we've been made more conscious of how realism can draw on the unconscious. And I think a very good example is certain work done by Picasso in the years around 1930, such as the small paintings he did at Dinard – I think it was in 1928 – of figures on the beach. As Picasso, I believe, absorbed everything, he absorbed Surrealism, and those images are profoundly unillustrative but profoundly real about figures. For instance, a curious curved image unlocking the door of a bathing cabin is far more real than if it was an illustration of a figure unlocking the door of a bathing cabin.
(P. 170.)

DS: *Now, does the reality which that Picasso image has for you owe something to the contrast between the quite literal rendering of the key and the keyhole and the invented character of the figure? I mean, does this contrast throw into relief the force of the gesture?*
FB: I think so. I think that it brings in not only the external reality but it brings in the unconscious reality of turning the key in the lock, which has subjective implications, and these are what gives a poignancy to the key being inserted into the lock. I believe that realism has to be re-invented.
(P. 172.)

FB: I think it's the reason I have always been so much more interested in Picasso. Because Matisse never had the – what can one say? – the brutality of fact which Picasso had. I don't think he ever had the invention of Picasso and I think he turns fact into lyricism. He doesn't have Picasso's brutality of fact. (P. 182.)

9. Francis Bacon on Photography and Eadweard Muybridge:

FB: Well, I think one's sense of appearance is assaulted all the time by photography and by the film. So that, when one looks at something, one's not only looking at it directly but one's also looking at it through the assault that has already been made on one by photography and film. And 99 per cent of the time I find that photographs are very much more interesting than either abstract or figurative painting. I've always been haunted by them.
(P. 30.)

FB: [...] the thing of doing series may possibly have come from looking at those books of Muybridge with the stages of a movement shown in separate photographs.
(P. 31.)

FB: I've also always had a book that's influenced me very much called *Positioning in Radiography*, with a lot of photographs showing the positioning of the body for the X-ray photographs to be taken, and also the X-rays themselves.
(P. 31–32.)

FB: Actually, Michelangelo and Muybridge are mixed up in my mind together, and so I perhaps could learn about positions from Muybridge and learn about the ampleness, the grandeur of form from Michelangelo, and it would be very difficult for me to disentangle the influence of Muybridge and the influence of Michelangelo.
(P. 114.)

FB: I very often think of people's bodies that I've known, I think of the contours of those bodies that have particularly affected me, but then they're grafted very often onto Muybridge's bodies. I manipulate the Muybridge bodies into the form of the bodies I have known.
(P. 116.)

10. Francis Bacon on Michelangelo Buonarroti:

FB: And I've always thought about Michelangelo; he's always been deeply important in my way of thinking about form. But although I have this profound admiration for all his work, the work that I like most of all is the drawings. For me he is one of the very greatest draughtsmen, if not the greatest.
DS: *I've often suspected, since as far back as 1950, that, with many of your nude figures, certain Michelangelo images had been there in the back of your mind at least, as prototypes of the male figure. Do you think this has been the case?*
FB: Actually, Michelangelo and Muybridge are mixed up in my mind together, and so I perhaps could learn about positions from Muybridge and learn about the ampleness, the grandeur of form from Michelangelo, and it would be very difficult for me to disentangle the influence of Muybridge and the influence of Michelangelo. But, of course, as most of my figures are taken from the male nude, I am sure that I have been influenced by the fact that Michelangelo made the most voluptuous male nudes in the plastic arts.
(P. 114.)

11. Francis Bacon on Paul Cézanne:

DS: *Does a Cézanne still life or landscape ever move you as much as a Cézanne portrait of nude?*
FB: No, it doesn't, although I think that Cézanne's landscapes are very much better than his figures, generally. I think that there are one or two figure-paintings which are marvellous, but generally speaking I think the landscapes are better.
DS: *Nevertheless, the figures say more to you?*
FB: They do, yes.
(P. 63.)

FB: I always hope to be able to make a great number of figures without a narrative.
DS: As Cézanne does in the bathers?
FB: He does.
(P. 63–64.)

12. Francis Bacon on Vincent van Gogh:

FB: I believe that realism has to be re-invented. It has to be continuously re-invented. In one of his letters Van Gogh speaks of the need to make changes in reality, which become lies that are truer than the literal truth. This is the only possible way the painter can bring back the intensity of the reality which he is trying to capture.
(P. 172.)

DS: *But isn't it the case, when we look at a great work of art and are moved by it, that we don't make such comparisons, that the work has a kind of power of its own which speaks to us?*
FB: Yes, certainly, of course it has. It has its own Power. Because it has re-invented its own realism. And Van Gogh is one of my great heroes because I think that he was able to be almost literal and yet by the way he put on the paint give you a marvellous vision of the reality of things. I saw it very clearly when I was once in Provence and going through that part of the Crau where he did some of his landscapes, and one just saw in this absolutely barren country that by the way he put on the paint he was able to give it such an amazing living quality, give that reality the Crau has of just plain, bare land. The living quality is what you have to get.
(P. 173–174.)

13. Francis Bacon on the triptych-form:

DS: *Triptychs have been a very large part of your output in recent years. Of course, your very first major work was a triptych, back in 1944. [...] What attracts you so much to the form?*
FB: I see images in series. And I suppose I could go on long beyond the triptych and do five or six together, but I find the triptych is a more balanced unit.
(P. 84.)

FB: Well, there was something very unsatisfactory, for instance, when I had the show in Paris and the Guggenheim lent their *Crucifixion* triptych and the canvases were all together in one frame. It absolutely ruined the whole picture. I wrote and told them that if I'd wanted them all to be together I would have put them together. I wanted them to be in separate frames. It ruins the balance putting them together, because, if I'd wanted to do that, I would have painted them a different way.
(P. 86.)

Excerpts from: Michel Archimbaud, *Francis Bacon. In Conversation with Michel Archimbaud*, Phaidon Press, London 1993.

1. Francis Bacon on Diego Rodriguez de Silva y Velázquez:

FB: [...] Indeed, I have literally been obsessed by works of great painters from the past.
MA: *Are you thinking, for example, of* Pope Innocent X *by Velázquez?*
FB: Yes.
MA: *But that was later, and it wasn't the case of copying, but rather an interpretation of that famous portrait.*
FB: Yes, perhaps I should have been satisfied with just copying it after all. I tried to re-create it, but I don't think it worked.
MA: *But everyone agreed that those canvases are amongst you most important works.*
FB: Perhaps they are for some people, but not for me. I really consider it a mistake to have done those paintings. I was haunted by that work, by the reproductions that I saw of it. It's such an extraordinary portrait that I wanted to do something based on it. It's an example of what I've already described to you; I was quite overcome by it and I felt compelled to do what I did. I felt overwhelmed by that image. Unfortunately, the result was far from satisfactory.
MA: *I believe you've never seen the original, is that right?*
FB: Yes, that's right. When I had the opportunity to see it during a stay in Rome, I was not at all well. Being ill at the time, I didn't feel that I was in a fit state to go. (P. 157-159.)

2. Francis Bacon on Film Director Sergej Eisenstein:

FB: [...] There are some films that I've liked a lot. Perhaps they've had an influence on me. The *Battleship Potemkin* by Eisenstein, for example, made a great impact on me when I saw it. You remember that scene where the child's pram rolls down the steps, that screaming woman, and the rest of the film [...] Oh, yes, cinema is great art! Of course, during the silent era, the image had tremendous force. The images of silent film were sometimes very powerful, very beautiful.
(P. 16.)

MA: *Apart from Eisenstein, are there any other film makers that you respect?*
FB: Well, he really was a great director. Buñuel too, of course. There are some very powerful images in Buñuel's work.
(P. 19.)

3. Francis Bacon on Edgar Degas:

FB: [...] It's his pastels that I particularly like. They are extraordinary. Especially the interiors with women and their toilet, the nudes rather than the dancers.
Generally speaking, his bodies of women are superb. He really is the only artist to have known how to handle pastels like that, with those lines between the colours.
(P. 43.)

4. Francis Bacon on Rembrandt Harmenszoon van Rijn:

FB: [...] The self-portraits of the end of his life are superb. He had done others earlier, but the later works are even more beautiful. The way in which it's always Rembrandt that you see, in an image which changes each time, is really astonishing, magnificent.
(P. 38.)

5. Francis Bacon on Alberto Giacometti:

FB: [...] I have always loved Giacometti's portraits, particularly those done in pencil or charcoal. I know he once said that the most exciting thing for him was to see some unknown quality materialize every day on the same face. I know exactly what he meant, and I've always thought that his portraits were very interesting. Of everything he's done, I much prefer his drawings to his sculpture. He is very much better known for his sculptures; they've been reproduced so much throughout the world. It's thanks to them that Giacometti is so well known today. I think people have failed to appreciate his drawings for a long time and, in my opinion, they're the strongest things he's done. I do like some of his sculptures, but certainly not those from the surrealist period, nor the famous works such as *The Nose* or *The Hand* which don't work. I think there are some sculptures by Picasso which are much more important than many of Giacometti's sculptures, but I definitely prefer his drawings.
(P. 70–71.)

6. Francis Bacon on Pablo Picasso:

FB: It was after staying in Paris, where I saw an exhibition of Picasso, that I said to myself that I was going to paint.
(P. 23.)

FB: [...] At a certain time in my life I was very much influenced by Picasso. Perhaps 'influence' isn't quite the right word, I certainly don't think Picasso would have used it. Let's perhaps say that Picasso helped me to see [...] No, not to see, it isn't even

that [...] Whatever it is, I admired Picasso greatly. For me, he was the genius of the century. Everything of his that I saw at that time had an huge effect on me. It changed me a lot. It was, as I told you, seeing an exhibition of his work at Rosenburg's that made me decide to begin to try and paint. Some of the things that I did then were very much influenced by him. Later on, I don't know. I think I've been influenced by everything I've seen. But it is true that Picasso was also influenced by everything. That's what I am thinking of when I talk about influence; something like that phenomenon of a sponge that absorbs everything.
(P. 31–32.)

FB: [...] I believe that Picasso had a great gift as a draughtsman, and more than anything it was his capacity always to do something new that was so extraordinary. There are many of his works that I don't like, nine-tenths of what he did, but he produced remarkable works at all periods of his life, and came up with something quite new each time. That is what's extraordinary. With such a vast output, one can't like everything anyway. For example, what he did from Velázques' *Las Meninas*, I don't like at all. I don't think it worked. But variations on a theme aren't that straightforward. I remember having a discussion with Giacometti on this subject. He asked me, 'But why all these variations?' I don't think he was really against the principle; in raising the question he simply wanted to explore the matter. In fact, some of Picasso's variations have been of interest, though what he did from Manet's *Dejeuner sur l'herbe*, like the *Meninas,* I don't really think was successful.
(P. 33.)

FB: [...] I don't like most of the works from the Cubist period either: I find them too decorative, they do absolutely nothing for me. They are variations again, a mixture based on the work of Cézanne and discoveries from African art. It's not a period I like.
(P. 34.)

FB: I don't like *Guernica* either. People have gone crazy over that work. Of course the work is of considerable importance as an historical event, but I don't think it's one of Picasso's best works. I don't know really, at any rate, it doesn't affect me. I think that his best works come from between 1926 and 1932. That's the period when he painted figures on beaches at Juan-les-Pins and other places in the north of France. He has invented some very interesting images in these pictures. It is said to be the period during which he was influenced by Surrealism, but he wasn't a Surrealist. He was Spanish. Perhaps in a way the Spanish are always Surrealists? It's also the period when he carried out a series of works inspired by meeting Marie-Thérèse Walter.
(P. 34–35.)

FB. [...] In a certain sense the Picassos that I like are violent, but not in their subject matter; they are violent in the colours and forms that they use, and it's because these pictures are so remarkably well executed that one could say that they are violent in a certain sense. They are violent because of the incredible emotional charge which they produce, and that is an impressive sort of violence.
MA: *It's not a violence that destroys, it's a constructive violence in some way.*
FB: Yes, that's how I see it. Certain works of Picasso have not only unlocked images for me, but also ways of thinking, and even ways of behaving. It doesn't happen often, but I have experienced it. They released something in me, and made way for something else. Let's say that it wasn't fruitless violence.
(P. 151–152.)

7. Francis Bacon on Michelangelo Buonarroti:

FB: [...] I like certain works by Michelangelo enormously, especially the drawings with their grandeur of form and grandeur of image.
(P. 37.)

8. Francis Bacon on Théodore Géricault:

MA: *I believe you've been to see the Géricault exhibition which is on at the Grand Palais in Paris. Do you like Géricault?*
FB: Yes. The impressive thing about Géricault is the sense of movement in everything. Especially the representation of the human body and of horses; everything is captured in an incredible sense of movement. But when I talk about movement, I don't mean the representation of speed, that's not what it's about at all. Géricault somehow had movement pinned to the body. He was fascinated by it.
(P. 41.)

9. Francis Bacon on Paul Cézanne:

FB: [...] I only like certain of his works. I have to choose them very carefully. I'm not sure what place he really has in the history of painting. I can see that he has been important, but I must admit I'm not madly enthusiastic about him, as many people are. All things considered, I think that I only like the works from the end of his life. [...] It's the period when there is almost nothing on the canvas, when the subjects have almost completely disappeared, are hardly there any more, when one has the impression that they have barely been sketched and that they're about to disappear.
(P. 42.)

10. Francis Bacon on Georges Seurat:

FB: I admire Seurat a lot. We have perhaps one of his best pictures here in London, *Bathers at Asnières,* which I think is a magnificent work [...]. But above all I like his sketches.
(P. 44.)

11. Francis Bacon on Vincent van Gogh:

FB: [...] His way of treating the material is quite different from the technique of the Impressionists. You know, his use of that very thick paint, that very thick material. His manner was unique. He is one of the great geniuses of painting. For me Van Gogh is the greatest. He really did find a new way of depicting reality, even for the simplest things, and that method wasn't realist, but was much more powerful than simple realism. It was really a work of re-creating reality.
(P. 42.)

12. Francis Bacon on Jean-Auguste-Dominique Ingres:

FB: I'm very fond of certain portraits by Ingres and I also like The Turkish Bath, but I don't see any value at all in history painting.
(P. 40.)

13. Francis Bacon on Surrealism:

MA: *We were talking about Leiris. He was part of the surrealist movement,*

between 1924 and 1929. Were you influenced either by surrealist writers or painters?
FB: No, I've never liked Surrealist painting. I'm not interested in Dali or Ernst. I think that it's the writers of this movement who were the best. All the texts, manifestos and reviews that they wrote, dreamed up and published and the great interest in reading and writing amongst Breton and his circle – that, in my opinion, constitutes the most interesting aspect of Surrealism.
MA: *In 1936, you were not accepted for a Surrealist exhibition?*
FB: That's true; my pictures were in fact refused because they were not sufficiently Surrealist! As a matter of fact, my relationship with Surrealism is a little complicated. I think that I've been influenced by what the movement represented in terms of revolt against the establishment, in politics, religion and the arts, but my pictures haven't really shown any direct influence. Well perhaps a little in my early work. Even in *Painting* of 1946. But in the end, my painting certainly has nothing to do with Surrealist painting. With hindsight, one could say that those who turned down my work for the 1936 exhibition were right. I'm not a Surrealist painter.
(P. 122–128.)

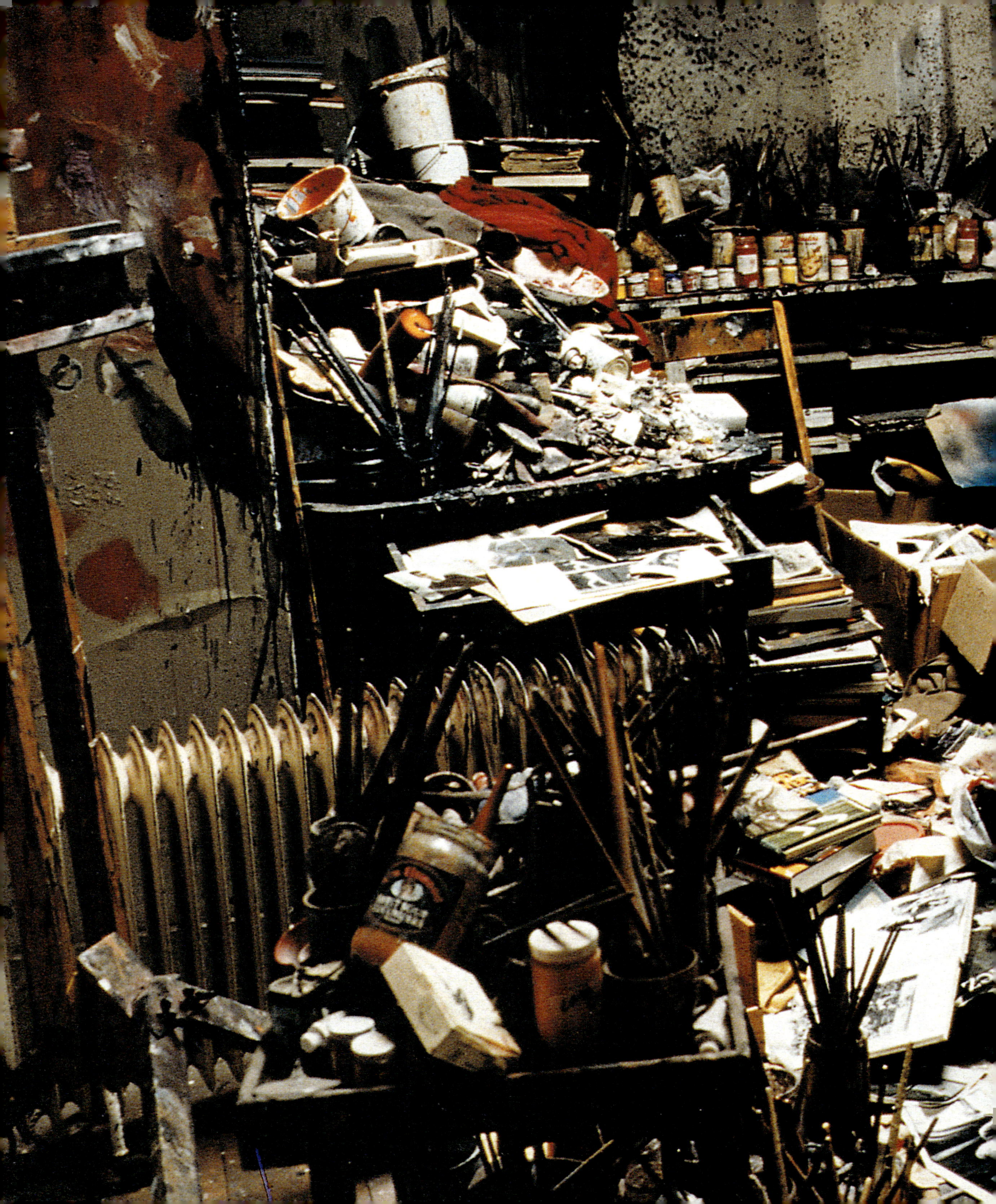

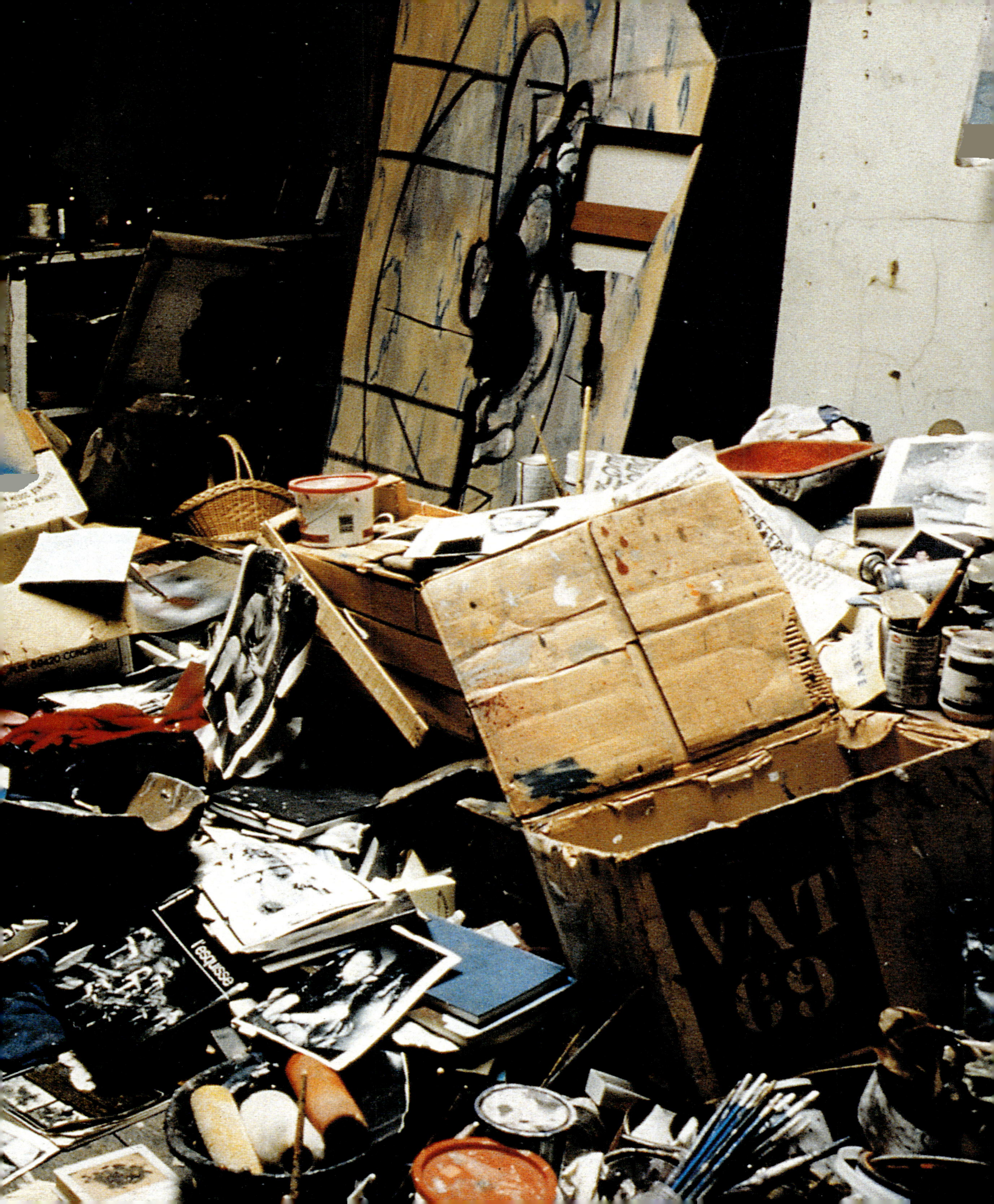
l'esquisse
VAT
69

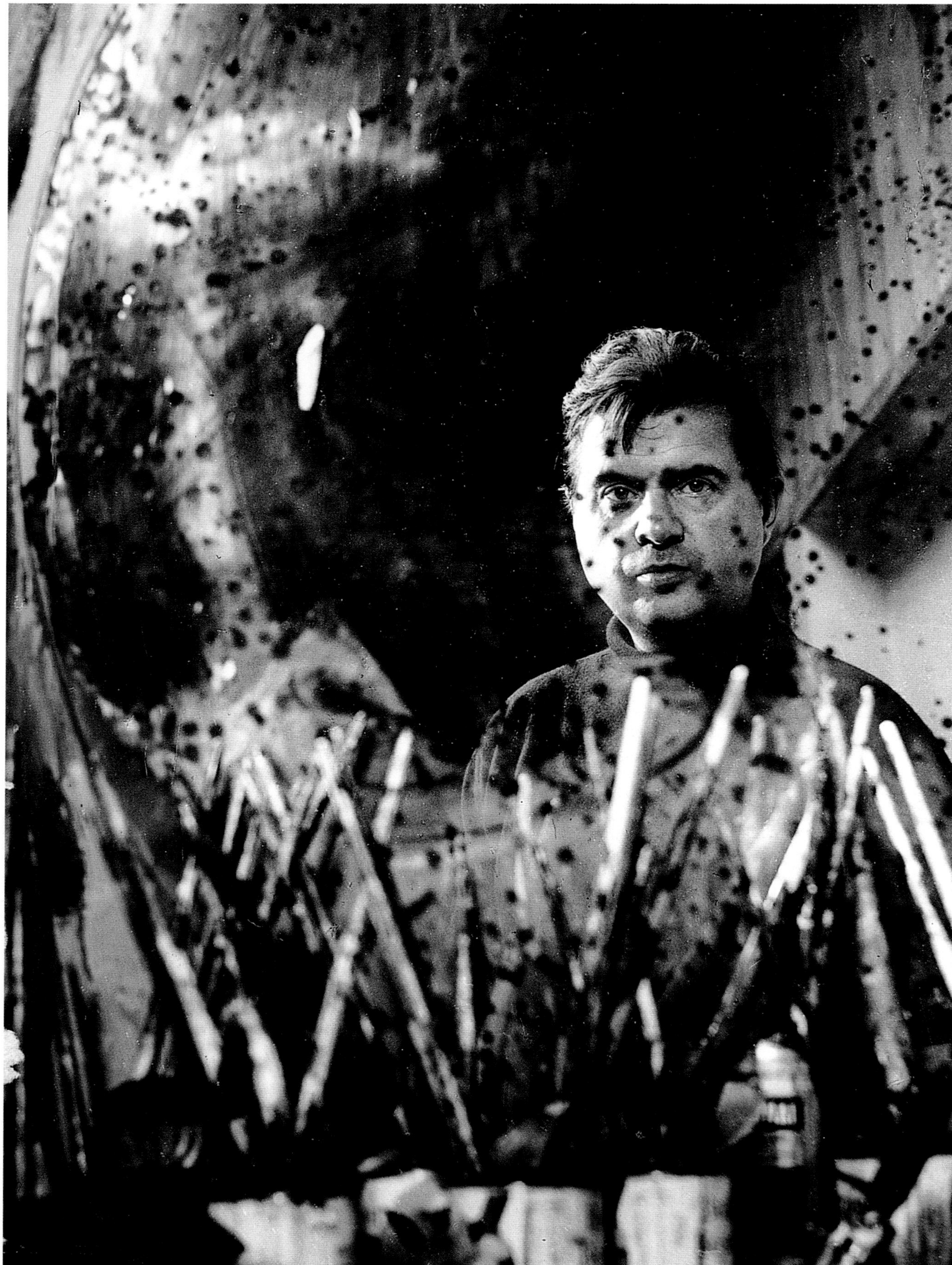

Biography and List of Solo Exhibitions

Biography

1909
Francis Bacon was born on 28 October 1909 in Dublin, the son of English parents. He was the second of the five children of Christina Winifred Bacon, née Firth, and of Edward Anthony Mortimer Bacon. His father, formerly in the army, was a racehorse trainer and claimed to be a descendant of the philosopher Sir Francis Bacon (1561–1626). From early childhood, Bacon suffered severe asthma.

1914–1925
At the start of the War, the family moved to London, and the father took up a position in the War Office. Towards the end of the War, the family lived between London and Ireland. Because of his asthma, frequent changes in residence and the upset of war, Francis Bacon never attended school regularly. Vehement quarrels with his father caused Bacon to leave his family at the age of sixteen. He spent several months in London, living on three pounds a week given him by his mother.

1926–1928
The father entrusted his son's education to a friend of his, a certain Harcourt-Smith. Accompanied by this new tutor, Bacon spent a few months in Berlin, followed by several months in Paris. Here he produced his first drawings and water-colours, after he had seen an exhibition of Picasso's drawings in the Galerie Paul Rosenberg in the summer of 1927.

1929
After returning to London, Bacon moved into 17 Queensbury Mews in South Kensington, a workshop turned into a studio. He worked as an interior designer, designed wall hangings and furniture in tubular shapes of steel and glass similar to those of Le Corbusier. He produced his first oil paintings, strongly influenced by cubism and surrealism. At the end of the year he held the first exhibition of his works, which were published the following year in the magazine *The Studio* as *The Look in British Decoration.* Bacon is spoken of as one of the most promising designers of his generation.

1930
Bacon meets Roy de Maistre, an Australian artist living in London, and they organise an exhibition together in November.

1931–1932
Bacon moves to Fulham Road and gradually gives up his work as a designer in favour of painting. He earns his living with casual jobs (telephonist, cook, valet, etc.).

1933
In April, Bacon moves to a new studio in Chelsea, at 71 Royal Hospital Road, where he stays until 1936. He paints his first significant pictures, including several *Crucifixions,* which are shown in two joint exhibitions in the Mayor Gallery. *Crucifixion* is reproduced in the influential book by Herbert Read *Art Now – An Introduction to the Theory of Modern Painting and Sculpture* which appears at the same time as the exhibition is showing at the Mayor Gallery. Read places Bacon's painting opposite Picasso's painting *Man bathing, with arm raised,* 1929. The painting is immediately bought by Sir Michael Sadler, a leading English collector.

1934/35
In February 1934 Bacon himself organises an exhibition of his works in a friend's house in Curzon Street. Here, in what Bacon calls the Transition Gallery, he shows seven paintings and six gouaches. His first self-organised exhibition is neither a success with the public nor with the media. Subsequently, Bacon paints less and less and begins to gamble in casinos. In 1935 Bacon sees Eisenstein's film *Battleship Potemkin* for the first time, and is hugely impressed.

1936
Bacon rents a house in Gelbe Street, S.W.3 and sets up his studio on the top floor. Herbert Read and Roland Penrose visit him in order to select works for the *International Surrealist Exhibition* in the New Burlington Galleries, but reject his style as being "not surrealistic enough" for the exhibition.

1937
In January, Bacon takes part in the joint exhibition *Young British Painters,* organised by his patron Eric Hall in the gallery of Thomas Agnew and Sons in London. Bacon and Hall select – among others – works by Victor Pasmore, Roy de Maistre and Graham Sutherland. Bacon himself shows three canvasses, among them *Figures in a Garden* of 1936.
Bacon's father dies on 1 June in Bradford Peverell, near Dorchester.

1941–1943
For a year, Bacon lives in a cottage in Petersfield in Hampshire. At the end of 1942 he returns to London and installs his studio at 7 Cromwell Place, South Kensington, previously occupied by the pre-Raphaelite painter John Everett Millais. He is spared military service on account of his asthma. At this time, Bacon destroys the majority of the works he has achieved up to now. Only fifteen pictures from the period 1929–1944 survive.

1944–1945
From now on Bacon devotes himself exclusively to painting. He completes *Three Studies for Figures at the Base of a Crucifixion* which he had begun a few years earlier. For him, this triptych represents the beginning of his

work, and is shown in April 1945 in the Lefevre Gallery together with *Figures in a Landscape* beside more recent works by Francis Hodgkins, Henry Moore, Matthew Smith and Graham Sutherland. Eric Hall purchases the triptych *Three Studies for Figures at the Base of a Crucifixion* (1944) and donates it to the Tate Gallery in 1953.

1946–1947

Bacon takes part in numerous joint exhibitions in the Lefevre Gallery, the Redfern Gallery and the Tate Gallery. He travels to Paris in order to show *Painting 1946* in the British section of the international exhibition of modern art, organised by Jean Cassou for UNESCO in the Musée d'art moderne in November 1946. Following the advice of his friend Graham Sutherland, Erika Brausen, future director of the Hanover Gallery, visits Bacon's studio and purchases *Painting 1946*. Bacon makes use of the unexpected financial windfall and travels to Monte Carlo, where he often stayed until 1950, mainly devoting himself to his passion for gambling.

1948

Erika Brausen sells *Painting 1946* to the director of the Museum of Modern Art in New York, Alfred J. Barr.

1949

With the prospect of his first exhibition in the Hanover Gallery, Bacon returns to London in order to complete the series of the six *Heads* he had begun the previous year. In the last picture *(Head VI)* the figure of the screaming pope appears for the first time. Wyndham Lewis, one of the leading English painters and art theoreticians of the 20th century and leader of the so-called Vorticists, writes in the magazine The Listener: "Not one of the contemporary young artists paints as grandiosely as Bacon. Some of his paintings remind me of Velázquez and, like the Master, he prefers black." (Wyndham Lewis in The Listener, 17 November 1949, p. 860.) In the late 1940's and early 1950's Bacon finds many new friends and drinking companions, among them artists such as Robert Colquhoun, John Minton, Denis Wirth-Miller, Richard Chopping, Lucian Freud, Michael Wishart, Isabel Lampert (later Rawsthorne), Robert Buhler, Rodrigo Moynihan and, a few years later, Frank Auerbach and Michael Andrews. A few of these friendships are short-lived, others survive. The most important are those with Wirth-Miller, Freud and Isabel Rawsthorne. Some of these artists belong to the teaching staff of the Royal College of Art. Among other friends and acquaintances from this time are Peter Watson, Sonia Orwell, Muriel Belcher, Henrietta Law (later Moraes), John Deakin, David Sylvester and Dan Farson.

Favourite meeting-places are: in Soho the "Colony Room," a Bar owned and run by Muriel Belcher; the "Gargoyle," a nightclub founded in the 1920's for which Matisse designed the decoration; "Wheelers," a fish restaurant and the "York Minster," today known as "The French House;" in South Kensington a pub known as the "Queen's Elm" and – at lunchtime – the "Senior Common Room" at the Royal College of Art.

1950

In preparation for an exhibition entitled *Francis Bacon: Recent Paintings* to be held in September and October in the Hanover Gallery, Bacon begins a series of three pope figures after the painting *Pope Innocent X* by Velázquez. He paints only the first two pictures which are destroyed after the exhibition. In the same year, Bacon takes part in several joint exhibitions in Great Britain and the USA. In the autumn, Bacon teaches for a few weeks at the Royal College of Art in London as a substitute for John Milton. In November, Bacon travels to South Africa to visit his mother. He stays for a few days in Cairo and is inspired by the art of ancient Egypt. Bacon meets the young art critic David Sylvester, with whom he has many conversations between 1962 and 1986.

1951

Bacon sells his studio at 7 Cromwell Place. He moves several times until 1955. For some time he lives in the Carlyle Studios in Chelsea and then works in a studio lent to him by his friend Rodrigo Moynihan of the Royal College of Art until the autumn of 1953. He paints the first *Portrait of Lucian Freud* – inspired by a Kafka photograph – and a series of three popes which are shown in his first exclusive exhibition at the Hanover Gallery.

1952

In the spring, Bacon travels for a second time to South Africa and Kenya. Lucian Freud paints a portrait of Bacon which will later be purchased by the Tate Gallery. The photographer and friend John Deakin is equally impressed by Bacon's face and is at the same time making a close-up study of the painter.

Bacon meets Peter Lacy, a test pilot who had fought in the Battle of Britain.

In July and August, he takes part in the joint exhibition *Recent Trends in Realist Painting* organised by Robert Melville and David Sylvester at the Institute of Contemporary Arts in London. At the end of the year Bacon presents, in an exclusive exhibition at the Hanover Gallery, landscapes inspired by Africa and the South of France, as well as two dogs painted after photographs by Muybridge.

1953

For a short time Bacon installs himself at 6 Beaufort Gardens in Chelsea, then rents accommodation for the summer at Hurst near Henley-on-Thames next door to Peter Lacy. During 1953, Bacon paints more than twenty pictures, among them two *Sphinx* paintings, inspired by his visit to Cairo and photos of marching Nazis in the stadium at Nürnberg. *Two Figures,* showing two figures on a bed, painted after photos of wrestlers by Muybridge, causes a scandal when it is shown in 1953 in the Hanover Gallery. Bacon paints a *Study after Velázquez' Portrait of Pope Innocent X* and the series of eight *Studies for Portrait.* The eight canvasses are sent to New York for Bacon's first exclusive exhibition outside Great Britain, which takes place in the Durlacher Gallery in October. David Sylvester introduces Bacon to the director of the Beaux-Arts Gallery in London (Bruton Street), Helen Lessore, who plans an exhibition for Bacon in November.

Bacon lives for a few weeks at Apollo Place 9, where David Sylvester lives.

1954

In February, Bacon lives in a furnished room at 19 Cromwell Place and in March in the Hotel Imperial at Henley-on-Thames. The series *Men in Blue* is produced and is to be shown in the summer in an exclusive exhibition in the Hanover Gallery.

On a trip to Italy, Bacon visits Ostia and Rome, but does not see *Pope Innocent X*, the Velázquez picture that he admires so much, in the Palazzo Doria Pamphilij. He also does not visit the Biennale in Venice, where twelve of his pictures are presented by David Sylvester in the British pavilion, together with pictures by Ben Nicholson and Lucian Freud. With Barbara Hepworth and William Scott, Bacon participates in a joint exhibition at the Martha Jackson Gallery in New York.

1955

In January, the Institute of Contemporary Arts in London organises the first retrospective exhibition with thirteen pictures by Francis Bacon. He moves into an apartment near Sloane Street and works in a studio in Mallord Street in Chelsea, where Michael Astor had worked before him. In March, he is commissioned by Lisa Sainsbury to portrait her husband, Sir Robert Sainsbury. Between the autumn of 1955 and the spring of 1957 Bacon begins a series of eight portraits of Lisa Sainsbury, of which only three have survived. In May, Bacon participates in a joint exhibition *The New Decade* in the Museum of Modern Art in New York. In the framework of a joint exhibition in the Hanover Gallery he shows a series of portraits after the life mask of William Blake, which is kept in the National Portrait Gallery in London. In the autumn, he moves into an apartment at 9 Overstrand Mansions in Battersea, which he shares with Paul Danquah, an internationally renowned lawyer, and Peter Pollock. He stays here for six years.

1956

In the spring, Bacon paints the first of six pictures, inspired by the self-portrait *The Street Painter of Tarascon* by Vincent van Gogh (1888). This picture was destroyed in Germany during the Second World War, but Bacon knew it from reproductions. In the summer, Francis Bacon and Peter Pollock are invited to Tangiers by Peter Lacy. After staying in various hotels, Bacon rents an apartment which he uses during his numerous visits until the 1960's. In Tangiers, Bacon meets the *Beat* writers. Back in London, he paints his first self-portrait.

1957

In February, Jean Larcade, director of the Gallery Rive Droite, arranges with Erika Brausen Bacon's first exhibition in Paris. This is followed in March by an exhibition in the Hanover Gallery in London, and this includes the six *Studies for a Portrait of Van Gogh.*

Bacon leaves in May to meet Peter Lacy in Tangiers, staying there throughout the summer. In October, he takes part in a joint exhibition entitled *La peinture britannique contemporaine*, organised by Eric Newton in the Galerie Raymond Creuze in Paris.

1958

At the beginning of 1958, exhibitions of Bacon's works were shown in Italy for the first time. These were in the Galleria Galatea in Turin, then in the Galleria dell'Ariete in Milan and finally in the Galleria dell'Obelisco in Rome. The Arts Council of Great Britain organises a major travelling exhibition *Three Masters of Modern British Painting*, in which besides Francis Bacon, Victor Pasmore and Matthew Smith participate.

Bacon suddenly leaves the Hanover Gallery and signs a contract with the Marlborough Fine Art Gallery (at that time at 18 Old Bond Street).

1959

In June, the last exhibition of Bacon's works takes place in the Hanover Gallery. In July, the Richard Feigen Gallery in Chicago presents a mini-retrospective, containing twelve paintings. Three of Bacon's works are shown at the Dokumenta II in Kassel, twelve at the V. Biennale in San Paulo and five in the joint exhibition *New Image of Man* in the Museum of Modern Art in New York.

1960

At the beginning of the year Bacon participates in the exhibition *Antagonismes* in the Musée des arts décoratifs in Paris and presents a *Lying Figure* in the XVI Salon du Mai in the Musée de l'art moderne de la Ville de Paris. He is represented in this salon also in the years 1961, 1962 and 1964. The Marlborough Fine Arts Gallery in London organises for the first time an exhibition of Francis Bacon's works, at which more than thirty paintings from the years 1959–60 are shown. The exhibition is a huge success. Two pictures are shown in a joint exhibition in Moscow and Leningrad.

1961

In the autumn, Bacon moves into Reece Mews in South Kensington, with a studio above a former stable. He is to live here until the end of his life. The studio is abandoned to chaos, which Bacon says is necessary for his work.

1962

Participation in *Art since 1950* at the World Exhibition in Seattle. In May, John Rothenstein organises in the Tate Gallery in London a large-scale retrospective of Francis Bacon's works. 92 paintings are displayed, almost half those existing at this time. For this occasion, in great haste Bacon paints his first large triptych *Three Studies for a Crucifixion,* which is still damp when he delivers it to the Tate. After the exhibition, the left-hand panel is painted over and the work is acquired by the Guggenheim Museum in New York. On the opening day of the exhibition, Bacon receives a telegram with the news of the death of Peter Lacy in Tangiers. The exhibition achieves sensational success. Subsequently it is shown in the Kunsthalle in Mannheim, in the Galeria Civica d'Arte Moderna in Turin, in the Kunsthaus in Zurich and in the Stedelijk Museum in Amsterdam. Bacon meets Alberto Giacometti through Isabel Rawsthorne, a former model and lover of the sculptor. In 1964 Giacometti comes to London in order to prepare his retrospective, planned for 1965. In October, Sylvester records a conversation with Bacon for a BBC broadcast, the start of a series of nine interviews he will have with Bacon until 1986.

1963

Bacon paints *Landscape near Malabata, Tangiers* in memory of his friend Peter Lacy who had died shortly before, and the *Portrait of Henrietta Moraes* after a series of photographs which John Deakin had been commissioned to make, showing a young woman in various poses naked on a bed. These photographs form the basis for many paintings from the 1960's. His works are shown in Naples in 1965 at the side of those by Graham Sutherland. In July, the Marlborough Gallery places works by Bacon side by side with those of Henry Moore. In 1965 a further exhibition will unite Bacon and Moore. After the exhibition in the Tate Gallery, the Guggenheim Museum in New York itself organises a Bacon retrospective with 64 works. The exhibition is subsequently shown at the Art Institute in Chicago and in the Contemporary Arts Association in Houston.

1964

Bacon paints the great triptych *Three Figures in a Room*, bought by the Centre national d'art contemporaine in 1969, and the first portrait of Isabel Rawsthorne. He participates in numerous joint exhibitions in Great Britain and abroad, including the Dokumenta III in Kassel, where a whole room is devoted to his works.

Roland Alley publishes in the edition

Thames and Hudson a list of Bacon's works with a foreword by John Rothenstein, director of the Tate Gallery. The work numbers 300 pages and includes 221 known, 13 unfinished and 9 destroyed pictures. Bacon paints the first portrait of his friend and model George Dyer.

1965

Bacon paints *Crucifixion,* a large triptych, which is acquired by the Staatsgalerie moderner Kunst in Munich.

In July, he meets Michel Leiris at the opening of Alberto Giacometti's retrospective in the Tate Gallery in London. A long and fruitful friendship develops between the French writer and the painter. A few days before the private viewing of the Giacometti exhibition, the Marlborough Gallery opens an exhibition with new works by Bacon. The "new" Bacons are displayed in the Marlborough Gallery parallel to the largest retrospective of Giacometti's works of the time in the Tate Gallery. They are old friends, and more than one of Bacon's compositions remind one of the cage which had pursued Giacometti since his childhood. They both have an obsession for the impossible and a great tendency to destroy their works. For both artists, and also for us, it was an enriching experience to go from one exhibition to the other "(Giacometti, by the way, spent the duration of his own private viewing in the Marlborough Gallery)" (Russell 1965, p. 51).

1966

In November, an exhibition with more than fifteen new pictures opens in the Galerie Maeght in Paris. Bacon is present at the private viewing and is very pleased with the success of his exhibition in Paris. Michel Leiris writes his first text on Francis Bacon in the magazine Derrière le miroir, which the Galerie Maeght publishes in conjunction with the exhibition. The exhibition is then shown in the Marlborough Gallery in Rome, and in an expanded version in the Marlborough Gallery in London. On this occasion, Bacon befriends the photographer Peter Beard. George Dyer is more and more frequently the model of the numerous pictures Bacon produces. *Portrait George Dyer, Crouching, Portrait George Dyer Riding a Bicycle, George Dyer Staring at a Blind Card.*

1967

Bacon receives two international prizes; the Carnegie Institute Award in Painting of the Pittsburgh World Exhibition, which he refuses, and the Rubens Prize. The latter is awarded in June at Siegen, Rubens' birthplace. He donates the prize money for the restoration of art works in Florence following the severe flooding of the city.

In the summer, an exhibition of his works at the Marlborough Gallery in London includes for the first time small portraits, often put together as triptychs.

1968

At Kooning's wish, Bacon meets him as Kooning passes through London in the company of Xavier Fourcarde. Bacon spends several weeks with his sick mother in South Africa. For his first exhibition in the Marlborough Gallery in New York, he travels to the USA for the first time. Twenty new pictures are shown, all are sold during the first week. The triptych inspired by T.S. Elliot's poem *Sweeney Agonistes,* painted in 1967, is acquired for the Joseph H. Hirschhorn Foundation in Washington, which already owns eight other pictures by Bacon. For six months he enjoys the advantages of a large studio in the Royal College of Art in London.

1969

Bacon paints three studies on a bullfight. His 1964 triptych is shown in the exhibition of new acquisitions at the Centre national d'art contemporaine in Paris.

1970

Bacon moves into a house in Narrow Street on the bank of the Thames in Limehouse in the East End of London. The movement of the river and the resulting restlessly flickering light make it impossible for him to work there. To do his work, he therefore returns immediately to Reece Mews. In September, Bacon is arrested for the illegal possession of marihuana, but for lack of evidence is released immediately.

1971

On 14 April, Francis Bacon's mother dies in South Africa. In October, Blaise Gautier organises the first retrospective of Francis Bacon in France. Originally planned for the Musée des arts décoratifs, the exhibition finally takes place in rooms at the Grand Palais, at the same time as an exhibition of the works of Fernand Léger. It consists of 108 pictures, including 12 triptychs. Because the conservators of the Museum of Modern Art decline the loan of *Painting 1946* on account of its fragility, Bacon paints a second version. Following restoration, at which Bacon himself is present, the painting is finally taken to Paris and both versions can be hung side by side.

Two evenings before the opening of the exhibition, George Dyer commits suicide in the room he shares with Bacon in the Hotel Saint-Pères. On the occasion of the exhibition, a monograph by John Deakin appears, which is published in London the same year. In a ranking published every five years by the magazine Connaissances des Arts, Bacon leads the ten most significant living artists; Picasso is granted a position of honour. In November and December Bacon paints the triptych *In Memory of George Dyer.*

1972–1973

Following the exhibition in the Grand Palais, the retrospective is shown in the Kunsthalle Dusseldorf. John Deakin, who had accompanied Bacon to his exhibition in the Grand Palais, dies in May in Brighton, where Bacon had sent him for his health. Bacon paints more and more self-portraits, as well as numerous portraits from photos great photographers had taken of him, as well as from some taken in automatic photo booths. "I have made a number of self-portraits, simply because people around me have been dying like flies and there is nothing else to paint except myself" (Sylvester 1997, p. 129). He produces a series of large triptychs, which Hugh Davies assembles under the title *Black Triptychs.*

1974

Bacon meets John Edwards, who will become his model and best friend, and who will later inherit his estate. John Edwards takes over the role of photographer previously filled by John Deakin, and takes the photos required by the painter.

1975

The day of the exhibition in the Grand Palais, the Metropolitan Museum in New York suggests to Bacon that they will organise an exhibition of his newest works. *Francis Bacon, Recent Paintings 1968–1974* includes 35 paintings and opens in March, it is the first exhibition this museum has devoted to a contemporary English artist. Curator of the exhibition is Henry Geldzahler. During the exhibition, the collection of the four first interviews David Sylvester made with Bacon between

1962 and 1974 appears in New York and in London. Bacon is now more and more in Paris, where he moves into rooms at 14 Rue de Birague, near the Place des Vosges, which he also uses as a studio.

1976

Bacon paints the first portrait of Michel Leiris. Marielle Latour, director of the Marseilles museums, presents sixteen new works in the Musée Cantini, including six triptychs. Five conversations with David Sylvester are translated into French by Michael Peppiatt and Michel Leiris, the latter also writing the foreword. They are published by Edition Skira with the title *L'Art de l'Impossible.*

1977

In January, the Galerie Claude Bernard organises an important exhibition of Bacon's new works. A catalogue with a foreword by Michel Leiris appears, who sees his own portrait only shortly before the opening of the exhibition. Bacon, who comes to Paris for all his exhibitions there, says later that this one showed the best of his pictures that had ever been seen in a gallery. The exhibition is a sensational success and attracts so many visitors that the police have to close the road. Bacon spends a short time in Rome where, through Isabel Rawsthorne, he meets Balthus in the Villa Medici.

At the end of the year an exhibition of his works takes place in Mexico, later in the Museo de arte contemporáneo in Caracas. Participation in Dokumenta VI in Kassel.

1978

Bacon paints a second portrait of Michel Leiris.

Inspired by two verses from *The Waste Land* by T.S. Elliot ("I heard the turning of the key in the lock once, in the castle only once") he produces *Painting 1978* (Russell 1971/94, p. 182). In the spring, an exhibition is organised in Madrid by the Fondación Juan March, which is then shown in the Fondación Joan Miró in Barcelona. The city of Frankfurt offers Bacon the Max Beckmann Prize, which he however declines.

1979–1980

Following the death of Muriel Belcher at the end of October 1979, Bacon paints *Sphinx – Portrait of Muriel Belcher.*

In April 1980, an exhibition opens in the Marlborough Gallery in New York, showing his new paintings.

1981

His younger sister Winifred dies at the end of March. In May, Michel Leiris publishes *Bacon, le hors-la-loi (Bacon, the outlaw)* in the magazine Critique. Leiris devotes a short text to Bacon in a special number of the magazine L'ire des vents. The book *Francis Bacon – Logique de la Sensation* by Gilles Deleuze is published by Edition La Différence.

1982

Inspired by Ingres, Bacon paints two pictures: in 1982 the *Study of the Human Body – after a Drawing by Ingres,* based on a sketch by Ingres for *The Turkish Bath* and *Oedipus and the Sphinx after Ingres,* 1983.

1983

The Musée national d'art moderne in Tokyo organises Bacon's first exhibition in Japan. It will be seen later in Kyoto and Nagoya.

1984

In January, Bacon returns to Paris for the opening of an exhibition in the Galerie Maeght-Lelong. Michel Leiris' essay *Francis Bacon, en face et en profil* is seen for the first time in the framework of this exhibition. In May, Bacon is in New York for an exclusive exhibition in the Marlborough Gallery. Louise and Michel Leiris donate four portraits by Bacon to the Centre Georges Pompidou (Collection Kahnweiler-Leiris); a self-portrait (1971), two portraits of Michel Leiris (1976 and 1978) and a portrait of Isabel Rawsthorne (1966). For an exhibition of John Deakins' photographs at the Victoria and Albert Museum in London, Bacon writes a short text in memory of his deceased friend.

1985–1986

The Tate Gallery in London organises another Bacon retrospective. This includes 125 pictures from the period 1944 to 1984. Subsequently, the exhibition is shown in Stuttgart and Berlin. The National Gallery in London asks Bacon to select works from its collection for an exhibition with the title *The Artist's Eye.* He declines, as besides the works selected by him, some of his own works were to be shown, which is actually what the organisers had intended. For an exhibition in the Neue Nationalgalerie, Bacon travels to Berlin, where he had not been since 1926.

1987

In May, an exhibition of Bacon's works takes place in the Marlborough Gallery in New York; in June there is a retrospective in the Galerie Beyeler. In September, an exhibition in the Galerie Lelong in Paris follows and Bacon attends the private viewing. The daily newspaper Le Monde reports extensively on the exhibition on its first page, and the media speaks of the "Bacon Myth." Bacon paints a large triptych with a bullfight as the subject. He had already started it in 1969. Later, Bacon dismantles the triptych and keeps only the right-hand panel. A third impression of the interview with David Sylvester appears in London, *The Brutality of Fact,* expanded by four new interviews.

1988

James Birch, owner of a gallery in Soho, organises a Bacon exhibition in Moscow, with the support of a Soviet diplomat Serge Klokhov, the British Council and the Marlborough Gallery – this is a premiere for a living artist from the West. It takes place in the Central House of Art and shows 22 pictures from the period 1945 to 1988. For a retrospective prepared by the Hirschhorn Museum in Washington, Bacon paints a *Second Version of Triptych 1944* on learning that the first version is too fragile to transport.

1989

Before the *Second Version of Triptych 1944* is seen in the American exhibition, it is shown in the Marlborough Fine Art in the framework of the exhibition *Auerbach, Bacon, Kitaj,* then for a few days in the Galerie Lelong and in the Librairie Seguier in Paris. In October, James T. Demetrion, director of the Hirschhorn Museum in Washington, opens the painter's first American retrospective since his 1963 exhibition in the Guggenheim Museum. Subsequently it is shown in Los Angeles and in New York.

A further exclusive exhibition takes place in October in the Marlborough Gallery in Tokyo.

1990

Bacon travels to Madrid to see the Velázquez exhibition in the Prado. Michel Leiris dies on 30 September. The Marlborough shows Bacon's painting in May, the Tate Gallery in Liverpool at the end of the year.

1991

Bacon paints *Study of the Human Body* with John Edwards as model. The Tate Gallery devotes a whole room in its new extension to Bacon's works. In October, Michel Archimbaud starts a series of interviews with Bacon, to be published in 1992.

1992
Isabel Rawsthorne dies at the end of the year. During a visit to Madrid in April, Bacon contracts pneumonia due to his asthma and is taken to hospital. He dies six days later of a heart attack on 28 April, at the age of 82.

Exhibitions

1929
London, in his studio, 7 Queensberry Mews West, winter
1934
London, Transition Gallery, Sunderland House, Curzon Street, February
1951
London, Hanover Gallery, December 1951 – February, 1952
1952
London, Hanover Gallery, December 1952 – January, 1953
1953
New York, Durlacher Bros., 20 October – 14 November
London, Beaux-Arts Gallery, *Francis Bacon: New Paintings,* 12 November – 9 December
1954
London, Hanover Gallery, June – July
1955
London, Institute of Contemporary Arts (ICA). *Paintings by Francis Bacon.* 20 January – 19 February
1957
Paris, Galerie Rive Droite, 12 February – 10 March
London, Hanover Gallery, 21 March – 26 April
1958
Turin, Galleria Galatea, 23 January – 10 February/Milan, Galleria dell'Ariete, 17 February – 5 March/Rome, Galleria l'Obelisco, March
1959
London, Hanover Gallery, 9 June – 6 July
Chicago, Richard L. Feigen Gallery, *Francis Bacon, 12 paintings 1947–1958,* 6 July – 1 August
1960
London, Marlborough Fine Art, *Francis Bacon, Paintings 1959–1960,* 23 March – April
1961
Nottingham, Nottingham University, Department of Fine Art, 16 February – 17 March
1962
London, Tate Gallery, *Francis Bacon,* 24 May – 1 July/Mannheim, Städtische Kunsthalle, 18 July – 26 August/Turin, Galleria civica d'arte moderna, 11 September – 14 October/Zurich, Kunsthaus, 27 October – 25 November/Amsterdam, Stedelijk Museum, 11 January – 18 February, 1963
Milan, Galleria Galatea, 10 October – 6 November
1963
New York, Granville Gallery, 3 October – 2 November
New York, Solomon R. Guggenheim Museum, *Francis Bacon,* 18. October 1963 – 12 January 1964/Chicago, Art Institute, 24 January – 23 February, 1964
1964
Houston, Contemporary Arts Association, 24 September – 1 November
1965
Hamburg, Hamburger Kunstverein, *Francis Bacon,* 23 January – 21 February/Stockholm, Moderna Museet, *Francis Bacon, Mälningar 1945–1964,* 27 February – 4 April/Dublin, Municipal Gallery of Modern Art, April – May
1966
Milan, Galleria Toninelli Arte Moderna, *Francis Bacon: Mostra di undici dipinti,* January – February
Paris, Galerie Maeght, 15 November – 31 December/Rome, Marlborough Galleria d'Arte, January 1967/Milan, Galleria Toninelli Arte Moderna, *Francis Bacon, opere recenti,* 2–18 February 1967/London, Marlborough Fine Art, *Francis Bacon: Recent Paintings,* March – April, 1967/Siegen, Upper Castle, 28 June – 23 July, 1967
1968
New York, Marlborough-Gerson Gallery, *Francis Bacon: Recent Paintings,* 11 November – 7 December
1970
Turin, Galleria Galatea, March – April
1971
Paris, Galeries nationales du Grand Palais, *Francis Bacon: Rétrospective,* 26 October 1971 – 10 January, 1972/Düsseldorf, Städtische Kunsthalle, 7 March – 7 May, 1972
1972
Milan, Galleria del Milione, 16 December 1972 – 18 January, 1973
1975
New York, Metropolitan Museum of Art, *Francis Bacon: Recent Paintings 1968–1974,* 20 March – 29 June
Zurich, Galerie Marlborough, 7 May – 26 July
1976
Marseille, Musée Cantini, *Francis Bacon, oeuvres récentes,* 9 July – 30 September
1977
Paris, Galerie Claude Bernard, *Francis Bacon, oeuvres récentes,* 19 January – 26 March
Mexico, Museo de arte moderno, *Francis Bacon: oleos de 1970–1977,* October – December/Caracas, Museo de arte contemporaneo de Caracas, February, 1978
1978
Madrid, Fundación Juan March, April – May/Barcelona, Fundación Juan Miró, 2 June – 16 July
1980
Mannheim, Städtische Kunsthalle, *Francis Bacon: Schreiender Papst, 1951,* 8 March – 11 May
New York, Marlborough Gallery, *Francis Bacon, Recent Paintings,* 26 April – 7 June
1983
London, Marlborough Fine Art, *Francis Bacon*
Tokyo, National Museum of Modern Art, *Francis Bacon: Paintings 1945–1982,* 30 June – 14 August/Kyoto, National Museum of Modern Art, 13 September – 10 October/Nagoya, Aichi Prefectural Art Gallery, 12–28 November
1984
Paris, Galerie Maeght-Lelong, *Francis Bacon: peintures récentes,* 18 January – 25 February
Brüssel, Galerie Isy Brachot, *Francis Bacon, estampes, pour la première fois en Belgique,* 2 May – 30 June
New York, Marlborough Gallery, *Francis Bacon: Recent Paintings,* 5 May – 5 June
London, Thomas Gibson Gallery, June
1985
London, Marlborough Fine Art, *Francis Bacon, Paintings,* May – June
London, Tate Gallery, *Francis Bacon,* 22 May – 18 August/Stuttgart, Staatsgalerie, 18 October 1985 – 5 January 1986/Berlin, Nationalgalerie, 7 February – 31 March, 1986
1987
New York, Marlborough Gallery, *Francis Bacon, Paintings of the Eighties,* 7 May – 31 July
Basel, Galerie Beyeler, *Francis Bacon Retrospektive,* 12 June – 12 September
Paris, Galerie Lelong, *Francis Bacon, peintures récentes,* 30 September – 14 November
1988
Moscow, Central House of Art, New Tretjakow Gallery, *Francis Bacon,*

23 September – 6 November
Tokyo, Marlborough Fine Art, *Francis Bacon: Paintings,* 18 October 1988 – 21 January 1989
1989
Paris, Librairie Séguier (Presentation of the new 1988 version of the 1944 triptych by Francis Bacon in conjunction with the publication of the album by Dominique Jameux, dedicated to Pierre Boulez), 24 April
Paris, Galerie Lelong (Second version of the 1944 triptych: Francis Bacon's new picture is only displayed for two days), 20–21 May
Washington, Hirshhorn Museum and Sculpture Garden, Smithsonian Institution, *Francis Bacon,* 12 October 1989 – January 1990/Los Angeles, County Museum, 11 February – 29 April/New York, Museum of Modern Art, 24 May – 28 August
London, Marlborough Fine Art, "Francis Bacon: Loan Exhibition in Celebration of his 80th Birthday", 27 October – 18 November
1990
Glasgow, Barbizon Gallery, 2–25 April/Amsterdam, Bogard Fine Arts, 29 April – 1 June
New York, Marlborough Gallery, *Francis Bacon, Paintings,* 23 May – 29 June
Liverpool, Tate Gallery, *Francis Bacon,* 20 February 1990 – 13 January, 1991
1992
Madrid, Galeria Marlborough, *Francis Bacon, Pinturas 1981–1991,* 8 October – 14 November/New York, Marlborough Gallery, Francis Bacon, *Paintings 1981–1990,* April, 1993
1993
Lugano, Museo d'arte moderna, *Francis Bacon,* 7 March – 30 May
Venice, XLV Biennale di Venezia, Museo Correr, *Figurabile Francis Bacon,* 13 June – 10 October
London, Marlborough Fine Art, Francis Bacon 1909–1992: Small Portrait Studies, Loan Exhibition, 21 October – 3 December
1994
Berlin, Charlottenburg, Fine Art Rafael Vostell, *Francis Bacon, Einblicke in das graphische Werk,* 12 March – 28 May
1996
Paris, MNAM Centre Georges Pompidou, *Francis Bacon,* 27 June – 14 October/Munich, Haus der Kunst, 1 November 1996 – 26 January 1997
1998
Humlebaek, Louisiana Museum for Modern Art, *Francis Bacon,* 23 January – 26 April
London, Hayward Gallery, *Francis Bacon: The Human Body,* 5 February – 5 April
New York, Tony Shafrazi Gallery, *Francis Bacon: Important Paintings from The Estate,* 31 October 1998 – 16 January 1999
1999
New Haven, The Yale Center for British Art, *Francis Bacon. A Retrospective,* 25 January – 21 March/Minneapolis, The Minneapolis Institute of Arts, 8 April – 27 May/San Francisco, The Fine Arts Museums of San Francisco, 13 June – 2 August/Fort Worth, Modern Art Museum of Fort Worth, 20 August – 15 October
San Diego, Museum of Contemporary Art, *Francis Bacon: The Papal Portraits of 1953,* 17 January – 28 March
London, Tate Gallery, *Francis Bacon: Works on Paper,* 15 February – 2 May
Paris, Galerie Lelong, *Francis Bacon. Papes et Autres Figures,* 15 December, 1999–30 January, 2000
2000
Dublin, The Hugh Lane Municipal Gallery, *Francis Bacon in Dublin,* 1 June – 31 August
2001
The Hague, Gemeentemuseum Den Haag, *Francis Bacon,* 27 January – 13 May
Dublin, Hugh Lane Municipal Gallery of Modern Art, *Francis Bacon Studio* (permanent exhibition, opened on 31 May)
2002
London, Faggionato Fine Arts, *Francis Bacon: Last Paintings,* 4 April – 3 May
New York, Tony Shafrazi Gallery, *Francis Bacon: Paintings,* 6 April – 18 May
Arles, Fondation Vincent Van Gogh, *Van Gogh vu par Bacon,* 4 July – 6 October
New York, Marlborough Gallery, *Francis Bacon: Paintings,* 4 November – 7 December
2003
Porto, Museu de Arte Contemporânea de Serralves, *Francis Bacon: Caged – Uncaged,* 24 January – 20 April
Vienna, Kunsthistorisches Museum, *Francis Bacon und die Bildtradition,* 15 October 2003 – 18 January 2004/Riehen/Basel, Fondation Beyeler, 8 February – 20 June
2004
Valencia, IVAM, *The Sacred and the Profane,* 11 December, 2003 – 21 March, 2004/Paris, Musée Mayllol, 7 June, 2004 – 30 June, 2004

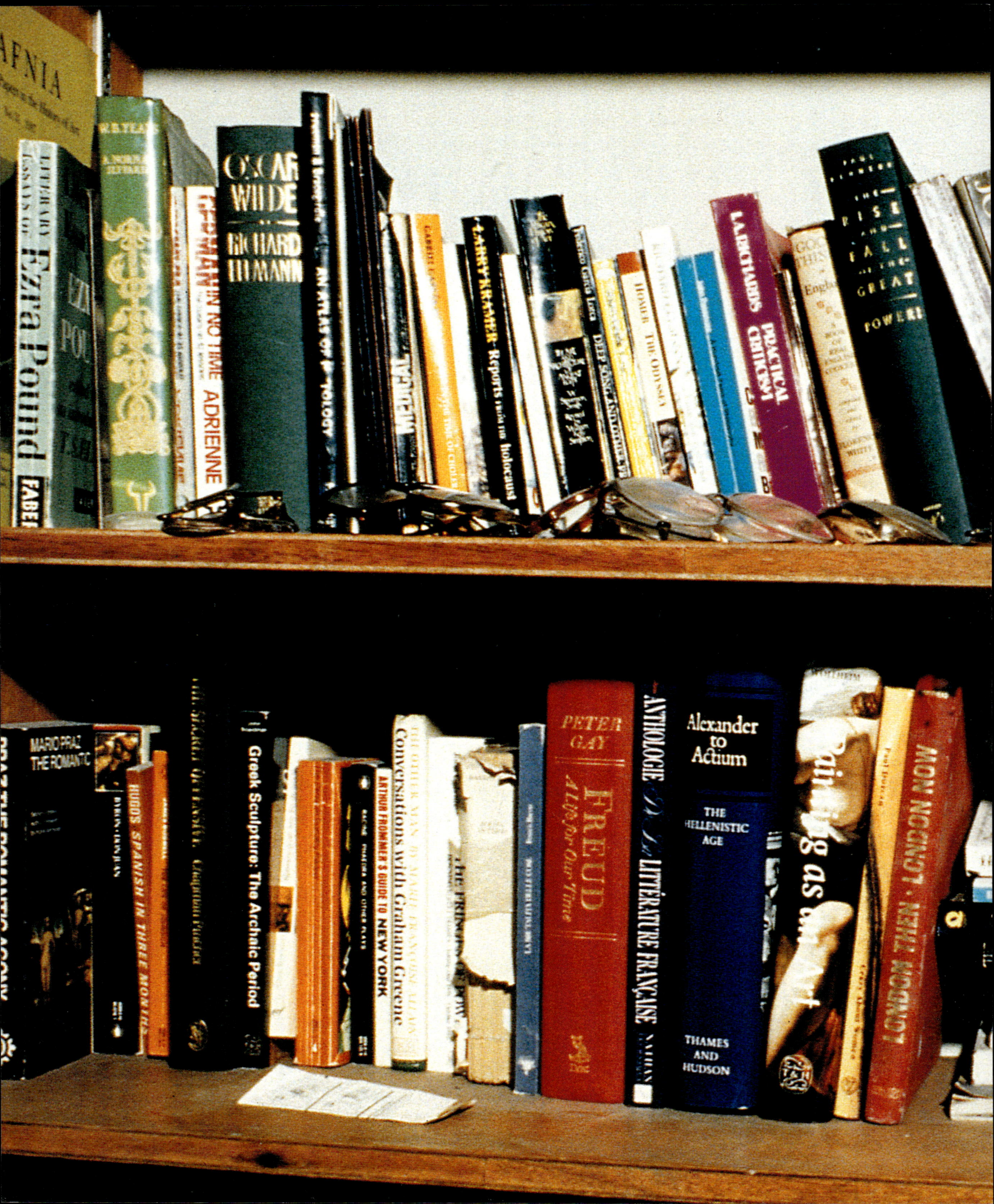

Ezra Pound
FABER
OSCAR WILDE
RICHARD ELLMANN
ADRIENNE
LARRY KRAMER
HOMER THE ODYSSEY
I.A. RICHARDS PRACTICAL CRITICISM
THE RISE AND FALL OF THE GREAT POWERS
MARIO PRAZ THE ROMANTIC
HUGO SPANISH IN THREE MONTHS
Greek Sculpture: The Archaic Period
ARTHUR FROMMER'S GUIDE TO NEW YORK
Conversations with Graham Greene
PETER GAY
FREUD
A Life for Our Time
ANTHOLOGIE
LITTÉRATURE FRANÇAISE
Alexander to Actium
THE HELLENISTIC AGE
THAMES AND HUDSON

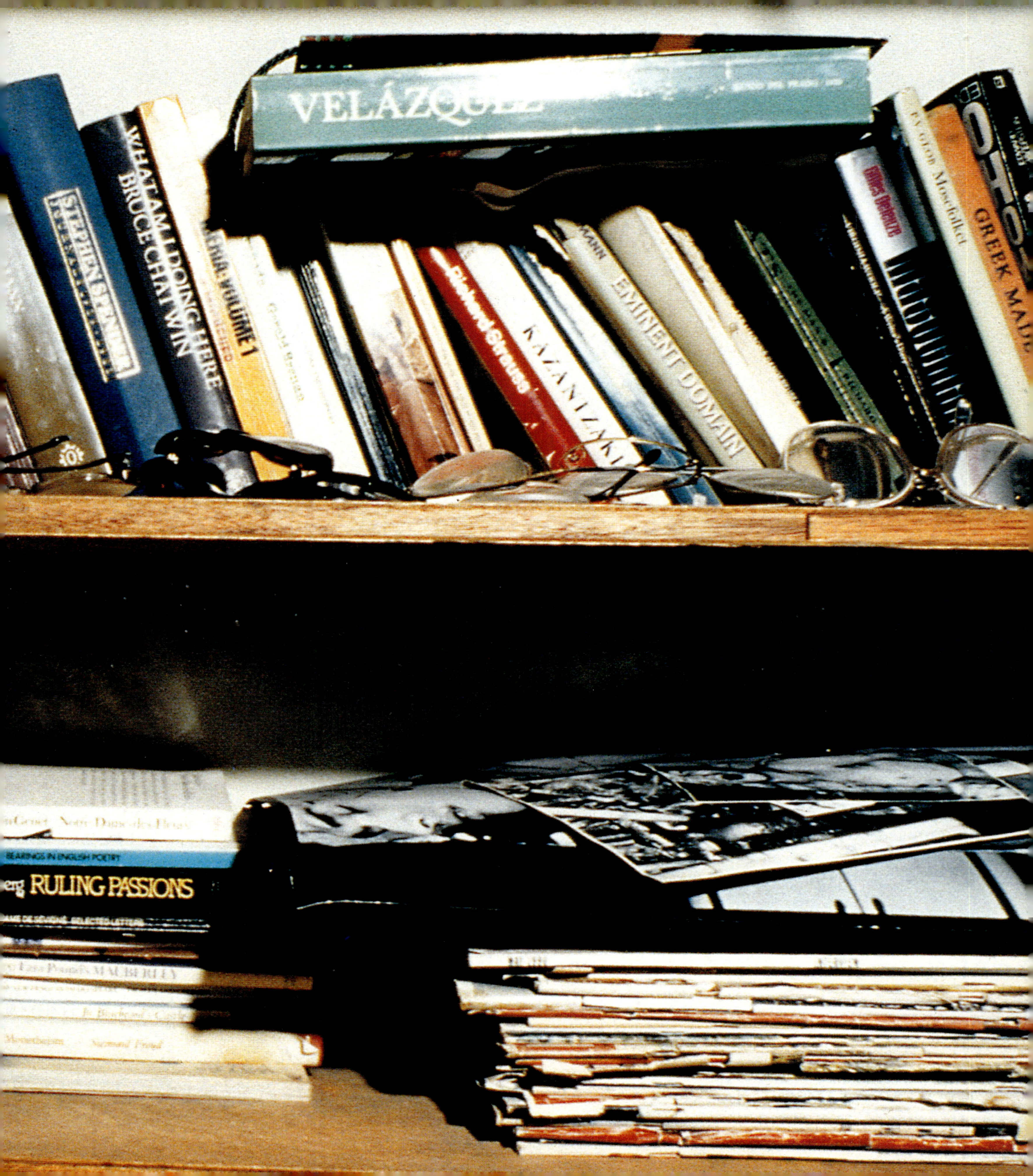
STEPHEN SPENDER
WHAT AM I DOING HERE
BRUCE CHATWIN
EMINENT DOMAIN
BEARINGS IN ENGLISH POETRY
RULING PASSIONS

Bibliography

Exhibition Catalogues Bacon

Francis Bacon. Recent Paintings, Marlborough Fine Art, London, July – August 1965
Francis Bacon, Paris (Galerie nationale du Grand Palais) and Düsseldorf (Städtische Kunsthalle) 1971–1972
Francis Bacon. Recent Paintings 1968–1974, New York (The Metropolitan Museum of Art) 1975
Francis Bacon, London (Tate Gallery) 1985
The Artist's Eye, curator: Francis Bacon, London (The National Gallery) 1985
Jean Clair (ed.), *The Body on the Cross,* Paris (Musée Picasso) and Montréal (Musée des Beaux-Arts) 1992
Rudi Chiappini (ed.), *Francis Bacon,* Lugano (Museo d'Arte Moderna) 1993
Bacon – Freud Expressions, St. Paul (Fondation Maeght) 1995
Trapping Appearance, Portraits by Francis Bacon and Alberto Giacometti from the Robert and Lisa Sainsbury Collection, Sainsbury Center for the Visual Arts, University of East Anglia, Norwich, 1996
Christoph Vitali (ed.), *Francis Bacon. 1909–1992. Retrospektive,* Munich (Haus der Kunst) and Paris (MNAM Centre Georges Pompidou) 1996
David Sylvester (ed.), *Francis Bacon: The Human Body,* London (Hayward Gallery) – Berkeley – Los Angeles 1998
Francis Bacon: Important Paintings from the Estate, New York (Tony Shafrazi Gallery) 1998
Dennis Farr (ed.), *Francis Bacon: A Retrospective,* New Haven (CT) (Yale Center for British Art) – Fort Worth 1999
Face to Face to Cyberspace, Riehen/Basel (Fondation Beyeler) 1999
Matthew Gale (ed.), *Francis Bacon: Working on Paper,* London (Tate Gallery) 1999
Francis Bacon, Paintings from The Estate 1980–1991, London (Faggionato Fine Arts) 1999
Francis Bacon in Dublin, Dublin (Hugh Lane Municipal Gallery of Modern Art) 2000
David Allan Mellor (ed.), *The Barry Joule Archive-Works on paper attributed to Francis Bacon,* Dublin (Irish Museum of Modern Art) 2000
Francis Bacon's Studio at the Hugh Lane, Dublin (Hugh Lane Municipal Gallery of Modern Art) 2001
Hugh M. Davies (ed.), *Francis Bacon. The Papal Portraits of 1953,* San Diego (Museum of Contemporary Art) 2001
Francis Bacon, Den Haag (Gemeentemuseum) – Zwolle (Gemeentemuseum) 2001
Maurice Tuchman (ed.), *The impact of Chaim Soutine: de Kooning, Pollock, Dubuffet, Bacon,* Cologne (Galerie Gmurzynska) 2002
The violence of Reality, Francis Bacon, New York (Tony Shafrazi Gallery) 2002
David Allan Mellor (ed.), *Van Gogh vu par Bacon,* Arles (Fondation Vincent van Gogh) Actes du Sud/Fondation Vincent van Gogh 2002
William Feaver (ed.), *Lucian Freud,* London (Tate Gallery) 2002
Francis Bacon. Caged. Uncaged, Porto (Museu de Arte Contemporânea de Serralves) 2003

Exhibition Catalogues of Other Artists:

Exposition de cent dessins par Picasso, Paris (Galerie Rosenberg) Juni – Juli 1927
Soutine, New York (The Museum of Modern Art) 1950
Picasso: A Retrospective, New York (The Museum of Modern Art) 1980
Paul Cézanne. Die Badenden, Basel (Kunstmuseum) – Zürich 1989
Judith Zilczer (ed.), *Willem de Kooning from the Hirshhorn Museum Collection,* Washington D. C. (Hirshhorn Museum and Sculpture Garden, Smithsonian Institution) 1993
¿Bunuel! Auge des Jahrhunderts, Bonn (Kunst- und Ausstellungshalle der Bundesrepublik Deutschland in Bonn) 1994
Peter-Klaus Schuster (ed.), *Picasso und seine Zeit. Die Sammlung Berggruen,* Berlin (Staatliche Museen zu Berlin Preußischer Kulturbesitz) 1996
Beat Wismer (ed.), *Degas – Cézanne – Picasso. Meisterwerke aus Schweizer Privatbesitz,* Vienna (Bank Austria Kunstforum) 1996
Im Reich der Phantome. Fotografie des Unsichtbaren, Krems (Kunsthalle) – Winterthur (Fotomuseum Winterthur) – Mönchengladbach (Städtisches Museum Abteiberg) 1997
Gary Tinterow and Philip Conisbee (eds.), *Portraits by Ingres. Images of an Epoch,* New York (The Metropolitan Museum of Art) – Washington D. C. (The National Gallery of Art) – London (National Gallery) 1999
Christopher White and Quentin Buvelot (eds.), *Rembrandts Selbstbildnisse,* Den Haag (Mauritshuis) – London (National Gallery) 1999/2000

Litterature Concerning Francis Bacon:

Alley 1964
Alley, Ronald, *Francis Bacon. Catalogue raisonné,* London (Thames and Hudson) 1964
Archimbaud 1993
Archimbaud, Michel, *Francis Bacon in conversation with Michel Archim-*

baud, London (Phaidon Press) 1993
Borel 1996
Borel, France, *Bacon: Portraits and Self-Portraits,* New York (Thames and Hudson) 1996
Brighton 2001
Brighton, Andrew, *Francis Bacon. British Artists,* London (Tate Publishing) 2001
Dagen 1996
Dagen, Philippe, *Francis Bacon,* Paris (Editions Cercle d'Art) 1996
Danto 1994
Danto, Arthur C., *Francis Bacon. Embodied Meanings – Critical Essays and Aesthetic Meditations,* New York (The Noonday Press) – Farrar (Strauss and Giroux) 1994
Davies 1978
Davies, Hugh M., *Francis Bacon: The Early and Middle Years, 1928–1958,* New York – London (Garland Publishing) 1978
Davies – Yard 1986
Davies, Hugh – Yard, Sally, *Francis Bacon,* New York – London – Paris (Abbeville Press) 1986
Deleuze 1995
Deleuze, Gilles, *Logik der Sensation,* Munich (Fink Verlag) 1995
Deleuze 2003
Deleuze, Gilles, *The Logic of Sensation,* Continuum International Publishing Group – Mansell 2003 (1981, 1989)
Domino 1996
Domino, Christophe (ed.), *Francis Bacon "Taking reality by surprise",* Paris (Gallimard/Centre Georges Pompidou) 1996 – London (New Horizons, Thames and Hudson) 1997
Domino 1997
Domino, Christophe, *Francis Bacon: Painter of a Dark Vision,* New York (Harry N. Abrams) 1997
Farson 1993
Farson, Daniel, *The Gilded Gutter Life of Francis Bacon,* London (Century) 1993
Giacobetti 2003
Giacobetti, Francis, *"Francis Bacon: I painted to be loved",* Interview, in: The Art Newspaper Nr. 137, Juni 2003
Hunter 1952
Hunter, Sam, *Francis Bacon: The anatomy of horror,* in: Magazine of Art, vol. 45, January 1952
Kudielka 1999
Kudielka, Robert, *Die Gier, der Zufall und das Rote. Zur Malerei von Francis Bacon,* in: Konrad Paul Liessmann (ed.), *Im Rausch der Sinne. Kunst zwischen Animation und Askese,* vol. 2 of the Philosophicum Lech, Vienna (Paul Zsolnay) 1999
Kundera 1996
Kundera, Milan, *Die Brutale Geste des Malers,* in: *Francis Bacon, Portraits und Selbstportraits,* Munich – Paris – London (Schirmer – Mosel) 1996
Leiris 1989
Leiris, Michel, *Francis Bacon heute,* in: id., *Bacon, Picasso, Masson,* Frankfort/Main (Fischer) 1989
Leiris 1983
Leiris, Michel, *Francis Bacon. Meine Bilder,* Munich (Prestel Verlag) 1983
Meinhart 1999
Meinhart, Hedwig, *Das Portrait im Werk Francis Bacons und sein Bezug zur Bildtradition. Eine kunstpädagogische Annäherung,* University of Salzburg 1999
Molony 1977
Molony, Doreen, *Unclaimed genius from county Kildare,* in: The Irish Press, 28 March 1977
Ogden 2001
Francis Bacon's Studio, 7 Reece Mews, London (Thames and Hudson) 2001
Peppiatt 1997
Peppiatt, Michael, *Francis Bacon: Anatomy of an Enigma,* London (Weidenfeld & Nicolson) 1997 (1989, 1996)
Peppiatt 2000
Peppiatt, Michael, *Francis Bacon. Anatomie eines Rätsels,* Cologne (DuMont) 2000 (1996)
Peppiatt
Peppiatt, Michael, *Les rêves décomposés de Francis Bacon,* in: Connaissance des Arts, no. 351, Paris
Ratcliff 2002
Ratcliff, Carter, *Francis Bacon, The violence of Reality,* in: *Francis Bacon, Paintings,* Exhibition Catalogue New York (Tony Shafrazi Gallery) 2002
Russell 1993
Russell, John, *Francis Bacon,* London (Thames and Hudson) 1993 (1971, 1979)
Russell 1998
Russell, John, *Francis Bacon,* Munich (Lichtenberg) 1998
Schmied 1996
Schmied, Wieland, *Francis Bacon, Das Bewußtsein der Gewalt,* Munich – New York (Prestel) 1996
Schmied 1996
Schmied, Wieland, *Francis Bacon: Commitment and Conflict,* Munich – New York (Prestel) 1996
Schönmayr 1993
Schönmayr, Renate Brigitta, *Francis Bacon und Thomas Bernhard: Ein Vergleich,* University of Salzburg 1993
Sinclair 1993
Sinclair, Andrew, *Francis Bacon. His Life and Violent Times,* London (Sinclair/Stevenson) 1993
Sylvester 1997
Sylvester, David, *Gespräche mit Francis Bacon,* Munich – New York (Prestel) 1997 (1982)
Sylvester 1999
Sylvester, David, *Interviews with Francis Bacon,* New York (Thames and Hudson) 1999 (1975, 1980, 1987)
Sylvester 2000
Sylvester, David, *Looking Back at Francis Bacon,* New York (Thames and Hudson) 2000
Trucchi 1975
Trucchi, Lorenza, *Francis Bacon,* New York (Harry N. Abrams) 1975
Van Alphen 1998
Van Alphen, Ernst, *Francis Bacon and the Loss of Self,* London (Reaktion Books) 1998 (1992)
Zimmermann 1986
Zimmermann, Jörg, *Kreuzigung. Versuch, eine gewalttätige Wirklichkeit neu zu sehen,* Frankfort/Main (Fischer) 1986

Literature Concerning the Exhibition:

Adriani 1993
Adriani, Götz, *Cézanne. Gemälde,* Cologne (DuMont) 1993
Bal 1999
Bal, Mieke, *Quoting Caravaggio: Contemporary Art. Preposterous History,* Chicago (University of Chicago Press) 1999
Baxandall 1990
Baxandall, Michael, *Ursachen der Bilder. Über das historische Erklären der Kunst,* Berlin (Reimer) 1990
Beaton 1976
Beaton, Cecil, *The Restless Years,* London (Weidenfeld and Nicolson) 1976
Beyeler 1998
Beyeler, Ernst, *Fondation Beyeler,* Munich (Prestel) 1998
Bordwell 1993
Bordwell, David, *The Cinema of Eisenstein,* Cambridge (Mass.) (Harvard University Press) 1993
Brown 1986
Brown, Jonathan, *Velázquez, painter and courtier,* New Haven and London (Yale University Press) 1986
Bryson 1990
Bryson, Norman, *Tradition and Desire,* Cambridge, Mass. (Cambridge University Press) 1990
Bryson 2001
Bryson, Norman, *Das Sehen und die Malerei. Die Logik des Blicks,* Munich (Fink Verlag) 2001
Bryson – Holly – Moxey 1994
Bryson, Norman – Holly, Michael Ann – Moxey, Keith (eds.), *Visual*

Culture. Images and Interpretations, Hanover and London (Wesleyan University Press and University Press of New England) 1994

Carluccio 1976
Carluccio, Luigi, *Alberto Giacometti, Begegnung mit der Vergangenheit,* Zurich (Ernst Scheidegger) 1967

Chapman 1990
Chapman, H. Perry, *Rembrandt's Self-Portraits: a Study in seventeenth-century Identity,* Princeton (NJ) (Princeton University Press) 1990

Chastel 1990
Chastel, André, *Leonardo da Vinci, Sämtliche Gemälde und die Schriften zur Malerei,* Munich (Schirmer – Mosel) 1990

Châtelet 1999
Châtelet, Albert (ed.), *Rogier van der Weyden, problèmes de la vie et de l'oeuvre,* Straßburg (Presses Univ. de Strasbourg) 1999

Coll 1998
Coll, Simone, *Aspekte der Intermedialität im frühen Werk Luis Bunuels; mit einer Filmanalyse von „Un chien andalou",* Vienna (University of Vienna) 1998

Davies 1972
Davies, Martin, *Rogier van der Weyden,* 1972

De Vos 1999
De Vos, Dirk, *Rogier van der Weyden. Das Gesamtwerk,* Munich (Hirmer) 1999

Eco 1988
Eco, Umberto, *Über Spiegel und andere Phänomene,* Munich – Vienna (Carl Hanser) 1988

Eitner 1983
Eitner, Lorenz, *Géricault. His life and his work,* London (Orbis) 1983

Eliot 1975
Eliot, T.S., *Tradition and Individual Talent,* in: *Selected Prose of T.S. Eliot,* ed. and with an introduction by Frank Kermode, London (Faber und Faber) 1975, S. 37–44

Eliot 1995
Eliot, T.S., *Tradition und individuelle Begabung,* Berlin 1995

Freud 1998
Freud, Sigmund, *Abriß der Psychoanalyse,* Frankfort/Main (Fischer Verlag) 1998

Gasman 1981
Gasman, Lydia, *Mystery, Magic and Love in Picasso, 1925–1938: Picasso and the Surrealist Poets,* PhD dissertation, New York (Columbia University Press) 1981

Gerwen 2001
van Gerwen, Rob (ed.), *Richard Wollheim on the Art of Painting,* Cambridge, Mass. (Cambridge University Press) 2001

Gilman 1995
Gilman, Sander, *Freud, Identität und Geschlecht,* Frankfort/Main (Fischer Verlag) 1995

Goldschneider 1966
Goldschneider, Ludwig, *Michelangelo Drawings,* London (Phaidon) 1966

Gould 1966
Gould, Cecil, *Michelangelo. Battle of Cascina,* Newcastle upon Tyne (University of Newcastle upon Tyne), Charlton Lecture, 1966

Haas 1976
Haas, Robert Bartlett, *Muybridge: man in motion,* Berkeley – Los Angeles – London (University of California Press) 1976

Haidacher 1965
Haidacher, Anton, *Geschichte der Päpste in Bildern,* Heidelberg (F. H. Kerle Verlag) 1965

Hartt 1971
Hartt, Frederick, *The Drawings of Michelangelo,* London (Thames and Hudson) 1971

Herbert 1962
Herbert, Robert L., *Seurat's Drawings,* London 1962

Holeczek 1992
Holeczek, Bernhard, *Zufall als Prinzip,* Heidelberg (Edition Braus) 1992

Hughes 1988
Hughes, Robert, *Lucian Freud Paintings,* London – New York (Thames and Hudson) 1988

Janecke 1995
Janecke, Christian, *Kunst und Zufall. Analyse und Bedeutung,* Nuremberg (Verlag für Moderne Kunst) 1995

Janson 1961
Janson, H. W., *The image made by Chance in Renaissance Thought,* in: Millard Meiss (ed.), *Essays in Honor of Erwin Panofsky,* 2 vols., New York (New York University Press) 1961, p. 254–266

Jochims 1996
Jochims, Reimer, *Kunst und Identität. Visuelle Erkenntnis als Lebenserfahrung,* Ostfildern-Ruit (Edition Tertium) 1996

Kaminski 1998
Kaminski, Marion, *Tiziano Vecellio, Tizian 1488/1490,* Cologne (Könemann Verlag) 1998

Kemp 1986
Kemp, Wolfgang, *Rembrandt. Die Heilige Familie oder die Kunst, einen Vorhang zu lüften,* Frankfort/Main (Fischer Verlag) 1986

Koepplin 1995
Koepplin, Dieter, *Warum kopierte Alberto Giacometti ältere Kunst,* Basel (Wiese Verlag) 1995

Lacan 1991
Lacan, Jacques, *Schriften I,* Berlin (Quadriga Verlag) 1991

Lachman 1992
Lachman, Charles, *The Image made by Chance,* in: *China and the West: Ink Wang meets Jackson Pollocks Mother,* in: Art Bulletin, vol. LXXI, no. 3, September 1992, p. 455–510

Lankheit 1959
Lankheit, Klaus, *Das Triptychon als Pathosformel,* Heidelberg 1959

Lebel 1961
Lebel, Robert, *Géricault. Ses ambitions monumentales et l'inspiration italienne,* Paris 1961

Lem 1985
Lem, Stanislaw, *Philosophie des Zufalls. Zu einer empirischen Theorie der Literatur,* vol. 2, Frankfort/Main (Insel Verlag) 1985

Levita 1971
Levita, David J. de, *Der Begriff der Identität,* Frankfort/Main (Suhrkamp Verlag) 1971

Lomas 2001
Lomas, David, *The Haunted Self – Surrealism Psychoanalysis, Subjectivity,* New Haven (CT) (Yale University Press) 2001

Lopez-Rey 1999
Lopez-Rey, José, *Velázquez, Werkverzeichnis,* Cologne 1999

Muybridge 1955
Muybridge, Eadweard, *The human figure in motion,* New York (Dover Publ.) 1955

Muybridge 1984
Muybridge, Eadweard, *The male and female figure in motion: 60 classic photographic sequences,* New York (Dover Publ.) 1984

Muybridge 1985
Muybridge, Eadweard, *Horses and other animals in motion: 45 classic photographic sequences,* New York (Dover Publ.) 1985

Osborne 2000
Peter Osborne (ed.), *From an Aesthetic Point of View – Philosophy, Art and the Senses,* London (Serpent's Tail) 2000

Pedrocco 2000
Pedrocco, Filippo, *Tizian,* Munich (Hirmer) 2000

Preimesberger – Baader – Suthor 1999
Preimesberger, Rudolf – Baader, Hannah – Suthor, Nicola, *Portrait,* Berlin (Reimer) 1999

Radatz
Radatz, Fritz J., *Süchtig nach Kunst. Bekenntnisse zur Figuration,* Regensburg (Lindinger + Schmid Verlag) 1995

Rich 1958
Rich, Daniel Catton, *Seurat, Paintings and Drawings,* London 1958
Ronte 1989
Ronte, Dieter, *Hess Collection*, Bern and Stuttgart (Verlag Paul Haupt) 1989
Rosenblum 1990
Rosenblum, Robert, *Jean-Auguste-Dominique Ingres,* New York (Harry N. Abrams) 1990
Russoli 1970
Russoli, Franco (ed.), *Opera completa di Degas,* Milan (Rizzoli) 1970
Schäublin 1991
Schäublin, Christoph (ed.), *Cicero. Über die Wahrsagung (De Divinatione),* Munich and Zürich (Artemis und Winkler) 1991
Schopenhauer 1996
Schopenhauer, Arthur, *Die Welt als Wille und Vorstellung,* vol. I and II, Frankfort (Insel Verlag) 1996
Schrenck-Notzing 1923
von Schrenck-Notzing, Albert, *Materialisationsphänomene,* Munich (Ernst Reinhardt) 1923
Seesslen 1994
Seesslen, Georg, *David Lynch und seine Filme,* Marburg (Schüren Verlag) 1994
Smith 1836
Smith, John, *A Catalogue Raisonné of the works of the Most Eminent Dutch, Flemish and French Painters*, vol. VII: *Rembrandt,* London 1836
Schmid 1988
Schmid, Wilhelm (ed.), *Wege zu Degas,* Munich (Matthes & Seitz) 1988
Spiess 1995
Spiess, Werner, *Pablo Picasso, Wege zur Skulptur,* Munich (Prestel Verlag) 1995
Steiner – Pöschl – Wegner
Steiner, Reinhard – Poeschl, Sabine – Wegner, Reinhard (eds.), *Kunsthistorische Beiträge aus Anlaß des 65. Geburtstags von Herwarth Roettgen*
Sylvester 1994
Sylvester, David, *Looking at Giacometti,* London (Chatto and Windus) 1994
Tesson 1995
Tesson, Charles, *Luis Bunuel,* Paris (Cahiers du Cinéma) 1995
Tomlinson 1994
Tomlinson, Janis, *Francisco Goya y Lucientes,* London (Phaidon) 1994
Vigne 1995
Vigne, Georges, *Jean-Auguste-Dominique Ingres,* Munich (Hirmer) 1995
Vigne 1995
Vigne, Georges, *Dessins d'Ingres: catalogue raisonné des dessins du Musée de Montauban,* Paris (Gallimard) 1995
Volpe 1980
Volpe, Carlo (ed.), *L'Opera completa di Sebastiano del Piombo*, Milan (Rizzoli) 1980
Wethey 1971
Wethey, Harold E., *The paintings of Titian, The Portraits*, vol. 2, London (Phaidon) 1971
Wildenstein 1954
Wildenstein, Georges, *Jean-Auguste-Dominique Ingres,* London (Phaidon) 1954
Wollheim 1987
Wollheim, Richard, *Painting as an Art,* The A. W. Mellon Lectures in the Fine Arts, 1984, Washington, D. C. (The National Gallery of Art) – Princeton (NJ) (Princeton University Press) 1987
Woodall 1997
Woodall, Joanna (ed.), *Portraiture: Facing the Subject,* Manchester (Manchester University Press) 1997
Zaloscer 1985
Zaloscer, Hilde, *Der Schrei, Signum einer Epoche,* Vienna (Edition Brandstätter) 1985
Zelger 1994
Zelger, Franz, *Diego Velázquez,* Reinbeck bei Hamburg (Rowohlt) 1994

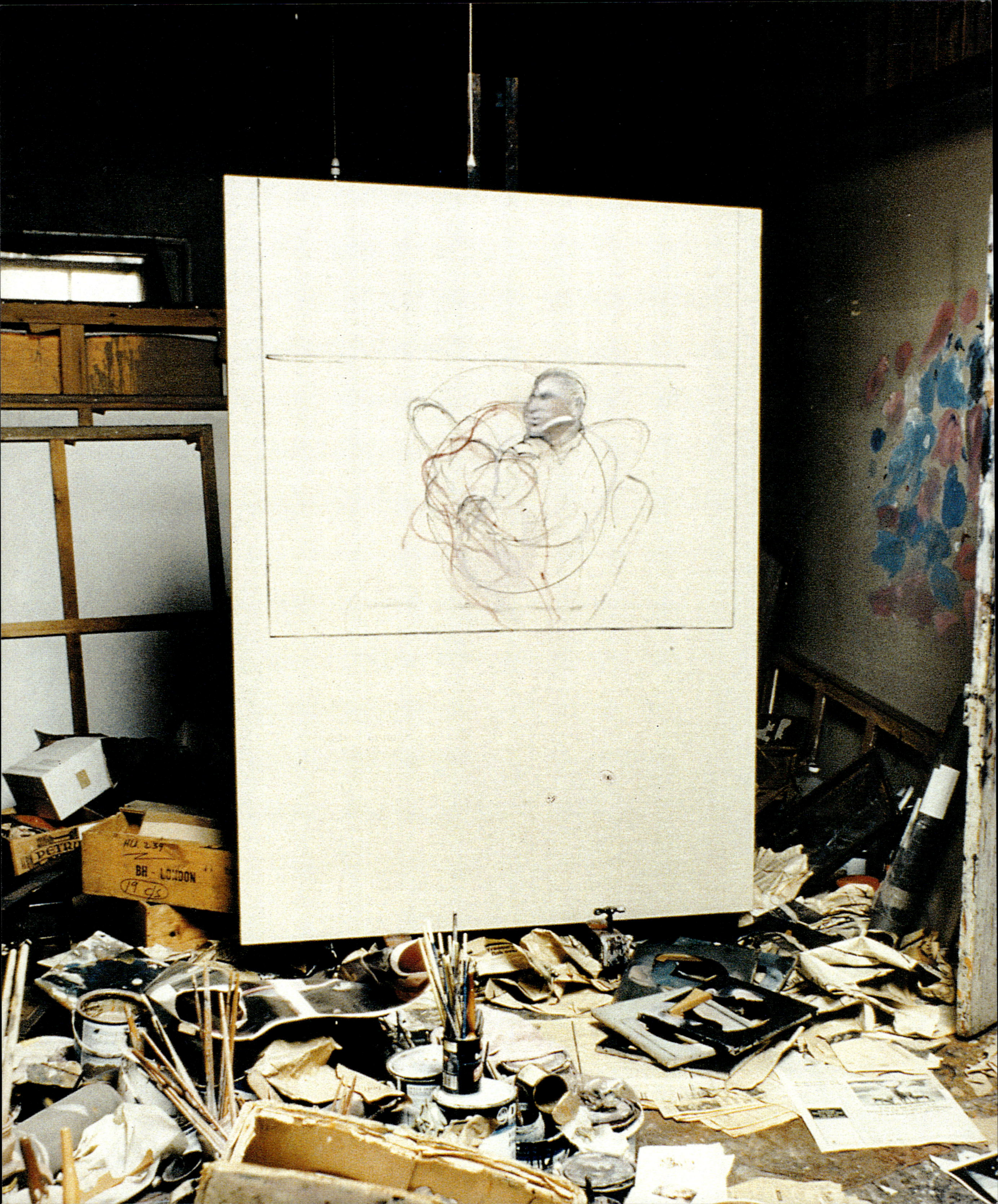
BH - LONDON

Picture credits

Aberdeen, City Art Gallery and Museums Collections: cat. no. 4
Aix-en-Provence, Musée Granet: cat. no. 80B (photo: Bernard Terlay)
Amsterdam, Stedelijk Museum: cat. no. 57
Basel/Riehen, Fondation Beyeler: cat. nos. 15 (photo: Robert Bayer LAC AG), 31, 54, 58, 60, 93, 110, 121 (photo: Peter Schibli), 111 (photo: Christian Baur)
Basel, Galerie Beyeler: cat. no. 75 (photo: Peter Schibli)
Belfast, Ulster Museum: cat. no. 26
Bergamo, Accademia Carrara di Belle Arti: cat. no. 3
Berlin, SMPK, Neue Nationalgalerie: cat. no. 59 (photo: Jörg P. Anders)
Berlin, SMPK, Nationalgalerie, Sammlung Berggruen: cat. no. 92
Brussels, Private Collection: cat. no. 8
Chicago, The Art Institute of Chicago: cat. no. 136
Chicago, Museum of Contemporary Art: cat. no. 50
Des Moines, Des Moines Art Center: cat. no. 14 (photo: Michael Tropea)
Dublin, Dublin City Gallery The Hugh Lane: cat. nos. 10–12, 21–25, 33–41, 46–49, 55, 56, 66–71, 77–79, 86–88, 94, 95, 103–107, 112–117, 122–126, 130, 133, 139–144, 148–155
Frankfort/Main, Städelsches Kunstinstitut und Städtische Galerie: cat. nos. 27, 53 (photo: Ursula Edelmann)
Freiburg/Breisgau, Institut für Grenzgebiete der Psychologie und Psychohygiene e. V.: cat. nos. 18–20
Lisbon, The Berardo Collection – Sintra Museum of Modern Art: cat. no. 97
London, Arts Council Collection and Hayward Gallery: cat. no. 129
London, National Gallery: cat. no. 96
London, Tate Gallery: cat. no. 132
London, Private Collection: cat. no. 52
Los Angeles, Collection Franklin and Susanne Konigsberg: cat. nos. 81, 137 (photo: Brian Forrest)
Lyon, Musée des Beaux-Arts: cat. no. 61 (photo: RMN©Ojeda/Le Mage)
Madrid, Museo Nacional Centro de Arte Reina Sofia: cat. nos. 29, 30 (photo: Museo Nacional Centro de Arte Reinas Sofia Photographic Archive, Madrid)
Madrid, Fundación Collección Thyssen-Bornemisza: cat. no. 120
Melbourne, National Gallery of Victoria: cat. no. 17
Minneapolis, Minneapolis Institute of Arts: cat. no. 135
Montauban, Musée Ingres: cat. nos. 98, 99, 100, 101
Napa/Bern, Hess Collection: cat. no. 89
New Haven, Yale Center for British Art: cat. no. 28 (photo: Richard Caspole)
New York, Collection of Samuel and Ronnie Heyman: cat. no. 5
New York, Collection of Mr. and Mrs. J. Tomilson Hill: cat. no. 74
New York, Museum of Modern Art: cat. no. 7
New York, Solomon R. Guggenheim Museum: cat. nos. 51, 91, 147 (photo: David Heald©The Solomon R. Guggenheim Foundation, New York)
New York, Private Collection: cat. no. 43, 62
Norwich, University of East Anglia: cat. nos. 85 (photo: James Austin), 109
Otterlo, Stiftung Kröller-Müller Museum: cat. no. 127
Paris, Musée National d'Art Moderne, Centre de création industrielle Georges Pompidou: cat. nos. 83 (photo: RMN©Bertrand Prévost/ADAGP), 84 (photo: RMN©Service de documentation photo/ADAGP)
Paris, Musée Picasso: cat. nos. 9 (photo: RMN©ADAGP), 45 (photo: RMN©R.G.Ojeda)
Philadelphia, Philadelphia Museum: cat. no. 13
Rouen, Musée des Beaux-Arts: cat. no. 108 (photo RMN © P. Bernard)
Switzerland, Private Collection: cat. nos. 76, 90, 131, 138
Switzerland, Private Collection: cat. no. 16
Vaduz, Marlborough International Fine Art: cat. nos. 42, 44 (photo: Herbert Michel)
Vienna, Albertina: cat. nos. 63–65
Vienna, Kunsthistorisches Museum: cat. nos. 1, 2, 72, 73, 80A, 82, 118, 119, 134, 145, 146
Vienna, Leopold Museum – Privatstiftung: cat. no. 3
Washington D.C., Hirshhorn Museum and Sculpture Garden, Smithsonian Institution: cat. nos. 6 (photo: Ricardo Blanc), 102, 128 (photo: Lee Stalsworth)